Tolley's Tax [illegible]ons 2018/19

Tolley's Tax Computations 2018/19

by

Tolley's Editorial Team

Tolley®

Members of the LexisNexis Group worldwide

United Kingdom	RELX (UK) Limited, trading as LexisNexis, Lexis House, 30 Farringdon Street, London EC4A 4HH
Australia	LexisNexis Butterworths, Chatswood, New South Wales
Austria	LexisNexis Verlag ARD Orac GmbH & Co KG, Vienna
Benelux	LexisNexis Benelux, Amsterdam
Canada	LexisNexis Canada, Markham, Ontario
China	LexisNexis China, Beijing and Shanghai
France	LexisNexis SA, Paris
Germany	LexisNexis Deutschland GmbH, Munster
Hong Kong	LexisNexis Hong Kong, Hong Kong
India	LexisNexis India, New Delhi
Italy	Giuffrè Editore, Milan
Japan	LexisNexis Japan, Tokyo
Malaysia	Malayan Law Journal Sdn Bhd, Kuala Lumpur
New Zealand	LexisNexis NZ Ltd, Wellington
Singapore	LexisNexis Singapore, Singapore
South Africa	LexisNexis Butterworths, Durban
USA	LexisNexis, Dayton, Ohio

First Published in 1987

Published by LexisNexis

A CIP Catalogue record for this book is available from the British Library.

ISBN for this volume: 9780754554950

Printed and bound by Hobbs the Printers Ltd, Totton, Hampshire

About This Book

Tolley's Tax Computations is an established annual publication, having been first published in the early 1980s in response to interest shown by Tolley tax subscribers in worked examples, both to assist in understanding UK tax legislation and to provide guidance as to layout. The book is divided into six parts covering income tax, corporation tax, capital gains tax, inheritance tax, value added tax and national insurance contributions. In each part, chapters are arranged in alphabetical order by subject to assist reference. Most of the computations have explanatory notes, and statutory references are given wherever appropriate. The book also includes a table of statutes and an index.

This 2018/19 edition has been fully updated to take account of the provisions of the Finance Act 2018 and other relevant information.

Comments on this annual publication and suggestions for improvements and additional computations are always welcome.

Contents

Contents

Abbreviations

ACT	=	Advance Corporation Tax
Art	=	Article
BPR	=	Business Property Relief
b/f	=	brought forward
C & E	=	Customs and Excise
CA	=	Court of Appeal
CAA	=	Capital Allowances Act
CCAB	=	Consultative Committee of Accountancy Bodies
Ch D	=	Chancery Division
c/f	=	carried forward
CGT	=	Capital Gains Tax
CGTA	=	Capitals Gains Tax Act
CRCA	=	Commissioners for Revenue and Customs Act
CT	=	Corporation Tax
CTA	=	Corporation Tax Act
CTT	=	Capital Transfer Tax
CVS	=	Corporate Venturing Scheme
CY	=	Current Year
DTR	=	Double Tax Relief
EIS	=	Enterprise Investment Scheme
ESC	=	Extra-Statutory Concession
ESP	=	Expected Selling Price
FA	=	Finance Act
F(No 2)A	=	Finance (No 2) Act
FIFO	=	First In, First Out
FII	=	Franked Investment Income
FY	=	Financial Year
FYA	=	First-Year Allowance
HL	=	House of Lords
HMRC	=	Her Majesty's Revenue and Customs
IBA	=	Industrial Buildings Allowance
ICTA	=	Income and Corporation Taxes Act
IRPR	=	Inland Revenue Press Release
IHT	=	Inheritance Tax
IHTA	=	Inheritance Tax Act
IT	=	Income Tax
ITA	=	Income Tax Act
ITEPA	=	Income Tax (Earnings and Pensions) Act
ITTOIA	=	Income Tax (Trading and Other Income) Act
LEL	=	Lower Earnings Limit
LIFO	=	Last In, First Out
LLPA	=	Limited Liability Partnerships Act
NBV	=	Net Book Value
NIC	=	National Insurance Contributions
para	=	paragraph
PAYE	=	Pay As You Earn
P/e	=	Period ended
PET	=	Potentially Exempt Transfer
PR	=	Personal Representative

Abbreviations and References

PY	=	Previous Year
Reg	=	Regulation
RNRB	=	Residence nil rate band
s	=	section
SC/S	=	Scottish Court of Session
Sch	=	Schedule
SI	=	Statutory Instrument
SSAP	=	Statement of Standard Accounting Practice
TCGA	=	Taxation of Chargeable Gains Act
TIOPA	=	Taxation (International and Other Provisions) Act
TPA	=	Taxation of Pensions Act
TMA	=	Taxes Management Act
UEL	=	Upper Earnings Limit
VAT	=	Value Added Tax
VATA	=	Value Added Tax Act
VCT	=	Venture Capital Trust
WDA	=	Writing-down Allowance
WDV	=	Written-down Value
Y/e	=	Year ended

References

STC	=	Simon's Tax Cases (LexisNexis, 30 Farringdon Street, London EC4A 4HH)
TC	=	Official Tax Cases (H.M. Stationery Office, P.O. Box 276, SW8 5DT)

Table of Statutes

Table of Statutes

Table of Statutory Instruments

Income Tax

1 Allowances and Tax Rates

Cross-reference. See also **16.1** MARRIED PERSONS AND CIVIL PARTNERS for transfer of married couple's allowance.

1.1 DIVIDEND ALLOWANCE

[*ITA 2007, ss 8, 13, 13A, 16, 19; FA 2016, s 5(3)(5)(10); F(No 2)A 2017, s 8*]

(A)

Cicero has property income of £33,850, bank interest of £800 and UK dividends of £2,200 for 2018/19. Cicero is a not a Scottish taxpayer.

His taxable income and tax liability are computed as follows

	£
Property income	33,850
Savings income	800
Dividend income	2,200
Total and net income	36,850
Personal allowance	(11,850)
Taxable income	£25,000
Tax payable:	
22,000 @ 20% (basic rate on property income)	4,400.00
800 @ 0% (personal savings allowance)	—
2,000 @ 0% (dividend allowance)	—
200 @ 7.5% (dividend ordinary rate)	15.00
£25,000	
Tax payable	£4,415.00

Notes

(a) The dividend allowance for individuals for 2018/19 is £2,000. It was £5,000 for tax years 2016/17 and 2017/18. The dividend allowance is not a deduction in arriving at total income or taxable income. Instead, the first £2,000 of dividend income attracts a zero rate of income tax (the 'dividend nil rate').

(b) Dividends no longer carry a dividend tax credit as was the case for 2015/16 and earlier years.

(c) Dividend income in excess of the dividend allowance is charged at special rates. Where taxable income does not exceed the basic rate limit the rate applied is the 'dividend ordinary rate', 7.5%. To the extent that dividend income exceeds the basic rate limit but not the higher rate limit of £150,000, the rate is the 'dividend upper rate', 32.5%.

To the extent that dividend income exceeds the higher rate limit, the rate is the 'dividend additional rate', 38.1%. In determining the extent to which dividend income does fall above the basic rate or higher rate limit, dividend income is treated as the top slice of income (with certain limited exceptions).

(d) See **1.2** below for the personal savings allowance.

(B)

Terentia has employment income of £9,850, savings income of £7,000 and dividends of £3,500 for 2018/19. She is not a Scottish taxpayer.

	Savings income	Dividend income	Other income	Total income
	£	£	£	£
Total and net income	7,000	3,500	9,850	20,350
Deduct Personal allowance	(1,000)	(1,000)	(9,850)	(11,850)
Taxable income	£6,000	£2,500	—	£8,500
Tax payable:				
£5,000 @ 0% (starting rate for savings)	—			—
£1,000 @ 0% (personal savings allowance)	—			—
£2,000 @ 0% (dividend allowance)		—		—
£500 @ 7.5% (dividend ordinary rate)		37.50		37.50
Tax payable	–	£37.50		£37.50

Note

(a) The personal allowance is treated as reducing income of different descriptions in such manner as will result in the greatest reduction in tax liability. [*ITA 2007, s 25(2)*]. In this example, what remains of the personal allowance (£2,000) is set firstly against savings income but only to the extent necessary to produce a nil liability on that income. If the £2,000 were set wholly against savings income there would a total liability of £112 (£1,500 @ 7.5%) on the dividend income. If the £2,000 were set wholly against dividend income it would wipe out the liability on dividend income but produce a liability of £200 on savings income (£1,000 @ 20%).

(C)

Crassus has trading income of £43,650, bank interest of £700, UK dividends of £1,300 and overseas dividends £2,550 (net of 15% foreign withholding tax) for 2018/19. He is not a Scottish taxpayer.

His taxable income and tax liability are computed as follows

	Non–savings income	Savings income	Divi-dend income	Total income
	£	£	£	£
Trading income	43,650			43,650
Bank interest		700		700
Dividend income:				
UK dividends			1,300	1,300
Overseas dividends £2,550 × 100/85			3,000	3,000
Total and net income	43,650	700	4,300	48,650
Personal allowance	(9,350)	(200)	(2,300)	(11,850)
Taxable income	£34,300	500	2,000	36,800
Tax payable:				
34,300 @ 20% (basic rate on trading income (note (a))	6,860.00			6,860.00
500 @ 0% (personal savings allowance)		—		—
2,000 @ 0% (dividend allowance)			—	—
	6,860.00			
Less: Foreign withholding tax £3,000 @ 15%	(450.00)	–		(450.00)
Tax payable	£6,410.00	–		£6,410.00

Tax on income excluding foreign dividends

		Non–savings income	Savings income	Dividend income	Total income
		£	£	£	£
Trading income		43,650			43,650
Bank interest			700		700
Dividend income:					
Dividend income (UK dividends only)				1,300	1,300
Total and net income		43,650	700	1,300	45,650
Personal allowance		(11,650)	(200)		(11,850)
Taxable income		£32,000	500	1,300	33,800
Tax payable:					
32,000	@ 20% (basic rate on trading income (note (b))	6,400.00			6,400.00
500	@ 0% (personal savings allowance)		—		—
1,300	@ 0% (dividend allowance)			—	—
Tax payable		£6,400.00	–		£6,400.00

The difference between the two calculations of tax payable (before withholding tax) is £460 (£6,860 – 6,400). This is greater than the foreign withholding tax of £450, so the withholding tax is deductible in full.

Notes

(a) The personal allowance is treated as reducing income of different descriptions in such manner as will result in the greatest reduction in tax liability. [*ITA 2007, s 25(2)*]. In this example, £2,300 of the personal allowance has been set against dividend income, £200 has been set against savings income, leaving £9,350 to be set against trading income. The advantage of doing this is that it removes £2,300 of dividend income that would otherwise be taxed at the dividend upper rate of 32.5% and £200 of savings income be taxed at higher rate of 40%. The cost is an additional £2,300 of non-dividend income chargeable at the basic rate of 20%. The tax saving is £287.50 (£2,300 @ (32.5% - 20%)).

(b) Overseas dividends are taxed at the same rates, and attract the dividend allowance in the same way, as UK dividends. Credit for the withholding tax on the overseas dividends is given against the UK tax due on them to the extent that it does not exceed that UK tax. See also **8.1** DOUBLE TAX RELIEF. In the calculation of tax on income excluding foreign dividends, the personal allowance is set entirely against trading income; there is no longer an advantage in setting it partly against dividend income as the latter is fully covered by the dividend allowance.

(c) The personal savings allowance is £500 as the taxpayer has income above the basic rate limit but not above the higher rate limit. See **1.2** below.

1.2 PERSONAL SAVINGS ALLOWANCE

[*ITA 2007, ss 7(2), 12A, 12B, 16; FA 2016, s 4(3)(5)(6)(17)*]

Servilia has pension income of £41,950, bank interest of £2,500 and dividends of £2,000 for 2018/19. She is not a Scottish taxpayer.

Her taxable income and tax liability are computed as follows

		£
Pension income		41,950
Savings income		2,500
Dividend income		2,000
Total and net income		46,450
Personal allowance		(11,850)
Taxable income		£34,600
Tax payable:		
30,100	@ 20% (basic rate on pension income)	6,020.00
500	@ 0% (personal savings allowance)	—
2,000	@ 20% (basic rate on savings income)	400.00
1,900	@ 0% (dividend allowance — part)	—
34,500	Basic rate limit	
100	@ 0% (dividend allowance — part)	—
£34,600		
Tax payable		£6,420.00

Notes

(a) A personal savings allowance was introduced for individuals for 2016/17 onwards. The allowance is £1,000 for basic rate taxpayers, i.e. individuals who have no income chargeable at the higher or additional rates or the dividend upper and additional rates. For individuals with income chargeable at the higher rate or dividend upper rate but not at the additional rate or dividend additional rate, the allowance is £500. Individuals with income chargeable at the additional rate or dividend additional rate are not entitled to the allowance. If dividend income is, in fact, chargeable at the dividend nil rate because of the dividend allowance but would otherwise have been chargeable at the dividend upper or additional rate, it is treated as if it had been chargeable at the dividend upper or additional rate for the purpose of determining the amount (if any) of the personal savings allowance.

(b) The personal savings allowance is not a deduction in arriving at total income or taxable income. Instead, the savings income covered by the allowance (whether the allowance be £500 or £1,000) attracts a zero rate of income tax (the 'savings nil rate') instead of the basic or higher rate (whichever would otherwise apply).

(c) For the purpose of applying these rules, savings income is treated as the highest part of an individual's total income apart from dividend income and other limited exceptions.

(d) The personal savings allowance operates in conjunction with the starting rate for savings where the latter is available (see **1.3** below).

(e) Deduction of basic rate tax at source by banks and building societies was abolished for 2016/17 onwards, so interest is receivable gross. [*ITA 2007, ss 851, 876; FA 2016, Sch 6 paras 1, 2, 28*].

(f) See **1.1** above for the dividend allowance.

1.3 STARTING RATE FOR SAVINGS

[*ITA 2007, ss 7(1), 12, 16; FA 2016, s 4(3)(6)(17); FA 2017, s 4*]

(A)

Catalina has earned income of £11,530, bank interest of £6,590 and UK dividends of £500 for 2018/19. Catalina is not a Scottish taxpayer.

His income tax position is as follows

	£
Earnings	11,530
Savings income	6,590
Dividends	500
Total and net income	18,620
Personal allowance	(11,850)
Taxable income	£6,770
Tax payable:	
5,000 @ 0% (starting rate for savings)	—
1,000 @ 0% (personal savings allowance)	—
270 @ 20% (basic rate on savings income)	54.00
500 @ 0% (dividend allowance)	—
£6,770	
Tax payable	£54.00

Notes

(a) To the extent that an individual's savings income (excluding dividends) does not exceed the starting rate limit, it is taxed at the 0% starting rate for savings instead of the basic rate. The starting rate limit for 2018/19 is £5,000. For the purpose of determining whether savings income exceeds the starting rate limit, it is treated as the highest part of the individual's total income apart from dividend income and other limited exceptions.

(b) It follows that wherever the amount of an individual's taxable income, apart from savings income and dividend income, equals or exceeds the starting rate limit, the starting rate for savings cannot apply to any of the income.

(c) The personal allowance is treated as reducing income of different descriptions in such manner as will result in the greatest reduction of the tax liability. [*ITA 2007, s 25(2)*]. In this example, it is set firstly against earnings and then against savings income, which gives the best result (see also **1.1**(B)(C) above).

(d) The starting rate for savings operates in conjunction with the personal savings allowance (see **1.2** above) but takes priority.

(e) Savings income includes interest, income from purchased life annuities, profits on deeply discounted securities, accrued income profits and chargeable event gains on life policies etc.

(B)

Clodia has a pension of £12,750, on which tax of £180 has been paid under PAYE, and building society interest of £5,350 for 2018/19. She is not a Scottish taxpayer.

Her income tax position is as follows

	£
Pension income	12,750
Savings income	5,350
Total and net income	18,100
Personal allowance	(11,850)
Taxable income	£6,250
Tax payable:	
900 @ 20% (basic rate on pension income)	180.00
4,100 @ 0% (starting rate for savings)	—
1,000 @ 0% (personal savings allowance)	—
250 @ 20% (basic rate on savings income)	50.00
Tax payable (of which £180 already collected under PAYE)	£230.00

Notes

(a) The building society interest is the highest part of the individual's income, and £4,100 of this interest is within the 0% starting rate band of £5,000. The personal allowance has been set against the pension income as this gives the best result.

(b) See also the notes to (A) above.

1.4 USE OF LOSSES

[*ITA 2007, s 25(2)*]

Hortensius has traded for a number of years. He prepares accounts to 30 June, and his tax-adjusted profits for the year ended 30 April 2018 are £20,880. His other 2018/19 income consists of building society interest of £2,500, interest on UK company loan stock of £1,200 (net of basic rate tax deducted at source) and dividends of £4,500.

For the year to 30 April 2019 Hortensius sustains a tax-adjusted trading loss of £3,228 and makes a claim under *ITA 2007, s 64(2)(b)* to carry it back against general income of 2018/19. He is not a Scottish taxpayer.

His 2018/19 tax liability after loss relief is computed as follows

		£
Trading income		20,880
Building society interest		2,500
Loan stock interest (£1,200 × 100/80)		1,500
Dividends		4,500
Total income		29,380
Loss relief under *ITA 2007, s 64(2)(b)*		(3,228)
Net income		26,152
Personal Allowance		(11,850)
Taxable income		£14,302
Tax payable:		
5,802	@ 20% (basic rate on net trading income)	1,160.40
1,000	@ 0% (personal savings allowance)	—
3,000	@ 20% (basic rate on savings income)	600.00
2,000	@ 0% (dividend allowance)	—
2,500	@ 7.5% (dividend ordinary rate)	187.50
14,302		1,947.90
Less: tax deducted at source		(300.00)
Net tax liability		£1,647.90

Notes

(a) Although dividend income is generally regarded as the top slice of income and savings income as the next slice, this does not mean that a loss must be set against those types of income first. Deductions allowable in computing net income are treated as reducing income of different descriptions in such manner as will result in the greatest reduction of the tax liability. Here the loss has been set against trading income. Savings income and dividend income are left intact, and attract the personal savings allowance and dividend allowance respectively.

(b) In this example, the whole of the personal allowance is also set against trading income as this gives the best result, but see **1.1**(B)(C) above as regards optimum use of the personal allowance in other cases in accordance with the principle stated in (a) above.

1.5 RESTRICTION OF PERSONAL ALLOWANCE

[*ITA 2007, ss 35(2)–(4), 58; F(No 2)A 2015, s 5*].

Cato has employment income of £118,200 for 2018/19 (and no other income) and makes Gift Aid donations of £4,800. He is not a Scottish taxpayer.

His 2018/19 tax liability is computed as follows

	£	£
Employment income		118,200
Total and net income		118,200
Deduct Personal allowance	11,850	
Less reduction for excess adjusted net income over £100,000 (½ × 12,200) (note (b))	6,100	(5,750)
Taxable income		£112,450
Tax liability:		
£40,500 @ 20% (note (c))		8,100.00
£71,950 @ 40%		28,780.00
Tax payable		£36,880.00

Notes

(a) The personal allowance is reduced by one-half of the excess of adjusted net income over £100,000.

(b) Net income of £118,200 is reduced to adjusted net income of £112,200 by deducting the grossed up amount of the Gift Aid donations (£4,800 x 100/80 = £6,000).

(c) Whilst the Gift Aid donations are deductible in arriving at adjusted net income, they are not deductible in arriving at taxable income. Instead, the basic rate band is extended by the grossed up amount of the donations. See **5.1**(C) CHARITIES.

1.6 TRANSFERABLE TAX ALLOWANCE

[*ITA 2007, ss 55A–55E; TMA 1970, s 42(10A); FA 2014, s 11(2)(10)(12); FA 2015, ss 3(4)(5), 5(8)(9)(11); FA 2016, ss 4(8)(17), 5(6)(7)(10)*].

Irina, a married woman with small children receives income (net of allowable expenses) of £10,860 in 2018/19 from occasional freelance proofreading. She has no other taxable income. Irina elects under *ITA 2007, s 55C* to transfer part of her personal allowance to her husband. Her husband, Arkady, has employment income of £43,350 but no other taxable income. The couple are not eligible for married couple's allowance and neither is a Scottish taxpayer.

	£	£
Arkady		
Net income		43,350
Deduct Personal allowance		(11,850)
Taxable income		£31,500
Tax on £31,500 @ 20% (basic rate)		6,300.00
Deduct Transferable tax allowance £1,190 @ 20%		238.00
		£6,062.00

Irina			
Net income			10,860
Deduct	Personal allowance	11,850	
	Less transferable tax allowance	(1,190)	
			(10,660)
Taxable income			£200
Tax liability: £200 @ 20% (basic rate)			£40.00

Notes

(a) An individual may elect to transfer part of his or her personal allowance to a spouse or civil partner. The amount transferable (known as the '*transferable tax allowance*' or '*marriage allowance*') is equivalent to 10% of the basic personal allowance for the year, e.g. it is £1,190 for 2018/19. Relief is given to the transferee by means of a tax reduction.

(b) The election is valid only if neither the transferor nor the transferee are liable to income tax at the higher or additional rate or the dividend upper or additional rate. It cannot be made if either the transferor or transferee claims married couple's allowance for the year.

(c) This couple save tax of £198 by electing to use the transferable tax allowance. Arkady makes the maximum saving of £238.00 (£1,190 @ 20%) while Irina has to pay tax of £40.00 to which she would not otherwise have been liable. If Irina's income had been £10,660 (90% of the personal allowance) or less, the couple would have achieved the maximum saving of £238.00.

1.7 MARRIED COUPLE'S ALLOWANCE

[*ITA 2007, ss 42–55, 58*]

(A)

Vlad and Nadia are a married couple born in 1934 and 1942 respectively. Vlad's net income for 2018/19 amounts to £30,950 and Nadia's to £34,650. Neither spouse has any dividend income or savings income. Nadia elected under *ITA 2007, s 47* before 6 April 2018 to be given half the basic married couple's allowance for 2018/19 onwards. The couple have been married for many years and have not elected to be brought within the rules for couples marrying on or after 5 December 2005. Neither is a Scottish taxpayer.

Taxable income and tax payable are calculated as follows

	Vlad	Nadia
	£	£
Net income	30,950	34,650
Deduct Personal allowance	11,850	11,850
Taxable income	£19,100	£22,800

Tax payable:		
19,100/22,800 @ 20%	3,820.00	4,560.00
Reduction for married couple's allowance:		
5,990/1,680 (see below) @ 10%	(599.00)	(168.00)
Total liabilities	£3,221.00	£4,392.00
Calculation of married couple's allowance		
Unrestricted married couple's allowance	8,695	
Deduct 1/2 × £2,050 (excess of net income over £28,900)	1,025	
	7,670	
Transfer from husband to wife (£3,360 × 1/2)	(1,680)	£1,680
	£5,990	

Notes

(a) The restriction in the married couple's allowance is by reference to the husband's income only.

(b) Married couple's allowance is available only where at least one of the spouses/civil partners was born before 6 April 1935. The transfer to the wife in this example under *ITA 2007, s 47* is restricted to one half of the basic allowance, i.e. the minimum amount below which the age-related allowance may not be reduced by reference to the income of the claimant. For 2018/19 this amount is £3,360. [*ITA 2007, ss 43, 47*].

(c) If the wife, but not the husband, had been born before 6 April 1935, the husband would still qualify for the married couple's allowance.

(B)

The facts are as in (A) above except that Vlad and Nadia have elected under *ITA 2007, s 44* to be treated in the same way as couples who married on or after 5 December 2005. The result of this, as regards the year 2018/19, is that the married couple's allowance is initially given to *Nadia* as she has the higher net income for that year. They have elected under *ITA 2007, s 47* for half of the basic allowance to be then transferred to Vlad.

Taxable income and tax payable are calculated as follows

	Vlad	Nadia
	£	£
Net income	30,950	34,650
Deduct Personal allowance	11,850	11,850
Taxable income	£19,100	£22,800
Tax payable:		
19,100/22,800 @ 20%	3,820.00	4,560.00

Restriction for married couple's allowance:		
1,680/4,140 (see below) @ 10%	(168.00)	(414.00)
Total liabilities	£3,652.00	£4,146.00
Calculation of married couple's allowance		
Unrestricted allowance		8,695
Deduct 1/2 × £5,750 (i.e. excess over £28,900)		2,875
		5,820
Transfer from wife to husband (£3,360 × 1/2)	£1,680	(1,680)
		£4,140

Notes

(a) *ITA 2007, s 46* applies to all couples who get married on or after 5 December 2005 and to all civil partners. Couples who married before that date may elect into this regime; the election must be made before the start of the first tax year to which it is to have effect and is irrevocable. [*ITA 2007, ss 44, 46*].

(b) Under *section 46*, the married couple's allowance is given to the partner with the higher net income instead of automatically to the husband. The allowance is then restricted by reference to that partner's income. If the couple were married before 5 December 2005 and the wife has the higher net income, an election into the *section 46* regime may reduce the allowance, as is the case in this example. There are no circumstances in which an election can result in an increased allowance.

(c) It remains possible for husband and wife (and civil partners) to elect to transfer half of the basic allowance between them.

1.8 SCOTTISH RATES OF INCOME TAX

[*ITA 2007, s 11A; Scotland Act 1998, Pt 4A; Scotland Act 2016, ss 13, 14(8)–(10)(15); FA 2014, Sch 38 paras 5, 12; SI 2016 No 1161*].

Duncan is a Scottish taxpayer (within the definition at *Scotland Act 1998, ss 80D–80F*). For 2018/19 he has earnings of £43,650, bank interest of £1,400 and no other taxable income.

Duncan's taxable income and tax liability are computed as follows

	£
Employment income	43,650
Savings income	1,400
Total and net income	45,050
Personal allowance	(11,850)
Taxable income	£33,200

Tax payable:

2,000	@ 19% (Scottish starter rate on non-savings/non-dividend income)	380.00
10,150	@ 20% (Scottish basic rate on non-savings/non-dividend income)	2,030.00
19,430	@ 21% (Scottish intermediate rate on non-savings/non-dividend income)	4,080.30
220	@ 41% (Scottish higher rate on non-savings/non-dividend income)	90.20
1,000	@ 0% (personal savings allowance)	—
400	@ 20% (basic rate on savings income)	80.00
£33,200		
Tax payable		£6,660.50

Notes

(a) With effect for 2017/18 onwards, the Scottish Parliament is empowered to set its own income tax rates and thresholds for Scottish taxpayers independently of, and not linked to, UK rates. The Scottish rates and thresholds apply only for the purpose of calculating tax on income that is neither savings income nor dividend income; UK rates and thresholds still apply to those types of income. The Scottish rates for 2018/19, as set by the Scottish Parliament on 20 February 2018, are divided into five different tax rates and bands as follows: .

- Starter rate — £0 – £2,000 @ 19%
- Basic rate — £2,001 – £12,150 @ 20%
- Intermediate rate — £12,151 – £31,580 @ 21%
- Higher rate — £31,581 – £150,000 @ 41%
- Top rate — Over £150,000 @ 46%

(b) In this example, the personal allowance is set against employment income as this gives the best result. This leaves taxable non-savings/non dividend income of £31,800 which is taxed at the rates in (a) above. However, the savings income falls entirely within the UK basic rate band and is thus chargeable at the basic rate (to the extent that it exceeds the personal savings allowance).

(c) In determining the amount of the personal savings allowance (PSA), a Scottish taxpayer is assumed to pay income tax by reference to UK rate thresholds. [*ITA 2007, s 12B*]. In this example, the PSA is £1,000 because taxable income does not exceed the UK basic rate limit of £34,500 and the taxpayer would not be liable above basic rate if he were not a Scottish taxpayer. See **1.2** above for the PSA generally.

2 Accrued Income Scheme

[*ITA 2007, ss 615–681*]

2.1 The following transactions take place between individuals during the year ended 5 April 2019.

Settlement day	Sale by	Purchase by	Securities
14.8.18	X (cum div)	Y	£4,000 6¼% Treasury Loan 2022
17.9.18	X (ex div)	P	£4,000 8% Treasury Loan 2020
4.4.19	S (cum div)	Y	£2,500 4% Treasury Loan 2021

Interest payment days are as follows

6¼% Treasury Loan 2022	25 May, 25 November
8% Treasury Loan 2020	27 March, 27 September
4% Treasury Loan 2021	7 March, 7 September

Both X and Y owned chargeable securities with a nominal value in excess of £5,000 at some time in either 2017/18 or 2018/19, and both are resident in the UK. P is non-resident in the UK throughout 2018/19. The maximum value of securities held by S at any time in 2018/19 and 2019/20 is £4,000.

14.8.18 transaction

The transaction occurs in the interest period from 26.5.18 to 25.11.18 (inclusive).

Number of days in interest period	184
Number of days in interest period to 14.8.18	81
Interest payable on 25.11.18	£125

The deemed payment is

$$£125 \times \frac{81}{184} = £\underline{55}$$

X is treated as receiving a payment of £55 on 25.11.18. Assuming no other transfers in this kind of security in the interest period, this will also be the figure of accrued income profit chargeable.

Y is treated as making a payment of £55. Assuming no other transfers in this kind of security in the interest period, this will also be the figure of accrued income loss to set against the interest of £125 he receives on 25.11.18. £70 remains taxable.

17.9.18 transaction

The transaction occurs in the interest period from 28.3.18 to 27.9.18 (inclusive).

Number of days in interest period	184
Number of days in interest period from 17.9.18	10
Interest payable on 27.9.18	£160

The deemed payment is

$$£160 \times \frac{10}{184} = \underline{£9}$$

X is treated as making a payment of £9. Assuming no other transfers in this kind of security in the interest period, this will also be the figure of accrued income loss to set against the interest of £160 he receives on 27.9.18. £151 remains taxable. P is an excluded transferee (see note (a)).

4.4.19 transaction

The transaction occurs in the interest period from 8.3.19 to 7.9.19 (inclusive)

Number of days in interest period	184
Number of days in interest period to 4.4.19	28
Interest payable on 7.9.19	£50

The deemed payment is

$$£50 \times \frac{28}{184} = \underline{£7}$$

S is an excluded transferor as his holdings do not exceed £5,000 at any time in 2018/19 or 2019/20 (the year in which the interest period ends).

Y is treated as making a payment of £7. Assuming no other transfers in this kind of security in the interest period, this will also be the figure of accrued income loss to set against the interest of £50 he receives on 7.9.19. £43 remains taxable.

Note

(a) P is an excluded transferee as he is non-resident in the UK throughout the tax year in which the transfer is made (2018/19). Different rules apply where a non-UK resident is trading in the UK through a branch or agency. [*ITA 2007, s 643*].

3 Capital Allowances

Cross-reference. See also 4 CAPITAL ALLOWANCES ON PLANT AND MACHINERY.

3.1 BUSINESS PREMISES RENOVATION

[*CAA 2001, ss 360A–360Z4; FA 2014, s 66; SI 2007 No 945*]

Mickey is a jeweller who has been in business for many years and makes up accounts to 30 June each year. On 1 July 2015, he purchased the freehold of a building in the Speke ward in Liverpool. The building had been empty since June 2013, having been used before that time as a pawnbrokers. In the year ended 30 June 2016, Mickey incurs capital expenditure of £40,000 in renovating the building for use as his business premises. Mickey claims a reduced business premises renovation initial allowance of 40% of the expenditure for the year ended 30 June 2016.

The renovation is completed on 1 August 2016, and Mickey starts to use the building for the purposes of his trade on that date. In September 2017 he sells the freehold for £260,000. Of the net sale proceeds, £45,000 can be attributed to assets representing the renovation expenditure.

Mickey's allowances are as follows

			Residue of expenditure
		£	£
2016/17	Qualifying expenditure		40,000
	Initial allowance (maximum 100%)	16,000	(16,000)
2017/18	Writing-down allowance		
	(25% of £40,000)	10,000	(10,000)
			14,000
2018/19	Writing-down allowance		
	Sale proceeds		(45,000)
	Excess of sale proceeds over residue of expenditure		£31,000
	Balancing charge (restricted to allowances made, £16,000 + £10,000)		£26,000

Notes

(a) For expenditure incurred before 6 April 2017, subject to conditions, capital allowances (known as business premises renovation allowances) are available for qualifying expenditure incurred by individuals and companies on the conversion or renovation of vacant business premises in designated development areas of the UK for the purpose of bringing those premises back into business use. The premises must have been unused for at least one year before the date the work begins. Certain trades are excluded.

(b) No writing-down allowance is available for the year ended 30 June 2016 as the building is not in use for the purposes of the trade (and hence is not qualifying business premises) on 30 June 2016. It becomes qualifying business premises on 1 August 2016, so that a writing-down allowance is available for the year ended 30 June 2017. Mickey does not hold the relevant interest in the building on 30 June 2018, having sold it in September 2017, so no writing-down allowance is available for the year ended 30 June 2018.

(c) A balancing adjustment is made for the chargeable period in which the relevant interest in the building is sold (or in which certain other events occur) if the sale (or other event) occurs within five years of the after the time the building was first used, or suitable for letting, for qualifying purposes. For expenditure incurred before 6 April 2014, the stipulated period is seven years rather than five. There is no provision for the transfer of allowances to a purchaser. [*CAA 2001, ss 360M–360P; FA 2014, s 66(9)(10)(12)*]. If the proceeds from the event are only partly attributable to assets representing expenditure for which a business premises renovation allowance can be made, only that part of the proceeds as is so attributable, on a just and reasonable apportionment, is brought into account. [*CAA 2001, s 360Z2*].

(d) If the person entitled to business premises renovation allowances or liable to charges carries on a trade or occupies the qualifying building for the purposes of a trade, profession or vocation, the allowances/charges are treated as expenses/receipts of the trade etc. Otherwise, allowances and charges are given effect by treating them as expenses/receipts of a UK property business. If the relevant interest in the building is not an asset of such a business, the claimant is treated as if he were carrying on such a business and allowances and charges made accordingly. [*CAA 2001, ss 360Z, 360Z1*]. See also **15.6** LOSSES.

3.2 DREDGING

[*CAA 2001, ss 484–489*]

D is the proprietor of an estuary maintenance business preparing accounts to 30 June. Expenditure qualifying for dredging allowances is incurred as follows

	£
Year ended 30.6.17	4,000
Year ended 30.6.18	5,000

On 2 January 2019, D sells the business to an unconnected third party.

The allowances available are

Date of expenditure	Cost	Residue brought forward	Allowances WDA 4%	Residue carried forward
	£	£	£	£
2017/18 (year ended 30.6.17)				
2017	4,000	—	160	3,840
2018/19				
Year ended 30.6.18				
2017	4,000	3,840	160	3,680
2018	5,000	—	200	4,800
			£360	£8,480
Six months ended 2.1.19				
Balancing allowance note (a)			£8,480	
Total allowances 2018/19 (£360 + £8,480)			£8,840	

Note

(a) On permanent cessation of the trade by the person carrying it on, including a sale other than one falling within *CAA 2001, s 488(4)(5)*, a balancing allowance is given and is equal to the excess of expenditure over writing-down allowances previously made. There are no provisions for a balancing charge or a transfer of allowances to a purchaser.

3.3 MINERAL EXTRACTION

[*CAA 2001, Pt 5; FA 2014, ss 67, 68*]

X has for some years operated a mining business with two mineral sources, G and S. Accounts are prepared to 30 September. On 31 December 2017 the mineral deposits and mineworks at G are sold at market value to Z for £80,000 and £175,000 respectively. A new source, P, is purchased on 30 April 2018 for £170,000 (including land with an undeveloped market value of £70,000) and the following expenditure incurred before the end of the period of account ended 30 September 2018.

	£
Plant and machinery	40,000
Construction of administration office	25,000
Construction of mining works which are likely to have little value when mining ceases	50,000
Staff hostel	35,000
Winning access to the deposits	150,000
	£300,000

During the year to 30 September 2018, X incurred expenditure of £20,000 in seeking planning permission to mine a further plot of land, Source Q. Permission was refused.

Residue of expenditure brought forward		
(based on accounts to 30 September 2017)		£
Mineral exploration and access	– Source G	170,000
	– Source S	200,000
Mineral assets	– Source G	95,250
	– Source S	72,000

The mineral extraction allowances due for the year ending 30.9.18 are as follows.

Source G	£	£
Mineral exploration and access		
WDV b/f	170,000	
Deduct: Proceeds	175,000	
Balancing charge	£5,000	(5,000)
Mineral assets		
WDV b/f	95,250	
Deduct: Proceeds	80,000	
Balancing allowance	£15,250	15,250
Total allowances		
Source S		
Mineral exploration and access		
WDV b/f	200,000	
WDA 25%	(50,000)	50,000
WDV c/f	£150,000	
Mineral assets		
WDV b/f	72,000	
WDA 10%	(7,200)	7,200
WDV c/f	£64,800	
Source P		
Mineral exploration and access		
Expenditure	150,000	
WDA 25%	(37,500)	37,500
WDA c/f	£112,500	
Mineral assets		
Expenditure	100,000	
WDV 10%	(10,000)	10,000
WDV c/f	£90,000	

Mining works		
Expenditure	50,000	
WDA 25%	(12,500)	12,500
WDV c/f	£37,500	
Source Q		
Mineral exploration and access		
Expenditure	20,000	
WDA 25%	(5,000)	5,000
WDV c/f	£15,000	
Total allowances (net of charges)		£132,450

Notes

(a) Expenditure on the acquisition of mineral assets, which includes expenditure on the acquisition of, or of rights in or over, both the site of a source and of mineral deposits, qualifies for a 10% writing-down allowance. Other types of expenditure qualify for a 25% writing-down allowance. [*CAA 2001, s 418(1)*].

(b) Allowances are not due on either the office or staff hostel. The plant and machinery qualify for plant and machinery allowances under *CAA 2001, Pt 2* rather than for mineral extraction allowances.

(c) Abortive expenditure on seeking planning permission is qualifying expenditure by virtue of *CAA 2001, s 396(2)(3); FA 2014, s 68(2)(4)* as if it were expenditure on mineral exploration and access.

(d) The undeveloped market value of land is excluded from qualifying expenditure and from disposal receipts. [*CAA 2001, ss 404, 424*].

3.4 PATENT RIGHTS

[*CAA 2001, ss 464–483*]

P, who prepares accounts to 31 December, acquires two new patent rights for trading purposes

	Date	Term	Cost
Patent 1	19.4.17	15 years	£4,500
Patent 2	5.10.18	5 years	£8,000

On 1.12.18 P sold part of his rights under patent 1 for £2,000.

3.4 IT Capital Allowances

The allowances for each patent are

	Pool	WDA
Y/e 31.12.17	£	£
Expenditure (patent 1)	4,500	
WDA 25%	(1,125)	£1,125
	3,375	
Y/e 31.12.18		
Expenditure (patent 2)	8,000	
Disposal proceeds (patent 1)	(2,000)	
	9,375	
WDA 25%	(2,344)	£2,344
WDV c/f	£7,031	

3.5 RESEARCH AND DEVELOPMENT

[*CAA 2001, ss 437–451*]

C is in business manufacturing and selling cosmetics, and he prepares accounts annually to 30 June. For the purposes of this trade, he built a new laboratory adjacent to his existing premises, incurring the following expenditure

		£
April 2016	Laboratory building	50,000
June 2016	Technical equipment	3,000
March 2017	Technical equipment	4,000
July 2017	Plant	2,500
August 2018	Extension to existing premises comprising 50% further laboratory area and 50% sales offices	30,000

In September 2017 a small fire destroyed an item of equipment originally costing £2,000 in June 2016; insurance recoveries totalled £3,000. In March 2018, the plant costing £2,500 in July 2017 was sold for £1,800.

The 100 per cent R&D allowances due are

Y/e 30.6.16	£
Laboratory building	50,000
Technical equipment	3,000
	£53,000
Y/e 30.6.17	
Technical equipment	4,000
	£4,000

Y/e 30.6.18	
Net allowance on plant sold (note (a))	£700
Balancing charge on equipment destroyed (note (b))	(£2,000)
Y/e 30.6.19	
Extension (note (d))	£15,000

Notes

(a) As the plant was sold in the period of account in which the expenditure was incurred, the disposal value of £1,800 is set against the expenditure of £2,500, resulting in a net allowance of £700.

(b) The destruction of the equipment in the year to 30 June 2018 results in a balancing charge limited to the allowance given. The charge accrues in the period of account in which the event occurs.

(c) A capital gain of £1,000 (£3,000 – £2,000) will also have arisen on the destruction of equipment and insurance recovery. However, the gain will be exempt from capital gains tax under the chattels exemption. [*TCGA 1992, s 262*].

(d) Capital expenditure which is only partly for research and development is apportioned on a just basis to arrive at the amount qualifying for allowances. [*CAA 2001, s 439(4)*].

4 Capital Allowances on Plant and Machinery

Cross-reference. See also **31** TRADING INCOME — CASH BASIS FOR SMALLER BUSINESSES.

4.1 PERIODS OF ACCOUNT

[*CAA 2001, s 6*]

(A) General

James commenced business on 1 October 2015 preparing accounts initially to 30 September. He changed his accounting date in 2017, preparing accounts for the 15 months to 31 December 2017. The following capital expenditure is incurred

	Plant	Car
	£	£
Year ended 30 September 2016	74,400	4,000 (no private use)
1 October 2016 to 31 December 2017	7,500	
Year ended 31 December 2018	4,000	

An item of plant was sold for £500 (original cost £1,000) on 25 September 2017. All of the expenditure on plant additions is AIA qualifying expenditure. (AIA = Annual Investment Allowance.) The expenditure on the car is not special rate expenditure. James chooses to claim a reduced AIA of £60,000 for the year ended 30 September 2016.

Profits *before* capital allowances but otherwise as adjusted for tax purposes are as follows

	£
Year ended 30 September 2016	96,000
Period ended 31 December 2017	81,000
Year ended 31 December 2018	100,000

4.1 IT Capital Allowances on Plant and Machinery

The capital allowances are

	AIA qualifying expenditure	Main pool	Allowances
	£	£	£
Year ended 30.9.16			
Qualifying expenditure	74,400	4,000	
AIA 100% (note (b))	(60,000)		60,000
Transfer to main pool	(14,400)	14,400	
		18,400	
WDA 18%		(3,312)	3,312
WDV at 30.9.16		15,088	
Total allowances			£63,312
15 months ended 31.12.17			
Additions	7,500	7,500	
AIA 100% (maximum £250,000 — note (c))		(7,500)	7,500
Disposals		(500)	
		14,588	
WDA 18% x 15/12 (note (d))		(3,281)	3,281
WDV at 31.12.17		11,307	
Total allowances			£10,781
Year ended 31.12.18			
Additions	4,000	4,000	
AIA 100% (maximum £200,000)		(4,000)	4,000
		11,307	
WDA 18%		(2,035)	2,035
WDV at 31.12.18		£9,272	
Total allowances			£6,035

Taxable profits for the periods of account concerned are

	Before CAs	CAs	After CAs
	£	£	£
Year ended 30 September 2016	96,000	63,312	32,688
Period ended 31 December 2017	81,000	10,781	70,219
Year ended 31 December 2018	100,000	6,035	93,965

Taxable profits for the first four tax years of the business are

	£	£
2015/16 (1.10.15–5.4.16) (£32,688 × 6/12)		16,344
2016/17 (y/e 30.9.16)		32,688
2017/18 (1.10.16–31.12.17)	70,219	
Deduct Overlap relief £16,344 × 3/6 note (e)	8,172	
		62,047
2018/19 (y/e 31.12.18)		93,965

Notes

(a) Capital allowances are calculated by reference to periods of account and are treated as expenses of the trade or other qualifying activity. [*CAA 2001, ss 2, 6, 247*]. For this purpose, a period of account may exceed 12 months (but cannot exceed 18 months — see (B) below).

(b) The maximum AIA for the twelve-month period of account to 30 September 2016 is £275,000 ((£500,000 x 3/12) + (£200,000 x 9/12)). All of James's qualifying expenditure of £74,400 would attract AIAs but he has chosen to claim only £60,000. The overriding rule, as regards expenditure incurred in the part of the chargeable period falling after 31 December 2015, is that no more than the appropriate proportion (9/12 in this case) of £200,000 can qualify for the AIA.

(c) The maximum AIA for the 15-month period of account to 31 December 2017 is £250,000 (£200,000 x 15/12).

(d) Where a period of account exceeds 12 months as is the case with the 15-month period to 31 December 2017 in this example, both the maximum AIA and the WDAs are proportionately increased. [*CAA 2001, ss 51A(6), 56(3)*].

(e) The overlap profit is £16,344 being the profit taxed twice under the commencement rules. This represents 6 months' profit (1 October 2015 to 5 April 2016). As the basis period for 2017/18 is 3 months greater than one year, 3/6 of the overlap profit is relieved in that year, the balance being carried forward. For further examples on the basis of assessment for businesses see **30.1–30.3** TRADING INCOME.

(B) **Period of account exceeding 18 months**

Anastasia commenced business on 1 October 2015 preparing accounts initially to 30 June. She changed her accounting date in 2017/18, preparing accounts for the 21 months to 31 March 2018. The following capital expenditure was incurred

	Plant	Motor Car
	£	£
9 months to 30 June 2016	60,000	20,000 (no private use)
21 months to 31 March 2018	10,600	
Year ended 31 March 2019	8,000	

4.1 IT Capital Allowances on Plant and Machinery

Of the £10,600 of expenditure incurred in the 21-month period of account to 31 March 2018, £3,600 was incurred in January 2017 and £7,000 in the nine months to 31 March 2018. Apart from the car, all expenditure is AIA qualifying expenditure. The expenditure on the car is special rate expenditure. Anastasia chooses to claim a reduced AIA of £48,000 for the nine-month period to 30 June 2016.

An item of plant was sold for £512 (original cost £1,100) on 3 November 2017.

Profits *before* capital allowances but otherwise as adjusted for tax purposes are as follows

	£
Period ended 30 June 2016	64,000
Period ended 31 March 2018	112,000
Year ended 31 March 2019	85,000

The capital allowances are

	AIA qualifying expenditure	Main pool	Car	Total allow-ances
	£	£	£	£
9 months ended 30.6.16				
Qualifying expenditure	60,000		20,000	
AIA (note (d))	(48,000)			48,000
	12,000			
Transfer to main pool	(12,000)	12,000		
WDA 18% ×9/12 (note (e))		(1,620)		1,620
WDA 8% × 9/12 (note (e))			(1,200)	1,200
WDV at 30.6.16		10,380	18,800	
Total allowances				£50,820
12 months ended 30.6.17				
Additions	3,600			
AIA 100% (note (d))	(3,600)			3,600
WDA 18%		(1,868)		1,868
WDA 8%			(1,504)	1,504
WDV at 30.6.17		8,512	17,296	
Total allowances				£6,972
9 months ended 31.3.18				
Additions	7,000			
AIA 100% (note (d))	(7,000)			7,000
Disposals		(512)		
		8,000		
WDA 18% × 9/12		(1,080)		1,080
WDA 8% × 9/12			(1,038)	1,038

	AIA qualifying expenditure	Main pool	Car	Total allowances
	£	£	£	£
WDV at 31.3.18		£6,920	£16,258	
Total allowances				£9,118
Year ended 31.3.19				
Additions	8,000			
AIA 100% (note (d))	(8,000)			8,000
WDA 18%		(1,246)		£1,246
WDA 8%			(1,301)	£1,301
WDV at 31.3.19		£5,674	£14,957	
Total allowances				£10,547

Taxable profits for the periods of account concerned are

	Before CAs	CAs	After CAs
	£	£	£
Period ended 30 June 2016	64,000	50,820	13,180
Period ended 31 March 2018	112,000	(6,972 + 9,118)	95,910
Year ended 31 March 2019	85,000	10,547	74,453

Taxable profits for the first four tax years of the business are

	£	£
2015/16 (1.10.15 − 5.4.16) (£13,180 × 6/9)		8,786
2016/17 (1.10.15 − 30.9.16):		
1.10.15 − 30.6.16	13,180	
1.7.16 − 30.9.16 (£95,910 × 3/21)	13,701	
		26,881
2017/18 (1.10.16 − 31.3.18) (£95,910 × 18/21)	82,209	
Deduct Overlap relief (note (f))	(8,786)	
		73,423
2018/19 (1.04.18 − 31.03.19)		74,453

Notes

(a) Where a period of account for capital allowances purposes would otherwise exceed 18 months, it is broken down into shorter periods, the first beginning on the first day of the actual period and each subsequent period beginning on an anniversary of the first day of the actual period. No period can therefore exceed 12 months. [*CAA 2001, s 6(6)*].

(b) The capital allowances computed for the notional periods of account referred to in (*a*) above are deductible in aggregate in arriving at the adjusted profit for the actual period of account.

(c) A period of account exceeding 18 months cannot normally result in an immediate change of basis period, because of *ITTOIA 2005, ss 216, 217(1)(3)*. However, the conditions of *ITTOIA 2005, s 217* do not have to be satisfied if the change of accounting period occurs in the second or third tax year of a new business, as in this example.

(d) The maximum AIA for the nine-month period of account ended 30 June 2016 is £225,000 ((£500,000 x 3/12) + (£200,000 x 6/12)). All of Anastasia's qualifying expenditure of £60,000 would attract AIAs but she has chosen to claim only £48,000. The overriding rule, as regards expenditure incurred in the part of the period falling after 31 December 2015, is that no more than the appropriate proportion of £200,000 (6/12 in this case) can qualify for the AIA.

The maximum AIA for the notional twelve-month period of account ended 30 June 2017 is £200,000.

The maximum AIA for the notional nine-month period of account ended 31 March 2018 is £150,000 (£200,000 x 9/12).

(e) Where the period of account is less than 12 months, WDAs are proportionately reduced. [*CAA 2001, s 56(3)*].

(f) In this example, the overlap profit is £8,786 being the profit taxed twice under the commencement rules. This represents 6 months' profit (1 October 2015 to 5 April 2016). As the basis period for 2017/18 is 6 months greater than one year, the whole of the overlap profit is relieved in that year. For further examples on the basis of assessment for businesses, including commencement and cessation rules, overlap relief and changes of accounting date, see **30.1–30.3** TRADING INCOME.

4.2 SUCCESSIONS

[*CAA 2001, ss 265–267, 268, 559*]

Michael, who had been in business for a number of years, decided to retire, and he transferred the business, as a gift, to his son, Alec, on 1 May 2018. Accounts, prepared by both Michael and Alec to 30 April annually, reveal the following expenditure on, and proceeds of, plant and machinery.

	Expenditure	(Disposal Proceeds)
	£	£
Michael		
Period 1.5.17 – 30.4.18	7,200	–
Alec		
Period 1.5.18 – 30.4.19	5,000	(600)

The plant and machinery disposed of by Alec was an item transferred to him by Michael. The market value of plant and machinery at 1.5.18 totalled £18,000. In no case did an item's market value exceed its cost. The written-down value brought forward at 1.5.17 was £10,000.

The capital allowances are as follows.

(i) **No election under CAA 2001, s 266**

	AIA qualifying expenditure	Main pool	Total allowances
	£	£	£
Michael			
Period of account y/e 30.4.18			
WDV b/f at 1.5.17		10,000	
Additions		7,200	
Disposals (at market value)		(18,000)	
		(800)	
Balancing charge		800	£(800)
Alec			
Period of account y/e 30.4.19			
Additions qualifying for AIA	5,000		
AIA 100%	(5,000)	—	5,000
Other additions		18,000	
Disposals		(600)	
		17,400	
WDA 18%		(3,132)	3,132
WDV at 30.4.19		£14,268	
Total allowances			£8,132

Note

(a) If no election is made under *CAA 2001, s 266* (see (ii) below), plant and machinery is treated as sold by the predecessor to the successor at market value, but no annual investment allowance is due to Alec on the assets transferred. [*CAA 2001, s 265*]. Similar rules apply for other assets. [*CAA 2001, s 559*]. No annual investment allowance is due for expenditure incurred in the period of account at the end of which Michael permanently ceases to carry on the trade. [*CAA 2001, ss 38B, 46(2)*].

(ii) **Election under CAA 2001, s 266**

	AIA qualifying expenditure	Main pool	Total allowances
	£	£	£
Michael			
Period of account y/e 30.4.18			
WDV b/f at 1.5.17		10,000	
Additions		7,200	
Disposals (at written-down value)		(17,200)	
Balancing allowance/charge		Nil	Nil
Alec			
Period of account y/e 30.4.19			
Additions qualifying for AIA	5,000		
AIA 100%	(5,000)	—	5,000
Other additions		17,200	
Disposals		(600)	
		16,600	
WDA 18%		(2,988)	2,988
WDV at 30.4.19		£13,612	
Total allowances			£7,988

Notes

(a) Under *CAA 2001, s 267*, plant and machinery passing to the successor is deemed to have been sold by the predecessor to the successor at such a price as to leave no balancing allowance or balancing charge. An election must be made (under *CAA 2001, s 266*) for these provisions to apply.

(b) An election under *CAA 2001, s 266* may be made only between connected persons, as defined by *section 266(5)*, must be made jointly by predecessor and successor and must be made within two years of the succession, i.e. by 1 May 2020 in this example.

(c) Annual investment allowances are not available to the successor on plant and machinery transferred under a *CAA 2001, s 266* election (by virtue of *CAA 2001, ss 214, 217*).

(d) For certain assets other than plant and machinery, a similar election is available under *CAA 2001, s 569* for certain transfers between connected persons.

4.3 POOLING, ANNUAL INVESTMENT ALLOWANCE, WRITING-DOWN ALLOWANCES, CARS, PARTIAL NON-BUSINESS USE, ACQUISITIONS FROM CONNECTED PERSONS AND BALANCING ADJUSTMENTS

A has for some years been in business as a builder and demolition contractor. He makes up his accounts to 31 March. The accounts for the year to 31 March 2019 reveal the following additions and disposals.

	£
Additions	
Plant	
Wagon	30,000
Concrete mixer	45,000
Excavator 1	32,000
Excavator 2	50,000
Dumper Truck	5,000
Bulldozer	20,000
Fittings	
Office furniture and equipment	52,000
Motor Vehicles	
Van	7,000
Car 2	21,000
Car 3	2,000
Car 4	15,000

Disposals	Cost	Proceeds
	£	£
Excavator 1	32,000	30,000
Digger loader	15,000	4,000
Car 1	14,200	3,600
Fittings	3,500	500

The dumper truck was bought second-hand from Q, brother of A, but had not been used in a trade or other qualifying activity. The truck had originally cost Q £6,000, but its market value at sale was only £2,000.

Excavator 1 was sold without having been brought into use.

The bulldozer and Car 3 were both purchased from P, father of A and had originally cost P £25,000 and £3,500 respectively. Both assets had been used for the purposes of a qualifying activity. In both cases the price paid by A was less than the market value.

Car 1 sold and the new Car 2 are both used for private motoring by A. Private use has always been 30%. Car 2 has CO_2 emissions of over 110g/km. Car 3 is occasionally borrowed by A's daughter, and the private use proportion is 20%. Car 3 has CO_2 emissions of less than 110g/km.

4.3 IT Capital Allowances on Plant and Machinery

Car 4 was purchased new and unused on 1 July 2018 and is used for business purposes only. It is a car with low CO_2 emissions and qualifies for 100% first-year allowances under *CAA 2001, s 45D.*

The written-down values at 1 April 2018 of the main plant and machinery pool and Car 1 are £80,500 and £3,225 respectively.

The capital allowances for 12-month period of account to 31.3.19 are as follows

	Expenditurequalifying for AIA	Main pool	Car 1 partial use pool	Car 2 partial use pool	Car 3 partial use pool	Total allowances
	£	£	£	£	£	£
WDV b/f		80,500	3,225			
Additions						
Wagon	30,000	30,000				
Concrete mixer	45,000	45,000				
Excavator 1 (note (a))	32,000	32,000				
Excavator 2	50,000	50,000				
Dumper truck (notes (b)(c)(d))		2,000				
Bulldozer (notes (b)(d)(e))		20,000				
Furniture	52,000	52,000				
Van	7,000	7,000				
Cars	£216,000			21,000	2,000	
Car 4	15,000					
FYA 100%	15,000					15,000
AIA (100% on £200,000)		(200,000)				200,000
Disposals						
Excavator		(30,000)				
Digger		(4,000)				
Fittings		(500)				
Car 1			(3,600)			
		84,000	(£375)	21,000	2,000	
WDA (18%)		(15,120)			(360)	15,480
WDA (8%)				(1,680)		1,680
Private use restriction:						
Car 2 — £1,680 @ 30%						(504)
Car 3 — £360 @ 20%						(72)
WDV c/f		£68,880		£19,320	£1,640	
Total allowances						£231,584
Balancing charge (Car 1) £375 less 30% private use						£263

Notes

(a) The annual investment allowance (AIA) and writing-down allowances are available even though an item of plant or machinery is disposed of without being brought into use, always provided that the expenditure is, respectively, AIA qualifying expenditure and general qualifying expenditure.

(b) If an AIA is made in respect of an amount of AIA qualifying expenditure, the expenditure is nevertheless added to the appropriate pool (or pools). Such allocation is necessary to enable a disposal value to be properly brought into account when a disposal event occurs in relation to the item in question. Following the allocation, the available qualifying expenditure in the pool (or in each pool) is reduced by the amount of the AIA on the expenditure allocated. [*CAA 2001, s 58(4A)*]. It follows that any excess of the AIA qualifying expenditure over the AIA made will qualify for WDAs beginning with the chargeable period in which the expenditure is incurred.

(c) No AIA is available in respect of an item of plant or machinery purchased from a connected person (within *CAA 2001, s 575*). [*CAA 2001, ss 213, 214, 217*].

(d) Qualifying expenditure (and AIA qualifying expenditure) on the dumper truck is restricted to the lowest of

(i) market value;

(ii) capital expenditure incurred by the vendor (or, if lower, by a person connected with him);

(iii) capital expenditure incurred by the purchaser.

[*CAA 2001, ss 213, 214, 218(3)*].

(e) Qualifying expenditure on the bulldozer is the lesser of A's actual expenditure and the disposal value brought into account in the vendor's computations. [*CAA 2001, ss 213, 214, 218(2)*]. (The vendor's disposal value would have been market value but for the fact that the purchaser is himself entitled to claim capital allowances on the acquisition. [*CAA 2001, s 61(2)(4)*].) A's qualifying expenditure is thus equal to his actual expenditure. The same applies to the purchase of Car 3.

(f) Cars 2 and 3 are allocated to separate single asset pools by virtue their being partly used for non-business purposes. [*CAA 2001, s 206*]. Car 2 qualifies for writing-down allowances at the special rate of 8% because of its CO_2 emissions level. [*CAA 2001, ss 104A, 104AA; FA 2009, Sch 11 paras 7, 8, 26–28; FA 2013, s 68(3)(6)(8)*]. See note (e) above as regards the amount of qualifying expenditure to be brought into account in respect of Car 3. Car 4 qualifies for 100% first-year allowances under *CAA 2001, s 45D*; if the full 100% had not been claimed, the balance of the expenditure would have entered the main pool.

4.4 SHORT-LIFE ASSETS

[*CAA 2001, ss 83–89*]

A prepares trading accounts to 30 September each year and buys and sells machines for use in the trade as follows

4.4 IT Capital Allowances on Plant and Machinery

	Cost	Date of acquisition	Disposal proceeds	Date of disposal
Machine X	£40,000	30.4.10	£13,000	1.12.11
Machine Y	£25,000	1.9.10	£3,000	1.12.17
Machine Z	£35,000	15.12.17	N/A	N/A

A elects under *CAA 2001, s 83* for these machines to be treated as short-life assets. It is assumed for the purposes of the example that no annual investment allowance is claimed for any of the expenditure. His pool of qualifying expenditure brought forward at the beginning of period of account 1.10.09–30.9.10 is £80,000.

A's capital allowances are as follows

	Main pool	Short-life asset pools		Total allowances
		Machine X	Machine Y	
	£	£	£	£
Period of account 1.10.09–30.9.10				
WDV b/f	80,000			
Additions		40,000	25,000	
WDA 20%	(16,000)	(8,000)	(5,000)	£29,000
	64,000	32,000	20,000	
Period of account 1.10.10–30.9.11				
WDA 20%	(12,800)	(6,400)	(4,000)	£23,200
	51,200	25,600	16,000	
Period of account 1.10.11–30.9.12				
Disposal		(13,000)		
Balancing allowance		£12,600		12,600
WDA 19.03% (note (e))	(9,743)		(3,045)	12,788
				£25,388
	41,457		12,955	
Period of account 1.10.12–30.9.13				
WDA 18%	(7,462)		(2,332)	£9,794
	33,995		10,623	
Period of account 1.10.13–30.9.14				
WDA 18%	(6,119)		(1,912)	£8,031
	27,876		8,711	

Period of account 1.10.14–30.9.15				
Transfer to main pool	8,711		(8,711)	
	36,587			
WDA 18%	(6,586)			£6,586
	30,001			
Period of account 1.10.15–30.9.16				
WDA 18%	(5,400)			5,400
	24,601			
Period of account 1.10.16–30.9.17				
WDA 18%	(4,428)			4,428
	20,173			
Period of account 1.10.17–30.9.18				
Disposal	(3,000)			
	17,173			
		Machine Z		
Addition		35,000		
WDA 18%	(3,091)	(6,300)		£9,391
WDV c/f	£14,082	£28,700		

Notes

(a) Only plant and machinery which is not specified in *CAA 2001, s 84* is eligible to be treated as short-life assets.

(b) Where separate identification of short-life assets is impracticable, a form of pooling may be adopted (HMRC Statement of Practice SP 1/86).

(c) The fourth anniversary of the end of the chargeable period in which the expenditure on the first two machines is incurred is 30.9.14 (the cut-off date). The balance of expenditure on Machine Y is thus transferred to the main pool in the period of account 1.10.14–30.9.15, this being the first chargeable period ending after the cut-off date. [*CAA 2001, s 86(2)(3)*].

(d) The expenditure on Machine Z is incurred after 5 April 2011, so an eight-year cut-off applies. [*FA 2011, s 12*]. If the machine is not disposed of in the meantime, the balance of expenditure will be transferred to the main pool in the period of account 1.10.26–30.9.27.

(e) The hybrid rate of writing-down allowance for the year to 30 September 2012 is 19.03%, computed as follows (where 188 is the number of days from 1 October 2011 to 5 April 2012, 178 is the number of days from 6 April 2012 to 30 September 2012 and 366 is the total number of days in the period of account).

$$R = \left(20 \times \frac{188}{366}\right) + \left(18 \times \frac{178}{366}\right) = \qquad 19.03\%$$

4.5 LONG-LIFE ASSETS AND SPECIAL RATE POOL

[*CAA 2001, ss 90–104, 104A–104E*]

B prepares trading accounts to 31 December. In the year to 31 December 2007, he has new factory premises built for use in his trade, which include a building mainly in use as offices (on which 20% of the cost of the premises is expended). The main plant and machinery pool written-down value at 1 January 2007 is £800,000, and the disposal value brought into account in respect of plant and machinery in B's previous premises is £720,000. Machines installed in the new factory cost £920,000. No first-year allowances were available.

B also claims, for the year to 31 December 2007, plant and machinery allowances for expenditure of £520,000 incurred on fixtures integral to the new premises, which are agreed to have an expected life in excess of 25 years. Of this expenditure, it is agreed £120,000 should be apportioned to the offices.

On 1 May 2008 B incurs additional expenditure on upgrading the fixtures of £19,000, none of it relating to office fixtures.

On 1 May 2018 he moves to new premises, disposing of the old premises for a consideration including £425,000 relating to the integral fixtures (of which £95,000 relates to the office fixtures) and £510,000 relating to other plant and machinery.

Plant and machinery in the new premises costs £1,460,000, of which £180,000 is agreed to be long-life asset expenditure and £620,000 relates to integral features as defined by *CAA 2001, s 33A*. The full £1,460,000 is AIA (annual investment allowance) qualifying expenditure.

The plant and machinery allowances computations for relevant periods are as follows

	Main pool	Long-life asset pool	Special rate pool	Total allow-ances
	£	£	£	
Year ending 31.12.07				
WDV b/f	800,000	—		
Additions (see note (b))	1,040,000	400,000		
Disposals	(720,000)			
	1,120,000	400,000		
WDA 25%/6%	280,000	24,000		304,000
WDV c/f	840,000	376,000		
Year ending 31.12.08				
Addition (see note (c))		19,000		
	840,000	395,000		
WDA (see note (f))	179,004	35,353		214,357
	660,996	359,647		
Transfer to special rate pool		359,647	359,647	
WDV c/f	660,996	—	359,647	
b/f	660,996		359,647	
Year ending 31.12.09				
WDA 20%/10%	132,199		35,965	168,164
WDV c/f	528,797		323,682	
Years 2010 to 2017 inclusive				
WDA	426,578		165,605	592,183
WDV c/f at 31.12.17	102,219		158,077	
Year ending 31.12.18				
Additions	660,000		800,000	
	762,219		958,077	
AIA 100% (see note (e))			200,000	200,000
			758,077	
Disposals	(605,000)		(330,000)	
	157,219		428,077	
WDA 18%/8%	28,300		34,246	62,546
				£262,546
WDV c/f at 31.12.18	£128,919		£393,831	

Notes

(a) Long-life asset expenditure incurred on or before 5 April 2008 was allocated to a class pool known as the long-life asset pool. Long-life asset expenditure incurred thereafter is allocated to the special rate pool in *CAA 2001, s 104C*.

(b) Expenditure on fixtures provided for use in offices is excluded from being on long-life assets. (Such expenditure is nevertheless special rate expenditure if it relates to integral features as defined by *CAA 2001, s 33A*.)

(c) Additional expenditure on existing long-life assets is within the provisions even if within the annual £100,000 *de minimis* limit.

(d) The balance of the long-life asset pool at the end of the period of account straddling 5 April 2008 is transferred to the special rate pool, and the long-life asset pool ceases to exist. [*FA 2008, s 83(4), (5)*].

(e) The maximum AIA of £200,000 has been allocated to special rate expenditure as this maximises the WDA available in subsequent years.

(f) The WDAs in the main pool and long-asset pool are at a hybrid rate for periods of account straddling 5 April 2008, calculated as follows.

Main pool (where 96 is the number of days from 1 January 2008 to 5 April 2008, 270 is the number of days from 6 April 2008 to 31 December 2008 and 366 is the total number of days in the period of account)

$$R = \left(25 \times \frac{96}{366}\right) + \left(20 \times \frac{270}{366}\right) = 21.31\%$$

[*FA 2008, s 80(9)–(12)*].

Long-life asset pool

$$R = \left(6 \times \frac{96}{366}\right) + \left(10 \times \frac{270}{366}\right) = 8.95\%$$

[*FA 2008, s 83(1)–(3)*].

4.6 ANNUAL INVESTMENT ALLOWANCE — PERIODS STRADDLING 1 JANUARY 2016

[*CAA 2001, ss 38A, 38B, 51A; FA 2014, s 10, Sch 2 para 4; F(No 2)A 2015, s 8*].

Olga is a trader making up accounts to 30 April each year. For the year ended 30 April 2016, she incurs expenditure of £400,000 on plant and machinery. £80,000 of this amount was incurred after 31 December 2015. All the expenditure is AIA qualifying expenditure.

Olga's maximum annual investment allowance for the year ended 30 April 2016 is computed as follows

Period 1.5.15 to 31.12.15 (245 days)

$\text{Maximum£}500,000 \times \frac{245}{366}$	334,700

Period 1.1.16 to 30.4.16 (121 days)

$\text{Maximum£}200,000 \times \frac{121}{366}$	66,120
Maximum qualifying for AIAs for the year	£400,820

Further adjustment

However, there is an overriding rule, as regards expenditure incurred in the part of the period of account falling after 31 December 2015, that no more than the appropriate proportion of £200,000 can qualify for the AIA. The appropriate proportion is the figure of 66,120 above.

Therefore, of the expenditure of £80,000 in the period 1.1.16 to 30.4.16, only £66,120 qualifies. The remaining expenditure of £320,000 qualifies in full, as the resulting maximum AIA for the year of £386,120 (320,000 + 66,120) is within the overall maximum of £400,820.

If the total expenditure of £400,000 had been split as to £335,000 incurred before 1 January 2016 and £65,000 thereafter, the overriding rule would not have come into play and the whole expenditure would have qualified for AIAs.

4.7 VAT CAPITAL GOODS SCHEME

[*CAA 2001, ss 234–246, 546–551*]

T Ltd carries on a trade which is partially exempt for VAT purposes, and draws up accounts to 31 March each year. Its partial exemption year also runs to 31 March. On 1 May 2015, the company acquired computer equipment at a cost of £340,000 plus VAT of £68,000. The company had a written-down value of £143,000 on its plant and machinery main pool at 1 April 2015 and, for the purposes of this example, it is assumed that there are no other acquisitions and no disposals during the period covered.

T Ltd's claimable percentage of non-attributable input tax for the partial exemption years ended 31 March 2016, 2017, 2018 and 2019 is as follows

Year ended	
31.3.16	75%
31.3.17	80%
31.3.18	65%
31.3.19	65%

4.7 IT Capital Allowances on Plant and Machinery

The input tax position is as follows

	Computer
Year ended 31.3.16	
Initial input tax claim:	
£68,000 × 75%	£51,000
Year ended 31.3.17	
Additional VAT rebate:	
$\frac{68,000}{5} \times (80-75)\%$	£680
Year ended 31.3.18	
Additional VAT liability:	
$\frac{68,000}{5} \times (75-65)\%$	£1,360
Year ended 31.3.19	
Additional VAT liability:	
$\frac{68,000}{5} \times (75-65)\%$	£1,360

T Ltd deals with the appropriate VAT capital goods scheme adjustments in its quarterly VAT return to 30 September following each partial exemption year.

The capital allowances computations are as follows

Plant and machinery

	Qualifying for AIAs	Main pool	Total allowances
	£	£	£
Year to 31.3.16			
WDV at 1.4.15		143,000	
Addition (£340,000 + £(68,000 – 51,000))	357,000		
AIA 100% (maximum £425,000)	(357,000)		357,000
WDA 18%		(25,740)	25,740
			£382,740
		117,260	
Year to 31.3.17			
WDA 18%		(21,107)	£21,107
		96,153	
Year to 31.3.18			
Disposal value		(680)	

Plant and machinery			
		95,473	
WDA 18%		(17,185)	£17,185
		c/f 78,288	
		b/f 78,288	
Year to 31.3.19			
Addition	1,360		
AIA 100%	(1,360)	—	1,360
WDA 18%		(14,092)	14,092
		64,196	
			£51,452
Year to 31.3.20			
Addition	1,360		
AIA 100%	(1,360)	—	1,360
WDA 18%		(11,555)	11,555
WDV at 31.3.20		£52,641	
			£12,915

Notes

(a) For the purpose of determining the chargeable period in which capital allowances are to be adjusted by reference to any additional VAT rebate/liability, the rebate/liability is treated as accruing on the last day of the VAT return period in which the adjustment is made (i.e. the return for the quarter to 30 September in the chargeable period). [*CAA 2001, s 549*].

(b) Where expenditure was AIA qualifying expenditure (i.e. it qualified for the annual investment allowance), any additional VAT liability incurred in respect of that expenditure at a time when the plant or machinery is provided for the purposes of the qualifying activity, is also AIA qualifying expenditure — for the chargeable period in which the liability accrues. [*CAA 2001, s 236(3A)–(3C)*].

5 Charities

5.1 DONATIONS TO CHARITY

[*ITA 2007, ss 414, 415, 423–425; FA 2016, Sch 1 paras 63(4), 73*]

(A) Higher rate taxpayer

Ronan has total income of £47,775 for 2018/19, which consists entirely of employment income. During that year, he makes a number of payments to charity, all of them qualifying donations, amounting in total to £600. Ronan is not a Scottish taxpayer.

Ronan's income tax liability for 2018/19 is as follows

			£
Total and net income			47,775
Less Personal allowance			11,850
Taxable income			£35,925
Tax liability			
	35,250	at 20%	7,050.00
	675	at 40%	270.00
	£35,925		£7,320.00

Notes

(a) The basic rate limit of £34,500 is increased by the grossed up amount of the qualifying donations (£600 × 100/80 = £750) and becomes £35,250. Ronan thereby saves tax of £150 (£750 × 20% (40% − 20%)). The charities will reclaim basic rate tax of £150 (£750 × 20%) and will thus receive £750 in all. The net cost to Ronan is £450 (£600 − £150), a saving of 40%. (The tax relief can, in fact, exceed 40% where the effect of extending the basic rate limit is that an additional amount of dividend income falls within the basic rate band and is taxed at 7.5% instead of at 32.5% (see (B) below).

(b) Gift aid donations may, by election, be treated as made in the preceding year of assessment. The election must be made on or before the date the donor submits his tax return for that preceding year and not later than 31 January following that year. An election cannot be made if insufficient income tax or capital gains tax was payable for the preceding year to cover the tax deducted from the payment. [*ITA 2007, ss 426, 427*].

(B) Higher rate taxpayer with dividend income

The facts are as in (A) above except that £7,000 of Ronan's income is dividend income.

Ronan's income tax liability for 2018/19 is as follows

	£
Employment income	40,775
Dividend income	7,000
Total and net income	47,775
Less Personal allowance	11,850
Taxable income	£35,925

Tax liability			
	28,925	at 20%	5,785.00
	2,000	at 0% (dividend nil rate)	—
	4,325	at 7.5% (dividend ordinary rate)	324.37
	35,250		
	675	at 32.5%	219.37
	£35,925		£.6,328.74

Note

(a) As in (A) above, the basic rate limit (£34,500) is increased by the grossed up amount of the qualifying donations (£750) and thus becomes £35,250. But this time the tax saving is £187.50; this reflects the fact that the donation has the effect of pushing £750 of dividend income back into the basic rate band, a saving of 25% (32.5% − 7.5%) instead of the usual 20% (40% − 20%). Ronan's relief at source is still £150 (£750 − £600). His total relief is thus £337.50 which gives him total relief of 45% (not 40%) on the grossed up amount of the gift (£750).

(C) Additional rate taxpayer

Rikki has total income of £175,000 for 2018/19, none of which is dividend income. During that year, he makes qualifying donations to charity of £2,400. Rikki is not a Scottish taxpayer.

Rikki's income tax liability for 2018/19 is as follows

	£
Total and net income	175,000
Less Personal allowance (note (b))	Nil
Taxable income	£175,000

Tax liability		
37,500	at 20%	7,500.00
115,500	at 40%	46,200.00
22,000	at 45%	9,900.00
£175,000		£63,600.00

Notes

(a) Both the basic rate limit of £34,500 and the higher rate limit of £150,000 are increased by the grossed up amount of the qualifying donations (£2,400 × 100/80 = £3,000) and become £37,500 and £153,000 respectively. Rikki thereby saves tax of £750 (£3,000 × 25% (45% – 20%)). [*ITA 2007, s 414(2)(b)*]. The charities will reclaim basic rate tax of £600 (£3,000 × 20%) and will thus receive £3,000 in all. The net cost to Rikki is £1,650 (£2,400 – £750), a saving of 45%.

(b) No personal allowance is available in this example as income is too far above the £100,000 income limit. [*ITA 2007, s 35*].

(D) Low income taxpayer

Rod, a single person, has a State pension of £10,200 and UK dividends of £2,000. He makes a qualifying donation of £400 to charity. Rod is not a Scottish taxpayer.

Rod's income tax liability for 2018/19 is as follows

		£
Pension income		10,200
Dividends		2,000
Total and net income		12,200
Less Personal allowance	11,850	
Restricted by (see note (a))	2,150	(9,700)
Taxable income		£2,500

Tax liability		
£500	at 20% (basic rate)	100.00
£2,000	at 0% (dividend nil rate)	—
		£100.00

Note

(a) The personal allowance is restricted by such amount as is necessary to leave tax of £100.00 in charge.

6 Compensation for Loss of Employment

6.1 TAXATION OF POST-EMPLOYMENT NOTICE PAY

[*ITEPA 2003, ss 402, 402A–402E, 403, 404, 415, 416; F(No 2)A 2017, s 5(3)–(5)(10)*].

Yujin is a monthly-paid employee on a salary of £66,000 per annum (£5,500 per month). On 10 April 2018 her employment is terminated. She is given three months notice as required by her employment contract, and it is agreed that she will receive a £35,000 termination payment. On 1 May 2018 the employer asks her to leave immediately and pays her a PILON (payment in lieu of notice) of £12,200, which was not required under the terms of her contract. It is assumed for the purposes of the example that Yujin is not entitled to a statutory redundancy payment.

'*Post-employment notice pay*' is given by the formula:

$$\left(\frac{BP \times D}{P}\right) - T$$

where:

BP	=	the employee's basic pay (as defined) from the employment in respect of the last pay period to end before the trigger date (as defined);
P	=	the number of days in that pay period;
D	=	the number of days in the post-employment notice period (as defined); and
T	=	the total amount of any payments or benefits received in connection with the termination which are already taxable as earnings apart from these provisions, but excluding bonuses and holiday entitlement pay for a period before the employment ends. The purpose of deducting T in the formula is to avoid any double charge.

Applying the formula to Yujin's circumstances:

BP	=	£5,500 (Yujin's basic pay for the last monthly pay period ended before 10 April 2018 (the trigger date)
P	=	31 (the number of days in that pay period)
D	=	69 (the number of days in the post-employment notice period, which runs from 2 May to 9 July 2018 inclusive)
T	=	Nil

		£
Post-employment notice pay	$\left(\frac{5,500 \times 69}{31}\right) - 0$	£12,241

The post-employment notice pay of £12,241 is less than the total termination awards of £47,200. Therefore, £12,241 is treated as taken out of the special provisions for termination payments (*ITEPA 2003, s 403*) and into the charge on general earnings. The balance of the termination awards is £34,959, and this is taxable under the special provisions for termination payments and thus subject to an exemption for the first £30,000. Therefore, £12,241 is taxable as earnings and £4,959 under the special provisions.

Notes

(a) The income tax treatment of termination payments is amended with effect for 2018/19 onwards. Whether or not they are entitled to a contractual payment in lieu of notice, employees pay tax on the amount of basic pay that they would have received had they worked their notice in full.

(b) If the post-employment notice pay had equalled or exceeded the total termination awards, the full amount of the termination awards would have been treated as taken out of the special provisions for termination payments and into the charge on general earnings. The exemption for the first £30,000 would not have been available at all. For these purposes, a termination award does not include a statutory redundancy payment.

(c) An amount of payments and benefits within the charge to income tax under the special provisions for termination payments (or that would be in the charge were it not for the £30,000 exemption) is not currently subject to either employer or employee national insurance contributions (NICs). For 2019/20 onwards, under legislation to be included in a 2018 National Insurance Contributions Bill, any excess over the £30,000 threshold will be liable to employer Class 1A NICs (but the exemption for employer NICs on the first £30,000 will remain in place, as will the exemption for employee NICs on the full amount). For 2017/18 onwards, any amount of post-employment notice pay treated as taken out of the special provisions and into the charge on general earnings is thereby subject to employer and employee Class 1 NICs. See www.gov.uk/government/publications/autumn-budget-2017-overview-of-tax-legislation-and-rates-ootlar/autumn-budget-2017-overview-of-tax-legislation-and-rates-ootlar at para 2.13.

7 Deceased Estates

[*ITTOIA 2005, ss 649–680A, 681, 682*]

7.1 ESTATE INCOME: ABSOLUTE INTEREST

C died on 5 July 2016 leaving his estate of £400,000 divisible equally between his three children. The income arising and administration expenses paid in the administration period which ends on 25 January 2019 are as follows

	Period to 5.4.17		*Year to 5.4.18*		*Period to 25.1.19*	
	£	£	£	£	£	£
UK dividends		16,875		9,900		3,720
Dividend ordinary tax thereon payable by personal representatives		(1,266)		(743)		(279)
		15,609		9,157		3,441
Administration expenses chargeable to income		(1,500)		(750)		(366)
		14,109		8,407		3,075
Other income (gross)	10,000		3,200		975	
Basic rate tax thereon payable by personal representatives	(2,000)		(640)		(195)	
		8,000		2,560		780
Net residuary income		£22,109		£10,967		£3,855
Each child's share		£7,370		£3,656		£1,285

Dates and amounts of payments to each child are as follows

	Payment
	£
30.4.17	5,000
16.10.17	3,500
21.6.18	2,500
22.1.19	1,000
30.7.19	311

Each child's assumed income entitlement is as follows

	2016/17	2017/18	2018/19
	£	£	£
Cumulative income entitlement (net)	7,370	11,026	12,311
Deduct net equivalents of amounts			
taxed in previous years	Nil	Nil	8,500
Assumed income entitlement	£7,370	£11,026	£3,811

For all years other than the final tax year (i.e. the year in which the administration period ends), compare the assumed income entitlement with the payments made.

	2016/17	2017/18
Assumed income entitlement	£7,370	£11,026
Payments made	Nil	£8,500
Lower amount is the taxable amount		
(subject to grossing up)	Nil	£8,500

For the final tax year (2018/19), the taxable amount (subject to grossing up) is the amount of the assumed income entitlement (£3,811).

The children's income from the estate for tax purposes is as follows

	2016/17	2017/18	2018/19
Each child's share of income (net)	Nil	£8,500	£3,811
Each child's share of basic rate income	Nil	3,520*	260
Basic rate tax	Nil	880	65
Grossed up basic rate income	Nil	£4,400	£325
* £(8,000 + 2,560) × $^1/_3$ = £3,520.			
Each child's share of dividend income	Nil	4,980	3,551
Dividend ordinary rate tax (7.5/92.5)	Nil	404	288
Gross dividend income	Nil	£5,384	£3,839

Notes

(a) A beneficiary with an absolute interest is chargeable to income tax on income treated as arising in a tax year from the interest if he has an 'assumed income entitlement' (see *ITTOIA 2005, s 665)* for the year and a payment is made in respect of the interest in the year and before the end of the administration period. For the year in which the administration period ends (the '*final tax year*'), income is treated as arising if the beneficiary has an assumed income entitlement for the year (whether or not any payments are made). [*ITTOIA 2005, s 652*].

(b) Payments to a beneficiary of an estate are deemed to be made out of his share of income bearing tax at the basic rate in priority to his share of income bearing tax at the dividend ordinary rate. [*ITTOIA 2005, s 679*]. Therefore, administration expenses chargeable to income are effectively relieved primarily against dividend income.

(c) Each beneficiary would receive tax certificates (Forms R185 (Estate Income)) showing the gross amount of his entitlement and the tax paid by the personal representatives. Where the estate has dividend income bearing tax at the dividend ordinary rate, the tax certificate shows such income separately from income which has borne tax at the basic rate.

(d) Estate income which has borne tax at the dividend ordinary rate is treated as dividend income in the hands of a beneficiary. [*ITTOIA 2005, s 680A*]. For example, such income will attract the dividend allowance for 2016/17 onwards.

(e) The beneficiaries' shares of income are grossed up at the rate for the year in which the income is treated as arising to them, rather than, if different, the year in which the income is received, and tax accounted for, by the trustees. [*ITTOIA 2005, s 656*].

(f) Personal representatives are not entitled to the dividend allowance.

7.2 ESTATE INCOME: LIMITED INTEREST

Mrs D died on 5 January 2017 leaving her whole estate with a life interest to her husband and then the capital to her children on his death. The administration of the estate was completed on 7 February 2019. Mr D received payments on account of income of £1,200 on 30 September 2017, £2,500 on 31 December 2018, £1,050 on 7 February 2019 and £360 on 31 May 2019.

The actual income and deductible expenses of the estate were as follows

	2016/17 (from 6.1.17)	2017/18	2018/19 (to 7.2.19)
	£	£	£
Bank interest received	750	3,000	2,500
Basic rate tax thereon payable by personal representatives	(150)	(600)	(500)
	600	2,400	2,000
Other income (gross)	500	600	200
Basic rate tax thereon payable by personal representatives	(100)	(120)	(40)
Expenses	(80)	(150)	(400)
Net income available for distribution	£920	£2,430	£1,760

D's income from the estate for tax purposes is calculated as follows

	2016/17	2017/18	2018/19
	£	£	£
Net income	Nil	1,200.00	3,910.00
Basic rate tax	Nil	300.00	977.50
Gross income	Nil	£1,500.00	£4,887.50

Notes

(a) Subject to note (b) below, the beneficiary's net income is equal to distributions received in each tax year.

(b) The £360 paid to D in May 2019 remains payable on completion of administration and is thus treated as income of the beneficiary for the tax year in which the administration period ends, i.e. 2018/19. [*ITTOIA 2005, ss 654(3), 661*].

(c) For 2018/19, D is also likely to have taxable income from his life interest in his wife's settlement. This will be income covering the period 8 February 2019 to 5 April 2019. It does not enter into the above calculations, but is dealt with as in **27.3**(A) SETTLEMENTS.

(d) Personal representatives are not entitled to the personal savings allowance.

(e) See generally notes (b) to (f) to **7.1** above.

8 Double Tax Relief

8.1 RELIEF BY CREDIT

[*TIOPA 2010, ss 18–41*].

(A)

A UK resident non-Scottish taxpayer has, for 2018/19, UK earnings of £23,305 and foreign income from property of £2,000 on which foreign tax of £300 has been paid.

(i) *Tax on total income*

	£
Employment income	23,305
Income from property (foreign tax £300)	2,000
	25,305
Deduct Personal allowance	11,850
Taxable income	£13,455
Tax on £13,455 @ 20%	£2,691.00

(ii) *Tax on total income less foreign income*

	£
Employment income	23,305
Deduct Personal allowance	11,850
Taxable income	£11,455
Tax on £11,455 @ 20%	£2,291.00

The difference in tax between (i) and (ii) is £400. The foreign tax is less than this and full credit of £300 is available against the UK tax payable. If the foreign tax were £600, the credit would be limited to £400 and the balance of £200 would be unrelieved.

Note

(a) For a further example, involving overseas dividends, see **1.1**(C) ALLOWANCES AND TAX RATES.

(B)

A UK resident non-Scottish taxpayer has the following income, allowances and UK tax liability for the year 2018/19 before double tax relief

Earned income	£
UK directorship	34,565
USA directorship (foreign tax £1,200)	6,000
Dutch partnership (foreign tax £3,750)	7,500
	48,065
Unearned income	
UK dividends	1,600
Foreign bank interest (foreign tax £250)	2,500
Total income	52,165
Deduct Personal allowance	11,850
Taxable income	£40,315
Tax on £34,500 at basic rate (20%)	6,900.00
£1,715 at higher rate on earnings (40%)	686.00
£500 at savings nil rate (0%)	—
£2,000 at higher rate on savings (40%)	800.00
£1,600 at dividend nil rate (0%)	—
Tax borne before double tax relief	£8,386.00

The maximum double tax relief is obtained by progressively taking relief for each foreign source with the source with the highest rate of foreign tax being eliminated first. [*TIOPA 2010, s 36*].

	£	£	£
Taxable income from all sources	40,315	40,315	40,315
Deduct foreign income			
Dutch partnership	(7,500)	(7,500)	(7,500)
USA directorship		(6,000)	(6,000)
Interest			(2,500)
	£32,815	£26,815	£24,315
Tax thereon (see note (a))	6,043.00	4,843.00	4,543.00
Tax on income before eliminating foreign source under review	8,386.00	6,043.00	4,843.00
Tax attributable to that source (A)	£2,343.00	£1,200.00	£300.00
Foreign tax suffered (B)	£3,750.00	£1,200.00	£250.00
Double tax relief i.e. lesser of (A) and (B)	£2,343.00	£1,200.00	£250.00
The UK income tax borne after credit for double tax relief is			
As computed before double tax relief		£8,386.00	
Deduct Double tax relief		3,793.00	
		£4,593.00	

Note

(a) The recalculation of tax after each element of foreign income has been deducted is as follows

	£	£	£
Earned income	40,565	34,565	34,565
Deduct Personal allowance	11,850	11,850	11,850
	28,715	22,715	22,715
Savings income	2,500	2,500	
Dividend income	1,600	1,600	1,600
	£32,815	£26,815	£24,315
Basic rate tax (20%) on net earned income	5,743.00	4,543.00	4,543.00
Personal savings allowance £1,000 at 0%	—	—	
Basic rate tax (20%) on savings income	300.00	300.00	
Dividend allowance £1,600 at 0%	—	—	—
	£6,043.00	£4,843.00	£4,543.00

In the first two of these calculations, the personal savings allowance is £1,000 as there is now no income above the basic rate limit.

9 Employment Income

Cross-reference. See also 6 COMPENSATION FOR LOSS OF EMPLOYMENT.

9.1 DUTIES PERFORMED ABROAD — TRAVEL COSTS AND EXPENSES

[*ITEPA 2003, ss 370, 371; FA 2013, Sch 46 paras 35, 72*]

M, a married man resident in the UK, is employed by Bigbuild Ltd in Milnrow at a salary of £50,000 per annum and is involved in the management of the following construction projects.

29.8.18 – 30.11.18	Office block in Philippines
9.12.18 – 15.1.19	Factory in Germany
19.3.19 – 27.6.19	Housing development in Spain

Details of travel expenses incurred in 2018/19 are

		Paid by M	Reimbursed by Bigbuild	Paid by Bigbuild
		£	£	£
28.8.18	Milnrow – Heathrow Airport (M)	40		
29.8.18	Heathrow – Philippines (M)			400
20.10.18	Milnrow – Philippines (wife and children)			1,000
30.10.18	Philippines – Milnrow (wife and children)			1,000
30.11.18	Philippines – Milnrow (M)	500	500	
9.12.18	Milnrow – Manchester Airport (M)	10	10	
9.12.18	Manchester – Germany (M)			100
10.12.18	Milnrow – Germany (wife and children)			300
3. 1.19	Germany – Milnrow (wife and children)	300	300	
15.1.19	Germany – Milnrow (M)			100
19.3.19	Milnrow – Spain (M)	150	150	
31.3.19	Milnrow – Spain (wife)	60	—	150
		£1,060	£960	£3,050

9.1 IT Employment Income

M's 2018/19 taxable income is as follows

		£	£
Salary			50,000
Cost of expenses incurred by Bigbuild			3,050
Reimbursed travel expenses			960
			54,010
	Allowable part of expenses incurred by Bigbuild (note (a))	2,750	
	Allowable expenses incurred by M (note (a))	700	
	Personal allowance	11,850	(15,300)
			£38,710

Note

(a) A deduction is allowed for travelling expenses of the employee from any place in the UK to take up the overseas employment. In addition where the employee is out of the UK for 60 days or more continuously, an allowance is available for up to two outward and two return trips per fiscal year for the employee's wife and minor children provided the expense is borne or reimbursed by the employer. As M is away for less than 60 days in Germany, he cannot deduct the cost of his family's Christmas and New Year trip. The part of the cost of his wife's trip to Spain not reimbursed cannot be deducted.

9.2 ALLOWABLE DEDUCTIONS

(A) Mileage allowances

[*ITEPA 2003, ss 229–236; SI 2011 No 896*]

D is employed as a buyer by CB Ltd and uses his own car for business. CB Ltd pays its employees a standard mileage allowance of 62 pence per business mile for 2018/19. D's business mileage is 18,000 in 2018/19.

The amount to be included in D's taxable employment income for 2018/19 is as follows

	£	£
Mileage allowances received 18,000 × 62p		11,160
Tax free rates:		
First 10,000 business miles at 45p	4,500	
Balance of 8,000 miles at 25p	2,000	(6,500)
Taxable amount		£4,660

Notes

(a) Mileage allowance payments are taxable only to the extent that, in total for the year, they exceed the approved rates. The approved rates for cars and vans are 45 pence per mile for the first 10,000 miles and 25 pence per mile thereafter. The same rates apply to all cars and vans, regardless of cylinder capacity. [*ITEPA 2003, ss 229, 230; SI 2011 No 896*].

(b) Where no mileage allowance payments are made, or payments are made at a rate lower than the approved rates, the employee may claim a deduction ('mileage allowance relief') for business mileage of an amount equal to the approved rates or, as the case may be, equal to the excess of the approved rates over the payments. [*ITEPA 2003, ss 231, 232*].

(c) In addition to the mileage allowances, employers can make 'approved passenger payments', taxable only to the extent that they exceed 5 pence per mile. If no such payment is made, however, the employee may not claim a deduction as in (*b*) above. [*ITEPA 2003, ss 233, 234*].

(d) Relief as in (a) and (b) above is also available in respect of business use of a cycle or motorcycle. The approved rates are 20 pence per mile for cycles and 24 pence per mile for motorcycles.

(e) No other method can be used to calculate relief for business use of an employee's own vehicle, and capital allowances are not available. [*CAA 2001, s 36(1)(a)*].

(B) Travelling expenses generally

[*ITEPA 2003, ss 336–340*]

Three employees of Fixit Ltd, which has offices in Central London and a main depot in Chelmsford in Essex, incur travelling expenses as follows in 2018/19.

(1) A, who lives in Surrey, normally works in the London office, travelling in by train. She has to attend a monthly meeting of managers in Chelmsford, to which she travels direct by car. She is able to claim a deduction for the costs of travel to Chelmsford.

(2) B, who lives in North London and normally drives to work in the Chelmsford office, occasionally calls in at the London office to pick up urgent packages. He also frequently visits, on his way to the Chelmsford office, a customer whose offices are close to Fixit Ltd in Chelmsford, to check on work in progress. He is allowed the costs of travel on days when he visits the London office. It is unlikely that he will be allowed the costs of travel when he visits the customer in Chelmsford; an employee cannot turn what is really an ordinary commuting journey into a business journey simply by arranging a business appointment along the way (HMRC Employment Income Manual EIM32060).

(3) C is an operative living in a defined area of Kent, in which he has responsibility for serving all the company's customers. He occasionally calls at the Chelmsford office to discuss new contracts, but generally arranges call-outs by telephone. He is allowed in full the costs of travel within the defined area, the whole of which is defined as his 'permanent workplace'. He is also allowed the costs of travel to the Chelmsford office, as this is not a permanent workplace.

9.3 THE BENEFITS CODE

(A) Cars and fuel

[ITEPA 2003, ss 114–153; FA 2014, s 25(1)(3); FA 2015, ss 7–9; FA 2016, ss 8–10]

(i) *Example*

A, B and C are employees of D Ltd. Each is provided with a company car throughout 2018/19. The company also bears at least part of the cost of petrol for private motoring.

A is provided with a 1,800 cc car first registered in January 2015 with a list price (including VAT, car tax (but not road tax), delivery charges and standard accessories) of £19,000. The car was made available to A in April 2015. It has a diesel engine and a CO2 emissions figure of 155 g/km. An immobilisor was fitted in September 2015 at a cost of £200. A is required to pay the company £250 per year as a condition of using the car for private motoring, and duly pays this amount in 2018/19.

B is provided with a 1,400 cc car first registered in March 2014 with a list price of £9,000. It has an emissions figure of 90g/km. B was required to make a capital contribution of £1,000 on provision of the car in January 2015. B leaves the company in March 2019 and returns the car to D Ltd on 16 March. B was required to pay the company £50 per year as a condition of using the car for private motoring, and duly paid this amount in 2018/19.

C is provided with a luxury car first registered in February 2017 with a list price of £88,000 (which includes the list price of non-standard accessories). He made a capital contribution of £3,000 in 2016/17. The car's CO2 emissions figure is 280g/km.

Car and fuel benefits for in 2018/19 are as follows

	A	B	C
	£	£	£
List price	19,000	9,000	88,000
Later accessories	200	—	—
	19,200		
Capital contributions	—	(1,000)	(3,000)
Price of car	£19,200	£8,000	£85,000
Cash equivalent — 36% (32% + 4%)			
(including diesel supplement — note (d))	6,912		
— 19%		1,520	
— 37%			31,450
Deduction for unavailability			
(£1,520 × 20/365)		(83)	
		1,437	
Contribution for private use	(250)	(50)	—
Car benefit	6,662	1,387	31,450

Fuel benefit (£23,400 @ 36%)	8,424		
(£23,400 @ 19%)		4,446	
(£23,400 @ 37%)			8,658
Deduction for unavailability			
(£4,446 × 20/365)		(244)	
Total car and fuel benefits	£15,086	£5,589	£40,108

Notes

(a) For cars which have an approved carbon dioxide emissions figure, the benefit is a percentage of the car's list price determined by reference to the level of those emissions. [*ITEPA 2003, ss 133–142*].

(b) The price of the car is ascertained under *ITEPA 2003, ss 122–132.*

(c) The fuel benefit charge is computed by taking the car benefit percentage ascertained in (a) above and applying it to a set figure of £23,400 (£22,600 for 2017/18). [*ITEPA 2003, ss 149–153; SI 2015 No 1979; SI 2016 No 1174*].

(d) The diesel supplement for company cars is 4% from 2018/19 onwards. (3% for 2017/18).

(ii)

J is Managing Director of K Ltd and during the year ended 5 April 2019 the company provided two cars for his use. Car 1 was a two-year old car (2,200 cc with CO2 emissions of 175g/km and a list price of £20,000) and it was used by J for both business and private purposes until 31 October 2018 when it was written off as a result of an accident. J was subsequently prosecuted for dangerous driving, banned for one year and incurred legal costs of £800 which were ultimately paid for by K Ltd. In the period 6 April 2018 to 31 October 2018 J had paid the company £30 per month as a contribution towards private fuel. J was then provided with the use of a new 2-litre car (Car 2) and, since at first he had injuries which prevented him from driving and later lost his licence, a chauffeur. This replacement car was to be used for business purposes only.

J's benefits for 2018/19 relating to the cars are

	£
Car 1	
Car benefit £20,000 @ 36%	7,200
Fuel benefit £23,400 @ 36%	8,424
	£15,624
Proportion for period 6.4.18–31.10.18	
($^{209}/_{365}$ × £15,624)	8,946
Legal costs	800
Car 2	
Annual scale charge	—
Provision of chauffeur	—
	£9,746

Notes

(a) For 2018/19 the percentage used to compute the car and fuel benefits is 20% at carbon dioxide emissions levels of 95g/km or more, plus 1% for each additional 5g/km up to a maximum of 37%. The maximum is reached at 180g/km.

(b) The car benefit and car fuel scale charges for Car 1 are reduced because the car was not available for use for part of the year. [*ITEPA 2003, ss 143, 152*].

(c) Since J makes a contribution only towards private fuel as distinct from private use, a reduction in the car benefit under *ITEPA 2003, s 144* will not be available. As J is not *required* to make good the *whole* of the expense incurred by K Ltd in providing fuel for private use, his contributions do not reduce the fuel benefit. [*ITEPA 2003, s 151*].

(d) The legal costs will be taxable as a benefit following *Rendell v Went HL 1964, 41 TC 641*. No relief is available under *ITEPA 2003, ss 346–350* (employee liabilities) as the expenses are incurred in connection with a criminal conviction. [*ITEPA 2003, s 346(2)*].

(e) Since Car 2 is not available for private use, no benefits will arise. [*ITEPA 2003, ss 114, 118*]. No benefit arises in respect of the chauffeur's wages as they relate to business travel only and J would have been eligible for a deduction had he incurred and paid the equivalent expense himself. [*ITEPA 2003, ss 289A–289E; FA 2015, s 11*].

(f) K Ltd will be liable to employers' Class 1A NIC for 2018/19 in respect of Car 1, under *Social Security Contributions and Benefits Act 1992, s 10.*

(B) Vans

[*ITEPA 2003, ss 155–164, 170(1A)(2)(5); FA 2014, s 25(2)(3); FA 2015, s 10; FA 2016, s 11*]

W is an employee of C Ltd, earning £37,000 per annum. From 1 October 2018 to 5 April 2019, W is provided by his employer with exclusive use of a one-year old company van (Van A) on terms such that the restricted private use requirements are not met and which provide for a deduction of £4 per month to be made from his net salary at the end of each month in consideration for private use. Van A was off the road and incapable of use for a three-week period in January 2019; no replacement was provided.

X, Y and Z are also employees of C Ltd, each earning £32,500 per annum. Throughout 2018/19, a single two-year old company van (Van B) is made available to the three of them. The terms are such that the restricted private use requirements are met in relation to X but not in relation to Y and Z. No payment for private use was required from any of them. Van B was damaged and incapable of use for 40 consecutive days in February/ March 2019; no replacement was provided. The facts show that a just and reasonable allocation of the benefit for 2018/19 is 0% to X (whose private use was insignificant), 60% to Y and 40% to Z.

Both vans have a normal laden weight not exceeding 3,500 kilograms.

It is not the policy of C Ltd to provide fuel for private travel in its vans. All employees are required to make good the full cost of any fuel used for private purposes and have done so in 2018/19.

The taxable benefits to W, X, Y and Z for 2018/19 of company vans are calculated as follows.

	£
W	
Cash equivalent of benefit before adjustment	3,350
Exclude Period of unavailability (see note (b) below):	
$£3,350 \times \frac{178}{365}$ (6.4.18 – 30.9.18)	(1,634)
	1,716
Deduct Payment for private use (6 × £4 per month)	24
Cash equivalent of benefit	£1,692
X	
Cash equivalent of benefit	Nil
Y	
Cash equivalent of benefit before adjustment	3,350
Exclude Period of unavailability:	
$£3,350 \times \frac{40}{365}$	(367)
	2,983
Exclude Reduction for sharing (40%)	(1,193)
Cash equivalent of benefit	£1,790
Z	
Cash equivalent of benefit before adjustment	3,350
Exclude Period of unavailability (same as for Y):	(367)
	2,983
Exclude Reduction for sharing (60%)	(1,790)
Cash equivalent of benefit	£1,193

Notes

(a) The cash equivalent of the benefit is £3,350 (£3,230 for 2017/18). [*ITEPA 2003, s 155(1); SI 2015 No 1979; SI 2016 No 1174*].

(b) In W's case, the period of unavailability in January 2019 does not count towards the reduction as it is a period of less than 30 consecutive days.

(c) No fuel benefit arises in this example due to C Ltd's policy on fuel for private travel and the fact that the employees have reimbursed the company for any private fuel used.

(C) Assets given and leased

[*ITEPA 2003, ss 203–208*]

During 2018/19 P Ltd transferred to R a television set which it had previously leased to him for a nominal rent of £4 per month. The company also leased a suit to R under similar arrangements but at a rent of £2 per month.

Television

First leased to R on 6 April 2017 (when its market value was £860); transferred to R on 1 March 2019 for £100, the market value at that time being £375.

R's benefits are			£	£
2017/18				
Cost of benefit	20% × £860			172
Deduct Rent paid by R				48
Cash equivalent of benefit				£124
2018/19				
Cost of benefit	20% × £860 × 330/365 (note (a))			155
Deduct Rent paid by R (11 months)				44
Cash equivalent of benefit				111
Greater of				
(i)	Market value at transfer		375	
	Deduct Price paid by R		100	
			£275	
	and			
(ii)	Original market value		860	
	Deduct Cost of benefits	note (b)	327	
			533	
	Deduct Price paid by R		100	
			£433	
				433
Total				£544

Suit

First leased to R on 31 July 2018 (when its market value was £580).

R's benefit for 2018/19 is		
Cost of benefit	20% × £580 × 249/365 (note (a))	79
Deduct Rent paid by R (8 months)		(16)
Cash equivalent of benefit		£63

Notes

(a) For 2017/18 onwards, where the benefit consists in the use (without transfer) of an asset, the cost of the benefit is time-apportioned by reference to the number of days in the tax year on which the asset is available for private use. An asset is *unavailable* for private use on any day if, inter alia, that day falls before the day on which the asset is first available to the employee (without any transfer of property) or after the day on which it is last so available. [*ITEPA 2003, ss 205(1B)–(1D), 205A, 205B; FA 2017, s 8(1)–(3)(5)*]. Before 2017/18, where an asset was not available for the whole of a tax year, only a corresponding proportion of the cost of the benefit was brought into charge, but this had effect purely on a non-statutory basis (see HMRC Employment Income Manual EIM21200, 21637).

(b) On the transfer of the television set, the cost of the benefits to date (£172 + £155), not the cash equivalents, is deducted from the original market value. [*ITEPA 2003, s 206*].

(c) It is assumed that the television set and suit have been bought by P Ltd and are not goods provided from within its own business. If the latter was the case, R would be taxed on the marginal or additional cost to P Ltd in providing the benefit (*Pepper v Hart* HL 1992, 65 TC 421).

(D) Cheap loan arrangements

[*ITEPA 2003, ss 173–191*]

D, who is an employee of A Ltd earning £40,000 per annum, obtained a loan of £10,000 from the company on 10 October 2007 for the purpose of buying a car. Interest at a nominal rate is charged annually on the outstanding balance while the principal is repayable by instalments of £1,000 on 31 December and 30 June commencing 31 December 2007. The interest paid by D in 2007/08 amounted to £50 and in 2008/09 to £250. The official rate of interest is 6.25% p.a. until 28 February 2009 and 4.75% p.a. thereafter. The average rate for 2008/09 is 6.1%.

D will be chargeable for 2007/08 as follows

Normal method (averaging)	£
Average balance for period $\dfrac{£10{,}000 + £9{,}000}{2}$	£9,500
£9,500 × $^{5}/_{12}$	£3,958
£3,958 × 6.25%	247
Deduct Interest paid in year	50
Cash equivalent of loan benefit	£197

Alternative method

Period	Balance of loan in period	Interest at official rate on balance	
	£		£
10.10.07 – 31.12.07	10,000	£10,000 × 6.25% × 83/365	142
1.1.08 – 5.4.08	9,000	£9,000 × 6.25% × 95/365	146
			288
Deduct Interest paid in year			50
Cash equivalent of loan benefit			£238
Amount chargeable to tax	note (b)		£238

D will be chargeable for 2008/09 as follows

Normal method (averaging)

	£
Average balance for year $\frac{£9,000 + £7,000}{2}$	£8,000
£8,000 × 6.1%	488
Deduct Interest paid in year	250
Cash equivalent of loan benefit	£238

Alternative method

Period	Balance of loan in period	Interest at official rate on balance	
	£		£
6.4.08 – 30.6.08	9,000	£9,000 × 6.25% × 86/365	132
1.7.08 – 31.12.08	8,000	£8,000 × 6.25% × 184/365	252
1.1.09 – 28.2.09	7,000	£7,000 × 6.25% × 59/365	71
1.3.09 – 5.4.09	7,000	£7,000 × 4.75% × 95/365	33
			488
Deduct Interest paid in year			250
Cash equivalent of loan benefit			£238
Amount chargeable to tax	note (b)		£238

Notes

(a) The period 10 October 2007 to 5 April 2008 is, for the purpose of calculating the average balance, five complete months (months begin on the sixth day of each calendar month). However, for the purpose of applying interest rates, the actual number of days (178) during which the loan was outstanding is taken into account.

(b) HMRC will probably require the alternative method to be applied for 2007/08. For 2008/09, both methods happen to give the same result.

(c) Note that a loan is exempt from the cheap loan provisions for a tax year if it and other employment-related loans (excluding qualifying loans) do not exceed £10,000 in aggregate at any time in the year (£5,000 for 2013/14 and earlier years). [*ITEPA 2003, s 180; FA 2014, s 22*].

(d) There is no taxable benefit in respect of a loan where, if interest were paid on it, the whole of the interest would qualify for tax relief. [*ITEPA 2003, s 178*]. Where such interest only partly qualifies, a benefit continues to arise, with relief being given for the qualifying part of the interest.

(e) In order for interest paid by the employee to be taken into account, it need not be paid *in* the tax year, only *for* the tax year. See HMRC Employment Income Manual, EIM26250–26258 for a useful discussion on this.

(f) This example illustrates the year 2008/09 as that was the latest year in which the official rate was changed in-year. The principles continue to apply for subsequent years.

9.4 BENEFITS — LIVING ACCOMMODATION

[*ITEPA 2003, ss 97–113, 313–315; FA 2016, s 7(2)(3)(9)*]

(A) Expenses

N is employed by the G Property Co Ltd, earning £13,850 p.a. He occupies, rent-free, the basement flat of a block of flats for which he is employed as caretaker/security officer. The annual value of the flat is determined at £250. In 2018/19, G Ltd incurred the following expenditure on the flat

	£
Heat and light	700
Decoration	330
Repairs	210
Cleaning	160
	£1,400
Conversion of large bedroom into two smaller bedrooms	£3,000

In addition, the company pays N's council tax which amounts to £500.

N pays a personal pension premium of £160 net of tax (equivalent to £200 gross) into a registered scheme on 31 October 2018, but, apart from his personal allowance, he has no other reliefs.

N's taxable income for 2018/19 is

Salary	13,850
Annual value of flat	—
Heat and light, decoration, repairs, cleaning	
£1,400 restricted to (note (c))	1,365
	15,215
Deduct Personal allowance	(11,850)
Taxable	£3,365

Notes

(a) N is not chargeable to income tax on the annual value of the flat if he can show that it is necessary for the proper performance of his duties for him to reside in the accommodation. [*ITEPA 2003, s 99(1)*]. He might equally well be able to claim under *ITEPA 2003, s 99(2)*.

(b) The structural alterations costing £3,000 will not be regarded as a benefit. [*ITEPA 2003, s 313*].

(c) The earnings treated as having arisen in respect of the heat and light, decoration, repairs and cleaning costs will be restricted by *ITEPA 2003, s 315* to the lesser of

(i)	the expenses incurred	£1,400
(ii)	10% × £13,650 (net earnings)	£1,365

The contribution to a registered pension scheme is deductible in arriving at net earnings for this purpose. [*ITEPA 2003, s 315(5)*]. (The contribution is not shown above as a deduction from taxable income as basic rate relief has been given at source and higher/additional rate relief is not applicable.)

(d) Where the benefit of living accommodation is exempt under *ITEPA 2003, s 99(1), s 99(2) or s 100* (accommodation provided as result of security threat), the payment by the employer of the employee's council tax (and/or water rates) is also exempt. [*ITEPA 2003, s 314*].

(B) **Normal and additional charge**

S, the founder and managing director of S Ltd, a successful transport company, has since April 2013 occupied a house owned by S Ltd. The house was acquired by S Ltd in August 2007 for £150,000 and, since acquisition, but before 6 April 2017, £80,000 has been spent by S Ltd on alterations and improvements to the house. The gross annual value of the house for rating purposes before 1 April 1990 (when the community charge replaced general rates) was £1,663. S pays annual rental of £2,000 to the company for 2018/19 only. He pays all expenses relating to the property.

S's taxable benefits in respect of his occupation of the house for 2017/18 and 2018/19 are as follows

		£	£
2017/18			
Gross annual value			1,663
Additional charge			
Acquisition cost of house		150,000	
Cost of improvements		80,000	
		230,000	
Deduct		75,000	
Additional value		£155,000	
Additional value at 2.5%%	note (b)		3,875
			£5,538
2018/19			
Gross annual value	note (a)		Nil
Additional charge			
Acquisition cost of house		150,000	
Cost of improvements		80,000	
		230,000	
Deduct		75,000	
Additional value		£155,000	
Additional value at 2.5%	note (b)		3,875
			3,875
Rental payable by S		2,000	
Deduct Gross annual value		1,663	
			(337)
			£3,538

Notes

(a) No taxable gross annual value arises in 2018/19 because the rental of £2,000 payable by S exceeds the gross annual value of £1,663. The excess is deductible from the amount of the benefit arising under the additional charge.

(b) The percentage to be used in determining the amount of the benefit is that in force for the purposes of taxing cheap loan arrangements (see **9.3**(D) above) at the beginning of the tax year.

(c) If S had moved into the house on, say, 6 April 2014 (more than six years after its acquisition by S Ltd), market value at that date would be substituted for cost plus improvements to date. If, however, original cost plus cost of improvements had not exceeded £75,000, the additional charge would not apply (regardless of market value at the date of first occupation by S). [*ITEPA 2003, s 107*].

9.5 REMOVAL BENEFITS AND EXPENSES, INCLUDING CHEAP LOAN ARRANGEMENTS

[*ITEPA 2003, ss 271–289*]

Mr R E Locate lives in Chelsea and is employed as a store manager by T Ltd, a department store chain, at one of their London branches. In June 2018, he is asked by T Ltd to take up a similar position at their main Birmingham store with effect from 1 August 2018. The company agrees to pay Mr Locate's expenses, up to a ceiling of £7,500, in connection with his moving house to the Birmingham area. In the event, the expenses paid or reimbursed by the company amount to £7,000, all paid in 2018, all eligible expenses within *ITEPA 2003, ss 272, 277–285* and all reasonably incurred by the employee in connection with his change of residence. As he is unable to move into his new home until 15 August 2018, T Ltd provides Mr Locate with temporary living accommodation near his new place of employment. The accommodation is rented by the company and would give rise to a taxable benefit on the employee of £300 under *ITEPA 2003, s 105*, but no charge under *ITEPA 2003, s 106* (see 9.4 above).

T Ltd also provides Mr Locate with an interest-free bridging loan of £50,000 in connection with the change of residence. The loan is made on 1 August 2018 and is repaid on 10 April 2019 when the sale of the employee's former residence is completed. The official rate of interest under *ITEPA 2003, s 181* is assumed to remain at 2.5% throughout. Mr Locate's salary for 2018/19 amounts to £44,000.

Mr Locate's taxable benefits for 2018/19 in respect of removal expenses and benefits plus cheap loans are calculated as follows

	£
Qualifying removal expenses	7,000
Qualifying removal benefits	300
	£7,300

The total is less than the qualifying limit of £8,000 under *ITEPA 2003, s 287(1)* and is thus exempt from tax by virtue of *ITEPA 2003, s 271(1)*.

Cheap loan arrangements

The interest-free loan is treated by *ITEPA 2003, s 289* as having been made on a date later than that on which it was actually made, as follows.

Number of days in the 'exempted discharge period' = $\dfrac{A}{B \times C} \times 365$

A = 700 (unused qualifying limit, i.e. £8,000 - £7,300)

B = 50,000 (maximum loan outstanding between the actual date of the loan, 1.8.18, and 5.4.20, the latter being the 'limitation day' — see *ITEPA 2003, s 274* and note (a) below)

C = 2.5% (the official rate of interest as at the actual date of the loan, 1.8.18, disregarding any subsequent changes of rate)

$$\frac{700}{50{,}000 \times 2.5\%} \times 365$$

= 204.4 rounded up to 204 days

[*ITEPA 2003, s 288(4)*].

The 'exempted discharge period' of 204 days runs from 1.8.18 to 20.2.19 inclusive. The loan is deemed to have been made on 20.2.19. [*ITEPA 2003, s 289(1)–(3)*].

Calculation of benefit:

(i) Averaging method

$\frac{£50{,}000 + £50{,}000}{2} \times \frac{1}{12} \times 2.5\% =$	£104

(ii) Alternative method

20.2.19–5.4.19 = 45 days	
£50,000 × 2.5% × $^{45}/_{365}$	£154
Amount chargeable to tax (on the assumption that the alternative method is applied)	£154

Notes

(a) Eligible expenses and benefits which are reasonably incurred or provided in connection with the change in the employee's residence are qualifying expenses or benefits only if they are incurred or provided on or before the end of the tax year following that in which the employment, new duties or duties at the new location commence, i.e. by 5 April 2020 in this example.

(b) 'Subsistence' provided for the employee is an eligible benefit by virtue of *ITEPA 2003, s 281(4)*. For this purpose, 'subsistence' includes temporary living accommodation as well as food and drink. [*ITEPA 2003, s 281(6)*].

(c) See also **9.3**(D) above as regards cheap loans.

9.6 BENEFITS — MISCELLANEOUS

T earns £6,000 p.a. and during the year ended 5 April 2019 his employer provided him with, or paid on his behalf, or reimbursed, the following

	£
BUPA contributions (self and family) of which 25% reimbursed by T	600
Special medical insurance for overseas business visit lasting four nights	250
Voucher exchangeable for rail season ticket	500
Gift token exchangeable for goods at local department store	75

Holiday pay scheme voucher, exchangeable for cash	350
Overnight incidental expenses (telephone, laundry etc.) relating to above-mentioned overseas trip	36

The rail ticket voucher was purchased in March 2018 but was not handed to T until after 6 April 2018. The holiday pay voucher was received by T in June 2018 at which time PAYE was applied. The gift token was received in December 2018.

T's chargeable earnings for 2018/19 are

	£
Salary	6,000
BUPA contributions (£600 less 25% reimbursed) (note (a))	450
Rail ticket voucher (note (c))	500
Gift token (note (d))	75
Holiday pay scheme voucher (note (e))	350
	£7,375

Notes

(a) For 2016/17 onwards, the earlier concept of 'lower-paid' employment is abolished, with the result that all provisions of the benefits code apply in full to all employees (including directors) whatever their level of earnings, subject to special rules for ministers of religion and an exemption for home care workers. [*ITEPA 2003, ss 216–220; FA 2015, s 13(1)(4)*]. The BUPA contributions are now a chargeable benefit, which would not previously have been the case for a 'lower-paid' employee.

(b) The special medical insurance for the overseas business trip is exempted from charge by *ITEPA 2003, s 325.*

(c) The rail ticket voucher is chargeable in 2018/19 being the later of the year of receipt by the employee and the year of expense incurred by the employer. [*ITEPA 2003, s 88*].

(d) The gift token is a non-cash voucher chargeable under *ITEPA 2003, s 87.*

(e) The holiday pay voucher, being a 'cash voucher' within *ITEPA 2003, s 75* is taxable under PAYE by virtue of *ITEPA 2003, s 693.*

(f) The reimbursement of incidental overnight expenses is not taxable as the amount does not exceed £10 for each night of absence (£5 for absences within the UK). [*ITEPA 2003, ss 240, 241*].

10 Enterprise Investment Scheme

[ITA 2007, ss 156–257; TCGA 1992, ss 150A, 150B; FA 2014, s 56(2)–(4)(8); FA 2015, Sch 6 paras 2–5, 10, 14; F(No 2)A 2015, ss 25, 27, 28, Sch 5; FA 2016, ss 28–30; FA 2018, ss 14–16, Sch 4]

10.1 CONDITIONS FOR AND FORM OF RELIEF

(A)

Marshal Ney is a UK resident with a salary of £185,000 for 2017/18 and no other income. For 2017/18, he is entitled to full income tax relief on an investment of £200,000 in a venture capital trust.

In 2017/18 he subscribes for ordinary shares in two unquoted companies issuing shares under the enterprise investment scheme (EIS).

A Ltd was formed by some people in Ney's neighbourhood to publish a local newspaper. 200,000 ordinary £1 shares were issued at par in August 2017 and the company started trading in September 2017. Ney subscribed for 16,000 of the shares. Ney becomes a director of A Ltd in September 2017, and receives director's fees of £3,222 in 2017/18, a level of remuneration which is considered reasonable for services rendered by him to the company in his capacity as a director.

B Ltd, which is controlled by an old friend of Ney, has acquired the rights to manufacture in the UK a new type of industrial cleaning solvent and requires additional finance. Ney subscribed for 8,000 ordinary £1 shares at a premium of £1.50 per share in October 2017. The issue increases the company's issued share capital to 25,000 ordinary £1 shares.

Ney will obtain tax relief in 2017/18 as follows

Amount eligible for relief

		£
A Ltd	note (a)	16,000
B Ltd	note (b)	Nil
Total (being less than the maximum of £1,000,000)		£16,000

	£
Salary	185,000
Director's remuneration (A Ltd)	3,222
Total income	188,222
Personal allowance (restricted due to level of income)	Nil
Taxable income	£188,222
Tax payable:	
33,500 @ 20%	6,700.00
116,500 @ 40%	46,600.00
38,222 @ 45%	17,200.00

	70,500.00
VCT relief £200,000 @ 30%	60,000.00
	10,500.00
Deduct EIS relief £16,000 @ 30%	4,800.00
Net tax liability 2017/18	£5,700.00

Notes

(a) Marshal Ney is entitled to relief on the full amount of his investment in A Ltd. The fact that he becomes a paid director of A Ltd *after* an issue to him of eligible shares does not prevent his qualifying for relief in respect of those shares providing his remuneration as a director is reasonable and he is not otherwise connected with the company. [*ITA 2007, s 169*].

(b) Ney is not entitled to relief against his income for his investment of £20,000 in B Ltd. As a result of the share issue he owns more than 30% of the issued ordinary share capital (8,000 out of 25,000 shares) and is therefore regarded as connected with the company and denied relief. [*ITA 2007, s 170*].

(c) EIS relief is given at the EIS rate of tax (30%) and by way of an income tax reduction. The relief cannot exceed what would otherwise be the income tax liability (no restriction being necessary in this example). For this purpose, the income tax liability is before taking into account any married couple's allowance, double tax relief and certain other specified items. However, the VCT investment relief must be deducted before the EIS relief. [*ITA 2007, ss 26, 27, 29, 158*].

(B)

In 2018/19 Marshal Ney subscribes for shares in three more unquoted UK companies issuing shares under the EIS. None of the companies are knowledge-intensive companies.

C Ltd is a local company engaged in the manufacture of car components. It issues a further 540,000 ordinary £1 shares at £2 per share in June 2018 and Ney subscribes for 14,800 shares costing £29,600, increasing his stake in the company to 10%. He had originally held 24,300 shares, acquired by purchase at arm's length in May 2016 for £32,400.

D Ltd has been trading as a restaurateur for several years and requires an injection of capital to finance a new restaurant. Ney and three other unconnected individuals each subscribe for 75,000 ordinary £1 shares at par in November 2018. The balance of 480,000 shares are held by Ney's sister and niece. D Ltd has the equivalent of 80 full-time employees in November 2018 when the new shares are issued.

E Ltd is an electronics company, with 60 employees, controlled by two cousins of Marshal Ney. The company has not issued any shares in the previous twelve months but is now seeking £5 million extra capital for expansion, and raises it via the EIS. Ney subscribes for 950,000 ordinary £1 shares at par in December 2018.

Ney's salary is increased by bonus to £277,000 for 2018/19. His director's fees from A Ltd amount to £5,320, which again is considered reasonable for services rendered. He makes a claim to treat 9,500 of his C Ltd shares (costing £19,000) to be regarded as issued in 2017/18, thus eliminating his tax liability for that year.

Ney will obtain tax relief as follows

2017/18

C Ltd note (a) £19,000 @ 30% =	£5,700

2018/19

Amount eligible for relief

	£
C Ltd (£29,600 − £19,000 carried back)	10,600
D Ltd	75,000
E Ltd	950,000
Total amount subscribed	£1,035,600
But amount eligible for relief restricted to subscriptions of	£1,000,000

Relief given

	£
Salary	277,000
Director's remuneration	5,320
Total income	282,320
Personal allowance (restricted due to level of income)	Nil
Taxable income	£282,320
Tax payable:	
34,500 @ 20%	6,900.00
115,500 @ 40%	46,200.00
132,320 @ 45%	59,544.00
	112,644.00
Deduct EIS relief:	
£1,000,000 @ 30% = £300,000, but restricted to	112,644.00
Net tax liability 2018/19	Nil

Attribution of relief to shares note (b)

	£
C Ltd shares $\frac{10,600}{1,035,600} \times £112,644$	1,153
D Ltd shares $\frac{75,000}{1,035,600} \times £112,644$	8,158
E Ltd shares $\frac{950,000}{1,035,600} \times £112,644$	103,333
	£112,644

Notes

(a) The investor may claim relief as if any number of the shares had been issued in the preceding tax year. The only restriction (not relevant in this example) is that relief in any one tax year may not be given on subscriptions of more than the annual maximum for that year. The relief will be given in addition to that previously claimed for 2017/18 (see (A) above). [*ITA 2007, s 158(4)*].

(b) Relief is restricted in this example by (i) the £1,000,000 maximum, (ii) the available EIS rate (i.e. 30%) and (iii) an insufficiency in Ney's tax liability. The relief attributable to each issue of shares (which will be relevant in the event of a disposal of the shares or withdrawal of relief — see **10.2** below) is found by apportioning the income tax reduction by reference to the amounts subscribed for each issue. (For this purpose, 9,500 of the C Ltd shares are regarded as having been separately issued in the previous year.) The relief so attributed to each issue is then apportioned equally between all the shares comprised in that issue. [*ITA 2007, ss 201, 210(2)*].

(c) An issuing company under the EIS scheme must have fewer than the equivalent of 250 full-time employees (500 for knowledge-intensive companies) when the EIS shares are issued. [*ITA 2007, s 186A; FA 2012, Sch 7 paras 12, 23*].

(d) With effect in accordance with provision to be made by Treasury regulations, but not so as to affect shares issued before 6 April 2018, the upper limit on the amount in respect of which an individual may obtain income tax relief for a tax year operates as follows:

(i) if the shares do not include any 'KIC shares', the limit is £1 million;

(ii) if the total amount subscribed for KIC shares is £1 million or more, the limit is £2 million; and

(iii) in any other case, the limit is £1 million plus total amount subscribed for KIC shares.

'*KIC shares*' are shares in any company which is a knowledge-intensive company (as defined) at the time the shares are issued.

Prior to the above taking effect the upper limit is in all cases £1 million.

[*ITA 2007, s 158(2)(2ZA)(2ZB); FA 2018, Sch 4 paras 1(2)–(4), 10*].

10.2 WITHDRAWAL OF RELIEF/GAINS AND LOSSES ON EIS SHARES

(A)

In June 2019, Marshal Ney, the investor in **10.1** above, sells 38,100 ordinary £1 shares in C Ltd (see **10.1**(B) above), in an arm's length transaction, for £90,000, leaving him with 1,000 shares.

The position is as follows
Income Tax

2017/18	£
Relief attributable to 9,500 shares treated as issued in 2017/18:	
9,500 shares at £2 per share = £19,000 @ 30%	5,700
Consideration received $\left(\frac{9,500}{38,100} \times £90,000\right) = £22,441$ @ 30%	6,732
Excess of tax at the EIS rate on consideration over relief	£1,032
Relief withdrawn by assessment for 2017/18	£5,700

2018/19	£
Relief attributable to 4,300 shares	
4,300/5,300 × £1,153	935
Consideration received	
$\left(\frac{4,300}{38,100} \times £90,000\right) = £10,157 \times 935 / (8,600\ @\ 30\%) = £3,681$ @ 30%	1,104
Excess of tax at the EIS rate on adjusted consideration over relief	£169
Relief withdrawn by assessment for 2018/19	£935

Capital Gains Tax

2019/20	£	£
Disposal proceeds (38,100 shares)		90,000
Cost: 24,300 shares acquired May 2016	32,400	
13,800 shares acquired June 2018	27,600	60,000
Chargeable gain		£30,000

Notes

(a) For both income tax and capital gains tax purposes, a disposal is matched with acquisitions on a first in/first out basis. [*ITA 2007, s 246*]. Thus, the 38,100 shares sold in June 2019 are matched with 24,300 shares purchased in May 2016 and with 13,800 of the 14,800 EIS shares subscribed for in June 2018. For these purposes, 9,500 of the EIS shares are treated as having been issued in 2017/18 (by virtue of

Marshal Ney's carry-back claim — see note (a) to **10.1**(B) above). [*ITA 2007, s 201(6)*]. Therefore, those shares are treated as disposed of in priority to those on which relief was given in 2018/19.

(b) Following the disposal, Ney is left with 1,000 shares in C Ltd acquired in June 2018 for £2,000, to which the EIS relief attributable is £218 (1,153 – 935).

(c) EIS relief is withdrawn if shares are disposed of before the end of the requisite three-year period. In this example, relief attributable to the shares sold is fully withdrawn as consideration received, reduced as illustrated, exceeds the relief attributable. See (B) below for where the reverse applies. The consideration is reduced where the relief attributable (A) is less than tax at the 'EIS original rate' on the amount subscribed (B), and is so reduced by applying the fraction A/B. [*ITA 2007, ss 209, 210*]. The '*EIS original rate*' is the EIS rate for the tax year for which the relief was obtained, i.e. currently 30%.

(d) Relief is withdrawn by means of an assessment for the year(s) in which relief was given. [*ITA 2007, s 235*].

(e) The capital gain on the disposal is fully chargeable as the EIS shares are not held for the requisite three-year period.

(B)

In December 2019 Ney disposes of his 75,000 ordinary £1 shares in D Ltd (see **10.1**(B) above), in an arm's length transaction, for £60,000.

The position is as follows
Income Tax

2018/19

	£
Relief attributable to shares sold	8,158
$£60{,}000 \times \dfrac{8,158}{£75,000 \times 30\%} = 21,755 \ @\ 30\%$	6,527
Excess of relief over tax at the EIS rate on adjusted consideration	£1,631
Relief withdrawn by assessment for 2018/19	£6,527

Capital Gains Tax

2019/20

	£	£
Disposal proceeds (December 2019)		60,000
Cost (November 2018)	75,000	
Less Relief attributable to shares:		
£8,158 – £6,527	1,631	
		73,369
Allowable loss		£13,369

Notes

(a) See notes (*b*) and (*c*) to (A) above.

(b) The EIS relief withdrawn is limited to tax at the EIS original rate (see note (c) to (A) above) on the consideration received, reduced as illustrated. If the disposal had been made otherwise than by way of a bargain made at arm's length, the full relief would have been withdrawn. [*ITA 2007, s 209*].

(c) An allowable loss may arise for capital gains tax purposes on a disposal of EIS shares, whether or not the disposal occurs within the requisite three-year period. In computing such a loss, the allowable cost is reduced by EIS relief attributable to the shares (and not withdrawn). [*TCGA 1992, s 150A(1)*].

(d) A loss, as computed for capital gains tax purposes, may be relieved against income on a claim under *ITA 2007, s 132* (share loss relief — see **15.5** LOSSES). [*ITA 2007, s 131*].

(C)

(i) In September 2019, Marshal Ney receives from E Ltd (one of the companies in **10.1**(B) above) an asset with a market value of £38,000 but for which he pays the company only £2,000.

(ii) In March 2022, Ney sells his 950,000 shares in E Ltd for their market value of £1,190,000.

Income Tax

(i) The difference of £36,000 between the market value of the asset and the consideration given for it represents value (which is not insignificant value) received by the investor from the company within the period beginning one year before the issue of the shares and ending three years after the issue (or three years after the commencement of trade, if later). The value received (reduced in like manner as is mentioned in note (b) to (A) above) is compared to the relief attributable to the shares.

2018/19

		£
Relief attributable to 950,000 E Ltd shares (see **10.1**(B) above)		103,333
Value received		
	$£36{,}000 \times \dfrac{103{,}333}{£950{,}000 \times 30\%} = 13{,}053 @ 30\%$	3,916
Excess of relief over value received		£99,417
Relief withdrawn by assessment for 2018/19		£3,916

[*ITA 2007, ss 159(4), 213–217, 220, 234(1), 235*].

(ii) As Ney holds the shares for the requisite three-year period, there is no withdrawal of relief on disposal.

Capital Gains Tax

As Ney holds the shares for the requisite three-year period, and EIS relief has not been fully withdrawn, any gain on disposal is generally exempt from capital gains tax (although this does not prevent an allowable loss from arising). [*TCGA 1992, s 150A(2)(2A)*]. A proportion of the gain could become chargeable under *TCGA 1992, s 150A(3)* where the relief given was less than tax at the EIS rate on the amount subscribed but this does not apply where, as in Ney's case, the relief fell to be restricted due to his having insufficient income tax liability to cover it. [*TCGA 1992, s 150A(3)*].

A proportion of the gain does, however, become chargeable where value is received leading to a part-withdrawal of relief. [*TCGA 1992, s 150B*].

2021/22

	£
Disposal proceeds (March 2022)	1,190,000
Cost (December 2018)	950,000
Gain	240,000
Chargeable gain =	

$$\text{gain} \times \frac{\text{Relief withdrawn}}{\text{Relief attributable (before reduction)}}$$

i.e.

$£240{,}000 \times \dfrac{£3{,}916}{£103{,}333}$	£9,095
Exempt gain £(240,000 − 9,095)	£230,905

11 Herd Basis

[*ITTOIA 2005, ss 111–129*]

11.1 A farmer acquires a dairy herd and elects for the herd basis to apply. The movements in the herd and the tax treatment are as follows

Year 1

	No	*Value* £
Mature		
Bought @ £150	70	10,500
Bought in calf @ £180		
(Market value of calf £35)	5	900
Immature		
Bought @ £75	15	1,125

Herd Account

70	Friesians	10,500
5	Friesians in calf (5 × £(180 − 35))	725
75	Closing balance	£11,225

Trading Account

5 Calves (5 × £35)	175
15 Immature Friesians	1,125
Debit to profit and loss account	£1,300

Year 2

	No	*Value* £
Mature		
Bought @ £185	15	2,775
Sold @ £200	10	2,000
Died	3	—
Immature		
Born	52	—
Matured @ 60% of market value of £200 note (a)	12	1,440

Herd Account

75		Opening balance		11,225
		Increase in herd		
	15	Purchases	2,775	
	12	Transferred from trading stock	1,440	
	27		4,215	
	(13)	Replacement cost £4,215 × 13/27	(2,029)	
14		Non-replacement animals cost		2,186
89		Closing balance		£13,411

Trading Account

Sale of 10 mature cows replaced	(2,000)
Transfer to herd — 14 animals	(1,440)
Cost of 13 mature cows purchased to replace those sold/deceased ($^{13}/_{15}$ × £2,775)	2,405
Net credit to profit and loss account note (b)	£(1,035)

Year 3

	No	*Value* £
Mature		
Jerseys bought @ £250	70	17,500
Friesians slaughtered @ £175 (market value £185)	52	9,100
Immature		
Friesians born	20	—
Matured		
Friesians @ 60% of market value of £190 note (*a*)	15	1,710

Herd Account

89	Opening balance			13,411
	Increase in herd			
18	Jerseys			4,500
	52	Improvement Jerseys@	250	
	less	Market value of Friesians	185	
	52@		65	3,380
	Transfer from trading stock			
15	Friesians			1,710
122	Closing balance			£23,001

Trading Account	
Compensation	(9,100)
Transfer to herd	(1,710)
Purchase of replacements note (c) (52 × £185)	9,620
Net credit to profit and loss account	£(1,190)

Year 4

The farmer ceases dairy farming and sells his whole herd.

	No	*Value* £
Mature		
Jersey sold @ £320	70	22,400
Friesians sold @ £200	52	10,400
Immature		
Friesians sold @ £100	65	6,500

Herd Account		
	Opening balance	23,001
52	Friesians	
70	Jerseys	
(122)	Sales	(32,800)
–	Profit on sale note (d)	£(9,799)

Trading Account	
Sale of 65 immature Friesians	(6,500)
Credit to profit and loss account	£(6,500)

Notes

(a) The use of 60% of market value was originally by agreement between the National Farmers' Union and HMRC (see now HMRC Business Income Manual BIM55410). Alternatively, the actual cost of breeding or purchase and rearing could be used.

(b) As the cost of rearing the 12 cows to maturity will already have been debited to the profit and loss account, no additional entry is required to reflect that cost. Due to the fact that the animals were in opening stock at valuation and will not be in closing stock, the trading account will in effect be debited with that valuation.

(c) The cost of the replacements is restricted to the cost of replacing like with like.

(d) Provided these animals are not replaced by a herd of the same type within five years the proceeds will be tax-free.

(e) The herd basis is not available when profits are calculated using the cash basis for smaller businesses. [*ITTOIA 2005, s 111A; FA 2013, Sch 4 paras 24, 56*].

12 Intellectual Property

Cross-reference. See **3.5** CAPITAL ALLOWANCES for allowances for patent rights.

12.1 PATENT ROYALTIES

[*ITA 2007, s 461*].

An inventor received £24,920 after deduction of tax at source (i.e. £31,150 gross) on 1 June 2018, for the use of his patent over a four-year period ending on that date. His only other income for the four years was a salary as set out below.

In the absence of spreading provisions, the assessments for the four years to 5 April 2019 are

Tax year	2015/16	2016/17	2017/18	2018/19
	£	£	£	£
Salary	20,010	20,625	21,350	23,200
Patent rights				31,150
	20,010	20,625	21,350	54,350
Deduct Personal allowance	10,600	11,000	11,500	11,850
Taxable income	£9,410	£9,625	£9,850	£42,500
Tax thereon	1,882.00	1,925.00	1,970.00	10,100.00
Less tax deducted at source				£6,230.00
	£1,882.00	£1,925.00	£1,970.00	£3,870.00
Total tax payable				£9,647.00

The inventor may however claim under *ITA 2007, s 461* for the liability for 2018/19 to be limited to the tax payable if the royalties had been spread over the four-year period to which they relate. The tax payable would then have been

	£	£	£	£
Salary	20,010	20,625	21,350	23,200
Patent rights	7,787	7,787	7,787	7,787
	27,797	28,412	29,137	30,987
Deduct Personal allowance	10,600	11,000	11,500	11,850
Taxable income	£17,197	£17,412	£17,637	£19,137
Tax thereon	£3,439.40	£3,482.40	£3,527.40	£3,827.40
Total tax thereon				14,276.60
Less tax deducted at source				6,230.00
Total tax payable				£8,046.60

A claim is beneficial in this case as spreading would reduce the liability by £1,600.40. Upon a claim being made, the saving will be given effect by means of a tax reduction for the year in which the royalty is received (2018/19 in this example). Tax reductions are given effect at Step 6 of the calculation of income tax liability at *ITA 2007, s 23*.

13 Late Payment Interest and Penalties

13.1 PAYMENTS UNDER SELF-ASSESSMENT

(A) Interest and penalties arising on late payment

[*FA 2009, ss 101, 107, Sch 56*]

Mrs Worthington is a self-employed cook. Her self-assessment for 2015/16 shows a net income tax liability of £9,000. She makes the following interim payments for 2016/17:

31 January 2017	£4,500
31 July 2017	£4,500

Mrs Worthington's profits increase, and her self-assessment liability for 2016/17 amounts to £12,000. Mrs Worthington does not pay the additional income tax of £3,000 until 26 September 2018.

Mrs Worthington will have a liability to late payment interest computed as follows

31.1.18 – 25.9.18	£3,000 × 3%% × 238/365	£58.68

In addition as the tax is paid more than 30 days late a late payment penalty will arise on 2 March 2018 of £3,000 × 5% = £150.

As the tax is still unpaid more than five months after the initial penalty is incurred, a further late payment penalty will arise on 2 August 2018 of £3,000 × 5% = £150. See also note (b).

Notes

(a) Interest accrues from the due date until date of payment. [*FA 2009, s 101(3)(4)*].

(b) The interest rate on late paid income tax is 3% from 21 November 2017. It was 2.75% from 23 August 2016 to 20 November 2017.

(c) If the tax had remained unpaid on 2 February 2019 (i.e. eleven months after the initial penalty was incurred), there would have been a third late payment penalty of 5% of the amount unpaid). [*FA 2009, Sch 56 para 3*].

(d) A late payment penalty may arise in respect of unpaid tax due in respect of a final payment of income tax or capital gains tax under *TMA 1970, s 59B*. For other circumstances in which a late payment penalty may arise, see the Table in *FA 2009, Sch 56 para 1*.

(e) Late payment interest will accrue on an unpaid late payment penalty with effect from the expiry of 30 days beginning with the date of the notice imposing the penalty. [*FA 2009, s 101, Sch 56 para 11*].

(B) Interest arising on insufficient interim payment

[*FA 2009, s 101, Sch 53 para 1*]

Frank is a self-employed butcher with no other income or capital gains who draws up accounts to 31 October each year. His liability under self-assessment for 2016/17 amounts to £25,000. Frank forecasts that his profits for the accounting period ended 31 October 2017 will result in a liability under self-assessment of £10,000 for 2017/18. He makes a claim to that effect under *TMA 1970, s 59A(4)* and duly pays £5,000 each on 31 January 2018 and 31 July 2018. However, actual profits are in excess of his expectations and result in a self-assessment liability of £16,000. Frank pays an additional £6,000 income tax on 25 January 2019.

For each interim payment Frank's interest will be calculated on the difference between £5,000 and the lesser of:

£8,000 being the sum of £5,000 (actual interim payment) and £3,000 (50% of the final tax payment); and

£12,500 being the interim payment based on the preceding year's tax liability.

Interest will be as follows*

First interim payment

31.1.18 – 24.1.19	£3,000 × 3% × $^{359}/_{365}$	£88.52

Second interim payment

31.7.18 – 24.1.19	£3,000 × 3% × $^{178}/_{365}$	£43.89

* Assuming no further changes in interest rates before 25 January 2019

14 Life Assurance Policies

14.1 LIFE ASSURANCE GAINS AND NON-QUALIFYING POLICIES

[*ITTOIA 2005, ss 461–546*]

(A) Top slicing relief — single chargeable event

A single policyholder realises, in 2018/19, a gain of £2,600 on a non-qualifying policy which has been in existence for 2½ years. Her other income for 2018/19 comprises employment income of £41,370, bank interest of £1,900 and dividends amounting to £2,000. She is not a Scottish taxpayer.

The tax chargeable on the gain is calculated as follows

	Normal basis	Top slicing relief claim
	£	£
Policy gain	2,600	1,300
Earnings	41,370	41,370
Savings income	1,900	1,900
Dividends	2,000	2,000
	47,870	46,570
Less Personal allowance	11,850	11,850
	£36,020	£34,720

	Normal basis		Top slicing relief claim
	£		£
Tax applicable to policy gain			
Higher rate			
£1,520 at 40%	608.00		
£220 at 40%	—		88.00
	608.00		88.00
Deduct			
Basic rate			
£1,520 at 20%	304.00		—
£220 at 20%	—		44.00
			£44.00
Appropriate multiple 2 × £44.00			£88.00
Tax chargeable lower of	£304.00	and	£88.00
Top slicing relief (£304.00 − £88.00) =	£216.00		

Tax payable is therefore as follows

29,520	@ 20%	5,904.00
500	@ 0% (personal savings allowance)	—
1,400	@ 20% (basic rate on savings income)	280.00
2,000	@ 0% (dividend nil rate)	—
1,080	@ 20% (policy gain at basic rate)	216.00
34,500		
1,520	@ 40% (policy gain at higher rate)	608.00
£36,020		
		7,008.00
Deduct:	Top slicing relief (as above)	216.00
		6,792.00
Deduct:	Basic rate of tax on policy gain (£2,600 @ 20%)	520.00
	Tax liability (subject to PAYE deductions)	£6,272.00

Notes

(a) Tax is calculated by treating the policy gain as the top slice of income. Under the top slicing relief calculation, the total policy gain is divided by the number of complete years the policy has run (two) and the resulting tax multiplied by the same factor.

(b) If a qualifying policy is replaced by a new qualifying policy on a different life or lives then, if certain conditions are met, no chargeable event occurs on the surrender of the earlier policy. [*ITTOIA 2005, s 542*].

(c) Gains on certain offshore policies do not carry a notional tax credit, though top slicing relief is computed as if a notional tax credit were available. [*ITTOIA 2005, s 531*]. A similar rule applies to gains on policies issued by friendly societies as part of their tax exempt life or endowment business.

(B) Top slicing relief — multiple chargeable events in same tax year

[*ITTOIA 2005, s 537*]

On 1 May 2018, a policyholder realises a gain of £10,000 on the maturity of a four-year non-qualifying policy. On 1 March 2019, he realises a gain of £12,000 on the surrender of a non-qualifying policy which he took out on 1 October 2012. For 2018/19, his *taxable* income excluding the two policy gains is £33,300. He is not a Scottish taxpayer.

Tax on policy gains without top slicing relief

1,200	@ 20% (basic rate)	240.00
20,800	@ 40%	8,320.00
£22,000		8,560.00
Deduct Basic rate tax (£22,000 × 20%)		4,400.00
Tax payable on policy gains		£4,160.00

Tax on policy gains with top slicing relief

£10,000 divided by 4 years =	2,500
£12,000 divided by 6 years =	2,000
	£4,500

Tax on £4,500 as top slice of income:

1,200	@ 20% (basic rate)	240.00
3,300	@ 40%	1,320.00
£4,500		1,560.00
Deduct Basic rate tax (£4,500 × 20%)		900.00
		£660.00

$$£660.00 \times \frac{2,500}{4,500} = £\,366.67.\ £\,366.67 \times 4 = \qquad 1,466.68$$

$$£660.00 \times \frac{2,000}{4,500} = £\,293.33.\ £\,293.33 \times 6 = \qquad 1,760.00$$

Tax payable on policy gains £3,226.68

Note

(a) The basic rate limit for 2018/19 is £34,500, so the amount of policy gains falling within the basic rate band in this case is £1,200 (£34,500 – £33,300).

14.2 PARTIAL SURRENDERS OF LIFE POLICIES ETC.

[*ITTOIA 2005, s 507*]

Sheridan took out a policy on 4 February 2011 for a single premium of £15,000. The contract permits periodical withdrawals.

(i) Sheridan draws £750 p.a. on 4 February in each subsequent year.

There is no taxable gain because at the end of each insurance year the total value of rights surrendered (VRS) does not exceed the total allowable payments (TAP).

	£	
At 3.2.15 withdrawals have been	2,250	(VRS)
Deduct 4 × $^1/_{20}$ of the sums paid in	3,000	(TAP)
	No gain	

(ii) On 20.7.15 Sheridan withdraws an additional £3,500.

	£	
At 3.2.16 withdrawals have been	6,500	(VRS)
Deduct 5 × $^1/_{20}$ of the sums paid in	3,750	(TAP)
Chargeable 2015/16	£2,750	

(iii) Sheridan makes no annual withdrawal on 4.2.16 but on 4.2.17 makes a withdrawal of £1,000.

In the year 2017/18 the position is

	£	£	
At 3.2.18 withdrawals have been		7,500	
Deduct Withdrawals at last charge		6,500	
		1,000	(VRS)
Deduct 7 × $^1/_{20}$ of the sums paid in	5,250		
less amount deducted at last charge	3,750		
		1,500	(TAP)
		No gain	

(iv) Sheridan surrenders the policy on 1.7.18 for £13,250, having made a further £1,000 withdrawal on 4.2.18.

In the year 2018/19, the position is

	£	£
Proceeds on surrender		13,250
Previous withdrawals		8,500
		21,750
Deduct Premium paid	15,000	
Gains previously charged	2,750	
		17,750
Chargeable 2018/19		£4,000

Notes

(a) VRS is the total of all surrenders, withdrawals etc. for each insurance year since commencement *less* the total of such values which have been brought into account in earlier chargeable events.

(b) TAP is the total of annual fractions of one-twentieth (with a maximum of 20 twentieths) of the premiums, lump sums etc. paid for each insurance year since commencement *less* the total of such fractions which have been brought into account in earlier chargeable events.

(c) The chargeable event gain is generally treated as arising at the end of the insurance year and is thus chargeable to income for the tax year in which the insurance year ends. [*ITTOIA 2005, s 509*].

(d) An insurance year is a year ending twelve months from the commencement of the policy or from an anniversary thereof. [*ITTOIA 2005, s 499*].

(e) The gain on final surrender of the policy is calculated under *ITTOIA 2005, s 491*.

(f) The gains in (ii) and (iv) above are subject to any available top slicing relief (see **14.1** above).

14.3 ADJUSTMENTS FOR PERIODS OF NON-UK RESIDENCE

[*ITTOIA 2005, s 528; FA 2013, Sch 8 paras 3, 7, Sch 45 paras 86(2)–(6), 153(2)*]

Churchill took out a life policy on 1 May 2008 paying premiums of £100 per month. On 1 May 2014 he exercised a right under the policy to vary the policy so as to increase the benefits payable under it; the premiums then increase to £120 per month. On 31 March 2019 Churchill assigns all the rights under the policy to an unconnected third party for £15,520. Churchill was non-resident in the UK throughout the three years 2009/10 to 2011/12 but UK resident throughout 2008/09 and 2012/13. He was also UK resident for the six years 2013/14 to 2018/19. Subject to the chargeable event gain, his income for 2018/19 amounts to £46,250, consisting entirely of employment income. Churchill is not a Scottish taxpayer.

The chargeable event gain is calculated as follows

	£	£
Total benefit value (assignment proceeds)		15,520
Deduct: Total allowable deductions (premiums paid):		
1.5.08–30.4.14 (£100 x 72 months)	7,200	
1.5.14–1.3.19 (£120 x 59 months)	7,080	14,280
Chargeable event gain		1,240
Less: Reduction for periods of non-UK residence (note (b)):		
$£1,240 \times \frac{1,095\ (6.4.09 - 5.4.12)}{3,985\ (1.5.08 - 31.3.19)}$		340
Taxable gain		£900

Top slicing relief is calculated as follows

	Normal basis	Top slicing relief claim
	£	£
Taxable gain (note (c))	900	129
Earnings	46,250	46,250
	47,150	46,379
Deduct Personal allowance	11,850	11,850
	£35,300	£34,529

	Normal basis		Top slicing relief claim
	£		£
Tax applicable to policy gain			
Higher rate			
£800 at 40%	320.00		—
£29 at 40%	—		11.60
	320.00		11.60
Deduct			
Basic rate			
£800 at 20%	160.00		—
£29 at 20%	—		5.80
			£5.80
Appropriate multiple 7 × £5.80 (note (c))			£40.60
Tax chargeable lower of	£160.00	and	£40.60
Top slicing relief (£160.00 − £40.60) =	£119.40		

Notes

(a) As regards policies issued in respect of insurances made on or after 6 April 2013, a chargeable event gain is reduced to take account of any periods during which the policyholder was not resident in the UK. The reduction also applies in relation to an insurance made before 6 April 2013 if, on or after that date, the policy is varied so as to increase the benefits (an exercise of rights conferred by the policy being treated for this purpose as a variation), is assigned (in whole or in part) or becomes held as security for a debt.

(b) In the reduction fraction, the numerator is the number of days in the 'material interest period' when the individual was not UK resident. The denominator is the total number of days in the material interest period. The '*material interest period*' is broadly the policy period, i.e. the period for which the policy has run before the chargeable event occurs; see *ITTOIA 2005, s 528(5)(10)* for the full definition.

(c) In computing top slicing relief, the total policy gain is normally divided by the number of *complete* years the policy has run (10 years in this example) and the resulting tax multiplied by the same factor — see **14.1**(A) above. However, where a reduction has been made for periods of non-UK residence, that number is itself reduced by the number of complete years consisting wholly of days of non-UK residence (3 years in this example). Therefore, a factor of 7 (10 minus 3) applies in this example. [*ITTOIA 2005, s 536(6)–(8); FA 2013, Sch 8 paras 5, 7, Sch 45 paras 88(2)(3), 153(2)*].

(d) The calculation of tax payable would then proceed as in **14.1**(A) above with the top slicing relief given as a tax reduction.

15 Losses

Cross-references. See also **18.2–18.4** PARTNERSHIPS, and see **26.2** SELF-ASSESSMENT for the method of giving effect under self-assessment to the carry-back of losses to earlier years of assessment.

15.1 SET-OFF OF TRADING LOSSES AGAINST GENERAL INCOME

[*ITA 2007, ss 61(2), 64, 65*]

L, a single woman, commences to trade on 1 July 2014, preparing accounts to 30 June, and has the following results (as adjusted for tax purposes) for the first four years.

	Profit/(loss)
	£
Year ended 30 June 2015	27,000
Year ended 30 June 2016	9,000
Year ended 30 June 2017	(3,000)
Year ended 30 June 2018	(25,000)

L has other income of £19,500 for 2017/18 and £22,000 for 2018/19, having had no other income in the earlier years. The 2018/19 income includes dividend income of £3,000.

The taxable profits for the first four tax years of the business are as follows

	£
2014/15 (1.7.14–5.4.15) (£27,000 × $^{9}/_{12}$)	20,250*
2015/16 (y/e 30.6.15)	27,000
2016/17 (y/e 30.6.16)	9,000
2017/18 (y/e 30.6.17)	Nil
2018/19 (y/e 30.6.18)	Nil

* Overlap relief accruing – £20,250.

L claims relief under *ITA 2007, s 64(2)(a)* (set-off against income of the same year) for the 2017/18 loss (£3,000). She also claims relief under *ITA 2007, s 64(2)(b)* (set-off against income of the preceding year) for the 2018/19 loss (£25,000), with a further claim being made under *ITA 2007, s 64(2)(a)* for the balance of that loss.

The tax position for 2017/18 and 2018/19 is as follows

2017/18	£
Total income before loss relief	19,500
Deduct Claim under *ITA 2007, s 64(2)(a) note (b)*	3,000
	16,500
Deduct Claim under *ITA 2007, s 64(2)(b)*	16,500
Net income	Nil

2018/19	
Total income before loss relief	22,000
Deduct Claim under *ITA 2007, s 64(2)(a)*	8,500
Net income	13,500
Deduct Personal allowance	(11,850)
Taxable income	£1,650
Tax payable £1,650 @ 0% (dividend nil rate) (note (d))	—

Loss utilisation

	£
2017/18	
Loss available under *ITA 2007, s 64(2)(a)*	3,000
Deduct Utilised in 2017/18	3,000
Loss available under *ITA 2007, s 64(2)(b)*	25,000
Deduct Utilised in 2017/18	16,500
Loss available for relief in 2018/19 under *ITA 2007, s 64(2)(a)*	£8,500
2018/19	
Balance of loss available under *ITA 2007, s 64(2)(a)*	8,500
Deduct Utilised in 2018/19	8,500

Notes

(a) Under *ITA 2007, s 64*, relief is available for the tax year in which the loss arises (*section 64(2)(a)*) or the immediately preceding year (*section 64(2)(b)*).

(b) Where losses of two different years are set against the income of one tax year, then, regardless of the order of claims, relief for the current year's loss is given in priority to that for the following year's loss. [*ITA 2007, s 65(2)–(4)*]. This is beneficial to the taxpayer in this example as it leaves £8,500 of the 2018/19 loss to be relieved in that year.

(c) By making the claim under *ITA 2007, s 64(2)(b)* (set-off against income of the preceding year), L has avoided a tax liability for 2017/18 but has also wasted her personal allowance. This claim might not have been made in practice.

(d) Both the personal allowance and loss relief can be deducted in such way as will result in the greatest reduction in the taxpayer's liability to income tax (see **1.4** ALLOWANCES AND TAX RATES). It is assumed that for 2018/19 L will deduct these firstly from income other than dividend income. This leaves dividend income in charge which will attract the dividend allowance.

(e) See **15.3** below for losses in the opening years of a business.

15.2 SET-OFF OF TRADING LOSSES ETC. AGAINST CAPITAL GAINS

[*ITA 2007, s 71; TCGA 1992, ss 261B, 261C*]

M has carried on a trade for some years, preparing accounts to 30 June each year. For the year ended 30 June 2018 he makes a trading loss of £17,000. Taxable profit for 2017/18 is £5,000 and other income for 2017/18 and 2018/19 amounts to £2,000. He makes a capital gain of £15,900 and a capital loss of £1,000 for 2018/19 and has capital losses brought forward of £11,000. M makes claims for loss relief, against income of 2017/18 and income and gains of 2018/19, under *ITA 2007, s 64(2)(b), s 64(2)(a)* and *TCGA 1992, s 261B*.

Calculation of 'relevant amount'

	£
Trading loss — year ended 30.6.18	17,000
Relieved against other income for 2018/19	(2,000)
Relieved against income for 2017/18	(7,000)
Relevant amount	£8,000

Calculation of 'maximum amount'

	£
Gains for 2018/19	15,900
Losses for 2018/19	(1,000)
Unrelieved losses brought forward	(11,000)
Maximum amount	£3,900

Relief under *TCGA 1992, s 261B*

	£	£
Gains for the year		15,900
Losses for the year	1,000	
Relief under *TCGA 1992, s 261B*	3,900	
		4,900
Gain (covered by annual exemption)		£11,000
Capital losses brought forward and carried forward		£11,000

Loss memorandum

	£
Trading loss	17,000
Claimed under *ITA 2007, s 64(2)(a)*	(2,000)
Claimed under *ITA 2007, s 64(2)(b)*	(7,000)
Claimed under *TCGA 1992, s 261B*	(3,900)
Unutilised loss	£4,100

Notes

(a) Where relief is available under *ITA 2007, s 64* (set-off against general income) for a tax year and either a claim is made under that *section* or the person's total income for the year is nil, a claim may also be made to treat an amount of trading loss (determined as above) as an allowable capital loss for the year.

(b) The amount to be set against gains is restricted to so much of the 'relevant amount' as does not exceed the 'maximum amount'. The '*relevant amount*' is so much of the loss that cannot be set against income for the year and has not been otherwise relieved. The '*maximum amount*' is the amount chargeable to capital gains tax for the year, ignoring the annual exemption and the effect of *TCGA 1992, s 261B* itself.

(c) Capital losses brought forward are deducted in ascertaining the 'maximum amount', and thus the relief due under *TCGA 1992, s 261B*, but the relief itself is treated as an allowable loss for the year of claim and thus given in priority to capital losses brought forward.

(d) In this example, £700 of the capital gains tax annual exemption of £11,700 is wasted, but the brought forward capital losses are preserved for carry-forward against gains of future years. If M had *not* made the claim under *TCGA 1992, s 261B*, his net gains for the year of £14,900 would have been reduced to the annual exempt amount by deducting £3,200 of the losses brought forward. Only £7,800 of capital losses would remain available for carry-forward against future gains and a further £3,900 of trading losses would have been available for carry-forward against future trading profits. So the effect of the claim is to preserve capital losses at the expense of trading losses.

15.3 LOSSES IN EARLY YEARS OF A BUSINESS

(A) Losses carried back three years

[*ITA 2007, ss 72–74*]

F, a single person, commences to trade on 1 December 2015, preparing accounts to 30 November. The first four years of trading produce losses of £12,000, £9,000, £2,000 and £1,000 respectively, these figures being as adjusted for tax purposes. For each of the four tax years 2012/13 to 2015/16, F had other income of £8,000.

The losses for tax purposes are as follows

			£	£
2015/16	(1.12.15–5.4.16) (£12,000 × $^{4}/_{12}$)			4,000
2016/17	(y/e 30.11.16)		12,000	
	Less already allocated to 2015/16		4,000	8,000
2017/18	(y/e 30.11.17)			9,000
2018/19	(y/e 30.11.18)			2,000
2019/20	(y/e 30.11.19)	note (b)		1,000

Loss relief under *ITA 2007, s 72* is available as follows

	Losses available			
	2015/16	2016/17	2017/18	2018/19
	£	£	£	£
Losses available	4,000	8,000	9,000	2,000
Set against total income				
2012/13	4,000	—	—	—
2013/14	—	8,000	—	—
2014/15	—	—	8,000	—
2015/16	—	—	1,000	2,000
	£4,000	£8,000	£9,000	£2,000

Revised total income is thus £4,000 for 2012/13, nil for 2013/14 and 2014/15 and £5,000 for 2015/16.

Notes

(a) Losses are computed by reference to the same basis periods as profits. Where any part of a loss would otherwise fall to be included in the computations for two successive tax years (as is the case for 2015/16 and 2016/17 in this example), that part is excluded from the computation for the second of those years. [*ITA 2007, s 61(2)*].

(b) The loss for the year ended 30 November 2019 in this example is not available for relief under *ITA 2007, s 72* as it does not fall into the first four *tax years* of the business (even though it is incurred in the first four years of trading). It is of course available for relief under *ITA 2007, s 64* (depending on the level of other income for 2018/19 and 2019/20) or for carry-forward under *ITA 2007, s 83*.

(B) Computation of losses in early years

Q commenced trading on 1 February 2018 and prepared accounts to 31 December. He made a trading loss of £20,900 in the eleven months to 31 December 2018 and profits of £18,000 and £16,000 in the years to 31 December 2019 and 2020 respectively. He has substantial other income for 2017/18 and 2018/19 and makes claims under *ITA 2007, s 64* for both years.

Taxable profits/(allowable losses) are as follows

		£	£
2017/18	(1.2.18–5.4.18) (£20,900) × 2/11		(3,800)
2018/19	(1.2.18–31.1.19):		
	1.2.18–31.12.18	(20,900)	
	Less already allocated to 2017/18	3,800	
		(17,100)	
	1.1.19–31.1.19 £18,000 × 1/12	1,500	
			(15,600)
2019/20	(y/e 31.12.19)		18,000
	(Overlap relief accruing — £1,500)		
2020/21	(y/e 31.12.20)		16,000

Notes

(a) Losses are computed by reference to the same basis periods as profits. Where any part of a loss would otherwise fall to be included in the computations for two successive tax years (as is the case for 2017/18 and 2018/19 in this example), that part is excluded from the computation for the second of those years. [*ITA 2007, s 61(2)*].

(b) Losses available for relief for 2017/18 and 2018/19 are £3,800 and £15,600 respectively. If both years' losses are carried forward under *ITA 2007, s 83* instead of being set against other income (under either *ITA 2007, s 64* or *s 72*), the aggregate loss of £19,400 will extinguish the 2019/20 profit and reduce the 2020/21 profit by £1,400. Note that although the actual loss was £20,900, there is no further amount available for carry-forward: the difference of £1,500 has been used in aggregation in 2018/19.

(c) The net profit for the first three accounting periods is £13,100 (£18,000 + £16,000 – £20,900). The net taxable profit for the first four tax years is £14,600 (£18,000 + £16,000 – £3,800 – £15,600). The difference of £1,500 represents the overlap relief accrued, which will be given on cessation or on a change of accounting date resulting in a basis period of more than one year. Note that the overlap profit of £1,500 is by reference to an overlap period of *three* months, i.e. 1.2.18 to 5.4.18 (two months — overlap profit nil) and 1.1.19 to 31.1.19 (one month — overlap profit £1,500).

15.4 TERMINAL LOSS RELIEF

[*ITA 2007, ss 63, 89–91*]

B, a trader with a 30 September year end, ceases to trade on 30 June 2018. Tax-adjusted results for his last two periods of account are as follows

	Trading profit/(loss)
	£
Year ended 30 September 2017	28,000
Nine months to 30 June 2018	(9,000)

At cessation, there is unused overlap relief of £2,000.

The terminal loss relief available is as follows

	£	£
2018/19 (6.4.18 – 30.6.18)		
£9,000 × 3/9		3,000
plus unused overlap relief		2,000
Terminal loss		5,000
2017/18 (1.7.17 – 5.4.18)		
1.10.17 – 5.4.18 £9,000 × 6/9	6,000	
1.7.17 – 30.9.17 (£28,000) × 3/12	(7,000)	
Net profit	(1,000)	
Terminal loss		Nil
Terminal loss relief		£5,000

Notes

(a) In determining the terminal loss arising in a part of the final twelve months (a terminal loss period) that falls into any one tax year, a profit made in that period must be netted off against a loss in that period. In this example, no loss has been incurred in the terminal loss period that falls within 2017/18. However, two different tax years are looked at separately, so that the 'net profit' of £1,000 arising in the terminal loss period falling within 2017/18 does not have to be netted off against the 2018/19 loss and is instead disregarded.

(b) Available overlap relief is given as a deduction in computing the profit or loss of the final *tax year* and is thus included in a terminal loss in full. It does not fall to be apportioned between tax years in the same way as a loss sustained for a *period of account*.

(c) The losses which do not form part of the terminal loss claim may be relieved under *ITA 2007, s 64*, and in practice, where other income is sufficient, the whole of the losses would in many cases be claimed under *section 64*.

15.5 SHARE LOSS RELIEF

[*ITA 2007, ss 131–151*]

Over the years, X has acquired a number of shareholdings in unquoted companies and suffers the following losses.

(i) 500 shares in A Ltd (a qualifying trading company) which X subscribed for in 1996. Allowable loss for CGT purposes on liquidation in June 2017 — £12,000.

(ii) 500 shares in B Ltd which X subscribed for in 1997 at £10 per share. B Ltd traded as builders until 2007 when it changed its trade to that of buying and selling land. X received an arm's length offer for the shares of £3 per share in May 2017 which he accepted.

(iii) In 1997, X subscribed for 2,000 shares in C Ltd at £50 per share. In 2001, his aunt gave him a further 1,000 shares. The market value of the shares at that time was £60 per share. The company has been a qualifying trading company since 1993 but has fallen on hard times recently. X was offered £20 per share in June 2018 and accepted it to the extent of 1,500 shares.

The treatment of these losses in relation to income tax would be as follows

(i) Loss claim — *ITA 2007, s 132*, 2017/18 or 2016/17 — £12,000.

(ii) No loss claim possible under *ITA 2007, s 132* as the company does not meet the trading requirement.

(iii) *Step 1.* Compute the allowable loss for capital gains tax purposes.

Share pool

	Shares	Qualifying expenditure
		£
1997 subscription	2,000	100,000
2001 acquisition	1,000	60,000
	3,000	160,000
2018 disposal	(1,500)	(80,000)
Pool carried forward	1,500	£80,000

	£
Disposal consideration 1,500 × £20	30,000
Allowable cost $\frac{1,500}{3,000}$ × £160,000	80,000
Allowable capital loss	£50,000

Step 2. Applying a LIFO basis, identify the qualifying shares (500) and the non-qualifying shares (1,000) comprised in the disposal.

Step 3. Calculate the proportion of the loss attributable to the qualifying shares.

Loss referable to 500 qualifying shares 500/1,500 × £50,000	£16,667

Step 4. Compare the loss in *Step 3* with the actual cost of the qualifying shares, *viz*.

Cost of 500 qualifying shares 500/2,000 × £100,000	£25,000

No restriction is necessary as the cost of the qualifying shares exceeds the loss in *Step 3*.

Loss claim — *ITA 2007, s 132* for 2018/19 or 2017/18 — £16,667

(The loss not relieved against income (£50,000 - £16,667 = £33,333) remains an allowable loss for capital gains tax purposes.)

X makes all possible claims under *ITA 2007, s 132* so as to obtain relief against the earliest possible income. He is a single man and has total income of £7,000 for 2016/17, £11,500 for 2017/18 and £10,000 for 2018/19.

The losses available are as follows

	2017/18 disposals	2018/19 disposals
	£	£
A Ltd shares	12,000	
C Ltd shares		16,667

Claims are made as follows

	£
2016/17	
Total income	7,000
Claim under *ITA 2007, s 132(1)(b)*	(7,000)
Net income	Nil
2017/18	
Total income	11,500
Claim under *ITA 2007, s 132(1)(a)* note (b)	(5,000)
	6,500
Claim under *ITA 2007, s 132(1)(b)*	(6,500)
Net income	Nil
2018/19	
Total income	10,000
Claim under *ITA 2007, s 132(1)(a)*	(10,000)
Net income	Nil

Loss utilisation

	£
2017/18 loss	
Loss available	12,000
Relief claimed for 2016/17 *(ITA 2007, s 132(1)(b))*	(7,000)
Relief claimed for 2017/18 *(ITA 2007, s 132(1)(a))*	(5,000)
2018/19 loss	
Loss available	16,667
Relief claimed for 2017/18 *(ITA 2007, s 132(1)(b))*	(6,500)
Relief claimed for 2018/19 *(ITA 2007, s 132(1)(a))*	(10,000)
Unused balance note (c)	£167

Notes

(a) Losses may be set against current year's income (*ITA 2007, s 132(1)(a)*) or preceding year's income (*ITA 2007, s 132(1)(b)*). In this example, losses have been set against preceding year's income first, as X wished to obtain relief against earliest possible income, but this need not be the case.

(b) Where two years' losses are set against one year's income, the current year's loss is relieved in priority to that of the following year. [*ITA 2007, s 133(3)*].

(c) The unused balance of the 2018/19 loss cannot be relieved under *ITA 2007, s 132* due to insufficiency of income and therefore reverts to being a capital loss available to reduce chargeable gains.

15.6 PROPERTY BUSINESS LOSSES

[*ITA 2007, ss 120–124*]

Sergey purchases an empty shop in a disadvantaged area and converts it to offices which he leases out to a firm of solicitors. Sergey incurs conversion expenditure of £20,000 in each of the two years ended 5 April 2016 and 5 April 2017. It is accepted by HMRC that this expenditure qualifies for business premises renovation allowances under *CAA 2001, ss 360A–360Z4* (see **3.1** CAPITAL ALLOWANCES). Sergey claims a 100% initial allowance for both 2015/16 and 2016/17 on the conversion expenditure but is not entitled to any other capital allowances. Sergey makes the following taxable profits and losses in respect of his UK property business:

	Profit/(loss) before capital allowances	Capital allowances	Profit/(loss) after capital allowances
	£	£	£
2015/16	(4,000)	(20,000)	(24,000)
2016/17	10,000	(20,000)	(10,000)
2017/18	(3,000)	—	(3,000)
2018/19	19,000	—	19,000

Sergey has other income of £10,000 for 2015/16, £40,000 for 2016/17 and £42,000 for both 2017/18 and 2018/19. He makes a claim under *ITA 2007, s 120* in respect of the property business loss for 2015/16 to set against income of 2015/16 first, with any remaining amount to be set against income of 2016/17. He claims under *ITA 2007, s 120* for the2016/17 loss to be set against other income of 2016/17.

The tax position for 2015/16 to 2018/19 is as follows.

	£
2015/16	
Total income	10,000
Deduct claim under *ITA 2007, s 120* note (a)	(10,000)
Net income	Nil

	£
2016/17	
Total income	40,000
Deduct claims under *ITA 2007, s 120* note (b)	
2015/16 loss	(10,000)
2016/17 loss	(10,000)
Net income	£20,000

	£	£
2017/18		
Loss for the year	(3,000)	
Add 2015/16 loss b/fwd	(4,000)	
Loss c/fwd	(7,000)	
Other income		42,000
Net income		£42,000

	£	£
2018/19		
Property income	19,000	
Deduct loss b/wd	(7,000)	12,000
Other income		42,000
Net income		£54,000

Loss utilisation

	£
Loss for 2015/16	24,000
Used in 2015/16 under *ITA 2007, s 120*	(10,000)
Used in 2016/17 under *ITA 2007, s 120*	(10,000)
Used in 2018/19 under *ITA 2007, s 118*	(4,000)
Loss for 2016/17	10,000
Used in 2016/17 under *ITA 2007, s 120*	(10,000)
Loss for 2017/18	3,000
Used in 2018/19 under *ITA 2007, s 118*	(3,000)

Notes

(a) The amount of relief for 2015/16 in respect of the 2015/16 loss under *ITA 2007, s 120* is the lowest of:

(i) income of 2015/16 − £10,000;

(ii) the property business loss for 2015/16 = £24,000; and

(iii) the net capital allowances (after deducting any balancing charges) for 2015/16 = £20,000.

Relief is therefore restricted to £10,000. In practice, Sergey would be likely to claim relief for the 2015/16 loss for 2016/17 only, to avoid wasting personal allowances.

(b) The amount of relief for 2016/17 in respect of the 2015/16 loss under *ITA 2007, s 120* is the balance of the lower of (ii) and (iii) in note (a) above after deducting the relief given in 2015/16 (i.e. £10,000), or where lower the income of 2016/17.

The amount of relief for 2016/17 in respect of the 2016/17 loss under *ITA 2007, s 120* is the lowest of:

(A) income of the year less relief given for 2016/17 in respect of the 2015/16 loss (£40,000 − £10,000) = £30,000;

(B) the property business loss for 2016/17 = £10,000; and

(C) the net capital allowances for 2016/17 = £20,000.

Relief is therefore restricted to £10,000.

(c) A claim under *ITA 2007, s 120* must be made on or before the first anniversary of 31 January following the tax year for which relief is claimed.

(d) Any balance of a property business loss not claimed under *ITA 2007, s 120* is carried forward to be set against profits of the UK property business for subsequent years, earliest first. [*ITA 2007, ss 118, 119*]. The 2017/18 loss in this example is not available at all under *ITA 2007, s 120* and can be relieved only by carry-forward.

(e) Where a UK property business is carried on in relation to land consisting of or including an agricultural estate, a claim may be made under *ITA 2007, s 120* as above to the extent that the loss consists of 'allowable agricultural expenses', being expenses attributable to the estate which are deductible in respect of maintenance, repairs, insurance or management of the estate (and not in respect of interest on a loan). [*ITA 2007, ss 122, 123, 127B; FA 2012, s 10*]. In computing the amount of relief, the amount in (ii) in note (a) above would then be the net capital allowances plus the allowable agricultural expenses.

(f) A restriction applies if a loss arises in connection with tax avoidance arrangements and there is a net amount of capital allowances. No property loss relief against general income may be given to the person making the loss for so much of the available loss relief as is attributable to a plant and machinery annual investment allowance. [*ITA 2007, s 127A*].

(g) There is no relief against general income where the results of the property business are calculated on the cash basis. [*ITA 2007, s 127BA*].

16 Married Persons and Civil Partners

Cross-reference. See also **1.7** ALLOWANCES AND TAX RATES for the married couple's allowance, and see **1.6** ALLOWANCES AND TAX RATES for the transfer of personal allowances between spouses/civil partners.

16.1 TRANSFER OF PERSONAL RELIEFS

Cross-reference. See **1** ALLOWANCES AND TAX RATES for the starting rate for savings, the personal savings allowance and the dividend allowance.

(A) Election to transfer basic married couple's allowance

[*ITA 2007, ss 45, 47–50; FA 2015, s 2*]

Before 6 April 2018, Mr and Mrs Scarlet made a joint election under *ITA 2007, s 48* to transfer from husband to wife the whole of the basic married couple's allowance with effect for 2018/19 and later years. Mr Scarlet was born on 29 May 1934 and his wife on 6 January 1953. The couple married before 5 December 2005 and have not made the joint election under *ITA 2007, s 44* to be treated in the same way as couples marrying on or after that date. Neither is a Scottish taxpayer. For 2018/19, their incomes are as follows.

	Mr Scarlet	Mrs Scarlet
	£	£
Employment income	—	39,215
Pension income	11,530	—
Dividends	2,000	2,000
Building society interest	10,000	—

The couple's tax position for 2018/19 is as follows

	£	£
Employment income	—	39,215
Pension income	11,530	
Dividends	2,000	2,000
Building society interest	10,000	
Total and net income	23,530	41,215
Deduct Personal allowance	11,850	11,850
Taxable income	£11,680	£29,365
Tax payable:		
5,000 @ 0% (starting rate for savings)	—	
1,000 @ 0% (personal savings allowance)	—	
3,680 @ 20% (basic rate on savings income)	736.00	

2,000 @ 0% (dividend allowance)	—	
27,365 @ 20% (basic rate)		5,473.00
2,000 @ 0% (dividend allowance)		—
	736.00	5,473.00
Deduct Married couple's allowance (£8,695):		
£5,335 @ 10%	533.50	
£3,360 @ 10%		336.00
Tax liabilities (subject to PAYE deductions)	£202.50	£5,137.00

Notes

(a) Married couple's allowance is available only where one of the spouses/civil partners was born before 6 April 1935.

(b) A wife can elect to receive half the basic married couple's allowance (i.e. the minimum amount below which the age-related allowance may not be reduced by reference to the income of the claimant) or, as illustrated in this example, husband and wife can jointly elect for the whole of the basic amount to be allocated to the wife. An election is not dependent on levels of income but, except for the year of marriage, must be made before the start of the first year for which it is to apply (e.g. before 6 April 2018 to have effect for 2018/19). [*ITA 2007, ss 47–50*].

(c) If the wife's income is too low to fully utilise the married couple's allowance allocated to her, she may transfer the excess allowance back to the husband. [*ITA 2007, s 52*]. The transfer operates in the same way as a transfer of surplus married couple's allowance from husband to wife — see (B) below.

(d) As the married couple's allowance attracts tax relief at a fixed rate of 10%, an election to transfer the basic allowance does not save any tax, although the election may have cash flow advantages where the wife pays tax under PAYE and the husband does not.

(e) Civil partners and couples who marry on or after 5 December 2005 (or who married before that date and elect into the new rules) are also able to transfer the basic married couple's allowance between them. [*ITA 2007, ss 47–50*].

(f) As they have claimed married couple's allowance, no part of the personal allowance can be transferred between husband and wife as in **1.6** ALLOWANCES AND TAX RATES. [*ITA 2007, s 55B(2); FA 2014, s 11(2)*].

(B) Transfer of surplus married couple's allowance

[*ITA 2007, ss 45, 51, 53; FA 2015, s 2*]

Mr Grey, who was born on 19 July 1933, has pension income of £11,670 and building society interest of £3,900 for 2018/19, and his wife, who was born in 1953, has a salary of £21,815 and building society interest of £2,500. Mr and Mrs Grey receive interest of £2,800 in 2018/19 from a bank deposit account in their joint names. The couple have not made the joint election under *ITA 2007, s 44* to be treated in the same way as couples who marry on or after 5 December 2005. Neither have they made the election at (A) above to transfer the basic married couple's allowance between them. Neither is a Scottish taxpayer. Mr Grey gives notice under *ITA 2007, s 51* to transfer the unused balance of his married couple's allowance for 2018/19 to his wife.

The couple's tax position for 2018/19 is as follows

	Mr Grey	Mrs Grey
	£	£
Employment income	—	21,815
Pension income	11,670	—
Building society interest	3,900	2,500
Bank deposit interest (note (b))	1,400	1,400
Total and net income	16,970	25,715
Deduct Personal allowance	11,850	11,850
Taxable income	£5,120	£13,865
Tax payable:		
5,000 @ 0% (starting rate for savings)	—	
120 @ 0% (personal savings allowance)	—	
9,965 @ 20% (basic rate)		1,993.00
1,000 @ 0% (personal savings allowance)		—
2,900 @ 20% (basic rate on savings income)		580.00
	—	2,573.00
Deduct Married couple's allowance 8,695 @ 10% = £869.50, but restricted to nil	—	
Deduct Excess married couple's allowance		869.50
Tax liabilities (subject to PAYE)	Nil	£1,703.50

Notes

(a) Where the married couple's allowance is restricted to the amount that reduces the tax liability to nil (or where no married couple's allowance can be given as there is no tax liability), the unused part of the allowance (or all of it) can be transferred to the spouse. Married couple's allowance is available only where one of the spouses/civil partners was born before 6 April 1935.

(b) Income from property held in their joint names is normally divided equally between husband and wife (and civil partners). [*ITA 2007, s 836*]. Note that certain gifts and settlements between spouses (and civil partners) of property from which income arises are not valid transfers of income. [*ITTOIA 2005, s 626*]. This applies where the donor retains an interest in the property. Outright gifts comprising both income and capital should not be caught.

(c) Civil partners and couples who marry on or after 5 December 2005 (or who married before that date and elect into the new rules) are also able to transfer surplus married couple's allowance between them.

(d) As they have claimed married couple's allowance, no part of the personal allowance can be transferred between husband and wife as in **1.6** ALLOWANCES AND TAX RATES. [*ITA 2007, s 55B(2); FA 2014, s 11(2)*].

16.2 MAINTENANCE PAYMENTS

[*ITA 2007, ss 453–456, Sch 2 para 101*]

Mr Green, who was born on 7 October 1933, separated from his wife in June 2004 and, under a Court Order dated 15 July 2005, pays maintenance of £300 per month to his ex-wife and £100 per month to his daughter, payments being due on the first of each calendar month commencing 1 August 2005. Mr Green has pension income of £17,820 and dividends of £2,200 for 2018/19. He is not a Scottish taxpayer. He re-marries on 6 October 2018.

			£
2018/19			
Mr Green			
Earned income			17,820
Dividends			2,200
Total and net income			20,020
Deduct Personal allowance			11,850
Taxable income			£8,170
Tax payable:			
5,970	@ 20% (basic rate)		1,194.00
2,000	@ 0% (dividend nil rate)		—
200	@ 7.5% (dividend ordinary rate)		15.00
			1,209.00
Deduct	Maintenance relief — wife:		
	£3,600 paid, but restricted to £3,360 @ 10%		336.00
			873.00
Deduct	Married couple's allowance		
	£8,695 × $^{6}/_{12}$ = £4,348 @ 10%		434.80
Tax liability (subject to PAYE deductions)			£438.20

Notes

(a) Relief for qualifying maintenance payments is restricted to cases where at least one of the parties was aged 65 or over on 5 April 2000. The relief is restricted to an amount equal to a percentage of the basic married couple's allowance for the year. No relief is due for other maintenance payments. Relief is given by way of income tax reduction and is restricted to 10%.

(b) Maintenance payments are exempt from tax in the hands of the recipient.

(c) Tax relief for maintenance payments does not affect entitlement to the married couple's allowance either in the year of re-marriage or in later years. The allowance for the year of re-marriage is restricted in the normal way under *ITA 2007, s 54*.

17 Non-Residents

17.1 LIMIT ON LIABILITY TO INCOME TAX

[*ITA 2007, ss 56, 460, 810–828, Sch 2 paras 14–17; ITTOIA 2005, s 397(1)(4); FA 2013, Sch 45 para 152(5), Sch 46 paras 66, 72; FA 2016, Sch 1 paras 63(14)(15), 73*]

Hugh and Elizabeth are non-UK resident for 2018/19. They are each entitled to a UK personal allowance under *ITA 2007, s 56*. Their tax liabilities on total UK income for 2018/19, disregarding the limit under *ITA 2007, s 811*, are as follows

	Hugh	Elizabeth
	£	£
Net rental income (received gross)	2,150	7,550
Bank interest	18,100	7,230
Dividends	1,600	—
Total UK income	21,850	14,780
Deduct Personal allowance	11,850	11,850
Taxable UK income	£10,000	£2,930
Tax on total UK income:		
£5,000/2,930 @ 0% (starting rate for savings)	—	—
£1,000 @ 0% (personal savings allowance)	—	
£2,400 @ 20% (basic rate on interest)	480	
£1,600 @ 0% (dividend nil rate)	—	
	£480.00	—

But tax is limited under *ITA 2007, s 811* as follows

	£	£
Property income	2,150	7,550
(Bank interest and dividends are 'disregarded income'.)		
£2,150/7,550 @ 20% (basic rate)	£430.00	£1,510.00

Notes

(a) 'Disregarded income' includes interest and other annual payments, dividends from UK resident companies, purchased life annuity payments, profits from deeply discounted securities, distributions from unit trusts, some social security benefits (including state pensions), retirement annuities, certain UK-sourced employment-related annuities and any other income so designated by the Treasury, but generally excluding income from non-UK sources. [*ITA 2007, s 813*].

(b) Hugh's UK income tax liability is therefore restricted to £430.00. Elizabeth's liability remains at zero as in the normal computation.

17.2 NON-RESIDENT ENTERTAINERS AND SPORTSMEN

[*ITA 2007, ss 965–970; ITTOIA 2005, ss 13, 14; SI 1987 No 530; SI 2012 No 1359; SI 2013 No 605, Regs 2, 3*]

G, a professional golfer who is not resident in the UK, visits the UK in July 2018 to play in a tournament from which he earns £80,000 in appearance and prize money. He directs that the money be paid to a non-resident company which he controls. During his visit, he receives £8,000 from a UK television company for a series of interviews and £15,000 from a national newspaper for a number of exclusive articles. He arranges for 22.5% of the latter sum to be paid direct to his agent, also non-resident and who pays tax on his income at a rate not exceeding 25%, who arranged the deal. G incurs allowable expenses of £14,000 in connection with the trip. He has no other taxable income in the UK during 2018/19. He does not qualify for UK personal reliefs.

G's UK tax position for 2018/19 is as follows

		Taxable income		Tax with-held at source
		£		£
Prize and appearance money	note (b)	80,000		16,000
Fee from television company	note (c)	8,000		—
Fee for newspaper articles	note (d)	15,000		3,000
		103,000		19,000
Deduct Expenses		14,000		
		£89,000		
Tax payable			£	
34,500 at 20%			6,900	
54,500 at 40%			21,800	
£89,000				28,700
Tax payable				£9,700

Notes

(a) G is considered to have carried on a trade in the UK in respect of the payments received, or deemed to have been received, by him in connection with his UK activities. The trade is distinct from any other trade carried on by him. [*ITTOIA 2005, s 13*].

(b) A payment to a company under the entertainer's (or sportsman's) control (defined in accordance with *CTA 2010, ss 450, 451*) is treated as a payment to him and withholding tax at the basic rate must be deducted at source. [*ITTOIA 2005, s 14; SI 1987 No 530, Reg 7*].

(c) No withholding tax falls to be deducted from the television company fee as it does not exceed the de minimis limit. [*SI 1987 No 530, Reg 4(3)*]. The limit is equal to the amount of the basic personal allowance for the year in question (£11,850 for 2018/19). [*SI 2012 No 1359*].

(d) Although a percentage of the fee for newspaper articles was paid not to G but to his agent, it falls to be treated as G's income and is subject to withholding tax by virtue of his agent's being non-resident in the UK and liable to tax at a rate not exceeding 25% in his country of residence. [*SI 1987 No 530, Reg 7(2)(b)*].

(e) It is assumed in the above example that G would not have been able to agree with HMRC a reduced rate of withholding tax. He could have attempted to do so by making written application, under *SI 1987 No 530, Reg 5*, not later than 30 days before any payment fell to be made. However, the total reduced tax payment must represent, as nearly as can be, the actual liability of the performer.

18 Partnerships

18.1 BASIS OF ASSESSMENT

[ITTOIA 2005, ss 846–856, 863; FA 2014, Sch 17 paras 7, 11–13; FA 2016, Sch 1 paras 26, 73].

(A) Changes in partners etc.

P and Q commenced trading in partnership on 1 July 2013, making up accounts to 30 June. Under the partnership agreement P is to receive a salary of £10,000 per year and Q a salary of £5,000. Profits are to be shared in the ratio 3:2. On 1 July 2016 R becomes a partner, and profits for the year to 30 June 2017 are shared in the ratio 2:2:1 (P and Q continuing to receive their salaries). On 30 June 2017 P leaves the partnership and profits are thereafter shared between Q and R in the ratio 2:1 (Q continuing to receive his salary).

Results for relevant years up to 30 June 2018 are as follows

Year ended	Partners' salaries			Adjusted Profit
	P	Q	R	
	£	£	£	£
30.6.14	10,000	5,000	—	30,000
30.6.15	10,000	5,000	—	35,000
30.6.16	10,000	5,000	—	38,000
30.6.17	10,000	5,000	—	51,000
30.6.187	—	5,000	—	47,000

The adjusted profit figures above are after adding back partners' salaries, which are not deductible for tax purposes.

The tax position for the years 2013/14 to 2018/19 is as follows

	P	Q	R
	£	£	£
2013/14			
1.7.13–5.4.14			
Profits £(30,000 − 15,000) × $^{9}/_{12}$	6,750	4,500	
Salaries × $^{9}/_{12}$	7,500	3,750	
Trading income	£14,250	£8,250	

2014/15			
Y/e 30.6.14			
Profits £(30,000 − 15,000)	9,000	6,000	
Salaries	10,000	5,000	
Trading income	£19,000*	£11,000*	
*Overlap relief accrued: (1.7.13–5.4.14)	£14,250	£8,250	
2015/16			
Y/e 30.6.15			
Profits £(35,000 − 15,000)	12,000	8,000	
Salaries	10,000	5,000	
Trading income	£22,000	£13,000	
2016/17			
Y/e 30.6.16			
Profits £(38,000 − 15,000)	13,800	9,200	
Salaries	10,000	5,000	
1.7.16–5.4.17			
Profits £(51,000 − 15,000) × $^1/_5$ × $^9/_{12}$)			5,400
Trading income	£23,800	£14,200	£5,400
2017/18			
Y/e 30.6.17			
Profits £(51,000 − 15,000)	14,400	14,400	7,200
Salaries	10,000	5,000	—
	24,400	19,400	7,200
Less overlap relief			
(see 2014/15)	14,250		
Trading income	£10,150	£19,400	£7,200*
*Overlap relief accrued:			
(1.7.16–5.4.17)			£5,400
2018/19			
Y/e 30.6.18			
Profits £(47,000 − 5,000)		28,000	14,000
Salaries		5,000	
Trading income		£33,000	£14,000

Notes

(a) On a partnership change (e.g. the admission or retirement of a partner), the partnership is automatically regarded as continuing, providing there is at least one continuing partner.

(b) Profits are allocated between partners for tax purposes in accordance with the profit-sharing ratios in force during a period of account. Each partner is taxed on his own share, the partnership not being treated as a separate entity. The normal rules used to determine the basis periods for the early years and closing years of a business apply to individuals joining or leaving a partnership. [*ITTOIA 2005, ss 850(1), 852, 853*].

(B) Partnership trading and investment income

X and Y begin to trade in partnership on 1 July 2014 preparing first accounts to 30 September 2015 and sharing profits equally. Z joins the firm as an equal partner on 1 October 2016. Y leaves the firm on 31 March 2018. Accounts are prepared to that date to ascertain Y's entitlement but the accounting date then reverts to 30 September and the partnership does not give notice to HMRC of a change of accounting date, so there is no change of basis period. In addition to trading profits, the partnership had a source of lettings income which ceased in September 2017 and is in receipt of both bank deposit interest and untaxed interest, the latter from a source commencing in October 2015. The bank deposit interest is received on 31 March each year, but the March 2016 interest (£1,500) is the last from which tax is deducted at source. Relevant figures as adjusted for tax purposes are as follows.

	Trading income	Property income	Savings income (untaxed interest)	Savings income (taxed interest) (gross)
	£	£	£	£
15 months to 30.9.15	30,000	4,500	—	750
Year to 30.9.16	24,000	5,000	1,000	1,500
Year to 30.9.17	39,000	3,000	600	—
6 months to 31.3.18	19,500	—	225	—
6 months to 30.9.18	14,000	—	140	—

The partners' shares of taxable income from the partnership for the years 2014/15 to 2018/19 are as follows

	X	Y	Z
	£	£	£
Trading income			
2014/15			
1.7.14–5.4.15 (£30,000 × 9/15)	9,000	9,000	
2015/16			
1.10.14–30.9.15 (£30,000 × 12/15)	12,000*	12,000*	

	X £	Y £	Z £
* Overlap relief accrued			
1.10.14–5.4.15 (£30,000 × 6/15)	(6,000)	(6,000)	
2016/17			
Y/e 30.9.16	12,000	12,000	
1.10.16–5.4.17			
(£39,000 × 6/12 × 1/3)			6,500
2017/18			
Y/e 30.9.17	13,000	13,000	13,000*
1.10.17–31.3.18		6,500	
		19,500	
Less overlap relief		(6,000)	
		13,500	
* Overlap relief accrued			
1.10.16–5.4.17 (as above)			(6,500)
2018/19			
Y/e 30.9.18			
1.10.17–31.3.18	6,500		6,500
1.4.18–30.9.18	7,000		7,000
	13,500		13,500
Property income			
2014/15			
1.7.14–5.4.15 (£4,500 × 9/15)	1,350	1,350	
2015/16			
1.10.14–30.9.15 (£4,500 × 12/15)	1,800*	1,800*	
* Overlap relief accrued			
1.10.14–5.4.15 (£4,500 × 6/15)	(900)	(900)	
2016/17			
Y/e 30.9.16	2,500	2,500	
1.10.16–5.4.17			
(£3,000 × 6/12 × 1/3)			500
2017/18			
Y/e 30.9.17	1,000	1,000	1,000*
1.10.17–31.3.18		—	
		1,000	

	X	Y	Z
	£	£	£
Less overlap relief		(900)	
		100	
* Overlap relief accrued			
1.10.16–5.4.17 (as above)			(500)
Savings income (untaxed interest)			
2016/17			
Y/e 30.9.16	500	500	
1.10.16–5.4.17			
(£600 × $^6/_{12}$ × $^1/_3$)			100
2017/18			
Y/e 30.9.17	200	200	200*
1.10.17–31.3.18		75	
		275	
* Overlap relief accrued			
1.10.16–5.4.17 (as above)			(100)
2018/19			
Y/e 30.9.18			
1.10.17–31.3.18	75		75
1.4.18–30.9.18	70		70
	145		145
Savings income (bank interest)			
2014/15 (received 31.3.15)	375	375	
2015/16 (received 31.3.16)	750	750	

Notes

(a) As regards trading profits, see also (A) above.

(b) Untaxed investment income of a trading or professional partnership is taxed by reference to the same periods as the trading or professional profits with the same rules as to overlap relief, changes of accounting date (not illustrated here) etc. For this purpose, all sources of such income are regarded as a single source which commences when a partner joins the partnership and ceases when he leaves (regardless of when any source actually commences or ceases). Thus, the basis of assessment for any tax year will always follow that for the trading or professional income source. [*ITTOIA 2005, ss 851, 854, 855; FA 2016, Sch 1 paras 26, 73*].

(c) Any excess of investment income overlap relief over untaxed investment income for the tax year in which the relief falls to be given is deductible in arriving at the partner's total income for that year (not illustrated in this example). [*ITTOIA 2005, s 856*].

(d) The above rules do not apply to taxed investment income, which is taxed on a fiscal year basis as for an individual but is apportioned between partners according to their shares for the period of account in which the income arises. Nor do those rules apply to untaxed income receivable by a partnership not carrying on a trade or profession, such income being taxable on a fiscal year basis as for an individual.

(e) In this case there is no taxed investment income for 2016/17 onwards due to the abolition of deduction of tax at source from bank interest with effect in relation to interest paid or credited on or after 6 April 2016. Assuming that bank interest is received on 31 March each year (e.g. in the accounts for the year ending 30 September 2017 if received on 31 March 2017) it will be taxed on an accounts year basis as part of that year's assessment on untaxed interest (i.e. 2017/18 for interest received in the tax year ending 30 September 2017).

To give a further example, where a firm prepares accounts to, say, 31 July 2016 and has received bank or building society interest taxed at source on 31 March 2016 and untaxed interest on 30 June 2016, the March interest is taxable for 2015/16 on a fiscal year basis and the June interest is taxable for 2016/17 on an accounts year basis (as far as continuing partners are concerned); the March interest is not taxable on an accounts year basis for 2016/17 (which would give rise to double taxation) as it did not arise from a source of untaxed income.

(f) For convenience, income for accounting periods has been apportioned to tax years on a time basis in this example. However, *ITTOIA 2005, s 203* strictly permits a time basis to be used only where 'it is necessary'. It may be more appropriate to apportion untaxed interest, for example, according to the dates when it was received. For instance, if the £600 interest received in the year to 30 September 2017 had been received as to, say, £100 on 31 December 2016 and £500 on 30 June 2017, Z's taxable interest for 2016/17 (and his overlap relief) could be taken as a one-third share of £100 rather than a one-third share of £600 × 6/12.

18.2 UNUSUAL ALLOCATIONS OF PROFITS/LOSSES BETWEEN PARTNERS

[*ITTOIA 2005, s 850(2)–(5)*].

J, K and L are full equity partners, sharing profits and losses equally and preparing accounts to 30 April. The partnership agreement also makes provision for partners' salaries, and for the year to 30 April 2018, J and K are entitled to salaries of £12,000 and £5,000 respectively. However, the firm has an unexpectedly bad year and makes a loss of £13,000, this being the tax-adjusted figure after adding back non-deductible partners' salaries.

The initial allocation between partners is as follows

	Total	J	K	L
	£	£	£	£
Partnership loss	(13,000)			
Allocate salaries	17,000	12,000	5,000	—
Loss after salaries	(£30,000)	(10,000)	(10,000)	(10,000)
Allocation of loss	(£13,000)	£2,000	(£5,000)	(£10,000)

A reallocation must be made as follows

For tax purposes, a profit cannot be allocated to one partner (in this case J) if the partnership as a whole has made a tax loss. (Similarly, if the partnership had made a tax profit, no partner could have a tax loss.) J's allocation must be reduced to nil and the profit initially allocated to K and L must be proportionately reduced as follows.

$$\text{K's loss} = £13{,}000 \times \frac{5{,}000}{5{,}000 + 10{,}000} = \underline{£4{,}333}$$

$$\text{L's loss} = £13{,}000 \times \frac{10{,}000}{5{,}000 + 10{,}000} = \underline{£8{,}667}$$

	Total	J	K	L
Final allocation	(£13,000)	Nil	(£4,333)	(£8,667)

Note

(a) The losses allocated to K and L are losses of the basis period for 2018/19 and are therefore tax losses of that year. [*ITA 2007, s 62*]. It is up to each of K and L individually to decide what to do with his allocated loss, e.g. carry it forward, set it off against other income etc.

18.3 LIMITED PARTNERSHIPS — LOSSES

[*ITA 2007, ss 103–106, 113A, 114*]

R and S, who have been trading in partnership for several years preparing accounts to 30 June, share profits and losses equally. S is a limited partner. For the year ended 30 June 2018, the partnership made a loss of £12,000. Other relevant details are as follows

	R £	S £
Other income		
2018/19	10,000	8,000
Capital and accumulated profits		
At 30.6.18	4,000	5,000

R and S may claim loss relief under ITA 2007, s 64 for 2018/19 as follows

	R £	S £
Other income	10,000	8,000
Share of partnership loss (restricted for S)	(6,000)	(5,000)
	£4,000	£3,000
Loss carried forward against future partnership trading profits	—	£1,000

Notes

(a) The amount of partnership loss which a limited partner may set against general income and gains is restricted to the amount of his 'contribution to the firm' (broadly his capital contribution and accumulated profits) at the end of the basis period for the tax year in which the loss is sustained.

(b) Certain amounts must be excluded from a limited partner's contribution for these purposes, where the cost of providing those amounts is or could be borne by another person.

(c) The relief a limited partner can claim (against general income and gains) for what remains of the loss after applying the above restrictions is capped at £25,000. [*ITA 2007, ss 103, 103C, 103D; ITTOIA 2005, s 863(2)*].

18.4 LIMITED LIABILITY PARTNERSHIPS — LOSSES

[*ITA 2007, ss 107–109, 113A(2)–(4), 114; LLPA 2000, s 10(1)*]

Mr Wainwright becomes a member of a limited liability trading partnership on 6 April 2016. The partnership prepares accounts to 5 April each year. He introduces capital of £20,000 into the partnership on 6 April 2016, and on 1 April 2019 he makes a further capital contribution of £12,000.

His share of the partnership's trading losses are as follows

Y/e 5 April 2017	£12,000
Y/e 5 April 2018	£12,000
Y/e 5 April 2019	£6,000

Mr Wainwright claims relief under *ITA 2007, s 64* for these losses against his general income. The amounts available are as follows:

	£	£
2016/17		
Share of loss y/e 5.4.17		12,000
Capital contribution 6.4.16		20,000
Unrelieved capital contribution c/fwd		£8,000
ITA 2007, s 64 relief available		£12,000
2017/18		
Share of loss y/e 5.4.18		12,000
Unrelieved capital contribution b/fwd		8,000
Total unrelieved loss c/fwd		£4,000
ITA 2007, s 64 relief available		£8,000

2018/19		
Share of loss y/e 5.4.19	6,000	
Total unrelieved loss b/fwd	4,000	10,000
Capital contribution 1.4.19		12,000
Unrelieved capital contribution c/fwd		£2,000
ITA 2007, s 64 relief available		£10,000

Notes

(a) The amounts of partnership trading loss which a member of a limited liability partnership may set against general income and gains are restricted to the amount of his 'contribution to the LLP' (as defined) at the end of the basis period for the tax year in which the loss is sustained.

(b) Amounts relating to a trade carried on by a member of a limited liability partnership which are prevented from being given or allowed by (a) above are referred to as the member's 'total unrelieved loss'. In each subsequent tax year in which the member continues to carry on the trade and any of the total unrelieved loss remains outstanding, the balance of the total unrelieved loss is treated for the purposes of *ITA 2007, s 64*, *ITA 2007, s 72* and *TCGA 1992, s 261B*, and for the purposes of (a) above, as having been made in that subsequent tax year.

(c) 'Contribution to the LLP' falls to be restricted as in note (b) to **18.3** above.

19 Pension Provision

19.1 RELIEF FOR CONTRIBUTIONS BY INDIVIDUAL MEMBERS

[FA 2004, ss 188–195, 195A, Sch 36 paras 39, 40; ITA 2007, s 58; FA 2014, Sch 7 paras 13, 16]

(A) Henry

Henry carries on a trade in the UK in which he makes an allowable loss of £1,000 for 2016/17 (for which he claims relief against 2015/16 income), a taxable profit of £16,500 for 2017/18 and a taxable profit of £43,350 for 2018/19. His only other income consists of building society interest and UK dividends. Building society interest received amounted to £10,200 for 2016/17 and £10,700 for 2017/18 and 2018/19. UK dividends received amounted to £900 for each year. He makes net contributions to a registered pension scheme of £2,400 during the tax year 2016/17 and £4,000 during each of the tax years 2017/18 and 2018/19. He is not a Scottish taxpayer.

Henry's tax liabilities are as follows.

2016/17

	£
Trading income	Nil
Building society interest	10,200
UK dividends	900
Total and net income	11,100
Less Personal Allowance	11,000
Taxable Income	£100

Tax Liability

100 @ 0% (dividend allowance)

Henry has made gross pension contributions of £3,000 (£2,400 × 100/80). As his gross contributions do not exceed £3,600, he is entitled to tax relief even though he has no relevant UK earnings for the year. He is not required to repay the basic rate tax of £600 withheld at source from the contributions.

19.1 IT Pension Provision

2017/18

	£
Trading income	16,500
Building society interest	10,700
UK dividends	900
Total and net income	28,100
Less Personal Allowance	11,500
Taxable Income	£16,600

Tax Liability

5,000	@ 20% (basic rate)	1,000.00
1,000	@ 0% (personal savings allowance)	—
9,700	@ 20% (basic rate on savings income)	1,940.00
900	@ 0% (dividend allowance)	—
£16,600		
		2,940.00

Henry has made gross pension contributions of £5,000 (£4,000 × 100/80). His relevant UK earnings are £16,500, which is more than sufficient to cover the gross contributions. He is entitled to full tax relief, which he has already obtained by deduction at source.

2018/19

	£
Trading income	43,350
Building society interest	10,700
UK dividends	900
Total and net income	54,950
Less Personal Allowance	11,850
Taxable Income	£43,100

Tax Liability

31,500	@ 20% (basic rate on earnings)	6,300.00
500	@ 0% (personal savings allowance)	—
6,500	@ 20% (basic rate on savings income)	1,300.00
3,700	@ 40% (higher rate on savings income)	1,480.00
900	@ 0% (dividend allowance)	—
£43,100		
		£9,080.00

Henry has made gross pension contributions of £5,000 (£4,000 × 100/80). His relevant UK earnings are £43,350, which is more than sufficient to cover the gross contributions. He has obtained basic rate tax relief at 20% by deduction at source. He obtains higher rate relief by extension of the basic rate band; the normal basic rate limit of £34,500 is increased by £5,000 to £39,500. Without that increase, an additional £5,000 of savings income would have fallen into the 40% rate band. (Above the normal basic rate limit, the rate at which the pension contributions save tax will depend on the mix of taxable income, i.e. the extent to which it is dividend income, savings income or other income.)

Notes

(a) A 'relevant UK individual' (see *FA 2004, s 189(1)*) is entitled to relief on contributions to a registered pension scheme up to the total amount of his 'relevant UK earnings' (see *FA 2004, s 189(2)(3)*) within the charge to income tax for the year. Provided, however, the scheme operates tax relief at source, contributions of up to £3,600 (gross) attract relief even if total relevant UK earnings are less than that amount or if there are no such earnings.

(b) Provided the individual has sufficient relevant UK earnings to cover them there is no upper limit on the contributions that can be relieved in each year. Tax relief may, however, be effectively clawed back by the application of the lifetime allowance charge and/or the annual allowance charge.

(B) Celia

Celia is a self-employed professional with taxable profits of £200,000 for the year to 30 April 2018. She has bank deposit interest of £4,000 for 2018/19. She makes net contributions to a registered pension scheme of £16,000 during the tax year ending on 5 April 2019. She is not a Scottish taxpayer.

Celia's 2018/19 income tax liability is computed as follows.

	£
Professional income	200,000
Bank interest	4,000
Total and net income	204,000
Less Personal Allowance (note (b))	—
Taxable Income	£204,000

Tax Liability	
54,500 @ 20% (basic rate)	10,900.00
115,500 @ 40% (higher rate)	46,200.00
34,000 @ 45% (additional rate)	15,300.00
£204,000	
	£72,400.00

Notes

(a) Celia has made gross pension contributions of £20,000 (£16,000 × 100/80) and has obtained basic rate relief at source. She obtains additional rate relief by extension of the basic rate band; the normal basic rate limit of £34,500 is increased by £20,000 to £54,500. The higher rate limit of £150,000 is increased by the same amount, so that the higher rate band remains at £115,500. Without these adjustments, an additional £20,000 of income would have been taxable at 45% instead of 20% (a 25% saving).

(b) No personal allowance is due as income is too far in excess of the £100,000 limit. [*ITA 2007, s 35(2)–(4)*].

(c) No personal savings allowance is due as Celia is an additional rate taxpayer.

(d) As a high income individual, Celia may face an annual allowance charge for 2018/19. See the continuation of this example at **19.3**(C) below.

19.2 LIFETIME ALLOWANCE

[*FA 2004, ss 214–226; FA 2013, s 48, Sch 22; TPA 2014, Sch 1 paras 26, 27, 76, Sch 2 paras 19(2), 20–24; FA 2015, Sch 4 paras 4–7; F(No 2)A 2015, s 21(7)(10); FA 2016, s 19, Sch 4*]

(A) With no enhancement factor

Aisleyne starts to receive a pension from a registered pension scheme (a benefit crystallisation event) on 1 November 2006. The amount of benefit crystallised is £600,000. Aisleyne is entitled to the standard lifetime allowance of £1.5 million (for 2006/07). Thus, the crystallisation event does not give rise to a lifetime allowance charge, but Aisleyne has used up two-fifths of her lifetime allowance.

Aisleyne is also a member of another registered pension scheme, from which she receives a lump sum on 1 August 2018 and starts to draw a pension; these are benefit crystallisation events. The total amount of benefit crystallised is £515,000. The standard lifetime allowance for 2018/19 is £1.03 million. Aisleyne's unused lifetime allowance is three-fifths of this, i.e. £618,000. Thus, the crystallisation event does not give rise to a lifetime allowance charge, and Aisleyne has used up 90% of her lifetime allowance (40% + 50% (0.515/1.03 × 100)).

(B) With an enhancement factor

(i) Shabnam notified HMRC of her intention to benefit from **primary protection** by reference to relevant pre-2006/07 accrued pension rights of £2.5 million, and HMRC duly certified that she is entitled to a lifetime allowance enhancement factor of 0.667 ((£2.5 million – 1.5 million)/£1.5 million). This means that Shabnam can have benefits of 1.667 times the standard lifetime allowance before incurring any liability to the lifetime allowance charge.

In 2018/19 Shabnam receives a lump sum from the registered scheme and starts to draw a pension; these are benefit crystallisation events. The total amount of benefit crystallised is £2.95 million. Shabnam's enhanced lifetime allowance in 2018/19 is £3 million (£1.8 million × 1.667) (see note (d)). Therefore, she will not become liable to the lifetime allowance charge.

(ii) Winston has primary protection by reference to relevant pre-2006/07 accrued pension rights of £2.25 million and has a lifetime allowance enhancement factor of 0.5 ((£2.25 million – 1.5 million)/£1.5 million). In 2011/12, he took benefits valued at £0.9 million. At this time his enhanced lifetime allowance was £2.7 million (£1.8 million × 1.5), so the benefit crystallisation did not give rise to a lifetime allowance charge.

In 2018/19 Winston takes the remainder of his benefits then worth £1.9 million. The standard lifetime allowance is then £1.03 million. Winston's enhanced lifetime allowance remains at £2.7 million (£1.8 million × 1.5) (see note (d)).

The amount of lifetime allowance used up by Winston's 2011/12 benefit crystallisation is found by multiplying the then crystalised amount of £0.9 million by:

$$\frac{\text{SLA at time of current } (2018/19) \text{ event } (\text{but see note } (e))}{\text{SLA at time of previous } (2011/12) \text{ event}}$$

So the used amount is:

$$£900{,}000 \times \frac{1.5}{1.8} = £750{,}000$$

Winston has used up £0.75 million and has £1.95 million (£2.7 million – £0.75 million) still available. As Winston's 2018/19 benefit crystallisation is worth £1.9 million, he does not become liable to the lifetime allowance charge.

Notes

(a) Any excess of crystallised benefits over the unused lifetime allowance is chargeable to income tax at 55% if paid as a lump sum or at 25% otherwise. The charge is not dependent upon any person's being resident or domiciled in the UK. Although chargeable to income tax, the chargeable amount is not treated for any tax purposes as income, which means that, for example, losses, reliefs and allowances cannot be set against it and it does not count as income for the purposes of any double tax treaty.

(b) The tax will normally be paid by the scheme administrator. It will usually be recovered by deduction from the benefits paid by the scheme to the individual. If instead it is paid out of scheme funds, the tax itself is added to the chargeable amount. See, for example, HMRC Pensions Tax Manual PTM085000.

(c) See *FA 2004, Sch 36 paras 7–11D* as regards primary protection under the transitional rules for pension rights accrued at 5 April 2006.

(d) Despite the fall in the standard lifetime allowance from £1.8 million to £1.5 million, then to £1.25 million and to £1 million and with an inflation adjustment in 2018/19 to £1.03 million, where an individual's lifetime allowance falls to be enhanced under primary protection for 2012/13 or any subsequent year, the amount of the enhancement is computed by applying the primary protection factor to a lifetime allowance of £1.8 million (as long as this remains greater than the actual lifetime allowance). [*FA 2004, s 218(5B)*].

(e) When calculating the availability of the lifetime allowance for an individual with primary protection, where a benefit crystallisation event has occurred before 6 April 2014 and a further benefit crystallisation event occurs on or after that date, then in calculating the adjustment of the used amount, the current standard lifetime allowance (£1.03 million for 2018/19) is replaced by £1.5 million if greater. This ensures that those with primary protection do not benefit from an increase in their available lifetime allowance if the current standard lifetime allowance is less than £1.5 million when the adjustment is made. [*FA 2004, s 219(5A); FA 2013, Sch 22 para 7; FA 2014, Sch 6 para 10*].

19.3 ANNUAL ALLOWANCE

[FA 2004, ss 227–238A; FA 2011, Sch 17 paras 29–31; FA 2013, s 49; TPA 2014, Sch 1 paras 63–68, 88–91; F(No 2)A 2015, Sch 4]

(A) Carry-forward of annual allowance

Lily is self-employed and joins a registered pension scheme for the first time on 1 July 2014. The scheme's annual pension input period coincides with the fiscal year. Lily has fluctuating business profits and makes contributions to the scheme under deduction of basic rate tax at source as follows.

2014/15	£6,400 net (£8,000 gross)
2015/16	£40,000 net (£50,000 gross)
2016/17	£16,000 net (£20,000 gross)
2017/18	£44,000 net (£55,000 gross)
2018/19	£68,800 net (£86,000 gross)

No-one else makes contributions to Lily's pension arrangement under the scheme. Lily's total pension input amount for each year will be equal to the gross amount of her contributions. For each year, she will receive higher and additional rate tax relief, where appropriate, on the gross amount of her contributions provided she has sufficient relevant UK earnings to cover that amount, which it is assumed she does.

For 2014/15, Lily has unused annual allowance of £32,000 (£40,000 – £8,000). Note that if her total pension input had exceeded the annual allowance, there would have been no question of her bringing forward any unused annual allowance from earlier years as she was not a member of a registered pension scheme in those years.

For 2015/16, she has excess pension input amounts of £10,000 (£40,000 – £50,000). In the absence of a carry-forward facility, she would have been liable to an annual allowance charge on £10,000 at her marginal rate of tax for the year. However, £10,000 of her unused allowance for 2014/15 is brought forward to extinguish her liability. She still has £22,000 unused allowance remaining from 2014/15.

For 2016/17, she has unused annual allowance of £20,000 (£40,000 – £20,000).

For 2017/18, she has excess pension input amounts of £15,000 (£40,000 – £55,000). £15,000 of her unused allowance for 2014/15 is brought forward to extinguish her liability.

For 2018/19, Lily has excess pension input amounts of £46,000 (£40,000 – £86,000). Although £7,000 of her 2014/15 annual allowance remains unused, it cannot be carried forward more than three years. However, her unused allowance of £20,000 for 2016/17 is available in full. She is liable to an annual allowance charge on £26,000 at her marginal rate of tax for the year and has no more unused allowance to carry forward.

The position can be summarised as follows

	Annual allowance	Pension input amounts	Unused allowance b/fwd	Chargeable amount	Unused allowance c/fwd		Cumulative unused allowance c/fwd
	£	£	£	£	£		£
2014/15	(40,000)	8,000		Nil	32,000		32,000
2015/16	(40,000)	50,000	(10,000)	Nil			22,000
2016/17	(40,000)	20,000		Nil	20,000		42,000
2017/18	(40,000)	55,000	(15,000)	Nil			27,000
					3 year dropout		(7,000)
							20,000
2018/19	(40,000)	86,000	(20,000)	26,000			Nil

Notes

(a) A carry-forward facility was introduced by *FA 2011* whereby any unused part of the annual allowance for a tax year can be carried forward for up to three tax years. The first year for which unused allowance could be carried forward was 2008/09, but see (B) below as regards carry-forward from 2008/09, 2009/10 and/or 2010/11. Unused annual allowance is available for carry-forward only if it arises during a tax year in which the individual is a member of a registered pension scheme. If the amount of the annual allowance exceeds the total pension input amount (broadly the pension savings) for that year, the excess is unused allowance.

(b) The current year's annual allowance is deemed to be used first. If this is insufficient to avoid an annual allowance charge, any unused annual allowance from the three previous years can then be used; the earliest year's unused allowance is used first and so on. The carry-forward is automatic and does not have to be claimed.

(B) Carry-forward of annual allowance from before 2011/12 (transitional)

Alfie is a company director and has been a member of his employer's final salary scheme (a registered pension scheme) for a number of years. The scheme's annual pension input period coincides with the fiscal year. Alfie's total pension input amounts for the three years preceding 2011/12 were as follows.

	£
2008/09	39,000
2009/10	44,000
2010/11	46,000

For each of these years, Alfie's total pension input amounts were clearly well within his annual allowance, so there was no annual allowance charge. Alfie's total pension input amounts for the next two years are as follows.

	£
2011/12	55,500
2012/13	55,000

For 2011/12, in the absence of a carry-forward facility, Alfie would have been liable to an annual allowance charge on £5,500 at his marginal rate of tax for the year. Similarly, he would have been liable on £5,000 for 2012/13. In order to ascertain whether he has any unused annual allowance to bring forward to 2011/12 and beyond, his annual allowance is assumed to have been £50,000 for each of the years 2008/09 to 2010/11, and his total pension input amount for each of those years must be recomputed using post-2010/11 valuation methods. Alfie's revised total pension input amounts for those three years are as follows (and note that these figures are purely for illustration purposes and not necessarily realistic).

	£
2008/09	44,000
2009/10	49,000
2010/11	51,000

The position can now be summarised as follows (bearing in mind that the annual allowance and pension input amounts for years prior to 2011/12 are assumed figures only).

	Annual allowance	Pension input amounts	Unused allowance b/fwd	Chargeable amount	Unused allowance c/fwd		Cumulative unused allowance c/fwd
	£	£	£	£	£		£
2008/09	(50,000)	44,000		Nil	6,000		6,000
2009/10	(50,000)	49,000		Nil	1,000		7,000
2010/11	(50,000)	51,000		Nil			7,000
2011/12	(50,000)	55,500	(5,500)	Nil			1,500
					3 year dropout		(500)
							1,000
2012/13	(50,000)	55,000	(1,000)	4,000			Nil

Notes

(a) For the purpose of carrying forward unused annual allowances from 2008/09, 2009/10 and/or 2010/11, the unused amount is computed under post-2010/11 rules. Therefore, it is assumed for this purpose only that the annual allowance was only £50,000 for each of those years, and that pension input amounts for those years are to be calculated as if the post-2010/11 rules had already been in place. [*FA 2011, Sch 17 para 30*].

(b) Although in 2010/11 the assumed pension input amounts exceed the assumed annual allowance, none of the cumulative unused allowance brought forward need be set against this excess. This is in contrast to the position for 2011/12 and subsequent years. (HMRC Pensions Tax Manual PTM055300).

(C) Annual allowance taper

Celia, the additional rate taxpayer in **19.1**(B) above, has 'threshold income' of £184,000 (net income £204,000 less gross pension contributions of £20,000) for 2018/19. As her threshold income is over £110,000, she will be a high-income individual and subject to the annual allowance taper if her adjusted income is over £150,000. In fact, Celia's adjusted income is equal to net income in this case and is £204,000.

Her annual allowance of £40,000 is reduced by £27,000 (one-half of (204,000 – 150,000)) and is thus £13,000 (being above the £10,000 minimum). She has a £7,000 excess of pension input amount (£20,000) over annual allowance (£13,000) and is thus subject to an annual allowance charge for 2018/19 at her marginal tax rate (45%) on £7,000.

In practice Celia may well have some unused annual allowance brought forward (see (A) above) from 2015/16 (year before the taper took effect) and/or 2016/17, 2017/18 which would operate to reduce or eliminate the charge for 2018/19.

Notes

(a) For 2016/17 onwards, if an individual is a 'high-income individual' for a tax year, the annual allowance is reduced by £1 for every £2 by which 'adjusted income' exceeds £150,000, but cannot be reduced below £10,000. The £10,000 minimum thus takes effect where adjusted income is £210,000 or more. A 'high-income individual' is one whose 'threshold income' is over £110,000 and whose 'adjusted income' is over £150,000. [*FA 2004, ss 228ZA, 228ZB; F(No 2)A 2015, Sch 4 para 10*]

(b) 'Threshold income' is broadly net income (taxable income before deducting any personal allowance) less the gross equivalent of pension contributions for the year on which basic rate tax relief has been given at source. Certain amounts which would have been included in employment income were it not for salary sacrifice arrangements must be added, and any lump sum death benefits taxable on the individual as pension income for the year are excluded.

(c) 'Adjusted income' is broadly net income after adding back any deductions made for pension contributions and any employer contributions. Lump sum death benefits are excluded as in (b) above.

(D) Money purchase annual allowance

Kerensky had two money purchase pension arrangements at 6 April 2015.

He does not make any contributions to Arrangement A in 2015/16. In April 2015 he designates funds into a member flexi-access drawdown fund from which he makes the first income withdrawal on 15 May 2015. The withdrawal triggers the money purchase annual allowance test for 2015/16 and subsequent years.

Arrangement B has a pension input period ending on 5 April. Kerensky makes contributions of £16,000 net (equivalent to £20,000 gross) during 2015/16, of which £14,400 net (£18,000 gross) is paid after 15 May 2015.

Kerensky has taxable income of £140,000 for 2015/16, including all his income withdrawals from Arrangement A but excluding any annual allowance chargeable amount.

The calculation of the annual allowance charge proceeds as follows.

Compare (i) the 'alternative chargeable amount' with (ii) the 'default chargeable amount'. If (i) exceeds (ii), Kerensky's annual allowance charge for 2015/16 will be based on (i) rather than (ii).

(i) The '*alternative chargeable amount*' is the total of the amount by which 'defined benefit pension input amounts' (see *FA 2004, s 227B(3)–(5)*) exceed the 'alternative annual allowance' and the amount by which money purchase input amounts (see *FA 2004, s 227C–227F*) exceed £10,000. The '*alternative annual allowance*' is the normal annual allowance (£40,000) minus £10,000, i.e. it is £30,000 for 2015/16.

(ii) The '*default chargeable amount*' is the excess (if any) of pension input amounts over the normal annual allowance of £40,000.

Alternative chargeable amount

£(18,000 – 10,000) + £(2,000 – £30,000) =	£8,000

The pension input amounts of £2,000 for money purchase arrangements that are not tested against the £10,000 money purchase annual allowance are tested against the alternative annual allowance — see note (b). Kerensky has no defined benefit arrangements. If he did, pension input amounts for those arrangements would also be tested against the alternative annual allowance.

Default chargeable amount

£(20,000 – £40,000) =	Nil

Default chargeable amount = Nil.

The alternative chargeable amount thus exceeds the default chargeable amount.

Annual allowance charge

£8,000 @ 40% =	£3,200

The chargeable amount falls within Kerensky's higher rate band for the year.

Notes

(a) A reduced annual allowance applies for 2015/16 onwards where an individual has flexibly accessed his money purchase savings. [*FA 2004, ss 227, 227ZA, 227B–227G; TPA 2014, Sch 1 paras 63–65; F(No 2)A 2015, Sch 4 paras 4, 11*].

(b) Only the pension input amounts arising after the trigger date (15 May 2015 in this example) are tested against the money purchase annual allowance of £10,000. If the pension input period had ended before the trigger date, the pension input amount for the pension input period ending in 2015/16 would not have fallen to be tested against the money purchase annual allowance. Any pension input amounts that do not fall to be thus tested are tested instead against the alternative annual allowance. [*FA 2004, ss 227B(3)(c), 227E, 227F; TPA 2014, Sch 1 para 65; F(No 2)A 2015, Sch 4 para 4*].

(c) Unused money purchase annual allowance cannot be carried forward to subsequent tax years. Where the alternative chargeable amount applies to an individual for a tax year (instead of the default chargeable amount), the only amount capable of carry-forward from that year is the excess (if any) of the alternative annual allowance over 'defined benefit pension input amounts'. [*FA 2004, s 228A(8); TPA 2014, Sch 1 para 67*].

(d) As regards an individual's option to have his annual allowance charge paid from his pension benefits by the scheme administrator, the amount of the liability is computed *for this purpose only* as if the default chargeable amount applied to him instead of the alternative chargeable amount (i.e. in a case where the alternative chargeable amount does, in fact, apply). [*FA 2004, s 237B(2A); TPA 2014, Sch 1 para 68*].

(e) For examples on the operation of the money purchase annual allowance where a trigger event occurs during 2016/17 or a subsequent tax year, see HMRC Pensions Tax Manual PTM056540.

20 Personal Service Companies etc.

[*ITEPA 2003, ss 48–61; ITTOIA 2005, ss 163, 164; FA 2016, Sch 1 paras 61, 73*]

20.1 CALCULATION OF DEEMED EMPLOYMENT PAYMENT

Harry is a systems analyst trading through his own personal service company, ABC Ltd, in which he owns 99% of the ordinary shares. During 2018/19, he is engaged at different times by two independent companies, DEF Ltd and GHJ Ltd (the client companies), in each case under a contract between the client company and ABC Ltd. It is accepted that each engagement is in the nature of employment and is within the special tax and NIC rules for personal service companies and other intermediaries. ABC Ltd is paid £40,000 by DEF Ltd and £20,000 by GHJ Ltd for the services provided by Harry.

For 2018/19, Harry draws a salary of £28,000 from ABC Ltd which is taxed under PAYE and on which employer's NICs of, say, £2,800 are due. He is also provided with a company car on which the taxable benefit is £4,000 and on which Class 1A NICs of, say, £550 are due. ABC Ltd makes pension contributions of £3,100 into a registered pension scheme on Harry's behalf and reimburses expenses of £1,500 which, if Harry had been employed directly by the client companies, would have been qualifying travelling expenses within *ITEPA 2003, ss 337–340* and which do not cover any home-to-work travel (see note (c)). ABC Ltd pays a salary of £8,000 to Harry's wife who acts as company secretary and administrator.

ABC Ltd is deemed to make a payment to Harry on 5 April 2019, chargeable to tax as employment income and computed as follows

			£	£	£
Step (1)	Total amount from relevant engagements				60,000
	Deduct	5%			3,000
					57,000
Step (2)	*Add* payments and other benefits received other than from ABC Ltd				—
Step (3)	*Deduct*	(a) Expenses	1,500		
		(b) Capital allowances	—		
		(c) Pension contributions	3,100	4,600	
Step (4)	*Deduct*	Salary	28,000		
		Benefits	4,000		
		Employer's Class 1 NICs	2,800		
		Employer's Class 1A NICs	550	35,350	(39,950)
					£17,050
	Deemed employment payment $£17,050 \times \frac{100}{113.8}$				14,982
Employer's NICs due on deemed payment £14,982 @ 13.8%					2,068
Total as above					£17,050

Notes

(a) The salary paid by ABC Ltd to Harry's wife is not deductible in arriving at the deemed employment payment, except to the extent that it, and other expenses of the company, are covered by the 5% deduction at Step (1) above. (The salary may of course be deductible in computing ABC Ltd's taxable business profits.) The 5% deduction is a standard allowance intended to cover the company's running costs and is given automatically, regardless of the actual occurrence or amount of such costs. It is computed purely for the purpose of determining the deemed employment payment and is not deductible in computing ABC Ltd's taxable business profits.

(b) The deemed employment payment is generally treated in the same way as an actual payment of remuneration, so that the normal PAYE provisions apply. Subject to special rules where the intermediary is a partnership, the payment (and the related employer's NICs) is an allowable expense in computing the taxable business profits of the intermediary for the period of account in which it is deemed to be made (and for no other period). [*ITEPA 2003, s 56; ITTOIA 2005, ss 163, 164*].

(c) For 2016/17 onwards, and subject to conditions being met, relief is denied for home-to-work travel expenditure for engagements via personal service companies and other employment intermediaries. [*ITEPA 2003, s 339A; FA 2016, s 14(1)(6)*].

21 Post-Cessation Receipts and Expenditure

21.1 POST-CESSATION RECEIPTS

[*ITTOIA 2005, ss 241–257; FA 2013, Sch 4 paras 39(2), 56, Sch 5 paras 4, 6, Sch 45 paras 77, 153(2)*].

A trader retired and closed down his trade on 31 March 2018 and, in the year 2018/19, the following subsequent events occurred.

(i) He paid a former customer £100 as compensation for defective work.

(ii) In the accounts at the date of closure a specific provision was made against a debt for £722 and in addition there was a general bad debt provision of £2,000. All debts were recovered in full.

(iii) Stock in trade incorrectly taken to be valueless at the date of cessation was sold for £215.

(iv) He eventually sold a piece of machinery six months after cessation for £136. This had been valued at nil at cessation.

(v) At 31 March 2018, after obtaining maximum loss relief, there was a trading loss of £333 unrelieved.

The above will be subject to income tax for 2018/19 as follows

		£	£
Sales			215
Bad debts recovered			722
			937
Deduct	Compensation payment	100	
	Balance of losses	197	
			297
Taxable post-cessation receipts			£640

Notes

(a) The proceeds of sale of the plant are taken into the final capital allowances computation, i.e. for 2017/18 [*CAA 2001, s 61(2)*] and the loss carried forward of £333 has been reduced by the balancing charge to £197.

(b) An election could be made under *ITTOIA 2005, s 257* for the post-cessation receipts to be treated as having been received on the date of cessation and thus chargeable at 2017/18 rates. See also *TMA 1970, Sch 1B para 5*.

21.2 POST-CESSATION EXPENDITURE

[*ITA 2007, ss 96–101, 125, 126; TCGA 1992, ss 261D, 261E; ITTOIA 2005, ss 248(3)(4), 250, 255(4); FA 2012, s 9*]

Simcock ceased trading in February 2018. In 2018/198, the following events occur in connection with his former trade.

(i) Simcock pays a former customer £9,250 by way of damages for defective work carried out by him in the course of the trade.

(ii) He incurs legal fees of £800 in connection with the above claim.

(iii) He incurs debt collection fees of £200 in connection with trade debts outstanding at cessation and which were taken into account as receipts in computing profits.

(iv) He writes off a trade debt of £500, giving HMRC notice of his having done so.

(v) He incurs legal fees of £175 in relation to a debt of £1,000 owing by him to a supplier which, although disputed, was taken into account as an expense in computing his trading profits.

(vi) He eventually agrees to pay £500 in full settlement of his liability in respect of the debt in (v) above, paying £250 in March 2019 and the remaining £250 in May 2019.

In 2019/20, Simcock receives £3,000 from his insurers in full settlement of their liability with regard to the expense incurred in (i) above.

For 2018/19, Simcock's total income before taking account of the above events is £9,000 and he also has capital gains of £12,800 (with £900 capital losses brought forward from 2017/18).

Simcock makes a claim under *ITA 2007, s 96* (relief for post-cessation expenditure) for 2018/19 and a simultaneous claim under *TCGA 1992, s 261D* to have any excess relief set against capital gains.

Simcock's tax position for 2018/19 is as follows

		£	£
Income			
Total income before claim under *ITA 2007, s 96*			9,000
Deduct Post-cessation expenditure			
(i)		9,250	
(ii)		800	
(iii)		200	
(iv)		500	
(v)	not allowable under these rules	—	
(vi)	*less* unpaid expenses at 5.4.19	(750)	
		10,000	
Restricted to total income		(9,000)	(9,000)
Excess relief		£1,000	

Capital gains

Gains before losses brought forward and annual exemption		12,800
Deduct Post-cessation expenditure (excess as above)		1,000
Net gains for the year		11,800
Losses brought forward	900	
Used in 2017/18	(100)	(100)
Carried forward	£800	
Net gains (covered by annual exemption)		£11,700

For 2019/20, Simcock will have taxable post-cessation receipts of £3,000 arising from the insurance recovery. He will be able to offset expenses of £175 under (v) above, which, whilst not within these rules, should qualify as a deduction against post-cessation receipts. He will also have post-cessation expenditure of £250 in respect of the further payment in 2019/20 under (vi) above, the 2018/19 post-cessation expenditure having been restricted by at least that amount (see note (b)).

Notes

(a) Under *ITA 2007, s 96* relief is available against total income for specified types of expenditure and for bad debts where the expenditure is incurred or the debt proves to be bad within seven years after the date of cessation of the trade, profession or vocation. Any excess can be claimed against chargeable gains for the year. Any remaining excess relief cannot be carried forward against total income or gains of a subsequent year but is available as a deduction against any future post-cessation receipts.

(b) Allowable post-cessation expenditure is restricted to the extent that any expenses were taken into account in computing profits but remained unpaid at the end of the year to which the claim relates. Any subsequent payment is itself treated as a post-cessation expense to the extent that the unpaid expense previously caused post-cessation expenditure to be restricted.

22 Property Income

Cross-references. See **15.6** LOSSES for property business losses.

[*ITTOIA 2005, Pt 3*]

22.1 FURNISHED LETTINGS

[*ITTOIA 2005, ss 263–272ZA, 273, 274, 275, 276A, 307B–307F, 311A, 334B–334E; FA 2016, s 73(1)(8)(9); F(No 2)A 2017, Sch 2 paras 13–15, 17, 22, 23, 64; FA 2018, s 36*]

(A) Cash basis

Mrs C has a furnished cottage in a picturesque coastal village. She makes the cottage available for letting. Several lettings are for periods of more than 31 days, and the cottage does not qualify as 'furnished holiday accommodation' under **22.2** below. The letting does not constitute a trade. The rent charged is £800 per month from June to September inclusive and £550 per month for the rest of the year. Mrs A has no other letting income.

During 2018/19 the house was occupied from April until October, lay vacant during November, December and January and was let again for February and March. In March 2019, the tenant defaulted on two weeks' rent, which proved impossible to collect. All of the remaining rent was paid during 2018/19

Expenses paid in 2018/19 were as follows:

Business rates £680, Water rates £184, Electricity £520 (£500 received from tenants through coin operated meters), Advertising £300, Cleaning between lettings £280, House contents insurance £272, Repairs £220.

During the year Mrs C purchased for the cottage a fridge freezer for £400 and a microwave for £85. Both were like-for-like replacements for existing items. No value was received for the items replaced.

The property income computation for 2018/19 is as follows

	£	£
Rent received (4 × £800 + 4 × £550 + £275)		5,675
Business rates	680	
Water rates	184	
Electricity (520 − 500)	20	
Advertising	300	
Cleaning	280	
Insurance	272	
Repairs	220	
Replacement domestic items relief (note (d))	485	(2,441)
Taxable profit		£3,234

Notes

(a) For 2017/18 onwards, the profits of a property business for a tax year must be calculated on the cash basis unless one of the following conditions is met:

- an election to disapply the cash basis is made by the person carrying on the property business;
- the business is carried on at any time in the tax year by a company, a limited liability partnership, a partnership in which one or more partners is not an individual, or the trustees of a trust;
- the cash basis receipts, i.e. the amount that would be brought into account as receipts if the cash basis applied, exceed £150,000 (proportionately reduced if the property business is carried on for only part of the tax year);
  - the property business is carried on by an individual and includes a share of 'joint property income' (i,e, income to which spouses or civil partners are treated for income tax purposes as beneficially entitled in equal shares); and
  - a share of that joint property income is included in a property business carried on by that individual's spouse or civil partner for the same tax year, the profits of which are *not* calculated on the cash basis; or
- business premises renovation allowances have been made to the property business at any time and, if profits were to be calculated in accordance with generally accepted accounting practice (GAAP), a balancing event would give rise to a balancing allowance or balancing charge for the tax year.

Where a person has a UK property business and an overseas property business, the conditions apply separately to each.

(b) In calculating profits of a property business on the cash basis, receipts are brought into account at the time they are received, and expenses are brought into account at the time they are paid. This is subject to any adjustment required or authorised by law, and certain special rules apply to the cash basis. Otherwise, the general rule applies that the profits of a property business are calculated in the same way as the profits of a trade. All letting income from UK property, whether furnished or unfurnished, is taxed as income from a single UK property business carried on by the landlord.

(c) Although property income is computed similarly to trading income, it retains its nature as investment income as opposed to earnings and does not count as relevant earnings for pension contribution purposes (subject to the rules for furnished holiday lettings — see **22.2** below).

(d) With effect in relation to expenditure incurred on or after 6 April 2016, and subject to conditions being met, replacement domestic items relief enables landlords of residential property to deduct capital expenditure on domestic items, e.g. furniture, furnishings, appliances (including white goods) and kitchenware, where the expenditure is on a replacement item provided for use in the property. The relief applies to both furnished and unfurnished lettings, but not to furnished holiday lettings within **22.2** below. The deduction is made in computing the profits of the property business, and does not require the making of a claim. The amount of the deduction is the cost of the replacement item, but is limited to the cost of an equivalent item if the new item is not the same, or substantially the same, as the old. [*ITTOIA 2005, s 311A; FA 2016, s 73(1)(8)(9)*].

(e) See (B) below for profits calculated on the GAAP basis, i.e. on the accruals basis in accordance with generally accepted accounting practice.

(B) **GAAP basis**

Mrs A has a furnished cottage in a picturesque coastal village. She makes the cottage available for letting. Several lettings are for periods of more than 31 days, and the cottage does not qualify as 'furnished holiday accommodation' under **22.2** below. The letting does not constitute a trade. The rent charged is £800 per month from June to September inclusive and £550 per month for the rest of the year. Mrs A has no other letting income.

During 2018/19 the house was occupied from April until October, lay vacant during November, December and January and was let again for February and March. In March 2019, the tenant defaulted on two weeks' rent, which proved impossible to collect.

Expenses payable in respect of 2018/19 were as follows:

Business rates £680, Water rates £184, Electricity £520 (£500 received from tenants through coin operated meters), Advertising £300, Cleaning between lettings £280, House contents insurance £272, Repairs £220.

During the year Mrs A purchased for the cottage a fridge freezer for £400 and a microwave for £85. Both were like-for-like replacements for existing items. No value was received for the items replaced.

The property income computation for 2018/19 is as follows

Mrs A has elected under *ITTOIA 2005, s 271A(10)* to use the accruals basis to calculate the taxable profits of her property business. She must do so by 31 January 2021. As such, her profits are calculated in accordance with GAAP.

	£	£
Rent receivable (4 × £800 + 5 × £550)		5,950
Business rates	680	
Water rates	184	
Electricity (520 − 500)	20	
Advertising	300	
Cleaning	280	
Insurance	272	
Repairs	220	
Bad debt written off (550 ÷ 2)	275	
Replacement domestic items relief (note (c))	485	(2,716)
Taxable profit		£3,234

Notes

(a) All letting income from UK property, whether furnished or unfurnished, is taxed as income from a single UK property business carried on by the landlord. The profits of that business are computed according to trading income principles as if the business were a trade.

(b) Although property income is computed similarly to trading income, it retains its nature as investment income as opposed to earnings and does not count as relevant earnings for pension contribution purposes (subject to the rules for furnished holiday lettings — see **22.2** below).

(c) With effect in relation to expenditure incurred on or after 6 April 2016, and subject to conditions being met, replacement domestic items relief enables landlords of residential property to deduct capital expenditure on domestic items, e.g. furniture, furnishings, appliances (including white goods) and kitchenware, where the expenditure is on a replacement item provided for use in the property. The relief applies to both furnished and unfurnished lettings, but not to furnished holiday lettings within **22.2** below. The deduction is made in computing the profits of the property business, and does not require the making of a claim. The amount of the deduction is the cost of the replacement item, but is limited to the cost of an equivalent item if the new item is not the same, or substantially the same, as the old. [*ITTOIA 2005, s 311A; FA 2016, s 73(1)(8)(9)*].

(d) See (A) above for profits calculated on the cash basis.

22.2 FURNISHED HOLIDAY LETTINGS

[*ITA 2007, ss 127, 127ZA; ITTOIA 2005, ss 322–326, 326A, 327, 328, 328A, 328B; F(No 2)A 2015, s 24(6); FA 2016, ss 72(5)(8)(9), 73(1)(2)*]

Mr B owns and lets out furnished holiday cottages. None is ever let to the same person for more than 31 consecutive days. Three cottages have been owned for many years but Rose Cottage was acquired on 1 June 2018 (and first let on that day) while Ivy Cottage was sold on 30 June 2018 (and last let on that day).

In 2018/19 days available for letting and days let are as follows

	Days available	Days let
Honeysuckle Cottage	270	240
Primrose Cottage	195	150
Bluebell Cottage	225	90
Rose Cottage	225	90
Ivy Cottage	30	5

Additional information

Rose Cottage was let for 45 days between 6 April and 31 May 2019.

Ivy Cottage was let for 103 days in the period 1 July 2017 to 5 April 2018 and was available for letting for 180 days in that period.

Qualification as 'furnished holiday accommodation'

Honeysuckle Cottage qualifies as it meets both the 210-day availability test and the 105-day letting test.

Primrose Cottage does *not* qualify although it is let for more than 105 days as it fails to satisfy the 210-day test. Averaging (see below) is only possible where it is the 105-day test which is not satisfied.

Bluebell Cottage does not qualify by itself as it fails the 105-day test. However, it may be included in an averaging election.

Rose Cottage qualifies as furnished holiday accommodation. It was acquired on 1 June 2018 so qualification in 2018/19 is determined by reference to the period of twelve months beginning on the day it was first let, in which it was let for a total of 135 days.

Ivy Cottage was sold on 30 June 2018 so qualification is determined by reference to the period from 1 July 2017 to 30 June 2018 (the last day of letting). It qualifies as it was available for letting for 210 days and let for 108 in this period.

Averaging election for 2018/19

	Days let
Honeysuckle Cottage	240
Bluebell Cottage	90
Rose Cottage	135
Ivy Cottage	108

$$\frac{240 + 90 + 135 + 108}{4} = 143.25 \text{ days}$$

note (c)

Notes

(a) Income from the commercial letting of furnished holiday accommodation is treated as trading income for certain limited purposes; in particular it counts as relevant UK earnings for the purpose of obtaining relief for contributions to a registered pension scheme.

(b) In addition, the commercial letting of furnished holiday accommodation is treated as a trade for the purpose of various capital gains tax reliefs including ENTREPRENEURS' RELIEF (CGT 211) and business assets gifts hold-over relief (see CGT 213 HOLD-OVER RELIEFS). [*TCGA 1992, ss 241, 241A*].

(c) All four cottages included in the averaging election now qualify as furnished holiday accommodation as each is deemed to have been let for 143.25 days in the year 2018/19.

(d) If Bluebell cottage had still not qualified as a result of averaging but qualified in 2017/18, it would have been possible to make a 'period of grace' election, provided there had been a genuine intention to meet the 105-day letting condition for 2018/19. The same applies if the cottage had qualified for 2016/17 and a period of grace election had been made in respect of it for 2017/18. [*ITTOIA 2005, s 326A*].

22.3 'RENT-A-ROOM' RELIEF

[*ITTOIA 2005, ss 784–802; FA 2013, Sch 4 paras 40, 56*]

Frankie and Johnny are single persons sharing a house as their main residence. They have for some years taken in lodgers to supplement their income. As Frankie contributed the greater part of the purchase price of the house, she and Johnny have an agreement to share the rental income in the ratio 2:1, although expenses are shared equally. The house was acquired without a mortgage.

For the year ended 5 April 2013, gross rents amounted to £5,700 and allowable expenses were £1,100. In the year ended 5 April 2014, the pair face a heavy repair bill after uninsured damage to one of the rooms. Gross rents for that year amount to £3,600 and expenses to

£4,400. For the years ended 5 April 2015 and 5 April 2016, gross rents are £6,600 and expenses £2,200, and for the year ended 5 April 2017 they are £6,000 and £2,500 respectively. For the year ended 5 April 2018 they are £13,500 and £8,000 respectively. For the year ended 5 April 2019, they are £12,000 and £1,000 respectively.

For 2012/13, the position is as follows

Normal computation of property income

	Frankie	Johnny
	£	£
Gross rents (y/e 5.4.13)	3,800	1,900
Allowable expenses	(550)	(550)
Net rents	£3,250	£1,350

Johnny's share of *gross* rents is less than his one half share (£2,125) of the basic amount (£4,250). It is assumed that he would not make the election for full rent-a-room relief not to apply. His share of net rents is thus treated as nil.

Frankie's share of gross rents exceeds £2,125, so full rent-a-room relief cannot apply. She can, however, elect to apply the alternative method of calculation. Under that method, she is taxed on the excess of *gross* rents over £2,125. It is assumed that she will make the election as she will then be taxed on £1,675 rather than £3,250.

For 2013/14, the position is as follows

Normal computation of property income

	Frankie	Johnny
	£	£
Gross rents (y/e 5.4.14)	2,400	1,200
Allowable expenses	(2,200)	(2,200)
Net rents / (loss)	£200	£(1,000)

Johnny's share of gross rents continues to be less than £2,125. Under full rent-a-room relief, his share of net rents will be treated as nil. However, he will obtain no relief, by carry-forward or otherwise, for his loss. In order to preserve his loss, he could elect for full rent-a-room relief not to apply, the election having effect for 2013/14 only.

Frankie's share of gross rents exceeds £2,125. Therefore, her previous election for the alternative method will not be treated as automatically withdrawn. She will be taxed under the alternative method on £275 (£2,400 – £2,125). However, this is greater than the amount taxable on the normal property income computation (£200), so it is assumed she would withdraw the election with effect for 2013/14 and subsequent years. The notice of withdrawal does not prejudice the making of a fresh election for 2014/15 or any subsequent year.

For 2014/15, the position is as follows

Normal computation of property income

	Frankie	Johnny
	£	£
Gross rents (y/e 5.4.15)	4,400	2,200
Allowable expenses	(1,100)	(1,100)
Net rents	£3,300	£1,100

Johnny's share of gross rents now exceeds £2,125, so full rent-a-room relief will not apply. He could elect for the alternative method to apply, and his chargeable income will then be reduced to £75 (£2,200 − £2,125). This is further reduced to nil by the bringing forward of his £1,000 loss for 2013/14 Johnny then carries forward £925 of losses to 2015/16. If Johnny did not make the election, his chargeable income would be £100 with the whole of his 2013/14 loss having been utilised.

Frankie can make a fresh election for the alternative method, with effect from 2014/15, and she will then be taxed on £2,275 (£4,400 − £2,125).

For 2015/16, the position is as follows

The normal computation of property income is as for 2014/15. Assuming Frankie and Johnny both elected to apply the alternative method for 2014/15, the elections will continue to apply for 2015/16, so that their respective chargeable property incomes are £2,275 and £75. Johnny's profit is reduced to nil by utilising £75 of his brought forward losses (with his remaining losses of £850 being carried forward to 2016/17).

For 2016/17, the position is as follows

Normal computation of property income

	Frankie	Johnny
	£	£
Gross rents (y/e 5.4.17)	4,000	2,000
Allowable expenses	(1,250)	(1,250)
Net rents	£2,750	£750

Johnny's share of gross rents is below £3,750, i.e. half of the increased £7,500 limit which was introduced in 2016/17, so that the election to apply the alternative method is treated as having been withdrawn, and full rent-a-room relief applies instead (assuming he makes no election to disapply it). The balance of £850 of his 2013/14 loss is carried forward to 2017/18.

Frankie's election to apply the alternative method will continue to have effect (unless withdrawn), so that her chargeable property income will be £250 (£4,000 − £3,750).

For 2017/18, the position is as follows

Normal computation of property income

	Frankie	Johnny
	£	£
Gross rents (y/e 5.4.18)	9,000	4,500
Allowable expenses	(4,000)	(4,000)
Net rents	£5,000	£500

For both Frankie and Johnny their shares of gross rents now exceed £3,750, i.e. half of the £7,500 limit, so that full rent-a-room relief will not apply, and since their share of the expenses also exceeds £3,750, the election to apply the alternative method will be unfavourable. It is therefore assumed that Frankie withdraws her election (by 31 January 2020). They are accordingly both charged to tax on the basis of the normal property income computation, with Johnny's £850 loss brought forward being set against his share, the balance of £350 being carried forward to 2018/19.

For 2018/19, the position is as follows

Normal computation of property income

	Frankie	Johnny
	£	£
Gross rents (y/e 5.4.19)	8,000	4,000
Allowable expenses	(500)	(500)
Net rents	£7,500	£3,500

For both Frankie and Johnny, their share of gross rents exceeds £3,750, so that full rent-a-room relief will not apply. Both could now elect to apply the alternative method of calculation (the election to be made by 31 January 2021). Frankie's chargeable property income will be reduced to £4,250 (£8,000 − £3,750). Johnny's chargeable property income will be reduced to £250 (£4,000 − £3,750) and further reduced to nil by offsetting £250 of his remaining 2013/14 loss (of which the balance of £100 is carried forward to 2019/20).

Notes

(a) Rent-a-room relief covers receipts for meals, cleaning, laundry etc. as well as sums (i.e. rents) received for the use of the furnished accommodation. It applies equally where the provision of accommodation and services is chargeable as trading income or as miscellaneous income. [*ITTOIA 2005, s 786*].

(b) Where receipts accrue to more than one person in respect of the same residence in one income period, each of those persons who is a qualifying individual is entitled to a limit of one half of the 'basic amount' for the relevant tax year. The basic amount is £4,250 for years up to and including 2015/16 and £7,500 for 2016/17 onwards. [*ITTOIA 2005, ss 789, 790; SI 2015 No 1539*].

(c) The property allowance (see **22.6** below), which became available from 2017/18 onwards, cannot be used in conjunction with rent-a-room relief. [*ITTOIA 2005, s 783BM*].

22.4 MORTGAGE INTEREST AND OTHER FINANCE COSTS

[*ITTOIA 2005, ss 272A, 272B, 274A, 274AA, 274B, 274C; F(No 2)A 2015, s 24(2)(5); FA 2016, s 26*].

Jacob owns a property in Coventry which he acquired with the aid of a mortgage. Part of the building is rented out as office premises and part as residential accommodation. The latter is not furnished holiday accommodation. A comparison of the floor areas of the commercial and residential parts of the building shows that the latter comprise 64% of the total floor area of the building.

For 2018/19, the interest paid on the mortgage amounts to £5,600. The profits of Jacob's UK property business, before deducting any mortgage interest but otherwise as adjusted for tax purposes, amount to £32,000. There is an allowable loss of £3,200 brought forward from 2017/18 under *ITA 2007, s 118*. Jacob has no overseas property business. He is a lecturer with taxable profits of £25,858 for the year to 30 June 2018 but has no other source of taxable income. He has no children and will therefore be unaffected by the high income child benefit charge.

Jacob's property income for 2018/19 is calculated as follows

		£	£
Profits before deducting mortgage interest			32,000
Deduct:	Mortgage interest:		
	commercial accommodation £5,600 @ 36%	2,016	
	residential accommodation (£5,600 @ 64%) x 50%	1,792	
			(3,808)
			28,192
Deduct:	Loss brought forward		3,200
Taxable property income			£24,992

Jacob's income tax liability for 2018/19 is calculated as follows

			£	£
Professional income				25,858
Property income as above				24,992
Total and net income				50,850
Deduct:	Personal allowance			11,850
Taxable income				£39,000
Tax payable:				
	34,500	@ 20%		6,900.00
	4,500	@ 40%		1,800.00
	£39,000			—
				8,700.00
	Less:	Basic rate reduction (see below): £1,792 @ 20%		358.40
Tax payable				£8,341.60

The basic rate reduction is calculated as follows

The basic rate reduction is based on the lowest of the following:

		£
(i)	interest otherwise unrelieved (£5,600 – £2,016 – 1,792)	1,792
(ii)	the taxable profits of the property business for the year, net of losses brought forward	24,992
(iii)	the individual's 'adjusted total income' for the year, i.e. net income, exclusive of any savings income or dividend income, minus the personal allowance (and any blind person's allowance)	39,000

Notes

(a) Deductions for finance costs, including mortgage interest, incurred on or after 6 April 2017 are restricted in computing residential property income (other than from furnished holiday lettings). Only a percentage of otherwise allowable finance costs are deductible in computing property income, with the balance attracting basic rate relief only. The percentage is 50% for 2018/19 (it was 75% for 2017/18 and it will be 25% for 2019/20). For 2020/21 onwards, all finance costs will be relieved at basic rate only.

(b) Where a property business consists of the letting of both residential and other property, the restriction to basic rate applies only to the proportion of finance costs that relates to the residential letting. Any apportionment should be made on a just and reasonable basis. In this example, the mortgage interest has been apportioned by reference to floor space. One alternative would have been to apportion it by reference to the respective values of the different parts of the building. See HMRC Property Income Manual PIM2056.

(c) If the amount on which the basic rate deduction is based had been less than the figure given by option (i) (i.e. because option (ii) or (iii) gave a lower figure), the deficit would have been carried forward and added to the option (i) figure for the following tax year.

22.5 PREMIUMS ETC. ON LEASES OF UP TO 50 YEARS

[*ITTOIA 2005, ss 276–307*]

Cross-reference. See also CGT **216.3**(C)(H)(J) LAND.

(A)

Mr Green grants a 30-year lease of premises to a trader, Mr Indigo, on 1 March 2019 for a premium of £35,000.

The amount to be included in the profits of Mr Green's property business for 2018/19 is as follows

$$P \times \frac{50 - Y}{50}$$

where

P = the amount of the premium, and

Y = the number of complete periods of 12 months (other than the first) comprised in the effective duration of the lease.

[*ITTOIA 2005, s 277*].

Thus

$$£35{,}000 \times \frac{50 - 29}{50} = \underline{£\,14{,}700}$$

(B) **Allowance to lessee carrying on trade etc.**

[*ITTOIA 2005, ss 60–67*]

Assuming the same figures as in (A) above and that Mr Indigo prepares accounts to 31 March

Chargeable premium	£14,700
Number of days comprised in the lease period	10,958

The lessee will obtain relief as follows

$$\frac{£14{,}700}{10{,}958} = £\,1.34 \text{ per day treated as a deductible expense.}$$

i.e. £42 for period of account to 31.3.19 and £489 for period of account to 31.3.20 and so on.

(C) **Grant of sub-lease**

[*ITTOIA 2005, ss 64, 287, 288*]

On 1 May 2020, Mr Indigo in (A) and (B) above finds that the leased premises are now surplus to his trading requirements, and he grants a 10-year sub-lease at a premium of £12,500.

The amount to be included in the profits of Mr Indigo's property business for 2020/21 is computed as follows

	£
Chargeable premium before reduction	
$£12{,}500 \times \frac{50-9}{50} =$	10,250
Reduced by £14,700 × 10/30	4,900
Reduced chargeable premium	£5,350

The chargeable sub-lease premium is reduced by reference to the premium chargeable on the landlord.

The number of days in the 10-year receipt period of the sub-lease is 3,653. The daily amount of the relief given is therefore £4,900 divided by 3,653 = £1.34. This equals the daily expense computed in (B) above; as there is no deficit, Mr Indigo is not entitled to any deduction under (B) above for any of the 3,653 qualifying days covered by the sublease.

Supposing Mr Indigo had been able to obtain a premium of only £5,000 for the 10-year sub-lease. The amount to be included as a receipt in computing the profits of his property business for 2020/21 would then be as follows.

	£
Chargeable premium before reduction	
$£5{,}000 \times \frac{50-9}{50} =$	4,100
Reduced by	
$£14{,}700 \times \frac{10}{30} = £4{,}900$ but restricted to	4,100
	Nil

The daily amount of the relief given is now £4,100 divided by 3,653 = £1.12. This is less than the daily expense of £1.34 computed in (B) above, the deficit being £0.22. Mr Indigo would be entitled to a deduction of £0.22 under (B) above for each of the 3,653 qualifying days covered by the sub-lease.

22.6 PROPERTY ALLOWANCE

[*ITTOIA 2005, ss 783B–783BQ; F(No 2) 2017, Sch 3 paras 1, 8, 13*]

Ariadne is in employment earning £25,000 per annum but earns extra money by renting out a garage to a neighbour. For the year ended 5 April 2019 she receives rent of £1,300. She pays £200 for repairs to the garage roof.

Ariadne's taxable property business profits for the year to 5.4.19 are as follows

		£	£
Rent received (i.e. gross receipts)			1,300
Deduct:	Repairs expenses	500	(200)
Taxable profit			£1,100

Ariadne elects to use the property allowance and is instead taxed as follows

		£
Gross receipts		1,300
Deduct:	Property allowance	1,000
Taxable profit for 2018/19		£300

Notes

(a) A £1,000 allowance (the '*property allowance*') was introduced for property income with effect for the tax year 2017/18 onwards. It does not apply to property businesses carried on in partnership or where rent-a-room relief is available (see **22.3** above).

(b) Where an individual's gross receipts do not exceed the £1,000 allowance, profits are treated as nil ('*full relief*'). The individual can elect for full relief not to be given. Where, as in this example, gross receipts exceed the £1,000 allowance, the individual can elect to use an alternative method of calculating income ('*partial relief*'). Under this method the charge to tax is on the excess of gross receipts over £1,000.

23 Remittance Basis

23.1 REMITTANCES FROM MIXED FUNDS

[*ITA 2007, ss 809Q, 809R; FA 2013, Sch 6 para 5*]

Van Helsing is resident, but not domiciled or deemed domiciled in the UK. He has regular employment in both the UK and Transylvania and some non-UK shareholdings. He maintains a single bank account in Transylvania which he opened in August 2017. Previously all his transactions went through a UK bank account; part of his UK salary after tax continues to be paid into that account. Van Helsing has made a claim to pay UK tax on the remittance basis for 2017/18 and 2018/19.

Van Helsing's Transylvanian bank account statements show the following

		Debit	Credit	Balance
		£	£	£
30 August 2017	UK salary (part)		4,200	4,200
15 September 2017	overseas salary		12,000	16,200
30 September 2017	UK salary (part)		4,200	20,400
6 October 2017	overseas dividends		11,000	31,400
30 October 2017	UK salary (part)		4,200	35,600
30 November 2017	UK salary (part)		4,200	39,800
15 December 2017	overseas salary		12,000	51,800
30 December 2017	UK salary (part)		4,200	56,000
30 January 2018	UK salary (part)		4,500	60,500
28 February 2018	UK salary (part)		4,500	65,000
15 March 2018	overseas salary		12,000	77,000
30 March 2018	UK salary (part)		4,500	81,500
4 April 2018	overseas dividends		21,500	103,000
30 April 2018	UK salary (part)		4,500	107,500
30 April 2018	bank interest		6,000	113,500
15 May 2018	sale proceeds of overseas shareholding		794,000	907,500
30 May 2018	UK salary (part)		4,500	912,000
15 June 2018	overseas salary		13,000	925,000
21 June 2018	transfer to UK bank account	450,000		475,000

All amounts of overseas income other than the bank interest were subject to deduction of tax at source in their country of origin. The investment sold in May 2018 was originally inherited from Van Helsing's great aunt's estate; the chargeable gain on disposal is £350,000.

Applying the rules in ITA 2007, s 809Q(3)

Step 1

For each of the categories of income and capital in paragraphs (a) to (i) below, find the amount of income or capital for the tax year in question in the mixed fund immediately before the transfer to the UK. The tax year in question is the tax year in which the transfer occurs, i.e. 2018/19. The categories are:

(a) employment income (other than income within (b), (c) or (f));

(b) relevant foreign earnings (other than income within (f));

(c) foreign specific employment income (other than income within (f));

(d) relevant foreign income (other than income within (g));

(e) foreign chargeable gains (other than gains within (h));

(f) employment income subject to a foreign tax;

(g) relevant foreign income subject to a foreign tax;

(h) foreign chargeable gains subject to a foreign tax;

(i) income or capital not within any of the above.

		£
employment income not subject to a foreign tax — (a) above	UK salary	9,000
relevant foreign income not subject to a foreign tax — (d) above	bank interest	6,000
foreign chargeable gains not subject to a foreign tax — (e) above	overseas shareholding	350,000
employment income subject to a foreign tax — (f) above	overseas salary	13,000
relevant foreign income subject to a foreign tax — (g) above	overseas dividends	Nil
		£378,000

Step 2

Identify the earliest category which has an amount of income or gain in the mixed fund. This is category (a) which has £9,000.

Step 3

As the amount of the transfer is greater than the amount identified at Step 2 the amount of the transfer is treated as reduced by the amount identified in Step 2.

£450,000 – £9,000 = £441,000

Step 4

Repeat Steps 2 & 3 for each category in turn until the transfer is reduced to nil or all categories are exhausted.

£441,000 – £6,000 – £350,000 – £13,000 = £72,000

Step 5

As the amount of the transfer is not exhausted, repeat steps 1 to 4 but this time in relation to the immediately preceding year, i.e. 2017/18.

		£
employment income not subject to a foreign tax — (a) above	UK salary	34,500
employment income subject to a foreign tax — (f) above	overseas salary	36,000
relevant foreign income subject to a foreign tax — (g) above	overseas dividends	32,500
		£102,500

Applying Steps 1 to 4 for 2017/18, all of the income in categories (a) and (f) and £1,500 of the income in category (g) is matched with the transfer.

£72,000 – £34,500 – £36,000 – £1,500 = Nil

Outcome

The £450,000 transfer is therefore regarded as a remittance of:

	2018/19	2017/18	Total
	£	£	£
UK employment income – category (a)	9,000	34,500	43,500
relevant foreign income not subject to foreign tax — category (d)	6,000		6,000
foreign chargeable gains not subject to foreign tax — category (e)	350,000		350,000
employment income subject to a foreign tax — category (f)	13,000	36,000	49,000
relevant foreign income subject to a foreign tax — category (g)		1,500	1,500
			£450,000

Conclusions

All of Van Helsing's UK employment income for both years to date (£43,500) is included in the transfer. This is not a taxable remittance as it is taxable in the UK on an arising basis.

£56,500 of overseas income is included in the transfer and treated as remitted to the UK. It is chargeable income for 2018/19, the year in which it is remitted, with credit being available under the double tax relief provisions for foreign taxes paid.

The remaining £350,000 of the £450,000 transfer is taxable as a chargeable gain for 2018/19, the year in which it is remitted.

The balance of £475,000 carried forward in the Transylvanian bank account consists of £31,000 of 2017/18 overseas dividends and £444,000 (£794,000 – £350,000) of capital originally represented by the overseas shareholding sold in May 2018. The capital is 'clean capital', having come from an inheritance, and will not be chargeable to tax when remitted to the UK.

Notes

(a) The remittance basis can only apply to an individual for a particular tax year if, for that tax year, the individual is resident but not domiciled in the UK. In most cases it requires the making of a claim; there are certain exceptions where the amounts involved are small. [*ITA 2007, ss 809B–809D; FA 2013, Sch 45 para 152(2)–(4), Sch 46 paras 3–5, 25, 27*].

(b) The abolition of the concept of ordinary residence for 2013/14 onwards means that the remittance basis no longer applies on the grounds that an individual is not ordinarily resident in the UK. However, transitional provisions have effect where an individual was resident in the UK for 2012/13 but was not ordinarily resident there at the end of that year. These provisions are intended to reflect the fact that an individual, unless having established an intention to settle in the UK, would have been regarded as not ordinarily resident for a maximum of three years of UK residence (typically straddling four tax years). See *FA 2013, Sch 46 para 26*.

(c) Where, for any tax year, an individual makes a *claim* for the remittance basis to apply, he loses entitlement to UK personal reliefs for that year and, if he is a 'long-term UK resident' (as defined), he is also liable to an additional tax charge. [*ITA 2007, ss 809G, 809H; FA 2015, s 24*].

(d) All chargeable income and gains are taxable for the year in which they are remitted and not, if different, the year in which they arose. [*ITEPA 2003, s 22; ITTOIA 2005, s 832; TCGA 1992, s 12*].

(e) If Van Helsing had claimed the remittance basis for 2018/19 but not for 2017/18, his 2017/18 foreign income would have been taxed on the arising basis in that year and would not have been taxable when remitted. If, on the other hand, he had claimed the remittance basis for 2017/18 but not for 2018/19, his 2017/18 foreign income would still have been chargeable when remitted in 2018/19 or any later year.

(f) Subject to conditions, individuals performing the duties of a *single* employment both inside and outside the UK may calculate their tax liability by reference to the total amount transferred out of a mixed fund during a tax year, rather than by reference to individual transfers. The rules are then applied to the total amount transferred out of the fund to the UK in the tax year as if it were a single transfer. This has effect only if the mixed fund account is credited with nothing other than earnings from employment, consideration for the disposal of employment-related securities/options or interest on the account. [*ITA 2007, ss 809RA–809RD; FA 2013, Sch 6 paras 6, 8*].

(g) Note that individuals who become deemed domiciled by virtue of being UK-resident for at least 15 out of the previous 20 tax years under rules introduced by *F(No 2)A 2017* and are on remittance basis may rearrange their overseas mixed funds to allow them to remit clean capital from overseas ahead of taxable income and gains provided they do so before 6 April 2019. [*F(No 2)A 2017 Sch 8 paras 44–46*].

24 Savings and Investment Income

24.1 DEEPLY DISCOUNTED SECURITIES

[*ITTOIA 2005, ss 427–460*]

(A) Profit on disposal.

On 28 June 2002 Mr Knight subscribed for £10,000 3% loan stock issued by DDS plc at a price of £55 per £100 stock incurring costs of £60. He sold these same securities on 6 July 2018 for £80 per £100 stock and incurred costs of £90. The 3% loan stock in DDS plc is quoted on the Stock Exchange, was issued on 1 July 2000 at £80 and is redeemable on 30 June 2030 at £100.

Mr Knight's tax position for 2018/19 on the disposal is

			£	£
Disposal proceeds				8,000
Less acquisition cost				(5,500)
				2,500
Deduct	Costs of acquisition	note (b)	60	
	Costs of disposal	notes (b), (c)	—	
				(60)
Taxable income				£2,440

Notes

(a) Subject to certain exceptions, a security is a '*deeply discounted security*' if, at the time it is issued, the amount payable on maturity (or any possible occasion of redemption) exceeds (or may exceed) the issue price by more than R × 0.5% × Y, where R is the amount payable on maturity etc. and Y is the period between issue and redemption, expressed in years (and fractions of years) but with a maximum value of 30. In this example, R = £100 and Y = 30. £100 × 0.5% × 30 = £15. The difference between issue price and redemption price is £20. Thus, the loan stock is a deeply discounted security. Exceptions include company shares, gilts (but not strips), excluded indexed securities, life assurance policies, capital redemption policies and securities issued under the same prospectus as other securities issued previously but not themselves deeply discounted securities. [*ITTOIA 2005, ss 430–436*].

(b) Subject to note (c), relief is available for costs incurred in connection with the acquisition of the security or with its transfer or redemption, but only if incurred before 27 March 2003 or, if incurred on or after that date, the person transferring or redeeming the security had held it continuously since before that date *and* the security was listed on a recognised stock exchange (within *ITA 2007, s 1005*) at some time before that date. [*FA 1996, Sch 13 para 1(2)–(4); ITTOIA 2005, ss 453, 455*].

(c) Such costs as are referred to in note (b) are not deductible where incurred on or after 6 April 2015. [*ITTOIA 2005, s 455; FA 2012, Sch 39 para 48*]. Thus the disposal costs are not deductible in this example.

(B) **Loss on disposal.**

On the assumption that Mr Knight in (A) above sells the loan stock for £40 per £100 stock instead of £80 the following will apply:

Mr Knight's tax position for 2018/19 on the disposal is

		£	£
Disposal proceeds			4,000
Less acquisition cost			(5,500)
			(1,500)
Deduct	Costs of acquisition	60	
	Costs of disposal	—	
			(60)
Allowable loss			(£1,560)

Notes

(a) Mr Knight will be able to claim loss relief of £1,560 as a deduction in computing net income for 2018/19. The relief must be claimed no later than 31 January 2021.

(b) Loss relief is available only if the person sustaining the loss had held the security continuously since before 27 March 2003 *and* the security was listed on a recognised stock exchange (within *ITA 2007, s 1005*) at some time before that date. [*ITTOIA 2005, ss 453, 454*].

25 Seed Enterprise Investment Scheme

25.1 INCOME TAX INVESTMENT RELIEF

[ITA 2007, ss 257A–257EG; FA 2013, s 56(4)(6); FA 2014, s 54; FA 2018, s 14(2)(4)(5)].

For 2018/19 Ben has taxable earnings of £225,000, dividends of £20,000 and bank interest of £15,000. He makes the following qualifying investments by subscription in companies issuing shares via the Seed Enterprise Investment Scheme (SEIS). He is not a Scottish taxpayer.

	Date shares acquired	Shares acquired (all at par)	Acquisition cost £
X Ltd	25 August 2018	10,000 ordinary £1	10,000
Y Ltd	15 December 2018	40,000 ordinary 50p	20,000
Z Ltd	1 February 2018	30,000 ordinary £1	30,000
			£60,000

On 29 April 2018 Ben also made a qualifying investment of £5,000 under the enterprise investment scheme (EIS).

Ben's investment in Z Ltd represents 25% of that company's issued share capital. He becomes a director of the company and receives director's fees of £6,000 in 2018/19. This is in addition to his earnings quoted above.

Ben will obtain tax relief for 2018/19 as follows

Amount eligible for SEIS relief

	£
X Ltd	10,000
Y Ltd	20,000
Z Ltd note (c)	30,000
Total (being less than the maximum of £100,000)	£60,000

	£
Earnings (including director's fees)	231,000
Dividends	20,000
Bank interest	15,000
Total income	266,000
Personal allowance (restricted due to level of income)	Nil
Taxable income	£266,000

Tax payable:		
34,500	@ 20%	6,900.00
115,500	@ 40%	46,200.00
96,000	@ 45%	43,200.00
2,000	@ 0% (dividend allowance)	—
18,000	@ 38.1% (dividend additional rate)	6,858.00
		103,158.00
Deduct EIS relief £5,000 @ 30%		(1,500.00)
		101,658.00
Deduct SEIS relief £60,000 @ 50%		(30,000.00)
Net tax liability 2018/19 (subject to PAYE deductions)		£71,658.00

Notes

(a) The SEIS is a tax-advantaged venture capital scheme. Income tax relief is available for investment in small companies (i.e. those with 25 or fewer employees and assets of up to £200,000) that are carrying on, or preparing to carry on, a new qualifying business. The relief is available on share subscriptions of up to £100,000 per individual per tax year. The shares must be retained for at least three years.

(b) SEIS relief is given at the SEIS rate of tax (50%) and by way of an income tax reduction. The relief cannot exceed what would otherwise be the income tax liability (no restriction being necessary in this example). For this purpose, the income tax liability is before taking into account any married couple's allowance, double tax relief and certain other specified items. However, the EIS investment relief must be deducted before the SEIS relief. [*ITA 2007, ss 26, 27, 29, 257AB*].

(c) The fact that Ben is a director of Z Ltd and in receipt of director's remuneration does not invalidate his claim for relief. If, however, he had been an employee *other than a director* of the company at any time in the requisite three-year holding period, he would not have been eligible for SEIS income tax relief. [*ITA 2007, ss 257AC, 257BA*].

(d) Though not illustrated in this example, any amount of SEIS investment relief can be carried back to the preceding tax year, provided the £100,000 maximum is not thereby exceeded for that year.

(e) Ben is not entitled to a personal savings allowance in respect of his bank interest as he is an additional rate taxpayer.

25.2 WITHDRAWAL OF RELIEF/CAPITAL LOSSES

[*ITA 2007, ss 257F–257GI, 257HA*].

(A) Withdrawal of income tax relief

[*ITA 2007, ss 257F–257GI, 257HA*].

On 1 March 2021 Ben, the investor in **25.1** above, needs to raise some funds urgently and sells half his X Ltd shares at arm's length to another shareholder for £4,250.

The position is as follows

SEIS investment relief falls to be reduced or withdrawn as the shares have not been held for the requisite period of three years.

The tax reduction in 2018/19 is attributed to the three share issues subscribed for according to the amounts claimed for each issue.

The relief attributable to the 10,000 X Ltd shares subscribed for is 10,000/60,000 x £30,000 = £5,000.

The relief attributable to the 5,000 shares sold is therefore £2,500.

If the relief attributable is greater than an amount equal to tax at the SEIS rate on the disposal consideration, the relief is reduced by that amount. Otherwise, the relief is withdrawn in full.

Tax at the SEIS rate on the disposal consideration:

50% x £4,250 = £2,125

This is less than £2,500 so the relief given is reduced by £2,125 by the making of an assessment to income tax for 2018/19.

Notes

(a) If the disposal had not been at arm's length, the relief would have been withdrawn in full.

(b) The disposal consideration would fall to be treated as reduced for the purposes of the above calculation where the relief attributable (A) is less than tax at the SEIS rate on the amount subscribed (B). It is so reduced by applying the fraction A/B. [*ITA 2007, ss 209, 210*]. This works the same way as for withdrawal of relief under the EIS scheme; see **10.2** ENTERPRISE INVESTMENT SCHEME for an illustration.

(B) **Capital losses**

[*TCGA 1992, s 150E*].

The disposal in (A) above is also a disposal for capital gains tax purposes

The capital gains position is as follows

2020/21

	£	£
Disposal proceeds (March 2021)		4,250
Cost (August 2018)	5,000	
Less Relief attributable to shares:		
£2,500 − £2,125	(375)	
		(4,625)
Allowable loss		(£375)

25.2 IT Seed Enterprise Investment Scheme

Note

(a) An allowable loss may arise for capital gains tax purposes on a disposal of SEIS shares, whether or not the disposal occurs within the requisite three-year period. In computing such a loss, the allowable cost is reduced by SEIS relief attributable to the shares (and not withdrawn).

26 Self-Assessment

Cross-references. See also **13.1** LATE PAYMENT INTEREST AND PENALTIES.

26.1 CALCULATION OF INTERIM PAYMENTS

[*TMA 1970, s 59A*]

For 2017/18, Kylie's self-assessment shows the following.

	£
Gross income tax liability	8,164
Capital gains tax liability	2,122
Class 4 NIC liability	198
PAYE tax deducted (all relating to 2017/18)	3,740

The payments on account for 2018/19 (unless, on a claim, Kylie chooses to pay different amounts) are based on relevant amounts as follows.

	£
Income tax (£8,164 − £3,740 =)	4,424
Class 4 NIC	198

Half of the relevant amounts is due on each of 31 January 2019 and 31 July 2019. No payment on account is required in respect of capital gains tax liability.

26.2 CLAIMS INVOLVING MORE THAN ONE YEAR

[*TMA 1970, s 42(11A), Sch 1B*]

(A) Carry-back claim made after 31 January in the later year

Ant files his 2017/18 tax return at the end of January 2019. His self-assessment shows an income tax liability of £8,640, of which £2,400 represents higher rate tax charged on the top £6,000 of income. Ant subsequently makes a claim to carry back from 2018/19 (the later year) to 2017/18 a trading loss of £5,000 for the year to 31 December 2018, producing a tax saving of £2,000 (£5,000 @ 40%). All tax due has been paid on the due dates.

If the claim is made on, say, 1 April 2019, a repayment of £2,000 will be made.

If the claim is made on, say, 1 July 2019, the relief of £2,000 will be set against the second 2018/19 interim payment on account (POA) of £4,320 (half of £8,640) due on 31 July 2019 (see note (a)).

If the claim is made on, say, 1 September 2019, and the 31 July 2019 POA has been duly made, a repayment of £2,000 will be made. If the claim is made on 1 September 2019, and the 31 July 2019 POA has *not* been made, the relief of £2,000 will be set against the POA (see note (a)), which is then regarded to that extent as having been paid on 1 September 2019 (see note (b)).

In no case will repayment interest be due, as the relief is given before 31 January 2020 (see note (c)).

As he has made no trading profit for 2018/19, Ant might make a separate claim to reduce or dispense with his POAs for that year (see *TMA 1970, s 59A(3)(4)*).

Notes

(a) Once a valid claim involving more than one year, e.g. a carry-back claim, has been made, HMRC will give effect to it as soon as possible, subject to the following policies:

- no repayment of tax will be made for the earlier year unless tax for the earlier year has been paid in full; and
- where liability for any year is outstanding (or will become due within 35 days after HMRC process the claim), relief will be given by set-off rather than by repayment.

(Revenue Tax Bulletins December 1996 361–365, June 1997 p 443; HMRC Self Assessment Claims Manual SACM11020).

(b) Where the tax saving arising from a loss carry-back claim is set against an outstanding tax liability, the effective date of settlement of that liability, for the purpose of calculating any charge to late payment interest or penalties, is the date on which the valid carry-back claim is made (Revenue Tax Bulletins December 1996 p 364, August 2001 p 879).

(c) On a repayment or set-off arising from a loss carry-back claim, repayment interest accrues only from 31 January following the later year (i.e. the year of loss). It follows that if in this example the repayment or set-off is made before 31 January 2020, no repayment interest will be due. [*FA 2009, s 102, Sch 54 para 7*].

(d) For loss relief carry-backs generally, see **15.1**, **15.3**, **15.4** LOSSES.

(B) Carry-back claim made after 31 July but before 31 January in the later year

Dec files his 2017/18 tax return in October 2018. On 1 November 2018, he makes a claim to carry back from 2018/19 (the later year) to 2017/18 a trading loss of £5,000 for the year to 30 April 2018. Dec's POAs for 2017/18 (based on his 2016/17 liability) were £3,000 each. All tax due has been paid on the due dates.

What if Dec's self-assessment for 2017/18 shows an income tax liability of £8,640, of which £2,400 represents higher rate tax charged on the top £6,000 of income? The loss produces a tax saving of £2,000 (£5,000 @ 40%). This will be available to set off against the 2017/18 balancing payment (due on 31 January 2019), reducing it from £2,640 to £640. The 2018/19 POAs will be £4,320 each.

What if Dec's self-assessment for 2017/18 shows an income tax liability of £5,500, which represents tax charged at 20%? The 2017/18 POAs will have been adjusted to £2,750 each, and repayments made of £250 in respect of each POA. The loss produces a tax saving of £1,000 (£5,000 @ 20%). As all the tax for 2017/18 has been paid and there are no outstanding liabilities for any year, the £1,000 will be repaid. No repayment interest is due. The 2018/19 POAs will be £2,750 each.

Say the carry-back claim had instead been made on 3 January 2019 (assuming all other facts are as immediately above), the £1,000 tax saving would have been set against the first 2018/19 POA of £2,750 due on 31 January 2019, reducing it to £1,750.

As he has made no trading profit for 2018/19, Dec might make a separate claim to reduce or dispense with his POAs for that year (see *TMA 1970, s 59A(3)(4)*).

(C) **Carry-back claim made before 31 July in the later year**

The facts are as in (B) above except that Dec files his 2017/18 return on 25 April 2018 and makes his carry-back claim on 31 May 2018. As accounts for the year to 30 April 2018 are not finalised at this stage, the trading loss of £5,000 is a 'best estimate' but does turn out to be an accurate figure. Dec could not have made the claim in the return as the period of account in which the loss is sustained had not yet come to an end when he filed the return.

What if Dec's self-assessment for 2017/18 shows an income tax liability of £8,640, which £2,400 represents higher rate tax charged on the top £6,000 of income? The loss produces a tax saving of £2,000 (£5,000 @ 40%). This will be available to set off against the 2017/18 balancing payment (due on 31 January 2019), reducing it from £2,640 to £640. The 2018/19 POAs will be £4,320 each.

What if Dec's self-assessment for 2017/18 shows an income tax liability of £5,500, which represents tax charged at 20%? The 2017/18 POAs will be adjusted to £2,750 each and there will be no balancing payment due on 31 January 2019. A repayment of £250 will be made from the first POA paid on 31 January 2018. The tax saving of £1,000 (£5,000 @ 20%) will be set against the second POA due on 31 July 2018, reducing it from £2,750 to £1,750. The 2018/19 POAs will be £2,750 each.

What if the facts were as immediately above but Dec has failed to pay the first POA for 2018/19 due on 31 January 2019? The tax saving of £1,000 (£5,000 @ 20%) will be set against this outstanding liability, reducing the payment required from £2,750 (originally £3,000) to £1,750. The effective date of payment for interest purposes is 31 May 2018, the date of the valid claim (see note (b) to (A) above). The balance of £1,750 is already overdue, and a further POA of £2,750 is due on 31 July 2018. No balancing payment for 2017/18 is due on 31 January 2019. The 2018/19 POAs will be £2,750 each.

As he has made no trading profit for 2018/19, Dec might make a separate claim to reduce or dispense with his POAs for that year (see *TMA 1970, s 59A(3)(4)*).

27 Settlements

27.1 TAX PAYABLE BY TRUSTEES

A is sole life-tenant of a settlement which has income and expenses in the year 2018/19 as follows

	£
Property income	500
Bank interest	1,500
Dividends	1,000
	£3,000
Expenses chargeable to income	£400

The tax payable by the trustees under self-assessment is as follows:

	£
Property income — £500 @ 20% (basic rate)	100.00
Bank interest — £1,500 @ 20% (basic rate)	300.00
Dividends — £1,000 @ 7.5% (dividend ordinary rate)	75.00
	£475.00

The expenses are not deductible in arriving at the tax payable by the trustees. The starting rate for savings, personal savings allowance and dividend allowance are not available to trustees.

Notes

(a) By prior arrangement, where there is a sole life-tenant in a trust, HMRC may allow the interest to be assessed directly on that beneficiary.

(b) For treatment of the trust income in the hands of the beneficiary, see **27.3**(A) below.

27.2 SPECIAL TRUST RATES OF TAX

[*ITA 2007, ss 9, 479–487, 491–498; FA 2016, s 5(4)(10), Sch 1 paras 63(5)–(7), 73*]

(A) Standard rate band

For 2018/19, a small discretionary trust has property income of £500, building society interest of £300 and UK dividends of £600. It has no other income or expenses. The settlor has made no other settlements.

The tax liability of the trust for 2018/19 is as follows

	£
Standard rate band	
Property income — £500 @ 20% (basic rate)	100.00
Interest — £300 @ 20% (basic rate)	60.00
Dividends — £200 @ 7.5% (dividend ordinary rate)	15.00
	£175.00
Income exceeding standard rate band	
Dividends — £400 @ 38.1% (dividend trust rate)	152.40
	£327.40

Notes

(a) The property income and building society interest form the lowest slice of the total income; thus, it all falls within the standard rate band and is charged at basic rate. £800 of the £1,000 standard rate band is now used up; thus, £200 of the dividend income falls within the standard rate band and is charged at the dividend ordinary rate. The remainder of the dividend income is charged at the dividend trust rate.

(b) Note that if the trustees were to distribute the whole of the net income of £1,072.60 (£500 + £300 + £600 − £327.40) to beneficiaries, they will have further tax to pay (assuming no balance, or insufficient balance, brought forward from earlier years in the trustees' tax pool). The total tax payable will be £877.58 (£1,072.60 × 45/55), from which can be deducted tax paid of £327.40, leaving a further £550.18 to pay (if no balance is brought forward in the pool). See also note (c) to (B) below and, for an illustration of the pool, (C) below.

(c) The standard rate band of £1,000 is divided between all settlements made by the same settlor, subject to a minimum band of £200 for each settlement. [*ITA 2007, ss 491, 492*].

(B) General

An accumulation and maintenance settlement (the 'XYZ trust') set up by W for his grandchildren in 1998 now comprises quoted investments and an industrial property. The property is let to an engineering company. Charges for rates, electricity etc. are paid by the trust and recharged yearly in arrears to the tenant. As a result of the delay in recovering the service costs, the settlement incurs overdraft interest. There are no other settlements in existence in relation to which W is the settlor.

The relevant figures for the year ended 5 April 2019 are as follows

	£
Property rents	40,500
Dividends	5,000
Bank interest	3,500
	£49,000
Trust administration expenses — proportion chargeable to income	1,350
Overdraft interest	1,050
	£2,400

Tax is payable by the trustees of a discretionary trust (including an accumulation and maintenance trust) at the trust rate (45%) or, in the case of dividend income, at the dividend trust rate (38.1%).

The tax liability of the trust for 2018/19 is as follows

		£	£
Property income	£1,000 at 20%	200.00	
	£39,500 at 45%	17,775.00	17,975.00
Bank interest £3,500 at 45%			1,575.00
Dividends		5,000	
Deduct Expenses (£2,400 grossed at $^{100}/_{92}$)		2,595	
		£2,405	
Tax on £2,595 @ 7.5% (dividend ordinary rate)		194.63	
Tax on £2,405 @ 38.1% (dividend trust rate)		916.31	1,110.94
Tax payable			£20,660.94

Notes

(a) Expenses (including in this example the overdraft interest) are set firstly against UK dividends and similar income, then against dividends from non-UK resident companies (not illustrated in this example), then against other savings income and finally against non-savings income. [*ITA 2007, ss 484–486*]. In this example, all the expenses are set against UK dividends. The effect of the calculation is that the expenses, grossed-up at 7.5%, save tax at 30.6% (the difference between the 7.5% dividend ordinary rate and the 38.1% dividend trust rate).

(b) The net income available for distribution to the beneficiaries, at the trustees' discretion, will be £25,939.06 (see (C) below).

(c) If the whole of the distributable income is in fact distributed, then unless there is sufficient balance brought forward from earlier years in the trustees' tax pool, there will be insufficient tax in the pool to frank the distribution (£25,939.06 × 45/55 =

£21,222.87). The tax paid of £20,660.94 will partly cover this, but the trustees will have a further liability which they may not have the funds to settle. See also (C) below.

(d) The property income and savings income form the lowest slice of the total income. Thus, the first £1,000 of such income falls within the standard rate band; as it is basic rate income in nature, that £1,000 is chargeable at the basic rate of 20%.

(e) See note (c) to (A) above as regards the standard rate band.

(f) For treatment of the trust income in the hands of a beneficiary, see **27.3**(B) below.

(C) Trustees' tax

[*ITA 2007, ss 496–498; FA 2016, Sch 1 paras 63(7), 73*]

The trustees of the XYZ trust in (B) above have distributed to beneficiaries all available income arising before 6 April 2018, and there is no balance brought forward in the trustees' tax pool created under *ITA 2007, s 497*.

The trustees' additional tax liability for 2018/19 are computed as follows

	£
Total income	49,000
Less expenses	2,400
	46,600
Less tax payable by trustees as in (B) above	20,661
Distributable income	£25,939
Tax added to trustees' tax pool (Y)	£20,661
Position if all income distributed	
Beneficiaries' income	25,939.00
Add tax at $^{45}/_{55}$ (see **27.3**(B) below) (X)	21,222.81
Beneficiaries' gross income	£47,161.81
Additional tax due from trustees (X) − (Y)	£561.81
Optimum position	
Income distributed (£46,600 (income net of expenses) @ 55%)	25,630.00
Tax credit $^{45}/_{55}$	20,970.00
Beneficiaries' gross income	£46,600.00
Additional tax due from trustees £(20,970 − 20,661)	£309.00
Funds available £(25,939 − 25,630)	£309.00

Note

(a) If the trustees distribute the whole of the distributable income, they will have no funds available from income to pay the additional tax due of £561.81.

27.3 INCOME OF BENEFICIARIES

(A) Interests in possession

A, as sole life-tenant of the settlement in **27.1** above, is absolutely entitled to receive the whole settlement income.

A's income from the trust for 2018/19 is computed as follows

		£	£	£
Trust dividend income		1,000		
Trust savings income			1,500	
Other trust income				500
Deduct:	dividend ordinary rate tax (7.5%)	(75)		
	basic rate tax (20%)		(300)	(100)
		925	1,200	400
Deduct Expenses (note (b))		400		
Net income entitlement		£525	£1,200	£400
Beneficiary's entitlement				
Grossed-up amounts:	£525 × $^{100}/_{92}$	£567.56		
	£1,200 × $^{100}/_{80}$		£1,500.00	
	£400 × $^{100}/_{80}$			£500.00
Tax deducted at source		£42.56	£300.00	£100.00

Notes

(a) This income falls to be included in A's return even if it is not actually paid to him, as he is absolutely entitled to it. He will receive a tax certificate (form R185 (Trust Income)) from the trust agents, showing three figures each for gross income, tax deducted and net income, as illustrated above.

(b) Trust expenses are deductible firstly from UK dividends and similar income, then from dividends from non-UK resident companies (not illustrated in this example), then from savings income and finally from non-savings income. [*ITA 2007, s 503*].

(c) That part of A's trust income which is represented by dividend income (£567) is treated in A's hands as if it were dividend income received directly by A. A is entitled to a credit against his tax liability for the £42 dividend ordinary rate tax deducted by the trustees, and this is repayable to him if he has insufficient liability to cover it.

(d) Similarly, that part of A's trust income which is represented by savings income (£1,500) is treated in A's hands as if it were such income received directly by A. It will thus qualify wholly or partly for the 0% starting rate for savings to the extent (if any) that A's other taxable income is less than the starting rate limit of £5,000, and for the personal savings allowance if A is not an additional rate taxpayer.

(B) Accumulation or discretionary trusts

M, the 17-year old grandson of W, is one of the five beneficiaries to whom the trustees can pay the settlement income in **27.2**(B) above. The trustees make a payment of £6,737 to M on 31 January 2019. He has no other income in the year 2018/19.

M's income from the trust is

	£
Net income	6,737.00
Tax at $^{45}/_{55}$	5,513.00
Gross income	£12,250.00

He can claim a tax repayment for 2018/19 of

	£
Total income	12,250
Deduct Personal allowance	11,850
	£400
Tax payable:	
£400 × 20% (basic rate)	80.00
Tax accounted for by trustees	(5,512.00)
Repayment due	£(5,432.00)

Notes

(a) If no income was actually paid to M from the settlement, nothing would fall to be included in his return.

(b) Unlike the position with interest in possession trusts (see (A) above), no distinction is made between dividend income, savings income and other income in the beneficiary's hands, the full amount of the payment to him being treated as having suffered tax at a single rate of 45% in the hands of the trustees. The beneficiary is not entitled to the dividend allowance, the starting rate for savings or the personal savings allowance as a payment from a discretionary trust is neither dividend income nor savings income in his hands.

(c) For treatment of trust income where the beneficiary is an infant under a parent's settlement, see **27.4** below.

27.4 SETTLEMENT BY PARENT IN FAVOUR OF OWN CHILD

[*ITTOIA 2005, ss 629, 631, 632, Sch 2 para 133*]

L set up an accumulation and maintenance trust for his two children, aged 5 and 3, in 2003. On 31 December 2004 and 31 December 2005, school fees of £990 were paid on behalf of each child. In January 2019 the trust was wound up and the assets transferred to the two beneficiaries, then aged 21 and 19, in equal shares. At that time there was £6,000 of undistributed income.

The income to be treated as the settlor's income will be as follows

2004/05	$£1,980 \times \frac{100}{60}$	£3,300
2005/06	$£1,980 \times \frac{100}{60}$	£3,300
2018/19 note (b)		Nil

Notes

(a) The payments for 2004/05 and 2005/06 are grossed up in accordance with the 'rate applicable to trusts' for each of those years, i.e. 40% for both the years.

(b) Income is not treated as that of the parent settlor if, at the time of payment, the children have either married or reached the age of eighteen.

27.5 LOANS BY SETTLEMENT TO SETTLOR

[*ITTOIA 2005, ss 633–638*]

The trustees of a settlement with undistributed income of £1,340 at 5 April 2014 made a loan of £30,000 to B, the settlor, on 30 September 2014.

B repays the loan on 31 December 2018. Undistributed income of £3,500 arose in 2014/15, £6,490 in 2015/16, £4,510 in 2016/17, £10,450 in 2017/18 and £9,200 in 2018/19. The trustees duly settle all their liabilities to tax on trust income.

The following income amounts will be treated as part of B's total income

		£
2014/15	£4,840 × $^{100}/_{55}$	8,800
2015/16	£6,490 × $^{100}/_{55}$	11,800
2016/17	£4,510 × $^{100}/_{55}$	8,200
2017/18	£10,450 × $^{100}/_{55}$	19,000
2018/19	£3,710 × $^{100}/_{55}$ note (b)	6,745

The notional tax credit available to B is

		£
2014/15	£8,800 @ 45%	3,960.00
2015/16	£11,800 @ 45%	5,310.00
2016/17	£8,200 @ 45%	3,690.00
2017/18	£19,000 @ 45%	8,550.00
2018/19	£6,745 @ 45%	3,035.25

Notes

(a) Where in any tax year the trustees of a settlement pay any capital sum (including by way of loan) to the settlor, a corresponding amount (grossed up at the trust rate) is treated as income of the settlor to the extent that it falls within the amount of available income in the settlement up to the end of that tax year or, to the extent that it does not fall within that amount, to the end of the next and subsequent tax years (up to a maximum of ten years).

(b) The amount treated as income in 2018/19 is limited to the amount of the loan less amounts previously treated as income (£30,000 – (£4,840 + £6,490 + £4,510 + £10,450)).

28 Share-Related Employment Income and Exemptions

28.1 SHARE OPTIONS — CHARGE TO TAX

[*ITEPA 2003, ss 471–484*]

An employee is granted an option exercisable within 5 years to buy 1,000 shares at £5 each. The option costs 50p per share. He exercises the option on 15 June 2018 when the shares are worth £7.50. The option is not granted under a tax-advantaged scheme. The employee does not incur any expenses in connection with the acquisition of the shares.

The amount taxable as employment income in 2018/19 is as follows

	£	£
Open market value of shares 1,000 × £7.50		7,500
Price paid 1,000 × £5 – shares	5,000	
1,000 × 50p – option	500	
		5,500
Amount taxable as employment income		£2,000

Notes

(a) The result would be the same if, instead of exercising the option, the employee transferred his option to a third party for £2,500.

(b) The capital gains tax base cost of the shares will be £7,500 being the aggregate of the price paid for the shares, the price paid for the option and the amount chargeable to income tax. [*TCGA 1992, ss 119A, 144(3)*].

(c) A share option acquired on or after 2 December 2004 is taken outside these rules (and into the convertible shares regime at **28.3** below) if it is a right to acquire securities that is itself acquired pursuant to a right or opportunity made available under arrangements having as one of their main purposes the avoidance of tax or national insurance contributions. This may also apply to a share option acquired before 2 December 2004 if 'something is done on or after that date as part of the arrangements under which it was made available'. [*ITEPA 2003, s 420(8)*].

28.2 RESTRICTED SHARES

[*ITEPA 2003, ss 422–432; FA 2014, Sch 9 para 36*]

Edward and Andrew are employees of Perks Ltd.

Edward is given 2,000 shares in the company on 1 October 2014 on the understanding that he cannot sell them for at least three years. This has the practical effect of restricting the market value by 30 pence per share.

Andrew is given 3,000 shares in the company on the same date on the understanding that they will be forfeited if he leaves the company before 1 January 2019. This has the practical effect of restricting the market value by 50 pence per share. Andrew does not leave the company and thus holds the shares with full rights as from 1 January 2019.

The above awards are not made under a tax-advantaged scheme.

The market value per share, disregarding the above restrictions, is as follows.

At 1.10.14	£2.00
At 1.10.17	£4.00
At 1.1.19	£5.00

The following amounts are chargeable to tax as employment income

2014/15

Edward — 2,000 × £1.70 (restricted market value at 1.10.14) =	£3,400
Andrew — no charge, as provision for forfeiture persists for no more than five years (see *ITEPA 2003, s 425*)	Nil

2017/18

Edward — chargeable event occurs on 1.10.17 when the shares cease to be restricted shares.

Taxable amount = UMV × (IUP − PCP − OP) − CE (see *ITEPA 2003, s 428*)

UMV (Unrestricted Market Value) = (2,000 × £4) £8,000

$$\text{IUP (Initial Uncharged Proportion)} = \frac{4{,}000\ (2{,}000 \times £2) - 3{,}400}{4{,}000}$$

PCP (Previously Charged Proportion) = Nil (as there has been no previous chargeable event)

OP (Outstanding Proportion) = Nil (as unrestricted market value and actual market value are the same after the event)

CE (employee's expenses) = Nil

Taxable amount = £8,000 × 15% (600/4,000) = £1,200

2018/19

Andrew — chargeable event occurs on 1.1.19 when the shares cease to be restricted shares.

Taxable amount = UMV × (IUP − PCP − OP) − CE

UMV = (3,000 × £5) £15,000

$$\text{IUP (Initial Uncharged Proportion)} = \frac{6{,}000\ (3{,}000 \times £2) - \text{Nil}}{6{,}000}$$

Other values = Nil

Taxable amount = £15,000 × 100% (6,000/6,000) = £15,000

Available elections and their effect

Andrew could have elected, jointly with his employer, to disapply the exemption on acquisition. The election would have had to be made by 15 October 2014. [*ITEPA 2003, s 425*]. The chargeable amount for 2014/15 would have been 3,000 × £1.50 = £4,500. The chargeable amount in 2018/19 would then have been £15,000 × 25% (1,500/6,000) = £3,750.

Edward and/or Andrew could also (or alternatively) have elected, jointly with the employer, to ignore the restrictions in computing the chargeable amount on acquisition. The election(s) would have had to be made by 15 October 2014. [*ITEPA 2003, s 431*]. The chargeable amounts for 2014/15 would have been £4,000 for Edward (2,000 × £2) and £6,000 for Andrew (3,000 × £2) but there would have been no further charge in subsequent years.

Note

(a) The elections mentioned above are implemented by way of an agreement (between employer and employee), in a form approved by HMRC; there is no requirement for them to be submitted to HMRC. Once made, the elections are irrevocable.

28.3 CONVERTIBLE SHARES

[*ITEPA 2003, ss 435–444*]

Missy is an employee of XYZ Ltd. Under a non-tax-advantaged employee share scheme, she is awarded 1,000 'B' shares in the company on 1 December 2016 which are convertible in exactly two years' time into 1,200 'A' shares. Under the terms of the scheme, Missy is required to pay the company £150 for the conversion. She duly converts the shares on 1 December 2018. Relevant market values (MV) per share are as follows.

MV per 'B' share at 1.12.16 with right to convert after 2 years	£2.00
MV per 'B' share at 1.12.16 ignoring right to convert	£1.80
MV per 'A' share at 1.12.18	£3.75
MV per 'B' share at 1.12.18 ignoring right to convert	£3.00

Chargeable amount on acquisition of 'B' shares (2016/17)

1,000 × £1.80 (conversion right ignored — *ITEPA 2003, s 437*)	£1,800

Chargeable amount on conversion into 'A' shares (2018/19) *(ITEPA 2003, ss 440, 441)*

	£	£
1,200 × £3.75 (MV of 'A' shares)		4,500
Less 1,000 × £3.00 (MV of 'B' shares)	3,000	
Consideration given for the conversion	150	(3,150)
Chargeable amount		£1,350

Note

(a) Immediately after the conversion, Missy has shares worth £4,500 for which she has paid £150, a benefit of £4,350 of which only £3,150 has been taxed. The capital growth in the 'B' shares between acquisition and conversion is not charged to income tax.

28.4 TAX-ADVANTAGED SHARE INCENTIVE PLANS

[*ITEPA 2003, ss 488–515, Sch 2; FA 2016, Sch 3 para 2(3)(4)*]

GB plc operates a share incentive plan self-certified as a tax-advantaged plan in August 2018. The plan provides for free shares, partnership shares, matching shares and dividend shares. The following table illustrates the permissible benefits and the tax position of participating employees as regards each of these kinds of share.

	Free shares	Partnership shares	Matching shares	Dividend shares
Brief description	Shares appropriated (without payment) to employees	Shares acquired on employees' behalf from sums deducted from their salary	Shares appropriated (without payment) to employees in proportion to their partnership shares	Shares acquired on employees' behalf out of dividends received on their plan shares
Maximum limits per participant	Shares worth £3,600 (per tax year) at time of award	Salary deductions must be lower of £1,800 per tax year and 10% of salary (plan may specify lower limits)	Two matching shares for each partnership share acquired (plan may specify lower ratio)	No statutory limit but the amount of cash dividends to be reinvested (or how such an amount is to be determined) is at the direction of the company.
Minimum limits — note (a)	N/A	£10 on any occasion or such lesser amount as is specified in the plan	N/A	N/A
Holding period (i.e. period during which shares must remain in plan) — note (b)	As specified by company — must be at least three years but not more than five, from time of award	None — employee may withdraw shares from plan at any time (see below for tax position)	As specified by company — must be at least three years but not more than five, from time of award	Three years from acquisition

	Free shares	Partnership shares	Matching shares	Dividend shares
Tax on award of shares	None	None — deductions from salary allowable for income tax	None	None — dividends applied in acquiring shares are not taxable
Income tax on shares leaving the plan (note (c)) within less than three years of award (subject to note (d))	On market value of shares when they leave the plan	On market value of shares when they leave the plan	On market value of shares when they leave the plan	Original dividend becomes taxable, but in tax year in which shares leave plan
Income tax on shares leaving the plan (note (c)) after three years or more, but less than five years, after award (subject to note (d))	On lower of market value at time of award and market value on leaving the plan	On lower of salary used to acquire the shares and market value on leaving the plan	On lower of market value at time of award and market value on leaving the plan	None
Income tax on shares leaving the plan (note (c)) five or more years after award	None	None	None	None
Capital gains tax on shares leaving the plan (note (c)) at any time— note (f)	None	None	None	None

Notes

(a) It is at the option of the company whether or not to include in the plan a minimum limit for partnership shares. [*ITEPA 2003, Sch 2 para 47*].

(b) Shares appropriated to employees, or acquired on their behalf, are held within the plan by trustees until leaving the plan as in (d)) below. In all cases, the stipulated holding period automatically ends if the participating employee ceases to be in relevant employment. [*ITEPA 2003, Sch 2 paras 36, 61, 67*].

(c) References to shares leaving the plan are to their ceasing to be subject to the plan. Shares cease to be subject to the plan if they are withdrawn by the participant (i.e. transferred by the plan trustees on his instructions or sold by them on his instructions and his account) or the participant leaves the relevant employment. [*ITEPA 2003, Sch 2 paras 95–97*].

(d) There is no income tax charge on shares ceasing to be subject to the plan *at any time* by reason of the participant's ceasing to be in relevant employment due to death, injury, disability, redundancy, retirement and other specified reasons beyond his control. [*ITEPA 2003, s 498, Sch 2 paras 98, 99; FA 2013, Sch 2 paras 2, 5, 17(1)*].

(e) The income tax exemptions do not apply if the shares are awarded or acquired under arrangements one of the main purposes of which is the avoidance of tax or national insurance contributions. [*ITEPA 2003, s 489(4)*].

(f) For capital gains tax purposes, shares ceasing to be subject to the plan at any time are deemed to have been disposed of and immediately reacquired by the participant at that time at their then market value, but no chargeable gain or allowable loss arises on that deemed disposal. [*TCGA 1992, Sch 7D para 5*].

28.5 ENTERPRISE MANAGEMENT INCENTIVES

[*ITEPA 2003, ss 527–541, Sch 5*]

Keyman, an executive director of HIP Company Ltd, is granted on 1 September 2016, by reason of his employment, an option, exercisable within ten years, to acquire 8,000 ordinary shares in the company at £2.50 per share. No price is payable for the option itself. The market value of the company's ordinary shares at the date the option is granted is £3.50 per share. Keyman exercises the option on 11 October 2017 when the market value is £4.50 per share. On 19 September 2018, he sells half his holding (i.e. 4,000 shares) for net proceeds of £24,900. No other options have been granted to Keyman by reason of his employment with the company.

HIP Company Ltd is a qualifying company for the purposes of the Enterprise Management Incentives provisions, and gives HMRC notice of the grant of the option by 1 December 2016 (i.e. within 92 days). It obtained a Stock Market quotation in March 2018. Keyman is an eligible employee and, at the time of grant, the total value of shares in the company in respect of which options existed was well below £3 million.

Income tax

2016/17

No charge arises on receipt of the option. [*ITEPA 2003, ss 475, 528*].

2017/18

Charge on exercise of option (note (c))

Lower of		
		£
Market value of 8,000 shares at time option granted (8,000 × £3.50)	£28,000	
Market value of 8,000 shares at time option exercised (8,000 × £4.50)	£36,000	28,000
Deduct Option Price (8,000 × £2.50)		(20,000)
Amount chargeable to income tax as employment income		£8,000

Capital gains tax

2018/19

		£	£
Net disposal proceeds (4,000 shares)			24,900
Deduct	Cost of shares (4,000 × £2.50)	10,000	
	Amount charged to income tax: (note (c))		
	£8,000 × 4,000/8,000	4,000	(14,000)
Chargeable gain (within £11,700 annual exemption)			£10,900

Notes

(a) Under the Enterprise Management Incentives provisions, the company may be quoted or unquoted but must be an independent company carrying on (or preparing to carry on) a qualifying trade, whose gross assets do not exceed £30 million and which has less than 250 full-time employees and a permanent establishment in the UK. Broadly, an employee is eligible if he is employed by the company for at least 25 hours per week or, if less, at least 75% of his total working time, and he controls no more than 30% of the company's ordinary share capital.

(b) Companies are able to grant options over shares worth (at time of grant) up to £250,000 to eligible employees.

(c) The discount (i.e. the excess of market value at date of grant over the aggregate of any amount paid for the option itself and the option price) is chargeable to income tax under *ITEPA 2003, s 476*. If market value had fallen by the time of exercise, the amount so chargeable is reduced (or extinguished) accordingly. [*ITEPA 2003, s 531*]. The amount chargeable to income tax is deductible for capital gains tax purposes by virtue of *TCGA 1992, s 119A*. It is allocated pro rata to the shares sold, under the normal part disposal rules for shares.

(d) If the option had been a non-tax-advantaged share option, the income tax charge would have been on £16,000 (£36,000 – £20,000) (see computation at **28.1** above).

(e) Chargeable gains realised on shares acquired by the exercise of qualifying options may be eligible for capital gains tax entrepreneurs' relief. The twelve-month minimum holding period required for entrepreneurs' relief begins when the option is granted rather than when the shares are acquired. The normal requirement for entrepreneurs' relief that the individual must hold at least 5% of the company's ordinary share capital does not apply. [*TCGA 1992, s 169I(7A)–(7R); FA 2013, Sch 24 paras 1, 5, 6*].

(f) HMRC has advised companies to consider delaying the grant of enterprise management incentive (EMI) share options on or after 7 April 2018, until the EU reaches a decision on renewing state aid approval for the EMI scheme. The UK government has acknowledged that there will be a delay between expiry of the existing approval on 6 April and any new approval. See www.gov.uk/government/publications/employment-related-securities-bulletin/employment-related-securities-bulletin-no-27-april-2018.

29 Social Security Income

29.1 HIGH INCOME CHILD BENEFIT CHARGE

[*ITEPA 2003, ss 681B–681H; Social Security Administration Act 1992, s 13A; Social Security Administration (Northern Ireland) Act 1992, s 11A*].

Jill is a single parent of one child and is entitled to child benefit of £20.70 per week throughout 2017/18 and 2018/19. Her adjusted net income is less than £50,000 for both those tax years. On 11 May 2018 she moves in with her boyfriend Jack, who has an adjusted net income of £56,344 for 2018/19. They continue to live together beyond 5 April 2019.

The income tax consequences for 2017/18 and 2018/19 are as follows

Jill has no liability to the high income child benefit charge for either year as her adjusted net income does not exceed £50,000. Jack is liable to the charge in respect of Jill's child benefit entitlement for the week beginning Monday 15 May 2018 and all subsequent weeks throughout the tax year 2018/19.

The charge is 1% of the amount of child benefit entitlement for every £100 of the chargeable person's adjusted net income above £50,000. The amount of the charge on Jack is computed as follows. Child benefit entitlement for the 47 weeks beginning Monday 15 May 2018 is £20.70 x 47 = £972.90 which is rounded down to £972. Adjusted net income is rounded down to £56,300. The tax charge is:

£972 x 1% x 6,300/100 = £612.36

This is rounded down to £612, which is added to Jack's income tax liability for the year.

Notes

(a) An income tax charge (the '*high income child benefit charge*') is imposed on an individual whose adjusted net income exceeds £50,000 in a tax year and who is, or whose partner is, in receipt of child benefit. In the event that both partners have an adjusted net income that exceeds £50,000, the charge applies only to the partner with the highest income.

(b) The maximum charge is an amount equal to the full amount of child benefit entitlement and applies where the chargeable person's adjusted net income is £60,000 or more.

(c) Child benefit itself is non-taxable but the high income child benefit charge effectively claws back the benefit from high income taxpayers.

(d) Adjusted net income is broadly taxable income before deducting personal reliefs but adjusted by deducting the gross equivalent of any Gift Aid donations or any pension contributions paid net of basic rate tax. [*ITA 2007, s 58*].

30 Trading Income

Cross-reference. See also **31** TRADING INCOME — CASH BASIS FOR SMALLER BUSINESSES.

30.1 OPENING YEARS OF ASSESSMENT

[*ITTOIA 2005, ss 199, 200, 204*].

Simon commences trade on 1 September 2017 and prepares accounts to 30 April, starting with an eight-month period of account to 30 April 2018. His profits (as adjusted for tax purposes) for the first three periods of account are as follows

	£
Eight months to 30 April 2018	24,000
Year to 30 April 2019	39,000
Year to 30 April 2020	40,000

His taxable profits for the first four tax years are as follows

	Basis period		£	£
2017/18	1.9.17 – 5.4.18	£24,000 × $^{7}/_{8}$		21,000
2018/19	1.9.17 – 31.8.18:			
	1.9.17 – 30.4.18		24,000	
	1.5.18 – 31.8.18	£39,000 × $^{4}/_{12}$	13,000	
				37,000
2019/20	Y/e 30.4.19			39,000
2020/21	Y/e 30.4.20			40,000

Overlap relief accrued:	
1.9.17 – 5.4.18 – 7 months	21,000
1.5.18 – 31.8.18 – 4 months	13,000
Total overlap relief accrued note (b)	£34,000

Notes

(a) The taxable profits for the first tax year are those from the commencement date to 5 April. [*ITTOIA 2005, s 199(1)*]. In the second tax year, the period from commencement to the accounting date in that year is less than 12 months, so the basis period is the 12 months from commencement. [*ITTOIA 2005, s 200(2)*]. In the third tax year, there is a period of account of 12 months to the normal accounting date, so the basis period is that period of account. [*ITTOIA 2005, s 198*]. Assessments then continue on that basis.

(b) The overlap relief accrued (by reference to an aggregate overlap period of 11 months) will be given on cessation (see **30.3** below) or on a change of accounting date resulting in a basis period exceeding 12 months (the relief given depending on the extent of the excess) (see **30.2**(B) below).

30.2 CHANGE OF ACCOUNTING DATE

[*ITTOIA 2005, ss 214–220*]

(A) Change to a date earlier in the tax year

Miranda commenced trade on 1 September 2015, preparing accounts to 31 August. In 2018, she changes her accounting date to 31 May, preparing accounts for the nine months to 31 May 2018. The conditions of *ITTOIA 2005, s 217* are satisfied in relation to the change. Her profits (as adjusted for tax purposes) are as follows

	£
Year ended 31 August 2016	18,000
Year ended 31 August 2017	21,500
Nine months to 31 May 2018	17,000
Year ended 31 May 2019	23,000

Taxable profits for the first five tax years are as follows

	Basis period		£	£
2015/16	1.9.15 – 5.4.16	£18,000 × 7/12		10,500
2016/17	Y/e 31.8.16			18,000
2017/18	Y/e 31.8.17			21,500
2018/19	1.6.17 – 31.5.18:			
	1.6.17 – 31.8.17	£21,500 × 3/12	5,375	
	1.9.17 – 31.5.18		17,000	
				22,375
2019/20	Y/e 31.5.19			23,000

Overlap relief accrued:	
1.9.15 – 5.4.16 — 7 months	10,500
1.6.17 – 31.8.17 — 3 months	5,375
Total overlap relief accrued note (c)	£15,875

Notes

(a) For a change of accounting date to result in a change of basis period, the conditions in *ITTOIA 2005, s 217* must normally be satisfied. [*ITTOIA 2005, s 216*].

(b) In this example, the 'relevant period' is that from 1 September 2017 (the day following the end of the basis period for 2017/18) to 31 May 2018 (the new accounting date in the year 2018/19 — the year of change). As the relevant period is less than 12 months, the basis period for 2018/19 is the 12 months ending on the new accounting date. [*ITTOIA 2005, s 216(2)*].

(c) The overlap relief accrued (by reference to an aggregate overlap period of 10 months) will be given on cessation (see **30.3** below) or on a change of accounting date resulting in a basis period exceeding 12 months (the relief given depending on the extent of the excess) (see (B) below).

(B) **Change to a date later in the tax year**

Dennis starts a business on 1 July 2015, preparing accounts to 30 June. In 2018, he changes his accounting date to 31 December, preparing accounts for the six months to 31 December 2018. The conditions of *ITTOIA 2005, s 217* are satisfied in relation to the change. His profits (as adjusted for tax purposes) are as follows

	£
Year ended 30 June 2016	18,000
Year ended 30 June 2017	21,500
Year ended 30 June 2018	23,000
Six months to 31 December 2018	12,000
Year ended 31 December 2019	27,000

Taxable profits for the first five years are as follows

	Basis period		£	£
2015/16	1.7.15 – 5.4.16	£18,000 × $^{9}/_{12}$		13,500
2016/17	Y/e 30.6.16			18,000
2017/18	Y/e 30.6.17			21,500
2018/19	1.7.17 – 31.12.18:			
	1.7.17 – 30.6.18		23,000	
	1.7.18 – 31.12.18		12,000	
			35,000	
	Deduct Overlap relief		9,000	
				26,000
2019/20	Y/e 31.12.19			27,000

Overlap relief accrued:	
1.7.15 – 5.4.16 — 9 months	13,500
Less utilised in 2018/19 — 6 months	9,000
Carried forward — 3 months	£4,500

Utilisation of overlap relief in 2018/19

$$\text{Apply the formula: } A \times \frac{B - C}{D}$$

where

A = aggregate overlap relief accrued (£13,500);

B = length of basis period for 2018/19 (18 months);

C = 12 months; and

D = the length of the overlap period(s) by reference to which the aggregate overlap profits accrued (9 months).

Thus, the deduction to be given in computing profits for 2018/19 is

$$£13{,}500 \times \frac{18 - 12}{9} = £9{,}000$$

Notes

(a) For a change of accounting date to result in a change of basis period, the conditions in *ITTOIA 2005, s 217* must normally be satisfied. [*ITTOIA 2005, s 216*].

(b) In this example, the 'relevant period' is that from 1 July 2017 (the day following the end of the basis period for 2017/18) to 31 December 2018 (the new accounting date in the year 2018/19 — the year of change). As the relevant period is more than 12 months, the basis period for 2018/19 is equal to the relevant period. [*ITTOIA 2005, s 216(3)*]. Note that a basis period of 18 months results in this case, even though accounts were prepared for a period of only 6 months to the new date.

(c) The overlap relief accrued (by reference to an overlap period of 9 months) is given on cessation (see **30.3** below) or, as in this example, on a change of accounting date resulting in a basis period exceeding 12 months (the relief given depending on the extent of the excess). The balance of overlap relief (£4,500) is carried forward for future relief on the happening of such an event. [*ITTOIA 2005, s 220*]. If Dennis had changed his accounting date to 31 March or 5 April (instead of 31 December), the overlap relief of £13,500 would have been given in full in 2018/19.

(C) Change of accounting date carried forward

[*ITTOIA 2005, s 219*]

Sharon has been trading since 1 September 1992, preparing accounts to 31 August. She has transitional overlap relief of £21,000 brought forward by reference to an overlap period of seven months. She decides to change her accounting date to 30 April, preparing accounts for a period of 20 months from 1 September 2015 to 30 April 2017. Results for relevant periods of account are as follows.

	£
Year ended 31 August 2015	60,000
1 September 2015 to 30 April 2017 (20 months)	90,000
Year ended 30 April 2018	67,500
Year ended 30 April 2019	73,500

The first year of change is 2016/17 being the first year in which accounts are not made up to the old date of 31 August. [*ITTOIA 2005, s 214(1)*]. However, a period of account exceeding 18 months cannot result in a change of basis period. [*ITTOIA 2005, s 217(1)(3)*]. The position is then looked at with regard to 2017/18, but again the period of account ending with the new date in that year, 30 April 2017, is a period exceeding 18 months, so the basis period cannot change. Moving on to 2018/19, however, there is a period of account of less than 18 months to the new date in that year, i.e. the year to 30 April 2018, so there *can* be a change of basis period provided the other conditions of *ITTOIA 2005, s 217* are satisfied.

The assessments are as follows

	Basis period		£	£
2015/16	Y/e 31.8.15			60,000
2016/17	1.9.15 – 31.8.16	(90,000 × $^{12}/_{20}$)		54,000
2017/18	1.9.16 – 31.8.17:			
	1.9.16 – 30.4.17	(£90,000 × $^{8}/_{20}$)	36,000	
	1.5.17 – 31.8.17	(£67,500 × $^{4}/_{12}$)	22,500	58,500
2018/19	1.5.17 – 30.4.18*			67,500
2019/20	Y/e 30.4.19			73,500

*The relevant period is the 8 months from 1.9.17 – 30.4.18. As this is less than 12 months, the basis period for 2018/19 is the 12 months ending on 30.4.18, the new date in the year.

Notes

(a) The period 1.5.17 – 31.8.17 is an overlap period of 4 months for which there is an overlap profit of £22,500 (as computed for the 2017/18 assessment). Thus, the aggregate overlap profit carried forward is increased to £43,500 by reference to an overlap period of 11 months.

(b) The fact that the original overlap relief is transitional relief (applicable only to businesses commenced before 6 April 1994) is of no relevance. Such relief is carried forward, and eventually relieved, in the same way as any other overlap relief.

(c) For the calculation of capital allowances for a period of account exceeding 18 months, see **4.1**(B) CAPITAL ALLOWANCES ON PLANT AND MACHINERY.

30.3 CLOSING YEAR OF ASSESSMENT

[*ITTOIA 2005, s 202*].

Robin commenced to trade on 1 May 2014, preparing accounts to 30 April. He permanently ceases to trade on 30 June 2018, preparing accounts for the two months to that date. His profits (as adjusted for tax purposes) are as follows

	£
Year ended 30 April 2015	24,000
Year ended 30 April 2016	48,000
Year ended 30 April 2017	96,000
Year ended 30 April 2018	36,000
Two months ended 30 June 2018	5,000
	£209,000

Taxable profits for the five tax years of trading are as follows

	Basis period		£	£
2014/15	1.5.14 – 5.4.15	(£24,000 × $^{11}/_{12}$)		22,000
2015/16	Y/e 30.4.15			24,000
2016/17	Y/e 30.4.16			48,000
2017/18	Y/e 30.4.17			96,000
2018/19	1.5.17 – 30.6.18:			
	1.5.17 – 30.4.18		36,000	
	1.5.18 – 30.6.18		5,000	
			41,000	
	Deduct Overlap relief		22,000	19,000
				£209,000

Overlap relief accrued:	
1.5.14 – 5.4.15 — 11 months	22,000
Utilised in 2018/19	(22,000)

Notes

(a) The basis period for the tax year of cessation is the period beginning immediately after the end of the basis period for the penultimate tax year and ending on the date of cessation. Note that profits taxed over the lifetime of the business equate to profits earned (as adjusted for tax purposes).

(b) The overlap relief accrued as a result of the application of the opening years rules is given in full on cessation (in the absence of an earlier change of accounting date resulting in a basis period exceeding 12 months — see **30.2**(B) above). [*ITTOIA 2005, s 205*].

30.4 PROFIT COMPUTATIONS

A UK trader commences trading on 1 October 2017. His profit and loss account for the year to 30 September 2018 is

	£	£
Sales		110,000
Deduct Purchases	75,000	
Less Stock and work in progress at 30.9.18	15,000	
		(60,000)
Gross profit		50,000
Deduct		
Salaries (all paid by 30.6.19)	15,600	
Rent and rates	2,400	
Telephone	500	
Heat and light	650	
Depreciation	1,000	
Motor expenses	2,700	
Entertainment	600	
Bank interest	900	
Hire-purchase interest	250	
Repairs and renewals	1,000	
Accountant's fee	500	
Bad debts	200	
Sundries	700	
		(27,000)
Net profit		23,000
Gain on sale of fixed asset		300
Rent received		500
Bank interest received		150
Profit		£23,950

Further Information

(i) Rent and rates. £200 of the rates bill relates to the period from 1.6.17 to 30.9.17.

(ii) Telephone. Telephone bills for the trader's private telephone (included in the accounts) amount to £150. It is estimated that 40% of these calls are for business purposes.

(iii) Motor expenses. All the motor expenses are in respect of the proprietor's car. 40% of the annual mileage relates to private use and home to business use.

			£
(iv)	Entertainment	Staff	100
		UK customers	450
		Overseas customers	50
			£600

(v) Hire-purchase interest. This is in respect of the owner's car.

(vi) Repairs and renewals. There is an improvement element of 20% included.

(vii) Bad debts. This is a specific write-off.

(viii) Sundries. Included is £250 being the cost of obtaining a bank loan to finance business expenditure, £200 for agent's fees in obtaining a patent for trading purposes and a £50 inducement to a local official.

(ix) Other. The proprietor obtained goods for his own use from the business costing £400 (resale value £500) without payment.

(x) Capital allowances for the year to 30 September 2018 amount to £1,520.

Computation of taxable trading income — Year to 30.9.18

		£	£
Profit per the accounts			23,950
Add			
Repairs — improvement element			200
Hire-purchase interest (40% private)			100
Entertainment	note (e)		500
Motor expenses (40% private)			1,080
Depreciation			1,000
Telephone (60% × £150)			90
Goods for own use			500
Illegal payment	note (g)		50
			27,470
Deduct			
Bank interest received (savings income)		150	
Rent received (property income)		500	
Gain on sale of fixed asset		300	
			(950)
			26,520
Less Capital allowances			1,520
Chargeable trading income			£25,000

Notes

(a) Costs of obtaining loan finance are specifically allowable. [*ITTOIA 2005, s 58*].

(b) Capital allowances are deductible as a trading expense.

(c) The adjusted profit of £25,000 would be subject to the commencement provisions for assessment purposes. See **30.1** above.

(d) Pre-trading expenses are treated as incurred on the day on which trade is commenced if they are incurred within seven years of the commencement and would have been allowable if incurred after commencement. [*ITTOIA 2005, s 57*].

(e) All entertainment expenses, other than staff entertaining, are non-deductible. [*ITTOIA 2005, ss 45–47*].

(f) If wages and salaries remain unpaid nine months after the end of the period of account, they are disallowed. A deduction is then allowable for the period of account in which they are paid. [*ITTOIA 2005, ss 36, 37*].

(g) Trading stock appropriated for personal use must be accounted for at market value. [*ITTOIA 2005, s 172B*].

(h) Expenditure in making a payment which itself constitutes the commission of a criminal offence (or would do if made in the UK) is specifically disallowed. This includes payments which are contrary to the Prevention of Corruption Acts. [*ITTOIA 2005, s 55*].

30.5 TRADING ALLOWANCE

[*ITTOIA 2005, ss 783A-783AR; F(No 2) 2017, Sch 3 para 1*]

Jennifer is in employment earning £25,000 per annum but for the last few years has been earning extra money by buying and selling rare DVDs online. After taking advice she accepts that her online activities amount to the carrying on of a trade, and she calculates profits to 5 April each year on the cash basis. For the year ended 5 April 2019 she has online sales of £2,100. Her purchases amount to £500 and she has allowable expenses of £100.

Jennifer's taxable profits for the year to 5.4.19 are as follows

		£	£
Sales (i.e. gross receipts)			2,100
Deduct:	Purchases	500	
	Expenses	100	
			600
Taxable profit			£1,500

Jennifer elects to use the trading allowance and is instead taxed as follows

		£
Gross receipts		2,100
Deduct:	Trading allowance	1,000
Taxable profit for 2018/19		£1,100

Notes

(a) A £1,000 allowance (the '*trading allowance*')was introduced for trading income with effect for the tax year 2017/18 onwards. It applies to trades, professions and vocations, but not to businesses carried on in partnership. The allowance also covers certain miscellaneous income. A similar, but entirely separate, £1,000 allowance was introduced simultaneously for property income — see **22.3** PROPERTY INCOME.

(b) Where an individual's gross receipts do not exceed the £1,000 allowance, profits will be treated as nil ('*full relief*'). The individual will be able to elect for full relief not to be given. Where, as in this example, gross receipts exceed the £1,000 allowance, the individual can elect to use an alternative method of calculating income ('*partial relief*'). Under this method the charge to tax is on the excess of gross receipts over £1,000.

(c) Although the taxpayer in this example uses the cash basis to calculate profits, the trading allowance is not restricted to such cases.

30.6 CREATIVE ARTISTS — AVERAGING

[*ITTOIA 2005, ss 221, 222, 223–225; FA 2016, s 25(2)(4)–(7)(12)*]

Richard is an established author by profession and has the following profits/losses as adjusted for income tax purposes (including a deduction for capital allowances) for the five years mentioned.

Year ended	Profit/loss £
31.12.12	35,000
31.12.13	30,000
31.12.14	6,000
31.12.15	25,000
31.12.16	13,000
31.12.17	10,000
31.12.18	(2,000)

Averaged profits for all years would be

		No averaging claims	Averaging claims for all possible years
		£	£
2012/13	note (a)	35,000	35,000
2013/14	note (b)	30,000	18,000
2014/15	note (c)	6,000	20,250
2015/16	note (d)	25,000	17,875
2016/17	note (e)	13,000	13,938
2017/18	note (f)	10,000	6,969
2018/19	note (f)	Nil	6,969
		£119,000	£119,000

Notes

(a)

2012/13	35,000
2013/14	30,000
	£65,000

As £30,000 is not less than 75% of £35,000, no averaging claim is possible.

(b)

2013/14	30,000	
2014/15	6,000	
	£36,000	÷ 2 = £18,000

As £6,000 does not exceed 70% of £30,000, straight averaging applies. Still no claim can be made to average 2013/14 (as adjusted) with 2012/13, even though this would now be possible purely on the figures.

(c)

2014/15	18,000
2015/16	25,000
	£43,000

As £18,000 exceeds 70% of £25,000 (but is less than 75%), the adjustment proceeds as follows

Difference £7,000 × 3	21,000	
Deduct 75% × £25,000	18,750	
Adjustment	2,250	(2,250)
Existing 2014/15	18,000	
Existing 2015/16		25,000
Averaged profits 2014/15 & 2015/16	£20,250	£22,750

Note that this methodology is no longer valid where the second of the two years in question is 2016/17 or a later year. Straightforward averaging applies instead [*ITTOIA 2005, s 223(4); FA 2016, s 25(5)(12)*].

(d)

2015/16	22,750	
2016/17	13,000	
	£35,750	÷ 2 = £17,875

As £13,000 is less than 75% of £22,750, straight averaging applies.

(e)

2016/17	17,875	
2017/18	10,000	
	£27,875	÷ 2 = £13,938

As £10,000 is less than 75% of £22,750, straight averaging applies.

(f)

2017/18	13,938	
2018/19	Nil	
	£13,938	÷ 2 = £6,969

The loss of £2,000 for 2018/19 does not enter into the averaging claim, but is available to reduce either the 2017/18 or the 2018/19 averaged profits of £6,969 on a claim under *ITA 2007, s 64* (see **15.1** LOSSES).

The 2018/19 averaged profits of £6,969 may themselves be averaged with 2019/20 profits if the 75% rule is satisfied. Any loss claim against income of 2018/19 is disregarded for this purpose.

(g) Averaging does not apply in calculating profits using the cash basis for smaller businesses. [*ITTOIA 2005, ss 221–221A; FA 2013, Sch 4 paras 32, 56*].

30.7 FARMING AND MARKET GARDENING — AVERAGING

[*ITTOIA 2005, ss 221, 222, 222A, 223–225; FA 2016, s 25(2)–(7)(12)*]

(A) Five-year averaging

Boycie has been carrying on a farming trade for ten years. In December 2017 the farm suffered heavy flooding. The farm initially had taxable profits as follows for the six years to 30 June 2018.

Year ended	£
30.6.13	34,000
30.6.14	52,000
30.6.15	44,000
30.6.16	50,000
30.6.17	47,000
30.6.18	26,000

Boycie made an averaging claim for the two years 2013/14 and 2014/15. The profits for the first of those years did not exceed 70% of the profits of the other, meaning both that a claim was possible and that straightforward averaging applied. The taxable profit of each of those two years was adjusted to £43,000.

For 2017/18 and 2018/19 a two-year averaging claim is possible, the profits of one year being clearly less than 75% of the profits of the other. If such a claim were made, the taxable profit of each of those two years would be adjusted to £36,500.

As an alternative, after taking into account his other income and his tax rates and allowances for each year, Boycie decides to make a five-year averaging claim for the years 2014/15 to 2018/19 inclusive. The average of the profits of the first four years is £(43,000 + 44,000 + 50,000 + 47,000) divided by 4 = £46,000. (The 2014/15 profit is taken to be £43,000, i.e. the averaged profit resulting from the earlier claim.) The profits of the fifth year are clearly less than 75% of £46,000, so five-year averaging is possible. Following the claim, the taxable profit of each of the five years is now £(43,000 + 44,000 + 50,000 + 47,000 + 26,000) divided by 5 = £42,000.

Notes

(a) As an alternative to two-year averaging, where in relation to five consecutive tax years:

- either A or B is less than 75% of the other (where A is the average of the profits of the first four years and B is the profits of the fifth year); or
- the profits for one or more years, but not all five years, are nil,

a five-year averaging claim may be made under *ITTOIA 2005, s 222A* by a UK farmer or market gardener. This has effect where the last of the five years is 2016/17 or a subsequent year.

(B) Two-year averaging

Giles, who has been farming for several years, has the following profits as adjusted for income tax purposes.

Year ended	Profit/(loss)
	£
30.9.11	8,500
30.9.12	12,000
30.9.13	15,000
30.9.14	10,000
30.9.15	4,000
30.9.16	(1,000)
30.9.17	(10,000)
30.9.18	1,600

Two-year averaged profits for all years would be

		No averaging claims	Averaging claims for all years
		£	£
2011/12	note (a)	8,500	10,000
2012/13	notes (a)(b)	12,000	12,750
2013/14	notes (b)(c)	15,000	12,750
2014/15	notes (c)(d)	10,000	7,000
2015/16	notes (d)(e)	4,000	3,500
2016/17	notes (e)(f)	Nil	1,750
2017/18	notes (g)(h)	Nil	1,750
2018/19	note (j)	1,600	1,600
		£51,100	£51,100

Notes

(a)

2011/12	8,500
2012/13	12,000
	£20,500

As £8,500 exceeds 70% of £12,000 but does not exceed 75%, the adjustment is computed as follows

Difference £3,500 × 3	10,500	
Deduct 3/4 × £12,000	9,000	
Adjustment	1,500	(1,500)
Existing 2011/12	8,500	
Existing 2012/13		12,000
Revised averaged profits 2011/12 & 2012/13	£10,000	£10,500

Note that this methodology is no longer valid where the second of the two years in question is 2016/17 or a later year. Straightforward averaging applies instead. [*ITTOIA 2005, s 223(4); FA 2016, s 25(5)(12)*].

(b)

2012/13	10,500	
2013/14	15,000	
	£25,500	÷ 2 = £12,750

As £10,500 does not exceed 70% of £15,000, the straight average applies.

(c)

2013/14	12,750
2014/15	10,000
	£22,750

As £10,000 is not less than 75% of £12,750, no averaging is permitted.

(d)

2014/15	10,000	
2015/16	4,000	
	£14,000	÷ 2 = £7,000

As £4,000 does not exceed 70% of £10,000, the straight average applies.

(e)

2015/16	7,000	
2016/17	Nil	
	£7,000	÷ 2 = £3,500

(f) The loss for the year to 30 September 2016 is not taken into account for averaging, but would be available to eliminate the averaged profits for 2016/17 on a claim under *ITA 2007, s 64*.

(g)	2016/17	3,500	
	2017/18	Nil	
		£3,500	÷ 2 = £1,750

(h) The loss for the year to 30 September 2017 is not taken into account for averaging, but would be available to set off against the balance of the averaged profits for 2016/17 and against the averaged profits for 2017/18 on a claim under *ITA 2007, s 64*, with the balance being carried forward.

(j)	2017/18	1,750
	2018/19	1,600
		£3,350

As £1,600 is not less than 75% of £1,750, a two-year averaging claim is not possible. See (A) above as regards five-year averaging.

(l) Averaging does not apply in calculating profits using the cash basis for smaller businesses. [*ITTOIA 2005, ss 221–221A; FA 2013, Sch 4 paras 32, 56*].

30.8 ADJUSTMENT ON CHANGE OF BASIS — BARRISTERS

[*ITTOIA 2005, ss 227, 228, 231, 238, 239*]

Olivia commenced practice as a barrister on 1 October 2004, preparing accounts to 30 June on a cash basis as permitted by *ITTOIA 2005, s 160* (and earlier equivalents). As required by that *section*, she switches to an earnings basis for the year to 30 June 2012, preparing accounts in accordance with *ITTOIA 2005, s 25* (note (a)). She accordingly brings in opening work-in-progress of £43,000, opening debtors of £10,000 (for fees billed, but not received, before 1 July 2011 and opening creditors of £2,000 (for expenses invoiced to her, but not paid, before 1 July 2011). She also brings in a £1,000 opening creditor for cash received in advance (and included in the accounts to 30 June 2011) in respect of a fee billed in the year to 30 June 2012.

Without an adjustment, the £43,000 opening work-in-progress would be relieved twice and the £10,000 fees reflected in debtors would never be taxed. On the other hand, the expenses of £2,000 would never be relieved and the £1,000 payment in advance would be taxed twice.

The adjustment income required to be brought into account under ITTOIA 2005, s 232 is

£(43,000 + 10,000) − £(2,000 + 1,000) = £50,000

(i) Olivia's profits before capital allowances and balancing charges are as follows.

Y/e 30 June 2012	30,000
Y/e 30 June 2013	45,000
Y/e 30 June 2014	40,000
Y/e 30 June 2015	48,000
Y/e 30 June 2016	52,000

Y/e 30 June 2017	56,000
Y/e 30 June 2018	47,000
Y/e 30 June 2019	51,000
Y/e 30 June 2020	53,000
Y/e 30 June 2021	46,000

The £50,000 adjustment will be taxed as follows

		£
2012/13	(£30,000 × 10%)	3,000
2013/14	(£45,000 × 10%)	4,500
2014/15	(£40,000 × 10%)	4,000
2015/16	(£48,000 × 10%)	4,800
2016/17	(£50,000 × 10%)	5,000
2017/18	(£50,000 × 10%)	5,000
2018/19	(£47,000 × 10%)	4,700
2019/20	(£50,000 × 10%)	5,000
2020/21	(£50,000 × 10%)	5,000
2021/22	(balance)	9,000
		£50,000

(ii) Supposing Olivia ceased to practice on 30 June 2014. The catching-up charge would be taxed as above for years up to and including 2014/15. Thereafter, it would be £5,000 for each of the six years up to and including 2020/21, leaving a balance of £8,500 to be taxed in 2021/22.

(iii) Supposing that Olivia continued to practice as in (i) above but she had extraordinary expenditure in the year to 30 June 2018 and made a tax loss of £9,000 (after capital allowances) instead of the profit in (i) above, all figures for other years remaining the same. The catching-up charge for 2018/19 would then be nil (i.e. 10% of nil profits). On the assumption that her other income is covered by her personal allowance, she might elect to increase the catching-up charge by £9,000 (see note (c)), so as to relieve the loss in that year by means of a claim under *ITA 2007, s 64*.

The £50,000 adjustment will then be taxed as follows

		£
2012/13	(£30,000 × 10%)	3,000
2013/14	(£45,000 × 10%)	4,500
2014/15	(£40,000 × 10%)	4,000
2015/16	(£48,000 × 10%)	4,800
2016/17	(£50,000 × 10%)	5,000
2017/18	(£50,000 × 10%)	5,000
2018/19	(nil + £9,000)	9,000
2019/20	(£20,000 × 10%) note (d)	2,000

2020/21	(£20,000 × 10%) note (d)	2,000
2021/22	(balance)	10,700
		£50,000

Notes

(a) *ITTOIA 2005, s 25* requires that profits be calculated in accordance with generally accepted accounting practice (GAAP), subject to any adjustment required or authorised by law in calculating profits for income tax purposes. This in turn requires (among other things) profits to be calculated on an earnings basis rather than a cash basis. For 2012/13 and earlier years (and see note (e) below), *ITTOIA 2005, s 160* provides an exemption for barristers for periods of account ending no more than seven years after they commence practice. The exemption is not compulsory but once a particular basis has been adopted it must be applied consistently.

(b) Adjustment income is treated as arising on the last day of the first period of account for which the new basis is adopted. [*ITTOIA 2005, s 232*].

(c) The election in (iii) above must be made in writing on or before the first anniversary of 31 January following the tax year for which the charge is to be increased. [*ITTOIA 2005, s 239(2)*].

(d) In (iii) above, for years subsequent to 2018/19 (apart from the tenth year) the catch-up charge is calculated as if the adjustment income (£50,000) were reduced by £9,000 (the additional amount taxed in 2018/19) multiplied by 10 and divided by 3 (the number of tax years remaining). Thus the maximum charge for 2019/20 and 2020/21 is 10% of £20,000 (the revised amount of adjustment income) as this is less than 10% of profits.

(e) *ITTOIA 2005, s 160* is repealed for 2013/14 onwards in light of the introduction of the cash basis for smaller businesses. By way of transition, where a barrister's profits for a period of account ending in the tax year 2012/13 were calculated under *section 160*, they can continue to be so calculated for any subsequent period of account for which *section 160* would have been applied had it not been repealed, i.e. any periods within the seven years mentioned in (a) above, assuming the barrister does not choose to adopt an earnings basis before the end of those seven years. [*ITTOIA 2005, s 160; FA 2013, Sch 4 paras 51, 56, 57(1)*].

The spreading rules illustrated in this example are also repealed for 2013/14 onwards but the repeal does not apply in a case where, as in this example, advantage was taken of *ITTOIA 2005, s 160* for any period(s) of account ending in or before the tax year 2012/13. [*ITTOIA 2005, ss 238, 239; FA 2013, Sch 4 paras 52, 56, 57(2)*].

30.9 FOSTER CARE RELIEF

[*ITTOIA 2005, ss 803–828*]

Dave and Holly, a couple living together, provide foster care by way of trade. Each prepares accounts to 31 December. Foster children are placed with them by their local authority. During the calendar year 2018, they provide care to a twelve-year old (child 1) for the full 52 weeks and to a nine-year old (child 2) for 15 weeks. Their total foster care receipts for the year (before deduction of expenses) are £25,000 each. Their allowable expenses are £14,000 each.

Each of Dave and Holly's individual limits for 2018/19 is computed as follows

		£
Fixed amount for 2018/19: £10,000 ÷ 2		5,000
Amounts per child (y/e 31.12.18):	child 1 (52 × £250)	13,000
	child 2 (15 × £200)	3,000
		£21,000

For 2018/19, their income tax position is as follows

Normal trading income computation

	Dave	Holly
	£	£
Total foster care receipts (y/e 31.12.18)	25,000	25,000
Allowable expenses	(14,000)	(14,000)
Net taxable profit (subject to below)	£11,000	£11,000

Alternative calculation under ITTOIA 2005, ss 815–819

Each could now elect, under *ITTOIA 2005, s 818*, for his or her taxable profits from foster care to be taken as the excess of total foster care receipts over his or her individual limit computed as above. Such an election for any tax year must be made on or before the first anniversary of 31 January following that year and has effect for that tax year only. Under the election, Dave and Holly's taxable profits for 2018/19 will each be reduced to £4,000 (£25,000 - £21,000).

Notes

(a) Foster care receipts are exempt if they do not exceed a limit computed by reference to the individual recipient. If, as in this example, they do exceed that limit, and the recipient so elects, they are subject to the alternative computation above. It is up to each individual recipient whether to make the election.

(b) Some HMRC offices are believed to have taken the view that, in a case such as that illustrated in this example, the amounts per child must be divided between the couple instead of being available separately to each individual. In this example, this would have the effect of reducing each individual's limit by £8,000. In the author's opinion, the legislation does not support such a view. If, however, a couple were trading in partnership (clearly not the case here) it does then become arguable that the partnership takes the place of the individual for the purpose of computing the limits, in which case only one amount per child would be available to the partnership.

30.10 CEMETERIES AND CREMATORIA

[*ITTOIA 2005, ss 169–172*]

GR, who operates a funeral service, owns a cemetery for which accounts to 31 December are prepared. The accounts to 31.12.18 reveal the following

(i)	Cost of land representing 110 grave spaces sold in period	£3,400
(ii)	Number of grave spaces remaining	275
(iii)	Residual capital expenditure on buildings and other land unsuitable for interments	£18,250

The allowances available are		£
(A) Item (i)		3,400
(B)	$\frac{110}{110+275} \times £18,250$	5,214
		£8,614

Note

(a) £8,614 will be allowed as a deduction in computing GR's trading profits for the period of account ending on 31 December 2018.

31 Trading Income — Cash Basis for Smaller Businesses

Cross-reference. See also **30** TRADING INCOME.

31.1 CASH BASIS

[*ITTOIA 2005, ss 25A, 31A–31F; FA 2013, Sch 4; SI 2017 No 293*]

Keith has been running a one-man business for a number of years, preparing accounts to 30 September. For the year ended 30 September 2018, his turnover is £95,000 and he elects for his trading profits to be calculated on the cash basis for 2018/19 onwards as provided for by *ITTOIA 2005, s 25A*. His accounts for the year ended 30 September 2017 showed closing stock of £6,300, trade and other creditors of £2,400 and trade debtors of £300.

Keith uses a motor vehicle in the business. On 15 October 2017 he sold his car (Vehicle 1) for £1,400 to an unconnected individual and purchased instead a van (Vehicle 2) for £3,500. Expenditure in connection with Vehicle 1 for the period from 1 October to date of sale amounted to £300, and it had always been accepted that the car was used as to 20% for private purposes. Keith chooses to use the fixed rate deduction scheme (under *ITTOIA 2005, ss 94D–94G*) to calculate allowable expenditure on Vehicle 2. Business mileage was 6,200 miles for the period from date of purchase to 30 September 2018.

Keith also uses a room in his home as an office, working there for 60 hours each month. He chooses to use the fixed rate deduction scheme (under *ITTOIA 2005, s 94H*) to calculate allowable expenditure for use of home for business purposes.

Keith pays out £27,000 on purchases and £4,400 on business overheads in the year to 30 September 2018. The business overheads are all allowable revenue expenses but the figure excludes bank overdraft interest and all expenses connected with the car and van. In addition, Keith spends £2,094 on office furniture and equipment; it is accepted that this is capital expenditure. In the year to 30 September 2018, he is charged interest of £700 on a bank overdraft; the bank account in question includes some personal as well as business transactions.

At 30 September 2017, there were written-down values of £1,560 on the plant and machinery main pool and £2,200 on the pool for Vehicle 1 (which is a single asset pool due to the private use). The main pool includes a computer used only for business purposes which Keith sells for £150 in June 2018 to an acquaintance.

An adjustment expense required to be brought into account under ITTOIA 2005, s 233 as follows

Without an adjustment, the value of £6,300 placed on the previous year's closing stock would be taxed twice, once in the previous year and again when the stock is sold. The £300 brought forward as trade debts would also be taxed twice, once in the previous year and again when the debts are settled. Similarly, the £2,400 brought forward as trade and other creditors would be relieved twice. See note (d).

The adjustment expense is: £(6,300 + 300) – £2,400 = £4,200.

This is treated as an expense of the trade arising on the last day of the year ending 30.9.18, i.e. the first period of account for which the new basis is adopted.

The capital allowances computation for 2018/19 is as follows

	Main pool	Vehicle 1	Allow-ances
	£	£	£
Year ended 30.9.18			
WDV at 30.9.17	1,560	2,200	
Expenditure removed from pool (note (e))	(1,560)		
WDV brought forward at 1.10.17	Nil	2,200	
Disposal proceeds		(1,400)	
		800	
Private use adjustment 20%		(160)	
Balancing allowance		£640	640
Total allowances			£640
WDV carried forward	Nil		

The allowable expenditure for Vehicle 2 is

$$M \times R$$

where M is the number of miles of business journeys made by a person (other than as a passenger) using the vehicle in the period; and

R is the rate applicable for that kind of vehicle. The rate applicable to a goods vehicle is 45p per mile up to 10,000 miles and 25p thereafter. See note (f).

6,200 x 45p = £2,790.

The allowable expenditure for use of home as business is as follows

The amount of the fixed rate deduction for the period is the sum of the applicable amounts for each month (or part of a month) falling within the period. The applicable amounts is based on the number of hours worked; it is £18 where the number of hours worked is 51 hours or more but less than 101 hours. See note (f).

£18 x 12 months = £216.

Taxable profits for the year to 30.9.18 are computed as follows

	£	£
Turnover		95,000
Deduct Purchases		27,000
Gross profit		68,000
Deduct		
Business overheads	4,400	
Expenses relating to Vehicle 1 (£300 x 80% business use)	240	
Fixed rate deduction for Vehicle 2 (see above)	2,790	
Fixed rate deduction for use of home as business (see above)	216	
Capital expenditure (note (g))	3,654	
Interest (note (h))	500	
Adjustment expense (see above)	4,200	
		(16,000)
		52,000
Add Capital receipt (note (i))		150
Net profit		52,150
Deduct Capital allowances on Vehicle 1 (see above)		640
Taxable profit		£51,510

Notes

(a) The cash basis is optional, and is available to unincorporated trades, professions and vocations (including those carried on in partnership) with an annual turnover not exceeding the turnover limit. For 2017/18 onwards, the turnover limit is £150,000; previously it was equal to the VAT registration threshold (e.g. £83,000 for 2016/17). Certain types of business are excluded from using the cash basis (see *ITTOIA 2005, s 31C*). Businesses must leave the cash basis the year after their receipts exceed £300,000 (previously twice the VAT registration threshold) unless they once again meet the turnover limit.

(b) The cash basis is an alternative to preparing accounts for tax purposes on an earnings basis and in accordance with generally accepted accounting practice (GAAP).

(c) In practice, elections to adopt the cash basis are made via the self-assessment tax return by ticking a box.

(d) An adjustment must be made upon entering or leaving the cash basis in the same way as for any other change of accounting basis. [*ITTOIA 2005, s 227A; FA 2013, Sch 4 paras 36, 56*]. This is to ensure that no receipt is taxed twice and no allowable payment is deducted twice, and similarly that neither receipts nor payments fall out of tax.

(e) No capital allowances are available to a person carrying on a trade in relation to which a cash basis election is in force, other than an allowance for capital expenditure on a car.

When a person enters the cash basis for a tax year (Year Z), any qualifying expenditure on plant or machinery which is unrelieved at the end of the basis period for the preceding tax year (Year Y) is allowable as a deduction under the cash basis in Year Z, provided that it would be an allowable deduction were it incurred in Year Z. The rule does not apply where the asset had not been fully paid for as at the end of the basis period for Year Y. [*ITTOIA 2005, ss 240A–240D; FA 2013, Sch 4 paras 38, 56*]. See also note (g) below.

(f) The fixed rate deduction schemes are entirely optional and are not restricted to those using the cash basis. If a fixed rate deduction is made for a period of account in respect of qualifying expenditure incurred in relation to a particular vehicle, no other deduction is allowed for such qualifying expenditure. As regards subsequent periods of account, the fixed rate deduction scheme is then compulsory for that vehicle for every period for which it is used for the purposes of the trade. 'Qualifying expenditure', in relation to a vehicle, means expenditure incurred in respect of the acquisition, ownership, hire, leasing or use of the vehicle (other than incidental expenses incurred in connection with a particular journey). [*ITTOIA 2005, ss 94B–94I; CAA 2001, s 38ZA; FA 2013, Sch 5 paras 2, 5, 6; FA 2016, s 24*].

For cars and goods vehicles, the 10,000 mile limit for the 45p rate takes into account the business mileage of *all* such vehicles used in the trade for which a fixed rate deduction is made; it is not 10,000 miles per vehicle.

For use of home as business, HMRC regard the number of hours worked as relating to hours worked wholly and exclusively for the purposes of the trade on core business activities, i.e. providing goods and/or services, maintaining business records and marketing/obtaining new business. The fixed rate deduction covers heat, light, power, telephone and internet connection. A separate deduction can still be claimed for fixed costs, such as council tax (or domestic rates in NI), insurance and mortgage interest, if an identifiable proportion can be attributed to business use. (HMRC Business Income Manual BIM75010).

(g) Under the cash basis there is no general prohibition on deductions for expenditure of a capital nature. Instead, there is a list of capital expenditure for which no deduction is allowed. This list includes expenditure on acquiring a business, education, training, assets that are not depreciating assets, non-business assets, cars, land, non-qualifying intangible assets and financial assets. Any capital expenditure on the provision of a car is therefore prohibited. [*ITTOIA 2005, s 33A*].

The deduction of £3,654 for capital expenditure comprises both the plant and machinery bought in the year (totalling £2,094) and the brought forward written-down value capital allowances for plant and machinery bought in earlier years (£1,560). This is an allowable deduction provided that it would be allowed were it purchased in the current tax year. It is assumed that all the assets purchased constitute depreciating assets. These are defined in *ITTOIA 2005, s 33A(6)* as an asset which can reasonably be expected to have a useful life of less than 20 years or be worth only 10% of its original value in 20 years' time. No deduction is allowed for the van, as explained in note (f) due to the use of the fixed rate deduction. [*ITTOIA 2005, s2 240B–240C*].

(h) Interest paid on cash borrowings is deductible up to a limit of £500. It does not matter whether or not the interest was paid wholly and exclusively for the purposes of the trade. [*ITTOIA 2005, ss 51A, 57B; FA 2013, Sch 4 paras 10, 14, 56*].

(i) Where a person using the cash basis receives amounts that would be capital in nature, these may be taxed under the cash basis. Of relevance to this particular example, capital receipts are brought into account where the person receives disposal proceeds in relation to capital expenditure that has been deducted under the cash basis, or would be were it incurred in the current year. [*ITTOIA 2005, ss 96A–96B*; *FA 2013, Sch 4 paras 20, 56*; *F(No 2)A 2017, s 16, Sch 2, paras 1,4*].

32 Venture Capital Trusts

[*ITA 2007, ss 258–332; TCGA 1992, ss 151A, 151B, Sch 5C; FA 2014, s 56(5)–(7)(9), Sch 10; FA 2015, Sch 6 paras 6–9, 11, 14; F(No 2)A 2015, ss 26–28, Sch 6; FA 2016, ss 28–31; FA 2018, ss 14–17, Schs 4, 5*]

32.1 INCOME TAX INVESTMENT RELIEF

(A) Form of relief

On 1 May 2018, Miss K, who has annual earnings of £82,000, subscribes for 100,000 eligible £1 shares issued at par to raise money by VCT plc, an approved venture capital trust. On 1 September 2018 she purchases a further 225,000 £1 shares in VCT plc for £175,000 on the open market. The VCT makes no distribution in 2018/19. Miss K's other income for 2018/19 consists of dividends of £18,000. PAYE tax deducted is £21,160.00. She is not a Scottish taxpayer.

Miss K's tax computation for 2018/19 is as follows

		£
Employment income		82,000
Dividends		18,000
Total and net income		100,000
Deduct Personal allowance		(11,850)
Taxable income		£88,150
Tax payable:		
34,500	@ 20%	6,900.00
35,650	@ 40%	14,260.00
2,000	@ 0% (dividend allowance)	—
16,000	@ 32.5% (dividend upper rate)	5,200.00
£88,150		26,360.00
Deduct VCT investment relief:		
£100,000 @ 30% = £30,000 but restricted to		26,360.00
Income tax liability		Nil
Deduct: PAYE		21,160.00
Income tax repayable		£21,160.00

Note

(a) VCT investment relief is available at the rate of 30% on the amount *subscribed for* up to a maximum subscription of £200,000 per tax year. The relief is restricted to the income tax liability (before taking into account certain reductions etc.). [*ITA 2007, ss 261–263*].

(B) Withdrawal of relief

[*ITA 2007, ss 266–270*]

On 1 May 2020, Miss K in (A) above, who has since 2018/19 neither acquired nor disposed of any shares in VCT plc, gives 62,500 shares to her son. On 1 January 2021, she disposes of the remaining 262,500 shares on the open market for £212,500.

The relief given as in (A) above is withdrawn as follows

Disposal on 1 May 2020

The shares disposed of are identified, on a first in, first out basis, with 62,500 of the 100,000 shares subscribed for in May 2018. Since the disposal was not at arm's length, the relief given on those shares is fully withdrawn.

$$\text{Relief withdrawn } \frac{62{,}500}{100{,}000} \times £26{,}360 = \qquad \underline{£16{,}475}$$

Disposal on 1 January 2021

The balance of £9,885 of the relief originally given was in respect of 37,500 of the 262,500 shares disposed of. The disposal consideration for those 37,500 shares is

$$£212{,}500 \times \frac{37{,}500}{262{,}500} = \qquad \underline{£30{,}357}$$

As the disposal was at arm's length, the relief withdrawn is the lesser of the relief originally given (£9,885) and 30% of the consideration received, i.e. 30% of £30,357 = £9,107. Relief withdrawn is therefore £9,107.

The 2018/19 assessment on relief withdrawn will therefore charge tax of £(16,475 + 9,107) £25,582

Notes

(a) VCT investment relief is withdrawn on a disposal (or deemed disposal) within five years following the issue of the shares. Withdrawal of relief is by assessment for the tax year for which the relief was given.

(b) If the disposal is at arm's length, the relief given by reference to those shares is reduced by the appropriate percentage of the consideration received for the disposal and is withdrawn entirely if thereby reduced to nil. The appropriate percentage is 30%, i.e. the rate at which investment relief was available.

32.2 INCOME TAX DIVIDEND RELIEF

On 1 June 2017, W subscribes for 100,000 eligible £1 shares issued at par to raise money by XYZ plc, an approved venture capital trust. On 1 October 2017, he purchases on the open market a further 200,000 shares in XYZ plc for £120,000. On 30 June 2018 W receives a distribution from XYZ plc of 2p per share. W's other income in 2018/19 is a salary of £87,850 and dividends from other companies of £20,000. Tax paid under PAYE amounts to £23,500.00. W is not a Scottish taxpayer.

W's taxable distribution from XYZ plc is arrived at as follows

The shares in XYZ plc were acquired in 2017/18 for £220,000. Distributions in respect of shares representing the £20,000 excess over the permitted maximum are not exempt. The 100,000 shares first acquired for £100,000 are first identified, so that the shares representing the excess are one-sixth of the 200,000 shares subsequently acquired for £120,000, i.e. 33,333 of those shares. The taxable dividend is therefore 33,333 @ 2p per share = £666.66. The dividend on the balance of 266,667 shares (266,667 @ 2p = £5,333.34) is exempt.

W's tax computation for 2018/19 is as follows

	£	£
Employment income		87,850
Dividends (other than from XYZ plc)		20,000
Taxable dividends from XYZ plc		666
Total and net income		108,516
Deduct Personal allowance	11,850	
Restricted by excess of income over £100,000: (£8,516 x /)	4,258	£7,592
Taxable income		£100,924
Tax payable:		
34,500 @ 20%		6,900.00
45,758 @ 40%		18,303.20
2,000 @ 0% (dividend allowance)		—
18,666 @ 32.5% (dividend upper rate)		6,066.45
£100,924		31,269.65
Deduct: PAYE		23,500.00
Net income tax liability		£7,769.65

Notes

(a) Dividends paid to a qualifying individual from a VCT are exempt from tax to the extent that they are made in respect of shares *acquired* (not necessarily subscribed for) for up to £200,000 in any tax year [*ITTOIA 2005, ss 709–712*].

(b) The personal allowance is reduced by one-half of the excess of 'adjusted net income' over £100,000. [*ITA 2007, s 35*]. '*Adjusted net income*' is broadly net income less the grossed up amount of any allowable pension contributions and Gift Aid donations. [*ITA 2007, s 58*].

32.3 CAPITAL GAINS TAX RELIEF ON DISPOSAL

On the disposals in **32.1**(B) above, a chargeable gain or allowable loss arises only on the disposal of shares acquired in excess of the permitted maximum (£200,000) for 2018/19. The 100,000 shares first acquired for £100,000 are first identified, so that the shares representing the excess are three-sevenths (75,000/175,000) of the 225,000 shares acquired for £175,000 on 1 September 2018, i.e. 96,429 of those shares. The disposal identified with those shares (on a first in, first out basis) is a corresponding proportion of the 262,500 shares disposed of for a consideration of £212,500 on 1 January 2021.

Miss K's capital gains tax computation for 2020/21 is therefore as follows

	£
Disposal consideration for 96,429 shares:	
$£212,500 \times \frac{96,429}{262,500} =$	78,061
Deduct Cost of 96,429 shares:	
$£175,000 \times \frac{96,429}{225,000} =$	75,000
Chargeable gain	£3,061

Notes

(a) On disposals by an individual of VCT shares (whether or not they were subscribed for), capital gains are exempt and losses not allowable to the extent that the shares disposed of were not acquired in excess of the £200,000 maximum in any tax year. [*TCGA 1992, s 151A*].

(b) The capital gains tax share identification provisions are disapplied as regards VCT shares within the above exemption. [*TCGA 1992, s 151B(1)*].

Corporation Tax

Contents

101 Accounting Periods

101.1 THE START AND END OF AN ACCOUNTING PERIOD

[*CTA 2009, ss 9, 10, 12*]

Plantagenet Ltd is incorporated on 1 January 2018. The company opens a bank account on 1 March 2018 which pays interest at 1%. It begins to trade on 1 June 2018. The company prepares its first set of accounts to 31 August 2019 and adopts 31 August as its annual accounting date.

Plantagenet Ltd's first three accounting periods are:

1 March 2018 – 31 May 2018 (beginning on the day on which the company comes within the charge to corporation tax and ending immediately before the day on which the company begins to trade).

1 June 2018 – 31 May 2019 (beginning immediately after the end of the previous accounting period and ending on the expiration of twelve months).

1 June 2019 – 31 August 2019 (beginning immediately after the end of the previous accounting period and ending on the company's accounting date).

Notes

(a) An accounting period of a company begins:

- when the company comes within the charge to corporation tax; or
- immediately after the end of the previous accounting period, if the company is still within the charge to corporation tax; or
- in the case of a company being wound up, when the winding up starts.

[*CTA 2009, ss 9(1), 12(3)*].

(b) An accounting period of a company comes to an end on the first occurrence of any of the following:

- the expiration of twelve months from the beginning of the accounting period;
- an accounting date of the company;
- if there is a period for which the company does not make up accounts, the end of that period;
- the company's beginning or ceasing to trade;
- if the company carries on a single trade, its coming, or ceasing to be, within the charge to corporation tax in respect of that trade;
- if the company carries on more than one trade, its coming, or ceasing to be, within the charge to corporation tax in respect of all the trades;
- the company's becoming, or ceasing to be, UK resident;
- the company's ceasing to be within the charge to corporation tax;

- the company's entering administration (in which case the accounting period is treated as ending immediately before the day on which the company enters into administration); or
- the company's ceasing to be in administration under *Insolvency Act 1986, Sch B1* (or any corresponding event otherwise than under that Act).

[*CTA 2009, s 10*].

101.2 EFFECT OF AN ACCOUNTING PERIOD OVERLAPPING TWO FINANCIAL YEARS HAVING DIFFERENT RATES OF CORPORATION TAX

[*CTA 2009, ss 5, 6, 8; FA 2015, s 6; F(No 2)A 2015, s 7*]

For the year ended 30 June 2017, the following information is relevant to A Ltd.

	£
Trading income	1,200,600
UK property income	350,000
Income from non-trading loan relationships	30,000

The main rate of corporation tax for the financial year 2016 is 20% and the rate for the financial year 2017 is 19%.

The corporation tax computation of A Ltd for the 12-month accounting period ended on 30.6.17 is

	£	
Trading income	1,200,600	
UK property income	350,000	
Income from non-trading loan relationships	30,000	
Total taxable profits	£1,580,600	
Total profits apportioned		
1.7.16 – 31.3.17	$^{9}/_{12}$ × £1,580,600	£1,185,450
1.4.17 – 30.6.17	$^{3}/_{12}$ × £1,580,600	£395,150
Tax chargeable		
20% × £1,185,450		237,090
19% × £395,150		75,079
Total tax charge		£312,169

Notes

(a) Where an accounting period does not coincide with a financial year, apportionment is necessary to calculate the tax payable. Apportionment is on a time basis, between the financial years which overlap the accounting period. Corporation tax is then charged on each proportion so computed at the rate fixed for the financial year concerned. [*CTA 2009, s 8*].

(b) In order to illustrate the effect of time apportionment, the example above deals with FY 2016 and FY 2017, as the main rate of corporation tax was different for these two years (20% and 19% respectively). Where two financial years have the same rate (as is the case for FY 2017 and FY 2018), there is no practical necessity to perform the time apportionment calculation – therefore, for a tax year ended 30 June 2018 where the total taxable profits are £1,580,600, the tax charge is £300,314 (19% × £1,580,600).

101.3 PERIODS OF ACCOUNT EXCEEDING 12 MONTHS

[*CTA 2009, ss 10(1), 53, 1307; CTA 2010, s 1172*]

B Ltd prepares accounts for 16 months ending on 31 March 2019. The following information is relevant

	£
Profit for 16 months	950,000
Capital gain (after indexation calculated to 31 December 2017) arising on 1.6.18	100,000
Tax written down value of plant and machinery main pool	
At 1.12.17	40,000
Plant purchased 1.4.18	200,000
Plant purchased 1.2.19	246,000
Proceeds of plant sold 31.12.18 (less than cost)	4,000

B Ltd has no related 51% group companies

B Ltd will be chargeable to corporation tax as follows

	Accounting period 12 months to 30.11.18	Accounting period 4 months to 31.3.19
	£	£
Adjusted profits (apportioned 12:4)	712,500	237,500
Deduct: Capital allowances	(207,200)	(79,155)
Trading income	505,300	158,345
Chargeable gain	100,000	
Chargeable profits	£605,300	£158,345

Notes

(a) Capital allowances

12 months to 30 November 2018

	AIA	Main pool	Allow-ances
	£	£	£
Main pool		40,000	
Additions	200,000	—	
AIA	(200,000)		200,000
		40,000	
WDA 18%		(7,200)	7,200
Total allowances			£207,200
WDV c/f		£32,800	

4 months to 31 March 2019

	AIA	Main pool	Allow-ances
	£	£	£
WDV b/f		32,800	
Additions	66,667	179,333	
Disposals		(4,000)	
AIA	(66,667)		66,667
		208,133	
WDA 18% x 4/12		(12,488)	12,488
Total allowances			£79,155
WDV c/f		£195,645	

Writing-down allowances, but not first-year allowances, are a proportionately reduced percentage of 18% if the accounting period is only part of a year. [*CAA 2001, s 56(3)*].
Annual investment allowance on £200,000 is available in a 12-month period. It is proportionately reduced for shorter periods or where there are related companies. [*CAA 2001, s 51A; FA 2013, s 7; FA 2014, s 10*]. See IT 4 CAPITAL ALLOWANCES ON PLANT AND MACHINERY.

(b) The capital gain is not apportioned on a time basis, but is included for the period in which it arises. [*TCGA 1992, s 8(1)*].

(c) The tax for the two accounting periods ended 30.11.18 and 31.3.19 will be due for payment on 1.9.19 and 1.1.20 respectively. [*TMA 1970, s 59D*]. The CT return(s) for both accounting periods will be due by 31.3.20, i.e. the first anniversary of the last day of the sixteen-month period of account, or, if later, three months after the issue of the notice requiring the return. [*FA 1998, Sch 18 para 14*]. See also **118** RETURNS.

102 Capital Allowances

102.1 TRANSFER OF TRADE WITHIN GROUP: PERIOD OF ACCOUNT EXCEEDING 12 MONTHS

[*CTA 2010, ss 938–953; CAA 2001, ss 55, 56, 310–313*]

A Ltd owns 80% of the ordinary share capital of both B Ltd and C Ltd, the latter companies carrying on similar trades.

A Ltd and C Ltd prepare accounts annually to 31 July. B Ltd which previously prepared accounts to 30 April each year has prepared accounts for 15 months ending on 31 July 2018.

On 31 December 2017, C Ltd transferred the whole of its trade to B Ltd under circumstances covered by *CTA 2010, ss 938–953*.

The following information is relevant to B Ltd

		£
Trading profit for 15 months to 31.7.18 before deduction of capital allowances		200,000
1.5.17	Tax written-down value of plant and machinery main pool	10,800
11.6.17	Plant purchased	3,000
3.9.17	Plant purchased	2,000
4.10.17	Plant sold (original cost £9,000)	6,800
1.3.18	Plant purchased	8,000
10.5.18	Plant sold (original cost £40,000)	9,560
15.6.18	Plant purchased	30,000
1.8.17	Tax written-down value of plant and machinery main pool owned by C Ltd	9,216

B Ltd will have chargeable profits as follows

	Accounting period 12 months to 30.4.18	Accounting period 3 months to 31.7.18
	£	£
Trading profits	160,000	40,000
Capital allowances on plant and machinery	(14,231)	(30,078)
Chargeable profits	£145,769	£9,922

Capital allowances

Plant and machinery

12 months to 30.4.18

	AIA	Main Pool	Total allow-ances
	£	£	£
WDV b/f		10,800	
Additions	13,000		
Transfer from C Ltd note (a)		8,525	
		19,325	
Disposals		(6,800)	
		12,525	
AIA £13,000 × 100% note (e)	(13,000)		13,000
WDA on assets transferred from C Ltd £8,525 × 18% × 4/12 note (a)		(511)	511
WDA on balance of expenditure £(12,525 – 8,525) × 18%		(720)	720
WDV c/f		£11,294	
Total allowances			£14,231

3 months to 31.7.18

	AIA	Main Pool	Total allow-ances
	£	£	£
WDV b/f		11,294	
Additions	30,000		
Disposals		(9,560)	
		1,734	
AIA (note (e))	(30,000)		30,000
WDA (18% × 3/12)		(78)	78
WDV c/f		£1,656	
Total allowances			£30,078

Notes

(a) Where a trade is transferred part-way through an accounting period, HMRC take the view that writing-down allowances are calculated for the predecessor for a notional accounting period ending on the date of the transfer. The successor is then treated, in relation to the assets transferred, as having a chargeable period starting on that date and running to the end of its accounting period. (HMRC Capital Allowances Manual CA15400.)

The transfer value of machinery and plant obtained from C Ltd is	£
Tax written-down value at 1.8.17	9,216
WDA due to C Ltd (£9,216 × 18% × $^{5}/_{12}$)	(691)
	£8,525

(b) The 'successor' company (B Ltd) is entitled to the capital allowances which the 'predecessor' company (C Ltd) would have been able to claim if it had continued to trade. [*CTA 2010, s 948(2)*].

(c) No annual investment allowance, first-year or initial allowance is available to the successor on assets transferred to it by the predecessor. [*CTA 2010, s 948(3)*].

(d) Writing-down allowances are reduced proportionately where the accounting period is less than one year. [*CAA 2001, ss 56(3), 310(2)*].

(e) A Ltd's group is entitled to only one annual investment allowance between all the companies, which can be allocated as the companies think fit. [*CAA 2001, s 51C*]. For the year ended 30 April 2018 it is assumed that B Ltd is allocated £13,000 to allow all of its expenditure in the period to qualify. For the three months to 31 July 2018 it is assumed that B Ltd is allocated £30,000 to allow all of its expenditure in the period to qualify.

102.2 NO CLAIM FOR ANNUAL INVESTMENT, FIRST-YEAR AND WRITING-DOWN ALLOWANCES

[*CAA 2001, ss 52(4), 56(5)*]

D Ltd is a company with one wholly-owned subsidiary, E Ltd, and there are no other group companies. Both companies prepare accounts to 30 September. For the year ended 30 September 2018, D Ltd has trading profits of £100,000 before capital allowances, whilst E Ltd incurs a trading loss of £100,000. E Ltd also incurred trading losses in the previous year and is unlikely to have any taxable profits in the foreseeable future. D Ltd spent £50,000 on plant and machinery on 26 March 2018 which qualifies for annual investment allowance at 100%. There was a written-down value of £70,000 on the plant and machinery main pool at 1 October 2017 and there were no disposals during the year.

Assuming a group relief claim is made under *CTA 2010, s 130* and that D Ltd claims the full capital allowances to which it is entitled, D Ltd's trading profits computation for the year to 30 September 2018 will be as follows

	£
Trading profit	100,000
Less capital allowances (see below)	(62,600)
	37,400
Less loss surrendered by E Ltd	(37,400)
Taxable profit	Nil

E Ltd has unrelieved losses carried forward of £62,600 (£100,000 — £37,400) available to be carried forward.

D Ltd's capital allowances computation is as follows

	AIA £	Main pool £	Total allowances £
WDV b/f		70,000	
Additions	50,000		
AIA	50,000		50,000
		70,000	
WDA 18%		(12,600)	12,600
WDV c/f		57,400	
Total allowances			£62,600

If D Ltd does not claim capital allowances, the position is as follows

	£
Trading profit	100,000
Less loss surrendered by E Ltd	100,000
Taxable profit	Nil

Capital allowances computation

	Expenditure qualifying for AIA £	Main pool £	Total allowances £
WDV b/f		70,000	
Additions	—	50,000	—
		120,000	
WDA – not claimed		—	—
WDV c/f		£120,000	
Total allowances			Nil

Notes

(a) A company may claim the whole, a part, or none of the allowances to which it is entitled. [*CAA 2001, ss 52(4), 56(5)*]. If a company does not claim annual investment allowance or claims part only, where available, the balance of the expenditure qualifies for writing-down allowances in the same accounting period. Capital allowances claims may be withdrawn within the same time limits as apply to the making of claims. [*FA 1998, s 117, Sch 18 paras 78–83*]. Expenditure on plant and machinery qualifies for annual investment allowance or first-year allowances only for the accounting period in which it is incurred. If no such allowance is claimed, the expenditure qualifies for writing-down allowances in subsequent periods.

(b) As a result of the allowances not being claimed, all of E Ltd's current year losses have been relieved, and D Ltd has a higher written-down value to carry forward on its plant and machinery main pool.

(c) See **106** GROUP RELIEF for group relief generally.

103 Capital Gains

103.1 CAPITAL LOSSES

[*TCGA 1992, s 8(1)*]

P Ltd has the following capital gains/(losses)

Year ended		£
31.7.15	Gains	27,000
	Losses	(7,000)
31.7.16	Losses	(12,000)
31.7.17	Gains	5,000
	Losses	(13,000)
31.7.18	Gains	40,000
	Losses	(30,000)

The gains and losses would be dealt with as follows in the CT computations of P Ltd

	£	£
31.7.15		
Gains chargeable to CT		£20,000
31.7.16		
Unrelieved losses carried forward	£(12,000)	Nil
31.7.17		
Losses (net)	(8,000)	Nil
Add Unrelieved losses brought forward	(12,000)	
Unrelieved losses carried forward	£(20,000)	
31.7.18		
Chargeable gains (net)	10,000	
Deduct Unrelieved losses brought forward	(20,000)	
Unrelieved losses carried forward	£(10,000)	Nil

Notes

(a) Unrelieved losses cannot be set off against trading profits, but are available to relieve future gains.

(b) Gains otherwise chargeable to CT may be covered by trading losses for the same accounting period or trading losses carried back from a succeeding period under *CTA 2010, s 37(3)*—see **114** LOSSES.

(c) See also **103.3(A)** below.

103.2 CLOSE COMPANY TRANSFERRING ASSET AT UNDERVALUE

[*TCGA 1992, s 125*]

(A)

G Ltd (a close company) sold a building in 2017 to an associated company Q Ltd, which is not a member of the same group as G Ltd, at a price below market value at the time. Relevant values relating to the asset were

	£
Cost 1999	45,000
Market value at date of disposal	95,000
Sale proceeds received	75,000

The issued share capital of G Ltd was held at the time of disposal as follows

	£1 ordinary shares	Value prior to sale of asset
		£
C	25,000	50,000
D	30,000	60,000
E	20,000	40,000
F	25,000	50,000
	100,000	£200,000

Sale proceeds on subsequent sale (at market value) in July 2018 of C's total shareholding (originally purchased at £0.80 per share in 1993) in G Ltd were £55,000.

G Ltd's chargeable gain on the sale of the building in 2017 is

	£
Market value (note (b))	95,000
Cost	(45,000)
Unindexed gain	50,000
Indexation allowance at, say, 40% on £45,000 (note (c))	(18,000)
Chargeable gain	£32,000

C's gain on the disposal of the shares in July 2018 is

		£	£
Sale proceeds			55,000
Deduct	Allowable cost:		
	Purchase price (25,000 × £0.80)	20,000	
	Less Apportioned undervalue (note (a))	(5,000)	(15,000)
Chargeable gain			£40,000

Notes

(a) The apportionment of undervalue on disposal is

	£
Market value at time of sale	95,000
Sale proceeds	(75,000)
	£20,000

Proportion of shareholding		Value apportioned
		£
C	$^{25}/_{100} \times$ £20,000	5,000
D	$^{30}/_{100} \times$ £20,000	6,000
E	$^{20}/_{100} \times$ £20,000	4,000
F	$^{25}/_{100} \times$ £20,000	5,000
		£20,000

(b) In the computation of the company's gain, market value is substituted for proceeds under *TCGA 1992, s 17*.

(c) Indexation allowance is frozen at its December 2017 level. No indexation allowance is available in respect of expenditure incurred after 31 December 2017, and for expenditure incurred on or before that date and falling to be deducted on a disposal after that date, indexation allowance is computed up to and including December 2017 only. [*TCGA 1992, ss 53(1)(1B), 54(1B); FA 2018, s 26(2)(3)(6)*].See **CGT 214.1** INDEXATION.

(B)

Assume the same facts as in (A) above except that the building had a market value of £155,000 at the date of disposal and the market value of C's shares on the subsequent disposal was £40,000. Assume now also that C purchased his shares at £0.70 per share before 31 March 1982 and that their value on that date was £21,000.

G Ltd's chargeable gain will be computed under the same principles as in (A) above. C's gain on the disposal of the shares will be as follows

		£	£
Sale proceeds			40,000
Deduct Allowable cost:			
31 March 1982 value		21,000	
Less Apportioned undervalue	(note (a))	(20,000)	
			(1,000)
Chargeable gain			£39,000

Notes

(a) The apportionment of undervalue on disposal is

	£
Market value at time of sale	155,000
Deduct Sale proceeds	(75,000)
	£80,000

Proportion of shareholding		Value apportioned
		£
C	$^{25}/_{100}$ × £80,000	20,000
D	$^{30}/_{100}$ × £80,000	24,000
E	$^{20}/_{100}$ × £80,000	16,000
F	$^{25}/_{100}$ × £80,000	20,000
		£80,000

(b) Transfers of assets on or before 31 March 1982 are disregarded in respect of disposals after 5 April 1988 to which re-basing applies (not illustrated in this example). [*TCGA 1992, s 125(1)(5)*].

(c) Indexation allowance is frozen at its December 2017 level. No indexation allowance is available in respect of expenditure incurred after 31 December 2017, and for expenditure incurred on or before that date and falling to be deducted on a disposal after that date, indexation allowance is computed up to and including December 2017 only. [*TCGA 1992, ss 53(1)(1B), 54(1B); FA 2018, s 26(2)(3)(6)*].See **CGT 214.1** INDEXATION.

103.3 GROUPS OF COMPANIES

(A) Re-allocation of gains and losses within a group

[*TCGA 1992, ss 171A–171C*]

A Ltd and B Ltd are members of the same group of companies, preparing accounts each year to 31 March. On 30 September 2018, A Ltd sold an asset (asset 1) to an unconnected third party for £100,000. The asset had been acquired in June 2013 for £40,000. On 29 January 2019 B Ltd sold an asset (asset 2), which had cost £70,000 in January 2011, for £50,000 to C Ltd, an unconnected third party. B Ltd incurred costs on the disposal of £2,000. Neither company disposes of any other assets in the year ended 31 March 2019.

A Ltd and B Ltd jointly elect before 31 March 2021 under *TCGA 1992, s 171A* for the chargeable gain or loss on asset 2 to be treated as accruing to company A at the time it would otherwise have accrued to B.

The chargeable gains computations for the year ended 31 March 2019 for A Ltd and B Ltd are as follows.

B Ltd

Deemed disposal of asset 2 in April 2018: consideration deemed to be such that neither gain nor loss arises.

	£
Deemed consideration	84,000
Cost of asset to B Ltd	(70,000)
Indexation allowance £70,000 × say 20%	(14,000)
Gain	—

A Ltd

Disposal of asset 1 in September 2018

	£
Consideration	100,000
Cost	(40,000)
Indexation allowance £40,000 × say 10%	(4,000)
Chargeable gain	£56,000

Disposal of asset 2 in January 2019

	£
Consideration	50,000
Cost to A Ltd	(70,000)
Cost of disposal incurred by B Ltd	(2,000)
Allowable loss	£(22,000)

Net chargeable gains £56,000 − £22,000 = £34,000

Notes

(a) The election under *TCGA 1992, s 171A* must be made in writing to HMRC within two years after the end of the accounting period of A Ltd in which the gain accrued. The election can only be made if a disposal of asset 2 by B Ltd to A Ltd would have been a no gain, no loss disposal within *TCGA 1992, s 171*.

(b) Indexation allowance is frozen at its December 2017 level. No indexation allowance is available in respect of expenditure incurred after 31 December 2017, and for expenditure incurred on or before that date and falling to be deducted on a disposal after that date, indexation allowance is computed up to and including December 2017 only. [*TCGA 1992, ss 53(1)(1B), 54(1B); FA 2018, s 26(2)(3)(6)*].See **CGT 214.1** INDEXATION.

(B) **Intra-group transfers of assets which are trading stock of one company but not of the other — transfer from a 'capital asset' company to a 'trading stock' company**

[*TCGA 1992, ss 161, 173(1)*]

In June 2018, X Ltd transfers an item classed as a fixed asset to another group company Y Ltd, which treats it as trading stock.

The following information is relevant

	Case (i)	Case (ii)
	£	£
Original cost (after 31.3.1982)	100,000	100,000
Market value at date of transfer	120,000	40,000
Eventual sale proceeds	140,000	140,000
Indexation allowance due on original cost at date of transfer	17,000	17,000

The position of Y Ltd will be as follows if there is no election under *TCGA 1992, s 161(3)*

Chargeable gain/(allowable loss) on appropriation		
Market value	120,000	40,000
Deemed cost of asset (note (a))	(117,000)	(117,000)
Gain/(loss)	3,000	(77,000)
Deduct Indexation allowance included in cost (note (b))	—	17,000
Chargeable gain/(allowable loss)	£3,000	£(60,000)
Trading profit at date of sale		
Sale proceeds	140,000	140,000
Deemed cost of asset	(120,000)	(40,000)
Trading profit	£20,000	£100,000

With an election under *TCGA 1992, s 161(3)*

No chargeable gain arises on appropriation

	£	£
Trading profit at date of sale		
Sale proceeds		140,000
Market value at appropriation	120,000	
Adjustment for (gain)/loss otherwise (chargeable)/allowable	(3,000)	117,000
Trading profit		£23,000

Notes

(a) The intra-group transfer by X Ltd to Y Ltd is treated as a disposal on which neither a gain nor a loss accrues after taking account of any indexation allowance due. X Ltd has no liability on the transfer and Y Ltd has a deemed acquisition cost of £117,000 on the appropriation to stock. [*TCGA 1992, ss 56(2), 171(1)*].

(b) The indexation allowance on a no gain/no loss transfer must be excluded on a subsequent disposal to the extent that it would otherwise contribute to an allowable loss. [*TCGA 1992, s 56(3*].

(c) With effect for appropriations on or after 8 March 2017 an election under *TCGA 1992, s 161(3)* can only be made where the appropriation would, in the absence of the election, result in a chargeable gain. Previously an election could be made where either a chargeable gain or an allowable loss would otherwise arise.

(d) Indexation allowance is frozen at its December 2017 level. No indexation allowance is available in respect of expenditure incurred after 31 December 2017, and for expenditure incurred on or before that date and falling to be deducted on a disposal after that date, indexation allowance is computed up to and including December 2017 only. [*TCGA 1992, ss 53(1)(1B), 54(1B); FA 2018, s 26(2)(3)(6)*].See **CGT 214.1** INDEXATION.

(C) Intra-group transfers of assets which are trading stock of one company but not of the other — transfer from a 'trading stock' company to a 'capital asset' company

[*TCGA 1992, ss 161, 173(2)*]

P Ltd acquires from another group company Q Ltd as a fixed asset an item previously treated as trading stock.

	£
Cost to Q Ltd (after 31.3.1982)	100,000
Market value at date of transfer	150,000
Eventual sale proceeds	200,000
Indexation allowance due on transfer value from date of transfer to date of sale	10,000

The group will have the following trading profits and chargeable gains

	£	£
Q Ltd trading profit [*TCGA 1992, s 161(2)*]		
Deemed sale proceeds		150,000
Cost to Q Ltd		(100,000)
Trading profit		£50,000

P Ltd chargeable gain [*TCGA 1992, s 171(1)*]

Sale proceeds		200,000
Cost of asset	150,000	
Indexation allowance	10,000	
		(160,000)
Chargeable gain		£40,000

Notes

(a) Indexation allowance is frozen at its December 2017 level. No indexation allowance is available in respect of expenditure incurred after 31 December 2017, and for expenditure incurred on or before that date and falling to be deducted on a disposal after that date, indexation allowance is computed up to and including December 2017 only. [*TCGA 1992, ss 53(1)(1B), 54(1B); FA 2018, s 26(2)(3)(6)*].See **CGT 214.1** INDEXATION.

(D) Rollover relief on the replacement of business assets

[*TCGA 1992, ss 152, 153, 155, 175*]

M Ltd and N Ltd are 75% subsidiaries of H Ltd. On 1 February 2017 M Ltd sold a showroom for £200,000, realising a chargeable gain of £110,000. N Ltd purchased a factory for £150,000 in March 2019, within three years after the date of sale of the showroom.

Rollover relief could be claimed as follows

	£	£
Gain otherwise chargeable to corporation tax		110,000
Deduct Unrelieved gain:		
Sale proceeds	200,000	
Less Amount reinvested	(150,000)	
Chargeable gain	£50,000	50,000
Rollover relief		£60,000
New base cost of factory		
Purchase price		150,000
Deduct Rollover relief		(60,000)
		£90,000

Notes

(a) To qualify for relief, the two companies concerned need not be members of the same group throughout the period between the transactions but each must be a member at the time of its own particular transaction.

(b) N Ltd will be entitled to indexation allowance, based on the deemed cost of £90,000, on a subsequent sale (to the extent that such sale produces an unindexed gain).

(c) See also CGT **205.2** ASSETS HELD ON **31** MARCH **1982** and CGT **226** ROLLOVER RELIEF.

(E) **Degrouping charge**

A Ltd had the following transactions

1.3.80 Purchased a freehold property £10,000.

31.3.82 Market value £25,000.

1.3.86 Purchased the entire share capital of B Ltd for £120,000.

1.12.12 Sold the freehold to B Ltd for £20,000 (market value £80,000).

31.9.18 Sold its shares in B Ltd (at which time B Ltd continued to own the freehold property) for £1 million.

Both companies prepare accounts to 30 April.

Relevant values of the RPI are: March 1982: 79.44, March 1986: 96.73, December 2012: 246.8, December 2017: 278.1.

The taxation consequences are

(i) There will be no chargeable gain on A Ltd's disposal of the property to B Ltd as the disposal is one on which, after taking account of indexation allowance, neither gain nor loss arises. [*TCGA 1992, ss 56(2), 171(1)*].

Indexation factor (246.8 – 79.44)/79.44 = 2.107

		£
Cost to A Ltd		10,000
Indexation allowance	£25,000 × 2.107 (note (a))	52,675
Deemed cost to B Ltd		£62,675

(ii) On the sale of A Ltd's shares in B Ltd on 31.9.18 (i.e. within six years after the transaction in (i) above), *A Ltd* will have a deemed disposal as follows.

Deemed disposal on 1.12.12

	£	£	£
Market value at 1.12.12		80,000	80,000
Cost (as above)	62,675		
Less indexation to date	(52,675)		
		(10,000)	
Market value at 31.3.82			(25,000)
Unindexed gain		70,000	55,000
Indexation allowance			
£25,000 ×2.107		(52,675)	(52,675)
Indexed gain		£17,325	£2,325
Deemed gain			£2,325

The deemed gain is not charged to corporation tax directly, but is treated as follows.

A Ltd's chargeable gain on disposal of B Ltd shares on 31.9.18

	£
Consideration	1,000,000
Add degrouping gain	2,325
	1,002,325
Less acquisition cost	(120,000)
Unindexed gain	882,325
Indexation allowance (278.1 – 96.73/96.73) × £120,000	(225,001)
Chargeable gain subject to note (b)	£657,324

Notes

(a) Indexation allowance is frozen at its December 2017 level. No indexation allowance is available in respect of expenditure incurred after 31 December 2017, and for expenditure incurred on or before that date and falling to be deducted on a disposal after that date, indexation allowance is computed up to and including December 2017 only. [*TCGA 1992, ss 53(1)(1B), 54(1B); FA 2018, s 26(2)(3)(6)*].See **CGT 214.1** INDEXATION.

(b) Where the conditions listed below are satisfied, a degrouping gain or loss is not treated as a separate gain or loss accruing to the transferee company, but instead the gain or loss accruing on a 'group disposal' (see below) is adjusted to take account of the degrouping gain or loss. The conditions are as follows:

(A) the transferee company ceases to be a member of the group as a result of one or more disposals ('*group disposals*') by a group member of the transferee's shares or those of another group member;

(B) either:

(i) the company making the group disposal (or, if there is more than one such disposal, at least one of them) is UK resident at the time of disposal, the shares are within the charge to corporation tax (or would be but for the substantial shareholdings exemption — see **103.4**), or any part of the gains or loss on the disposal (or at least one of them) is treated as accruing to a person under *TCGA 1992, s 13(2)* (attribution of gains to members of non-resident companies), or

(ii) had (i) above applied to the group disposal or to each of them, any gain arising would not have been a chargeable gain as a result of the substantial shareholdings exemption; and

(C) *CTA 2010, s 535* (UK real estate investment trusts: exemption of gains) would not apply to the degrouping gain or loss.

Where the conditions are satisfied, a chargeable gain or allowable loss on a single group disposal is calculated by adding any degrouping gain which would otherwise have arisen but for these provisions to the consideration for the group disposal (and a degrouping loss is treated as an allowable deduction).

[*TCGA 1992, s 179(3A)–(3H); FA 2011, Sch 10 para 3(6)*].

(c) Where a company is treated as making a gain under the degrouping charge provisions or such a gain is taken into account in calculating a gain on a disposal of shares as illustrated in this example, a claim can be made to defer part of the gain. Where the degrouping gain is taken into account in calculating a gain on a disposal of shares, the claim can be made by the company making the share disposal or, if there is more than one such disposal, the companies making those disposals acting jointly. In any other case the claim is to be made by the company to whom the degrouping gain is deemed to accrue. The effect is to reduce the amount of the gain by the amount specified in the claim. The reduction must be just and reasonable with regard to any transaction as a direct or indirect result of which the asset to which the gain relates was acquired. Where a gain is reduced in this way, the consideration for the deemed reacquisition of the asset by the transferee company is taken to be its market value less the amount of the adjustment to the gain. In effect the part of the gain excluded is deferred until final disposal of the asset by the transferee company (to whom the liability will then fall). [*TCGA 1992, s 179ZA; FA 2011, Sch 10 paras 4, 9(1)*].

(F) Restriction on set-off of pre-entry losses on or after 19 July 2011

[*TCGA 1992, s 177A, Sch 7A; FA 2011, s 46, Sch 11*]

Wooster Ltd, the holding company of a group, acquires the entire share capital of House Ltd on 1 January 2011. At that date, House Ltd is trading as a gun seller and has an unrelieved allowable pre-entry loss of £150,000. House Ltd makes no further disposals of assets until, in accounting period ended 31 March 2019, it disposes of four assets as follows.

	Date of acquisition	Chargeable gain/ (allowable loss)
Asset A	31/3/09	£50,000
Asset B	1/5/12	£30,000
Asset C	1/11/11	£100,000
Asset D	8/6/07	£(25,000)

Asset B was acquired from an unconnected company and has been used throughout the period of House Ltd's ownership for the purposes of the company's gun selling trade. Asset C is a building which has been leased to an unconnected company throughout. House Ltd had not carried on a property business before acquiring the asset.

House Ltd's total taxable gains for the year ended 31 March 2019 are as follows.

	£	£
Asset A (note (b))		
Chargeable gain	50,000	
Less pre-entry loss (part)	(50,000)	—
Asset B (note (b))		
Chargeable gain	30,000	
Less pre-entry loss (part)	(30,000)	—

Asset C (note (b))		
Chargeable gain	100,000	
Less loss on Asset D (note (b))	(25,000)	75,000
Total taxable gains		£75,000

The pre-entry loss has been utilised as follows.

Loss brought forward	150,000
Set against gain on Asset A	50,000
Set against gain on Asset B	30,000
Unrelieved loss carried forward	£70,000

Notes

(a) Broadly, the provisions of *TCGA 1992, Sch 7A* restrict the use of losses realised by a company before it joins a group and remaining unrelieved at that time. Such pre-entry losses can be set only against gains on assets held by the company at the time it joined the group or subsequently acquired by the company from outside the group and used by it in a continuing trade.

(b) The pre-entry loss in this example can be set off against the gain on Asset A as Asset A was owned by House Ltd before it joined Wooster Ltd's group. The loss can also be set off against the gain on Asset B as, although Asset B was acquired by House Ltd after it joined the group, it was acquired by the company from outside the group and has been used by it in a continuing trade throughout its period of ownership. Asset C fails to meet either of these conditions and so the loss cannot be set against the gain arising on its disposal.

(c) Although Asset D was acquired before House Ltd joined the group, the loss is not a pre-entry loss because it accrues on or after 19 July 2011. Had Asset D been disposed of before that date, the pre-entry proportion of the loss would have been subject to the pre-entry loss restrictions until that date. The loss would have been treated on and after that date as if it had accrued immediately before the company became a member of the group (and therefore as a pre-entry loss).

(d) The provisions do not apply where *TCGA 1992, s 184A* (restrictions on buying losses: avoidance schemes) applies. [*TCGA 1992, Sch 7A para 1(1)*].

103.4 SUBSTANTIAL SHAREHOLDING EXEMPTION

[*TCGA 1992, Sch 7AC; F(No 2)A 2017, ss 27, 28*]

Swallow Ltd acquired 1,500 shares in Summer Ltd in April 1994. Swallow Ltd holds no other investments in any company, has been a trading company throughout its existence, and is not a member of a group. Summer Ltd has 10,000 issued shares and has been a trading company since its formation. Swallow Ltd makes the following disposals of Summer Ltd shares. All disposals are to persons who are not connected with Swallow Ltd.

31 May 2012	600 shares
30 April 2012	400 shares
30 June 2018	500 shares

The effect of the disposals for the purposes of corporation tax on chargeable gains is as follows

31 May 2012 disposal

Swallow Ltd has held at least 10% of the ordinary share capital of Summer Ltd throughout the two years prior to the disposal. The disposal is therefore of part of a substantial shareholding and no chargeable gain or allowable loss arises on the disposal.

30 April 2012 disposal

Although Swallow Ltd did not hold at least 10% of the shares in Summer Ltd immediately before the disposal (the remaining holding being only 900 of 10,000 shares), there is a twelve month period beginning within two years prior to the disposal throughout which it did hold at least 10%. That period is 1 June 2015 to 31 May 2016. Accordingly, the substantial shareholding exemption applies and no chargeable gain or allowable loss arises on the disposal.

30 June 2018 disposal

Swallow Ltd holds only 5% of the share capital of Summer Ltd immediately before the disposal. In the period from 1 July 2011 to 30 June 2018, the company held at least 10% of Summer Ltd's shares only from 1 July 2011 to 31 May 2012. This is not a continuous twelve month period beginning within six years prior to the disposal, and therefore the substantial shareholding exemption will not apply. A gain on the disposal of 500 shares will be a chargeable gain, and a loss an allowable loss.

Note

(a) For disposals on or after 1 April 2017, a gain on a disposal by a company of shares in another company is not a chargeable gain (and a loss is not an allowable loss) if, broadly, the company held at least 10% of the other company's ordinary share capital throughout a twelve month period beginning within six years prior to the disposal. For disposals before 1 April 2017, the company must have held at least 10% of the other company's ordinary share capital throughout a twelve month period beginning within two years prior to the disposal, and both companies had to be trading companies.

104 Close Companies

104.1 CLOSE COMPANY — DEFINITION

[*CTA 2010, ss 439–453*]

(A)

A plc is a quoted company whose ordinary share capital is owned as follows

		%
B	a director	10
C	wife of B	5
D	father of B	4
E		17
F	business partner of E	2
G	a director	10
H		8
I Ltd	a non-close company	30
J		7
100	other shareholders	7
		100

It can be shown that A plc is a close company by considering the following three steps

(i) Is A plc controlled by five or fewer participators or by its directors?

		%	%
I Ltd			30
B	own shares	10	
	C's shares	5	
	D's shares	4	
			19
E	own shares	17	
	F's shares	2	
			19
			68

As A plc is controlled by three participators, the initial conclusion is that the company is close. [*CTA 2010, s 439(2)*].

(ii) Is A plc a quoted company, with at least 35% of the voting power owned by the public?

		%
I Ltd		30
J		7
100	other shareholders	7
		44

As at least 35% of the voting power is owned by the public it appears that A plc is exempt from close company status, subject to step (iii). [*CTA 2010, s 446(1)*].

(iii) Is more than 85% of the voting power in A plc owned by its principal members?

	%
I Ltd	30
B	19
E	19
G	10
H	8
	86

Because the principal members own more than 85% of the voting power A plc is a close company. [*CTA 2010, s 446(2)-(4)*].

Note

(a) Although J owns more than 5% of the share capital, he is not a principal member because five other persons each hold more than J's 7% and so themselves constitute the principal members. [*CTA 2010, s 446(4)*].

(B)

The ordinary share capital of A Ltd (an unquoted company) is owned as follows

		%
B	a director	9
C	son of B	9
D	works manager	5
E	wife of D	15
F	a director	9
G	a director	1
H	a director	1
J	a director	1
K	a director	1
49	other shareholders with 1% each	49
		100

A Ltd is a close company because it is controlled by its directors, thus

		%	%
B	own shares	9	
	C's shares	9	
			18
D	own shares	5	
	E's shares	15	
			20
F			9
G			1
H			1
J			1
K			1
			51

Note

(a) A manager is deemed to be a director if he and his associates own 20% or more of the ordinary share capital. [*CTA 2010, s 452(2)*].

(C)

The ordinary share capital of A Ltd is owned as follows

		%
B	a director	9
C	a director	9
D	a director	9
E		9
F		9
G Ltd	a close company	8
47	other shareholders with 1% each	47
		100

The ordinary share capital of G Ltd is owned as follows

		%
B	a director	50
C	a director	50
		100

A Ltd is not a close company under the control test because it is not under the control of five or fewer participators. The five largest shareholdings comprise only 45% of the share capital. [*CTA 2010, ss 439(2), 450(3)*].

A Ltd is a close company under the distribution of assets test because B and C would each become entitled to one-half of G Ltd's share of the assets of A Ltd. [*CTA 2010, s 439(3)*]. The shares of assets attributable to the five largest shareholdings become

		%	%
B	own share	9	
	50% of G Ltd's share	4	
			13
C	own share	9	
	50% of G Ltd's share	4	
			13
D			9
E			9
F			9
			53

(D)

A Ltd is an unquoted company with the following capital structure, owned as shown

	£1 ordinary shares	£1 non-participating preference shares (no votes attached)
B	6,000	—
C	15,000	25,000
D	6,000	19,000
E	5,000	10,000
F	1,600	13,000
G	2,000	—
Other shareholders owning less than 1,000 shares each	64,400	33,000
	100,000	100,000

The company is close by reference to share capital as follows

	Control by votes	Control of issued capital
B	6,000	6,000
C	15,000	40,000
D	6,000	25,000
E	5,000	15,000
F	—	14,600
G	2,000	—
	34,000	100,600

Note

(a) Control of the company includes control of more than one-half of:

(i) voting power; or

(ii) issued share capital.

[*CTA 2010, s 450(3)*].

104.2 LOANS TO PARTICIPATORS

[*CTA 2010, ss 455–464D; FA 2013, Sch 30; FA 2016, ss 50, 51*]

(A)

P is a participator in Q Ltd, a close company which makes up accounts to 30 September. Q Ltd loaned P £80,000 on 29 August 2016. On 24 May 2018 P repays the loan.

The effect of these transactions on Q Ltd is as follows

1 July 2017	The company is liable to pay corporation tax of £80,000 × 32.5%	£26,000
30 June 2019	On a claim, Q Ltd is entitled to a repayment of	£26,000

Notes

(a) An amount equal to 32.5% of the loan (25% for loans or advances made before 6 April 2016) must be self-assessed by the company as if it were corporation tax chargeable for the accounting period in which the loan was made.

(b) The tax is due on the day following the expiry of nine months after the end of the accounting period in which the loan or advance was made.

(c) Where loans or advances are repaid after the due date on which tax is charged, relief by claim in respect of the repayment is not given at any time before the expiry of nine months from the end of the accounting period in which the repayment takes place.

(d) Where a loan is repaid on or after 20 March 2013, the tax, or part of the tax, is not repaid if either:

- within a period of 30 days, a repayment of £5,000 or more is made by a participator and the company makes further chargeable payments (i.e. loans or benefits chargeable under *CTA 2010, s 464A*) of at least £5,000 to the participator, provided that the further chargeable payments are made in an accounting period after that in which the original loan was made; or
- the amount outstanding is at least £15,000, arrangements have been made at the time of the repayment for one or more chargeable payments to be made to replace some or all of the loan, and further chargeable payments of at least £5,000 are made by the company to the participator.

In either case, the repayment is treated as a repayment of the further chargeable payments and only any excess amount is treated as a repayment of the original loan.

[*CTA 2010, ss 464C, 464D; FA 2013, Sch 30 para 6*].

(B)

T is a participator in (but not an employee of) V Ltd, a close company. V Ltd loaned T £100,000 on 10 May 2017. On 2 March 2018, T repays £73,000 and on 15 February 2019, V Ltd agrees to waive the balance of the loan. V Ltd has a year end of 31 March and is not a large company or very large company for instalment payment purposes. T is a higher rate (but not an additional rate) taxpayer for 2018/19.

The effect of these transactions is as follows

V Ltd

On 1.1.2019	The company becomes liable to pay corporation tax of (£100,000 − £73,000) £27,000 × 32.5%	£8,775
On 31.12.2019	The company is due a repayment of £27,000 × 32.5%	£8,775

T

On 15.2.2019	T's 2018/19 taxable income is increased by	£27,000
	As T pays tax at the higher rate, the deemed income will be subject to tax at the dividend upper rate of 32.5% on £27,000	£8,775

Notes

(a) Where a loan or advance which gave rise to a charge under *CTA 2010, s 455* is released or written off, a claim can be made for repayment of the tax. [*CTA 2010, s 458(2)(b)*].

(b) Companies are required to include *section 455* tax in their self-assessment.

104.3 BENEFITS IN KIND FOR PARTICIPATORS

[*CTA 2010, ss 1064–1069; FA 2016, s 50*]

R is a participator in S Ltd, a close company, but he is neither a director nor an employee. For the whole of 2018/19, S Ltd provided R with a new petrol fuelled car of which the 'price' for tax purposes (i.e. under *ITEPA 2003, ss 122–124)* was £21,200, and the carbon dioxide emission figure for which was 180g/km. R was required to, and did, pay S Ltd £500 a year for the use of the car. The cost of providing the car, charged in S Ltd's accounts for its year ended 31 March 2019, was £5,000.

Deemed distribution

If the benefit of the car were assessable to tax as income from employment, the cash equivalent would be

	£
£21,200 @ 37%	7,844
Less contribution	(500)
Income of R for 2018/19	£7,344

S Ltd's taxable profits

In computing S Ltd's profits chargeable to corporation tax, the actual expenditure charged (£5,000) must be added back.

105 Double Tax Relief

105.1 MEASURE OF RELIEF

[*TIOPA 2010, ss 2–6, 18–20, 31–34, 42–56*]

The following facts relate to A Ltd's accounting period for the year ended 31 March 2019.

	£
Trading profits	1,500,000
Overseas chargeable gain (tax 40%)	80,000

A Ltd's tax liability is

		Trading income	Overseas gain	Total
		£	£	£
Profits		1,500,000	80,000	1,580,000
CT at 19%		285,000	15,200	300,200
Relief for foreign tax	(note (a))	—	(15,200)	(15,200)
		£285,000	—	£285,000

Note

(a) The maximum amount of relief for foreign tax is the amount of the gain multiplied by the company's corporation tax rate (£80,000 × 19% = £15,200). [*TIOPA 2010, s 42*]. The unrelieved foreign tax (£32,000 – £15,200 = £16,800) cannot be relieved by way of deduction from the gain under *TIOPA 2010, s 113*. [*TIOPA 2010, s 31*].

105.2 EXEMPTION FOR PROFITS OF FOREIGN PERMANENT ESTABLISHMENTS

[*CTA 2009, ss 18A–18S; FA 2011, s 48, Sch 13; FA 2012, Sch 20 paras 3–7, 55; FA 2016, ss 76(7), 81(1)*]

(A) Exclusion of permanent establishment profits

Wiggo Ltd is a UK company trading as a bike wholesaler. The company also operates through a permanent establishment in Tourland and has made an election under *CTA 2009, s 18A* which took effect at the start of the accounting period ending 31 December 2018. For the accounting period ending 31 December 2018, Wiggo Ltd's total taxable profits, before applying the foreign permanent establishments exemption, consists of trading profits of £5,000,000 and non-trading loan relationships income of £120,000. The company had no opening negative amount (see (B) below) and its foreign permanent establishments amount for the accounting period is calculated as follows.

	£
Profits amount	
Trading profits	250,000
Losses amount	
Non-trading loan relationship deficit	(40,000)
Foreign permanent establishments amount	£210,000

Exemption adjustments under *CTA 2009, s 18A* are made to Wiggo Ltd's total taxable profits for the year ended 31 December 2018 as follows.

	£	£
Trading profits	5,000,000	
Less Tourland trading profits	(250,000)	4,750,000
Non-trading loan relationship income	120,000	
Add Tourland non-trading loan relationship deficit	40,000	160,000
Total taxable profits		£4,910,000

Notes

(a) A company can make an election for profits arising from its foreign permanent establishments, including chargeable gains, to be exempt from corporation tax (and for losses from those permanent establishments to be excluded). This election can be made by UK resident companies and non-UK resident companies which expect to become UK resident. An election will apply to all accounting periods of the company beginning on or after the 'relevant day'. The 'relevant day' is the day on which, at the time of the election, the next or first accounting period is expected to begin or, in the case of a non-resident company, the day on which the company becomes UK resident. If, in the event, an accounting period begins before and ends on or after the relevant day, then for corporation tax purposes that period is treated as two accounting periods, the first ending immediately before the relevant day and the second starting on that day. Profits and losses are to be apportioned to the two periods on a just and reasonable basis. An election can only be revoked before the relevant day; otherwise it is irrevocable. Profits and losses are not left out of account if they are (for disposals of land on or after 5 July 2016), profits or losses of a company's trade of dealing in or developing UK land or would be such profits or losses if the company were non-UK resident. [*CTA 2009, ss 18A(1)–(3), 18F; FA 2011, Sch 13 paras 4, 31; FA 2012, Sch 20 paras 3, 5, 55; FA 2016, ss 76(7), 81(1)*].

(b) The '*foreign permanent establishments amount*' is the aggregate of the 'profits amount' for each territory outside the UK in which the company carries on, or has carried on, business through a permanent establishment, less the aggregate of the 'losses amount' for each such territory. Where there is a double tax treaty between the territory and the UK which includes a provision non-discrimination provision, the '*profits amount*' is the profits which would be taken to be attributable to the permanent establishment in ascertaining the amount of any credit relief for foreign tax. The '*losses amount*' is calculated on the same basis. If an amount of credit relief does not depend on the profits taken to be attributable to the permanent establishment because, under the treaty, the foreign tax is not charged by reference to such profits, then only profits which would be taken to be attributable to the permanent establishment if the foreign tax were charged by reference to such profits are included in the profits amount (and only such losses are included in the losses amount). Where there is no such treaty, the profits amount and losses amount are the amounts which would be taken to be so attributable to the permanent establishment if there were such a treaty and it was in the terms of the OECD model tax convention. [*CTA 2009, ss 18A(4)–(10), 18R; FA 2011, Sch 13 para 4*].

(c) Although profits amounts and losses amounts are aggregated in computing the foreign permanent establishments amount, they nevertheless retain their identity for the purpose of making the necessary adjustments to the company's total taxable profits.

(B) Pre-entry losses

A company with three foreign permanent establishments makes an election under *CTA 2009, s 18A* which takes effect for the accounting period ending 31 December 2018. The profits amounts and losses amounts (excluding chargeable gains and allowable losses) for the three territories in the preceding six years are as follows.

Year ended 31 December	Territory 1	Territory 2	Territory 3	Foreign permanent establishments amount
2012	2,000	0	(6,000)	(4,000)
2013	1,000	(2,000)	1,000	0
2014	(5,000)	(2,000)	2,000	(5,000)
2015	2,000	4,000	(3,000)	3,000
2016	(10,000)	1,000	2,000	(7,000)
2017	2,000	2,000	2,000	6,000
Opening negative amount				£7,000

The opening negative amount must be extinguished by matching with the aggregate profits amount (see note (b) to (A) above) for each subsequent accounting period, starting with the first period for which the election takes effect (i.e. the year ended 31 December 2018). No adjustments can be made to the company's total taxable profits under *CTA 2009, s 18A* until the opening negative amount has been so extinguished.

Alternatively, the company could have elected for the opening negative amount for territory 1 to be streamed, so that it need be matched only with profits amounts for that territory. The opening negative amount is calculated as follows.

Year ended 31 December	Territory 1
2012	2,000
2013	1,000
2014	(5,000)
2015	2,000
2016	(10,000)
2017	2,000
Total	(£8,000)

The streamed negative amount for that territory is the lower of £8,000 and the aggregate total opening negative amount, i.e. £7,000. The company streams no other territory, so the residual negative amount is the difference between the aggregate negative amount £7,000 and the streamed negative amount £7,000, i.e. nil. The profits amounts for Territory 1 must therefore be matched with the negative amount £7,000 before exemption can apply (i.e. the first £7,000 of such amounts are not exempt), but there is no restriction on exemption for profits amounts of Territories 2 and 3.

Notes

(a) Where losses have arisen in any of the company's foreign permanent establishments in the six-year period ending at the end of the accounting period in which the election is made, and those losses have not been eliminated by profits from those establishments before the end of that period, then the company will have an 'opening negative amount' and no adjustments can be made to the company's total taxable profits until that amount has been eliminated. The '*opening negative amount*' is ascertained by calculating the foreign permanent establishments amount (excluding chargeable gains and allowable losses) for each accounting period ending less than six years before the end of the accounting period in which the election is made and for that accounting period. The earliest negative amount is carried forward to the next period where it is either increased by another negative amount or reduced or eliminated by a positive amount, but not so as to cause the result to be positive. This process continues through each accounting period and if there is a negative amount remaining after applying it to the last period, that amount is the opening negative amount. The period for which this process must be carried out is extended if there is a losses amount of more than £50 million in an accounting period beginning within the six-year period ending on 18 July 2011, if that period would not otherwise fall within the normal six-year period. Where the period is extended in this way, the process must be carried out for the period of the losses amount and each subsequent accounting period up to and including that in which the election is made. [*CTA 2009, ss 18J, 18K; FA 2011, Sch 13 paras 4, 31, 34*].

(b) Alternatively, the company can elect for the opening negative amount to be streamed. If such an election is made then, in effect, the above provisions are applied separately to losses in a particular territory so that they do not delay the application of the exemption to other permanent establishments which would otherwise have no, or a shorter, transitional period. The election must be made at the same time as the exemption election and can only be revoked before the first accounting period to which the exemption election applies. It must specify the territories which are to be streamed. Where not all of the negative opening amount is streamed in this way, the residual amount must be eliminated against the residual profits amounts (i.e. for each accounting period, the total profits amount less the streamed profits amounts) in the same way. [*CTA 2009, ss 18L–18N; FA 2011, Sch 13 para 4*].

106 Group Relief

106.1 CALCULATION OF GROUP RELIEF

[*CTA 2010, ss 97–156*]

A Ltd has a subsidiary company, B Ltd, in which it owns 75% of the ordinary share capital. Relevant information for the year ended 31 March 2019 is as follows

		£
A Ltd	Trading profit	30,000
	Property income	10,000
	Chargeable gain	15,000
	Qualifying charitable donations	2,000
B Ltd	Trading loss	48,000
	Qualifying charitable donations	2,000

In addition, B Ltd has trading losses brought forward of £25,000 which arose in the year ended 31 March 2017.

Group relief is available as follows

	£	£
A Ltd		
Trading profit		30,000
Property income		10,000
Chargeable gain		15,000
		55,000
Deduct Charitable donation		(2,000)
Profits		53,000
Deduct Loss surrendered by B Ltd		(50,000)
Chargeable profits		£3,000
B Ltd		
Losses brought forward		25,000
Trading loss for the year	48,000	
Charitable donation	2,000	
	50,000	
Deduct Loss surrendered to A Ltd	(50,000)	—
Losses carried forward		£25,000

Note

(a) B Ltd's loss brought forward £25,000 cannot be surrendered as group relief for carried-forward losses as it arose before 1 April 2017. See further **106.6** below.

106.2 KINDS OF GROUP RELIEF

[*CTA 2010, s 99(1)(2), 100–104*]

A Ltd is an investment company which has three trading subsidiaries, B Ltd, C Ltd and D Ltd in which it owns 100% of the share capital. The companies have the following results for the two years ending 31 March 2017 and 31 March 2018.

			Year ended	Year ended
			31.3.17	31.3.18
			£	£
A Ltd	Profits		10,000	20,000
	Management expenses		(20,000)	(50,000)
B Ltd	Trading loss		(10,000)	(10,000)
	Property income (after capital allowances)			30,000
	Non-trading loan relationship deficit			(10,000)
C Ltd	Trading profit/(loss)		(10,000)	30,000
	Property income			1,000
	Capital allowances	— trading assets		(5,000)
		— property assets		(2,000)
	Management expenses			(40,000)
D Ltd	Profits			70,000

Group relief may be claimed for trading losses, management expenses and property business losses as follows

		Year ended	Year ended
		31.3.17	31.3.18
		£	£
A Ltd			
Profits		10,000	20,000
Management expenses		(20,000)	(50,000)
Excess management expenses		(10,000)	(30,000)
Deduct Surrendered to D Ltd		—	30,000
Management expenses carried forward to year ended 31.3.18	(note (a))	£(10,000)	—
B Ltd			
Trading loss brought forward		—	(10,000)
Trading loss		(10,000)	(10,000)
Trading loss carried forward		£(10,000)	—
			(20,000)
Deduct Surrendered to D Ltd	(note (b))		10,000

		Year ended	Year ended
		31.3.17	31.3.18
		£	£
Trading loss carried forward*			£(10,000)
*(not available for group relief or set-off against non-trading income as it arose before 1 April 2017)			
Non-trading loan relationship deficit	(note (b))		(10,000)
Deduct Surrendered to D Ltd			10,000
Profits chargeable to corporation tax			£30,000
C Ltd			
Trading loss brought forward		—	(10,000)
Trading loss		(10,000)	
Trading loss carried forward		£(10,000)	
Trading profit (£30,000) *less* trade capital allowances (£5,000)			25,000
			15,000
UK property income (£1,000) less UK property capital allowances (£2,000) less surrendered to D Ltd (£1,000)	(note (c))		—
			15,000
Management expenses (£40,000) less surrendered to D Ltd (£15,000)	(note (c))		(25,000)
Management expenses carried forward			£(10,000)
D Ltd			
Profits			70,000
Deduct Surrendered by A Ltd			(30,000)
Surrendered by B Ltd:			
– trading loss			(10,000)
– loan relationship deficit			(10,000)
Surrendered by C Ltd			
– UK property losses and management expenses			(16,000)
Profits chargeable to corporation tax			£4,000

Notes

(a) It is not possible in the year ended 31 March 2018 to deduct the excess management expenses brought forward from the year ended 31 March 2017 before deducting the current year management expenses to arrive at the amount available for group relief. The excess management expenses of £10,000 arising in the year ended 31 March

2017 are carried forward to the year ended 31 March 2018 but may not be surrendered and are, therefore, treated as carried forward from the year ended 31 March 2018. [*CTA 2010, ss 103, 1223*]. See **106.6** below for group relief for carried-forward losses (including management expenses arising after 31 March 2017).

(b) Although a company might normally relieve a trading loss and a non-trading loan relationship deficit against other income of the year before surrendering the loss or deficit, it is not obliged to do so. Thus, B Ltd could have reduced its chargeable profits in the year ended 31 March 2018 by £20,000 instead of surrendering that amount to D Ltd. [*CTA 2010, s 99(3)*].

(c) Qualifying charitable donations, UK property losses, management expenses and non-trading losses on intangible assets can be surrendered as group relief only to the extent that in aggregate they exceed the surrendering company's 'gross profits' (plus any CFC profits apportioned to it) for the accounting period. The 'gross profits' of the accounting period are, broadly, the profits of the period without any deduction for any amounts qualifying for group relief relating to that period or any amounts of any other period. [*CTA 2010, ss 99(4), 105; FA 2013, s 29*]. Therefore, the amount which C Ltd can surrender as group relief is restricted as follows

Management expenses	40,000
UK property loss	1,000
	41,000
Deduct gross profits (before *CTA 2010, s 45* relief)	25,000
Group relief	£16,000

The amount surrendered is taken to consist first of qualifying charitable donations, then of UK property losses, then of management expenses, and finally of losses on intangible assets. The amount surrendered by C Ltd is therefore identified as the UK property loss of £1,000 and management expenses of £15,000.

C Ltd's management expenses have been relieved as follows

Management expenses		40,000
Deduct	Management expenses relieved against income	(15,000)
	Surrendered to D Ltd	(15,000)
Excess management expenses carried forward		£10,000

106.3 'OVERLAPPING PERIODS'

[*CTA 2010, ss 138–142*]

D Ltd has several wholly owned subsidiaries, including E Ltd and F Ltd. D Ltd prepares accounts to 30 September, the other two companies to 31 December. Their results were

			£
D Ltd	year ended 30.9.18	loss	(240,000)
E Ltd	year ended 31.12.18	profit	120,000
F Ltd	year ended 31.12.18	profit	150,000

D Ltd makes a profit for the year ended 30.9.19. None of the companies have any brought-forward losses or other unrelieved amounts.

The overlapping period is the nine months to 30.9.18. The surrenderable amount of D Ltd's loss for the overlapping period is $^9/_{12}$ × £240,000 = £180,000. D Ltd surrenders the loss as follows

(i) Surrender to E Ltd — see note (a)

Surrender the smaller of:		£
Unused part of the surrenderable amount for the overlapping period		180,000
Unrelieved part of E Ltd's total profits for the overlapping period	$^9/_{12}$ × £120,000	90,000
Surrender		£90,000

(ii) Surrender to F Ltd — see note (b)

Surrender the smaller of:		£	£
Unused part of the surrenderable amount for the overlapping period			
surrenderable amount		180,000	
deduct amount surrendered to E Ltd		(90,000)	90,000
Unrelieved part of F Ltd's total profits for the overlapping period	$^9/_{12}$ × £150,000		112,500
Surrender			£90,000

Notes

(a) The effect of the rules is to restrict the overall surrender by D Ltd to $^9/_{12}$ of its loss for the year ended 30 September 2018.

(b) Where more than one claim relates to the whole or part of the same overlapping period, the claims must be considered in the order in which they are made (determined by the date on which the claim ceases to be capable of being withdrawn). Where, as in this case, two or more claims are deemed to be made at the same time, they are treated as made in such order as the companies involved may elect. In the absence of such an election, HMRC may direct. [*CTA 2010, ss 139–141*].

106.4 COMPANIES JOINING OR LEAVING THE GROUP

[*CTA 2010, ss 138–142*]

On 1 April 2018 B Ltd was held as to 90% by A Ltd and 10% by a non-resident.

On 1 September 2018 C Ltd became a 75% subsidiary of A Ltd.

On 31 December 2018 A Ltd sells 30% of the shares in B Ltd (retaining 60%). A Ltd, B Ltd and C Ltd all prepare accounts to 31 March each year. During the year ended 31 March 2019 the results of the companies are as follows

A Ltd	Profit	£60,000
B Ltd	Loss	£(240,000)
C Ltd	Profit	£30,000

None of the companies have any carried-forward loses or other unrelieved amounts.

Group relief for the loss sustained by B Ltd in the year ended 31.3.19 is available as follows

During the year ended 31 March 2019, B Ltd was a '75% subsidiary' of A Ltd only in the nine-month period 1 April 2018 to 31 December 2018. The period during which both B Ltd and C Ltd were '75% subsidiaries' of A Ltd was the four months 1 September 2018 to 31 December 2018.

Calculation of loss relieved
(i) Against profits of A Ltd

Smaller of:		
Unused part of the surrenderable amount for the overlapping period	$^9/_{12}$ × £240,000	£180,000
Unrelieved part of A Ltd's total profits for the overlapping period	$^9/_{12}$ × £60,000	£45,000
Therefore, loss relieved		£45,000

(ii) Against profits of C Ltd

Smaller of:			
Unused part of the surrenderable amount for the overlapping period			
surrenderable amount	$^4/_{12}$ × £240,000	80,000	
deduct proportion of amount surrendered to A Ltd relating to overlapping period	$^4/_9$ × £45,000	(20,000)	£60,000
Unrelieved part of C Ltd's total profits for the overlapping period	$^4/_{12}$ × £ 30,000		10,000
Therefore, loss relieved			£10,000

Summary

	A Ltd	B Ltd	C Ltd
	£	£	£
Profit/(loss)	60,000	(240,000)	30,000
Group relief (claim)/surrender	(45,000)	55,000	(10,000)
Chargeable profit/(loss carried forward)	£15,000	£(185,000)	£20,000

Notes

(a) When a company joins or leaves a group, the profit or loss is apportioned on a time basis unless this method would work unreasonably or unjustly. In the latter event a just and reasonable method of apportionment must be used. [*CTA 2010, s 141(3)*].

(b) See notes (a) and (b) to **106.3** above.

106.5 RELATIONSHIP TO OTHER RELIEFS

[*CTA 2010, ss 37, 45, 45A, 99, 105*]

B Ltd is a subsidiary of A Ltd and commenced trading on 1 April 2004. Both companies prepare accounts to 31 March each year. The results for the three years ended 31 March 2019 were as follows.

				£
A Ltd	Year ended 31 March	2017	Loss	(4,000)
		2018	Loss	(3,000)
		2019	Loss	(5,000)
B Ltd	Year ended 31 March	2017	Loss	(5,000)
		2018	Profit	10,000
		2019	Loss	(20,000)
		2017	UK property income	1,000
		2018	UK property income	1,000
		2019	UK property income	1,000
		2019	Chargeable gains	5,000

The losses can be used as follows

	Year ended 31.3.17	Year ended 31.3.18	Year ended 31.3.19
	£	£	£
B Ltd			
Trading profit/(loss)	(5,000)	10,000	(20,000)
Trading income	—	10,000	—
CTA 2010, s 45 loss relief	—	(4,000)	—
UK property income	1,000	1,000	1,000
Income	1,000	7,000	1,000
Chargeable gains	—	—	5,000
CTA 2010, s 37(3)(a) loss relief	(1,000)	—	(6,000)
Profits subject to group relief	—	7,000	—
Losses surrendered by A Ltd	—	(3,000)	—
	—	4,000	—
CTA 2010, s 37(3)(b) loss relief	—	(4,000)	—
Chargeable profits	—	—	—
Losses brought forward	—	(4,000)	—
Loss of the period	(5,000)	—	(20,000)
CTA 2010, s 45 relief	—	4,000	—
CTA 2010, s 37(3)(a) relief	1,000	—	6,000
CTA 2010, s 37(3)(b) relief	—	—	4,000
Losses carried forward	£(4,000)	—	£(10,000)
A Ltd			
Trading loss	4,000	3,000	5,000
Deduct Surrendered to B Ltd	—	(3,000)	—
Loss for the period	4,000	—	5,000
Loss brought forward	—	4,000	4,000
Loss carried forward	£4,000	£4,000	£9,000

Note

(a) The trading losses arising before 1 April 2017 which are not utilised or group relieved in the current period are to be carried forward and utilised against future trading profits of the company. Pre 1 April 2017 losses that are carried forward cannot be group relieved. [*CTA 2010, s 45*].

(b) The trading losses arising on or after 1 April 2017 which are not utilised or group relieved in the current period are to be carried forward and can be utilised against future total profits of the company (not just trading profits) or group relieved as carried forward losses. [*CTA 2010, s 45A*].

(c) Losses brought forward from previous periods must be used before claiming group relief, as must losses incurred in the current period and available for set-off under *CTA 2010, s 37(3)(a)*. However, group relief takes priority to losses carried back from subsequent periods under *CTA 2010, s 37(3)(b)*.

106.6 GROUP RELIEF FOR CARRIED-FORWARD LOSSES

[*CTA 2010, ss 188AA–EK; F(No 2)A 2017, Sch 4 paras 23, 190–192*].

A Ltd has a subsidiary company, B Ltd, in which it owns 75% of the ordinary share capital. The companies commence trading on 1 April 2017 and have the following results for the two years ending 31 March 2018 and 31 March 2019.

		Year ended	Year ended
		31.3.18	31.3.19
		£	£
A Ltd	Trade profits/(loss)	(20,000)	110,000
	Property income		30,000
B Ltd	Trade profits/(loss)	(150,000)	10,000

Group relief may be claimed for B Ltd's carried-forward trade loss as follows.

	Year ended	Year ended
	31.3.18	31.3.19
	£	£
A Ltd		
Trade profit/(loss)	(20,000)	110,000
Property income	—	30,000
	—	140,000
Deduct trade loss carried forward	—	(20,000)
Trade loss surrendered by B Ltd	—	(120,000)
Total taxable profits	£Nil	£Nil
B Ltd		
Trade profit/(loss)	(150,000)	10,000
Deduct trade loss carried forward	(150,000)	(10,000)
Total taxable profits	£(150,000)	£Nil

	Year ended	Year ended
	31.3.18	31.3.19
	£	£

D Ltd loss memoranda

	Year ended
	31.3.18
	£
Trade loss	150,000
Carried forward against total profits of y/e 31.3.19	(10,000)
Surrendered to A Ltd for y/e 31.3.19	(120,000)
Unrelieved loss c/fwd to y/e 31.3.20	£20,000

Notes

(a) The following carried-forward amounts can be surrendered as group relief for carried-forward losses for accounting periods beginning on or after 1 April 2017:

- post-1 April 2017 non-trading deficits from loan relationships;
- non-trading losses on intangible fixed assets;
- expenses of management of investment business;
- post-1 April 2017 trade losses; and
- losses of a UK property business.

Where an accounting period straddles 1 April 2017 it is treated for this purpose as two separate accounting periods, the first ending on 31 March 2017 and the second beginning on 1 April 2017. Apportionments between the two accounting periods are made on a time basis unless that would produce an unjust or unreasonable result, in which case the apportionment must be made on a just and reasonable basis.

(b) A company can only surrender carried-forward losses that it is unable to deduct from its own profits during the accounting period of surrender. Similarly, a company can only claim group relief for carried-forward losses after it has used its own carried-forward losses to the full extent possible.

(c) Group relief for carry-forward losses is subject to restriction where the total set-off of carried-forward amounts exceeds £5,000,000. See **114.7** LOSSES.

106.7 CONSORTIUM RELIEF

(A) Loss by company owned by consortium

[CTA 2010, ss 130, 132, 133]

On 1 April 2018 the share capital of E Ltd was owned as follows

	%
A Ltd	40
B Ltd	40
C Ltd	20
	100

All the companies were UK resident for tax purposes.

During the year ended 31 March 2019 the following events took place

On 1.7.18	D Ltd bought	20% from A Ltd
On 1.10.18	C Ltd bought	10% from B Ltd

The companies had the following results for the year ended 31 March 2019

		£
A Ltd	Profit	40,000
B Ltd	Profit	33,000
C Ltd	Profit	10,000
D Ltd	Profit	18,000
E Ltd	Loss	(100,000)

All the member companies claim consortium relief in respect of the loss sustained by E Ltd. The companies elect that the claims be treated as made first by A Ltd, then by B Ltd, C Ltd and finally by D Ltd. For each company the consortium relief available is the lowest of the following three amounts:

(i) the unused part of the surrenderable amount for the overlapping period;

(ii) the unrelieved part of the claimant company's total profits for the overlapping period; and

(iii) the surrenderable amount for the overlapping period multiplied by the claimant member's share in the consortium in that period.

[*CTA 2010, ss 139, 140, 143*]

A Ltd

The overlapping period is the twelve months to 31.3.19. The amounts are

	£
(i)	100,000
(ii)	40,000
(iii) 100,000 × 25% (40% × $^{3}/_{12}$ + 20% × $^{9}/_{12}$)	25,000
Therefore, loss relieved	£25,000

B Ltd

The overlapping period is the twelve months to 31.3.19. The amounts are

	£	£
(i) Surrenderable amount	100,000	
Deduct loss previously surrendered	(25,000)	75,000
(ii)		33,000
(iii) 100,000 × 35% (40% × $^6/_{12}$ + 30% × $^6/_{12}$)		35,000
Therefore, loss relieved		£33,000

C Ltd

The overlapping period is the twelve months to 31.3.19. The amounts are

	£	£
(i) Surrenderable amount	100,000	
Deduct losses previously surrendered (£25,000 + £33,000)	(58,000)	42,000
(ii)		10,000
(iii) 100,000 × 25% (20% × $^6/_{12}$ + 30% × $^6/_{12}$)		25,000
Therefore, loss relieved		£10,000

D Ltd

As D Ltd only became a member of the consortium on 1.7.18, the overlapping period is the nine months to 31.3.19. The amounts are

	£	£
(i) Surrenderable amount 100,000 × $^9/_{12}$	75,000	
Deduct $^9/_{12}$ × losses previously surrendered (£25,000 + £33,000 + £10,000)	(51,000)	24,000
(ii) 18,000 × $^9/_{12}$		13,500
(iii) 100,000 × $^9/_{12}$ × 20%		15,000
Therefore, loss relieved		£13,500

Summary

	A Ltd	B Ltd	C Ltd	D Ltd
	£	£	£	£
Profits for the year ended 31.3.19	40,000	33,000	10,000	18,000
Deduct Loss surrendered by E Ltd	(25,000)	(33,000)	(10,000)	(13,500)
Chargeable profits	£15,000	—	—	£4,500

E Ltd

		£	£
Loss for the year ended 31.3.19			100,000
Deduct Loss surrendered to	A Ltd	(25,000)	
	B Ltd	(33,000)	
	C Ltd	(10,000)	
	D Ltd	(13,500)	(81,500)
Not available for consortium relief			£18,500

(B) **Loss by company owned by consortium: claim by member of consortium company's group**

[*CTA 2010, ss 133, 146, 148*]

A Ltd owns 100% of the share capital of B Ltd

B Ltd owns 40% of the share capital of D Ltd

C Ltd owns 60% of the share capital of D Ltd

D Ltd owns 100% of the share capital of E Ltd

D Ltd owns 100% of the share capital of F Ltd

This can be shown as follows

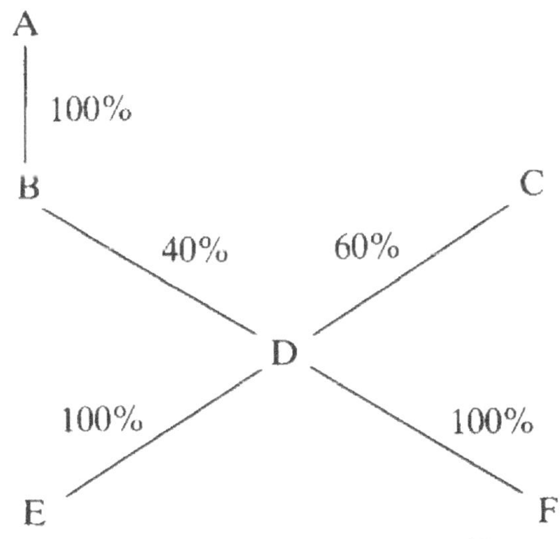

There are two groups, A and B, and D, E and F. D is owned by a consortium of B and C. This relationship has existed for a number of years with all companies having the same accounting periods. None of the companies has any losses brought forward.

The companies have the following results for year ended 31 July 2018

A Ltd	£100,000	profit
B Ltd	£(30,000)	loss
C Ltd	£Nil	
D Ltd	£(20,000)	loss
E Ltd	£10,000	profit
F Ltd	£(3,000)	loss

E Ltd claims group relief as follows

			£	£
Profit				10,000
Deduct	Group relief: loss surrendered by F Ltd	(note (b))	(3,000)	
	Group relief: loss surrendered by D Ltd	(note (b))	(7,000)	(10,000)
				—

A Ltd can claim group relief and consortium relief as follows

			£	£
Profit				100,000
Deduct	Group relief: loss surrendered by B Ltd	(note (c))	(30,000)	
	Consortium relief: loss surrendered by D Ltd	(note (d))	(5,200)	(35,200)
Chargeable profit				£64,800

Notes

(a) Where a company owned by a consortium is also a member of a group, its losses may be surrendered partly as group relief and partly as consortium relief.

(b) Where a loss of a company owned by a consortium or of a company within its group may be used both as group relief and consortium relief, the consortium relief is restricted. In determining the amount of consortium relief available, it is assumed that the maximum possible group relief is deducted after taking account of any other actual group relief claims within the consortium owned company's group. [*CTA 2010, s 148*]. As F Ltd has surrendered losses of £3,000 to E Ltd, D Ltd can only surrender £7,000 to E Ltd as group relief. The surrenderable amount for the period for the purpose of consortium relief is restricted to the balance of D Ltd's loss, i.e. £13,000. If E Ltd had not claimed £3,000 group relief for F Ltd's loss, D Ltd could have surrendered £10,000 to E Ltd by way of group relief and this would have reduced D Ltd's surrenderable amount for consortium relief purposes to £10,000.

(c) Group relief available to A Ltd is the lower of £100,000 and £30,000.

(d) Consortium relief available to A Ltd is the lower of £13,000 (the unused surrenderable amount for the period), £70,000 (its unrelieved profits for the period (£100,000 less £30,000 group relief previously claimed) and £5,200 (40% of £13,000). The relief available to A Ltd is the same as that which B Ltd could have claimed if it had had sufficient profits. A Ltd could also have claimed consortium relief in respect of F Ltd's loss if that had exceeded the £10,000 necessary to cover E Ltd's profit. [*CTA 2010, s 133(1), 146*].

(C) Loss by subsidiary of company owned by consortium

[*CTA 2010, ss 143, 151(4), 153(3)*]

Throughout 2018 and 2019 the share capital of E Ltd was owned as follows

	%
A Ltd	35
B Ltd	30
C Ltd	25
D Ltd	10
	100

E Ltd owned 90% of the share capital of F Ltd, a trading company. The companies had the following results for the year ended 31 March 2019.

		£
A Ltd	Profit	100,000
B Ltd	Loss	(40,000)
C Ltd	Profit	30,000
D Ltd	Profit	80,000
E Ltd	Profit	40,000
F Ltd	Loss	(240,000)

All the above companies were UK resident for tax purposes. Group relief of £40,000 of the loss sustained by F Ltd is claimed by E Ltd (note (c)).

Consortium relief for the loss sustained by F Ltd would be available as follows

	A Ltd	B Ltd	C Ltd	D Ltd
	£	£	£	£
Profits for the year ended 31.3.19	100,000	—	30,000	80,000
Deduct Loss surrendered by				
F Ltd (note (a))	(70,000)	—	(30,000)	(20,000)
Chargeable profits	£30,000	—	—	£60,000

			Losses
F Ltd		£	£
Loss for the year ended 31.3.19			240,000
Deduct Loss surrendered to E Ltd			(40,000)
Available for consortium relief			200,000
Deduct Loss surrendered to	A Ltd	(70,000)	
	C Ltd	(30,000)	
	D Ltd	(20,000)	(120,000)
Losses carried forward			£80,000

Notes

(a) Loss relief for each consortium member is the lower of

(i) the unused part of the surrenderable amount for the year;

(ii) the unrelieved part of the claimant company's total profits for the year; and

(iii) the surrenderable amount for the year multiplied by the claimant member's share in the consortium.

In this instance, the order in which the claims are deemed to be made does not affect the amounts which can be claimed, as (i) is greater than (ii) and (iii) in all cases.

(b) The surrenderable amount (see note (c)) multiplied by the share in the consortium appropriate to each member is

	%	£
A Ltd	35	70,000
B Ltd	30	60,000
C Ltd	25	50,000
D Ltd	10	20,000
	100	£200,000

(c) The loss available for consortium relief (the surrenderable amount) is reduced by any potentially available group relief. See also notes (a) and (b) to (B) above.

(D) Loss by consortium member

[*CTA 2010, ss 132, 144*]

A Ltd, B Ltd, C Ltd and D Ltd have for many years held 40%, 30%, 20% and 10% respectively of the ordinary share capital of E Ltd. All five companies are UK resident and have always previously had taxable profits. However, for the year ending 30 June 2018 D Ltd has a tax loss of £100,000, followed by taxable profits of £40,000 for the subsequent year. E Ltd's taxable profits are £80,000 and £140,000 for the two years ending 31 December 2017 and 31 December 2018 respectively.

With the consent of A Ltd, B Ltd and C Ltd, D Ltd can (if it wishes) surrender the following part of its loss of £100,000 to E Ltd (assuming no other group/consortium relief claims are made involving either company)

Overlapping period 1.7.17 to 31.12.17		
Unused part of the surrenderable amount for the overlapping period	6/12 × £100,000	£50,000
Unrelieved part of E Ltd's total profits for the overlapping period	6/12 × £80,000	£40,000
E Ltd's total profits for the overlapping period multiplied by D Ltd's share in consortium	6/12 × £80,000 × 10%	£4,000
Overlapping period 1.1.18 to 30.6.18		
Unused part of the surrenderable amount for the overlapping period	6/12 × £100,000	£50,000
Unrelieved part of E Ltd's total profits for the overlapping period	6/12 × £140,000	£70,000
E Ltd's total profits for the overlapping period multiplied by D Ltd's share in consortium	6/12 × £140,000 × 10%	£7,000

The lowest figures for the two periods are £4,000 and £7,000.

Therefore, E Ltd can claim £4,000 of D Ltd's loss against its own profits for the year ended 31.12.17 and £7,000 against its profits for the year ending 31.12.18.

107 Income Tax in Relation to a Company

107.1 ACCOUNTING FOR INCOME TAX ON RECEIPTS AND PAYMENTS

[*ITA 2007, ss 874–938; CTA 2010, s 967; FA 2016, ss 39–41, Sch 6; FA 2017, Sch 5*]

S Ltd, a company with two related 51% group companies, prepares accounts each year to 31 October. During the two years ending 31 October 2017 and 31 October 2018 it pays and receives several sums (not being interest) from which basic rate income tax is deducted.

The following items are shown net

	Receipts (£)	Payments (£)
21.12.16		8,000
4.1.17	4,000	
9.8.17	8,000	
24.10.17	12,000	
25.3.18		8,000
14.8.18		9,600

The adjusted profits (*before* taking account of the gross equivalents of the above amounts) were

Year ended 31.10.17	£630,000
Year ended 31.10.18	£860,000

S Ltd will use the following figures in connection with the CT61 returns rendered to HMRC and will also be able to set off against its corporation tax liability the income tax suffered as shown

Return period	Payments	Receipts	Cumulative payments less receipts	Income tax paid/ (repaid) with return
Year ended 31.10.17	£	£	£	£
1.11.16 to 31.12.16	8,000		8,000	2,000
1.1.17 to 31.3.17		4,000	4,000	(1,000)
1.4.17 to 30.6.17 (No return)			4,000	
1.7.17 to 30.9.17		8,000	(4,000)	(1,000)
1.10.17 to 31.10.17		12,000	(16,000)	
				—

Return period		Payments	Receipts	Cumulative payments less receipts	Income tax paid/ (repaid) with return
Year ended 31.10.18					
1.11.17 to 31.12.17	(No return)				
1.1.18 to 31.3.18		8,000		8,000	2,000
1.4.18 to 30.6.18	(No return)			8,000	
1.7.18 to 30.9.18	(No return)	9,600		17,600	2,400
1.10.18 to 31.10.18	(No return)			17,600	
					£4,400

Taxable profits

	Year ended 31.10.17	Year ended 31.10.18
	£	£
Adjusted profits as stated	630,000	860,000
Add Cumulative receipts		
£16,000 + tax £4,000	20,000	
Deduct Cumulative payments		
£17,600 + tax of £4,400		(22,000)
Taxable profits	£650,000	£838,000

Tax payable

		Year ended 31.10.17	Year ended 31.10.18
		£	£
CT @ 20%/19% on profits		126,209	159,220
Deduct Income tax suffered	(note (a))	(4,000)	
Net liability		£122,209	£159,220

Notes

(a) This represents tax suffered on receipts, less that which has been offset against tax deducted from payments.

	£
Tax on receipts	6,000
Tax deducted from payments and recovered from HMRC	2,000
	£4,000

(b) Payments made by companies under the following provisions do not have to be made under deduction of income tax where the company reasonably believes that, at the time of payment, the recipient is a UK company (or a partnership of such companies), a non-UK resident company trading in the UK through a permanent establishment and in computing whose profits the payment falls to be brought into account or one of certain specified bodies or persons. The provisions concerned are:

(i) *ITA 2007, s 874(2)* (payments of yearly interest);

(ii) *ITA 2007, s 889(4)* (payments in respect of building society securities);

(iii) *ITA 2007, s 901(4)* (annual payments by persons other than companies);

(iv) *ITA 2007, s 903(7)* (patent royalties);

(v) *ITA 2007, s 906(5)* (royalty payments etc. where the owner lives abroad);

(vi) *ITA 2007, s 910(2)* (proceeds of sale of patent rights paid to non-UK residents);

(vii) *ITA 2007, s 919(2)* (manufactured interest on UK securities: payments to UK residents etc.); and

(viii) *ITA 2007, s 928(2)* (chargeable payments connected with exempt distributions).

108 Intangible Assets

108.1 DEBITS AND CREDITS

[*CTA 2009, 726–744*]

(A) Writing-down on accounting basis

On 1 April 2015, Oval Ltd purchased an intangible asset from an unrelated company, Edgbaston Ltd, for £100,000. The asset is to be used for trading purposes and has a remaining useful economic life of 15 years. The cost of the asset is capitalised in Oval Ltd's accounts and in accordance with generally accepted accounting practice is amortised on a straight-line basis over the remaining 15 year life. On 1 April 2018, the company sells the asset to another unrelated company, Riverside Ltd, for £150,000.

Oval Ltd will bring into account for tax purposes the following debits and credits in respect of the intangible asset.

	£
Y/e 31.3.16	
Cost of asset	100,000
Debit for year (1/15 of cost)	(6,667)
WDV at 31.3.16	93,333
Y/e 31.3.17	
Debit for year (1/15 of cost)	(6,667)
WDV at 31.3.17	86,666
Y/e 31.3.18	
Debit for year (1/15 of cost)	(6,666)
WDV at 31.3.18	£80,000
Y/e 31.3.19	
Proceeds of realisation	150,000
Less Tax written-down value	(80,000)
Taxable credit	£70,000

As the asset was held for trading purposes, the debits of £6,667 for each of the years ended 31 March 2016, 2017 and 2018 are allowable trading deductions, and the credit of £70,000 for the year ended 31 March 2019 is a trading receipt.

Notes

(a) See **108.3** below for the rollover relief available on reinvestment of disposal proceeds in new intangible assets.

(b) No debits, other than realisation debits, are allowable in respect of goodwill or certain other customer-related intangible assets which are acquired on or after 8 July 2015. Realisation debits arising on such assets are treated as non-trading debits. [*CTA 2009, s 816A; F(No 2)A 2015, s 33*]. Similar restrictions also applied, in certain circumstances, where such assets were acquired from a related individual on or after 3 December 2014. [*CTA 2009, ss 849B–849D; FA 2015, s 26; F(No 2)A 2015, s 33(7)*].

(B) Writing-down at fixed rate

M Ltd is a UK subsidiary of a multi-national group and prepares its accounts under IFRS. On 1 January 2014, M Ltd, which draws up accounts each year to 31 December, purchases the trade of X Ltd, an unrelated company. It is agreed that, of the purchase price, £500,000 is allocated to X Ltd's brand name, which is particularly well established in the UK and the USA. The brand name is considered to have an indefinite economic life and accordingly the expenditure is not amortised in M Ltd's accounts. Before 31 December 2017 M Ltd elects to write down the cost at the fixed rate of 4% per year. On 1 January 2017, M Ltd sells its rights to the brand name in the USA for £400,000 to Z plc, an unrelated company. £250,000 of the book value of the brand name in the accounts is set off against the disposal, giving an accounting profit of £150,000, and leaving the remaining book value as £250,000. On 1 January 2019, M Ltd sells the remaining rights in the brand name to Z plc for £200,000.

M Ltd must bring into account in calculating its trading profits the following debits and credits in respect of the brand name.

	£
Y/e 31.12.15	
Cost of brand name	500,000
Debit for year (4% of cost)	(20,000)
WDV at 31.12.15	480,000
Y/e 31.12.16	
Debit for year (4% of cost)	(20,000)
WDV at 31.12.16	£460,000
Y/e 31.12.17	
Part-realisation proceeds	400,000
Less Adjusted WDV (note (b))	(230,000)
Gain on part realisation (credit)	£170,000
Adjusted WDV of asset after part realisation (note (c))	230,000
Debit for year (4% of cost of remaining asset (note (d))	(10,000)
WDV at 31.12.17	220,000
Y/e 31.12.18	
Debit for year (4% of remaining cost)	(10,000)
WDV at 31.12.18	£210,000

Y/e 31.12.19	
Realisation proceeds	200,000
Less WDV at 31.12.18	(210,000)
Loss on realisation (debit)	£(10,000)

Notes

(a) A company may elect for the tax cost of an intangible asset to be written down for tax purposes at a fixed rate. The election must be made in writing to HMRC within two years after the end of the accounting period in which the asset is created or acquired by the company and is irrevocable. Where the election is made, a debit of 4% of the cost (or, if less, the balance of the written-down value) is brought into account in each accounting period beginning with that in which the expenditure is incurred. The debit is proportionately reduced for accounting periods of less than twelve months. [*CTA 2009, ss 730, 731*].

(b) On the part realisation of an asset, a proportion of the written-down value of the asset is deducted from the proceeds to arrive at the amount of the credit or debit arising. The proportion is that given by dividing the reduction in accounting value (i.e. the accounting value immediately before the realisation less the accounting value immediately afterwards) by the accounting value immediately before the realisation. [*CTA 2009, s 737*]. In this case, the reduction in accounting value is (£500,000 − £250,000) = £250,000, and the accounting value immediately before the realisation is £500,000. The amount to be deducted from the proceeds in this case is therefore £460,000 × (£250,000/£500,000) = £230,000.

(c) Following a part realisation, the written-down value of the remaining part of the asset is reduced to that proportion of it that is equal to the accounting value immediately after the realisation divided by the accounting value immediately before the realisation. [*CTA 2009, s 744*]. In this case, therefore, the adjusted written-down value is £460,000 × (£250,000/£500,000) = £230,000.

(d) Following a part realisation, the fixed rate debit is calculated by reference to 4% of the value of the asset recognised for accounting purposes immediately after the realisation (plus the cost of any subsequent capitalised expenditure on the asset). [*CTA 2009, s 731(6)*].

108.2 NON-TRADING LOSS ON INTANGIBLE ASSETS

[*CTA 2009, ss 751–753; F(No 2)A 2017, Sch 4 paras 5, 190*]

A Ltd is an investment company drawing up accounts each year to 31 March. The following figures are relevant for the two years ended 31 March 2018 and 2019.

	Y/e 31.3.18	Y/e 31.3.19
	£	£
UK property income	15,000	16,000
Income from non-trading loan relationships	5,000	20,000
Overseas income (foreign tax paid £3,600)	20,000	—

	Y/e 31.3.18	Y/e 31.3.19
	£	£
Management expenses	(5,000)	(5,000)
Non-trading profit/(loss) on intangible fixed assets	(55,000)	11,000

A Ltd wishes to make the most tax-efficient use of the non-trading loss, and so makes a claim to set off £15,000 against profits of the year ended 31 March 2018 under *CTA 2009, s 753(1)*. The corporation tax computations for the two years ended 31 March 2019 are as follows.

	£
Y/e 31.3.18	
UK property income	15,000
Income from non-trading loan relationships	5,000
overseas income	20,000
	40,000
Deduct Management expenses	(5,000)
Non-trading loss	(15,000)
Profits chargeable to CT	£20,000
Corporation tax: £20,000 @ 19%	3,800
Deduct Double tax relief	(3,600)
Corporation tax payable	200

	£
Y/e 31.3.19	
UK property income	16,000
Income from non-trading loan relationships	20,000
Income from non-trading intangible assets (see below)	11,000
	47,000
Deduct Management expenses	(5,000)
Non-trading loss	(40,000)
Profits chargeable to CT	£2,000
Corporation tax: £2,000 @ 19%	£380

Use of non-trading loss

	£
Loss y/e 31.3.18	55,000
Set-off against profits for y/e 31.3.18	(15,000)
Set-off against profits for y/e 31.3.19	(40,000)
Carry-forward as non-trading loss	Nil

Notes

(a) A non-trading loss on intangible fixed assets for an accounting period may be set off against the company's total profits for the period. The company must make a claim for relief within two years after the end of the accounting period, or within such further period as HMRC may allow. Relief for the whole or part of the loss may be claimed in this way. [*CTA 2009, s 753(1)(2)*].

(b) A non-trading loss may alternatively be surrendered as group relief. See **106.2** GROUP RELIEF.

(c) To the extent that a non-trading loss is not set off against profits of the current accounting period or surrendered as group relief, it is carried forward to the next accounting period and treated as a non-trading loss of that period. [*CTA 2009, s 753(3)*]. The carried-forward loss is available for set-off against profits of that accounting period or alternatively may be surrendered as group relief for carried-forward losses (see **106.6** GROUP RELIEF). A loss cannot be carried forward to the accounting period in which the company ceases to be a company with investment business (or to any subsequent accounting period).

(d) The rules for the carry forward of losses illustrated in this example apply to accounting periods beginning on or after 1 April 2017. For this purpose, where an accounting period straddles that date it is treated as two separate accounting periods, the first ending on 31 March 2017 and the second beginning on 1 April 2017. Apportionments between the two accounting periods are made on a time basis unless that would produce an unjust or unreasonable result, in which case the apportionment must be made on a just and reasonable basis [*F(No.2)A 2017, Sch 4 para 190*]. Previously, to the extent that a non-trading loss was not set off against profits of the current accounting period or surrendered as group relief, it was carried forward to the next accounting period and treated as a non-trading debit of that period. The carried-forward loss was therefore included in the computation of any profit or loss on intangible fixed assets for that period. Where a loss resulted, the whole loss was available for set-off against total profits of the period. However, the debit carried forward had to be excluded from the loss for the period in calculating any amount available for surrender as group relief. [*CTA 2010, s 104(2)*].

(e) The carry-forward of non-trading losses is subject to restriction where the total set-off of carried-forward amounts exceeds £5,000,000. See **114.7** LOSSES.

108.3 ROLLOVER RELIEF ON REINVESTMENT

[*CTA 2009, ss 754–763*]

Oval Ltd, the company in **108.1(A)** above, purchases a new intangible fixed asset (asset 2) on 1 April 2019 for £165,000 and claims rollover relief in respect of the asset disposed of in that example (referred to below as asset 1).

The effect of the claim for tax purposes is as follows.

	£
Disposal proceeds of asset 1	150,000
Tax cost of asset 1	(100,000)
Rollover relief available	£50,000

The taxable credit on disposal of asset 1 for the year ended 31.3.19 is therefore recalculated as follows

		£
Proceeds of realisation		150,000
Less	Tax written-down value	(80,000)
	Amount rolled over	(50,000)
Taxable credit		£20,000

The cost for tax purposes of asset 2 is adjusted as follows

	£
Cost of asset 2	165,000
Less amount rolled over on asset 1	(50,000)
Adjusted cost for tax purposes	£115,000

Notes

(a) A company which realises a chargeable intangible asset and incurs expenditure on other chargeable intangible assets within the period beginning one year before the date of realisation and ending three years after that date, may, subject to meeting detailed conditions, claim rollover relief under *CTA 2009, Pt 8 Ch 7*. The claim must specify the old assets to which the claim relates, the expenditure on other assets by reference to which relief is claimed, and the amount of relief claimed. [*CTA 2009, s 757*].

(b) On making the claim, the proceeds of realisation of the old asset and the cost recognised for tax purposes of the other assets are both reduced by the amount available for relief. Where the expenditure on the other assets is equal to or exceeds the realisation proceeds the amount available for relief is the excess of the proceeds over the tax cost of the original asset. Where the expenditure on other assets is less than the realisation proceeds, the amount available for relief is the excess of the expenditure over the tax cost of the original asset. The relief does not affect the tax treatment of the other parties to the transactions. [*CTA 2009, s 758*].

(c) In this case, the relief available is £50,000, leaving £20,000 of the gain on realisation chargeable. This effectively recovers the debits previously given in respect of the asset (£6,667 × 3 = £20,000, see **108.1(A)** above). Only the profit element is rolled over.

109 Interest on Overpaid Tax

[*ICTA 1988, ss 825, 826; FA 1989, s 178; FA 1991, Sch 15 para 22, 23; SI 1989 No 1297; SI 1993 No 2212*]

109.1 (A) REPAYMENT OF TAX: GENERAL

[*SI 1998 No 3175; SI 1998 No 3176*]

X Ltd prepares accounts to 31 December. On 15 June 2018 it submits its tax return for the year ended 31 December 2017 showing a corporation tax liability for the period of £14,000, and accompanied by a payment of £7,000. On 1 October 2018 it makes a further payment of £7,000. It subsequently submits an amended return showing a reduced liability of £12,500, and £1,500 is repaid to the company on 1 December 2018.

X Ltd will be entitled to interest on overpaid tax, calculated as follows

		£
15.6.18 to 30.9.18	£7,000 × 0.5% × $^{108}/_{365}$ =	10.36
1.10.18 to 30.11.18	£1,500 × 0.5% × $^{61}/_{365}$ =	1.26
Total interest		£11.62

Notes

(a) The rate of interest on corporation tax paid early is the special (usually) higher rate applying to overpaid instalment payments (see (B) below). The special rate does not apply to overpaid tax after nine months after the end of the accounting period, from which date the (usually) lower normal rate applies. At the time of writing the two rates were the same: 0.5%. This is the minimum possible rate.

(b) The unified repayment interest provisions of *FA 2009, s 102, Sch 54* do not yet apply to corporation tax.

(B) REPAYMENT OF TAX: INSTALMENT PAYMENTS

[*SI 1998 No 3175; SI 1998 No 3176; SI 2017 No 1072*]

Z Ltd has no related 51% group companies and had taxable profits in excess of £1,500,000 for the year ended 31 March 2016. For the year ending 31 March 2017, Z Ltd pays £143,000 for the first instalment on 30 September 2016, this being equivalent to a quarter of its estimated corporation tax liability of £572,000. The same amount is paid on the due dates for the second and third instalments and on 5 July 2017 for the fourth instalment. On 3 September 2018, the tax liability is agreed at £506,800 and £65,200 is repaid to the company on 22 September 2018.

The interest on overpaid tax is calculated as follows

Instalments due on quarter dates £506,800 × $^1/_4$ = £126,700

Interest on overpaid tax

	£
14 October 2016 to 13 January 2017	
143,000 − 126,700 = £16,300 @ 0.5% × $^{91}/_{365}$	20.32
14 January 2017 to 13 April 2017	
286,000 − 253,400 = £32,600 @ 0.5% × $^{90}/_{365}$	40.19
14 April 2017 to 5 July 2017	
429,000 − 380,100 = £48,900 @ 0.5% × $^{83}/_{365}$	55.60
6 July 2017 to 13 July 2017	
572,000 −380,100 = £191,900 @ 0.5% × $^{8}/_{365}$	21.03
14 July 2017 to 31 December 2017	
572,000 − 506,800 = £65,200 @ 0.5% × $^{169}/_{365}$	150.94
1 January 2018 to 21 September 2018	
572,000 − 506,800 = £65,200 @ 0.5% × $^{264}/_{365}$	235.79
	£523.87

Notes

(a) Interest will not be payable before the due date of the first instalment.

(b) A special (usually) higher rate of interest for instalment payments applies from the date the excess arises to the earlier of nine months after the end of the accounting period and the date the tax is repaid. Interest is calculated using the usually lower normal rate from the date of nine months after the end of the accounting period to the date of issue of the repayment order. At the time of writing the two rates were the same: 0.5%. This is the minimum possible rate.

(c) Debit interest works in the same way as the credit interest illustrated in this example (see **110.1(C)**). For example, had Z Ltd paid less than the amount of tax due at any one of the above dates, the interest payable would be worked out on the same basis but using the relevant interest rates for unpaid tax.

(d) The instalment payment dates for very large UK companies (those with profits over £20 million) are to be changed. For such companies, instalments will be due in the third, sixth, ninth and twelfth months of each accounting period. The new rules will apply for accounting periods beginning on or after 1 April 2019.

(e) HMRC use a denominator of 365 in calculations of repayment interest regardless of whether or not a leap year is involved.

109.2 REPAYMENT ARISING FROM CARRY-BACK OF LOSSES UNDER *CTA 2010, SS 37, 39*: TERMINAL LOSSES

Y Ltd prepares accounts to 31 December. It has chargeable profits of £100,000 and £60,000 for the years to 31 December 2016 and 2017 respectively and pays corporation tax of £20,000 and £11,548 on the due dates (i.e. 1 October 2017 and 1 October 2018 respectively). The company ceases trading on 31 July 2018 and incurs a loss in its last period of £80,000. It claims loss relief under *CTA 2010, ss 37, 39* against profits of previous accounting periods. As a result of the claim, it receives a corporation tax repayment of £15,548 on 25 July 2019 comprising £4,000 for the year to 31 December 2016 and £11,548 for the year to 31 December 2017.

Interest on overpaid tax is calculated as follows

On tax of £11,548 for year ended 31.12.17:

Date of payment		1 October 2018
Material date		1 October 2018
Interest runs from		1 October 2018

Interest runs to 25 July 2019, a total of 297 days.

On tax of £4,000 for year ended 31.12.16:

Date of payment		1 October 2017
Material date	(note (a))	1 May 2019
Interest runs from		1 May 2019

Interest runs to 25 July 2019, a total of 85 days.

Notes

(a) Where, under a *section 37* claim, a loss is carried back to an accounting period not falling wholly within the twelve months preceding the period of loss, the resulting corporation tax repayment is effectively treated as a repayment of tax paid for the period *in* which the loss is incurred, rather than for the period *to* which the loss is carried back. [*ICTA 1988, s 826(7A)*].

(b) HMRC use a denominator of 365 in calculations of repayment interest regardless of whether or not a leap year is involved.

110 Interest on Unpaid Tax

110.1 SELF-ASSESSMENT

[TMA 1970, s 87A; SI 1998, No 3175; SI 1998 No 3176; SI 1999 No 1928; SI 1999 No 1929; SI 2017 No 1072]

(A) General

S Ltd (which has no related 51% group companies) prepares accounts to 31 July. On 31 May 2018, it makes a payment of £80,000 in respect of its corporation tax liability for the year to 31 July 2017, the due date being 1 May 2018. On completing its corporation tax return, the company ascertains its total tax liability for the year to be £105,000 and makes a further payment of £25,000 on 16 July 2018. The final CT liability is agreed at £107,500 on 27 November 2018 and the company pays a further £2,500 on 5 January 2019.

It is assumed that the interest rates remain unchanged after 21 November 2017.

Interest on unpaid tax will be payable as follows

1.5.18 to 31.5.18	£80,000 × 3% × $^{30}/_{366}$	=	196.72
1.5.18 to 16.7.18	£25,000 × 3% × $^{76}/_{366}$	=	155.73
1.5.18 to 5.1.19	£2,500 × 3% × $^{248}/_{366}$	=	50.82
Total interest charge			£403.27

Notes

(a) HMRC use a denominator of 366 in calculations of interest on unpaid tax regardless of whether or not a leap year is involved.

(b) The unified late payment interest provisions of *FA 2009, s 101, Sch 53* (see IT **13** LATE PAYMENT INTEREST AND PENALTIES) do not yet apply to corporation tax.

(B) Refund of interest charged

On 1 November 2018, T Ltd pays corporation tax of £100,000 for its year ended 31 December 2017. The due date for payment was 1 October 2018. The liability is finally agreed at £80,000 and a repayment of £20,000 is made to T Ltd on 1 May 2019.

The interest position will be as follows

(i) T Ltd will be charged interest on £100,000 for the period 1.10.18 to 1.11.18 (31 days). The charge will be raised following payment of the £100,000 on 1.11.18.

£100,000 × 3% × $^{31}/_{366}$ = £254.09

(ii) The company will be entitled to interest on overpaid tax of £20,000 for the period 1.11.18 (date of payment) to 1.5.19 (date of repayment) (181 days).

£20,000 × 0.5% × $^{181}/_{365}$ = £49.59

(iii) T Ltd will also receive a refund of interest charged on £20,000 for the period 1.10.18 to 1.11.18.

£20,000 × 3% × $^{31}/_{366}$ = £50.82

(C) **Instalment payments**

R Ltd has no related 51% group companies and had taxable profits in excess of £1,500,000 for the year ended 31 March 2016. For the year ending 31 March 2017, R Ltd makes instalment payments of £110,000 (this being equivalent to a quarter of its estimated corporation tax liability of £440,000) on the first three due dates. The last instalment is not paid until 24 July 2017. On 3 September 2018, the tax liability is finally agreed at £524,800. R Ltd pays the balance due of £84,800 on 10 September 2018.

The interest on unpaid tax is calculated as follows

Instalments due on quarter dates £524,800 × 1/4 = £131,200

	£
14 October 2016 to 13 January 2017	
131,200 – 110,000 = £21,200 @ 1.25% × $^{92}/_{366}$	66.61
14 January 2017 to 13 April 2017	
262,400 – 220,000 = £42,400 @ 1.25% × $^{90}/_{366}$	130.33
14 April 2017 to 13 July 2017	
393,600 – 330,000 = £63,600 @ 1.25% × $^{91}/_{366}$	197.66
14 July 2017 to 23 July 2017	
524,800 – 330,000 = £194,800 @ 1.25% × $^{10}/_{366}$	66.53
24 July 2017 to 12 November 2017	
524,800 – 440,000 = £84,800 @ 1.25% × $^{112}/_{366}$	324.37
13 November 2017 to 31 December 2017	
524,800 – 440,000 = £84,800 @ 1.5% × $^{49}/_{366}$	170.30
1 January 2018 to 9 September 2018	
524,800 – 440,000 = £84,800 @ 3% × $^{252}/_{366}$	1,751.61
Interest on underpaid tax	£2,707.41

Notes

(a) A special lower rate of interest for instalment payments applies from the due date of payment to the earlier of nine months after the end of the accounting period and the date the tax is paid. Interest is calculated using the higher normal rate from the date of nine months after the end of the accounting period to the date the tax is paid.

(b) Credit interest works in the same way as the debit interest illustrated in this example (see 109.1(B). For example, had R Ltd paid more than the amount of tax due at any one of the above dates, the interest payable by HMRC would be worked out on the same basis but using the relevant interest rates for overpaid tax.

(c) The instalment payment dates for very large UK companies (those with profits over £20 million) are to be changed. For such companies, instalments will be due in the third, sixth, ninth and twelfth months of each accounting period. The new rules will apply for accounting periods beginning on or after 1 April 2019.

(D) Surrenders of tax refunds within a group of companies

[*CTA 2010, ss 963–966; FA 1989, s 102*]

V Ltd has had, for some years, a 75% subsidiary, W Ltd, and both prepare accounts to 30 November. On 1 September 2017 (the due date), both companies make payments on account of their CT liabilities for the year ended 30 November 2016. V Ltd pays £250,000 and W Ltd pays £150,000. In August 2018, the liabilities are eventually agreed at £200,000 and £180,000 respectively. Before any tax repayment is made to V Ltd, the two companies jointly give notice under *CTA 2010, s 963(2)* that £30,000 of the £50,000 tax repayment due to V Ltd is to be surrendered to W Ltd. W Ltd makes a payment of £20,000 to V Ltd in consideration for the tax refund surrendered.

If no surrender had been made, and all outstanding tax payments/repayments made on, say, 1 September 2018, the interest position would have been as follows

		£
V Ltd		
Interest on CT repayment of £50,000		
for the period 1.9.17 to 1.9.18	£50,000 × 0.5% =	250
W Ltd		
Interest on late paid CT of £30,000		
for the period 1.9.17 to 20.11.17	£30,000 × 2.75% × 81/366	= 182.59
for the period 21.11.17 to 1.9.18	£30,000 × 3%×285/366	= 700.82
Net interest payable by the group		£633.41

The surrender has the following consequences

(i) Only £20,000 of the repayment (the unsurrendered amount) is actually made, and is made to V Ltd together with interest of £100 (at 0.5% for 365 days).

(ii) V Ltd, the surrendering company, is treated as having received a CT repayment of £30,000 (the surrendered amount) on the 'relevant date' which in this case is the normal due date of 1.9.17 V Ltd having made its CT payment on time. V Ltd is thus not entitled to any interest on this amount.

(iii) W Ltd, the recipient company, is deemed to have paid CT of £30,000 on the 'relevant date', 1.9.17 as above. It thus incurs no interest charge.

(iv) The group has turned a net interest charge of £633 into a net interest receipt of £100, a saving of £733. This arises from the differential in the rates of interest charged on unpaid and overpaid tax. (The surrendered amount (£30,000 × 2.25% (2.75 − 0.5) × 81 days = £149) + (£30,000 × 2.5% (3 − 0.5) × 285 days = £584) gives a total of £733.)

(v) The payment of £20,000 by W Ltd to V Ltd, not being a payment in excess of the surrendered refund, has no tax effect on either company.

Note

(a) V Ltd could have given notice to surrender its full refund of £50,000 to W Ltd, instead of just £30,000. There would, in fact, have been no point in doing so, but if W Ltd had made its original CT payment later than the due date, so as to incur an interest charge on the £150,000 originally paid, a full surrender would have produced a saving as the amount surrendered would be treated as having been paid on the due date.

111 Investment Companies and Investment Business

111.1 MANAGEMENT EXPENSES

[*CTA 2009 ss 1218–1220, 1223, 1248; CAA 2001, ss 18, 253*]

XYZ Ltd, an investment company, rents out rooms, halls and equipment to conference providers. It makes up accounts to 31 March. The following details are relevant

	31.3.17	31.3.18
	£	£
Rents receivable	38,000	107,000
Interest receivable accrued gross	10,000	5,000
Chargeable gains	18,000	48,000
Management expenses		
attributable to property	20,000	25,000
attributable to management	50,000	40,000
Capital allowances		
attributable to property	1,000	500
attributable to management	2,000	1,000

The corporation tax computations are as follows
Year ended 31.3.17

		£	£
Property income			
Rents			38,000
Deduct	Capital allowances	1,000	
	Management expenses	20,000	(21,000)
			17,000
Non-trading loan relationships			10,000
Chargeable gains			18,000
			45,000
Deduct	Management expenses	50,000	
	Capital allowances	2,000	(52,000)
Unrelieved balance carried forward			£(7,000)

Year ended 31.3.18

		£	£
Property income			
Rents			107,000
Deduct	Capital allowances	500	
	Management expenses	25,000	(25,500)
			81,500
Non-trading loan relationships			5,000
Chargeable gains			48,000
			£134,500
Deduct	Management expenses	40,000	
	Capital allowances	1,000	
	Unrelieved balance from previous accounting period	7,000	(48,000)
Profit chargeable to CT			£86,500

On 1 April 2018, XYZ Ltd diversified and began to provide conference services itself. The following details are relevant for the year ending 31 March 2019.

	31.3.19
	£
Income from conferences	65,000
Rents receivable	40,000
Interest receivable accrued (gross)	5,000
Conference costs	22,000
Management expenses	
attributable to property	20,000
attributable to management	73,000
Capital allowances	
attributable to conferences	2,000
attributable to property	400
attributable to management	800

The corporation tax computations are as follows.
Year ended 31.3.19

		£	£	£
Trading income				65,000
Deduct	Conference costs		22,000	
	Capital allowances		2,000	
				(24,000)
				41,000
Property income				
Rents			40,000	
Deduct	Capital allowances	400		
	Management expenses	20,000	(20,400)	
				19,600
Income from non-trading loan relationships				5,000
Deduct	Management expenses	73,000		
	Capital allowances	800		
				(73,800)
Unrelieved balance carried forward				£(8,200)

Notes

(a) Relief for management expenses is available to companies with investment business whether or not they are investment companies. Such expenses are deductible for corporation tax purposes for the accounting period in which they are charged to the accounts. [*CTA 2009, ss 1218–1231, 1248, 1255*]. A company with investment business is defined as 'any company whose business consists wholly or partly in the making of investments'. [*CTA 2009, s 1218*]. (It will include, for example, a trading company with shares in subsidiary companies.)

(b) The excess management expenses (including capital allowances) in the accounting period ended 31.3.17 are carried forward to the accounting period ended 31.3.18 and are set against total profits of that period. If profits in the year ended 31.3.18 had been insufficient, the excess management expenses could have been carried forward to subsequent periods until fully used. Similarly, the excess management expenses in the accounting period ended 31.3.19 can be carried forward to subsequent accounting periods. For accounting periods beginning on or after 1 April 2017, a claim is required for carried-forward management expenses to be set off against total profits of the next accounting period. A claim can be made for the whole or part of the excess carried forward. For this purpose, where an accounting period straddles 1 April 2017 it is treated as two separate accounting periods, the first ending on 31 March 2017 and the second beginning on 1 April 2017. Apportionments between the two accounting periods are made on a time basis unless that would produce an unjust or unreasonable result, in which case the apportionment must be made on a just and reasonable basis [*CTA 2009, s 1223; F (No 2) A 2017, Sch 4 paras 6, 190*]. See also note (d) below.

(c) Management expenses brought forward from earlier accounting periods beginning on or after 1 April 2017 (see note (b) above) can be included in a group relief for carried-forward losses claim. See **106.6** GROUP RELIEF.

(d) Surplus management expenses may not be carried forward if there is a change of ownership of a company with investment business and one of the following occurs:

(i) a significant increase (as defined) in the company's capital after the change of ownership,

(ii) a major change in the nature or conduct of the business of the company in the period beginning three years before the change and ending five years after (three years where either the change in ownership or the change in the nature or conduct of the business occurs before 1 April 2017),

(iii) a considerable revival of the company's business which before the change was small or negligible.

[*CTA 2010, ss 677–703; FA 2014, s 37(2)*].

(e) The carry-forward of excess management expenses is subject to restriction where the total set-off of carried-forward amounts exceeds £5,000,000. See **114.7** LOSSES.

112 Liquidation

112.1 ACCOUNTING PERIODS IN A LIQUIDATION

[*CTA 2009, ss 9, 12; CTA 2010, ss 626–629; FA 2014, Sch 1 para 15*]

On 31 August 2016 a resolution was passed to wind up X Ltd. The company's normal accounting date was 31 December.

It was later agreed between the liquidator and HMRC that 31 January 2018 would be the assumed date of completion of winding up. The actual date of completion is 30 April 2019.

The last accounting period of the company before liquidation is

1.1.16 to 31.8.16	—	8 months

The accounting periods during the liquidation are as follows

1.9.16 to 31.8.17	—	12 months
1.9.17 to 31.1.18	—	5 months
1.2.18 to 31.1.19	—	12 months
1.2.19 to 30.4.19	—	3 months

Note

(a) If the rate for the financial year in which the winding-up is completed (the 'final year') has not been fixed or proposed by Budget resolution before completion of the winding-up, the rate for the penultimate financial year will apply to the income of that year. In this case, the final and penultimate financial years for the above accounting periods are 2019 and 2018 respectively.

113 Loan Relationships

113.1 TRADING PURPOSE

[CTA 2009 ss 295–301, 304, 306A–310, 328; FA 2011, Sch 7 paras 6, 8; F(No 2)A 2015, Sch 7 paras 4, 5, 20, 103]

A Ltd requires additional trade finance and on 1 January 2017 enters into an agreement with XY Bank plc to borrow £100,000 for 3 years. Interest is payable every 6 months commencing 1 July 2017 at 6% per annum. Legal fees and negotiation expenses of £2,800 which were directly incurred in bringing this loan into existence were paid in December 2016. The company's accounting reference date is 31 March and it adopts an amortised cost basis for all loan relationships.

A Ltd's accounts for the year ended 31 March 2017 show the following

	£	£
Turnover		1,400,000
Purchases and expenses		
(all allowable for corporation tax purposes)	900,000	
Finance Charges		
XY Bank plc – interest to 31 March 2017	1,500	
Legal fees and negotiation expenses	2,800	
Depreciation*	120,000	
		1,024,300
Net profit per accounts		£375,700

*Capital allowances for the same year are £95,000.

The company's corporation tax computation for the same period is as follows

	£
Net profit per accounts	375,700
Add: Depreciation	120,000
Less: Capital allowances	(95,000)
Adjusted profit for corporation tax purposes	£400,700

For corporation tax purposes the accrued interest on the loan with XY Bank plc taken out for trading purposes is treated as a trading expense.

The profit and loss charge for each of the following accounting periods will be

	Year ended 31.3.17	Year ended 31.3.18	Year ended 31.3.19	Year ended 31.3.20
	£	£	£	£
'Debits'				
Expenses	2,800	—	—	—
Interest payable	1,500	6,000	6,000	4,500

This conforms to the amortised cost basis of accounting as interest will be allocated to the period to which it relates. Where the directly-incurred expenses are material then under GAAP they should be deducted from the proceeds of the loan and spread over the life of the loan within the overall finance charge.

Notes

(a) A company has a loan relationship whenever it stands in the position of debtor or creditor in respect of a money debt. (A money debt being any debt not arising in the normal course of purchase and sale of goods and services for resale.) [*CTA 2009 ss 302, 303*].

(b) The taxation of the loan relationship follows accounts drawn up in accordance with generally accepted accounting practice. [*CTA 2009, ss 306A–310; F(No 2)A 2015, Sch 7 paras 4, 5, 103*].

(c) Interest payments on current loans for trading purposes are treated as a trading expense. [*CTA 2009, ss 296, 297, 301*].

(d) Only expenses directly incurred in relation to the origination of a loan would be allowable under the loan relationships' code. [*CTA 2009, s 306A(2)(a)*].

113.2 NON-TRADING PURPOSES

Tradissimo Ltd, a non-financial trading company, bought £10,000 nominal of corporate bonds at £94 per £100 nominal stock as an investment on 1 January 2016. The bonds will be redeemed on 1 January 2019 at par. Interest at 5% is payable annually on 31 December each year. The company uses an amortised cost accounting method for all its loan relationships. The accounting reference date is 31 March.

As the purchase of the bonds does not relate to the company's trade, its income and expenditure is chargeable as income from a non-trading loan relationship. In addition to the interest, the company will also be taxable on the discount which will be spread over three years on an effective interest rate method. For illustration purposes, a straight-line method has been used below.

	Year ended 31.3.16	Year ended 31.3.17	Year ended 31.3.18	Year ended 31.3.19
	£	£	£	£
'Credits'				
Interest received	125	500	500	375
Discount	50	200	200	150
Income from non-trading loan relationships	£175	£700	£700	£525

Note

(a) Profits and losses from non-trading loan relationships are taxable as income from non-trading loan relationships. [*CTA 2009, s 299*].

113.3 NON-TRADING DEFICIT ON A LOAN RELATIONSHIP

(A) Deficit arising before 1 April 2017

[*CTA 2009, ss 456–463*]

The Beta Trading Co Ltd, which is a single company and not part of a group, made a loan to the PQR Company Ltd. This transaction did not form part of Beta's normal trade. PQR Company Ltd defaults on the loan on 1 October 2016 leaving a balance of £8,500 due to The Beta Trading Co Ltd. The accounting reference date is 31 March.

The Beta Trading Co Ltd's computations for relevant years are as follows

	Year ended 31.3.15	Year ended 31.3.16	Year ended 31.3.17	Year ended 31.3.18
	£	£	£	£
Trading income	10,000	11,000	800	12,000
Non-trading loan relationship income	2,000	2,000	100	400

The £8,500 debit is set against the non-trading loan relationship credit of £100 in the year ending 31 March 2017 and the remaining deficit of £8,400 may be relieved in whole or in part in three different ways (group relief not being available).

		£
Non-trading deficit		8,400
1.	Set off against total profits of the year ended 31 March 2017	(800)
2.	Carry back against profits from non-trading loan relationships of the preceding accounting period	(2,000)
3.	Carry forward against non-trading profits of the company for year ended 31 March 2018	(400)
Net deficit to carry forward against subsequent non-trading profits		£5,200

Notes

(a) Relief for a non-trading deficit may be claimed (to the extent not already surrendered as group relief) either:

(i) by set-off against profits of the company of whatever description for the deficit period; or

(ii) by carry back and set-off against profits of the preceding accounting period arising from non-trading loan relationships.

(b) Where relief is not claimed as in (a) above, the non-trading deficit is automatically carried forward for set-off against non-trading profits of the subsequent accounting period, subject to a claim for it to be not so carried forward, in which case it is treated as a non-trading deficit of that period to be carried forward for offset against non-trading profits of succeeding accounting periods.

(c) The £5,200 deficit balance (which income from non trading loan relationships for the year ended 31 March 2017 is insufficient to relieve) will be carried forward for relief against non-trading profits of the next and subsequent accounting periods subject to a claim as in (b) above. [*CTA 2009, s 457(1)(2)*].

(d) The rules illustrated in this example apply to non-trading deficits arising in accounting periods beginning before 1 April 2017. For this purpose, where an accounting period straddles that date it is treated as two separate accounting periods, the first ending on 31 March 2017 and the second beginning on 1 April 2017. Apportionments between the two accounting periods are made on a time basis unless that would produce an unjust or unreasonable result, in which case the apportionment must be made on a just and reasonable basis. See (B) below for the new rules. The rules illustrated here continue to apply, however, where the company is a charity. [*F (No 2) A 2017, Sch 4 para 190*].

(e) See note (e) to (B) below.

(B) **Deficit arising after 31 March 2017**

[*CTA 2009, ss 463A–463I; F(No 2)A 2017, Sch 4 paras 4, 190*]

Sigma Ltd, which is a single company and not part of a group, made a number of loans, including one to the JB Company Ltd. The loans did not form part of Sigma's normal trade. JB Company Ltd defaults on the loan on 1 October 2018 leaving a balance of £10,500 due to Sigma Ltd. The accounting reference date is 31 March.

Sigma Ltd's computations for relevant years are as follows

	Year ended 31.3.17	Year ended 31.3.18	Year ended 31.3.19	Year ended 31.3.20
	£	£	£	£
Trading income	10,000	11,000	800	2,500
Non-trading loan relationship income	2,000	2,000	2,000	2,000

The £10,500 debit is set against the non-trading loan relationship credit of £2,000 in the year ending 31 March 2019 and the remaining deficit of £8,500 may be relieved in whole or in part in three different ways (group relief not being available).

		£
Non-trading deficit		8,500
1.	Set off against total profits of the year ended 31 March 2019	(800)
2.	Carry back against profits from non-trading loan relationships of the preceding accounting period	(2,000)
3.	Carry forward against total profits of the company for year ended 31 March 2020	(4,500)
Net deficit to carry forward against subsequent total profits		£1,200

Notes

(a) The rules illustrated in this example apply to non-trading deficits arising in accounting periods beginning on or after 1 April 2017. For this purpose, where an accounting period straddles that date it is treated as two separate accounting periods, the first ending on 31 March 2017 and the second beginning on 1 April 2017. Apportionments between the two accounting periods are made on a time basis unless that would produce an unjust or unreasonable result, in which case the apportionment must be made on a just and reasonable basis. [*F (No 2) A 2017, Sch 4 para 190*].

(b) Relief for a non-trading deficit may be claimed (to the extent not already surrendered as group relief) either:

(i) by set-off against profits of the company of whatever description for the deficit period; or

(ii) by carry back and set-off against profits of the preceding accounting period arising from non-trading loan relationships.

(c) Where relief is not claimed as in (a) above or the deficit is not fully relieved, the company may make a claim for the whole or part of the remaining non-trading deficit to be carried forward for set-off against total profits of the subsequent accounting period. In relevant cases, the deficit may instead be surrendered as group relief for carried-forward losses. A claim cannot be made if either the company ceased to be a company with investment business in the period in which the deficit arose or (if it were such a company immediately before the deficit period) its investment business became small or negligible in the deficit period. In the latter case, the unrelieved deficit is automatically carried forward for relief against non-trading profits of the subsequent accounting period, subject to a claim for it to be not so carried forward, in which case it is carried forward for offset against non-trading profits of succeeding accounting periods. This treatment also applies where the company's investment business became small or negligible in an accounting period after the deficit period (but only in respect of that later period and subsequent accounting periods).

(d) The £1,200 deficit balance (which profits for the year ended 31 March 2020 are insufficient to relieve) can, on a claim, be carried forward for relief against total profits of the next accounting period subject to the provisions in (c) above.

(e) From 1 April 2017, the carry-forward of non-trading loan relationship deficits (whether arising pre- or post- April 2017) against total profits or non-trading profits is subject to restriction where the total set-off of carried-forward amounts exceeds £5,000,000. See **114.7** LOSSES.

114 Losses

114.1 CURRENT YEAR SET-OFF OF TRADING LOSSES

[*CTA 2010, s 37(3)(a)*]

A Ltd is a trading company with investment business (see **111.1** INVESTMENT COMPANIES AND INVESTMENT BUSINESS). Its results for the year ended 31 March 2019 show

	£
Trading loss	(100,000)
Property income	30,000
Income from non-trading loan relationships	40,000
Chargeable gains	72,000
Management expenses	(20,000)
Qualifying charitable donations	(10,000)

The loss may be relieved as follows

	£
Property income	30,000
Income from non-trading loan relationships	40,000
Chargeable gains	72,000
	142,000
Deduct Management expenses	(20,000)
	122,000
Deduct Trading loss	(100,000)
	22,000
Deduct Qualifying charitable donations	(10,000)
Taxable total profits	£12,000

Note

(a) Loss relief (other than group relief) against profits for the current year is given in priority to qualifying charitable donations. [*CTA 2010, s 189(1)(3)*].

114.2 CARRY-FORWARD OF TRADING LOSSES

[*CTA 2010, ss 45A–45E; F(No 2)A 2017, Sch 4 paras 10, 11, 190*]

(A) Loss arising before 1 April 2017

B Ltd has carried on the same trade for many years. The results for the years ended 30 September 2014, 2015 and 2016 are shown below

	2014	2015	2016
	£	£	£
Trading profit/(loss)	(25,000)	10,000	5,000
Property income	3,000	1,000	2,000
Income from non-trading loan relationships	2,000	2,000	3,000
Chargeable gains	5,600	4,700	4,000

B Ltd may claim under *CTA 2010, s 37* to set off the trading loss against other profits of the same accounting period. Assuming the claim is made (and that no claim is made to carry back the balance of the loss), the loss will be set off as follows

Year ended 30 September 2014		Loss memorandum
	£	£
Trading loss		(25,000)
Property income	3,000	
Income from non-trading loan relationships	2,000	
Chargeable gains	5,600	
	10,600	
Deduct Trading loss	(10,600)	10,600
Taxable total profits	—	
		(14,400)
Year ended 30 September 2015		
Trading income	10,000	
Deduct Loss brought forward	(10,000)	10,000
	—	(4,400)
Property income	1,000	
Income from non-trading loan relationships	2,000	
Chargeable gains	4,700	
Taxable total profits	7,700	
Year ended 30 September 2016		
Trading income	5,000	
Deduct Loss brought forward	(4,400)	4,400
	600	
Property income	2,000	
Income from non-trading loan relationships	3,000	
Chargeable gains	4,000	
Taxable total profits	9,600	

(B) **Loss arising after 31 March 2017**

Z Ltd, a trading company, has the following results for the years ended 31 March 2018 and 2019

	31.3.18	31.3.19
	£	£
Trading profit/(loss)	(52,000)	45,000
Income from non-trading loan relationships	2,000	4,000

The losses can be set off as follows

Y/e 31.3.18		Loss memo-randum
	£	£
Trading loss		(52,000)
Income from non-trading loan relationships		2,000
Loss carried forward		(£50,000)
Y/e 31.3.19		
Trading income	45,000	
Income from non-trading loan relationships	4,000	
	49,000	
Deduct Loss brought forward		(49,000)
Carried forward trading losses		(£1,000)

Notes

(a) Trading losses arising in accounting periods beginning on or after 1 April 2017 can be carried forward for set-off against total profits of the subsequent accounting period. In relevant cases, the loss may instead be surrendered as group relief for carried-forward losses. For this purpose, where an accounting period straddles that date it is treated as two separate accounting periods, the first ending on 31 March 2017 and the second beginning on 1 April 2017. Apportionments between the two accounting periods are made on a time basis unless that would produce an unjust or unreasonable result, in which case the apportionment must be made on a just and reasonable basis. A claim cannot be made if a claim for set-off against current year profits could not have been made in respect of the loss or if the trade became small or negligible in the loss-making period. In such cases, the loss is automatically carried forward for relief against trading profits of the subsequent accounting period, subject to a claim for it to be not so carried forward, in which case it is carried forward for offset against trading profits of succeeding accounting periods. This treatment also applies to pre-April 2017 losses carried forward to accounting periods beginning on or after 1 April 2017 and where the company's trade became small or negligible or the conditions for current-year set-off are not met in an accounting period after the loss-making period. (In the latter case, the restriction applies only in respect of that later period and subsequent accounting periods). [*CTA 2010, ss 45A–45E and Part 5A; F(No 2)A 2017, Sch 4 paras 11, 190*].

(b) The carry-forward of trading losses (whether pre- or post- April 2017) against total profits or trading profits is subject to restriction where the total set-off of carried-forward amounts exceeds £5,000,000. [*CTA 2010, Part 7ZA*] See **114.7** below.

114.3 CARRY-BACK OF TRADING LOSSES

[*CTA 2010, ss 37–44, and 45F–45G*]

(A) Terminal losses

X Ltd has the following results for the two years ending 31 December 2016 and 2017 and its final period to 30 September 2018 when it ceases trading.

	31.12.16	31.12.17	30.9.18
	£	£	£
Trading profit/(loss)	30,000	4,500	(30,000)
Property income	1,000	1,000	3,000
Income from non-trading loan relationships	500	500	4,000
Chargeable gains	—	1,500	2,250
Management expenses	—	(4,000)	(4,000)

The loss can be relieved as follows		Loss memorandum
	£	£
Period ended 30 September 2018		
Trading loss		(30,000)
Property income	3,000	
Income from non-trading loan relationships	4,000	
Chargeable gains	2,250	
	9,250	
Deduct Management expenses	(4,000)	
Trading loss (*CTA 2010, s 37(3)(a)*)	(5,250)	5,250
Taxable total profits	—	
		(24,750)

Year ended 31 December 2017		
Trading income	4,500	
Property income	1,000	
Income from non-trading loan relationships	500	
Chargeable gains	1,500	
	7,500	
Deduct Management expenses	(4,000)	
	3,500	
Deduct Loss carried back	(3,500)	3,500
(*CTA 2010, ss 37(3)(b), 39*)		
Taxable total profits	—	
		£(21,250)

Year ended 31 December 2016			
Trading income		30,000	
Property income		1,000	
Income from non-trading loan relationships		500	
		31,500	
Deduct Loss carried back		(21,250)	21,250
(*CTA 2010, ss 37(3)(b), 39*)			
Taxable total profits		£10,250	
Losses remaining	(note (a))		—

Notes

(a) Where a loss is incurred in the accounting period in which the trade is discontinued, it may be carried back for three years prior to the period in which the loss occurred. In this example, the losses are fully utilised in the year ended 31 December 2016 but if this were not the case, they could have been carried back to the year ended 31 December 2015. Similar relief is available where the loss is incurred in an accounting period ending within the 12 months immediately before the cessation but in this case the three year carry-back is limited to an apportioned part of the loss for that penultimate period. This apportionment is on a time basis, by reference to the proportion of the accounting period falling within the final 12-month period. The balance attributable to the earlier part of the accounting period can be carried back one year in the normal way. [*CTA 2010, s 39*].

(b) Losses must be set against current year profits before being carried back. If carried back, they must be carried back to the full extent possible, i.e. if losses are not fully relieved in the immediately preceding period, any balance must then be carried back to the period before that, and so on. [*CTA 2010, s 37(3)(4)*].

(c) Where a loss is incurred on or after 1 April 2017, an additional form of terminal loss relief is available. New-style terminal loss relief includes trading losses brought forward to the period of cessation under *CTA 2010, ss 45, 45A–45B* which can then be carried back three years from the end of the 'terminal period' on an unrestricted basis.[*CTA 2010, s 45F*]

The effect of this might be to negate the original 50% restriction that applied to losses carried forward into one or more of those periods. Losses carried back under a terminal loss relief claim can only be set off against the 'relevant profits' (i.e. trading profits or total profits) that would have been allowable when those losses were carried forward. The carry back period cannot include any of the following:

- the period in which the loss originated;
- any period before the period in which the loss originated;
- any period before 1 April 2017.

[*CTA 2010, s 45F; F(No 2)A 2017, Sch 4 paras 11, 190*].

(B) Accounting periods of different lengths

Y Ltd, which previously made up accounts to 31 March, changed its accounting date to 31 December. Its results for the three accounting periods up to 31 December 2018 were as follows

	12 months	9 months	12 months
	31.3.17	31.12.17	31.12.18
	£	£	£
Trading profit/			
(loss)	5,500	9,000	(66,000)
Income from non-trading loan relationships	2,500	3,000	—
Chargeable gains	—	—	2,000

Y Ltd makes all available loss relief claims so as to obtain relief against the earliest possible profits. The computations are summarised as follows—

	12 months	9 months	12 months
	31.3.17	31.12.17	31.12.18
	£	£	£
Trading income	5,500	9,000	—
Income from non-trading loan relationships	2,500	3,000	—
Chargeable gains	—	—	2,000
	8,000	12,000	2,000
Loss relief			
CTA 2010, s 37(3)(a)			(2,000)
CTA 2010, s 37(3)(b)	(2,000)	(12,000)	
Taxable total profits	£6,000	—	—

Loss memoranda

	12 months 31.12.18
	£
Trading loss	66,000
Relieved against current year profits	(2,000)
Relieved by carry-back:	
To p/e 31.12.16	(12,000)
To y/e 31.3.16	(2,000)
Carried forward under *CTA 2010, s 45*	£50,000

Note

(a) Relief under *CTA 2010, s 37(3)(b)* (carry-back of losses) is not restricted by reference to the length of the accounting period of loss. However, where a loss is carried back to an accounting period falling partly outside the carry-back period, relief is restricted to an appropriate proportion of profits. [*CTA 2010, s 38*]. In this example, the one-year period, as regards the loss for the year to 31 December 2018, begins on 1 January 2017 and, therefore, only three-twelfths of the profit for the year to 31 March 2017 can be relieved.

114.4 LOSSES ON UNLISTED SHARES

[*CTA 2010, ss 68–90*]

Z Ltd has been an investment company since its incorporation in 1973. It is not part of a trading group and has no associated companies. It makes up accounts to 31 December. On 6 February 2018, Z Ltd disposed of part of its holding of shares in T Ltd for full market value. Z Ltd makes no global re-basing election under *TCGA 1992, s 35(5)*.

Details of disposal	
Contract date	6.2.18
Shares sold	2,000 Ord
Proceeds (after expenses)	£4,500

Z acquired its shares in T Ltd as follows

				£
6.4.81 subscribed for	1,000	shares	cost (with expenses)	5,000
6.4.91 acquired	1,500	shares	cost (with expenses)	4,000
	2,500			£9,000

T Ltd shares were valued at £3 per share at 31 March 1982. T Ltd has been a UK resident trading company since 1980. Its shares are not quoted on a recognised stock exchange.

Z Ltd may claim that part of the loss incurred be set off against its income as follows

Identification on last in, first out basis

(i) Shares acquired 6.4.91 (not subscribed for)

	£
Proceeds of 1,500 shares	
$\frac{1,500}{2,000} \times £4,500$	3,375
Cost of 1,500 shares	(4,000)
Capital loss *not* available for set-off against income	£(625)

(ii) Shares acquired 6.4.81 (subscribed for)

	Cost basis	31.3.82 value basis
	£	£
Proceeds of 500 shares		
$\frac{500}{2,000} \times £4,500$	1,125	1,125
Cost of 500 shares	(2,500)	
31.3.82 value		(1,500)
	£(1,375)	£(375)
Capital loss available for set-off against income		£(375)

Notes

(a) A claim under *CTA 2010, s 70* is restricted to the loss in respect of the shares *subscribed* for.

(b) The claim must be submitted within two years of the end of the accounting period in which the loss was incurred.

(c) The loss of £(375) is available primarily against income of the year ended 31 December 2018, with any balance being available against, broadly speaking, income of the 12 months ended 31 December 2017.

(d) See IT **14.5** LOSSES and CGT **216.3** LOSSES for further examples on this topic.

114.5 RESTRICTION OF TRADING LOSSES ON RECONSTRUCTION WITHOUT CHANGE OF OWNERSHIP

[*CTA 2010, ss 940A–953; F(No 2)A 2017, Sch 4 paras 62–68*]

(A) Transfer of trade

A Ltd and B Ltd are two wholly-owned subsidiaries of X Ltd. All are within the charge to corporation tax, although A Ltd has accumulated trading losses brought forward and unrelieved of £200,000 and has not paid tax for several years. As part of a group reorganisation, A Ltd's trade is transferred to B Ltd on 31 October 2018.

A Ltd's balance sheet immediately before the transfer is as follows

	£		£
Share capital	100,000	Property	90,000
Debenture secured		Plant	20,000
on property	50,000	Stock	130,000
Group loan	10,000	Trade debtors	120,000
Trade creditors	300,000		
Bank overdraft	60,000		
	520,000		
Deficit on			
reserves	(160,000)		
	£360,000		£360,000

Book values represent the approximate open market values of assets. B Ltd takes over the stock and plant to continue the trade, paying £150,000 to A Ltd and taking over £15,000 of trade creditors relating to stock. A Ltd is to collect outstanding debts and pay remaining creditors.

B Ltd becomes entitled to A Ltd's trading losses as follows.

	£
Amount 'A' (i.e. broadly A Ltd's assets not transferred to B Ltd plus any consideration given for the transfer (in this case nil))	
Freehold property (£90,000 − £50,000)	40,000
Trade debtors	120,000
Consideration from B Ltd	150,000
	£310,000

	£
Amount 'L' (i.e. A Ltd's liabilities not transferred to B Ltd)	
Bank overdraft	60,000
Group loan	10,000
Trade creditors (£300,000 − £15,000)	285,000
	£355,000

Trading losses transferable with trade

£200,000 − £(355,000 − 310,000) = £155,000

Notes

(a) Where amount L exceeds amount A the amount of relief given to the successor for losses of the predecessor carried forward is reduced by the excess of L over A. [*CTA 2010, ss 945–947*].

(b) Assets taken over by the successor to the trade are not included in amount A. Loan stock is not included in amount L, but where the loan is secured on an asset which is not transferred, the value of the asset is reduced by the amount secured.

(c) The assumption by B Ltd of liability for £15,000 of trade creditors does not constitute the giving of consideration and is not, therefore, included in amount A. Amount L is, however, reduced by the amount taken over.

(B) **Transfer of part of a trade**

D Ltd and E Ltd are wholly-owned subsidiaries of X Ltd. On 1 November 2018 D Ltd transfers the manufacturing part of what has been an integrated trade to E Ltd. D Ltd has accumulated trading losses brought forward and unrelieved of £150,000, of which £50,000 are attributable to the manufacturing operations.

Immediately before the transfer D Ltd's balance sheet is as follows

	£			£
Share capital	100,000	Property	— shops	110,000
Share premium	18,000		— factory	70,000
Loan stock	50,000		Plant	45,000
Trade creditors	290,000		Vehicles	20,000
Bank overdraft	42,000		Stock	30,000
			Trade debtors	65,000
	500,000			
Deficit on reserves	(160,000)			
	£340,000			£340,000

Book values represent the approximate open market value of assets. E Ltd takes over the manufacturing business together with the factory, plant and £18,000 of stock for a total consideration of £134,000.

Approximately 60% of D Ltd's turnover relates to manufacturing, and it is agreed that trade debtors and creditors are proportional to turnover.

Amount A (see A above) apportioned to the trade transferred is

	£
Trade debtors (60%)	39,000
Consideration received from E Ltd	134,000
	£173,000

Amount L apportioned to the trade is

	£
Trade creditors (60%)	174,000
Overdraft (33%) note (a)	14,000
	£188,000

Tax losses transferable are restricted to

£50,000 − £(188,000 − 173,000) = £35,000

Notes

(a) On the transfer of part of a trade, such apportionments of receipts, expenses, assets or liabilities are made as may be just and reasonable. [*CTA 2010, s 952(1)*]. It is assumed that it is reasonable to apportion trade debtors and creditors in proportion to turnover and the overdraft in proportion to losses.

(b) Loan stock, share premium and share capital are not relevant liabilities unless they have arisen in replacing relevant liabilities within the preceding year.

(c) If the trade were transferred as a whole for market value of the assets, no restriction would apply to the losses transferable.

114.6 PROPERTY BUSINESS LOSSES

[*CTA 2010, ss 62–67; F(No 2)A 2017, Sch 4 paras 13, 14, 190*]

JW Ltd, an investment company which is not a member of a group, has the following results for the three years ended 30 April 2018:

	y/e 30.4.16	y/e 30.4.17	y/e 30.4.18
	£	£	£
Income from non-trading loan relationships	6,000	6,000	6,000
Property profit/(loss)	(7,500)	2,000	(8,500)
Management expenses	300	300	500

In view of the continuing losses, JW Ltd closes down its UK property business on 30 April 2018. It sells its properties in the year ended 30 April 2019, realising chargeable gains of £155,000. The company has income from non-trading loan relationships for that year of £6,000 and incurs management expenses of £3,600.

The company's profits chargeable to corporation tax for the four years are as follows.

	£	£
y/e 30.4.16		
Income from non-trading loan relationships		6,000
Deduct management expenses	300	
Property loss (restricted)	5,700	(6,000)
Taxable total profits		Nil
y/e 30.4.17		
Income from non-trading loan relationships		6,000
Property income		2,000
		8,000
Deduct management expenses	300	
Property loss (y/e 30.4.16)	1,800	(2,100)
Taxable total profits		£5,900
y/e 30.4.18		
Income from non-trading loan relationships		6,000
Deduct management expenses	500	
Property loss (restricted)	5,500	(6,000)
Taxable total profits		Nil
y/e 30.4.19		
Income from non-trading loan relationships		6,000
Chargeable gains		155,000
		161,000
Deduct management expenses		(3,600)
Taxable total profits		£157,400

Loss memorandum	£
Loss for y/e 30.4.16	7,500
Used y/e 30.4.16	(5,700)
Used y/e 30.4.17	(1,800)
	Nil
	£
Loss for y/e 30.4.18	8,500
Used y/e 30.4.18	(5,500)
Carried forward as management expenses (relieved y/e 30.4.19)	£3,000

Notes

(a) Relief for UK property business losses is only available where the UK property business is carried on as a commercial business or in the exercise of a statutory function.

(b) UK property business losses arising in accounting periods beginning on or after 1 April 2017 can be carried forward only on the making of a claim. The company can claim some or all of the amount available.

(c) As A Ltd is a company with investment business, on ceasing the UK property business, the unrelieved losses of £3,000 are treated as excess management expenses. [*CTA 2010, s 63*]. For losses arising in accounting periods beginning on or after 1 April 2017, a claim must be made for this treatment to apply. The company can claim some or all of the amount available.

(d) The carry-forward of UK property business losses (whether pre- or post- April 2017) against total profits is subject to restriction where the total set-off of carried-forward amounts exceeds £5,000,000. See **114.7** below. See also **106.6** GROUP RELIEF for group relief for carried-forward losses.

(e) For the purposes of the changes mentioned in notes (b) to (d) above, where an accounting period straddles 1 April 2017, it is treated as two separate accounting periods, the first ending on 31 March 2017 and the second beginning on 1 April 2017. Apportionments between the two accounting periods are made on a time basis unless that would produce an unjust or unreasonable result, in which case the apportionment must be made on a just and reasonable basis. [*F(No 2)A 2017, Sch 4, paras 190–192*].

[*F (No 2) A 2017, Sch 4*].

114.7 RESTRICTION ON DEDUCTIONS FOR CARRIED-FORWARD LOSSES

[*CTA 2010, ss 269ZA–269ZZB; F(No 2)A 2017, Sch 4 paras 16, 190*]

(A) Single company

Stephenson Ltd, which is not a member of a group, begins to trade on 1 April 2017. It has the following results for the two years ending 31 March 2018 and 2019.

	y/e 31.3.18 £	y/e 31.3.19 £
Trading profit/(loss)	(9,000,000)	8,000,000
Property income	—	2,000,000

Taxable profits for the two years are computed as follows

	y/e 31.3.18 £	y/e 31.3.19 £
Trading profit	—	8,000,000
Property income	—	2,000,000
	—	10,000,000
Less loss brought forward from y/e 31.3.18 (restricted)		(7,500,000)

Taxable profits	—	£2,500,000

The restriction on the set-off of the carried-forward loss against profits for the year ending 31 March 2019 is calculated as follows.

	£
Qualifying profits	10,000,000
Less deductions allowance	(5,000,000)
Relevant profits	5,000,000
Relevant profits × 50%	2,500,000
Add deductions allowance	5,000,000
Maximum set-off	£7,500,000

Loss memorandum

	£
Loss y/e 31.3.18	9,000,000
Less relieved y/e 31.3.19	(7,500,000)
Carried forward to y/e 31.3.20	£1,500,000

Notes

(a) For accounting periods beginning on or after 1 April 2017, the set-off of losses carried forward from previous accounting periods is restricted for companies with profits in excess of the 'deductions allowance'. Broadly, a company's profits after deduction of any current year reliefs and the deductions allowance can only be reduced by up to 50% by carried-forward losses. For this purpose, where an accounting period straddles 1 April 2017, it is treated as two separate accounting periods, the first ending on 31 March 2017 and the second beginning on 1 April 2017. Apportionments between the two accounting periods are made on a time basis unless that would produce an unjust or unreasonable result, in which case the apportionment must be made on a just and reasonable basis. [*CTA 2010, ss 269ZA–269ZZB; F(No 2)A 2017, Sch 4 paras 16, 190*].

(b) The restriction applies to the following carried-forward amounts: trade losses, losses of a UK property business, non-trading deficits from loan relationships, non-trading losses on intangible fixed assets and expenses of management of investment business.

It applies to both pre-April 2017 and post-April 2017 amounts and to amounts which can be set off against total profits or only against a profits of a particular type. Where the carried-forward amounts include losses which can only be set against particular types of profits, the maximum set-off must be computed separately for trading profits and non-trading profits. The company may decide how its deductions allowance should be allocated between trading and non-trading profits.

(c) If a company is not a member of a group, the deductions allowance is £5 million. If the accounting period is less than twelve months, the amount is reduced proportionally. If a company has profits for an accounting period that do not exceed the amount of the deductions allowance, carried-forward losses may be set against those profits without restriction.

(d) See also **106.6** GROUP RELIEF for group relief for carried-forward losses.

(B) Groups of companies

A Ltd is the ultimate parent company of B Ltd and C Ltd. All companies make up accounts to 31 March each year. The companies' results for the year ended 31 March 2019 are as follows.

		£
A Ltd	Trading profit	800,000
	Property income	185,000
	Chargeable gain	15,000
B Ltd	Trading profit	5,000,000
CLtd	Trading profit	400,000
	Non-trading loan relationships	100,000

In addition, each company has the following trading losses brought forward from the year ended 31 March 2018: A Ltd £1,000,000, B Ltd £5,000,000 and C Ltd £500,000. All of the carried-forward losses arose in the year ended 31 March 2018. A Ltd is the group's nominated company for the purpose of allocating the group deductions allowance.

If A Ltd allocates £1,000,000 of the group deductions allowance to itself and the remainder to B Ltd, the companies' taxable profits for the year ended 31 March 2019 are as follows.

	£
A Ltd	
Trading profit	800,000
Property income	185,000
Chargeable gain	15,000
	1,000,000
Deduct Loss brought forward from y/e 31.3.18	(1,000,000)
Chargeable profits	£Nil
B Ltd	
Trading profit	5,000,000
Deduct Loss brought forward from y/e 31.3.18	(4,500,000)
Chargeable profits	£500,000
C Ltd	
Trading profit	400,000

Non-trading loan relationships	100,000
	500,000
Deduct Loss brought forward from y/e 31.3.18	(250,000)
Chargeable profits	£250,000

The restriction on the set-off of the carried-forward losses against profits for the year ending 31 March 2019 is calculated as follows.

	£
A Ltd	
Qualifying profits	1,000,000
Less allocated group deductions allowance	(1,000,000)
Relevant profits	—
Relevant profits × 50%	—
Add allocated group deductions allowance	1,000,000
Maximum set-off	£1,000,000
B Ltd	
Qualifying profits	5,000,000
Less allocated group deductions allowance	(4,000,000)
Relevant profits	1,000,000
Relevant profits × 50%	500,000
Add allocated group deductions allowance	4,000,000
Maximum set-off	£4,500,000
C Ltd	
Qualifying profits	500,000
Less allocated group deductions allowance	—
Relevant profits	500,000
Relevant profits × 50%	250,000
Add allocated group deductions allowance	—
Maximum set-off	£250,000

Loss memoranda

	£
A Ltd	
Loss brought forward from y/e 31.3.18	1,000,000
Less relieved y/e 31.3.19	(1,000,000)
	–
B Ltd	
Loss brought forward from y/e 31.3.18	5,000,000

Less relieved y/e 31.3.19	(4,500,000)
Carried forward to y/e 31.3.20	£500,000

C Ltd

Loss brought forward from y/e 31.3.18	500,000
Less relieved y/e 31.3.19	(250,000)
Carried forward to y/e 31.3.20	£250,000

Notes

(a) A group of companies has a single deductions allowance known as the group deductions allowance and can allocate this to any company or companies in the group as it chooses. This is done through a nominated company. The maximum amount of the allowance that is available to be shared amongst all group companies is £5 million (reduced proportionately for accounting periods of less than twelve months). The nomination must be made by all the companies in the group that are within the charge to corporation tax and must state the date the nomination takes effect, which may be before the date the nomination is made. [*CTA 2010, s 269ZR; F(No 2)A 2017, Sch 4 para 16*].

(b) A group for this purpose is two or more companies where one company is the ultimate parent of each of the other companies and is not the ultimate parent of any other company. A company (A) is the ultimate parent of another company (B) if A is the parent of B and no company is the parent of both A and B. A is the parent of B if B is a 75% subsidiary of A, A is beneficially entitled to at least 75% of any profits available for distribution to equity holders of B or A would be beneficially entitled to at least 75% of the assets of B distributed to equity holders on a winding-up. [*CTA 2010, s 269ZZB; F(No 2)A 2017, Sch 4 para 16*].

(c) See also **106.6** GROUP RELIEF for group relief for carried-forward losses.

115 Payment of Tax

Cross-reference. See **109.1** and **110.1** for interest on overpaid and unpaid tax, and **118.1** and **118.2** for returns and filing dates.

115.1 PAYMENTS BY LARGE COMPANIES

[*TMA 1970, ss 59D, 59E; SI 1998 No 3175; SI 2014 No 2409; SI 2017 No 1072*]

(A) Large companies

BG Ltd, which has five related 51% group companies, draws up accounts to 31 December each year. Its taxable profits and tax liabilities are as follows. Note that the tax liabilities are assumed for the purposes of the example only.

Accounting period ended	Profits	Tax
	£	£
31.12.12	240,000	22,500
31.12.13	260,000	20,000
31.12.14	275,000	25,000
31.12.15	255,000	9,500
31.12.16	270,000	68,000
31.12.17	260,000	60,000
31.12.18	200,000	40,000

The upper limit is as follows

£1,500,000 ÷ 6 = £250,000

Year ended 31.12.12

The company is not large as its profits do not exceed the upper limit.

Year ended 31.12.13

Although the company's profits exceed the upper limit, it will not have to make quarterly instalments payments because it was not large during the previous twelve months.

Year ended 31.12.14

The company is a large company in this period as it would have been a large company in the previous year but for the exclusion in *SI 1998 No 3175, reg 3*.

Year ended 31.12.15

Although the company's profits exceed the upper limit, its tax liability does not exceed £10,000 so it is not a large company.

Year ended 31.12.16

Although the company's profits exceed the upper limit, it will not have to make quarterly instalment payments because it was not large during the previous twelve months.

Year ended 31.12.17

The company is a large company in this period as it would have been a large company in the previous year but for the exclusion in *SI 1998 No 3175, reg 3.*

Year ended 31.12.18

The company is not large as its profits do not exceed the upper limit.

Notes

(a) For accounting periods beginning on or after 1 April 2015, a company is 'large' for the purpose of quarterly instalment payments (see B below) if its augmented profits for an accounting period exceed the *CTA 2010, s 24* 'upper limit' which is in force at the end of that period. This is £1,500,000 divided by one plus the number of 'related 51% group companies' (as defined at *CTA 2010, s 279F*). For accounting periods beginning before 1 April 2015, the upper limit is fixed at £1,500,000 divided by one plus the number of associated companies. It is proportionately reduced where the accounting period is less than 12 months. 'Augmented profits' mean total profits chargeable to corporation tax plus 'exempt ABGH distributions' (as defined) (or, before 6 April 2016, franked investment income ('FII')) of the period other than any such distributions or FII received from fellow group members.

(b) A company is not large in an accounting period for which its total corporation tax liability (reduced by any deductions from payments in the period under the construction industry tax scheme) does not exceed £10,000, proportionately reduced if the accounting period is less than twelve months, or if its profits do not exceed £10,000,000 provided it was not a large company (disregarding this exclusion) in the previous 12-month period. The £10,000,000 threshold is reduced by dividing it by one plus the number of related 51% group companies (for accounting periods ending before 1 April 2015, associated companies) and is reduced proportionately where the accounting period is less than 12 months.

(B) Instalment payments

HP Ltd, a large company, draws up accounts to 30 September each year. The company's return for the year ended 30 September 2018 shows total taxable profits of £4,000,000 and corporation tax payable £760,000.

Tax is due and payable by the company for the year ended 30 September 2018 as follows.

Instalments due:	£
14.4.18	190,000
14.7.18	190,000
14.10.18	190,000
14.1.18	190,000
	£760,000

Notes

(a) Large companies (see (A) above) are required to pay corporation tax by instalments. Instalments are due at intervals of three months commencing six months and thirteen days from the start of the accounting period and culminating three months and fourteen days from its end. Therefore, for a twelve-month accounting period there will be four instalments.

(b) Instalment payments are calculated by reference to the total liability of the accounting period to which they relate. Where four instalments are due, each will be one quarter of the liability. Each instalment is calculated by reference to the formula $3 \times CTI/n$ where CTI is the total liability and n is the number of whole months in the accounting period plus the 'relevant decimal' (which adjusts for any odd days in the period). Clearly, an estimate of the liability will be required for making instalments before the final liability is known. Where those estimates turn out to be incorrect, interest will be charged to the extent that the instalment payments were insufficient (and interest will be paid on overpayments). Top-up payments may be made at any time. Where the company has grounds for believing that its instalment payments were excessive it may claim a repayment. For interest on instalment payments see **109.1(B)** INTEREST ON OVERPAID TAX and **110.1(C)** INTEREST ON UNPAID TAX.

(c) For accounting periods beginning on or after 1 April 2019, companies with profits exceeding £20 million will have to pay instalments in the third, sixth, ninth and twelfth months of the accounting period. The £20 million threshold will be divided between members of a group. See (C) below.

(C) Instalment payments by very large companies

KW plc, a very large company, draws up accounts to 31 March each year. The company's return for the year ended 31 March 2020 shows total taxable profits of £24,000,000 and corporation tax payable £4,560,000.

Tax is due and payable by the company for the year ended 31 March 2020 as follows.

Instalments due:	£
14.6.19	1,140,000
14.9.19	1,140,000
14.12.19	1,140,000
14.3.20	1,140,000
	£4,560,000

Notes

(a) For accounting periods beginning on or after 1 April 2019, the timing of instalment payments by a company depends on whether or not it is a 'very large' company. Where the company is very large, the first instalment is due two months and 13 days after the first day of the accounting period. The second, third and final instalments are then due at three-monthly intervals. If the accounting period is less than 12 months, the final instalment is generally due 14 days after the date falling one month before the end of the period. Earlier instalments are required only if they fall due before the final instalment date. If the accounting period does not end on the last day of the month and there is no day in the previous month with the same date, the final instalment is due 14 days after the last day of the previous month. Therefore, for a twelve-month accounting period there will be four instalments.

(b) Instalment payments are calculated by reference to the total liability of the accounting period to which they relate. Where four instalments are due, each will be one quarter of the liability. Each instalment is calculated by reference to the formula 3 × CTI/(*wm* + *wmd* where CTI is the total liability and *wm* is the number of whole months in the accounting period and *wmd* is a decimal which adjusts for any odd days in the period. Clearly, an estimate of the liability will be required for making instalments before the final liability is known. Where those estimates turn out to be incorrect, interest will be charged to the extent that the instalment payments were insufficient (and interest will be paid on overpayments). Top-up payments may be made at any time. Where the company has grounds for believing that its instalment payments were excessive it may claim a repayment. For interest on instalment payments see **109.1(B)** INTEREST ON OVERPAID TAX and **110.1(C)** INTEREST ON UNPAID TAX.

(c) A '*very large*' company is one whose profits (including UK dividend income, other than intra-group dividends) exceed £20,000,000 in an accounting period, divided by one plus the number of related 51% group companies (as defined at *CTA 2010, s 279F*). The threshold is proportionately reduced where the accounting period is less than 12 months. If a company is not a large company for an accounting period as a result of the rules described in note (b) to (A) above, it is not a very large company for that period.

116 Profit Computations

116.1 COMPUTATIONS

Y Ltd's accounts for the 12 months to 31 December 2018 show the following.

	£		£
Wages and salaries	77,500	Gross trading profit	209,160
Rent, rates and insurance	5,000	Net rents	1,510
Motor expenses	8,000	Government securities	340
Car hire	6,000	Dividend from UK company	
Legal expenses	2,000	(received 30.9.18)	4,500
Directors' remuneration	22,875	Profit on sale of investment	5,500
Audit and accountancy	2,500		
Miscellaneous expenses	2,600		
Debenture finance charges	2,450		
Ordinary dividend paid	15,000		
Depreciation	6,125		
Premium on lease written off	14,000		
Net profit	56,960		
	£221,010		£221,010

Analysis of various items gave the following additional information

		£
Legal expenses:		
Re staff service agreements		250
Re debt collecting		600
Re new issue of debentures (see (viii) below)		1,150
		£2,000
Miscellaneous expenses:		
Staff outing		400
Subscriptions:	Chamber of Commerce	250
	Political party	100
Interest on overdue tax		250
Contribution to training and enterprise council		350
Charitable donation to trade benevolent fund		150
Qualifying charitable donations		1,100
		£2,600

(ii) On 1 July 2018, Y Ltd was granted a lease on office accommodation for a period of seven years from that date for which it paid a premium of £14,000.

(iii) Car hire of £6,000 represents the hire, under a contract dated 1 July 2018, of a car with emissions 180g/km.

(iv) All wages and salaries were paid during the period of account apart from directors' bonuses of £20,000, accrued in the accounts, voted at the AGM on 1 November 2019 and not previously paid or credited to directors' accounts with the company.

(v) Profit on sale of investment is the unindexed gain arising from the sale of quoted securities on 28 February 2018. The chargeable gain after indexation is £2,070.

(vi) Capital allowances for the year to 31 December 2018 are £10,000.

(vii) Debenture finance charges relate to £50,000 nominal stock issued on 1 January 2018 for trade finance at £96 per £100, carrying interest at 4.5% payable annually in arrears, for redemption 31 December 2025. The charge to profit and loss comprises interest of £2,250 and redemption reserve costs of £200 on a straight line basis. As these are arrived at under an amortised cost basis, the charges are allowable for tax purposes. The issue costs included in legal expenses (see (i) above) are also allowable.

(viii) The £340 Government securities credit relates to £4,000 nominal stock acquired in May 2017 at £4,040 with two years to redemption. It represents gross interest £360 less £20 premium amortisation charge on a straight line basis. It is thus properly chargeable as income from a non-trading loan relationship. The interest was received gross on 31 March and 30 September.

The corporation tax computation is as follows

		£	£
Net profit			56,960
Add			
Depreciation		6,125	
Directors' remuneration	(note (a))	20,000	
Subscription to political party		100	
Charitable donations	(notes (c) and (d))	1,100	
Car hire	(note (e))	900	
Dividend paid		15,000	
Premium on lease written off	(note (f))	14,000	
Interest on overdue tax (note (g))		250	57,475
			114,435
Deduct			
Net rents		1,510	
Government securities		340	
Dividend received		4,500	
Profit on sale of investment		5,500	(11,850)
			102,585

Deduct		
Capital allowances	10,000	
Allowance for lease premium (note (f))		
$\frac{1}{7} \times \left(\frac{£14{,}000}{50} \times (50 - (7 - 1)) \right) \times \frac{6}{12}$	880	
		(10,880)
CT trading profit		91,705
Income from non-trading loan relationships (note (g))		90
Property Income		1,510
Chargeable gains		2,070
		95,375
Deduct Qualifying charitable donations (note (d))		(1,100)
Profits chargeable to corporation tax		£94,275

Notes

(a) Director's remuneration of £20,000 is disallowed as it remained unpaid nine months after the end of the period of account. It will, however, be allowable in the tax computation for the year to 31 December 2019, i.e. the period of account in which it is paid. See also *CTA 2009, s 1289; ITEPA 2003, s 18.*

(b) The contribution to a training and enterprise council is allowable under *CTA 2009, ss 82–86.*

(c) The charitable donation to trade benevolent fund is allowable under *CTA 2009, s 1300.*

(d) The qualifying charitable donations are deducted from the company's total profits under the Gift Aid provisions. [*CTA 2010, ss 189, 190*].

(e) The allowable proportion of the car hire expenditure is £6,000@85%

[*CTA 2009, s 56*].

(f) The proportion of the lease premium allowable is calculated under *CTA 2009 ss 217–220.*

(g) Interest on the overdue tax is treated as a non-trading loan relationship debit. The income from non-trading loan relationships for the year ended 31 December 2018 is therefore (£340 − £250 =) £90.

117 Research and Development

117.1 SMALL OR MEDIUM-SIZED ENTERPRISE

[*CTA 2009, ss 104B, 1044–1062; FA 2011, s 43; FA 2012, s 20, Sch 3; FA 2013, Sch 15 paras 12–15, 27–29; FA 2014, s 31; FA 2015, s 27*]

D Ltd is a small or medium-sized enterprise established on 1 January 2017. The company incurs qualifying research and development expenditure of £80,000 in the year ended 31 December 2017 , in addition to other revenue expenditure of £50,000 (all of which would have been allowable expenditure had the company been trading). On 1 January 2018 D Ltd commences a trade derived from the research and development expenditure, making a taxable profit (before adjustment for research and development relief or pre-trading expenditure) of £160,000 for the year ended 31 December 2018. Further qualifying research and development expenditure is incurred in that year of £41,000. If the company does not make a claim under *CTA 2009, s 104A* (see **117.2** below) the corporation tax position is as follows.

Y/e 31.12.17

D Ltd may elect, under *CTA 2009, s 1045*, by 31 December 2019, to be treated as having incurred a trading loss in the period of an amount equal to 230% of the qualifying research and development expenditure, i.e. £184,000 (£80,000 × 230%). There are then a number of possible alternatives open to D Ltd to make use of the loss. It may:

(1) set the loss against other profits for the accounting period under *CTA 2010, s 37(3)(a)*;

(2) surrender the loss as group relief under *CTA 2010, s 99*;

(3) claim a research and development tax credit equal to 14.5% of the loss (as reduced by any part of it relieved under (1) or (2)) under *CTA 2010, s 1060*; or

(4) carry the losses arising before 1 April 2017 forward for set-off against future trading income under *CTA 2010, s 45* ; or

(5) carry the losses arising after 31 March 2017 forward for set-off against future total profits or surrender as group relief under *CTA 2010, s 45B*.

D Ltd claims a tax credit as in (3) above in respect of the deemed loss for the year ended 31 December 2017. Assuming that all of the loss qualifies for the 14.5% tax credit rate, the credit is £184,000 × 14.5% = £26,680.

Y/e 31.12.18

D Ltd claims for the qualifying research and development expenditure to be treated as if it were 230% of the actual amount, i.e. £94,300. The company's taxable trading profits for the year are therefore as follows.

	£
Adjusted profit as above	160,000
Less Research and development relief	(94,300)
Other pre-trading expenditure	(50,000)
Trading profits chargeable to CT	£15,700

Note

(a) Relief for expenditure on research and development is available for expenditure of a revenue nature incurred by a 'small or medium-sized' company on qualifying 'research and development'. A 'small or medium-sized' enterprise is one that has less than 500 employees and either or both annual turnover not exceeding 100 million euros and annual balance sheet total not exceeding 86 million euros. A company is generally excluded if any company in which it holds, or which holds in it, more than 25% of the capital or voting rights, is not a small or medium-sized enterprise. For accounting periods ending before 1 April 2012 the company had to incur research and development expenditure of at least £10,000 (reduced pro-rata for accounting periods of less than 12 months) to qualify for enhanced relief.
For qualifying research and development expenditure incurred on or after 1 April 2015, where a claim is made, the expenditure is to be treated as if it were 230% of the actual amount. [*CTA 2009, s 1044; FA 2011, s 43(3)(13); FA 2012, Sch 3 para 2; FA 2015, s 27*].

117.2 ABOVE THE LINE R&D EXPENDITURE CREDITS

[*CTA 2009, ss 104A–104Y; FA 2013, Sch 15; FA 2015, s 27*].

R Ltd, a large company has trade profits of £6,000,000 before deducting research and development expenditure of £2,000,000 for the year ended 31 March 2019. The research and development expenditure is qualifying expenditure for the purposes of the above the line (ATL) expenditure credit. If R Ltd's claims relief, its corporation tax liability will be as follows.

	£'000
Trade profits before R&D expenditure	6,000
Qualifying R&D expenditure	(2,000)
	4,000
R&D expenditure credit ('above the line')	240
Additional R&D expenditure relief	–
Trade profits	4,240
Corporation tax at 19%	805.60
Deduct R&D expenditure credit (ATL)	(240.00)
Corporation tax payable	565.60

Notes

(a) 'Above the line' research and development tax credits may be claimed by companies for expenditure incurred on or after 1 April 2013. The scheme initially ran alongside the previous research and development reliefs for large companies, but those reliefs ceased to be available for expenditure incurred on or after 1 April 2016. A company could not claim relief under both schemes for the same expenditure, and once a company had made a claim under the new scheme it could make no further claims under the existing schemes. [*CTA 2009, ss 104A–104Y, 1040A; FA 2013, Sch 15*].

(b) Where a company claims ATL R&D expenditure credit, the amount of the credit is included as a receipt in the company's tax computation. The amount of the credit is 12% of the qualifying expenditure (11% for expenditure incurred before 1 January 2018, 10% for expenditure incurred before 1 April 2015; 49% in the case of a ring fence trade). [*CTA 2009, ss 104A, 104M*; *FA 2013, Sch 15 para 1*; *FA 2015, s 27*]. The tax credit is set off against the company's corporation tax liability for the period. If the credit exceeds the corporation tax liability then a specified order of set off applies, which allows for it to be surrendered as group relief, as well as carried forward, or back, against the company's tax liability for other accounting periods. See *CTA 2009, s 104N*.

118 Returns

118.1 RETURN PERIODS

[*FA 1998, Sch 18 paras 3–7*]

(A)

Aquarius Ltd has always prepared its accounts to 31 October. In 2018, it changes its accounting date, preparing accounts for the nine months to 31 July 2018. On 31 January 2018, HMRC issues a notice specifying a return period of 1 November 2016 to 31 October 2017. On 31 January 2019, they issue a notice specifying a return period of 1 November 2017 to 31 October 2018.

In respect of the first-mentioned notice, Aquarius Ltd is required to make a return for the period 1.11.16 to 31.10.17 accompanied by accounts and tax computations for that period.

In respect of the second of the above-mentioned notices, the company is required to make a return for the period 1.11.17 to 31.7.18 accompanied by accounts and tax computations for that period. [*FA 1998, Sch 18 para 5(1)(2)*].

(B)

Pisces Ltd has always prepared its accounts to 31 December. In 2018, it changes its accounting date, preparing accounts for the nine months to 30 September 2018. On 15 December 2018, HMRC issue a notice specifying a return period of 1 October 2017 to 30 September 2018.

Pisces Ltd is required to make returns both for the period 1.1.17 to 31.12.17 and for the period 1.1.18 to 30.9.18, each return being accompanied by accounts and tax computations for the period covered by it. [*FA 1998, Sch 18 para 5(1)(2)*].

(C)

Aries Ltd has always prepared accounts to 31 October. After 2017, it changes its accounting date, preparing accounts for the fifteen months to 31 January 2019. On 21 August 2018, HMRC issue a notice specifying a return period of 1 November 2016 to 31 October 2017. On 31 January 2018, they issue a notice specifying a return period of 1 November 2017 to 31 October 2018.

In respect of the first-mentioned notice, Aries Ltd is required to make a return for the period 1.11.16 to 31.10.17 accompanied by accounts and tax computations for that period.

In respect of the second of the above-mentioned notices, the company is required to make a return for the accounting period 1.11.17 to 31.10.18, accompanied by accounts and tax computations for the period of account 1.11.18 to 31.1.19. [*FA 1998, Sch 18 para 5(1)(3)*].

(D)

Taurus Ltd has always prepared accounts to 31 October. After 2017, it changes its accounting date, preparing accounts for the fifteen months to 31 January 2019. On 31 January 2018, HMRC issue a notice specifying a return period of 1 November 2016 to 31 October 2017. On 1 April 2018, HMRC issue a notice specifying a return period of 1 November 2017 to 31 January 2018.

In respect of the first-mentioned notice, the position is as in (C) above.

In respect of the second of the above-mentioned notices, Taurus Ltd is not required to make a return, but should notify HMRC of the correct accounting dates and periods. [*FA 1998, Sch 18 para 5(3)(5)*].

(E)

Gemini Ltd was incorporated on 1 July 2015 but remains dormant until 1 April 2017 when it begins to trade. The first trading accounts are prepared for the year to 31 March 2018 and the company retains that accounting date. On 1 May 2019, HMRC issue notices specifying return periods of 1 July 2015 to 30 June 2016, 1 July 2016 to 30 June 2017, 1 July 2017 to 30 June 2018 and 1 July 2018 to 31 March 2019.

In respect of the notice for the period 1.7.15 to 30.6.16, Gemini Ltd is required to make a return for that period.

In respect of the notice for the period 1.7.16 to 30.6.17, the company is required to make a return for the period 1.7.17 to 31.3.17.

In respect of the notice for the period 1.7.17 to 30.6.18, the company is required to make a return for the period 1.4.17 to 31.3.18 accompanied by accounts and tax computations for that period.

In respect of the notice for the period 1.7.18 to 31.3.19, the company is required to make a return for the period 1.4.18 to 31.3.19 accompanied by accounts and tax computations for that period. [*FA 1998, Sch 18 para 5(1)(2)*].

118.2 FILING DATES

[*FA 1998, Sch 18 para 14*]

The final dates for the filing with HMRC of the returns in **118.1** above, and for the payment of corporation tax (assuming none of the companies concerned falls within the definition of a 'large company' to which the instalment payment provisions apply—see **115.1** PAYMENT OF TAX), are as follows

Return period	Filing date		Payment date (note (f))
118.1(A) above			
1.11.16 – 31.10.17	31.10.18	(note (a))	1.8.18
1.11.17 – 31.7.18	31.7.19		1.5.19
118.1(B) above			
1.1.17 – 31.12.17	15.3.19	(note (b))	1.10.18
1.1.18 – 30.9.18	30.9.19		1.7.19
118.1(C) above			
1.11.16 – 31.10.17	21.11.18	(note (b))	1.8.18
1.11.17 – 31.10.18	31.1.20	(note (c))	1.8.19

Return period	Filing date	Payment date
118.1(D) above		
1.11.16 – 31.10.17	31.10.18	1.8.18
118.1(E) above		
1.7.16 – 30.6.16	1.8.19	—
1.7.16 – 31.3.17	1.8.19	—
1.4.17 – 31.3.18	1.8.19	1.1.19
1.4.18 – 31.3.19	31.3.20	1.1.20

Notes

(a) The normal filing date is the first anniversary of the last day of the return period.

(b) If later than the date in (a) above (or, where relevant, (c) below), the filing date is three months after the date on which the notice is issued by the Inspector.

(c) Where a company's period of account extends beyond the end of the return period, the filing date is extended to the first anniversary of the last day of that period of account. This is subject to a limit of 30 months from the beginning of the period of account, although this would come into play only in the exceptional case where accounts are prepared for a period exceeding 18 months.

(d) The time allowed for filing returns is effectively extended to the time allowed under the *Companies Act 2006* if this would give a later filing date than under (a)–(c) above. [*FA 1998, Sch 18 para 19*]. This will not be so in the majority of cases.

(e) HMRC may grant an extension, on an application by the company, if they are satisfied that the company has a 'reasonable excuse' for not being able to meet the filing date under (a)–(c) above. [*TMA 1970, s 118(2)*].

(f) Nothing in (a)–(e) above affects a company's liability to pay corporation tax within nine months and one day following the end of an accounting period. [*TMA 1970, s 59D(1)*]. See **115** PAYMENT OF TAX for the instalment payment provisions applicable to large companies.

119 Transfer Pricing

119.1 ADJUSTMENTS FOR TRANSFER PRICING

[*TIOPA 2010, ss 146–230; FA 2014, s 75; FA 2016, s 75*].

(A) Transfer pricing adjustment

A Ltd provides management and administrative services to a number of its wholly-owned subsidiaries. All companies in the group have accounting periods ending on 31 March and do not qualify as small or medium-sized enterprises for transfer pricing purposes. For the accounting period ending 31 March 2018, A Ltd makes a charge for its management and administrative services to B Ltd of £450,000. Following an enquiry into A Ltd's return for that period, it is agreed that the arm's length value of the services to A Ltd was £600,000. An adjustment is accordingly made of £150,000 to increase A Ltd's taxable profits by that amount.

B Ltd can claim to apply a corresponding adjustment (see note (c) below) to reduce its taxable profits for the same period by £150,000 (increasing its deductible expenses to £600,000). B Ltd may also make a balancing payment to A Ltd of up to £150,000 without it being treated as a distribution or otherwise taken into account for tax purposes.

Notes

(a) The transfer pricing rules apply broadly where transactions between connected parties take place at other than arm's length prices conferring an advantage to the parties in terms of a reduction in the liability to UK tax. A transfer pricing adjustment may then be made to restore the tax position to what it would have been had the transaction been at arm's length. The regime applies to both UK and cross-border transactions. Dormant companies and small and medium-sized enterprises will, in most circumstances, be exempt from applying the transfer pricing and thin capitalisation rules. Where an adjustment is required by the provisions to increase the profits of one party, the corresponding adjustment provisions apply so that the connected UK party can make a compensating reduction in their taxable profits, and provisions allow for a 'balancing payment' to be made tax-free up to the amount of the compensating adjustment.

(b) A 'dormant' company is one which is dormant (under the *Companies Act 2006, s 1169*) throughout the accounting period ending on 31 March 2004 (or if there is no such accounting period, the three-month period ending on that date); and has continued to be dormant at all times since the end of that period apart from any transfer pricing adjustments. Very broadly, a small enterprise is defined as a business with less than 50 employees and either turnover or assets of less than €10 million and a small or medium-sized enterprise as a business with less than 250 employees and either turnover of less than €50 million or assets of less than €43 million. A medium-sized enterprise can still be subject to a transfer pricing notice.

(c) Where a transfer pricing adjustment has been made by the advantaged party (either in the return or following a determination) the disadvantaged party may claim a corresponding adjustment in applying the arm's length rule rather than the actual provision. Claims must be made within two years of the making of the return or the giving of the notice taking account of the determination, and a claim based on a return which is subsequently the subject of such a notice may be amended within two years of the giving of the notice. (These time limits may be extended in certain cases where HMRC fails to give proper notice to disadvantaged persons under *TIOPA 2010, s 185*.) With effect, broadly, for amounts arising on or after 25 October 2013 a corresponding adjustment may not be claimed by a disadvantaged person which is not a company and which is within the charge to income tax if the advantaged person is a company.

(d) Where a transfer pricing adjustment is made, the disadvantaged company may make a corresponding balancing payment to the advantaged company. Provided the balancing payment does not exceed the amount of the 'available compensating adjustment', it is not taken into account when computing profits or losses for tax purposes or regarded as a distribution or charge on income. The '*available compensating adjustment*' is the difference between the profits and losses of the disadvantaged company computed on the basis of the actual provision and computed for the purposes of making a compensating adjustment (see note (c) above).

(B) Transfer pricing and thin capitalisation

On 1 July 2017, B Ltd is granted a loan of £5,000,000 at 6% interest p.a. from an unassociated bank. The loan is guaranteed by B Ltd's parent company, G plc. Both companies draw up accounts for the year ended 30 June and neither company qualifies as a small or medium-sized enterprise for transfer pricing purposes. Following an enquiry into B Ltd's return for the accounting period ending 30 June 2018, HMRC successfully maintain that, in the absence of the guarantee from G plc, the bank would not have advanced more than £1,000,000 to B Ltd. Accordingly, an adjustment is made to increase B Ltd's profits for the period by £240,000 in disallowing the interest on £4,000,000 of the loan.

G plc could make a claim (or B Ltd could claim on its behalf) for a corresponding adjustment before or after the transfer pricing adjustment is made in B Ltd's return, or following the determination so that it is treated as having paid the interest subject to the disallowance. Accordingly, provided the interest in G plc's case would not be subject to a transfer pricing adjustment, G plc could claim a deduction for £240,000 in respect of the interest paid by B Ltd. G plc can make a balancing payment of up to £240,000 to B Ltd without it being treated as a distribution or charge on income or otherwise taken into account for tax purposes.

Notes

(a) A compensating adjustment may be claimed by the disadvantaged party or by the advantaged person on his behalf before or after the arm's length provision has been applied in the case of the advantaged party (in his return or following a determination). Where a transfer pricing adjustment to disallow interest follows from the provision of a guarantee, the guarantor can claim a compensating adjustment as if it was the borrower and had paid the interest subject to the disallowance, and adjust its accounts accordingly. A claim can also be made by the lender on behalf of the guarantor. Claims must be made or amended before the expiry of the time limits in note (c) to (A) above.

(b) Where a transfer pricing adjustment applies to disallow interest and the lender claims a compensating adjustment under either *TIOPA 2010, ss 174–178* or *ss 181–184*, the interest disallowed as a deduction for the borrower is correspondingly not treated as from non-trading loan relationships income for the lending company.

(c) Where a transfer pricing adjustment applies in the case of the advantaged company, the guarantor company may make a corresponding balancing payment to the borrower. Provided such a balancing payment does not in aggregate exceed the amount of the compensating adjustment, it is not taken into account for corporation tax purposes when computing profits or losses of the guarantor or the borrower, or regarded as a distribution or charge on income. The compensating adjustment in this case is the total reduction in interest or other amounts payable under the loan subject to the guarantee (and thus treated as paid by the guarantor).

(d) For accounting periods commencing on or after 1 April 2017 (subject to transitional rules), the group would also be subject to the corporate interest restriction (CIR) rules in *TIOPA 2010, ss 372–498* and *Sch 7A*. These highly complex rules also incorporate a successor to the worldwide debt cap regime which has been repealed from the same date. Broadly, the CIR restricts interest and similar finance amounts to 30% of 'tax-EBITDA' ('the fixed ratio method') subject to a modified debt cap. There is also an election for an alternative group ratio method with its own modified debt cap. Groups with finance costs below £2m per annum will be unaffected by CIR. The CIR applies *after* transfer pricing and anti-hybrid rules, etc. but *before* the loss restriction rules. See CHAPTER **114** for details on loss restriction.

(e) See also the notes to (A) above.

Capital Gains Tax

201 Annual Rates and Exemptions

201.1 RATES OF TAX

[*TCGA 1992, ss 4, 4A, 4BA; FA 2016, ss 2, 83*]

(A)

Erica owns an established business and has taxable profits of £40,000 for her accounting year ended 5 April 2019. She has no other income for 2018/19 but she makes a chargeable gain (before deduction of the annual exemption) of £30,000. The gain is not an upper rate gain and does not qualify for entrepreneurs' relief. Her capital gains tax liability for 2018/19 is computed as follows.

			£
Trade profits			40,000
Deduct Personal allowance			(11,850)
Step 3 income			£28,150
Unused part of the basic rate band (£34,500 – £28,150)			£6,350
Chargeable gain			30,000
Deduct Annual exemption			(11,700)
Taxable gain			£18,300
	£		
	6,350	@ 10%	635
	11,950	@ 20%	2,390
	£18,300		£3,025

Notes

(a) Except for upper rate gains (see (C) below), an individual's gains are chargeable at a rate of 10%. However, to any extent that gains, if treated as the top slice of income, exceed the basic rate limit (£34,500 for 2018/19), they are chargeable at 20%. Note that for 2018/19, for Scottish taxpayers, the basic rate limit remains at £34,500 for the purpose of determining the applicable rate of capital gains tax. [*TCGA 1992, s 4(10); Scotland Act 2016, s 15(2)–(4); FA 2016, s 83(11)*].

(b) See (B) below for the 10% rate applicable to gains in respect of which a claim to entrepreneurs' relief is made.

(B)

Felix owns an established business and has taxable profits of £44,000 for his accounting year ended 31 March 2019. He has no other income for 2018/19 but he makes two chargeable gains (before deducting the annual exemption) of £17,000 each. Neither gain is an upper rate gain but one of them qualifies for entrepreneurs' relief. His capital gains tax liability for 2018/19 is computed as follows.

Disposal qualifying for entrepreneurs' relief

	£
Capital gains tax £17,000 × 10%	£1,700

Disposal not qualifying for entrepreneurs' relief

Chargeable gain	17,000
Deduct Annual exemption	(11,700)
Taxable gain	£5,300
Capital gains tax £5,300 × 20%	£1,060
Total capital gains tax for 2018/19 (£1,700 + £1,060)	£2,760

Notes

(a) Gains qualifying for entrepreneurs' relief are treated as the lowest part of the gains for the year. The unused part of the basic rate band, i.e. £2,350 (£34,500 – (£44,000 – £11,850)), is set against the gain qualifying for entrepreneurs' relief even though it does not affect the rate of tax for that gain. The whole of the gain not qualifying for entrepreneurs' relief is therefore chargeable to tax at 20%.

(b) It is assumed that Felix sets his annual exemption against the gain chargeable at 20% as this achieves the greater tax saving.

(C)

Marley owns an established business and has taxable profits of £44,000 for her accounting year ended 31 March 2019. She has no other income for 2018/19 but she makes two chargeable gains (before deducting the annual exemption) of £17,000 each. Neither gain qualifies for entrepreneurs' relief but one of them is an upper rate gain. Her capital gains tax liability for 2018/19 is computed as follows.

	£
Trade profits	44,000
Deduct Personal allowance	(11,850)
Step 3 income	£32,150
Unused part of the basic rate band (£34,500 – £32,150)	£2,350

Standard rate gain

£		£
2,350	@ 10%	235
14,650	@ 20%	2,930
£17,000		£3,165

Upper rate gain	
Chargeable gain	17,000
Deduct Annual exemption	(11,700)
Taxable gain	£5,300
Capital gains tax £5,300 × 28%	£1,484
Total capital gains tax for 2018/19 (£3,165 + £1,484)	£4,649

Notes

(a) 'Upper rate gains' are:

- gains by UK residents on disposals of interests in residential property (whether or not in the UK);
- NRCGT gains (i.e. gains by non-residents on disposals of interests in UK residential property); and
- carried interest gains (i.e. gains accruing under *TCGA 1992, s 103KA(2)(3)* (carried interest) or gains resulting from carried interest (other than a co-investment repayment or return) arising under arrangements not involving a partnership and under which the individual performs investment management services in respect of an investment scheme).

(b) An individual's upper rate gains are chargeable at a rate of 18%. However, to any extent that gains, if treated as the top slice of income, exceed the basic rate limit (£34,500 for 2018/19), they are chargeable at 28%. Note that for 2018/19, for Scottish taxpayers, the basic rate limit remains at £34,500 for the purpose of determining the applicable rate of capital gains tax. [*TCGA 1992, s 4(10); Scotland Act 2016, s 15(2)–(4); FA 2016, s 83(11)*].

(c) The taxpayer can choose to set the unused part of the basic rate band (£2,350) against either the upper rate gain or the other gain. In practice the effect is the same as there is a 10% reduction in the rate of CGT applicable to the gain falling within the unused part of the band. In this example the unused part is set against the standard rate gain for illustration purposes.

(d) It is assumed that Marley sets her annual exemption against the gain chargeable at 28% as this achieves the greater tax saving.

201.2 ANNUAL EXEMPTION

[*TCGA 1992, s 2(2)(4)–(8), s 3; FA 2012, s 34; FA 2015, Sch 7 para 5; FA 2018, Sch 10 para 1(2); SI 2018 No 244*]

(A) **Interaction with losses**

For 2018/19, R, who is UK-resident throughout the year, has chargeable gains of £17,000 and allowable losses of £4,000. He also has allowable losses of £14,000 brought forward.

	£
Adjusted net gains (£17,000 − £4,000)	13,000
Losses brought forward (part)	(1,300)
	11,700
Annual exempt amount	(11,700)
Taxable gains	Nil
Losses brought forward	14,000
Less utilised in 2018/19	(1,300)
Losses carried forward	£12,700

(B) **Interaction with losses and settlement gains attributed under TCGA 1992, s 87**

(i) *Example*

For 2018/19, P, who is resident in the UK, has the same gains and losses (including brought-forward losses) as R above, but is also a beneficiary of an offshore trust. Trust gains of £12,000 are attributed to her for 2017/18 under *TCGA 1992, s 87.*

	£
Adjusted net gains (£17,000 − £4,000 + £11,700 (note (a))	24,700
Losses brought forward (part)	(13,000)
	11,700
Annual exempt amount	(11,700)
	Nil
Add: section 87 gains not brought in above	300
Taxable gains	£300
Losses brought forward	14,000
Less utilised in 2018/19	(13,000)
Losses carried forward	£1,000

(ii) *Example*

Q is in the same position as P except that his attributed gains are only £6,300.

	£
Adjusted net gains (£17,000 − £4,000 + £6,300)	19,300
Losses brought forward (part)	(7,600)
	11,700
Annual exempt amount	(11,700)
Taxable gains	Nil
Losses brought forward	14,000
Less utilised in 2018/19	(7,600)
Losses carried forward	£6,400

Notes

(a) Attributed gains (as in (b) below) are included in adjusted net gains *only* to the extent that they do not exceed the annual exempt amount. Such gains cannot be covered by personal losses. The exempt amount is effectively allocated to attributed gains in priority to personal gains.

(b) For the purposes of (a) above, 'attributed gains' are non-resident settlement gains attributed to a beneficiary under *TCGA 1992, s 87* (as in this example) and those similarly attributed to a beneficiary or onward recipient under *TCGA 1992, ss 87K, 87L, 89(2)*.

202 Anti-Avoidance

202.1 VALUE SHIFTING

[*TCGA 1992, s 29*]

Jak owns all the 1,000 £1 ordinary shares of K Ltd. The shares were acquired on subscription in 1978 for £1,000 and had a value of £65,250 on 31 March 1982. In December 2018, the trustees of Jak's family settlement subscribed at par for 250 £1 ordinary shares in K Ltd, thereby acquiring 20% of the voting power in the company.

It is agreed that the value per share of Jak's holding immediately before the December 2018 share issue was £175 and immediately afterwards was £150. The value per share of the trust's holding, on issue, was £97 per share.

The proceeds of the deemed disposal are computed as follows

Value passing out of Jak's 1,000 shares is £25,000 (1,000 × £25 per share (£175 − £150)).

Value passing into the trust's 250 shares is £24,250 (250 × £97 per share) *less* the subscription price paid of £250 (250 × £1 per share) = £24,000.

The proceeds of the deemed disposal are equal to the value passing into the new shares, i.e. £24,000. (The trust's acquisition cost is £24,250, i.e. actual plus deemed consideration given.)

The disposal is a part disposal (see **208.2** COMPUTATION OF GAINS AND LOSSES), the value of the part retained being £150,000 (1,000 × £150 per share).

Jak will have a capital gain for 2018/19 as follows

	£
Proceeds of deemed disposal	24,000
Allowable cost $\frac{24{,}000}{24{,}000 + 150{,}000} \times £65{,}250$	(9,000)
Chargeable gain	£15,000

Note

(a) The legislation taxes the amount of value passing *into* the transferee holdings, not (if different) the amount passing from the transferor. The deemed proceeds are thus equal to the value received by the transferee(s). See HMRC Capital Gains Manual CG58855.

202.2 VALUE-SHIFTING TO GIVE TAX-FREE BENEFIT

[*TCGA 1992, s 30*]

M owns the whole of the issued share capital in C Ltd, an unquoted company. He is also a director of the company. M receives an offer from a public company for his shares. Prior to sale, C Ltd pays M £30,000 for loss of his office as director. M then sells the shares for £100,000.

On the sale of M's shares, HMRC may seek to adjust the consideration in computing M's chargeable gain on the grounds that M has received a tax-free benefit and the value of his shares has thereby been materially reduced.

202.3 ASSETS DISPOSED OF IN A SERIES OF TRANSACTIONS

[*TCGA 1992, ss 19, 20*]

L purchased a set of 6 antique chairs in June 1991 at a cost of £12,000. He gave 2 chairs to his daughter in February 2013, another pair to his son in November 2015, and sold the final pair to his brother for their market value in August 2018.

The market value of the chairs at the relevant dates were

	2 chairs	4 chairs	6 chairs
	£	£	£
February 2013	6,000	14,000	26,000
November 2015	7,800	18,000	34,200
August 2018	10,400	24,000	46,200

The capital gains tax computations are as follows
February 2013

Disposal to daughter

Deemed consideration	£6,000

As the consideration does not exceed £6,000, the disposal is covered by the chattel exemption (see note (a)).

November 2015

(i) 2012/13 disposal to daughter recomputed

Original market value (deemed disposal consideration at February 2013)	£6,000
Reasonable proportion of aggregate market value as at February 2013 of all assets disposed of to date	
£14,000 × 2/4	£7,000

	£
Deemed consideration (greater of £6,000 and £7,000)	7,000
Cost $\dfrac{7{,}000}{7{,}000 + 14{,}000} \times £12{,}000$	(4,000)
Chargeable gain 2012/13	£3,000

(ii) 2015/16 disposal to son

Original market value (deemed disposal consideration)	£7,800
Reasonable proportion of aggregate market value as at November 2015 of all assets disposed of to date	
£18,000 × 2/4	£9,000

	£
Deemed consideration (greater of £7,800 and £9,000)	9,000
Cost $\dfrac{9{,}000}{9{,}000 + 7{,}800} \times (£12{,}000 - £4{,}000)$	(4,286)
Chargeable gain 2015/16	£4,714

August 2018

(i) Gain on 2012/13 disposal to daughter recomputed

Original market value (deemed consideration in recomputation at November 2015)	£7,000
Reasonable proportion of aggregate market value as at February 2013 of all assets disposed of to date	
£26,000 × 2/6	£8,667
Deemed consideration (greater of £7,000 and £8,667)	£8,667
Cost $\frac{8,667}{8,667 + 14,000} \times £12,000$	(£4,588)
Revised chargeable gain 2012/13	£4,079

(ii) Gain on 2015/16 disposal to son recomputed

Original market value (deemed consideration in computation at November 2015)	£9,000
Reasonable proportion of aggregate market value as at November 2015 of all assets disposed of to date	
£34,200 × 2/6	£11,400
Deemed consideration (greater of £9,000 and £11,400)	11,400
Cost $\frac{11,400}{11,400 + 7,800} \times (£12,000 - £4,588)$	(4,401)
Revised chargeable gain 2015/16	£6,999

(iii) Gain on 2018/19 disposal to brother

Original market value (actual consideration)	£10,400
Reasonable proportion of aggregate market value as at August 2018 of all assets disposed of to date	
£46,200 × 2/6	£15,400
Deemed consideration (greater of £10,400 and £15,400)	£15,400
Cost (£12,000 − £4,588 − £4,401)	(£3,011)
Chargeable gain 2018/19	£12,389

Notes

(a) The disposal in February 2013 is at first covered by the chattel exemption of £6,000. As the second disposal in November 2015 is to a person connected with the recipient of the first disposal, the two must then be looked at together for the purposes of the chattel exemption, and, as the combined proceeds exceed the chattel exemption limit, the exemption is not available. [*TCGA 1992, s 262*]. See also **212.1(C)** EXEMPTIONS AND RELIEFS.

(b) The three disposals are linked transactions within *TCGA 1992, s 19* as they are made by the same transferor to persons with whom he is connected, and take place within a six-year period.

(c) It is assumed in the above example that it is 'reasonable' to apportion the aggregate market value in proportion to the number of items. In other instances a different basis may be needed to give the 'reasonable' apportionment required by *TCGA 1992, s 20(4)*.

202.4 DEPRECIATORY TRANSACTIONS: GROUPS OF COMPANIES

[*TCGA 1992, s 176; FA 2018, s 28*]

G Ltd owns 100% of the share capital of Q Ltd, which it acquired in June 1989 for £75,000. Q Ltd owns land which it purchased in 1985 for £50,000. In 2014, the land, then with a market value of £120,000, was transferred to G Ltd for £50,000. In April 2018, Q Ltd was put into liquidation, and G Ltd received liquidation distributions totalling £30,000.

The loss on the Q Ltd shares is £45,000 (£75,000 − £30,000). The whole or part of the loss is likely to be disallowed on the grounds that it resulted from the depreciatory transaction involving the transfer of land at less than market value.

Note

(a) Where the ultimate disposal of the shares or securities takes place on or after 22 November 2017 (or is treated as taking place before 22 November 2017 as a result of a negligible value claim (see **217.1**(B) LOSSES)) made on or after that date), any depreciatory transactions occurring on or after 31 March 1982 are taken into account. Previously, only depreciatory transactions occurring in the six years ending with that disposal were taken into account.

203 Assets

203.1 OPTIONS

[*TCGA 1992, ss 44, 46, 144, 144ZA–144ZD, 145*]

Cross-reference. See also **232.2** WASTING ASSETS.

On 1 February 2014 F granted an option to G for £10,000 to acquire freehold land bought by F for £50,000 in September 1996. The option is for a period of 5 years, and the option price is £100,000 plus 1% thereof for each month since the option was granted. On 1 February 2016, G sold the option to H for £20,000. On 30 June 2018, H exercises the option and pays F £141,000 for the land. Neither G nor H intended to use the land for the purposes of a trade.

2014 Grant of option by F

		£
Disposal proceeds		10,000
Allowable cost		—
Chargeable gain 2013/14		£10,000

2016 Disposal of option by G

	£	
Disposal proceeds		20,000
Allowable cost	10,000	
Less: Wasted — £10,000 × $^{2}/_{5}$	(4,000)	(6,000)
Chargeable gain 2015/16		£14,000

2018 Exercise of option

(i) Earlier assessment on F vacated	
(ii) Aggregate disposal proceeds	
(£10,000 + £141,000)	151,000
Allowable cost of land	(50,000)
Chargeable gain (on F) 2018/19	£101,000

H's allowable expenditure is

Cost of option	20,000
Cost of land	141,000
	£161,000

Note

(a) The wasting asset rules (see **232** WASTING ASSETS) apply on the disposal of the option by G (though certain options are exempted from these rules — see *TCGA 1992, s 144*). As these rules can only apply on a disposal, they cannot apply on the exercise of the option by H (as the exercise of an option is not treated as a disposal), so his acquisition cost remains intact.

204 Assets held on 6 April 1965

Note

The general re-basing rule for ASSETS HELD ON 31 MARCH 1982 (205) applies automatically and without exception for capital gains tax purposes, so that special rules for assets held on 6 April 1965 are not required. Accordingly, the provisions in this chapter apply only for the purposes of corporation tax on chargeable gains. [*TCGA 1992, s 35(9)*].

204.1 QUOTED SHARES AND SECURITIES

[*TCGA 1992, s 109(4)(5), Sch 2 paras 1–8*]

(A) Basic computation of gain

H Ltd acquired 3,000 U plc ordinary shares in 1962 for £15,000. Their market value was £10 per share on 6 April 1965 and £12 per share on 31 March 1982. In September 2018, H Ltd sells 2,000 of the shares for £45 per share. The indexation factor for the period March 1982 to December 2017 is 2.501.

	£	£	£
Sale proceeds	90,000	90,000	90,000
Cost	(10,000)		
6 April 1965 value		(20,000)	
31 March 1982 value			(24,000)
Unindexed gain	80,000	70,000	66,000
Indexation allowance:			
£24,000 × 2.501	(60,024)	(60,024)	(60,024)
Indexed gain	£19,976	£9,976	£5,976
Chargeable gain			£5,976

Notes

(a) The comparison is firstly between the gain arrived at by deducting cost and that arrived at by deducting 6 April 1965 value. The smaller of the two gains is taken. If, however, an election had been made under either *TCGA 1992, Sch 2 para 4* or *TCGA 1992, s 109(4)* for 6 April 1965 value to be used in computing all gains and losses on quoted shares held at that date, this comparison need not be made and the taxable gain, subject to (c) below, would be £10,000.

(b) The second comparison is between the figure arrived at in (a) above and the gain using 31 March 1982 value. As the latter is smaller, it is substituted for the figure in (b) above by virtue of *TCGA 1992, s 35(2)*. If, however, an election had been made under *TCGA 1992, s 35(5)* for 31 March 1982 value to be used in computing all gains and losses on assets held at that date, neither this comparison nor that in (a) above need be made and the taxable gain would still be £6,000.

(c) Indexation is based on 31 March 1982 value in all three calculations as this gives the greater allowance. [*TCGA 1992, s 55(1)(2)*].

(d) Indexation allowance is frozen at its December 2017 level. No indexation allowance is available in respect of expenditure incurred after 31 December 2017, and for expenditure incurred on or before that date and falling to be deducted on a disposal after that date, indexation allowance is computed up to and including December 2017 only. [*TCGA 1992, ss 53(1)(1B), 54(1B); FA 2018, s 26(2)(3)(6)*].See **214.1** INDEXATION.

(e) All comparisons are between gains *after* indexation.

(B) Basic computation—no gain/no loss disposals

J Ltd acquired a holding of quoted shares in 1956 for £1,000. The market value of the holding at 6 April 1965 and 31 March 1982 respectively was £19,000 and £20,000. J Ltd sells the holding in September 2018 for £18,000. The indexation factor for the period March 1982 to December 2017 is 2.501.

(i) Assuming no elections made to use 1965 value or 1982 value

	£	£
Sale proceeds	18,000	18,000
Cost	(1,000)	
6 April 1965 value		(19,000)
Unindexed gain/(loss)	17,000	(1,000)
Indexation allowance:		
£20,000 × 2.501 (see below) = £50,020 but restricted to	(17,000)	—
Indexed gain/(loss)	Nil	£(1,000)
Chargeable gain/allowable loss		Nil

As one computation shows no gain/no loss and the other a loss, the disposal is a no gain/no loss disposal. [*TCGA 1992, Sch 2 para 2(1)*]. There is no need to compute the gain or loss using 31 March 1982 value as re-basing cannot disturb a no gain/no loss position. [*TCGA 1992, s 35(3)(c)*].

(ii) Election made to use 6 April 1965 value

	£	£
Sale proceeds	18,000	18,000
6 April 1965 value	(19,000)	
31 March 1982 value		(20,000)
(Loss)	(1,000)	(2,000)
Allowable loss	£1,000	

The allowable loss is £1,000 as re-basing cannot increase a loss. [*TCGA 1992, s 35(3)(b)*].

(iii) Election made to use 31 March 1982 value

There is an allowable loss of £2,000.

(C) Parts of holding acquired at different times

L Ltd has the following transactions in shares of A plc, a quoted company

Date	Number of shares bought/(sold)	Cost/(proceeds)
9.1.57	1,500	1,050
10.11.62	750	600
15.7.69	1,200	3,000
12.10.80	1,400	5,000
16.12.83	850	5,950
17.9.95	1,150	5,200
19.12.18	(6,000)	(120,000)
	850	

Market value of A shares at 6 April 1965 was £1.60

Market value of A shares at 31 March 1982 was £4.00

Indexation factors	March 1982 to December 2017	2.501
	December 1983 to April 1985	0.091
	April 1985 to September 1995	0.589
	September 1995 to December 2017	0.847

(i) No election made to substitute 1965 market value

Identify 6,000 shares sold as follows

Section 104 holding	Shares	Qualifying Expenditure	Indexed Pool
		£	£
16.12.83 acquisition	850	5,950	5,950
£5,950 × 0.091			541
6.4.85 pool	850	5,950	6,491
Indexed rise: April 1985 to September 1995			
£6,491 × 0.589			3,823
17.9.95 acquisition	1,150	5,200	5,200
	2,000	11,150	15,514
Indexed rise: September 1995 to December 2017			
£15,514 × 0.847			13,140
			28,654

Section 104 holding	Shares	Qualifying Expenditure	Indexed Pool
		£	£
19.12.18 disposal	(2,000)	(11,150)	(28,654)
Balance of pool	—	—	—

	£
Sale proceeds (2,000 × £20)	40,000
Cost (as above)	(11,150)
Unindexed gain	28,850
Indexation allowance (£28,654 − £11,150)	(17,504)
Chargeable gain	£11,346

1982 holding	£	£
Sale proceeds (1,200 + 1,400) × £20	52,000	52,000
Cost (£3,000 + £5,000)	(8,000)	
Market value 31.3.82 (2,600 × £4)		(10,400)
Unindexed gain	44,000	41,600
Indexation allowance £10,400 × 2.501	(26,010)	(26,010)
Gain after indexation	£17,990	£15,590
Chargeable gain		£15,590

10.11.62 acquisition	£	£	£
Sale proceeds (750 × £20)	15,000	15,000	15,000
Cost	(600)		
Market value 6.4.65 (750 × £1.60)		(1,200)	
Market value 31.3.82 (750 × £4)			(3,000)
Unindexed gain	14,400	13,800	12,000
Indexation allowance £3,000 × 2.501	(7,503)	(7,503)	(7,503)
Gain after indexation	£6,897	£6,297	£4,497
Chargeable gain			£4,497

9.1.57 acquisition (part)	£	£	£
Sale proceeds (650 × £20)	13,000	13,000	13,000
Cost (650 × £0.70)	(455)		
Market value 6.4.65 (650 × £1.60)		(1,040)	
Market value 31.3.82 (650 × £4)			(2,600)
Unindexed gain	12,545	11,960	10,400
Indexation allowance £2,600 × 2.501	(6,503)	(6,503)	(6,503)
Gain after indexation	£6,042	£5,457	£3,897
Chargeable gain			£3,897

Summary of chargeable gains	Number of shares	Chargeable gain £
Section 104 holding	2,000	11,346
1982 holding	2,600	15,590
10.11.62 acquisition	750	4,497
9.1.57 acquisition (part)	650	3,897
	6,000	£35,330

Remaining shares
850 acquired on 9.1.57 for £595

(ii) Election made to substitute 1965 market value

Identify 6,000 shares as follows

Section 104 holding
Disposal of 2,000 shares as in (i) above £11,346

1982 holding	Shares		Pool cost £
9.1.57	1,500	× £1.60	2,400
10.11.62	750	× £1.60	1,200
15.7.69	1,200		3,000
12.10.80	1,400		5,000
	4,850		11,600
19.12.18 disposal	(4,000)	4,000/4,850 × £11,600	(9,567)
Remaining shares	850		£2,033

	£	£
Sale proceeds (4,000 × £20)	80,000	80,000
Cost (as above)	(9,567)	
Market value 31.3.82 (4,000 × £4)		(16,000)
Unindexed gain	70,433	64,000
Indexation allowance £16,000 × 2.501	(40,016)	(40,016)
Gain after indexation	£30,417	£23,984
Chargeable gain		£23,984

Summary of chargeable gains/allowable losses	Number of shares	Chargeable gain/ (loss) £
Section 104 holding	2,000	11,346
1982 holding	4,000	23,984
	6,000	£35,330

Notes

(a) Because re-basing to 31 March 1982 applies in this case, the result is the same whether or not the election to substitute 6 April 1965 value has been made, but with a lower 31 March 1982 value the computations could produce differing overall gains/losses.

(b) Note that indexation is based on 31 March 1982 value whenever this gives the greater allowance.

(c) Indexation allowance is frozen at its December 2017 level. No indexation allowance is available in respect of expenditure incurred after 31 December 2017, and for expenditure incurred on or before that date and falling to be deducted on a disposal after that date, indexation allowance is computed up to and including December 2017 only. [*TCGA 1992, ss 53(1)(1B), 54(1B); FA 2018, s 26(2)(3)(6)*]. See **214.1** INDEXATION.

204.2 LAND REFLECTING DEVELOPMENT VALUE

[*TCGA 1992, Sch 2 paras 9–15*]

K Ltd sells a building plot, on which planning permission has just been obtained, in November 2018 for £200,000. The company acquired the plot in 1958 when its value was £2,000. The market value was £5,000 at 6 April 1965 and £10,000 at 31 March 1982, and the current use value in November 2018 is £15,000. The indexation factor for the period March 1982 to December 2017 is 2.501.

	£	£	£
Sale proceeds	200,000	200,000	200,000
Cost	(2,000)		
Market value 6.4.65		(5,000)	
Market value 31.3.82			(10,000)
Unindexed gain	198,000	195,000	190,000
Indexation allowance			
£10,000 × 2.501	(25,010)	(25,010)	(25,010)
Gain after indexation	£172,990	£169,990	£164,990
Chargeable gain			£164,990

Notes

(a) Time apportionment would have substantially reduced the gain of £172,990, using cost, such that re-basing to 31 March 1982 would have given a greater gain than that based on cost and would not therefore have applied. However, as the plot has been sold for a price in excess of its current use value, no time apportionment can be claimed.

(b) Gains must be compared after applying the indexation allowance, which is based on 31 March 1982 value, this being greater than either cost or 6 April 1965 value.

(c) In this case, the gain is computed in accordance with the rules in 205 ASSETS HELD ON **31** MARCH **1982** as the gain by reference to 31 March 1982 value is lower than the gain by reference to 6 April 1965 value which in turn is lower than the gain by reference to cost.

(d) Indexation allowance is frozen at its December 2017 level. No indexation allowance is available in respect of expenditure incurred after 31 December 2017, and for expenditure incurred on or before that date and falling to be deducted on a disposal after that date, indexation allowance is computed up to and including December 2017 only. [*TCGA 1992, ss 53(1)(1B), 54(1B); FA 2018, s 26(2)(3)(6)*]. See **214.1** INDEXATION.

204.3 OTHER ASSETS

[*TCGA 1992, Sch 2 paras 16–19*]

(A) Chattels

M Ltd purchased a painting in 1942 for £5,000 to hang on the boardroom wall. On 5 October 2018 the company sold the painting for £470,000 net. The painting's value was £129,000 at 6 April 1965, but only £125,000 at 31 March 1982. The indexation factor for the period March 1982 to December 2017 is 2.501.

(i) Time apportionment

Period of ownership since 6 April 1945	(note (a))	73 years 6 months
Period of ownership since 6 April 1965		53 years 6 months
		£
Unindexed gain (£470,000 − £5,000)		465,000
Indexation allowance £125,000 × 2.501	(note (b))	(312,625)
		£152,375
Gain after indexation £152,375 × (53y 6m/73y 6m) (note (c))		£110,912

(ii) Election for 6.4.65 value

		£
Sale proceeds		470,000
Market value 6.4.65		(129,000)
Unindexed gain		341,000
Indexation allowance £129,000 × 2.501	(note (b))	(322,629)
Gain after indexation		£18,371

Election for 6.4.65 value is beneficial, subject to re-basing.

(iii) Re-basing to 1982

		£
Sale proceeds		470,000
Market value 31.3.82		(125,000)
Unindexed gain		345,000
Indexation allowance £129,000 × 2.501	(note (b))	(322,629)
Gain after indexation		£22,371

Re-basing cannot increase a gain. [*TCGA 1992, s 35(3)(a)*]. **Therefore, the gain of £18,371 stands and the election for 6.4.65 value is beneficial.**

Notes

(a) Under time apportionment, the period of ownership is limited to that after 5 April 1945.

(b) In (i) above, indexation is based on 31.3.82 value, being greater than cost — it cannot be based on 6 April 1965 value as this does not enter into the calculation. In (ii), indexation is on the higher of 31.3.82 value and 6.4.65 value. This is also the case in (iii) as one is comparing the position using 6.4.65 value and 31.3.82 value. See *TCGA 1992, s 55(1)(2)*.

(c) Indexation allowance is frozen at its December 2017 level. No indexation allowance is available in respect of expenditure incurred after 31 December 2017, and for expenditure incurred on or before that date and falling to be deducted on a disposal after that date, indexation allowance is computed up to and including December 2017 only. [*TCGA 1992, ss 53(1)(1B), 54(1B); FA 2018, s 26(2)(3)(6)*]. See **214.1** INDEXATION.

(d) The time apportionment calculation is applied to the gain *after* indexation (*Smith v Schofield HL 1993, 65 TC 669, [1993] STC 268*).

(B) Land and buildings

X Ltd acquired land on 5 June 1960 for £7,250. The company acquired access land adjoining the property for £2,750 on 1 January 1961 and, having obtained planning consent, on 30 July 1963 incurred expenditure of £15,000 in building houses on the land, which were let. On 6 September 2018, X Ltd sells the houses with vacant possession for £400,000, net of expenses. The value of the houses and land is £20,000 at 6 April 1965 and £100,000 at 31 March 1982. The indexation factor for the period March 1982 to December 2017 is 2.501.

The gain using time apportionment is

		£	£
Net proceeds of sale			400,000
Deduct Cost of land		7,250	
Cost of addition		2,750	
Cost of building		15,000	(25,000)
Unindexed gain			375,000
Indexation allowance £100,000 × 2.501			(250,100)
Gain after indexation			£124,900
Apportion to allowable expenditure	(note (c))		

	£	£
(i) Land 7,250/25,000 × £124, 900	36,221	
Time apportion £36,221 × (53y 5m/58y 3m)		33,215
(ii) Addition 2,750/25,000 × £124, 900	13,739	
Time apportion £13,739 × (53y 5m/57y 8m)		12,726
(iii) Building 15,000/25,000 × £124, 900	74,940	
Time apportion £74,940 × (53y 5m/55y 1m)		72,672
Gain after indexation and time apportionment		£118,613

The gain using re-basing to 1982 is

	£
Net proceeds of sale	400,000
Market value at 31.3.82	(100,000)
Unindexed gain	300,000
Indexation allowance	
£100,000 × 2.501	(250,100)
Gain	£49,900
Chargeable gain	£49,900

Notes

(a) An election for 6 April 1965 valuation could not be favourable, even were it not for the effect of re-basing, as the value is less than historic costs.

(b) It is the gain/loss *after* time apportionment that is compared with the gain/loss produced by re-basing. [*TCGA 1992, Sch 3 para 6*].

(c) The time apportionment calculation is applied to the gain *after* indexation (*Smith v Schofield HL 1993, 65 TC 669*, [*1993*] *STC 268*).

(d) Indexation allowance is frozen at its December 2017 level. No indexation allowance is available in respect of expenditure incurred after 31 December 2017, and for expenditure incurred on or before that date and falling to be deducted on a disposal after that date, indexation allowance is computed up to and including December 2017 only. [*TCGA 1992, ss 53(1)(1B), 54(1B); FA 2018, s 26(2)(3)(6)*]. See **214.1** INDEXATION.

(C) **Unquoted shares**

On 6 April 1953, A Ltd acquired 5,000 shares in C Ltd, an unquoted company, for £15,201. At 6 April 1965, the value of the holding was £15,000. A Ltd sells the shares (its entire holding in the company) on 6 April 2018 for £95,000.

The indexation factor for the period March 1982 to December 2017 is 2.501. No election for universal 31 March 1982 re-basing is made but the market value of the holding at that date is agreed at £17,000.

The gain using time apportionment is as follows

Total period of ownership:	65 years
Period after 6 April 1965:	53 years

	£
Proceeds	95,000
Cost	(15,201)
Unindexed gain	79,799
Indexation allowance:	
31.3.82 value £17,000 × 2.501	(42,517)
Gain after indexation	£37,282
Gain after time apportionment: £37,282 × 53/65	£30,399

The gain with an election to use 6.4.65 value is as follows

	£
Proceeds	95,000
6.4.65 value	(15,000)
Unindexed gain	80,000
Indexation allowance:	
31.3.82 value £17,000 × 2.501	(42,517)
Gain after indexation	£37,483

The gain with re-basing to 1982 is as follows

	£
Proceeds	95,000
31.3.82 value	(17,000)
Unindexed gain	78,000
Indexation allowance:	
31.3.82 value £17,000 × 2.501	(42,517)
Gain after indexation	£35,483

Time apportionment is more beneficial than an election for 6 April 1965 value. Re-basing does not apply as it cannot increase a gain. The chargeable gain is therefore £30,399.

(D) **Unquoted shares — share exchange before 6 April 1965**

[*TCGA 1992, Sch 2 para 19(1)(3)*]

N Ltd purchased 5,000 £1 ordinary shares in R Ltd, an unquoted company, on 1 January 1961. The purchase price was £3 per share, a total of £15,000. On 1 December 1964, R Ltd was acquired by D Ltd, an unquoted company, as a result of which N Ltd received 10,000 8% convertible preference shares in D Ltd in exchange for its holding of R shares. In November 2018, N Ltd sold the D Ltd shares for £8.45 per share.

The market value of the D Ltd shares was £2.03 per share at 6 April 1965 but only £1.50 per share at 31 March 1982. The indexation factor for the period March 1982 to December 2017 is 2.501.

The gain, disregarding re-basing, is

		£
Disposal consideration	10,000 at £8.45	84,500
Allowable cost	10,000 at £2.03	(20,300)
Unindexed gain		64,200
Indexation allowance £20,300 × 2.501		(50,770)
Gain after indexation		£13,430

The gain using re-basing to 1982 is

	£
Disposal consideration (as above)	84,500
Market value 31.3.82 10,000 at £1.50	(15,000)
Unindexed gain	69,500
Indexation allowance £20,300 × 2.501	(50,770)
Gain after indexation	£18,730
The overall result is	
Chargeable gain	£13,430

Notes

(a) Subject to re-basing, allowable cost *must* be taken as 6.4.65 value.

(b) Indexation is based on the greater of 31.3.82 value and 6.4.65 value. [*TCGA 1992, s 55(1)(2)*].

(c) Where the effect of re-basing would be to increase a gain, re-basing does not apply (but see note (e) below). [*TCGA 1992, s 35(3)(a)*].

(d) By concession (ESC D10), tax is not charged on a disposal of the *entire* new shareholding on more than the actual gain realised, i.e. by reference to original cost but without time apportionment.

(e) Indexation allowance is frozen at its December 2017 level. No indexation allowance is available in respect of expenditure incurred after 31 December 2017, and for expenditure incurred on or before that date and falling to be deducted on a disposal after that date, indexation allowance is computed up to and including December 2017 only. [*TCGA 1992, ss 53(1)(1B), 54(1B); FA 2018, s 26(2)(3)(6)*]. See **214.1** INDEXATION.

(E) Unquoted shares — share exchange after 5 April 1965

[*TCGA 1992, Sch 2 para 19(2)(3)*]

S Ltd acquired 10,000 £1 ordinary shares in L Ltd for £5,000 on 31 May 1959. The shares are not quoted, and their value at 6 April 1965 was £6,000. On 1 September 1989, the shares were acquired by R plc, in exchange for its own ordinary shares on the basis of 1 for 2. The offer valued L ordinary shares at £2.23 per share. In February 2019, S Ltd sells its 5,000 R shares for £14.60 per share. The agreed value of the L Ltd shares at 31 March 1982 was £2.05 per share.

Indexation factors	March 1982 to September 1989	0.468
	September 1989 to December 2017	1.385
	March 1982 to December 2017	2.501

The gain without re-basing to 1982 is computed as follows

(i) Using time apportionment

Deemed disposal at 1.9.89:

	£
Proceeds (market value £2.23 × 10,000)	22,300
Cost	(5,000)
Unindexed gain	17,300
Indexation allowance	
MV 31.3.82 10,000 × £2.05 × 0.468	(9,594)
Gain after indexation	£7,706
Gain after time apportionment:	
£7,706 × (24y 5m/30y 3m)	£6,219

Actual disposal in February 2019:

	£
Proceeds 5,000 × £14.60	73,000
Deemed acquisition cost at 1.9.89	(22,300)
Unindexed gain	50,700
Indexation allowance £22,300 × 1.385	(30,886)
Gain after indexation	£19,814
Total gain £(6,219 + 19,814)	£26,033

(ii) With election for 6.4.65 value

	£
Disposal consideration	73,000
Allowable cost	(6,000)
Unindexed gain	67,000
Indexation allowance 10,000 × £2.05 × 2.501	(51,271)
Gain	£15,729

Subject to re-basing, the election is beneficial.

The gain using re-basing to 1982 is

	£
Disposal consideration	73,000
Market value 31.3.82 10,000 × £2.05	(20,500)
Unindexed gain	52,500
Indexation allowance £20,500 × 2.501	(51,271)
Gain after indexation	£1,229
The overall result is	
Chargeable gain	£1,229

Re-basing applies as it produces a smaller gain than that using 6 April 1965 value.

Notes

(a) The deemed disposal on 1 September 1989 is *only* for the purposes of *TCGA 1992, Sch 2 para 16* (time apportionment).

(b) If an election is made for 6 April 1965 value, no valuation is required at 1 September 1989.

(c) Indexation allowance is frozen at its December 2017 level. No indexation allowance is available in respect of expenditure incurred after 31 December 2017, and for expenditure incurred on or before that date and falling to be deducted on a disposal after that date, indexation allowance is computed up to and including December 2017 only. [*TCGA 1992, ss 53(1)(1B), 54(1B); FA 2018, s 26(2)(3)(6)*]. See **214.1** INDEXATION.

(F) Part disposals after 5 April 1965

[*TCGA 1992, s 42, Sch 2 para 16(8)*]

H Ltd bought land for £15,000 on 31 October 1960. Its value at 6 April 1965 was £17,200. On 1 February 1988, H Ltd sold part of the land for £50,000, the balance being then worth £200,000. On 9 April 2018, H Ltd sells the remaining land for £450,000. The agreed value of the total estate at 31 March 1982 was £150,000 and H Ltd made a claim on the February 1988 disposal for that value to be used for indexation purposes under the law then in force.

Indexation factors	March 1982 to February 1988	0.305
	March 1982 to December 2017	2.501

1988 disposal

	£
Proceeds of part disposal	50,000
Deduct allowable cost $\frac{50,000}{50,000 + 200,000} \times £15,000$	(3,000)
Unindexed gain	47,000
Indexation allowance $£150,000 \times \frac{50,000}{50,000 + 200,000} = £30,000$	
£30,000 × 0.305	(9,150)
Gain after indexation	£37,850

Time apportionment

Chargeable gain $\frac{22y\ 10m}{27y\ 3m} \times £37,850$	£31,715

If an election were made to substitute 6 April 1965 valuation, the computation would be

	£
Proceeds of part disposal	50,000
Deduct allowable cost $\frac{50{,}000}{50{,}000 + 200{,}000} \times £17{,}200$	(3,440)
Unindexed gain	46,560
Indexation allowance $£150{,}000 \times \frac{50{,}000}{50{,}000 + 200{,}000} = £30{,}000$	
£30,000 × 0.305	(9,150)
Chargeable gain	£37,410

An election would not be beneficial.

2018 disposal
The gain without re-basing to 1982 is as follows

Computation of entire gain over period of ownership:

	£	
Proceeds	450,000	
Cost £(15,000 − 3,000)	(12,000)	
Unindexed gain	438,000	
Indexation allowance		
MV 31.3.82 £(150,000 − 30,000) × 2.501	(300,120)	
Gain after indexation	£137,880	(A)

Computation of gain for period 31.10.60 - 1.2.88:

	£	
Market value at date of part disposal	200,000	
Cost £(15,000 − 3,000)	(12,000)	
Unindexed gain	188,000	
Indexation allowance £(150,000 − 30,000) × 0.305	(36,600)	
Gain after indexation	£151,400	(B)
Time apportionment $£151{,}400 \times \frac{22y\ 10m}{27y\ 3m}$	£126,861	(C)
Balance of gain (1.2.88 to 9.4.18) ((A) – (B))	£(13,520)	(D)
Chargeable gain (subject to re-basing) ((C) + (D))	£113,341	

The gain using re-basing to 1982 is as follows

		£
Disposal proceeds		450,000
Market value 31.3.82 $£150{,}000 \times \frac{12{,}000}{15{,}000}$	(note (b))	(120,000)
Unindexed gain		330,000
Indexation allowance £120,000 × 2.501		(300,120)
Gain after indexation		£29,880

The overall result is

Chargeable gain	£29,880

Re-basing applies as it produces neither a larger gain nor a loss.

Notes

(a) The deemed disposal on 1 February 1988 is only for the purposes of *TCGA 1992, Sch 2 para 16(3)–(5)* (time apportionment). For re-basing purposes, the asset is still regarded as having been held at 31 March 1982.

(b) Where there has been a part disposal after 31 March 1982 and before 6 April 1988 of an asset held at 31 March 1982, the proportion of 31 March 1982 value to be brought into account in the re-basing calculation is that which the cost previously unallowed bears to the total cost, giving the same effect as if re-basing had applied to the part disposal. [*TCGA 1992, Sch 3 para 4(1)*].

(c) HMRC will also accept an alternative basis of calculation on the part disposal of land. Under this method, the part disposed of is treated as a separate asset and any fair and reasonable method of apportioning part of the total cost to it will be accepted e.g. a reasonable valuation of that part at the acquisition date. (HMRC Statement of Practice SP D1.)

(d) Indexation allowance is frozen at its December 2017 level. No indexation allowance is available in respect of expenditure incurred after 31 December 2017, and for expenditure incurred on or before that date and falling to be deducted on a disposal after that date, indexation allowance is computed up to and including December 2017 only. [*TCGA 1992, ss 53(1)(1B), 54(1B); FA 2018, s 26(2)(3)(6)*]. See **214.1** INDEXATION.

(e) The time apportionment calculation is applied to the gain *after* indexation (*Smith v Schofield HL 1993*, 65 TC 669, [1993] STC 268).

205 Assets held on 31 March 1982

205.1 CAPITAL GAINS TAX

[*TCGA 1992, s 35(1)(2)*]

Robbie sells an asset (which is neither tangible movable property nor otherwise exempt) on 25 April 2018 for £200,000. He had purchased the asset in 1979 for £50,000, and its value at 31 March 1982 was £42,000. The chargeable gain on the asset is computed as follows.

	£
Sale proceeds	200,000
31.3.1982 value	(42,000)
Chargeable gain 2018/19	£158,000

Notes

(a) The asset is deemed to have been sold and immediately re-acquired at its market value at 31 March 1982. For capital gains tax purposes (i.e. in relation to disposals by individuals, trustees and personal representatives), this rule (known as 're-basing') applies to all disposals. [*TCGA 1992, s 35(1)(2)*].

(b) Exceptions to re-basing apply for the purposes of corporation tax on chargeable gains. See 205.2 below.

205.2 CORPORATION TAX

[*TCGA 1992, s 35, Sch 3*]

(A)

R Ltd purchased a painting on 1 October 1979 for £50,000 (including costs of acquisition) and sold it at auction for £260,000 (net of selling expenses) on 15 August 2018. Its value at 31 March 1982 was £70,000 and the indexation factor for the period March 1982 to December 2017 is 2.501.

	£	£
Net sale proceeds	260,000	260,000
Cost	(50,000)	
Market value 31.3.82		(70,000)
Unindexed gain	210,000	190,000
Indexation allowance £70,000 × 2.501	(175,070)	(175,070)
Gain after indexation	£34,930	£14,930
Chargeable gain		£14,930

Notes

(a) The asset is deemed to have been sold and immediately re-acquired at its market value at 31 March 1982. [*TCGA 1992, s 35(1)(2)*].

(b) Re-basing does not apply if it would produce a larger gain or larger loss than would otherwise be the case, nor if it would turn a gain into a loss or vice versa, nor if the disposal would otherwise be a no gain/no loss disposal. [*TCGA 1992, s 35(3)(4)*].

(c) An *irrevocable* election may be made to treat, broadly speaking, *all* assets held on 31 March 1982 as having been sold and re-acquired at their market value on that date, in which case the restrictions in (b) above will not apply. [*TCGA 1992, s 35(5)*]. If the election had been made in this example, the gain would still be £14,930, but there would have been no need to compute the gain by reference to cost and make a comparison with that using re-basing.

There are some minor exclusions from the rule that the election must extend to all assets. [*TCGA 1992, Sch 3 para 7*]. There are also special rules for groups of companies. [*TCGA 1992, Sch 3 paras 8, 9*].

(d) Indexation is automatically based on 31 March 1982 value, without the need to claim such treatment, unless a greater allowance would be produced by reference to cost. [*TCGA 1992, s 55(1)(2)*]. See also **214.1(C)** INDEXATION.

(e) See also **204** ASSETS HELD ON **6** APRIL **1965** for the general application of the re-basing provisions to such assets. See **214.2(A)(C)** INDEXATION for the position as regards an asset acquired by means of a no gain/no loss transfer from a person who held it at 31 March 1982.

(f) For capital gains tax purposes (i.e. in relation to disposals by individuals, trustees and personal representatives), re-basing applies to all disposals with no exceptions. See **205.1** above.

(g) Indexation allowance is frozen at its December 2017 level. No indexation allowance is available in respect of expenditure incurred after 31 December 2017, and for expenditure incurred on or before that date and falling to be deducted on a disposal after that date, indexation allowance is computed up to and including December 2017 only. *[TCGA 1992, ss 53(1)(1B), 54(1B); FA 2018, s 26(2)(3)(6)]*. See **214.1** INDEXATION.

(B)

The facts are as in (A) above, except that net sale proceeds amount to £60,000.

	£	£
Net sale proceeds	60,000	60,000
Cost	(50,000)	
Market value 31.3.82		(70,000)
Unindexed gain/(loss)	10,000	(10,000)
Indexation allowance (as in (A))		
but restricted to	(10,000)	—
Gain/(loss)	Nil	£(10,000)
Chargeable gain/(allowable loss)	Nil	

Notes

(a) Re-basing does not apply as it cannot disturb a no gain/no loss position. [*TCGA 1992, s 35(3)(c)*].

(b) A universal re-basing election under *TCGA 1992, s 35(5)* would produce an allowable loss of £10,000 (but must extend to all assets).

(c) See **205.1** above for the application of re-basing for capital gains tax purposes.

(C)

The facts are as in (A) above, except that net sale proceeds amount to £230,000.

	£	£
Net sale proceeds	230,000	230,000
Cost	(50,000)	
Market value 31.3.82		(70,000)
Unindexed gain	180,000	160,000
Indexation allowance (as in (A))	(175,070)	
Indexation allowance (as in (A))		
but restricted to		(160,000)
Gain	£4,930	Nil
Chargeable gain/(allowable loss)		Nil

Note

(a) Re-basing applies as it produces a no gain/no loss position compared to a gain otherwise.

(b) Indexation allowance is frozen at its December 2017 level. No indexation allowance is available in respect of expenditure incurred after 31 December 2017, and for expenditure incurred on or before that date and falling to be deducted on a disposal after that date, indexation allowance is computed up to and including December 2017 only. *[TCGA 1992, ss 53(1)(1B), 54(1B); FA 2018, s 26(2)(3)(6)]*. See **214.1** INDEXATION.

(D)

A Ltd acquired a holding of D plc quoted shares for £11,000 net in January 1980. At 31 March 1982, their value had fallen to £8,000. On 29 April 2018, A Ltd sold the entire holding for £50,000 net. The indexation factor for the period March 1982 to December 2017 is 2.501.

	£	£
Proceeds	50,000	50,000
Cost	(11,000)	
Market value 31.3.82		(8,000)
Unindexed gain	39,000	42,000
Indexation allowance £11,000 × 2.501	(27,511)	(27,511)
Gain after indexation	£11,489	£14,489
Chargeable gain		£11,489

Notes

(a) Re-basing does not apply as its effect would be to increase a gain.

(b) Indexation is based on cost as that is greater than 31 March 1982 value.

(c) If a universal re-basing election had been made (under *TCGA 1992, s 35(5)*), the chargeable gain would have been £14,489.

(d) Indexation allowance is frozen at its December 2017 level. No indexation allowance is available in respect of expenditure incurred after 31 December 2017, and for expenditure incurred on or before that date and falling to be deducted on a disposal after that date, indexation allowance is computed up to and including December 2017 only. *[TCGA 1992, ss 53(1)(1B), 54(1B); FA 2018, s 26(2)(3)(6)]*. See **214.1** INDEXATION.

(E)

C Ltd acquired a holding of E Ltd shares for £14,000 net in January 1980. At 31 March 1982, their value stood at £17,000. C Ltd sold the shares in April 2018 for £10,000 net.

	£	£
Proceeds	10,000	10,000
Cost	(14,000)	
Market value 31.3.82		(17,000)
Unindexed loss (no indexation due)	£(4,000)	£(7,000)
Allowable loss	£(4,000)	

Notes

(a) Re-basing does not apply as its effect would be to increase a loss.

(b) Indexation is not available in either calculation as it cannot increase a loss.

(c) If a universal re-basing election had been made (under *TCGA 1992, s 35(5)*), the allowable loss would have been £7,000, but the election must extend to all assets.

205.3 DEFERRED CHARGES ON GAINS BEFORE 31 MARCH 1982

[*TCGA 1992, s 36, Sch 4*]

K Ltd, a farming company, purchased farmland for £25,000 in 1975. The company sold the land in August 1984 for £45,000 but purchased further farmland in September 1984 for £50,000 and claimed rollover relief in respect of the disposal of the original farmland. K Ltd sells the replacement farmland in April 2018 for £250,000 and claims relief under *TCGA 1992, Sch 4*. The relevant indexation factors are

March 1982 to August 1984	0.133
September 1984 to December 2017	2.086

The gain on the original farmland is rolled over as follows

	£
Allowable cost	25,000
Indexation allowance £25,000 × 0.133	3,325
	28,325
Actual consideration	45,000
Chargeable gain rolled over	£16,675
Cost of replacement farmland	50,000
Deduct amount rolled over	(16,675)
Deemed allowable cost	£33,325

K Ltd's chargeable gain on disposal of the replacement farmland in April 2018 is as follows

	£	£
Proceeds		250,000
Deemed allowable cost	33,325	
Add one-half of rolled-over gain	8,338	
	41,663	
Indexation allowance £41,663 × 2.086	86,909	(128,572)
Chargeable gain		£121,428

Notes

(a) K Ltd cannot benefit from re-basing to 1982 as it did not hold the replacement farmland on 31 March 1982. Instead, the company claims relief under *TCGA 1992, s 36, Sch 4* so that the reduction in the cost of the replacement farmland resulting from the rollover relief on the original farmland is itself reduced by one half. [*TCGA 1992, Sch 4 para 1*].

(b) Relief under *TCGA 1992, Sch 4* must be claimed within two years of the end of the accounting period in which the ultimate disposal takes place. [*TCGA 1992, Sch 4 para 9*].

(c) The relief applies only for the purposes of corporation tax on chargeable gains. [*TCGA 1992, s 36, Sch 4 para A1*].

(d) Indexation allowance is frozen at its December 2017 level. No indexation allowance is available in respect of expenditure incurred after 31 December 2017, and for expenditure incurred on or before that date and falling to be deducted on a disposal after that date, indexation allowance is computed up to and including December 2017 only. [*TCGA 1992, ss 53(1)(1B), 54(1B); FA 2018, s 26(2)(3)(6)*]. See **214.1** INDEXATION.

(e) For further rollover relief examples, see **226** ROLLOVER RELIEF — REPLACEMENT OF BUSINESS ASSETS.

206 Capital Sums Derived from Assets

206.1 GENERAL

[*TCGA 1992, s 22(1)*]

A Ltd holds the remainder of a 99-year lease of land, under which it has mineral rights. The lease, which commenced in 2000, was acquired in April 2009 by assignment for £80,000. Following a proposal to extract minerals, the freeholder pays A Ltd £100,000 in June 2018 in consideration of relinquishing the mineral rights, in order to prevent such development. The value of the lease after the alteration is £150,000.

	£
Disposal proceeds	100,000
Allowable cost $\frac{100,000}{100,000 + 150,000} \times £80,000$	(32,000)
Gain subject to indexation from April 2009 to December 2017	£68,000

206.2 DEFERRED CONSIDERATION

Z owns 2,000 £1 ordinary shares in B Ltd, for which he subscribed at par in August 2003. On 31 March 2014, he and the other shareholders in B Ltd sold their shares to another company for £10 per share plus a further unquantified cash amount calculated by means of a formula relating to the future profits of B Ltd. The value in March 2014 of the deferred consideration was estimated at £2 per share. On 30 April 2018, Z receives a further £4.20 per share under the sale agreement.

2013/14

		£	£
Disposal proceeds	2,000 at £10	20,000	
Value of rights	2,000 at £2	4,000	24,000
Cost of acquisition			(2,000)
Chargeable gain			£22,000

2018/19

Disposal of rights to deferred consideration	
Proceeds 2,000 × £4.20	8,400
Deemed cost of acquiring rights	(4,000)
Chargeable gain	£4,400

Notes

(a) A right to unquantified and contingent future consideration on the disposal of an asset is itself an asset, and the future consideration when received is a capital sum derived from that asset (*Marren v Ingles HL 1980, 54 TC 76* and *Marson v Marriage Ch D 1979, 54 TC 59*).

(b) See **229.4** SHARES AND SECURITIES for the position where deferred consideration is to be satisfied in shares and/or debentures in the acquiring company.

(c) See also **217.4** LOSSES for the election to treat a loss on disposal of a right to deferred unascertainable consideration as accruing in an earlier year.

206.3 RECEIPT OF COMPENSATION

[*TCGA 1992, ss 22, 23*]

(A)

C owns a freehold warehouse which is badly damaged by fire as a result of inflammable goods having been inadequately packaged. The value of the warehouse after the fire is £90,000, and it cost £120,000 in 1996. The owner of the goods is held liable for the damage and pays C £60,000 compensation in October 2018.

	£
Disposal proceeds	60,000
Allowable cost $\frac{60{,}000}{60{,}000 + 90{,}000} \times £120{,}000$	(48,000)
Chargeable gain 2018/19	£12,000

(B) **Restoration using insurance moneys**

A diamond necklace owned by D cost £100,000 in 2007. D is involved in a motor accident in which the necklace is damaged. Its value is reduced to £80,000. D receives £40,000 under an insurance policy in May 2018 and spends £45,000 on having the necklace restored.

(i) *No claim under TCGA 1992, s 23*

	£
Disposal proceeds	40,000
Allowable cost $\frac{40{,}000}{40{,}000 + 80{,}000} \times £100{,}000$	(33,333)
Chargeable gain 2018/19	£6,667
Allowable cost in relation to subsequent disposal	
£100,000 − £33,333 + £45,000	£111,667

(ii) *Claim under TCGA 1992, s 23*

No chargeable gain arises in 2018/19	
Allowable cost originally	100,000
Deduct Amount received on claim	(40,000)
	60,000
Add Expenditure on restoration	45,000
Allowable cost in relation to subsequent disposal	£105,000

(C) **Part application of capital sum received**

E Ltd is the owner of a large estate consisting mainly of parkland which it acquired for £150,000 in August 1995. It grants a one-year licence in August 2018 to an exploration company to prospect for minerals, in consideration for a capital sum of £50,000. The exploration proves unsuccessful and on expiry of the licence E Ltd spends £20,000 on restoration of the drilling sites to their former state. The market value of the estate after granting the licence is £350,000, and it is £400,000 after restoration.

(i) *No claim under TCGA 1992, s 23(3)*

	£
Disposal proceeds	50,000
Deduct Allowable cost $\frac{50,000}{50,000 + 350,000} \times £150,000$	(18,750)
Gain subject to indexation from August 1995 to December 2017	£31,250
Allowable expenditure remaining	
£150,000 − £18,750 + £20,000	£151,250

(ii) *Claim made under TCGA 1992, s 23(3)*

	£
Deemed disposal proceeds (£50,000 − £20,000)	30,000
Deduct	
Allowable cost $\frac{30,000}{30,000 + 400,000} \times £(150,000 + 20,000)$	(11,860)
Gain subject to indexation to December 2017	£18,140
Allowable expenditure remaining	
£150,000 − £20,000 − £11,860 + £20,000	£138,140

Note

(a) Indexation allowance is frozen at its December 2017 level. No indexation allowance is available in respect of expenditure incurred after 31 December 2017, and for expenditure incurred on or before that date and falling to be deducted on a disposal after that date, indexation allowance must be computed up to and including December 2017 only. *[TCGA 1992, ss 53(1)(1B), 54(1B); FA 2018, s 26(2)(3)(6)]*. See **214.1** INDEXATION.

(D) **Capital sum exceeding allowable expenditure**

F inherited a painting in 1980 when it was valued at £2,000. Its value at 31 March 1982 was £3,000. In March 1988, by which time its value had increased considerably, the painting suffered damage whilst on loan to an art gallery and F received £10,000 compensation. The value of the painting was then £30,000. It then cost F £9,800 to have the painting restored. In June 2018, he sells the painting for £50,000.

(i) *No election under TCGA 1992, s 23(2)*

	£
Disposal proceeds March 1988	10,000
Allowable cost $\dfrac{10{,}000}{10{,}000 + 30{,}000} \times £2{,}000$	(500)
Gain subject to indexation 1987/88	£9,500
Allowable cost in relation to subsequent disposal	
£2,000 − £500 + £9,800	£11,300

	£
Disposal proceeds June 2018	50,000
Allowable cost with re-basing	
$£3{,}000 \times \dfrac{30{,}000}{10{,}000 + 30{,}000} = £2{,}250 + £9{,}800$	(12,050)
Chargeable gain 2018/19	£37,950

(ii) *Election under TCGA 1992, s 23(2)*

	£
Disposal proceeds March 1988	10,000
Less allowable expenditure	(2,000)
Gain subject to indexation 1987/88	£8,000
Allowable cost in relation to subsequent disposal	
£2,000 − £2,000 + £9,800	£9,800

	£
Disposal proceeds June 2018	50,000
Allowable cost with re-basing (note (b))	
£3,000 − £2,000 + £9,800	(10,800)
Chargeable gain 2018/19	£39,200

Notes

(a) For capital gains tax purposes (i.e. in relation to disposals by individuals, trustees and personal representatives), re-basing applies to all disposals with no exceptions. See **205.1** ASSETS HELD ON **31** MARCH **1982**.

(b) Where there is a disposal after 5 April 1989 to which re-basing applies and, if re-basing had not applied, the allowable expenditure would have fallen to be reduced under *TCGA 1992, s 23(2)* by reference to a capital sum received after 31 March 1982 but before 6 April 1988, the 31 March 1982 value is reduced by the amount previously allowed against the capital sum. [*TCGA 1992, Sch 3 para 4(2)*].

207 Companies

Cross-references. See also **CT 103** CAPITAL GAINS.

207.1 BASIC COMPUTATION

A company, Crow Ltd, has an accounting date of 30 June. Crow Ltd acquired an asset in November 1987 for £28,000 and sells the asset on 11 June 2018 for £99,000. The company incurs allowable sale costs of £5,000. It makes no other disposals in the year ended 30 June 2018. The indexation factor for the period November 1987 to December 2017 is 1.690.. The company's taxable gain for the accounting period ended 30 June 2018 is as follows.

	£
Sale consideration	99,000
Less costs of sale	(5,000)
Cost of asset	(28,000)
Unindexed gain	66,000
Less indexation allowance £28,000 × 1.690	(47,320)
Chargeable (and taxable) gain	£18,680

Notes

(a) With two exceptions, companies do not pay capital gains tax. Instead they pay corporation tax on their chargeable gains. Gains are included in a company's profits liable to corporation tax and taxed at the applicable rate. [*TCGA 1992, s 1(2); CTA 2009, s 2*]. The exceptions are the capital gains tax charge on high value disposals of dwellings subject to the annual tax on enveloped dwellings under *TCGA 1992, ss 2B–2F* and the non-resident capital gains tax charge on disposals of UK residential property interests under *TCGA 1992, ss 14B–14H*.

(b) Chargeable gains and allowable losses are nevertheless computed according to capital gains tax principles, although there are now many important differences in the computational rules. The main differences are as follows.

(i) Computations are made by reference to accounting periods instead of tax years [*TCGA 1992, s 8(3)*].

(ii) Re-basing to market value at 31 March 1982 applies to individuals etc. automatically and without any exceptions for disposals on or after 6 April 2008, but the exceptions continue to apply to companies (see **205** ASSETS HELD ON **31** MARCH **1982**). The rules for ASSETS HELD ON **6** APRIL **1965** (**204**) therefore apply only to companies.

(iii) special provisions apply to tax as income gains and losses in respect of loan relationships, derivative contracts and intangible assets (see CT **108** INTANGIBLE ASSETS and CT **113** LOAN RELATIONSHIPS).

(iv) ENTREPRENEURS' RELIEF (**211**) applies to qualifying business disposals by individuals, etc., but not by companies;

(v) INVESTORS' RELIEF (**215**) applies to qualifying disposals of shares by individuals, etc., but not by companies;

(vi) indexation allowance is available to companies (see **214** INDEXATION) but is frozen at its December 2017 level. No indexation allowance is available in respect of expenditure incurred after 31 December 2017, and for expenditure incurred on or before that date and falling to be deducted on a disposal after that date, indexation allowance is computed up to and including December 2017 only. *[TCGA 1992, ss 53(1)(1B), 54(1B); FA 2018, s 26(2)(3)(6)]*;

(vii) the rules for matching shares and securities sold with those acquired are not the same for corporation tax as for capital gains tax (see **230.2** SHARES AND SECURITIES — IDENTIFICATION RULES);

207.2 CAPITAL LOSSES

P Ltd, which makes up accounts to 30 June annually, changes its accounting date to 31 December. It makes up 18-month accounts to 31 December 2018, and its chargeable gains and allowable losses are as follows

	Gains/(losses)
	£
31.7.17	4,600
19.10.17	11,500
1.12.17	3,500
28.3.18	(8,300)
21.7.18	8,500
1.9.18	(25,000)
20.12.18	7,000

The period of account is split into two accounting periods

1.7.17 – 30.6.18	
Net chargeable gain	£11,300
1.7.18 – 31.12.18	
Net allowable loss	£9,500

Notes

(a) The loss cannot be set off against the £11,300 net gain in the earlier accounting period (but *can* be carried forward against subsequent gains).

(b) A loss accruing to a company is not an allowable loss if it arises directly or indirectly in consequence of, or otherwise in connection with, any arrangements one of the main purposes of which is to secure a tax advantage. [*TCGA 1992, ss 8(2), 16A*].

(c) For a further example, see CT **103.1** CAPITAL GAINS.

208 Computation of Gains and Losses

208.1 ALLOWABLE AND NON-ALLOWABLE EXPENDITURE

(A) Allowable expenditure

[*TCGA 1992, s 38*]

In 2018/19 T sold a house which he had owned since 1992 and which was let throughout the period of ownership (other than as furnished holiday accommodation). The house cost £34,000, with legal costs of £900, in June 1992. T spent £2,000 on initial dilapidations in July 1992. In November 1999, he added an extension at a cost of £5,500 for which he received a local authority grant of £2,500 on completion. Legal costs of £500 were incurred on obtaining vacant possession at the end of the final tenancy in May 2018. The sale proceeds were £170,000 before deducting incidental costs (including valuation fees) of £1,200.

		£	£	£
Sale proceeds			170,000	
Deduct Costs of sale			(1,200)	168,800
Cost of house			34,000	
Add Incidental costs of purchase			900	
			34,900	
Improvement costs:				
Initial dilapidations	(note (a))	2,000		
Extension, less grant		3,000	5,000	
Cost of obtaining vacant possession				
(enhancement cost)			500	(40,400)
Chargeable gain 2018/19				£128,400

Note

(a) It is assumed that the cost of the initial dilapidations were disallowed for income tax purposes under the rule in *Law Shipping Co Ltd v CIR, CS 1923, 12 TC 621*. If any of the expenditure had been so allowed, a deduction would to that extent be precluded as an allowable deduction for CGT purposes by *TCGA 1992, s 39*.

(B) Non-allowable expenditure — capital allowances

[*TCGA 1992, s 41*]

S Ltd acquired land in March 2006 for £90,000 on which it constructed a factory for use in its manufacturing trade. The cost of construction was £45,000 incurred in June 2006. In April 2018, the company sold the freehold factory for £280,000, of which £200,000 related to the land and £80,000 to the building. Industrial buildings allowances of £9,000 had been given and, as the sale occurred after 20 March 2008, there was no balancing adjustment. The indexation factor for the period March 2006 to December 2017 is 0.426.

	Land	Building	
	£	£	£
Disposal consideration	200,000		80,000
Allowable cost	(90,000)	45,000	
Deduct net allowances given		9,000	(36,000)
Unindexed gain	110,000		44,000
Indexation allowance:			
£90,000 × 0.426	(38,340)		
£36,000 × 0.426			(15,336)
Chargeable gain	£71,660		£28,664
Total chargeable gain (£ 71,660+ £28,664)			£100,324

Note

(a) Indexation allowance is frozen at its December 2017 level. No indexation allowance is available in respect of expenditure incurred after 31 December 2017, and for expenditure incurred on or before that date and falling to be deducted on a disposal after that date, indexation allowance is computed up to and including December 2017 only. *[TCGA 1992, ss 53(1)(1B), 54(1B); FA 2018, s 26(2)(3)(6)]*. See **214.1** INDEXATION.

(C) Enhancement expenditure

[*TCGA 1992, s 38*]

Mr Hopkins bought a second home in August 1978 for £15,000. Mr Hopkins' neighbour, Mr Douglas, claimed that part of the garden of the house belonged to him. Mr Hopkins won the court case resulting, but incurred legal fees of £5,000 in September 1985.

In 2000 Mr Hopkins had a tennis court built for £5,000, but this was demolished in 2007.

Mr Hopkins sold the house in November 2018 for £126,000. It was agreed that the value of the house at 31 March 1982 was £25,000. The house has never been treated as Mr Hopkins' main residence.

The chargeable gain is as follows.

	£
Sale consideration	126,000
Less 31 March 1982 value	(25,000)
Legal fees re boundary dispute	(5,000)
Chargeable gain	£96,000

Notes

(a) The expenditure on the tennis court in 2000 is not allowable as it is not reflected in the state or nature of the asset at the time of disposal in November 2018 as required by *TCGA 1992, s 38(1)(b)*. HMRC consider that the demolition of the tennis court is not a deemed disposal within *TCGA 1992, s 24(1)* as it is not the 'entire loss, destruction, dissipation or extinction' of an asset because it is not an 'asset': it is only part of an asset, the land (see HMRC Capital Gains Manual CG15190).

(b) Expenditure wholly and exclusively incurred in establishing, preserving or defending title to, or to a right over, an asset is allowable expenditure. [*TCGA 1992, s 38(1)(b)*].

208.2 PART DISPOSALS

[*TCGA 1992, s 42*]

Note

See also **216.1** LAND for small part disposals of land.

(A)

T purchased a 300-acre estate in March 1988 for £1m plus legal and other costs of £50,000. In January 1991 he spent £47,000 on improvements to the main house on the estate (not his main residence), which he sells in September 2018 for £660,000. The costs of sale are £40,000. The value of the remaining land is £2.34m.

	£	£
Sale proceeds		660,000
Deduct incidental costs		(40,000)
		620,000
Cost $£1,050,000 \times \dfrac{660,000}{660,000 + 2,340,000}$	231,000	
Improvement costs	47,000	(278,000)
Chargeable gain		£342,000

Note

(a) The improvements expenditure is not apportioned as it relates entirely to the part of the estate being sold. [*TCGA 1992, s 42(4)*].

(B)

U inherited some land at a probate value of £500,000 in November 1981. Its market value at 31 March 1982 was £540,000. In November 1987, he sold part of the land for £240,000, the remaining land then being worth £480,000. He sells the remaining land in April 2018 for £600,000.

The gain, subject to indexation, on the part disposal in November 1987 is

	£
Proceeds	240,000
Cost $£500,000 \times \dfrac{240,000}{240,000 + 480,000}$	(166,667)
Gain subject to indexation	£73,333

The gain on the disposal in April 2018 is

	£
Proceeds	600,000
Market value 31.3.82	
$£540,000 \times \dfrac{480,000}{240,000 + 480,000}$	(360,000)
Chargeable gain	£240,000

Notes

(a) Where re-basing applies and there has been a part disposal after 31 March 1982 and before 6 April 1988, the proportion of 31 March 1982 value to be brought into account on the ultimate disposal is the same as the proportion of cost not allowed on the part disposal, as if the re-basing provisions had applied to the part disposal. [*TCGA 1992, Sch 3 para 4(1)*].

(b) For capital gains tax purposes (i.e. in relation to disposals by individuals, trustees and personal representatives), re-basing applies to all disposals with no exceptions. See **205.1** ASSETS HELD ON **31** MARCH **1982**.

(C)

V bought the film rights of a novel for £50,000 in May 2012. A one-third share of the rights was sold to W Ltd in March 2013 for £20,000, when the rights retained had a value of £45,000. In December 2018, V's rights were sold to a film company for £100,000 plus a right to royalties, such right being estimated to be worth £150,000.

March 2013	£
Sale proceeds	20,000
Cost $£50,000 \times \dfrac{20,000}{20,000 + 45,000}$	(15,385)
Chargeable gain 2012/13	4,615

December 2018	£
Sale proceeds (£100,000 + £150,000)	250,000
Cost (£50,000 − £15,385)	(34,615)
Chargeable gain 2018/19	£215,385

Note

(a) The right to royalties is itself an asset and could be the subject of a future disposal by V. See **206.2** CAPITAL SUMS DERIVED FROM ASSETS and, where applicable, **232** WASTING ASSETS.

(D)

C inherited land valued at £72,000 in May 1989. He granted rights of way over the land to a neighbouring landowner in March 1994, in consideration for a parcel of land adjacent to his, valued at £21,000. The value of the original land, subject to the right of way, was then £147,000. In March 2019, C sold the whole of the land for £170,000.

Indexation factor May 1989 to March 1994	0.239

Part disposal in March 1994	£
Disposal consideration	21,000
Allowable expenditure	
$\frac{21{,}000}{21{,}000 + 147{,}000} \times £72{,}000$	(9,000)
Unindexed gain	12,000
Indexation allowance £9,000 × 0.239	(2,151)
Chargeable gain 1993/94	£9,849

Disposal in March 2019		£
Disposal consideration		170,000
Deduct Original land £(72,000 − 9,000)	63,000	
Addition	21,000	(84,000)
Chargeable gain 2018/19		£86,000

Notes

(a) It is assumed that the additional land is merged with the existing land to give a single asset.

(b) A claim under *TCGA 1992, s 242* (small part disposals of land — see **216.1** LAND) could not be made in respect of the March 1994 part disposal as the consideration exceeded £20,000.

209 Double Tax Relief

209.1 RELIEF BY CREDIT

[*TIOPA 2010, ss 18–41*]

Lyra, a higher rate income tax payer, has the following chargeable gains for 2018/19.

UK gain	£30,200	
Foreign gain	£16,000	(Foreign tax £6,400)

Neither gain is an upper rate gain. Lyra claims credit relief for the foreign tax paid. Her capital gains tax liability for 2018/19 is as follows.

	UK gain	Foreign gain
	£	£
Chargeable gain	30,200	16,000
Less annual exempt amount	(11,700)	–
Gain chargeable to tax	18,500	16,000
Capital gains tax: £18,500/£16,000 × 20%	3,700	3,200
Less credit for foreign tax	—	3,200
Tax payable	£3,700	Nil

Notes

(a) No relief is available for the excess of the foreign tax over the CGT liability in respect of the foreign gain (£6,400 – £3,200 = £3,200).

(b) Strictly, the double tax relief is limited to the difference between the total CGT liability for the year before relief (i.e. £6,900) and what the CGT liability would be if the foreign gain were excluded (i.e. £3,700) [*TIOPA 2010, s 40*]. In practice, the effect of this provision is that the annual exempt amount is allocated against the UK gain. If Lyra had been a basic rate income tax payer, any unused part of the basic rate band would likewise have been allocated against the UK gain in priority to the foreign gain (gains within that unused part being chargeable to CGT at 10%).

(c) A claim for credit relief must normally be made not more than four years after the end of the tax year for which the gain is chargeable. The claim deadline is extended to 31 January following the tax year in which the foreign tax is paid, where this is later than the above deadline [*TIOPA 2010, s 19*].

210 Enterprise Investment Scheme

Cross-reference. See also **IT 10.2** ENTERPRISE INVESTMENT SCHEME.

210.1 DISPOSAL OF EIS SHARES MORE THAN THREE YEARS AFTER ISSUE

[*TCGA 1992, s 150A(2)(3); ITA 2007, s 159(2)*]

On 8 November 2018 P subscribes £1,350,000 for 900,000 shares in the EIS company, S Ltd. S Ltd is not a knowledge-intensive company and P obtains the maximum EIS income tax relief of £300,000 (£1,000,000 × 30%) for 2018/19. On 3 April 2023 he sells the entire holding for £2,790,000.

The chargeable gain arising is calculated as follows

	£
Disposal proceeds	2,790,000
Cost	(1,350,000)
Gain	1,440,000
Less TCGA 1992, s 150A(2)(3) exemption	
£1,440,000 × (£300,000/£405,000) (note (b))	(1,066,667)
Chargeable gain 2022/23	£373,333

Notes

(a) Gains arising on the sale more than three years after issue of shares qualifying for EIS income tax relief are not chargeable gains unless the EIS relief is fully withdrawn before disposal. The exemption begins three years after the date of commencement of the qualifying trade if this is later than three years after issue.

(b) Where the income tax relief is not given on the full EIS subscription (otherwise than because of insufficient income), capital gains tax relief is given on a proportion of the gain on the disposal or part disposal.

The gain is reduced by the multiple A/B where

A = the actual income tax reduction and

B = the tax at the EIS rate for the year of relief on the amount subscribed for the issue.

A = £1,000,000 × 30% = £300,000

B = £1,350,000 × 30% = £405,000

(c) With effect in accordance with provision to be made by Treasury regulations, but not so as to affect shares issued before 6 April 2018, the upper limit on the amount in respect of which an individual may obtain income tax relief for a tax year operates as follows:

(i) if the shares do not include any 'KIC shares', the limit is £1 million;

(ii) if the total amount subscribed for KIC shares is £1 million or more, the limit is £2 million; and

(iii) in any other case, the limit is £1 million plus total amount subscribed for KIC shares.

'*KIC shares*' are shares in any company which is a knowledge-intensive company (as defined) at the time the shares are issued.

Prior to the above taking effect the upper limit is in all cases £1 million.

[*ITA 2007, s 158(2)(2ZA)(2ZB); FA 2018, Sch 4 paras 1(2)–(4), 10*].

210.2 LOSS ON DISPOSAL OF EIS SHARES

[*TCGA 1992, s 150A(1)(2A)*]

(A) Disposal more than three years after issue

Assuming the facts otherwise remain the same as in 210.1 above but that the shares are sold for £1,100,000 on 3 April 2023.

The allowable loss arising is calculated as follows

	£	£
Disposal proceeds		1,100,000
Less Cost	1,350,000	
Less Income tax relief given (and not withdrawn)	300,000	(1,050,000)
Allowable loss 2022/23		£50,000

Note

(a) Any loss arising is reduced by deducting the amount of the EIS relief (given and not withdrawn) from the acquisition cost. On the question of income tax withdrawal, see note (b) to (B) below.

(B) Disposal within three years of issue

The facts are otherwise as in (A) above except that the shares are sold in an arm's length bargain on 6 April 2020, i.e. within three years after their issue.

Income tax relief given for 2018/19 is withdrawn as follows

Relief attributable (£1,000,000 @ 30%) £300,000 (1)

Consideration

$$£1,100,000 \times \frac{300,000\ (£1,000,000\ @\ 30\%)}{405,000\ \ (£1,350,000\ @\ 30\%)}\ @\ 30\% \qquad (£244,444)\ (2)$$

The amount at (1) is greater than that at (2), so income tax relief of £244,444 is withdrawn. [*ITA 2007, ss 209, 210*].

The relief not withdrawn is therefore £(300,000 − 244,444) =	£55,556

The allowable loss arising is calculated as follows

	£	£
Disposal proceeds		1,100,000
Less Cost	1,350,000	
Less Income tax relief not withdrawn	55,556	(1,294,444)
Allowable loss 2020/21		£194,444

Notes

(a) For the purposes of computing an allowable loss, the consideration is reduced by the relief attributable to the shares. [*TCGA 1992, s 150A(1)*]. The relief attributable is that remaining following any withdrawal of relief.

(b) A withdrawal of income tax relief arises on a disposal of EIS shares within period A under *ITA 2007, s 159(2)*, i.e. within three years after their issue or, if later, within the period ending immediately before the third anniversary of the date of commencement of the qualifying trade. [*ITA 2007, s 209*].

210.3 EIS DEFERRAL RELIEF

[*TCGA 1992, Sch 5B*]

On 1 June 2018, X realises a gain of £300,000 on the disposal of an asset he had owned since September 2005. X makes no other disposals in 2018/19. On 1 February 2020, X acquires by subscription 65% of the issued ordinary share capital of ABC Ltd at a total subscription price of £248,000. This is a qualifying investment for the purposes of EIS deferral relief. X makes a claim to defer the maximum £248,000 of the June 2018 gain against the qualifying investment.

On 1 July 2024, X sells 40% of his holding in ABC Ltd for £199,200. He makes no other disposals in 2024/25.

X's CGT position for 2018/19 is as follows

	£
Gain	300,000
Less EIS deferral relief	(248,000)
	52,000
Less annual exemption	(11,700)
Taxable gain 2018/19	£40,300

X's CGT position for 2024/25 is as follows

	£
Gain on ABC Ltd shares	
Disposal proceeds	199,200
Less cost (£248,000 @ 40%)	(99,200)
Chargeable gain	£100,000
Deferred gain brought into charge	
Total gain deferred	£248,000
Clawback restricted to expenditure to which disposal relates	£99,200
Taxable gains 2024/25 (subject to annual exemption) (£100,000 + £99,200)	£199,200
Gain remaining deferred until any future chargeable event (£248,000 − £99,200)	£148,800

Notes

(a) No part of X's subscription for ABC Ltd shares can qualify for EIS income tax relief. X is connected with the company by virtue of his shareholding being greater than 30%. (In practice, the holdings of his associates, e.g. wife and children, must also be taken into account in applying the 30% limit.) [*ITA 2007, ss 163, 166–171*].

(b) As the ABC Ltd shares do not qualify for income tax relief, there is no CGT exemption for the gain arising on disposal even though the shares were held for the requisite three-year period.

(c) Where a disposal on or after 3 December 2014 qualifies for both ENTREPRENEURS' RELIEF (**211**) and EIS deferral relief, deferral relief can be claimed and entrepreneurs' relief can then be claimed when the deferred gain comes back into charge on the happening of a chargeable event. [*TCGA 1992, ss 169T–169V; FA 2015, s 44*]. See **211.5** ENTREPRENEURS' RELIEF. Previously, the taxpayer had to choose between the reliefs.

211 Entrepreneurs' Relief

211.1 COMPUTATION OF RELIEF

[*TCGA 1992, ss 169L–169M*]

(A) Basic computation

In May 2018, Mr Henry sells his business, Joe's Toys, which he has owned since 1998, to an unrelated party, realising the following chargeable gains and allowable loss.

	Gain/(loss)
	£
Goodwill	700,000
Freehold shop 1	200,000
Freehold shop 2	200,000
Freehold shop 3	(150,000)

Mr Henry claims entrepreneurs' relief in respect of the sale of the business. He makes no other disposals in 2018/19 and has made no previous claim to entrepreneurs' relief.

Mr Henry's capital gains tax liability for 2018/19 is calculated as follows.

	£
Gains qualifying for entrepreneurs' relief	
Goodwill	700,000
Freehold shop 1	200,000
Freehold shop 2	200,000
	1,100,000
Less Loss on freehold shop 3	(150,000)
Deemed chargeable gain qualifying for entrepreneurs' relief	950,000
Annual exemption	(11,700)
Gain chargeable to tax	£938,300
Capital gains tax payable (£938,300 × 10%)	£93,830

Notes

(a) Entrepreneurs' relief can be claimed in respect of 'qualifying business disposals' (as defined in *TCGA 1992, ss 169H–169K*) made on or after 6 April 2008. Relief can also apply to certain chargeable gains deferred before that date which are deemed to accrue on or after that date — see *FA 2008, Sch 3 paras 7, 8*. The relief applies for capital gains tax purposes only and is not available to companies. For disposals on or after 23 June 2010, relief is given by deducting the aggregate losses arising on the disposal from the aggregate gains and, where the resulting amount is positive, charging it to tax at 10%. Previously, relief was given by deducting the aggregate losses arising on the disposal from the aggregate gains and, where the resulting amount was positive, reducing it by 4/9ths.

(b) Entrepreneurs' relief must be claimed on or before the first anniversary of the 31 January following the tax year in which the qualifying business disposal is made. In the case of a disposal of trust business assets, the claim must be made jointly by the trustees and the qualifying beneficiary. [*TCGA 1992, s 169M(1)–(3); FA 2008, Sch 3 para 2*]. Mr Henry must therefore make a claim on or before 31 January 2021.

(c) Where a disposal on or after 3 December 2014 qualifies for both entrepreneurs' relief and EIS deferral relief or social investment deferral relief, deferral relief can be claimed and entrepreneurs' relief can then be claimed when the deferred gain comes back into charge on the happening of a chargeable event. [*TCGA 1992, ss 169T–169V; FA 2015, s 44*]. See **211.5** below. Previously, the taxpayer had to choose between the reliefs.

(d) A disposal of goodwill on or after 3 December 2014 to a close company (or a non-UK resident company which would be a close company if it were UK-resident) does not qualify for entrepreneurs' relief if, immediately after the disposal, the person making the disposal (P) and any 'relevant connected person' together own 5% or more of the ordinary share capital or voting rights of the company or of any company in the same group. The exclusion does not, however, apply if P and any relevant connected person dispose of the close company's share capital to another company (company A) so that neither P nor any relevant connected person own any of the ordinary share capital immediately before the end of the period of 28 days beginning with the date of the qualifying business disposal (or such longer period as HMRC allow). If company A is itself a close company (or a non-UK resident company which would be a close company if it were UK-resident), P and any relevant connected person must, immediately before the end of that period, together own less than 5% of the ordinary share capital or voting rights of company A or of any company in the same group. A '*relevant connected person*' means a company connected with P or trustees connected with P.

A disposal of goodwill on or after 3 December 2014 is also excluded from relief if the person making the disposal is a party to arrangements one of the main purposes of which is to secure that the above exclusion does not apply to the goodwill.

TCGA 1992, s 169LA; FA 2015, s 42; FA 2016, s 85].

(B) Lifetime limit

In August 2018 Mr Robertson sells his entire shareholding in Robbie Ltd, realising a gain of £10,050,000, which qualifies for entrepreneurs' relief. Mr Robertson makes no other disposals in 2018/19 and has made no previous disposals qualifying for entrepreneurs' relief. He is an additional rate income tax payer for 2018/19.

Mr Robertson's capital gains tax liability for 2018/19 is calculated as follows.

	£
Deemed chargeable gain qualifying for entrepreneurs' relief (subject to lifetime limit £10,000,000)	10,050,000
Annual exemption	(11,700)
Gain chargeable to tax	£10,038,300

Capital gains tax payable	
£10,000,000 × 10%	1,000,000
£38,300 × 20%	7,660
	£1,007,660

Notes

(a) Entrepreneurs' relief is subject to a lifetime limit of £10 million (£5 million for disposals before 6 April 2011; £2 million for disposals before 23 June 2010; £1 million for disposals before 6 April 2010). The amount to which relief would otherwise apply in respect of a qualifying business disposal is added to any amounts to which relief applied in respect of earlier qualifying business disposals. Where the total exceeds the limit, only so much (if any) of the amount to which relief would otherwise apply in respect of the current disposal as, together with the earlier amounts, does not exceed the limit qualifies for the 10% rate (or $^4/_9$ths reduction). Any part of the deemed gain excluded by the application of this rule is chargeable at the normal rates of CGT. Where one of the previous lower lifetime limits was exceeded on disposals made before the increases, no further relief can be obtained for those disposals following the increases. Relief can, however, be obtained for qualifying business disposals on or after the dates of increase up to the appropriate new limit. See (D) below.

[*TCGA 1992, s 169N*].

(b) Disposals before 6 April 2008 do not affect the lifetime limit except in the case of deferred gains on which entrepreneurs' relief is claimed under the transitional rules of *FA 2008, Sch 3 paras 7, 8*.

(c) The annual exemption of £11,700 is allocated against the part of the gain chargeable to tax at 20% as this gives the greater tax saving. [*TCGA 1992, s 4B; FA 2015, Sch 7 para 7*].

(C) Lifetime limit — further example

In May 2018, Mr Helm sells his entire shareholding in Levon Ltd for £400,000. He had acquired the shares in March 2001 for £150,000 and has been a director of the company since that time. Levon Ltd is a trading company and qualifies as Mr Helm's personal company. He makes no other disposals in 2018/19 and claims entrepreneurs' relief in respect of the gain on the shares. He has made no previous entrepreneurs' relief claims.

Mr Helm's capital gains tax liability for 2018/19 is calculated as follows.

	£
Sale proceeds	400,000
Cost	(150,000)
Chargeable gain qualifying for entrepreneurs' relief	250,000
Annual exemption	(11,700)
Gain chargeable to tax 2018/19	£238,300
Capital gains tax payable (£238,300 × 10%)	£23,830

Following the disposal of his shares in Levon Ltd, Mr Helm buys a 25% shareholding in Amy Ltd, another trading company, for £200,000, and starts work as a director of the company. He continues as a director of the company until May 2022 when he sells his entire shareholding for £10,100,000. He claims entrepreneurs' relief in respect of the disposal. He makes no other disposals in 2022/23, but pays income tax at the additional rate. It is assumed for the purpose of this example only that the annual exemption for 2022/23 is £12,000 and the rates of tax remain as for 2018/19.

Mr Helm's capital gains tax liability for 2022/23 is calculated as follows.

	£
Sale proceeds	10,100,000
Cost	(200,000)
Chargeable gain qualifying for entrepreneurs' relief (subject to lifetime limit £10,000,000)	9,900,000
Annual exemption	(12,000)
Taxable gain 2022/23	£9,888,000
Capital gains tax payable (note (a))	
£9,750,000 × 10%	975,000
£138,000 × 20%	27,600
	£1,002,600

Notes

(a) The lifetime limit applies to restrict the amount of the gain in 2022/23 which qualifies for entrepreneurs' relief as follows. Of the limit of £10,000,000, £250,000 was used in 2018/19 leaving (£10,000,000 - £250,000 =) £9,750,000 unused. As the otherwise qualifying gain for 2022/23 is greater than the unused part of the limit, entrepreneurs' relief is restricted to £9,750,000.

(b) For a disposal of shares or securities (other than EMI shares — see (c) below) in a company to qualify for entrepreneurs' relief, the company must be the taxpayer's 'personal company' and must be either a 'trading company' or the 'holding company of a trading group' (both as defined). The taxpayer must be an officer or employee of the company or, where the company is a member of a trading group, of one or more companies which are members of the group. For this purpose, an individual's '*personal company*' is a company in which he holds at least 5% of the ordinary share capital (within *ITA 2007, s 989*) and in which he is able to exercise at least 5% of the voting rights by virtue of that holding. These conditions must be met throughout the one-year period ending with the date of disposal (or the one-year period ending with the date, within three years before the disposal, on which the company ceases to be a trading company without continuing to be or becoming a member of a trading group or ceases to be a member of a trading group without continuing to be or becoming a trading company). [*TCGA 1992, ss 169I, 169S(2)–(5); FA 2013, Sch 24 para 1; FA 2015, s 43*].

(c) A disposal of shares in a company on or after 6 April 2013 also qualifies for entrepreneurs' relief if the shares were acquired on or after 6 April 2012 as a result of the exercise of an option under the enterprise management incentives (EMI) scheme and the company is either a 'trading company' or the 'holding company of a trading group' (both as defined).The taxpayer must be an officer or employee of the company or, where the company is a member of a trading group, of one or more companies which are members of the group. These conditions must be met throughout the one-year period ending with the date of disposal (or the one-year period ending with the date, within three years before the disposal, on which the company ceases to be a trading company without continuing to be or becoming a member of a trading group or ceases to be a member of a trading group without continuing to be or becoming a trading company). The taxpayer does not have to have held the shares throughout the one year period, but the EMI option must have been granted on or before the first day of that period. For shares acquired on or after 6 April 2012 and before 6 April 2013 the taxpayer must elect before 31 January 2014 for the shares to qualify for entrepreneurs' relief if he disposed of any shares of the same class in 2012/13. [*TCGA 1992, s 169I; FA 2013, Sch 24 paras 1, 5*].

(d) The annual exemption of £12,000 is allocated against the part of the gain chargeable to tax at 20% as this gives the greater tax saving. [*TCGA 1992, s 4B; FA 2015, Sch 7 para 7*].

(D) Change in lifetime limit

If, in (C) above, Mr Helm's initial gain had been in May 2010 and had been, say, £2,500,000, his entrepreneurs' relief would have been restricted to the then lifetime limit of £2 million. Following the increases in the lifetime limit to £5 million with effect for disposals on or after 23 June 2010 and to £10 milliion for disposals on or after 6 April 2011, no further relief would have been due in respect of the 2010/11 gain. On the disposal in 2022/23, however, his unused lifetime limit would be £8 million (i.e. the new limit of £10 million less the £2 million in respect of which relief had previously been given).

211.2 PARTNERSHIPS

[*TCGA 1992, s 169I(8)*]

Martha has been a member of a trading partnership for ten years. In November 2018 she retires from the partnership and sells her interest in the partnership assets to the other partners, realising the following chargeable gains.

	£
Goodwill	100,000
Property	150,000
	£250,000

Martha claims entrepreneurs' relief in respect of the sale. She makes no other disposals in 2018/19 and has made no previous entrepreneurs' relief claims.

Martha's capital gains tax liability for 2018/19 is calculated as follows.

Gains qualifying for entrepreneurs' relief	£
Goodwill	100,000
Property	150,000
Deemed chargeable gain qualifying for entrepreneurs' relief	250,000
Annual exemption	(11,700)
Gain chargeable to tax	£238,300
Capital gains tax payable (£238,300 × 10%)	£23,830

Note

(a) A disposal by an individual of the whole or part of his interest in the assets of a partnership is treated for entrepreneurs' relief purposes as a disposal by him of the whole or part of the partnership business and may therefore be a qualifying business disposal where the necessary conditions are satisfied. [*TCGA 1992, s 169I(8)(b)*].

211.3 ASSOCIATED DISPOSALS

[*TCGA 1992, ss 169K, 169P; FA 2015, s 41; FA 2016, s 84*]

The facts are as in 211.2 above, except that Martha also sells an office which she owns personally and has let to the partnership rent-free since she first purchased it in 2006. The office has been used by the partnership for trade purposes throughout. The chargeable gain on the sale of the office is £56,000 and Martha claims entrepreneurs' relief.

Martha's capital gains tax liability for 2018/19 is calculated as follows.

Gains qualifying for entrepreneurs' relief	£
Goodwill	100,000
Property	150,000
Office	56,000
Deemed chargeable gain qualifying for entrepreneurs' relief	306,000
Annual exemption	(11,700)
Gain chargeable to tax	£294,300
Capital gains tax payable (£294,300 × 10%)	£29,430

Notes

(a) Where an individual makes a disposal of either all or part of his interest in the assets of a partnership or shares in or securities of a company (or an interest in such shares or securities) which qualifies for entrepreneurs' relief, an associated disposal of assets owned personally also qualifies for relief. The assets which are disposed of must have been in use for the purposes of the business of the partnership or company (or, where the company is a member of a trading group, the business of a member of the trading group) throughout the one-year period ending with the earlier of the date of the disposal of the partnership assets or shares etc. and the cessation of the business of the partnership or company. The disposal must be made as part of the individual's withdrawal from participation in the business. For disposals of assets acquired on or after 13 June 2016, the disposal must be of an asset or assets which the individual has owned throughout the three years ending with the date of disposal.

For disposals on or after 18 March 2015 where the disposal of business assets consists of the disposal of all or part of the individual's interest in the assets of a partnership, either:

- the disposed of interest must be at least a 5% interest in the partnership's assets and there must be no 'partnership purchase arrangements' at the date of the disposal; or
- if the disposed of interest is an interest of less than 5%, the individual must have held at least a 5% interest in the partnership's assets for a continuous period of at least three years in the eight years ending on the date of the disposal and there must be no partnership purchase arrangements at the date of the disposal.

For this purpose, '*partnership purchase arrangements*' are arrangements (other than the material disposal) under which the individual or a connected person is entitled to acquire an interest in, or an increased interest in, the partnership (including a share of its profits or assets or an interest in such a share). Arrangements are not, however, partnership purchase arrangements if they were made before both the material disposal and the associated disposal and without regard to either of them.

For disposals on or after 18 March 2015 where the disposal of business assets consists of the disposal of shares in a company (or an interest in such shares), all or some of which are ordinary shares, the ordinary shares disposed of must constitute at least 5% of the company's ordinary share capital and at least 5% of the voting rights in the company and there must be no 'share purchase arrangements' at the date of the disposal. For this purpose, '*share purchase arrangements*' are arrangements (other than the material disposal) under which the individual or a connected person is entitled to acquire shares or securities in the company or a company which is a member of the same trading group. Arrangements are not, however, share purchase arrangements if they were made before both the material disposal and the associated disposal and without regard to either of them. Two companies are treated as members of the same trading group if, at the date of the disposal, arrangements exist which it is reasonable to assume will result in them becoming such members. This requirement is not met if the disposal of shares is a deemed disposal in consideration of a capital distribution within *TCGA 1992, s 122* other than one made in the course of dissolving or winding up the company.

[*TCGA 1992, s 169K; FA 2015, s 41; FA 2016, s 84*].

(b) Entrepreneurs' relief in respect of an associated disposal is restricted where the assets were in use for the purposes of the business only for part of the period of ownership; where only part of the assets are in use for business purposes for that period; where the individual is concerned in carrying on the business (personally, in partnership or as an officer or employee of his personal company) for only part of the period in which the assets are in use for the purposes of the business; and where, for any part of the period for which the assets are in use for the purposes of the business (but ignoring any part of the period which falls before 6 April 2008), their availability is dependent on the payment of rent (which term includes any form of consideration given for the use of an asset). Relief is applied only to such part of the gain as is just and reasonable. [*TCGA 1992, ss 169P, 169S(5)*].

211.4 REORGANISATIONS ETC.

[*TCGA 1992, s 169Q*]

Mr Prosser is a shareholder in Oyster Ltd, a trading company which qualifies as his personal company for the purposes of entrepreneurs' relief. He acquired the shares in March 2002 for £150,000 and has been a director of the company since that time. In January 2019, the shareholders of Oyster Ltd accept an offer by a public company, Lobster plc, and Mr Prosser receives shares in Lobster plc in exchange for his entire shareholding in Oyster Ltd. His Lobster plc shares are valued at £550,000 at the time of the exchange, and the company does not qualify as his personal company. Mr Prosser makes no other disposals in 2018/19 and has made no previous claims to entrepreneurs' relief.

If Mr Prosser elects under *TCGA 1992, s 169Q* to disapply *TCGA 1992, s 127* in respect of the share exchange and claims entrepreneurs' relief in respect of the gain on the Oyster Ltd shares, his capital gains tax liability for 2018/19 is calculated as follows.

	£
Sale proceeds	550,000
Cost	(150,000)
Chargeable gain qualifying for entrepreneurs' relief	400,000
Annual exemption	(11,700)
Gain chargeable to tax	£388,300
Capital gains tax payable (£388,300 × 10%)	£38,830

Notes

(a) Where an exchange of securities (within *TCGA 1992, s 135*) takes place and *TCGA 1992, s 127* would otherwise apply to treat the 'original shares' and the 'new holding' (as defined for the purposes of that section) as the same asset, an election can be made to disapply that section so that entrepreneurs' relief can be claimed in respect of the disposal of the original shares.

(b) The election must be made on or before the first anniversary of the 31 January following the tax year in which the reorganisation takes place. In this case, therefore, the claim must be made by 31 January 2021 (which is the same date by which the claim to entrepreneurs' relief must be made). An election takes effect only where a claim to entrepreneurs' relief is also made; without such a claim, the election has no effect.

(c) Mr Prosser cannot claim entrepreneurs' relief on an eventual disposal of his shares in Lobster plc. If he had not made an election under *TCGA 1992, s 169Q* the opportunity to claim relief would have been lost.

(d) The above provisions apply also to reorganisations within *TCGA 1992, s 126* and to schemes of reconstruction within *TCGA 1992, s 136* to which *TCGA 1992, s 127* applies.

211.5 DEFERRED GAINS

[*TCGA 1992, ss 169T–169V; FA 2015, s 44*]

In May 2018, Charlotte sells her entire shareholding in Gochenauer Ltd, realising a gain of £137,000. The gain qualifies for entrepreneurs' relief. In August 2018, Charlotte acquires by subscription 51% of the issued ordinary share capital of Thorn Ltd for £137,000. This is a qualifying investment for the purposes of EIS deferral relief and Charlotte makes a claim to defer the whole of the May 2018 gain.

On 1 May 2022, Charlotte sells her shares in Thorn Ltd, realising a chargeable gain of £80,000, which qualifies for entrepreneurs' relief. She makes no other disposals in 2022/23 and has made no previous entrepreneur's relief claims.

If Charlotte claims entrepreneurs' relief in respect of both the deferred May 2018 gain and the May 2022 gain, her CGT position for 2022/23 is as follows. It is assumed that the annual exemption for 2022/23 is £12,000.

	£
Deferred May 2018 gain brought into charge	137,000
May 2022 gain	80,000
Chargeable gains qualifying for entrepreneurs' relief	217,000
Annual exemption	(12,000)
Gain chargeable to tax	£205,000
Capital gains tax payable (£205,000 × 10%)	£20,500

Notes

(a) Where a disposal on or after 3 December 2014 qualifies for both entrepreneurs' relief and EIS deferral relief or social investment deferral relief, deferral relief can be claimed and entrepreneurs' relief can then be claimed when the deferred gain comes back into charge on the happening of a chargeable event. A claim for relief must be made on or before the first anniversary of 31 January following the tax year in which the deferred gain comes back into charge. [*TCGA 1992, ss 169T–169V; FA 2015, s 44*].

(b) See **210.3** ENTERPRISE INVESTMENT SCHEME for a further example of EIS deferral relief.

212 Exemptions and Reliefs

Cross-references. See also **223** PRIVATE RESIDENCES, **224** QUALIFYING CORPORATE BONDS and **232** WASTING ASSETS.

212.1 CHATTELS

(A) Marginal relief

[*TCGA 1992, s 262(2)*]

On 1 April 1988, Y acquired by inheritance a painting valued for probate at £900. He sold it for £7,200 on 30 October 2018, incurring costs of £150.

	£	£
Disposal proceeds	7,200	
Incidental costs	(150)	7,050
Acquisition cost		(900)
Chargeable gain		£6,150
Marginal relief		
Chargeable gain limited to $^5/_3 \times$ (£7,200 − £6,000)		£2,000

(B) Loss relief

[*TCGA 1992, s 262(3)*]

Z bought a piece of antique jewellery for £7,000 in February 1991. In January 2019, he is forced to sell it, but at auction it realises only £1,500 and Z incurs costs of £100.

	£	£
Deemed disposal consideration		6,000
Cost of disposal	100	
Cost of acquisition	7,000	(7,100)
Allowable loss		£1,100

Note

(a) Where the disposal consideration for tangible movable property is less than £6,000 and there would otherwise be a loss, the consideration is deemed to be £6,000.

(C) Partial disposal of assets forming sets

[*TCGA 1992, s 262(4)*]

AB purchased a set of six 18th century dining chairs in 1985 for £1,200. After incurring restoration costs of £300 in 1991, he sold two of them in March 2014 to an unconnected person for £2,900. In August 2018, he sold the other four to the same buyer for £4,900.

The two disposals are treated as one for the purposes of the chattel exemption and marginal relief, the consideration for which is £7,800. Marginal relief on this basis would give a total chargeable gain of £3,000 ([£7,800 – £6,000] x $^5/_3$) which is to be compared with the following:

March 2014	£	£
Disposal proceeds		2,900
Acquisition cost	1,200	
Enhancement cost	300	
	1,500	
Cost of two chairs sold £1,500 × $^2/_6$		(500)
Chargeable gain		£2,400

August 2018	£
Disposal proceeds	4,900
Cost £1,500 × $^4/_6$	(1,000)
Chargeable gain	£3,900

Total chargeable gains (£2,400 + £3,900)	£6,300

The total gain of £6,300 compares with a gain of £3,000 using marginal relief. Marginal relief is therefore effective and the total chargeable gain is £3,000.

The gain is apportioned to tax years as follows (note (b))

2013/14	$£3{,}000 \times \frac{2{,}900}{7{,}800} =$	£1,115
2018/19	$£3{,}000 \times \frac{4{,}900}{7{,}800} =$	£1,885

Notes

(a) Prior to the second disposal, the first disposal would have been exempt, the proceeds being within the £6,000 chattel exemption.

(b) The gain as reduced by marginal relief is apportioned between tax years in the same ratio as the proportion of total sale proceeds applicable to each year (HMRC Capital Gains Manual, CG76637).

(c) See also **202.3** ANTI-AVOIDANCE.

213 Hold-Over Reliefs

213.1 RELIEF FOR GIFTS

[*TCGA 1992, s 260*]

(A) Chargeable lifetime transfers

B owns a house which he has not occupied as a private residence. He purchased the house for £15,200 inclusive of costs in 1979 and in January 2019 he gives it to a discretionary trust of which he is the settlor. The settlement is not a settlor-interested settlement for the purposes of *TCGA 1992, ss 169B–169G.* The market value of the house is agreed to be £200,000 at the date of transfer, and B incurs transfer costs of £1,000. The house had a value of £21,000 at 31 March 1982.

	£
Disposal consideration	200,000
Deduct Costs of disposal	(1,000)
	199,000
Market value 31.3.82	(21,000)
Chargeable gain	£178,000

If B elects under *TCGA 1992, s 260*, his chargeable gain is reduced to nil, and the trustees' acquisition cost of the house is treated as £22,000 (£200,000 - £178,000).

Notes

(a) Relief under *TCGA 1992, s 260* is restricted, generally, to transfers which are, or would but for annual exemptions be, chargeable lifetime transfers for inheritance tax purposes.

(b) Separate rules apply to transfers of assets between MARRIED PERSONS AND CIVIL PARTNERS **(218)**.

(c) Relief under *TCGA 1992, s 260* is not available on a disposal to the trustees of a settlor-interested settlement (as defined). [*TCGA 1992, ss 169B–169G*].

(B) Disposal consideration

[*TCGA 1992, s 260(5)*]

The facts are as in (A) above except that B sells the house to the trustees for £30,000.

	£	£
Chargeable gain (as above) (note (a))		178,000
Deduct		
Actual consideration passing	30,000	
B's allowable costs	(22,000)	
		(8,000)
Held-over gain		£170,000

(i) B's chargeable gain is reduced to £178,000 − £170,000	£8,000
(ii) The trustees' allowable cost is reduced to £200,000 − £170,000	£30,000

Note

(a) The disposal consideration is taken as the open market value of the house at the date of disposal because B and the trustees are connected persons. Thus, the computation of the gain is as in (A) above.

(C) **Relief for IHT**

[*TCGA 1992, s 260(7)*]

The facts are as in (A) above. Before transferring the house, B had made substantial chargeable transfers. Inheritance tax of £20,000 is payable on the transfer. The trustees sell the house in December 2019 for £195,000.

	£	£
Disposal proceeds		195,000
Acquisition cost	200,000	
Deduct held-over gain	178,000	
		(22,000)
Gain		173,000
IHT attributable to earlier transfer		(20,000)
Chargeable gain		£153,000

Notes

(a) Where the IHT attributable to the earlier transfer is greater than the gain, the IHT deduction is limited to the amount of the gain and cannot create or increase a loss. [*TCGA 1992, s 260(7)*].

(b) A similar inheritance tax relief operates where the original gain was held over under *TCGA 1992, s 165* or *FA 1980, s 79*. [*TCGA 1992, ss 67, 165(10)*].

213.2 RELIEF FOR GIFTS OF BUSINESS ASSETS

[*TCGA 1992, s 165, Sch 7*]

Zoë owns a freehold property which she lets to the family trading company, Sphere Ltd, in which she and her father each own half the shares and voting rights. Zoë inherited the property in April 1990 at a probate value of £50,000, and since then the whole of the property has been used for the purposes of the company's trade. In November 2018, Zoë transfers the property to her boyfriend. Its market value at that time is £115,000. The intention is that he should give sufficient consideration to leave Zoë with a chargeable gain exactly equal to the annual exempt amount (there being no other disposals in 2018/19).

Actual consideration should be £61,300 as shown by the following computation

	£
Deemed consideration	115,000
Deduct: Cost	(50,000)
Unrelieved gain	65,000
Held-over gain (see below)	(53,300)
Chargeable gain covered by annual exemption	£11,700

Computation of held-over gain

	£	£
Unrelieved gain		65,000
Actual consideration	61,700	
Less allowable expenditure	50,000	(11,700)
Held-over gain		£53,300

Note

(a) On a subsequent disposal of the property, the allowable expenditure would be £61,700 (deemed proceeds of £115,000 less held-over gain of £53,300).

213.3 TRANSFER OF BUSINESS TO A COMPANY — INCORPORATION RELIEF

[*TCGA 1992, s 162*]

W has carried on an antiquarian bookselling business for many years. He decides to form an unquoted company, P Ltd, to carry on the business. He transfers, in May 2018, the whole of the business undertaking, assets and liabilities to P Ltd, in consideration for the issue of shares, plus an amount left outstanding on interest-free loan. W becomes a director of P Ltd. The business assets and liabilities transferred are valued as follows

	£	Value £	Chargeable gain £
Freehold shop premises (acquired in 2000)		80,000	42,000
Goodwill		36,000	16,000
Fixtures and fittings		4,000	—
Trading stock		52,000	—
Debtors		18,000	—
		190,000	
Mortgage on shop	50,000		
Trade creditors	20,000	70,000	—
		£120,000	£58,000

The company issues 100,000 £1 ordinary shares, valued at par, to W in May 2018, and the amount left outstanding is £20,000.If W does not elect to disapply *TCGA 1992, s 162* treatment, the amount of the chargeable gain rolled over on transfer of the business is as follows.

$\frac{100,000}{120,000} \times £58,000$	£48,333

Of the chargeable gain, £9,667 (£58,000 − £48,333) remains taxable and is covered by the annual exemption.

The allowable cost of W's shares is £51,667 (£100,000 − £48,333).

213.4 DISINCORPORATION RELIEF

[*TCGA 1992, ss 162B, 162C; CTA 2009, s 849A; FA 2013, ss 58–61*]

(A) Goodwill outside intangible assets regime

W has owned all of the shares in B Ltd since the company was set up and began trading in 2000. On 31 July 2017, B Ltd transfers the trade as a going concern to W. The assets of the trade include land with a market value of £35,000 and goodwill with a market value of £27,000. The land cost £12,000 in 2000 and the goodwill, being internally generated, has no acquisition cost for chargeable gains purposes.

If W and B Ltd jointly make a claim for disincorporation relief before 31 July 2019, B Ltd's chargeable gains computation on the transfer is as follows.

Land

	£
Deemed disposal consideration	12,000
Deduct Costs of acquisition	(12,000)
Chargeable gain	£Nil

Goodwill

	£
Deemed disposal consideration	Nil
Deduct Costs of acquisition	Nil
Chargeable gain	£Nil

W's acquisition costs for the purposes of capital gains tax are £12,000 for the land and £Nil for the goodwill.

Notes

(a) Disincorporation relief is abolished for transfers of a business from a company after 31 March 2018.

(b) A claim to disincorporation relief must be made jointly by the company and all of the shareholders to whom the business is transferred. A claim is irrevocable and must be made within the two years beginning with the date of the transfer of the company's business. [*FA 2013, s 60*].

(c) A transfer of a business from a company to some or all of its shareholders qualifies for disincorporation relief if the business is transferred as a going concern and it is transferred together with all of the business assets (or all the assets other than cash). All of the shareholders to whom the business is transferred must be individuals and must have held shares in the company throughout the twelve months ending with the date of the transfer. The qualifying assets (see (c) below) must have a combined market value not exceeding £100,000. The business must be transferred between 1 April 2013 and 31 March 2018 inclusive. [*FA 2013, ss 58(1), 59(1)–(6)*].

(d) Qualifying assets are goodwill and interests in land which are not held as trading stock. [*FA 2013, s 59(10)*]. Goodwill within the INTANGIBLE ASSETS (CT 108) regime in the hands of the company is subject to specific rules under that regime. See (B) below. In this case, the goodwill is excluded from the intangible assets regime because the company's trade was carried on before 1 April 2002.

(e) Where a claim to disincorporation relief is made, the disposal consideration for each of the qualifying assets (and the shareholder's acquisition cost) is deemed to be equal to the lower of the allowable expenditure on the disposal and the market value of the asset. [*TCGA 1992, s 162B; FA 2013, s 61(1)*]. Where the market value is less than the allowable expenditure, the result is that an allowable loss accrues to the company; otherwise neither a gain nor a loss arises.

(B) Goodwill within intangible assets regime

[*TCGA 1992, s 260(5)*]

The facts are as in (A) above except that B Ltd was set up and the trade commenced in 2004.

If W and B Ltd jointly make a claim for disincorporation relief before 31 July 2019, B Ltd's chargeable gains computation on the transfer of the land is as follows.

	£
Deemed disposal consideration	12,000
Deduct Costs of acquisition	(12,000)
Chargeable gain	£Nil

W's acquisition cost for the purposes of capital gains tax is £12,000.

The goodwill falls within the INTANGIBLE ASSETS (CT 108) regime in the hands of the company. If a disincorporation relief claim is made, the realisation proceeds of the goodwill are treated as nil (see note (b)). W's acquisition cost for the purposes of capital gains tax is equal to the value at which the goodwill is treated as transferred by the company under the intangible assets regime, i.e. nil.

Notes

(a) Disincorporation relief is abolished for transfers of a business from a company after 31 March 2018.

(b) Where a claim to disincorporation relief is made and goodwill within the INTANGIBLE ASSETS (CT 108) regime is one of the qualifying assets, that regime applies to the company as follows:

- if the goodwill has been written-down for corporation tax purposes, the transfer is treated as being at the lower of the tax written-down value and the market value of the goodwill;
- if the goodwill has not been written down but is shown in the company's balance sheet, the transfer is treated as being at the lower of cost and market value;
- if the goodwill is not shown in the balance sheet, the transfer is treated as made for realisation proceeds of nil.

[*CTA 2009, s 849A; FA 2013, s 61(5)*].

214 Indexation

Note

Indexation allowance is available only for the purposes of corporation tax on chargeable gains.

214.1 INDEXATION ALLOWANCE — GENERAL RULES

[*TCGA 1992, ss 53–56*]

(A) Calculation of indexation factor — companies — disposal before 1 January 2018

M Ltd bought a freehold factory in December 1984 for £500,000. Further buildings are erected at a cost of £200,000 in May 1992. In May 2017 the factory is sold for £2m. The relevant values of the retail price index (RPI) are as follows

December 1984	90.87
May 1992	139.3
May 2017)	271.1

	£	£
Disposal consideration		2,000,000
Deduct Cost of factory and site	500,000	
Cost of additions	200,000	(700,000)
Unindexed gain		1,300,000
Indexation allowance		
(i) Factory and site		
Indexation factor		
$\frac{271.7 - 90.87}{90.87} = 1.990$		
Indexed rise		
£500,000 × 1.990	995,000	
(ii) Additions		
Indexation factor		
$\frac{271.7 - 139.3}{139.3} = 0.950$		
Indexed rise		
£200,000 × 0.950	190,000	1,185,000
Gain chargeable to corporation tax		£115,000

(B) Calculation of indexation factor — companies — disposal on or after 1 January 2018

The facts are as in (A) above , except that the factory is sold in May 201. The relevant values of the retail price index (RPI) are as follows

December 1984	90.87
May 1992	139.3
December 2017)	278.1

	£	£
Disposal consideration		2,000,000
Deduct Cost of factory and site	500,000	
Cost of additions	200,000	(700,000)
Unindexed gain		1,300,000
Indexation allowance		
(i) Factory and site		
Indexation factor		
$\frac{278.1 - 90.87}{90.87} = 2.060$		
Indexed rise		
£500,000 × 2.060	1,030,000	
(ii) Additions		
Indexation factor		
$\frac{278.1 - 139.3}{139.3} = 0.996$		
Indexed rise		
£200,000 × 0.996	199,200	1,229,200
Gain chargeable to corporation tax		£70,800

Note

(a) Indexation allowance is frozen at its December 2017 level. No indexation allowance is available in respect of expenditure incurred after 31 December 2017, and for expenditure incurred on or before that date and falling to be deducted on a disposal after that date, indexation allowance is computed up to and including December 2017 only. *[TCGA 1992, ss 53(1)(1B), 54(1B); FA 2018, s 26(2)(3)(6)]*.

(C) Disposal of asset held on 31 March 1982

X Ltd acquired an asset for £6,000 in August 1979. The company sold it for £29,000 in December 2018. The agreed market value of the asset at 31 March 1982 is £7,500. The indexation factor for March 1982 to December 2017 is 2.501.

	£	£
Disposal consideration	29,000	29,000
Deduct Cost	(6,000)	
Market value 31.3.82		(7,500)
Unindexed gain	23,000	21,500
Indexation allowance £7,500 × 2.501	(18,758)	(18,758)
Gain after indexation	£4,242	£2,742
Chargeable gain		£2,742

Notes

(a) In both the calculation using cost and that using 31 March 1982 value, indexation is automatically based on 31 March 1982 value. If, however, a greater allowance would have been produced by basing indexation on cost, that would automatically have applied instead. If, however, an irrevocable election were to be made under *TCGA 1992, s 35(5)* for all assets to be treated as sold and re-acquired at 31 March 1982, indexation must then be based on 31 March 1982 value whether it is beneficial or not. [*TCGA 1992, s 55(1)(2)*].

(b) Indexation allowance is frozen at its December 2017 level. No indexation allowance is available in respect of expenditure incurred after 31 December 2017, and for expenditure incurred on or before that date and falling to be deducted on a disposal after that date, indexation allowance is computed up to and including December 2017 only. *[TCGA 1992, ss 53(1)(1B), 54(1B); FA 2018, s 26(2)(3)(6)]*.

(c) See also **205.1 ASSETS HELD ON 31 MARCH 1982**.

(D) Losses — indexation allowance restriction

[*TCGA 1992, s 53(1)(b)(2A); FA 1994, s 93(1)–(3)(11)*]

In June 1993, M Ltd had purchased two assets, each for £25,000. In September 2018, the company sells the assets for £30,000 (A) and £23,000 (B) respectively. Incidental costs of purchase and sale are ignored for the purposes of this example. The indexation factor for the period June 1993 to December 2017 is 0.972.

The gains/losses on the sales are as follows

	(A)	(B)
	£	£
Proceeds	30,000	23,000
Cost	(25,000)	(25,000)
Unindexed gain/(loss)	5,000	(2,000)
Indexation allowance £25,000 × 0.972 = £24,300 but restricted to	(5,000)	Nil
Chargeable gain/(allowable loss)	Nil	£(2,000)

Note

(a) Indexation allowance can reduce an unindexed gain to nil but cannot create or increase a loss.

(b) Indexation allowance is frozen at its December 2017 level. No indexation allowance is available in respect of expenditure incurred after 31 December 2017, and for expenditure incurred on or before that date and falling to be deducted on a disposal after that date, indexation allowance is computed up to and including December 2017 only. *[TCGA 1992, ss 53(1)(1B), 54(1B); FA 2018, s 26(2)(3)(6)]*. See **214.1** INDEXATION.

214.2 NO GAIN/NO LOSS TRANSFERS

(A) Transfers between spouses or civil partners before 6 April 2008 — asset acquired by first spouse before 1 April 1982 — gain on ultimate disposal after 5 April 2008

[*TCGA 1992, s 35A, s 52A, s 55(5)(6), s 56(2), s 58; FA 2008, Sch 2 paras 59, 60, 65(2), 71, 78, 83*]

Mr N inherited a country cottage in 1977 at a probate value of £12,000. Its market value at 31 March 1982 was £30,000. In July 1988, Mr N incurred enhancement expenditure of £5,000 on the cottage. In May 1990, he gave the cottage to his wife. In November 2018, Mrs N sells it for £205,000. At no time was the cottage the main residence of either spouse. The relevant indexation factors are as follows

March 1982 to May 1990	0.589
July 1988 to May 1990	0.183

(i) *Disposal in May 1990*

Consideration deemed to be such that neither gain nor loss arises.

	£	£
Cost of cottage to Mr N		12,000
Enhancement expenditure		5,000
		17,000
Indexation allowance:		
£30,000 × 0.589	17,670	
£5,000 × 0.183	915	18,585
Cost of cottage to Mrs N		£35,585

(ii) *Disposal in November 2018*

Re-computation of Mrs N's acquisition cost

	£
Market value 31.3.82	30,000
Enhancement expenditure	5,000
	35,000
Indexation allowance (as above)	18,585
Cost of cottage to Mrs N	£53,585

Mrs N's chargeable gain

	£
Sale proceeds	205,000
Deduct cost	(53,585)
Chargeable gain 2018/19	£151,415

Notes

(a) The cottage having been acquired by Mrs N by means of a no gain/no loss disposal from her husband to which re-basing did not apply, in computing the gain on her disposal of the cottage after 5 April 2008 re-basing is assumed to have applied to the no gain/no loss disposal. [*TCGA 1992, s 35A; FA 2008, Sch 2 paras 59, 71*]. Therefore, in computing the gain or loss on the post-5 April 2008 disposal, the allowable expenditure includes the value of the cottage at 31 March 1982 and the indexation allowance due for the period from that date to the date on which Mrs N acquired the cottage (May 1990). This rule does not affect the position of Mr N.

(b) Indexation allowance is abolished for capital gains tax purposes (i.e. for disposals by individuals, trustees and personal representatives) for disposals on or after 6 April 2008. [*TCGA 1992, s 52A; FA 2008, Sch 2 paras 78, 83*]. No indexation allowance is due therefore on the disposal by Mrs N, but as a result of the rule in note (a) above, she effectively obtains indexation allowance up to the date on which she acquired the cottage (or April 1998 if earlier).

(c) See also (B) below and **218** MARRIED PERSONS AND CIVIL PARTNERS.

(B) Transfers between spouses or civil partners before 6 April 2008 — asset acquired by first spouse after 31 March 1982 — gain on ultimate disposal after 5 April 2008

[*TCGA 1992, s 56(2)*]

The facts are as in (A) above except that Mr N inherited the cottage in April 1982 at a probate value of £30,000. The relevant indexation factors are

April 1982 to May 1990	0.557
July 1988 to May 1990	0.183

(i) *Disposal in May 1990*

Consideration deemed to be such that neither gain nor loss arises.

	£	£
Cost of cottage to Mr N		30,000
Enhancement expenditure		5,000
		35,000
Indexation allowance:		
£30,000 × 0.557	16,710	
£5,000 × 0.183	915	17,625
Cost of cottage to Mrs N		£52,625

(ii) *Disposal in November 2018*

Sale proceeds	205,000
Cost (as above)	(52,625)
Chargeable gain 2018/19	£152,375

Notes

(a) For further examples on transfers between spouses or civil partners, see (A) above and **218** MARRIED PERSONS AND CIVIL PARTNERS.

(b) See note (b) to (A) above.

(C) **Intra-group transfers — asset acquired by group before 1 April 1982**

[*TCGA 1992, s 55(5)–(9), s 56(2), s 171*]

J Ltd and K Ltd are 75% subsidiaries of H Ltd. J Ltd acquired a property in 1980 for £20,000. Its market value at 31 March 1982 was £25,000. In May 1990, J Ltd transferred the property to K Ltd. In May 2018, K Ltd sells the property outside the group. The sale proceeds are (1) £90,000, (2) £18,000 or (3) £29,000. The relevant indexation factors are as follows

March 1982 to May 1990	0.589
March 1982 to December 2017	2.501

(i) *Disposal in May 1990*

Consideration deemed to be such that neither gain nor loss arises.

	£
Cost of asset to J Ltd	20,000
Indexation allowance £25,000 × 0.589	14,725
Cost of asset to K Ltd	£34,725

(ii) *Disposal in May 2018*

(1) Proceeds £90,000

	£	£	£
Proceeds		90,000	90,000
Cost	34,725		
Deduct Indexation allowance previously given	14,725	(20,000)	
Market value 31.3.82			(25,000)
Unindexed gain		70,000	65,000
Indexation allowance £25,000 × 2.501		(62,525)	(62,525)
Gain after indexation		£7,475	£2,475
Chargeable gain			£2,475

(2) Proceeds £18,000

	£	£	£
Proceeds		18,000	18,000
Cost	34,725		
Deduct Indexation allowance previously given	14,725	(20,000)	
Market value 31.3.82			(25,000)
		(2,000)	(7,000)
Add Rolled-up indexation		(14,725)	(14,725)
Loss after rolled-up indexation		£(16,725)	£(21,725)
Allowable loss		£16,725	

(3) Proceeds £29,000

	£	£	£
Proceeds		29,000	29,000
Cost	34,725		
Deduct Indexation allowance previously given	14,725		
		(20,000)	
Market value 31.3.82			(25,000)
Unindexed gain		9,000	4,000
Indexation allowance:			
£25,000 × 2.501 = £62,525 but restricted to		(9,000)	(4,000)

	Nil	Nil
Excess of rolled-up indexation (£14,725) over indexation allowance given above	(5,725)	(10,725)
Loss after rolled-up indexation	£(5,725)	£(10,725)
Allowable loss	£5,725	

Notes

(a) Having acquired the property by means of a no gain/no loss disposal from J Ltd, who held it at 31 March 1982, K Ltd is deemed to have held the asset at 31 March 1982 for the purposes of the re-basing provisions, and also the provisions under which indexation allowance is computed using value at 31 March 1982. [*TCGA 1992, s 55(5)(6), Sch 3 para 1*].

(b) In (2) and (3) above, as the ultimate disposal is after 29 November 1993 and indexation allowance is either unavailable in (2) above or restricted in (3) above, special provisions enable the person making the disposal to obtain the benefit of any indexation allowance already accrued on no gain/no loss transfers made *before* 30 November 1993 (called 'rolled-up indexation'). [*TCGA 1992, s 55(7)–(9)*].

(c) Indexation allowance is frozen at its December 2017 level. No indexation allowance is available in respect of expenditure incurred after 31 December 2017, and for expenditure incurred on or before that date and falling to be deducted on a disposal after that date, indexation allowance is computed up to and including December 2017 only. *[TCGA 1992, ss 53(1)(1B), 54(1B); FA 2018, s 26(2)(3)(6)]*. See **214.1** INDEXATION.

(D) Intra-group transfers — asset acquired by group after 31 March 1982 — loss on ultimate disposal

[*TCGA 1992, s 56(2)–(4), s 171*]

L Ltd, M Ltd and N Ltd are members of a 75% group of companies. L Ltd acquired a property in June 1990 for £50,000 and transferred it to M Ltd in June 1993. M Ltd transferred the property to N Ltd in June 1996, and N Ltd sold it outside the group in June 2018 for £55,000. The relevant indexation factors are as follows

June 1990 to June 1993	0.113
June 1993 to June 1996	0.085

(i) *Disposal in June 1993*

Consideration deemed to be such that neither gain nor loss arises.

	£
Cost of asset to L Ltd	50,000
Indexation allowance £50,000 × 0.113	5,650
Cost of asset to M Ltd	£55,650

(ii) *Disposal in June 1996*

Cost of asset to M Ltd	55,650
Indexation allowance £55,650 × 0.085	4,730
Cost of asset to N Ltd	£60,380

(iii) *Disposal in June 2018*

Proceeds	55,000
Cost (as above)	(60,380)
Loss before adjustment under *TCGA 1992, s 56(3)*	(5,380)
Deduct Indexation on June 1996 disposal	4,730
Allowable loss	£(650)

Note

(a) Where a loss accrues on the ultimate disposal, it is reduced by any indexation allowance included in the cost of the asset by virtue of a no gain/no loss disposal made *after* 29 November 1993. If this adjustment would otherwise convert a loss into a gain, the disposal is treated as giving rise to neither a gain nor a loss. [*TCGA 1992, s 56(3)*].

215 Investors' Relief

215.1 COMPUTATION OF RELIEF

[*TCGA 1992, ss 169VC, 169VK; FA 2016, Sch 14 para 2*]

(A) Basic computation

In May 2019, Sara sells her entire holding of shares in Watkins Ltd, an unlisted trading company, for £900,000. Sara subscribed for the shares in April 2016 for £200,000. She claims investors' relief in respect of the disposal. She has made no previous claim to the relief and makes no other disposals in 2019/20.

Sara's capital gains tax liability for 2019/20 is calculated as follows.

	£
Sale consideration	900,000
Less cost of shares	200,000
Chargeable gain	700,000
Annual exemption (assumed)	12,000
Gain chargeable to tax	£688,000
Capital gains tax payable (£688,000 × 10%)	£68,800

Notes

(a) Investors' relief can be claimed by individuals or trustees in respect of certain disposals on or after 6 April 2019 of qualifying ordinary shares in unlisted trading companies subscribed for on or after 17 March 2016. The relief applies for capital gains tax purposes only and is not available to companies. The investor must have held the shares continuously throughout the period beginning with the date they were issued and ending with the date of disposal. That period must be at least three years, or, where the share was issued before 6 April 2016, at least three years plus the period beginning with the date of issue and ending on 5 April 2016. With limited exceptions, the investor must not be an officer of employee of the company or a connected company. Relief is given by charging the gain to capital gains tax at 10%.

(b) Investors' relief must be claimed on or before the first anniversary of the 31 January following the tax year in which the qualifying business disposal is made. In the case of a disposal by trustees, the claim must be made jointly by the trustees and the eligible beneficiary or beneficiaries. [*TCGA 1992, s 169VM; FA 2016, Sch 14 para 2*]. Sara must therefore make a claim on or before 31 January 2022.

(c) There are provisions for the disqualification of shares from relief where the investor receives any value, other than insignificant value, from the company at any time in the period beginning one year before, and ending immediately before the third anniversary of, the date on which the shares were issued. See *TCGA 1992, Sch 7ZB*.

(B) **Qualifying and non-qualifying shares**

Charlie has the following transactions in ordinary 25p shares in Surf Ltd, an unlisted trading company.

Date		No. of shares acquired/(sold)	Cost/ (proceeds)
			£
1 May 2016	subscribes for	2,000	20,000
1 July 2016	purchases	2,000	25,000
1 August 2017	subscribes for	2,000	30,000
1 August 2019	sells	(3,000)	(120,000)
1 September 2020	sells	(3,000)	(200,000)

Charlie and the company meet all the conditions necessary for the shares issued to Charlie to qualify for investors' relief. Charlie makes no other disposals in 2019/20 or 2020/21. For the purpose only of this example it is assumed that the annual exempt amount for both years is £12,000. Charlie is a higher rate income tax payer for both years. If Charlie makes all of the available investors' relief claims, his capital gains liability is as follows

2019/20

Section 104 **holding**	Shares	Qualifying expenditure
		£
May 2016 acquisition	2,000	20,000
July 2016 acquisition	2,000	25,000
	4,000	45,000
August 2017 acquisition	2,000	30,000
	6,000	75,000
August 2019 disposal	(3,000)	(37,500)
Pool carried forward	3,000	£37,500

Calculation of chargeable gain	£
Disposal consideration	120,000
Allowable cost $\frac{3,000}{6,000} \times £75,000$	37,500
Chargeable gain	82,500
Annual exemption	12,000
Gain chargeable to tax	£70,500

Capital gains tax payable (see note (a))	
£55,000 × 10%	5,500
£15,500 × 20%	3,100
	£8,600

2020/21

Section 104 **holding**	Shares	Qualifying expenditure
		£
Pool brought forward	3,000	37,500
September 2020 disposal	(3,000)	(37,500)
Pool carried forward	—	—

Calculation of chargeable gain	£
Disposal consideration	200,000
Allowable cost	37,500
Chargeable gain	162,500
Annual exemption	12,000
Gain chargeable to tax	£150,500

Capital gains tax payable (see note (b))	
£108,333 × 10%	10,833
£42,167 × 20%	8,433
	£19,266

Notes

(a) Where only some of the shares in a holding are qualifying shares, only a corresponding proportion of the gain (after deduction of any allowable losses) is taxable at the rate of 10%. The proportion is the number of qualifying shares treated as disposed of divided by the total number of shares disposed of. For this purpose, qualifying shares are treated as disposed of in priority to non-qualifying shares. See (b) below where there has been a previous disposal of shares from the holding. [*TCGA 1992, s 169VD; FA 2016, Sch 14 para 2*].

In the case of the disposal in August 2019, Charlie's holding immediately before the disposal consists of 2,000 qualifying shares (the shares subscribed for in May 2016) and 4,000 non-qualifying shares. The non-qualifying shares consist of 2,000 excluded shares (i.e. shares which can never be qualifying shares) acquired in July 2016 and the 2,000 shares subscribed for in August 2017 which are potentially qualifying shares (i.e. shares which would be qualifying shares if they had been held by Charlie for sufficient time). Therefore 2,000 of the 3,000 shares disposed of are treated as qualifying shares. The part of the chargeable gain qualifying for investors' relief is therefore £82,500 × (2,000/3,000) = £55,000.

(b) Where, before a disposal in respect of which a claim to investors' relief is made, there have been one or more previous disposals of shares from the same holding, special rules apply, where needed, to determine which shares are treated as having been previously disposed of (and therefore which shares are treated as in the holding immediately before the current disposal). The rules operate to preserve the maximum potential relief for future disposals.

Where a claim to investors' relief was made in respect of the previous disposal:

(i) all of the qualifying shares in the holding immediately before the previous disposal are treated as having been disposed of or, if less, so many of the qualifying shares as equals the total number of shares disposed of;

(ii) if the number of qualifying shares in the holding immediately before the previous disposal was less than the total number of shares disposed of and excluded shares were in the holding at that time, then the excluded shares are also treated as having been disposed of, up to a maximum of the total number of shares in the disposal less those treated as having been disposed of in (i) above; and

(iii) if the total number of shares treated as having been disposed of under (i) and (ii) above is less than the total number of shares disposed of, so many of the potentially qualifying shares in the holding as make up the difference are treated as having been disposed of (on a last in first out basis).

If no claim to investors' relief was made in respect of the previous disposal that disposal is taken to consist of first excluded shares, then potentially qualifying shares and finally qualifying shares. [*TCGA 1992, ss 169VE–169VG; FA 2016, Sch 14 para 2*].

The August 2019 disposal is therefore taken to consist of 2,000 qualifying shares and 1,000 of the excluded shares acquired in July 2016. The remaining shares are taken to consist of 1,000 excluded shares and 2,000 potentially qualifying shares. By the time of the disposal in September 2020 the potentially qualifying shares have become qualifying shares. Applying the rules in (a) above to the September 2020 disposal, the part of the chargeable gain qualifying for investors' relief is £162,500 × (2,000/3,000) = £108,333

(c) The annual exemption of £12,000 is allocated against the part of the gain chargeable to tax at 20% as this gives the greater tax saving. [*TCGA 1992, s 4B*].

(C) Lifetime limit

In August 2020 Ms Moorer sells her entire shareholding in Alison Ltd, realising a gain of £10,050,000, which qualifies for investors' relief. Ms Moorer makes no other disposals in 2020/21 and has made no previous disposals qualifying for investors' relief. She is an additional rate income tax payer for 2020/21. Ms Moorer's capital gains tax liability for 2020/21 is calculated as follows.

	£
Chargeable gain	10,050,000
Annual exemption (assumed)	12,000
Gain chargeable to tax	£10,038,000
Capital gains tax payable	
£10,000,000 × 10%	1,000,000
£38,000 × 20%	7,600
	£1,007,600

Notes

(a) Investors' relief is subject to a lifetime limit of £10 million. The amount to which relief would otherwise apply in respect of a disposal is added to any amounts to which relief applied in respect of earlier disposals. Where the total exceeds the limit, only so much (if any) of the amount to which relief would otherwise apply in respect of the current disposal as, together with the earlier amounts, does not exceed the limit qualifies for the 10% rate. Any part of a gain excluded by the application of this rule is chargeable at the normal rates of CGT.

[*TCGA 1992, s 169VK; FA 2016, Sch 14 para 2*].

(b) The annual exemption of £12,000 is allocated against the part of the gain chargeable to tax at 20% as this gives the greater tax saving. [*TCGA 1992, s 1B; FA 2015, Sch 7 para 7*].

215.2 REORGANISATIONS ETC.

[*TCGA 1992, s 169VT; FA 2016, Sch 14 para 2*]

In May 2016, Mr W subscribed for 5,000 shares in Smith Ltd, an unlisted trading company for £10,000. The shares are potentially qualifying shares for the purposes of investors' relief. In January 2020, the shareholders of Smith Ltd accept an offer by a public company, Capaldi plc, and Mr W receives shares in Capaldi plc in exchange for his entire shareholding in Smith Ltd. His Capaldi plc shares are valued at £150,000 at the time of the exchange, and they are excluded from qualifying for investors' relief. Mr W makes no other disposals in 2019/20 and has made no previous claims to investors' relief.

If Mr W elects under *TCGA 1992, s 169VT* to disapply *TCGA 1992, s 127* in respect of the share exchange and claims investors' relief in respect of the gain on the Smith Ltd shares, his capital gains tax liability for 2019/20 is calculated as follows.

	£
Sale proceeds	150,000
Cost	10,000
Chargeable gain qualifying for investors' relief	140,000
Annual exemption (assumed)	12,000
Gain chargeable to tax	£128,000
Capital gains tax payable (£128,000 × 10%)	£12,800

Notes

(a) Where an exchange of securities (within *TCGA 1992, s 135*) takes place and *TCGA 1992, s 127* would otherwise apply to treat the 'original shares' and the 'new holding' (as defined for the purposes of that section) as the same asset, an election can be made to disapply that section so that investors' relief can be claimed in respect of the disposal of the original shares.

(b) The election must be made on or before the first anniversary of the 31 January following the tax year in which the reorganisation takes place. In this case, therefore, the claim must be made by 31 January 2022 (which is the same date by which the claim to investors' relief must be made). An election takes effect only where a claim to investors' relief is also made; without such a claim, the election has no effect.

(c) Mr W cannot claim investors' relief on an eventual disposal of his shares in Capaldi plc. If he had not made an election under *TCGA 1992, s 169VT* the opportunity to claim relief would have been lost.

(d) The above provisions apply also to reorganisations within *TCGA 1992, s 126* and to schemes of reconstruction within *TCGA 1992, s 136* to which *TCGA 1992, s 127* applies.

216 Land

216.1 SMALL PART DISPOSALS

[*TCGA 1992, s 242*]

C owns farmland which cost £134,000 in May 1988. In February 1996, a small plot of land is exchanged with an adjoining landowner for another piece of land. The value placed on the transaction is £18,000. The value of the remaining estate excluding the new piece of land is estimated at £250,000. In March 2019, C sells the whole estate for £300,000. He makes no other disposals in 2018/19. The indexation factor for May 1988 to February 1996 is 0.421

(i) **No claim made under TCGA 1992, s 242(2)**

		£	£
(*a*)	*Disposal in February 1996*		
	Disposal proceeds		18,000
	Allowable cost $\frac{18,000}{18,000 + 250,000} \times £134,000$		(9,000)
	Unindexed gain		9,000
	Indexation allowance £9,000 × 0.421		(3,789)
	Chargeable gain 1995/96		£5,211
(*b*)	*Disposal in March 2019*		
	Disposal proceeds		300,000
	Allowable cost		
	Original land £(134,000 − 9,000)	125,000	
	Exchanged land	18,000	(143,000)
	Chargeable gain 2018/19		£157,000

(ii) **Claim made under TCGA 1992, s 242(2)**

		£	£
(*a*)	*No disposal in February 1996*		
	Allowable cost of original land		134,000
	Deduct Disposal proceeds		(18,000)
	Adjusted allowable cost		£116,000
	Allowable cost of additional land		£18,000

(*b*) *Disposal in March 2019*

Disposal proceeds		300,000
Allowable cost		
Original land	116,000	
Additional land	18,000	(134,000)
Chargeable gain 2018/19		£166,000

Notes

(a) A claim under *TCGA 1992, s 242* may be made where the consideration for the part disposal does not exceed one-fifth of the value of the whole, up to a maximum of £20,000.

(b) If the second disposal had also been made in 1995/96 no claim under *section 242(2)* could have been made on the part disposal as proceeds of all disposals of land in the year would have exceeded £20,000.

(c) If the original land had been held at 31 March 1982 and the part disposal took place after that date, the disposal proceeds, on a claim under *section 242(2)*, would be deducted from the 31 March 1982 value for the purpose of the re-basing provisions.

216.2 COMPULSORY PURCHASE

[*TCGA 1992, ss 243–248*]

(A) Rollover where new land acquired

(i) *Rollover not claimed*

D owns freehold land purchased for £77,000 in 1978. Part of the land is made the subject of a compulsory purchase order. The compensation of £70,000 is agreed on 10 August 2018. The market value of the remaining land is £175,000. The value of the total freehold land at 31 March 1982 was £98,000.

	£
Disposal consideration	70,000
Market value 31.3.82	
$£98{,}000 \times \dfrac{70{,}000}{70{,}000 + 175{,}000}$	(28,000)
Chargeable gain 2018/19	£42,000

(ii) *Rollover claimed under TCGA 1992, s 247*

If, in (i), D acquires new land costing, say, £80,000 in, say, December 2018, relief may be claimed as follows.

	£
Allowable cost of land compulsorily purchased	28,000
Actual consideration	70,000
Chargeable gain rolled over	£42,000
Allowable cost of new land (£80,000 − £42,000)	£38,000

(B) **Small disposals**

(i) *No rollover relief claimed*

T inherited land in June 1988 at a probate value of £290,000. Under a compulsory purchase order, a part of the land is acquired for highway improvements. Compensation of £32,000 and a further £10,000 for severance, neither sum including any amount in respect of loss of profits, is agreed on 14 May 2018. The value of the remaining land is £900,000. Prior to the compulsory purchase, the value of all the land had been £950,000.

	£
Total consideration for disposal (£32,000 + £10,000)	42,000
Deduct Allowable cost $\frac{42,000}{42,000 + 900,000} \times £290,000$	(12,930)
Chargeable gain 2018/19	£29,070

(ii) *Rollover relief claimed under TCGA 1992, s 243*

Total consideration for disposal is £42,000, less than 5% of the value of the estate before the disposal (£950,000). T may therefore claim that the consideration be deducted from the allowable cost of the estate.

Revised allowable cost (£290,000 − £42,000)	£248,000

No chargeable gain then arises in 2018/19.

Note

(a) HMRC additionally regard consideration of £3,000 or less as 'small', whether or not it would pass the 5% test illustrated here. (Revenue Tax Bulletin February 1997, p 397).

216.3 LEASES

(A) Short leases which are not initially wasting assets

[*TCGA 1992, Sch 8 para 1*]

On 31 August 2013, N purchased the remaining term of a lease of commercial premises for £55,000. The lease was subject to a 25-year sub-lease granted on 1 July 1991 at a fixed rental of £1,000 a year. The market rental was estimated at £15,000 a year. The term of the lease held by N is 60 years from 1 April 1989. The value of the lease in 2016, when the sub-lease expired, was estimated at 31 August 2013 as being £70,000. Immediately upon expiry of the sub-lease, N has refurbishment work done at a cost of £50,000, of which £40,000 qualifies as enhancement expenditure. On 31 March 2019, N sells the lease for £130,000.

Term of lease at date of expiry of sub-lease	32 years 9 months
Relevant percentage 89.354 + $^{9}/_{12}$ × (90.280 − 89.354)	90.049%
Term of lease at date of assignment	30 years
Relevant percentage	87.330%

	£	£
Disposal consideration		130,000
Deduct Allowable cost	55,000	
Enhancement costs	40,000	
	95,000	
Less Wasted		
$\frac{90.049 - 87.330}{90.049} \times 95,000$	2,868	
		(92,132)
Chargeable gain 2018/19		£37,868

Note

(a) The head-lease becomes a wasting asset on the expiry of the sub-lease. [*TCGA 1992, Sch 8 para 1(2)*].

(B) Grant of long lease

[*TCGA 1992, s 42, Sch 8 para 2*]

In 1982, K acquired a long lease by assignment for £44,000. At the time he acquired it, the lease had an unexpired term of 95 years. On 10 April 2018, he granted a 55-year sublease for a premium of £110,000 and a peppercorn rent. The value of the reversion plus the capitalised value of the rents is £10,000. The value of the lease at 31 March 1982 was estimated at £54,000.

	£
Disposal consideration	110,000
Market value 31.3.82	
$£54{,}000 \times \dfrac{110{,}000}{110{,}000 + 10{,}000}$	(49,500)
Chargeable gain 2018/19	£60,500

(C) **Grant of short lease**

[*TCGA 1992, Sch 8 paras 2, 5; ITTOIA 2005, ss 277–281; CTA 2009, ss 215–218*]

L is the owner of a freehold factory which he leases for a term of 25 years commencing in December 2018. The cost of the factory was £100,000 in April 2000. The lease is granted for a premium of £30,000 and an annual rent. The reversion to the lease plus the capitalised value of the rents amount to £120,000.

	£	£
Amount chargeable to income tax		
Amount of premium		30,000
Deduct Excluded $\dfrac{25 - 1}{50} \times £30{,}000$		(14,400)
Amount chargeable to income tax		£15,600
Chargeable gain		
Premium received	30,000	
Deduct Charged to income tax	(15,600)	
		14,400
Allowable cost $\dfrac{14{,}400}{30{,}000 + 120{,}000} \times £100{,}000$		(9,600)
Chargeable gain 2018/19		£4,800

Notes

(a) A short lease is one the duration of which, at the time of grant, does not exceed 50 years.

(b) The amount chargeable to income tax is not deducted from the amount of premium appearing in the denominator of the CGT apportionment fraction.

(D) Disposal by assignment of short lease: without enhancement expenditure

[TCGA 1992, Sch 8 para 1]

X buys a lease for £200,000 on 1 October 2014. The lease commenced on 1 June 2005 for a term of 60 years. X assigns the lease for £300,000 at the end of March 2019.

Term of lease unexpired at date of acquisition	50 years 8 months
Relevant percentage	100%
Term of lease unexpired at date of assignment	46 years 2 months
Relevant percentage 98.490 + ($^2/_{12}$ × (98.902 − 98.490))	98.559%

	£	£
Disposal consideration		300,000
Allowable cost	200,000	
Deduct Wasted $\frac{100 - 98.559}{100} \times £200{,}000$	2,882	
		(197,118)
Chargeable gain 2018/19		£102,882

(E) Disposal by assignment of short lease held at 31 March 1982

[TCGA 1992, s 35, Sch 8 para 1]

A Ltd buys a lease for £100,000 on 1 March 1982. The lease commenced on 31 March 1972 for a term of 60 years. Its value at 31 March 1982 was estimated at £104,000. On 31 March 2019 A Ltd assigns the lease for £270,000. The indexation factor for the period March 1982 to December 2017 is 2.501

(i) *The computation without re-basing to 1982 is as follows*

Term of lease unexpired at date of acquisition (1.3.82)	50 years 1 month
Relevant percentage	100%
Term of lease unexpired at date of assignment	13 years 0 months
Relevant percentage	56.167%

	£	£
Disposal consideration		270,000
Cost	100,000	
Deduct Wasted $\frac{100 - 56.167}{100} \times £100{,}000$	(43,833)	(56,167)

Unindexed gain	213,833
Indexation allowance (see (ii) below)	(146,093)
Gain after indexation	£67,740

(ii) *The computation with re-basing to 1982 is as follows*

Term of lease unexpired at deemed date of acquisition (31.3.82)	50 years
Relevant percentage	100%
Term of lease unexpired at date of assignment	13 years
Relevant percentage	56.167%

	£	£
Disposal consideration		270,000
Market value 31.3.82	104,000	
Deduct Wasted $\dfrac{100 - 56.167}{100} \times £104{,}000$	(45,586)	(58,414)
Unindexed gain		211,586
Indexation allowance £58,414 × 2.501		(146,093)
Gain after indexation		£65,493
Chargeable gain		£65,493

Notes

(a) A Ltd is deemed, under *TCGA 1992, s 35*, to have disposed of and immediately re-acquired the lease on 31 March 1982 at its market value at that date.

(b) Both calculations produce a gain with the re-basing calculation producing the smaller gain. Therefore, re-basing applies. [*TCGA 1992, s 35(2)(3)(a)*].

(c) Indexation is based, in both calculations, on the assumption that the asset was sold and re-acquired at market value on 31 March 1982 since this gives a greater allowance than if based on original cost as reduced by the wasting asset provisions. [*TCGA 1992, s 55(1)(2)*].

(d) Indexation allowance is frozen at its December 2017 level. No indexation allowance is available in respect of expenditure incurred after 31 December 2017, and for that incurred on or before that date and falling to be deducted on a disposal after that date, indexation allowance is computed up to and including December 2017 only. *[TCGA 1992, ss 53(1)(1B), 54(1B); FA 2018, s 26(2)(3)(6)]*. **214.1** INDEXATION.

(F) Disposal by assignment of short lease: with enhancement expenditure

[*TCGA 1992, Sch 8 para 1*]. D Ltd acquires the lease of office premises for £100,000 on 1 July 2010. On 1 January 2012, the company contracts for complete refurbishment of the premises at a total cost of £180,000, of which £120,000 can be regarded as capital enhancement expenditure. Work is done at the beginning of January 2012, and money is payable in equal tranches in March 2012 and May 2012. The lease is for a 50 year term commencing 1 April 2003. On 1 January 2019, the lease is assigned to a new lessee for £450,000.

Indexation factors	July 2010 to December 2017	0.244
	March 2012 to December 2017	0.155
	May 2012 to December 2017	0.147

Term of lease unexpired at date of acquisition	42 years 9 months
Relevant percentage 96.593 + $^9/_{12}$ × (97.107 − 96.593)	96.979%
Term of lease unexpired at date of expenditure incurred (January 2012 — see note (a))	41 years 3 months
Relevant percentage 96.041 + $^3/_{12}$ × (96.593 − 96.041)	96.179%
Term of lease unexpired at date of assignment	34 years 3 months
Relevant percentage 91.156 + $^3/_{12}$ × (91.981 − 91.156)	91.362%

	£	£	£
Disposal consideration			450,000
Cost of acquisition	100,000		
Deduct Wasted			
$\frac{96.979 - 91.362}{96.979} \times 100{,}000$	(5,791)	94,209	
Enhancement expenditure	120,000		
Deduct Wasted			
$\frac{96.179 - 91.362}{96.179} \times 120{,}000$	(6,010)	113,990	(208,199)
Unindexed gain			241,801
Indexation allowance			
Cost of lease £94,209 × 0.244		22,987	
Enhancement costs			
March 2012 £56,995 × 0.155		8,834	
May 2012 £56,995 × 0.147		8,378	
			(40,199)
Chargeable gain			£201,602

Notes

(a) The wasting provisions apply to enhancement expenditure by reference to the time when it is first reflected in the nature of the lease. The indexation provisions apply by reference to the date the expenditure became due and payable. [*TCGA 1992, s 54(4)(b), Sch 8 para 1(4)(b)*].

(b) Indexation allowance is frozen at its December 2017 level. No indexation allowance is available in respect of expenditure incurred after 31 December 2017, and for expenditure incurred on or before that date and falling to be deducted on a disposal after that date, indexation allowance is computed up to and including December 2017 only. *[TCGA 1992, ss 53(1)(1B), 54(1B); FA 2018, s 26(2)(3)(6)]*. See **214.1** INDEXATION.

(G) Disposal of short lease where premium partly relieved as trading deduction

[*ITTOIA 2005, ss 60–67; CTA 2009, ss 62–67*]

Butcher acquired a 36-year lease of shop premises from Baker on 1 July 2011 at a premium of £33,000. Butcher prepares trading accounts to 30 June each year. On 1 July 2018, when the unexpired term of the lease is 29 years and property values have risen sharply in the locality, he assigns the lease for £76,000. He makes no other chargeable disposals in 2018/19.

The annual trading deduction under *ITTOIA 2005, ss 60–67* is computed as follows

	£
Premium on 36-year lease	33,000
Deduct (36 − 1) × 2% × £33,000	(23,100)
Premium chargeable on Baker	£9,900

In addition to actual rent payable under the lease, Butcher is entitled to a deduction in computing trading profits in respect of the part of the premium chargeable on Baker, accruing on a day-to-day basis for up to 36 years, of

$$\frac{£9,900}{36} = £275 \text{ p.a.}$$

In his seven accounting years to 30 June 2018, Butcher has thus received a total deduction of (£275 × 7) =	£1,925

The chargeable gain on disposal of the lease in July 2018 is computed as below.

Term of lease unexpired at date of acquisition	36 years
Relevant percentage	92.761%
Term of lease unexpired at date of disposal	29 years
Relevant percentage	86.226%

	£	£
Disposal consideration		76,000
Cost of acquisition	33,000	
Deduct Income tax relief given (see above) (note (a))	1,925	
	31,075	
Deduct Wasted $\dfrac{92.761 - 86.226}{92.761} \times £31,075$	(2,189)	(28,886)
Chargeable gain		47,114
Deduct Annual exemption		(11,700)
Taxable gain 2018/19		£35,414

Notes

(a) The allowable expenditure for CGT is reduced, by virtue of *TCGA 1992, s 39* (exclusion of double relief), by the amount on which income tax relief has been given. This reduction is made *before* the wasting asset reduction required by *TCGA 1992, Sch 8 para 1(4)* (HMRC Capital Gains Manual CG71200).

(b) For further examples on the *income tax* treatment of lease premiums, see (C) above, (H) and (J) below, and **IT 22.5** PROPERTY INCOME.

(H) Sub-lease granted out of short lease: premium not less than potential premium

[*TCGA 1992, Sch 8 paras 4, 5*]

On 1 November 2016, S purchased a lease of shop premises then having 50 years to run for a premium of £100,000 and an annual rental of £40,000. After occupying the premises for the purposes of his own business, S granted a sub-lease to N Ltd. The sub-lease was for a term of 21 years commencing on 1 August 2018, for a premium of £50,000 and an annual rental of £30,000. It is agreed that, had the rent under the sub-lease been £40,000, the premium obtainable would have been £20,000.

Term of lease at date granted	50 years
Relevant percentage	100%
Term of lease at date sub-lease granted	48 years 3 months
Relevant percentage $99.289 + {}^{3}/_{12} \times (99.657 - 99.289)$	99.381%
Term of lease at date sub-lease expires	27 years 3 months
Relevant percentage $83.816 + {}^{3}/_{12} \times (85.053 - 83.816)$	84.125%

Premium chargeable to income tax on S	£
Amount of premium	50,000
Deduct $\frac{21-1}{50} \times £50,000$	(20,000)
Amount chargeable	£30,000
Chargeable gain	
Disposal consideration	50,000
Allowable expenditure	
$£100,000 \times \frac{99.381 - 84.125}{100}$	(15,256)
Chargeable gain	34,744
Deduct Amount chargeable to income tax	(30,000)
Net chargeable gain 2018/19	£4,744

Note

(a) If the amount chargeable to income tax had exceeded the chargeable gain, the net gain would have been nil. The deduction cannot create or increase a loss. [*TCGA 1992, Sch 8 para 5(2)*].

(J) Sub-lease granted out of short lease: premium less than potential premium

[*TCGA 1992, Sch 8 paras 4, 5*]

C bought a lease of a house on 1 May 2014, when the unexpired term was 49 years. The cost of the lease was £20,000, and the ground rent payable is £500 p.a. C then let the house on a monthly tenancy until 30 November 2018 when he granted a 10-year lease for a premium of £5,000 and an annual rent of £8,000. Had the rent under the sub-lease been £500 a year, the premium obtainable would have been £40,000. C does not at any time occupy the house as a private residence.

Term of lease at date of acquisition	49 years
Relevant percentage	99.657%
Term of lease when sub-lease granted	44 years 5 months
Relevant percentage 97.595 + $^5/_{12}$ × (98.059 − 97.595)	97.788%
Term of lease when sub-lease expires	34 years 5 months
Relevant percentage 91.156 + $^5/_{12}$ × (91.981 − 91.156)	91.500%

Amount chargeable to income tax	£
Amount of premium	5,000
Deduct Exclusion $\frac{10-1}{50} \times £5,000$	900
Chargeable to income tax	£4,100
Chargeable gain	
Disposal consideration	5,000
Deduct Allowable expenditure	
$£20,000 \times \frac{97.788 - 91.500}{99.657} \times \frac{5,000}{40,000}$	158
Gain	4,842
Deduct Amount chargeable to income tax	4,100
Net chargeable gain 2018/19	£742

Note

(a) If the amount chargeable to income tax had exceeded the chargeable gain, the net gain would have been nil. The deduction cannot create or increase a loss. [*TCGA 1992, Sch 8 para 5(2)*].

216.4 NON-RESIDENT DISPOSAL OF INTEREST IN UK RESIDENTIAL PROPERTY

[*TCGA 1992, ss 14B–14H, Schs B1, 4ZZB; FA 2015, Sch 7; FA 2016, s 90*]

Mr Watkins purchased a residential property in March 1995 for £85,000, incurring £2,000 costs. He used the property as his main residence throughout the period from acquisition until he left the UK to retire abroad on 5 April 2010. The market value of the property at 5 April 2015 was £200,000. The property was sold for £290,000 (disposal costs £5,000) on 5 June 2020. Mr Watkins makes no other disposals giving rise to chargeable gains or losses in 2020/21. The property was let or available for let as a dwelling throughout the period 6 April 2010 to sale. For the purposes of this example, the annual exempt amount for 2020/21 is assumed to be £12,000.

	£
Disposal proceeds	290,000
Deduct incidental costs of sale	(5,000)
	285,000
Less: Market value on 5 April 2015	(200,000)
Notional post-April 2015 gain	85,000

Mr Watkins did not spend 90 nights in the property for any of the tax years 2015/16 to 2020/21 (the year of disposal) and so cannot nominate the property as his main residence for any of those years. Partial main residence exemption is, however, due for the last 18 months of ownership. Ownership from 6 April 2015 to 5 June 2020 is 62 months. The exemption is therefore 18/62 × £85,000 = £24,678. The notional gain attributable to letting (£85,000 – £24,678 = £60,322) is exempt to the extent that it does not exceed the lesser of £40,000 and the gain otherwise exempt (£24,678).The let property exemption is therefore £24,678. The taxable NRCGT gain for 2020/21 is therefore:

	£
Gain as above	85,000
Deduct Main residence exemption	(24,678)
Deduct Let property exemption	(24,678)
NRCGT gain	35,644
Annual exempt amount	(12,000)
Taxable NRCGT gain 2020/21	£23,644

Notes

(a) For 2015/16 onwards, capital gains tax is extended to disposals of UK residential property by non-residents. The CGT charge can apply to non-resident individuals (including on disposals in the non-resident part of a split tax year), non-resident trustees, personal representatives of non-resident deceased persons, certain non-resident companies, and any such person who is a partner in a partnership. [*TCGA 1992, s 14B; FA 2015, Sch 7 para 11*].

(b) Gains and losses are calculated as for CGT (or corporation tax) purposes but there are special rules for property interests held on 5 April 2015. Unless an election is made, only the gain arising after that date is charged. Alternatively an election can be made for time apportionment or (particularly where a loss arises) for the whole of the gain to be charged (or loss allowed). [*TCGA 1992, s 48A, Sch 4ZZB; FA 2015, Sch 7 paras 14, 39*].

(c) A person who makes a non-resident CGT ('NRCGT') disposal must, in most cases, make a special return reporting the disposal to HMRC within the thirty days following the day of the completion of the disposal. Tax on NRCGT gains is generally due 30 days after completion of sale (i.e. on the date the return reporting the disposal is due), except where the person is registered for self-assessment, in which case payment may be made on the normal payment date for CGT, though the disposal must still be reported in a return within 30 days. With effect from 15 September 2016, an NRCGT return is not required (but the taxpayer may choose to make a return) where the disposal is a no gain/no loss disposal or the grant of a lease at arm's length to an unconnected person for no premium. [*TMA 1970, ss 12ZAA–12ZG, 59AA; FA 2015, Sch 7 paras 43, 51; FA 2016, s 91*].

(d) For disposals on or after 6 April 2015 for the purposes of the main residence exemption, a dwelling-house is not treated as being occupied as a residence by an individual at any time in his period of ownership which falls into a 'non-qualifying' tax year or non-qualifying 'partial tax year'. A non-qualifying tax year can be a tax year before 2015/16 only if the disposal is a non-resident CGT disposal. A '*non-qualifying*' tax year is a tax year in the indiviudal's period of ownership where neither the individual nor their spouse or civil partner is tax resident in the territory in which the dwelling house is situated, and the individual does not meet the day count test for that year. Where only part of the tax year falls into the period of ownership that part is a '*partial tax year*' and the day count test is applied to the partial tax year. The day count test applies to any property that is occupied as a residence, wherever situated. The test is met if either the individual or his spouse or civil partner spends at least 90 days (prorated for a partial tax year, rounded up to the nearest whole day) in one or more houses which are situated in the same overseas territory, and which either the individual or his spouse or civil partner has an interest in. [*TCGA 1992, ss 222B, 222C; FA 2015, Sch 9 paras 3, 10*]. See **223** PRIVATE RESIDENCES for further examples on the main residence and let property exemptions.

217 Losses

Cross-references. See **IT 15.2** LOSSES for the set-off of trading losses against chargeable gains made by individuals. See **201.2** ANNUAL RATES AND EXEMPTIONS for the interaction between losses and the annual exemption.

217.1 RELIEF FOR ALLOWABLE LOSSES

[*TCGA 1992, ss 2, 24, 62(2); FA 2015, Sch 7 para 3*].

(A) General

On 30 April 2018 Q sells for £40,000 a part of the land which he owns. The market value of the remaining estate is £160,000. Q bought the land for £250,000 in March 1996.

	£
Disposal consideration	40,000
Allowable cost $\frac{40,000}{40,000 + 160,000} \times £250,000$	50,000
Allowable loss	£10,000

(B) Asset of negligible value

In June 2018, John sells an asset, realising a chargeable gain of £25,000. In December 2018, John learns that his shareholding in Jones Ltd has become worthless. He acquired the shares in 1995 for their then market value of £15,000. John makes no other disposals in 2018/19.

If John makes a negligible value claim under *TCGA 1992, s 24* no later than 5 April 2021, then his capital gains tax computation for 2018/19 is as follows.

	£
Chargeable gain	25,000
Less allowable loss	(15,000)
	10,000
Less annual exemption (£11,700 restricted to)	(10,000)
Gains chargeable to tax 2018/19	Nil

Notes

(a) Where the owner of an asset which has become of 'negligible value' makes a claim to that effect he is treated as if he had sold, and immediately reacquired, the asset for a consideration of an amount equal to the value specified in the claim. Such a claim can also be made if the disposal by which the claimant acquired the asset was a no gain/no loss disposal at the time of which the asset was of negligible value and, between the time at which the asset became of negligible value and that disposal, any other disposal of the asset was a no gain/no loss disposal. The deemed sale is treated as having occurred at the time of the claim or at an earlier time specified in the claim. An earlier time can be specified only if the claimant owned the asset at that time, the asset had become of negligible value at that time and that time is not more than two years before the beginning of the tax year in which the claim is made or, for corporation tax, is on or after the first day of the earliest accounting period ending not more than two years before the time of the claim. [*TCGA 1992, s 24*].

(b) '*Negligible value*' is not defined but is taken by HMRC to mean 'worth next to nothing' (HMRC Capital Gains Manual CG13125).

(C) Loss carried back from year of death

Rick dies on 30 March 2019. Before his death, he makes one disposal in 2018/19, realising an allowable loss of £20,000. In 2017/18 and 2016/17 he had realised chargeable gains of £16,000 and £27,000 respectively.

Following Rick's death his capital gains position for 2016/17 and 2017/18 is revised as follows.

2017/18	£
Chargeable gain	16,000
Less 2018/19 allowable loss carried back (part)	(4,700)
	11,300
Less annual exemption	(11,300)
Gains chargeable to tax 2017/18	Nil
2016/17	
Chargeable gain	27,000
Less 2018/19 allowable loss carried back (remainder)	(15,300)
	11,700
Less annual exemption	(11,100)
Taxable gain 2016/17	£600

Notes

(a) Allowable losses in excess of chargeable gains incurred by the deceased in the tax year in which death occurs can be carried back and set off against chargeable gains in the three preceding tax years. Chargeable gains accruing in a later year must be relieved before those of an earlier year. Losses carried back cannot be set against gains treated under *TCGA 1992, s 87* or *s 89(2)* as accruing to the individual as a beneficiary of a non-UK resident settlement. [*TCGA 1992, s 62(2)(2A)*].

(b) Any remaining unused losses *cannot* be carried forward and set off against gains made by the personal representatives or legatees.

217.2 PERSONAL LOSSES SET AGAINST ATTRIBUTED SETTLEMENT GAINS

[*TCGA 1992, ss 2(2)–(7), 86; FA 2015, Sch 7 para3; FA 2018, Sch 10 para 1*].

In May 2003, R created an offshore settlement in which he retained the reversionary interest. It is accepted that *TCGA 1992, s 86* applies to the settlement such that any chargeable gains accruing to the trustees are chargeable on R as settlor. In July 2018, the trustees realised a gain of £18,418 on a disposal of quoted securities which they had held since creation of the settlement. They made no other disposal in the year. R, meanwhile, made two disposals in 2018/19 on which he realised a chargeable gain of £4,000 and an allowable loss of £9,000. Neither the trustees nor R have any losses brought forward from earlier years. R pays income tax for 2018/19 at the higher rate

R's CGT position for 2018/19 is as follows.

	£
Personal gains	4,000
Attributed gains	18,418
Deduct Personal losses	9,000
	13,418
Deduct Annual exempt amount	(11,700)
Taxable gains 2018/19	£1,718
CGT payable by R at 20% (recoverable from trustees)	£343.60
Personal losses carried forward	Nil

Note

(a) Personal losses can be set against gains attributed to the taxpayer under *TCGA 1992, s 86* (charge on settlor of non-UK resident settlement in which he has an interest). Such losses cannot, however, be set off against gains treated under *TCGA 1992, ss 87, 87K, 87L* or *89(2)* as accruing to a beneficiary or the settlor of a non-UK resident settlement or the recipient of an onward gift from such a beneficiary — see **201.2(B)** ANNUAL RATES AND EXEMPTIONS.

217.3 LOSSES ON SHARES IN UNLISTED TRADING COMPANIES

[*TCGA 1992, s 125A; ITA 2007, ss 131–151*]

P subscribed for 3,000 £1 ordinary shares at par in W Ltd, a qualifying trading company, in June 1988. In September 1995, P acquired a further 2,200 shares at £3 per share from another shareholder. In December 2018, P sold 3,900 shares at 40p per share.

Procedure

Firstly, establish the '*section 104* holding' pool.

	Shares	Qualifying expenditure £
June 1988 subscription	3,000	3,000
September 1995 acquisition	2,200	6,600
	5,200	9,600
December 2018 disposal	(3,900)	(7,200)
Pool carried forward	1,300	£2,400

Step 1. Calculate the CGT loss in the normal way, as follows

	£
Disposal consideration 3,900 × £0.40	1,560
Allowable cost	(7,200)
Allowable loss	£(5,640)

Step 2. Applying a LIFO basis, identify the qualifying shares (1,700) and the non-qualifying shares (2,200) comprised in the disposal.

Step 3. Calculate the proportion of the loss attributable to the qualifying shares.

Loss referable to 1,700 qualifying shares $\frac{1,700}{3,900} \times £5,640$ £2,458

Step 4. Compare the loss in Step 3 with the actual cost of the qualifying shares, *viz.*

Cost of 1,700 qualifying shares $\frac{1,700}{3,000} \times £3,000$ £1,700

The loss available against income is restricted to £1,700 (being lower than £2,458).

The loss not relieved against income remains an allowable loss for CGT purposes.

£5,640 − £1,700 = £3,940

Note

(a) For further examples on this topic, see **IT 15.5** LOSSES and **CT 114.4** LOSSES.

217.4 DEFERRED UNASCERTAINABLE CONSIDERATION: ELECTION TO TREAT LOSS AS ARISING IN EARLIER YEAR

[*TCGA 1992, ss 279A–279D; FA 2008, Sch 2 paras 43, 56(2)*]

Tanya owns 2,000 £1 ordinary shares in Be Good Ltd, for which she subscribed at par in January 1995. On 31 March 2012, she and the other shareholders in Be Good Ltd sold their shares to another company for £20 per share plus a further unquantified cash amount calculated by means of a formula relating to the future profits of Be Good Ltd. The value in March 2012 of the deferred consideration was estimated at £5.10 per share. Tanya makes no other disposals of chargeable assets in 2011/12. On 30 April 2018, Tanya receives a further £3.60 per share under the sale agreement.

Without an election under *TCGA 1992, s 279A*, Tanya's capital gains position is as follows.

2011/12

	£	£
Disposal proceeds	40,000	
Value of rights	10,200	50,200
Cost of acquisition		(2,000)
Chargeable gain 2011/12		£48,200

2018/19

Disposal of rights to deferred consideration	
Proceeds 2,000 × £3.60	7,200
Deemed cost of acquiring rights	(10,200)
Allowable loss 2018/19	£(3,000)

If Tanya makes an election under *TCGA 1992, s 279A* by 31 January 2021 the 2018/19 loss is treated as arising in 2011/12 and can be set off against the gain of that year as follows.

2011/12

	£
Gain as above	47,842
Less Allowable loss	(3,000)
Chargeable gain 2011/12	£44,842

Notes

(a) Where a person within the charge to capital gains tax makes a disposal of a right to 'future unascertainable consideration' (as defined) acquired as consideration for the disposal of another asset, and a loss accrues, he may, subject to conditions, make an election for the loss to be treated as arising in the year in which that other asset was disposed of. Where the right was acquired as consideration for two or more disposals in different tax years (referred to as '*eligible years*'), the loss is utilised in the earliest year first. [*TCGA 1992, s 279A*].

(b) To the extent that the loss cannot be utilised in the earliest eligible year it may be carried forward for set-off against gains of later years. In the case of tax years falling between that year and the year of the loss, any remaining part of the loss can only be deducted if the year concerned is an eligible year. [*TCGA 1992, s 279C; FA 2008, Sch 2 paras 43, 56(2)*].

(c) The election is irrevocable and must be made by notice in writing to HMRC on or before the first anniversary of 31 January following the year of the loss. The notice must specify the amount of the relevant loss, the right disposed of, the tax year of the right's disposal, and, if different, the year of the loss, the tax year in which the right was acquired, the original asset or assets on disposal of which the right was acquired, the eligible year in which the loss is to be treated as accruing, and the amount to be deducted from gains of that year. [*TCGA 1992, s 279D*].

218 Married Persons and Civil Partners

218.1 TRANSFERS BETWEEN SPOUSES OR CIVIL PARTNERS

[*TCGA 1992, s 58*]

(A) No transfer between spouses or civil partners

Paul and Heidi are a married couple. For 2018/19 Heidi's taxable income (after personal allowance) is £50,000 and Paul's is £15,000. On 4 July 2018, Heidi sells two paintings which she had acquired in June 1994 at a cost of £5,000 each. Net sale proceeds amount to £16,000 and £25,000. Neither spouse disposed of any other chargeable assets during 2018/19.

Chargeable gains — Heidi

	£
Net proceeds of painting 1	16,000
Cost	(5,000)
Chargeable gain	£11,000
Net proceeds of painting 2	25,000
Cost	(5,000)
Chargeable gain	£20,000
Total chargeable gains (£11,000 + £20,000)	31,000
Annual exemption	(11,700)
Taxable gains 2018/19	£19,300
Tax payable £19,300 × 20%	£3,860.00

(B) Transfer between spouses or civil partners

The facts are as in (A) above except that in April 2018, Heidi gives painting 2 to Paul who then makes the sale on 4 July 2018.

Chargeable gains – Heidi

	£
Deemed consideration for painting 2 (April 2018) (note (a))	5,000
Cost	5,000
Chargeable gain	Nil
Net proceeds of painting 1	16,000
Cost	(5,000)
Chargeable gain	£11,000
Total chargeable gains	11,000
Annual exemption (restricted)	(11,000)
Taxable gains 2018/19	£Nil

Chargeable gain — Paul

	£
Net proceeds (4.7.18)	25,000
Cost (April 2018)	(5,000)
Chargeable gain	20,000
Annual exemption	(11,700)
Taxable gain 2018/19	£8,300
Capital gains tax £8,300 × 10%	£830.00
Tax saving compared with (A) above (£3,860 – £830)	£3,030

Notes

(a) The inter-spouse transfer is deemed to be for such consideration as to ensure that no gain or loss accrues. [*TCGA 1992, s 58*].

(b) The fact that transfers of assets between husband and wife or between civil partners are no gain/no loss transfers enables savings to be made by ensuring that disposals are made by a spouse or partner who has an unused annual exemption and/or pays CGT at a lower rate.

(c) A transfer between spouses or civil partners followed by a sale could be attacked by HMRC as an anti-avoidance device. To minimise the risk, there should be a clear time interval between the two transactions and no arrangements made to effect the ultimate sale until after the transfer. The gift should be outright with no strings attached and with no 'arrangement' for eventual proceeds to be passed to the transferor.

(C) **Transfer between spouses or civil partners before 6 April 2008**

The facts are as in (B) above except that Heidi gives painting 2 to Paul in January 2008. The indexation factor for the period June 1994 to April 1998 is 0.124.

Chargeable gains — Heidi

2007/08

	£
Deemed consideration for painting 2 (January 2008) (note (a))	5,620
Cost	(5,000)
Unindexed gain	620
Indexation allowance (to April 1998) £5,000 × 0.124	(620)
Chargeable gain	Nil

2018/19

Net proceeds of painting 1	16,000
Cost	(5,000)
Chargeable gain	11,000
Annual exemption (restricted)	(11,000)
Taxable gains 2018/19	£Nil

Chargeable gain — Paul

	£
Net proceeds (4.7.2018)	25,000
Cost (January 2008)	(5,620)
Chargeable gain	19,380
Annual exemption	(11,700)
Taxable gain	£7,680
Capital gains tax £7,680 × 10%	£768.00
Tax saving compared with (A) above (£3,860 − £768))	£3,092.00

Notes

(a) The consideration for the inter-spouse transfer is equal to cost plus indexation to April 1998. See **214.2** INDEXATION for further examples.

(b) The abolition of indexation allowance for capital gains tax purposes for disposals after 5 April 2008 does not affect the deemed consideration for which Paul is treated as acquiring painting 2.

218.2 EMPLOYEE SHAREHOLDER SHARES

[*TCGA 1992, s 58; FA 2013, Sch 23 para 17; FA 2016, s 88(7)–(10); FA 2017, s 13(2)(6)–(8)*]

In May 2020, Amy transfers shares with a market value of £90,000 to her husband Rory. The shares are exempt employee shareholder shares within *TCGA 1992, s 236B* acquired by Amy in May 2016 for £15,000. The capital gains tax consequences of the transfer are as follows.

(i) No previous disposals of exempt employee shareholder shares

Exempt gain — Amy

	£
Deemed consideration (market value)	90,000
Cost	(15,000)
Exempt gain	£75,000
Lifetime limit remaining unused (£100,000 – £75,000)	£25,000

Rory is deemed to have acquired the shares at market value for £90,000.

(ii) Lifetime limit previously used up

Chargeable gain — Amy

	£
Deemed consideration (no gain/no loss)	15,000
Cost	(15,000)
Exempt gain	£Nil

Rory is deemed to have acquired the shares for £15,000.

(iii) £60,000 of lifetime limit previously used

Balance of lifetime limit (£100,000 – £60,000)	£40,000

Chargeable gain — Amy

	£
Deemed consideration (amount resulting in gain equal to balance of lifetime limit)	55,000
Cost	(15,000)
Gain (exempt as equal to the balance of the lifetime limit)	£40,000

Rory is deemed to have acquired the shares for £55,000.

Notes

(a) The exemption for employee shareholder shares is abolished for such shares acquired under an employee shareholder agreement entered into on or after the 'relevant day'. The '*relevant day*' is in most cases 1 December 2016 but, where the individual received the necessary legal advice on 23 November 2016 before 1.30 pm, it is 2 December 2016. [*FA 2017, s 13(6)–(8)*]

(b) The no gain/no loss rule does not apply to a transfer of exempt employee shareholder shares between spouses or civil partners who are living together where any gain would be wholly exempt. [*TCGA 1992, s 58(2)(3); FA 2016, s 88(8)(9); FA 2017, s 13(2)(6)–(8)*].

(c) A lifetime limit of gains of £100,000 applies to disposals of exempt employee shareholder shares acquired under employee shareholder agreements entered into on or after 17 March 2016 and before the relevant day (see note (a) above). Gains falling partly within the limit are exempt to the extent that they do not exceed the unused balance of the limit. Gains on disposals of shares acquired under agreements entered into before that date do not count in applying the limit. [*TCGA 1992, s 236B(1A)–(1C)(3A); FA 2016, s 88(2)(3); FA 2017, s 13(4)(6)–(8)*].

(d) Where a transfer of employee shareholder shares would only be partly exempt as a result of the lifetime limit, the transfer is treated as made for a consideration equal to the amount (not exceeding market value) which results in a gain of an amount equal to the balance of the lifetime limit. [*TCGA 1992, s 58(4)(5); FA 2016, s 88(9); FA 2017, s 13(2)(6)–(8)*].

218.3 JOINTLY OWNED ASSETS

Derek and Raquel are a married couple. Derek had for many years owned an investment property which he purchased for £70,000 in May 1988. On 5 January 1996, he transferred to Raquel a 10% share in the property which was thereafter held in their joint names as tenants in common. At the time of the transfer, a 10% share of the property is worth £10,000 on the open market and a 90% share is worth £90,000. No declaration is made for income tax purposes under what is now *ITA 2007, s 837*, with the result that the rental income from the property is treated, by virtue of *ITA 2007, s 836*, as arising in equal shares. On 29 June 2018, the property is sold for £140,000. The indexation factor for May 1988 to January 1996 is 0.414.

(i) **Inter-spouse transfer**

	£
Deemed consideration (January 1996)	9,898
Cost £70,000 × $\frac{10,000}{10,000 + 90,000}$ (see note(*c*))	(7,000)
Unindexed gain	2,898
Indexation allowance £7,000 × 0.414	(2,898)
Chargeable gain 1995/96	Nil

(ii) **2018/19 disposal**

	Derek	Raquel
	£	£
Disposal proceeds	126,000	14,000
Cost: Derek (£70,000 − £7,000)	(63,000)	
Raquel (see (i) above)		(9,898)
Chargeable gains 2018/19	£63,000	£4,102

Notes

(a) Where a joint declaration of unequal beneficial interests is made under *ITA 2007, s 837* it is presumed that the same split applies for capital gains tax purposes. In the absence of a declaration, and regardless of the income tax treatment of income derived from the asset, a gain on an asset held in the joint names of husband and wife is apportioned in accordance with their respective beneficial interests at the time of disposal. (Revenue Press Release 21 November 1990).

(b) See **218.1(C)** above as to how the consideration for the inter-spouse transfer is arrived at.

(c) The allowable expenditure on the inter-spouse transfer is apportioned in accordance with the part disposal rules in *TCGA 1992, s 42* (see **208.2** COMPUTATION OF GAINS AND LOSSES).

219 Offshore Settlements

Cross-reference. See also **217.2** LOSSES.

219.1 CHARGE ON BENEFICIARY IN RECEIPT OF CAPITAL PAYMENTS

(A) Charge under TCGA 1992, s 87

C, resident and domiciled in the UK, is the sole beneficiary of a discretionary settlement created by his father in 2003 and administered in the Cayman Islands. The trustees are all individuals resident in the Cayman Islands. The trustees make no gains or capital payments in 2014/15 or any earlier year, but make the following capital payments to C in 2015/16 onwards.

	£
2015/16	50,000
2016/17	60,000
2017/18	50,000
2018/19	70,000

In 2018/19, the trustees sell two settlement assets (which are not UK residential property interests) realising a gain of £350,000 and a loss of £50,000. They make no other disposals in that year. C makes only one disposal in 2018/19, realising an allowable loss of £25,000. C pays income tax in 2018/19 at the higher rate.

The settlement's 'section 2(2) amount' for 2018/19 is:

	£
Gain	350,000
Less Loss	(50,000)
Section 2(2) amount for 2018/19	£300,000

The section 2(2) amount is matched with the capital payments made to C on a last in first out basis as follows.

	£
Section 2(2) amount	300,000
2018/19 capital payment	70,000
2017/18 capital payment	50,000
2016/17 capital payment	60,000
2015/16 capital payment	50,000
Unmatched amount carried forward	£70,000

C's liability to capital gains tax for 2018/19 is as follows.

	£
Matched section 2(2) amount (£70,000 + £50,000 + £60,000+ £50,000)	230,000
Less Annual exemption	(11,700)
Amount chargeable to capital gains tax 2017/18	£218,300
Capital gains tax (£. × 20%)	£43,660

Notes

(a) For 2013/14 and subsequent years, *TCGA 1992, s 87* applies to a settlement for a tax year if there is no time in the year when the trustees are resident in the UK. For 2012/13 and earlier years, *TCGA 1992, s 87* applies to a settlement for a tax year if the trustees are neither resident not ordinarily resident in the UK during any part of the year. [*TCGA 1992, s 87(1)(6); FA 2013, Sch 46 paras 92, 112*].

(b) There are detailed rules for matching gains with capital payments. Broadly, capital payments are matched with section 2(2) amounts on a last in first out basis by applying the five step process in *TCGA 1992, s 87A*.

(c) The '*section 2(2) amount*' for a tax year for which the settlement is within *TCGA 1992, s 87* is the amount which would have been chargeable on the trustees under *TCGA 1992, s 2(2)* (i.e. chargeable gains less current year and brought forward losses) had they been resident (and, for 2012/13 and earlier years, ordinarily resident) in the UK in that year *less*, if *TCGA 1992, s 86* (offshore settlement where settlor has interest) applies to the settlement for the year, any chargeable gains for the year under that section. The section 2(2) amount for a tax year for which *section 87* does not apply is nil. [*TCGA 1992, s 87(4)(5); FA 2013, Sch 46 paras 92, 112*].

(d) C's personal loss of £25,000 for 2018/19 cannot be relieved against gains chargeable under *TCGA 1991, s 87*.

(e) Subject to certain exceptions, capital payments received in 2018/19 or a subsequent year are disregarded for these purposes if received (or treated as received) from the trustee by a beneficiary who is non-UK resident throughout the tax year. This provision also applies for 2018/19 onwards to capital payments received before 2018/19 which have not been matched under the above provisions as they apply for 2017/18 and earlier years. [*TCGA 1992, ss 87D–87F, 87H; FA 2018, Sch 10 paras 1(1)(12)(13), 2*].

(f) Where a capital payment is received in 2018/19 or a later year by a beneficiary who is a close member (as above) of the settlor's family at the time of receipt and the settlor is resident in the UK in the tax year of receipt, the above provisions apply as if the payment were received by the settlor as a beneficiary (whether or not he is in fact a beneficiary) and not by the actual recipient. The settlor can recover any resulting tax from the actual recipient of the payment and can require HMRC to provide a certificate specifying the amount of the gains and the amount of tax for the purpose of recovering the tax. Any such certificate is conclusive evidence of the facts stated in it. [*TCGA 1992, s 87G; FA 2018, Sch 10 para 1(1)(13)*].

(g) *FA 2018* introduced provisions to tax capital payments by offshore settlements in circumstances where the beneficiary receiving the payment is not liable to CGT under these provisions (because he is non-UK resident or a remittance basis user) and he makes an onward gift of the proceeds to a UK resident. Broadly, the UK resident is treated as if they had received the payment from the trust as a beneficiary.

The provisions apply where the onward gift is made on or after 6 April 2018 (and do so even if the original capital payment is received before that date). [*TCGA 1992, ss 87I–87M; FA 2018, Sch 10 para 1(1)(14)*].

(B) Surcharge on CGT under TCGA 1992, s 87

[*TCGA 1992, s 91*]

D, resident and domiciled in the UK, is the sole beneficiary of a discretionary settlement created by his father in May 2010 and administered in the Cayman Islands. The trustees are all individuals resident in the Cayman Islands. In 2014/15, the trustees sell an asset realising a gain of £120,000, but otherwise make no disposals. In 2018/19, the trustees make a capital payment to D of £120,000, having made no previous capital payments. D makes no other disposals in 2018/19 but pays income tax for that year at the higher rate.

D's capital gains tax liability for 2018/19 is calculated as follows.

	£
CGT (subject to surcharge)	
(£120,000 − £11,700 annual exemption) × 20%	21,660
Surcharge £21,660 × 10% × 4 years (1.12.15–30.11.19)	8,664
Total tax payable 2018/19	£30,324

Notes

(a) The capital payment of £120,000 in 2018/19 is matched under *TCGA 1992, s 87A* with the section 2(2) amount for 2013/14 of £120,000. See (A) above.

(b) The surcharge is 10% per annum for a period beginning on 1 December following the end of the tax year the section 2(2) amount for which is matched with the capital payment and ending on 30 November in the tax year following that in which the capital payment is made but subject to a maximum period of six years. [*TCGA 1992, s 91(3)–(5)*].

220 Overseas Matters

220.1 COMPANY MIGRATION

[*TCGA 1992, ss 185, 187*]

Z Ltd is a company incorporated in Ruritania, but regarded as resident in the UK by virtue of its being managed and controlled in the UK. It is the 75% subsidiary of Y plc, a UK resident company. On 1 October 2018, the management and control of Z Ltd is transferred to Ruritania and it thus ceases to be UK resident, although it continues to trade in the UK, on a much reduced basis, via a UK permanent establishment.

Details of the company's chargeable assets immediately before 1 October 2018 were as follows.

	Market value	Capital gain after indexation (where applicable) if all assets sold
	£	£
Factory in UK	480,000	230,000
Warehouse in UK	300,000	180,000
Factory in Ruritania	350,000	200,000
Warehouse in Ruritania	190,000	100,000
UK quoted investments	110,000	80,000
Foreign trade investments	100,000	Loss (60,000)

The UK warehouse continues to be used in the UK trade. The UK factory does not, and is later sold. On 1 June 2019, the Ruritanian warehouse is sold for the equivalent of £210,000. On 1 October 2020, Y plc sells its shareholding in Z Ltd.

Prior to becoming non-UK resident, Z Ltd had unrelieved capital losses brought forward of £40,000.

The corporation tax consequences assuming no election under *TCGA 1992, s 187* are as follows

Chargeable gain accruing to Z Ltd on 1.10.18

	£
Factory (UK)	230,000
Factory (Ruritania)	200,000
Warehouse (Ruritania)	100,000
UK quoted investments	80,000
Foreign trade investments	(60,000)
	550,000
Losses brought forward	(40,000)
Net gain chargeable to corporation tax	£510,000

The later sale of the UK factory does not attract corporation tax as the company is non-resident and the factory has not, since the deemed reacquisition immediately before 1 October 2018, been used in a trade carried on in the UK through a permanent establishment. Similarly, the sale of the overseas warehouse, and of any other overseas assets, is outside the scope of corporation tax on chargeable gains. Any subsequent disposal of the UK warehouse *will* be within the charge to corporation tax, having been omitted from the deemed disposal on 1 October 2014, due to its being used in a trade carried on in the UK through a permanent establishment. On disposal, the gain will be computed by reference to original cost, or 31.3.82 value if appropriate, rather than to market value immediately before 1 October 2018 — see also note (d).

Y plc will realise a capital gain (or loss) on the sale of its shareholding in Z Ltd on 1 October 2019.

The corporation tax consequences if an election is made under *TCGA 1992, s 187* are as follows

Chargeable gain accruing to Z Ltd on 1.10.18

	£
Factory (UK)	230,000
UK quoted investments	(80,000)
	310,000
Losses brought forward	(40,000)
Net gain liable to corporation tax	£270,000

Postponed gain on foreign assets

	£
Factory (Ruritania)	200,000
Warehouse (Ruritania)	100,000
	300,000
Foreign trade investments	(60,000)
	£240,000

On 1 June 2019, a proportion of the postponed gain becomes chargeable as a result of the sale, within six years of Z Ltd's becoming non-resident, of one of the assets in respect of which the postponed gain accrued. The gain chargeable to corporation tax as at 1 June 2019 on Y plc is

$$\frac{100{,}000 \text{ (postponed gain on warehouse)}}{300{,}000 \text{ (aggregate of postponed gains)}} \times £240{,}000 = £80{,}000$$

On 1 October 2020, in addition to any gain or loss arising on the sale of the shares, Y plc will be chargeable to corporation tax on the remainder of the postponed gain, i.e. on £160,000 (£240,000 - £80,000), by virtue of Z Ltd having ceased to be its 75% subsidiary as a result of the sale of shares.

The position as regards the UK warehouse is the same as if no election had been made.

Notes

(a) The provisions of *TCGA 1992, s 185* apply where a company ceases to be resident in the UK. All companies incorporated in the UK are regarded as UK resident. As such a company cannot therefore cease to be resident, *section 185* can apply only to companies incorporated abroad which are UK resident. See also HMRC Statement of Practice SP 1/90 as regards company residence generally.

(b) If, with an election, Z Ltd's unrelieved capital losses had exceeded its chargeable gains arising on 1 October 2018, the excess could have been allowed against postponed gains at the time when they become chargeable on Y plc, subject to the two companies making a joint election to that effect under *TCGA 1992, s 187(5)*.

(c) *TMA 1970, ss 109B–109F* contain management provisions designed to secure payment of all outstanding tax liabilities on a company becoming non-UK resident. See also HMRC Statement of Practice SP 2/90.

(d) If the UK warehouse ceases to be a chargeable asset by virtue of Z Ltd's ceasing to carry on a trade in the UK through a permanent establishment, there will be a deemed disposal at market value at that time, under *TCGA 1992, s 25*. See **220.2** below.

(e) *FA 2013* introduced a facility for a company which becomes non-UK resident to enter into an exit charge payment plan, under which corporation tax arising under various exit charges, including *TCGA 1992, s 185* can be deferred. [*TMA 1970, s 59FA, Sch3ZB; FA 2013, s 229, Sch 49*].

220.2 NON-RESIDENTS CARRYING ON TRADE, ETC. THROUGH UK BRANCH OR AGENCY

[*TCGA 1992, ss 10, 25*]

X, who is not resident in the UK, practises abroad as a tax consultant and also practises in the UK through a London branch, preparing accounts to 5 April. The assets of the UK branch include premises bought in 1988 for £60,000 and a computer system acquired in March 2014 for £20,000. On 31 January 2019, the computer ceases to be used in the UK branch and is immediately shipped abroad, and on 28 February 2019, X closes down the UK branch. He sells the premises in June 2019 for £118,000. Capital allowances claimed on the computer up to and including 2017/18 were £20,000 and short-life asset treatment had been claimed.

Relevant market values of the assets are as follows

		£
Computer,	at 31 January 2019	11,000
Premises,	at 14 March 1989	65,000
	at 28 February 2019	110,000

The UK capital gains tax consequences are as follows

		£	£
Computer			
Market value 31.1.19			11,000
Deduct			
Cost		20,000	
Less capital allowances claimed	(note (f))	(9,000)	(11,000)
Chargeable gain			Nil

	£
Premises	
Market value 28.2.19	110,000
Deduct Market value 14.3.89	(65,000)
Chargeable gain	£45,000
Net chargeable gains 2018/19	£45,000

Notes

(a) X is within the charge to UK capital gains tax for disposals after 13 March 1989 by virtue of his carrying on a profession in the UK through a branch or agency. Previously, the charge applied only to non-residents carrying on a *trade* in this manner. X is deemed to have disposed of (with no capital gains tax consequences) and reacquired immediately before 14 March 1989 all chargeable assets used in the UK branch at market value, so that any subsequent CGT charge will be by reference only to post-13 March 1989 gains. [*FA 1989, s 126(3)–(5); TCGA 1992, s 10(5)*].

(b) There is a deemed disposal, at market value, of the computer on 31 January 2019 as a result of its ceasing to be a chargeable asset by virtue of its becoming situated outside the UK. [*TCGA 1992, s 25(1)*].

(c) There is a deemed disposal, at market value, of the premises on 28 February 2019 as a result of the asset ceasing to be a chargeable asset by virtue of X's ceasing to carry on a trade, profession or vocation in the UK through a branch or agency. [*TCGA 1992, s 25(3)(8)*]. See also note (g) below.

(d) There are no UK CGT consequences on the actual disposal of the premises in June 2019.

(e) X is entitled to the £11,700 annual exemption against UK gains, regardless of his residence status (but taxpayers who make a claim under *ITA 2007, s 809B* for the remittance basis are not entitled to the annual exemption).

(f) Where a chargeable asset has qualified for capital allowances and a loss accrues on its disposal, the allowable expenditure is restricted, under *TCGA 1992, s 41*, by the net allowances given, which in this example amount to £9,000 (annual investment allowance £20,000 less balancing charge £11,000 arising on the asset's ceasing to be used in the trade).

(g) *TCGA 1992, s 25(3)* (see note (c) above) does not apply in relation to an asset where a non-UK resident company transfers its trade (carried on through a UK permanent establishment) to a UK resident company in the same group. The asset is deemed to be transferred at no gain/no loss. [*TCGA 1992, s 171*].

220.3 TRANSFER OF ASSETS TO NON-RESIDENT COMPANY

[*TCGA 1992, s 140; FA 2018, s 27*]

Q Ltd, a UK resident company, carries on business in a foreign country through a branch there. In September 2012, it is decreed that all enterprises in that country be carried on by locally resident companies. Q Ltd forms a wholly-owned non-UK resident subsidiary R and transfers all the assets of the branch to R wholly in consideration for the issue of shares. The assets transferred include the following

	Value	Chargeable gains
	£	£
Goodwill	100,000	95,000
Freehold land	200,000	120,000
Plant (items worth more than £6,000)	50,000	20,000
Other assets	150,000	—
	£500,000	£235,000

On 1 January 2014, there is a compulsory acquisition of 50% of the share capital of R for £300,000 (market value). The value of the whole shareholding immediately before disposal is £750,000. The value of Q Ltd's remaining 50% holding is £300,000.

In June 2018, R is forced to sell its freehold land to the government.

Q Ltd's capital gains position is as follows

2012

The gain of £235,000 is deferred. The allowable cost of the shares in R is £500,000.

2014

	£
Consideration on disposal	300,000
Deduct	
Cost of shares sold £500,000 × $\frac{300,000}{300,000 + 300,000}$	(250,000)
Gain subject to indexation	£50,000
Proportion of deferred gain becoming chaargeable £235,000 × $\frac{300,000}{750,000}$	£94,000

2018

Proportion of deferred gain chargeable	£
Gain arising $\frac{120,000}{235,000} \times £235,000$	£120,000
Balance of gain still held over (£235,000 − £94,000 − £120,000)	£21,000

Notes

(a) The 2018 gain arises under *section 140(5)*. If the sale of freehold land had taken place more than six years after the original transfer of assets, no part of the deferred gain would have become chargeable as a result.

(b) The 2014 gain arises under *section 140(4)*. In this case, there is no time limit as in (a) above. The appropriate proportion of the deferred gain is treated as a separate chargeable gain.

220.4 INDIVIDUAL TEMPORARILY NON-RESIDENT IN THE UK

[*TCGA 1992, ss 10A, 10AA; FA 2013, Sch 45 paras 109–115, 119, 153(3)*]

Mr Stephenson, who has lived in the UK all his life, leaves the UK on 1 May 2013 for a four year employment contract abroad. Under the statutory residence test, Mr Stephenson is resident outside the UK for the whole of 2013/14 to 2017/18 inclusive. On 16 May 2015 he sells his entire shareholding in Snow plc for £30,000. He had purchased the shares for £10,000 in April 2005. Mr Stephenson returns to the UK on 6 April 2018 and, under the statutory residence test, is UK-resident from that date. He makes no other disposals in the period 1 May 2013 to 5 April 2019 inclusive.

No chargeable gain accrues on the disposal of the shares in 2015/16 as Mr Stephenson is not resident in the UK.

A chargeable gain is deemed to accrue in respect of the disposal of the shares in 2018/19, the year of Mr Stephenson's return to the UK, computed as follows.

	£
Proceeds	30,000
Acquisition cost	(10,000)
Chargeable gain	£20,000

Notes

(a) *TCGA 1992, s 10A* applies where an individual leaves the UK for a period of temporary residence outside the UK and four out of the seven tax years immediately preceding the year of departure were years for which the individual had sole UK residence or were split years which included a period for which the individual had sole UK residence, provided that the period of non-residence is five years or less. [*TCGA 1992, s 10A(1); FA 2013, Sch 45 paras 110–115*].

(b) Where the year of return is a split year under the statutory residence test, the deemed gain is treated as arising in the UK part of the year. [*TCGA 1992, s 10A(2)*].

(c) Slightly different rules applied where the year of departure was 2012/13 or an earlier year.

221 Partnerships

221.1 ASSETS

[*TCGA 1992, s 59*]

G, H and I trade in partnership. They share capital in the ratio 5:4:3. Land occupied by the firm is sold on 15 April 2018 for £240,000, having been acquired for £60,000 in 1981. The agreed market value of the land at 31 March 1982 is £54,000. G has personal gains in 2018/19 of £2,500, H has losses of £1,000 and I made no disposals of personal assets. None of the partners has any capital losses brought forward from earlier years.

The gains of G, H and I in respect of the land are as follows

	G($^5/_{12}$)	H($^4/_{12}$)	I($^3/_{12}$)
	£	£	£
Disposal consideration	100,000	80,000	60,000
Market value 31.3.82	(22,500)	(18,000)	(13,500)
Chargeable gain	£77,500	£62,000	£46,500

Summary

	G	H	I
	£	£	£
Share of partnership gain	77,500	62,000	46,500
Personal gains/(losses)	2,500	(1,000)	—
Chargeable gain	80,000	61,000	46,500
Annual exemption	(11,700)	(11,700)	(11,700)
Taxable gain 2018/19	£68,300	£49,300	£34,800

Notes

(a) Each partner is regarded as owning a fractional share of each partnership asset, which is calculated by reference to his capital sharing ratio.

(b) For capital gains tax purposes (i.e. in relation to disposals by individuals, trustees and personal representatives), re-basing to 31 March 1982 applies to all disposals with no exceptions. Market value at 31 March 1982 is therefore substituted for the actual cost, even where, as in this example, the cost is higher than that value. See **205.1** ASSETS HELD ON **31** MARCH **1982**.

221.2 CHANGES IN SHARING RATIOS

J and K have traded in partnership since 1990, sharing capital and income equally. The acquisition costs of the chargeable assets of the firm are as follows

	Cost
	£
Premises	60,000
Goodwill	10,000

The assets have not been revalued in the firm's balance sheet. On 1 June 2018, J and K admit L to the partnership, and the sharing ratio is J 35%, K 45% and L 20%.

J and K are regarded as disposing of part of their interest in the firm's assets to L as follows

	£
J	
Premises	
Deemed consideration	
£60,000 × (50% − 35%)	9,000
Allowable cost	(9,000)
Chargeable gain	—
Goodwill	
Deemed consideration	
£10,000 × (50% − 35%)	1,500
Allowable cost	(1,500)
Chargeable gain	—

	£
K	
Premises	
Deemed consideration	
£60,000 × (50% − 45%)	3,000
Allowable cost	(3,000)
Chargeable gain	—
Goodwill	
Deemed consideration	
£10,000 × (50% − 45%)	500
Allowable cost	(500)
Chargeable gain	—

The allowable costs of the three partners are now

	Freehold land	Goodwill
	£	£
J	21,000	3,500
K	27,000	4,500
L	12,000	2,000

Notes

(a) The treatment illustrated above is taken from HMRC Statement of Practice SP D12 (17.1.75), para 4 as extended by SP 1/89. Each partner's disposal consideration is equal to his share of current balance sheet value of the asset concerned and each disposal treated as producing no gain and no loss.

(b) L's allowable costs comprise 20% of original cost.

221.3 ACCOUNTING ADJUSTMENTS

A, B and C trade in partnership. They share income and capital profits equally. The firm's only chargeable asset is its premises which cost £51,000 in 1989. C decides to retire. The remaining partners agree to share profits equally. Before C retires (in May 2018), the premises are written up to market value in the accounts, agreed at £180,000. C does not receive any payment directly from the other partners on his retirement.

The capital gains tax consequences are

On retiring, C is regarded as having disposed of his interest in the firm's premises for a consideration equal to his share of the then book value.

		£
Disposal consideration	$^1/_3 \times$ £180,000	60,000
Acquisition cost	$^1/_3 \times$ £51,000	17,000
Chargeable gain, subject to entrepreneurs' relief		£43,000

A and B will each be treated as acquiring a $^1/_6$ ($^1/_2 \times {}^1/_3$) share in the premises, at a cost equal to one half of C's disposal consideration. Their acquisition costs are then

		A	B
		£	£
Cost of original share	$^1/_3 \times$ £51,000	17,000	17,000
Cost of new share	$^1/_2 \times$ £60,000	30,000	30,000
Total		£47,000	£47,000

221.4 CONSIDERATION OUTSIDE ACCOUNTS

D, E and F are partners in a firm of accountants who share all profits in the ratio 7:7:6. G is admitted as a partner in May 2018 and pays the other partners £10,000 for goodwill. The new partnership shares are D $^3/_{10}$, E $^3/_{10}$, F $^1/_4$ and G $^3/_{20}$. The book value of goodwill is £18,000, its cost on acquisition of the practice from the predecessor in 1990.

The partners are treated as having disposed of shares in goodwill as follows

	£	£
D		
7/20 − 3/10 = 1/20		
Disposal consideration		
Notional 1/20 × £18,000	900	
Actual 7/20 × £10,000	3,500	
		4,400
Allowable cost 1/20 × £18,000		(900)
Chargeable gain		£3,500
E		
7/20 − 3/10 = 1/20		
Disposal consideration (as for D)		4,400
Allowable cost (as for D)		(900)
Chargeable gain		£3,500
F		
6/20 1/4 = 1/20		
Disposal consideration		
Notional 1/20 × £18,000	900	
Actual 6/20 × £10,000	3,000	
		3,900
Allowable cost		(900)
Chargeable gain		£3,000
G's allowable cost of his share of goodwill is therefore		
Actual consideration paid		10,000
Notional consideration paid 3/20 × £18,000		2,700
		£12,700

221.5 SHARES ACQUIRED IN STAGES

Q is a partner in a legal practice. The partnership's only chargeable asset is a freehold house used as an office. The cost of the house to the partnership was £3,600 in 1998 and it was revalued in the partnership accounts to £50,000 in 2014. Q was admitted to the partnership in June 2000 with a share of 1/6 of all profits. As a result of partnership changes, Q's profit share altered as follows

2004	1/5
2012	1/4
2018	3/10

For capital gains tax, Q's allowable cost of his share of the freehold house is calculated as follows

		£
2000	$^1/_6$ × £3,600	600
2004	($^1/_5$ − $^1/_6$) × £3,600	120
2012	($^1/_4$ − $^1/_5$) × £3,600	180
2018	($^3/_{10}$ − $^1/_4$) × £50,000	2,500
		£3,400

Note

(a) On Q's acquisition of an increased share of the property in 2018 (subsequent to the revaluation in 2014), any partner with a reduced share will be treated as having made a disposal and thus a gain or loss.

221.6 PARTNERSHIP ASSETS DISTRIBUTED IN KIND

R, S and T are partners sharing all profits in the ratio 4:3:3. Farmland owned by the firm is transferred in November 2018 to T for future use by him as a market gardening enterprise separate from the partnership business. No payment is made by T to the other partners but a reduction is made in T's future share of income profits. The book value of the farmland is £50,000, its cost in 1995, but the present market value is £150,000.

		£
R		
Deemed disposal consideration	$^4/_{10}$ × £150,000	60,000
Allowable cost	$^4/_{10}$ × £50,000	(20,000)
Gain		£40,000
S		
Deemed disposal consideration	$^3/_{10}$ × £150,000	45,000
Allowable cost	$^3/_{10}$ × £50,000	(15,000)
Gain		£30,000
T		
Partnership share	$^3/_{10}$ × £50,000	15,000
Market value of R's share		60,000
Market value of S's share		45,000
Allowable cost of land for future disposal		£120,000

222 Payment of Tax

222.1 PAYMENT BY INSTALMENTS

(A) Consideration payable by instalments

[*TCGA 1992, ss 280, 281*]

Ian, a higher rate income tax payer, sells an asset on 31 March 2019 for £240,000. The consideration is to be paid by twelve annual instalments of £20,000 beginning on 31 March 2019. Ian originally purchased the asset for £15,000 in 1992 and his allowable costs of sale are £4,300. The gain is not an upper rate gain and does not qualify for entrepreneurs' relief. Ian has no other chargeable gains in 2018/19.

Ian's liability to capital gains tax for 2018/19 is as follows

	£
Consideration	240,000
Less costs of sale	(4,300)
Acquisition cost	(15,000)
Chargeable gain 2018/19	220,700
Annual exemption	(11,700)
Gain chargeable to tax	£209,000
Capital gains tax payable (£209,000 × 20%)	£41,800

If Ian opts under *TCGA 1992, s 280* to pay the tax by instalments, the following payments will be due.

31 January 2020	£10,000
31 March 2020	£10,000
31 March 2021	£10,000
31 March 2022	£10,000
31 March 2023	£1,800

Notes

(a) Where the whole or part of the consideration for a disposal is receivable by instalments over a period exceeding 18 months, beginning not earlier than the date of the disposal, the tax arising may at the option of the taxpayer by paid by such instalments as HMRC allows. The tax instalment period cannot exceed eight years and must end not later than the time at which the final instalment of the consideration is payable. [*TCGA 1992, s 280*].

(b) HMRC's practice is to ask for instalments of tax equal to half of each instalment of consideration until the total tax liability has been discharged. To the extent that instalments of consideration under the contract fall due on or before the normal due date for the payment of tax (31 January in the tax year following that in which the disposal occurred), the respective instalments of tax are payable on that normal due date. Where instalments of consideration fall due after that time, then the respective instalments of tax are payable on the dates when the taxpayer is contractually entitled to receive the consideration. (HMRC Capital Gains Manual CG14910).

(c) Interest on unpaid tax is charged on each instalment only if it is paid late and will run from the date when the instalment was due until the date of payment. (HMRC Self-Assessment Manual SAM80072).

(d) The above instalment provisions do not apply to deferred consideration which is unquantified and contingent. See **206.2** CAPITAL SUMS DERIVED FROM ASSETS.

(B) **Gifts of land or shares**

On 1 June 2018, Sean gives a parcel of land to his daughter, Erica. The market value of the land on that date is £316,000. Sean purchased the land in 1992 for £38,300, and makes no other disposals in 2018/19. He is a higher rate income taxpayer. For the purposes of this example only, the rate of interest on unpaid capital gains tax is taken to be 4% throughout.

Sean's liability to capital gains tax for 2018/19 is as follows

	£
Market value	316,000
Less acquisition cost	(38,300)
Chargeable gain 2018/19	277,700
Annual exemption	(11,700)
Gain chargeable to tax	£266,000
Capital gains tax payable (£266,000 × 20%)	£53,200

If Sean elects under *TCGA 1992, s 281*, before 31 January 2020 to pay the tax by instalments, the following payments will be due.

	£	£
1st instalment due 31.1.20		5,320
2nd instalment due 31.1.21	5,320	
Interest 4% × £47,880	1,915	7,235
3rd instalment due 31.1.22	5,320	
Interest 4% × £42,560	1,702	7,022
4th instalment due 31.1.23	5,320	
Interest 4% × £37,240	1,489	6,809
5th instalment due 31.1.24	5,320	
Interest 4% × £31,920	1,276	6,596
6th instalment due 31.1.25	5,320	
Interest 4% × £26,600	1,064	6,384
7th instalment due 31.1.26	5,320	
Interest 4% × £21,280	851	6,171
8th instalment due 31.1.27	5,320	
Interest 4% × £15,960	638	5,958
9th instalment due 31.1.28	5,320	
Interest 4% × £10,640	425	5,745
10th instalment due 31.1.29	5,320	
Interest 4% × £5,320	212	5,532
Total tax and interest		£62,772

Notes

(a) Capital gains tax chargeable on a gift of land or certain shares or securities can, on election in writing, be paid by ten yearly instalments. The first instalment is due on the ordinary due date. The outstanding balance together with accrued interest may be paid at any time. Where the gift is to a connected person, the tax (and accrued interest) are payable immediately if any part of the subject-matter of the gift is subsequently disposed of for consideration. [*TCGA 1992, s 281(2)(4)(6)(7)*].

(b) Payment by instalments is also available in respect of a deemed disposal by trustees under *TCGA 1992, s 71(1)* (person becoming absolutely entitled to settled property) or *s 72(1)* (termination of life interest on death) and, in certain cases, to a chargeable gain accruing under *TCGA 1992, s 169C(7)* (clawback of hold-over relief under *TCGA 1992, s 165* or *s 260* if settlement becomes settlor-interested). [*TCGA 1992, s 281(1)(8)*].

(c) The disposal must *either* be one to which neither *TCGA 1992, s 165(4)* nor *s 260(3)* (see **213.2** and **213.1** HOLD-OVER RELIEFS) applies (or would apply if a claim was made) *or* one to which either of those *sections* does apply but on which the held-over gain only partly reduces the gain otherwise arising or is nil. [*TCGA 1992, s 281(1)*].

(d) The assets on a disposal of which an election can be made are: land or any interest or estate in land; any shares or securities of a company which, immediately before the disposal, gave control to the person making or deemed to be making the disposal; and any other shares or securities of a company not listed on a recognised stock exchange. [*TCGA 1992, s 281(3)*].

(e) Interest on unpaid tax is charged as if no election had been made. The interest on the unpaid portion of the tax is added to each instalment and must be paid accordingly. [*TCGA 1992, s 281(5)*].

223 Private Residences

223.1 PERIODS OF OWNERSHIP QUALIFYING FOR EXEMPTION AND LET PROPERTY EXEMPTION

[*TCGA 1992, ss 222, 223; FA 2014, s 58; FA 2015, Sch 9 paras 2, 4, 10*]

(A)

P, who is resident in the UK, sold a house on 1 July 2018 realising an otherwise chargeable gain of £154,000. The house was purchased on 1 February 1981 and was occupied as a residence until 30 June 1990 when P moved to another residence, letting the house as residential accommodation. He did not re-occupy the house prior to its sale.

	£
Gain on sale	154,000
Deduct Exempt amount under main residence rules	
$\dfrac{8y\ 3m + 1y\ 6m}{36y\ 3m} \times £154,000$	(41,421)
	112,579
Deduct Let property exemption	(40,000)
Net chargeable gain	£72,579

Notes

(a) The final eighteen months of ownership are always included in the exempt period of ownership. For disposals before 6 April 2014, the final 36 months were so included. A 36-month period continues to apply where, at the time of the disposal:

- the taxpayer is a disabled person or a long-term resident in a care home and does not have any other right in a private residence; or
- the taxpayer's spouse or civil partner is a disabled person or a long-term resident in a care home and neither the individual nor the spouse or civil partner has any other right in a private residence.

'*Disabled person*' is defined for this purpose at *FA 2005, Sch 1A*. An individual is a '*long-term resident*' in a care home at the time of a disposal if at that time he is resident there and has been resident, or can reasonably be expected to be resident there, for at least three months. A '*care home*' is an establishment providing accommodation together with nursing or personal care *TCGA 1992, ss 223(1), 225E; FA 2014, s 58*].

(b) The period of ownership for the exemption calculation does not include any period before 31 March 1982. [*TCGA 1992, s 223(7)*].

(c) The gain attributable to the letting (£112,579) is exempt to the extent that it does not exceed the lesser of £40,000 and the gain otherwise exempt (£41,421 in this example). [*TCGA 1992, s 223(4)*].

(d) See also **216.4** LAND.

(B)

Q bought a house on 1 August 1981 for £40,000 and used it as his main residence. On 10 February 1982, he was sent by his employer to manage the Melbourne branch of the firm and continued to work in Australia until 4 August 1987, the whole of his duties being performed outside the UK. The house was let as residential accommodation during that period. Q took up residence in the house once again following his return to the UK, but on 30 September 2000 moved to Switzerland for health reasons. On this occasion, the property was not let. He returned to the UK in August 2003, but did not reside in the house at any time prior to it being sold on 31 December 2018 for £252,350. The house had a market value of £50,000 at 31 March 1982.

Computation of gain before applying exemptions

	£
Disposal consideration	252,350
Market value 31.3.82	(50,000)
Gain before exemptions	£202,350

The gain is reduced by the main residence exemptions as follows

Period of ownership (excluding period before 31.3.82)		36y 9m
Exempt periods since 31.3.82:		
31.3.82 – 30.9.00	18y 6m	
1.7.17 – 31.12.18 (last eighteen months)	1y 6m	20y 0m

		£
Gain as above		202,350
Deduct Exempt amount under main residence rules		
$\frac{20y\ 0m}{36y\ 9m} \times £202{,}350$		(110,122)
		92,228
Deduct Let property exemption:		
Period of letting 31.3.82 – 4.8.87	5y 4m	
Gain attributable to letting $\frac{5y\ 4m}{36y\ 9m} \times £202{,}350 =$	£29,366	
Exemption (note (e))		(29,366)
Net chargeable gain 2018/19		£(62,862)

Notes

(a) Periods of ownership before 31 March 1982 are excluded in applying the main residence exemptions. [*TCGA 1992, s 223(7)*].

(b) The period spent in Australia (regardless of its length but excluding that part of it before 31 March 1982) counts as a period of residence, as Q worked in an employment all the duties of which were performed outside the UK and used the house as his main residence at some time before and after this period of absence. [*TCGA 1992, s 223(3)(b)*].

(c) The period spent in Switzerland would have been exempt, having not exceeded three years, but the exemption is lost as Q did not occupy the property as a main residence at any time after this period. [*TCGA 1992, s 223(3)(a)*].

(d) The last eighteen months of ownership are always exempt providing the property has been used as the owner's only or main residence at some time during the period of ownership, and for this purpose, 'period of ownership' is not restricted to the period after 30 March 1982. See note (a) to (A) above.

(e) The let property exemption is the lesser of the gain attributable to the period of letting (£29,366), the gain otherwise exempt (£110,122) and £40,000. It cannot create a loss. It is available only if the property is let as residential accommodation. [*TCGA 1992, s 223(4)*].

223.2 ELECTION FOR MAIN RESIDENCE

[*TCGA 1992, s 222(5)*]

S, who is UK-resident throughout, purchased the long lease of a London flat on 1 June 2010. He occupied the flat as his sole residence until 31 July 2012 when he acquired a property in Shropshire. Both properties were thereafter occupied as residences by S until the lease of the London flat was sold on 28 February 2019, realising an otherwise chargeable gain of £75,000.

The possibilities open to S are

(i) **Election for London flat to be treated as main residence throughout**

Exempt gain	£75,000

(ii) **Election for Shropshire property to be treated as main residence from 31 July 2012 onwards**

$$\text{Exempt gain } £75{,}000 \times \frac{2\text{y } 2\text{m} + 1\text{y } 6\text{m}}{8\text{y } 9\text{m}} \qquad £31{,}429$$

(iii) **Election for London flat to be treated as main residence up to 31 August 2017, with election for the Shropshire property to be so treated thereafter**

$$\text{Exempt gain } £75{,}000 \times \frac{7y\ 3m + 1y\ 6m}{8y\ 9m} \qquad \underline{£75{,}000}$$

Note

(a) The elections in (iii) are the most favourable, provided they could have been made by 31 July 2014 in respect of the London flat, and by 31 August 2019 in respect of the Shropshire property. Note that the last eighteen months' ownership of the London flat is an exempt period in any case. The advantage of (iii) over (i) is that the period of ownership 1 September 2017 to 28 February 2019 of the Shropshire property will be treated as a period of residence as regards any future disposal of that property. HMRC practice is that the *initial* election (which can be varied) must be made within two years of acquisition of the second property, and this was upheld in *Griffin v Craig-Harvey Ch D 1993*, 66 TC 396, [1994] STC 54.

224 Qualifying Corporate Bonds

[*TCGA 1992, ss 115–117*]

224.1 DEFINITION

[*TCGA 1992, s 117*]

B has the following transactions in 5% unsecured loan stock issued in 1983 by F Ltd.

		£
11.11.83	Purchase £2,000	1,800
10.7.89	Gift from wife £1,000 (original cost £800)	—
30.9.97	Purchase £2,000	2,100
5.6.18	Sale £4,000	(3,300)

Apart from the gift on 10.7.89, all acquisitions were arm's length purchases. B's wife acquired her £1,000 holding on 11.11.83. Indexation allowance of £266 arose on the transfer from wife to husband.

For the purposes of the accrued income scheme, the sale is without accrued interest and the rebate amount is £20. The stock is a corporate bond as defined by *TCGA 1992, s 117(1)* and therefore a 'relevant security' as defined by *TCGA 1992, s 108(1)*.

Under the rules for matching relevant securities in *TCGA 1992, s 106A*, the stock disposed of is identified with acquisitions as follows.

(i) Identify £2,000 with purchase on 30.9.97 (LIFO)

	£
Disposal consideration $£3,300 \times \frac{2,000}{4,000}$	1,650
Add rebate amount $£20 \times \frac{2,000}{4,000}$	10
	1,660
Allowable cost	(2,100)
Loss	£(440)

The loss is *not* allowable as the £2,000 stock purchased on 30.9.97 is a qualifying corporate bond (note (a)). [*TCGA 1992, s 115*].

(ii) Identify £1,000 with acquisition on 10.7.89

	£
Disposal consideration $£3,300 \times \frac{1,000}{4,000}$	825
Add rebate amount $£20 \times \frac{1,000}{4,000}$	5
	830
Allowable cost (including indexation to 10.7.89)	(1,066)
Allowable loss	£(236)

The loss is allowable as the stock acquired on 10.7.89 is not a qualifying corporate bond (note (b)).

(iii) Identify £1,000 with purchase on 11.11.83

	£
Disposal consideration $£3,300 \times \frac{1,000}{4,000}$	825
Add rebate amount $£20 \times \frac{1,000}{4,000}$	5
	830
Allowable cost $£1,800 \times \frac{1,000}{2,000}$	(900)
Allowable loss	£(70)

The loss is allowable as the stock acquired on 11.11.83 is not a qualifying corporate bond (note (c)).

Notes

(a) The acquisition on 30.9.97 is a qualifying corporate bond as it was acquired after 13 March 1984 otherwise than as a result of an excluded disposal. [*TCGA 1992, s 117(7)(b)*].

(b) The acquisition on 10.7.89 was the result of an excluded disposal, being a no gain/no loss transfer between spouses where the first spouse had acquired the stock before 14 March 1984. It is therefore not a qualifying corporate bond. [*TCGA 1992, s 117(7)(b)(8)*].

(c) Securities acquired before 14 March 1984 cannot be qualifying corporate bonds in the hands of the person who so acquired them.

(d) See **IT 2** ACCRUED INCOME SCHEME for the income tax effects of the accrued income scheme.

224.2 REORGANISATION OF SHARE CAPITAL

[*TCGA 1992, s 116*]

D holds 5,000 £1 ordinary shares in H Ltd. He acquired the shares in April 1999 by subscription at par. On 1 August 2011, he accepted an offer for the shares from J plc. The terms of the offer were one 25p ordinary share of J plc and £10 J plc 10% unsecured loan stock (a qualifying corporate bond) for each H Ltd ordinary share. Both the shares and the loan stock are listed on the Stock Exchange. In December 2018, D sells £20,000 loan stock at its quoted price of £105 per cent.

The value of J plc ordinary shares at 1 August 2011 was £3.52 per share and the loan stock was £99.20 per cent.

The cost of the H Ltd shares must be apportioned between the J plc ordinary shares and loan stock.

	£
Value of J plc shares	
5,000 × £3.52	17,600
Value of J plc loan stock	
£50,000 × 99.2%	49,600
	£67,200

Allowable cost of J plc shares

$$\frac{17,600}{67,200} \times £5,000 \qquad £1,310$$

Allowable cost of J plc loan stock

$$\frac{49,600}{67,200} \times £5,000 \qquad £3,690$$

Chargeable gain on H Ltd shares attributable to J plc loan stock to date of exchange

	£
Deemed disposal consideration	49,600
Allowable cost	(3,690)
Deferred chargeable gain	£45,910

Deferred chargeable gain accruing on disposal of loan stock in December 2018

Loan stock sold (nominal)	£20,000
Total holding of loan stock before disposal (nominal)	£50,000
Deferred chargeable gain accruing in 2018/19	
$\frac{20,000}{50,000} \times £45,910$	£18,364

Notes

(a) The gain on the sale of J plc loan stock is exempt (as the stock is a qualifying corporate bond) except for that part which relates to the gain on the previous holding of H Ltd shares. [*TCGA 1992, s 115, s 116(10)*]. There will also be income tax consequences under the accrued income scheme (see **IT 2** ACCRUED INCOME SCHEME).

(b) The qualifying corporate bond is treated as acquired at the date of the reorganisation, so even if the original shares had been held at 31 March 1982, re-basing would *not* apply on the subsequent disposal of the loan stock.

(c) The exchange of J plc ordinary shares for H Ltd shares is dealt with under *TCGA 1992, ss 127–130*, and no gain or loss will arise until the J plc shares are disposed of. See **229.4** SHARES AND SECURITIES.

225 Remittance Basis

225.1 EFFECT OF ELECTION UNDER TCGA 1992, S 16ZA

[*TCGA 1992, ss 16ZA–16ZD; FA 2013, Sch 45 paras 98, 99; F(No 2)A 2017, Sch 8 paras 2–5*]

Kevin, who is domiciled in South Africa, comes to the UK on 6 April 2017 and is resident in the UK with effect from that date. He has substantial non-UK income and assets and makes claims under *ITA 2007, s 809B* for the remittance basis to apply for 2017/18 and 2018/19. Kevin disposes of two non-UK assets in 2017/18 realising a gain of £60,000 and a loss of £20,000. He also disposes of a UK asset on 1 May 2017, realising a gain of £10,000. He makes no disposals in 2018/19 but is treated as having remitted the £60,000 gain to the UK on 1 May 2018. Kevin is a higher rate income taxpayer for both years.

If Kevin makes an election under *TCGA 1992, s 16ZA* for 2017/18, his capital gains tax liabilities are as follows.

2017/18

	£
Gain on UK asset	10,000
Capital gains tax £10,000 × 20%	£2,000
Gain on non-UK asset	60,000
Deduct loss on non-UK asset	(20,000)
Net gain chargeable when remitted to UK	£40,000

2018/19

Net gain on non-UK asset remitted to UK	40,000
Capital gains tax £40,000 × 20%	£8,000

Notes

(a) Where an election has been made under *TCGA 1992, s 16ZA*, capital losses on non-UK assets arising in a tax year must be set against gains in the following order:

(I) foreign chargeable gains arising and remitted to the UK in the year or, if the year is a split year, in the UK part of the year;

(II) foreign chargeable gains arising in the year but not remitted to the UK in that year or, where the year is a split year, remitted to the UK in the overseas part of the year; and

(III) all other chargeable gains arising in the year (other than gains treated as accruing on the remittance to the UK of foreign chargeable gains arising in a previous year).

[*TCGA 1992, s 16ZC; FA 2013, Sch 45 para 99; F(No 2)A 2017, Sch 8 para 5*].

The 2017/18 loss cannot therefore be set against the UK gain arising in that year, as it must be set against the foreign gain within (II) above in priority.

(b) The election must be made within four years after the tax year to which it relates.

(c) If no election is made in respect of the first year for which a claim under *ITA 2007, s 809B* to the remittance basis is made (or, for 2017/18 onwards, the first year for which such a claim is made following a period in which the individual has been domiciled (or deemed domiciled) in the UK), losses accruing in that year and any subsequent year (other than one in which the taxpayer is domiciled in the UK) on the disposal of assets situated outside the UK are not allowable losses. [*TCGA 1992, s 16ZA*]. In this case, therefore, if no election had been made, the whole of the remitted gain of £60,000 would have been chargeable in 2018/19.

(d) No annual exemption is available for a tax year in respect of which a claim for the remittance basis under *ITA 2007, s 809B* has been made. [*TCGA 1992, s 3(1A)*].

(e) An individual who claims the remittance basis for a tax year incurs an additional tax charge of £30,000 for that year if he is 18 years of age or over in that tax year and he has been UK resident in at least seven of the nine tax years immediately preceding that tax year. For 2012/13 onwards, the charge is increased where the individual has been UK resident in at least twelve of the fourteen tax years immediately preceding the tax year in question. For 2012/13 to 2014/15 the increased charge is £50,000; for 2015/16 onwards it is £60,000. For 2015/16 and 2016/17 a higher charge of £90,000 applies where the individual has been UK resident in at least 17 of the 20 tax years immediately preceding the tax year. [*ITA 2007, ss 809C(3)(4), 809H; FA 2012, Sch 12 para 2; FA 2015, s 24; F(No 2)A 2017, Sch 8 paras 11, 14*].

(f) For 2017/18 onwards, an individual who is not domiciled in the UK is deemed to be so domiciled if either:

   (1) he was born in the UK with a UK domicile of origin and is resident in the UK; or

   (2) he has been UK-resident for at least 15 of the 20 preceding tax years. This provision does not apply if the individual is not UK-resident in the tax year in question and has not been UK-resident in any previous tax year beginning with 2017/18.

226 Rollover Relief — Replacement of Business Assets

Cross-reference. See also **205.2** ASSETS HELD ON **31** MARCH **1982** for relief under *TCGA 1992, s 36, Sch 4* for certain gains accruing before 31 March 1982.

[*TCGA 1992, ss 152–158*]

226.1 NATURE OF RELIEF

[*TCGA 1992, s 152*]

(A)

N Ltd carries on a manufacturing business. It makes the following disposals and acquisitions of assets during the company's accounting periods ended 31 December 2016, 31 December 2017 and 31 December 2018.

	Asset	Bought/ (sold)	Chargeable gains
		£	£
1.10.16	Freehold depot	18,000	—
12.12.16	Leasehold warehouse	(50,000)	28,000
19.7.16	Business formerly carried on by another (unrelated) company:		
	Goodwill (note (c))	20,000	—
	Freehold factory unit	90,000	—
1.2.18	Land adjacent to main factory, now surplus to requirements	(40,000)	19,000
8.9.18	Industrial mincer (fixed plant)	(30,000)	5,000
1.11.18	Extension to new factory	35,000	—

(i) *The gain on the leasehold warehouse may be rolled over against the following*

	Cost		Gain
	£		£
Freehold depot	18,000	$\frac{18,000}{50,000} \times £28,000$	10,080
Freehold factory (part)	32,000	$\frac{32,000}{50,000} \times £28,000$	17,920
	£50,000		£28,000

(ii) *The gain on the surplus land may then be rolled over as follows*

Freehold factory (part)	£40,000	Gain rolled over	£19,000

(iii) *The gain on the industrial mincer may be rolled over as follows*

Extension to new factory (part)	£30,000	Gain rolled over	£5,000

The position at 31 December 2018 is then as follows

	£
Freehold depot	
Cost	18,000
Deduct gains rolled over	(10,080)
Allowable cost	£7,920
Freehold factory	
Cost	90,000
Deduct gains rolled over (£17,920 + £19,000)	(36,920)
Allowable cost	£53,080
Extension to new factory	
Cost	35,000
Deduct gains rolled over	(5,000)
Allowable cost	£30,000

Notes

(a) The expenditure still available to match against disposal proceeds is

Extension to factory (£35,000 − £30,000)	£5,000

The expenditure is available only against disposals up to 31 October 2019.

(b) There is no statutory rule prescribing the way in which the gain on an asset must be rolled over against a number of different assets. The taxpayer's allocation of the rolled over gain against the cost of the new assets should be accepted by HMRC, providing specified amounts of consideration are positively earmarked and set against the cost of specified new assets (HMRC Capital Gains Manual, CG60770). In (i) the chargeable gain has been rolled over rateably to the costs of the items, but bringing in only part (i.e. the balance of proceeds) of the cost of the freehold factory.

(c) For corporation tax purposes, goodwill acquired from an unrelated party after 31 March 2002 falls within the intangible assets regime at *CTA 2009, ss 701–906* and is *not* a qualifying asset for chargeable gains rollover relief purposes. [*FA 2002, s 84, Sch 29 paras 132(5), 137*].

(B)

L Ltd carries on a vehicle repair business. In December 2003 it sells a workshop for £90,000 net of costs. The workshop had cost £45,000 inclusive in April 1995. A new workshop is purchased for £144,000 (including incidental costs of acquisition) on 11 January 2005 and sold for £168,000 on 14 January 2019.

Indexation factors	April 1995 to December 2003	0.232
	January 2005 to December 2017	0.472

L Ltd claims rollover of the chargeable gain on the disposal of the workshop.

	£
Allowable cost of original workshop	45,000
Indexation allowance £45,000 × 0.232	10,440
	55,440
Actual disposal consideration	90,000
Chargeable gain rolled over	£34,560
Cost of new workshop	144,000
Deduct Amount rolled over	(34,560)
Deemed allowable cost	£109,440
Disposal consideration, replacement workshop	168,000
Allowable cost	(109,440)
Unindexed gain	58,560
Indexation allowance £109,440 × 0.472	(51,656)
Chargeable gain (January 2019)	£6,904

(C)

The facts are as in (B) above except that the business is carried on by M, an individual. The indexation factor for the period April 1995 to April 1998 is 0.091.

	£
Allowable cost of original workshop	45,000
Indexation allowance £45,000 × 0.091	4,095
	49,095
Actual disposal consideration	90,000
Chargeable gain rolled over	£40,905
Cost of new workshop	144,000
Deduct Amount rolled over	(40,905)
Deemed allowable cost	£103,095
Disposal consideration, replacement workshop	168,000
Allowable cost	103,095
Chargeable gain 2018/19	£64,905

226.2 PARTIAL RELIEF

(A) Assets only partly replaced

[*TCGA 1992, s 153*]

G carries on an accountancy practice. In March 2018, he agrees to acquire the practice of another sole practitioner, who is about to retire. As part of the acquisition, G pays £20,000 for goodwill. In January 2019, G moves to new premises, acquiring the remaining 70 years of a 99-year lease for £50,000. The sale of his former office on 25 February 2019 realises £80,000, and a chargeable gain of £59,000 arises.

	£	£
Amount of proceeds of disposal of old office		80,000
Costs against which gains can be rolled over		
Goodwill	20,000	
Lease	50,000	
		(70,000)
Chargeable gain not rolled over		£10,000
Chargeable gain rolled over (£59,000 − £10,000)		£49,000
Allowable cost of assets (see note (a))		
Goodwill	20,000	
Gain rolled over $\frac{20,000}{70,000} \times £49,000$	(14,000)	
		£6,000
Lease	50,000	
Gain rolled over $\frac{50,000}{70,000} \times £49,000$	(35,000)	
		£15,000

Notes

(a) There is no statutory rule prescribing the way in which a gain is to be rolled over against more than one acquisition. See note (b) to **226.1**(A) above.

(b) It would not have been possible to roll over the gain only against the acquisition of the goodwill. The consideration not reinvested (£60,000) would be more than the gain (£59,000).

(B) **Partial business use**

[*TCGA 1992, s 152(7)*]

N carries on a consultancy business from commercial premises formerly used as a shop. N has owned the property since 1 July 1981, but it was let until 1 March 1995 when N moved in, following the expiry of the lease held by the former tenant. On 1 February 2019, N sells the property for £100,000, moving to a new office with a long lease which he acquires for £70,000 and which is wholly used for his business. The value at 31 March 1982 of the property sold was £40,000.

For rollover relief purposes, N is treated as having disposed of two separate assets, one representing his occupation and professional use of the property, the other his ownership of it as an investment. In practice, the proceeds and chargeable gain may be allocated by a simple time apportionment.

Proceeds attributable to business use	
£100,000 × 23y11m/36y10m (note (c))	£64,932
Chargeable gain attributable to business use	
[£100,000 – £40,000] = £60,000 × 23y11m/36y10m	£38,959

Notes

(a) The proceeds attributable to business use are less than the cost of the new office, so that the whole of the chargeable gain attributable to business use can be rolled over. The allowable cost of the new office is then £31,041 (£70,000 – £38,959).

(b) The balance of the chargeable gain, £21,041 (£60,000 – £38,959) is not eligible for rollover.

(c) The time apportionment takes into account only the period of ownership after 30 March 1982. [*TCGA 1992, s 152(9)*].

226.3 WASTING ASSETS

[*TCGA 1992, s 154*]

(A) **Crystallisation of held-over gain**

In March 2014, a father and son partnership carrying on a car dealing trade sold a freehold showroom for £400,000 realising a chargeable gain of £190,000. On 30 June 2014, the firm purchased for £450,000 the remaining term of a lease due to expire on 30 June 2044 and used the premises as a new showroom. The whole of the gain on the old asset was held over under *TCGA 1992, s 154* on the acquisition of the new asset. In consequence of the father's decision to retire from the business and the resulting need to downsize the operation, the firm assigns the lease for £490,000 on 1 July 2018.

The chargeable gains to be apportioned between the two partners for 2018/19 are as follows

	£	£
Proceeds of assignment		490,000
Cost (see note (a))	450,000	
Deduct Wasted $\frac{87.330 - 82.496}{87.330} \times$ £450,000	(24,909)	(425,091)
Chargeable gain 2018/19 (see also note (b))		£64,909
Held-over gain becoming chargeable under *TCGA 1992, s 154(2)(a)*		£190,000

Notes

(a) The gain of £190,000 is deferred as opposed to being rolled over and does not reduce the cost of the new asset.

(b) See also **216.3**(D)–(G) LAND for further examples on the assignment of short leases.

(B) **Rollover of held-over gain**

C Ltd, a manufacturing company, sells an item of fixed plant for £30,000 in February 2014. A chargeable gain of £7,200 arises. In 2016, the company buys storage facilities on a 20-year lease for £40,000. In 2018, an extension to the company's freehold factory is completed at a cost of £25,000.

The position is as follows

(i) The company may claim holdover of the £7,200 chargeable gain in 2014, against the cost of the lease.

(ii) In 2018, part of the chargeable gain can be rolled over against the cost of the factory extension, as follows

	£
Expenditure available for rollover	25,000
Maximum capable of rollover	
£7,200 – (£30,000 – £25,000)	(2,200)
Adjusted base cost of extension	£22,800

Notes

(a) The balance of the chargeable gain, £5,000 (£7,200 - £2,200) may continue to be held over against the cost of the lease, either until it crystallises or until further rollover is possible.

(b) Had the company not claimed holdover against the cost of the lease, a claim against the cost of the extension in 2018 would not have been possible, as the expenditure was incurred outside the normal three-year time limit.

226.4 FURNISHED HOLIDAY LETTINGS

In May 2014, Isobel sells Heene Cottage for £120,000. The cottage had qualified as furnished holiday accommodation throughout Isobel's period of ownership and had originally cost £55,000. The whole proceeds are invested in the acquisition in June 2014 of Croft Cottage at a cost of £150,000 and Isobel claims rollover relief under *TCGA 1992, s 152*. The new property is used as furnished holiday accommodation until June 2018 when it becomes Isobel's only residence. Croft Cottage is sold in June 2020 for £290,000. The chargeable gain on disposal is computed as follows.

Disposal of Heene Cottage

	£	£
Allowable cost		55,000
Actual disposal consideration		120,000
Chargeable gain rolled over		£65,000
Deemed allowable cost of Croft Cottage (£150,000 – £65,000)		£85,000

Disposal of Croft Cottage

Disposal consideration		290,000
Allowable cost		(85,000)
Gain before main residence relief		£205,000
Main residence relief		
Gain before relief	205,000	
Less amount of rolled-over gain	65,000	65,000
Gain eligible for relief	140,000	
Less relief (2/6 × £140,000)	(46,667)	93,333
Chargeable gain 2020/21		£158,333

Notes

(a) Commercial letting of furnished holiday accommodation is treated as a trade for the purposes of rollover relief. [*TCGA 1992, s 241(3), s 241A(4)(5); FA 2011, Sch 14 para 14*].

(b) Where main residence relief is available to any extent on the disposal of an asset and the acquisition cost has been reduced by rollover relief, the gain to which the main residence relief is applied is reduced by the amount of the rolled-over gain. [*TCGA 1992, s 241(6), s 241A(8); FA 2011, Sch 14 para 14*]. For main residence relief generally see **223** PRIVATE RESIDENCES.

(c) See also IT **22.2** PROPERTY INCOME for the rules which determine whether letting qualifies as the commercial letting of furnished holiday accommodation.

227 Seed Enterprise Investment Scheme

227.1 DISPOSAL OF SEIS SHARES MORE THAN THREE YEARS AFTER ISSUE

[*TCGA 1992, s 150E(2)(4)(5); FA 2012, Sch 6 paras 3, 23(1)*]

On 8 November 2018 P subscribes £130,000 for 65,000 shares in the SEIS company, S Ltd, and obtains the maximum SEIS income tax relief of £50,000 (£100,000 × 50%) for 2018/19. On 3 April 2022 he sells the entire holding for £240,000.

The chargeable gain arising is calculated as follows

	£
Disposal proceeds	240,000
Cost	(130,000)
Gain	110,000
Less TCGA 1992, s 150E(2)(4)(5) exemption	
$£110{,}000 \times \frac{50{,}000}{65{,}000}$ (note(b))	(84,615)
Chargeable gain 2021/22	£25,385

Notes

(a) Gains arising on the sale more than three years after issue of shares qualifying for SEIS income tax relief are not chargeable gains unless the SEIS relief is fully withdrawn before disposal.

(b) Where the income tax relief is not given on the full SEIS subscription (otherwise than because of insufficient income), capital gains tax relief is given on a proportion of the gain on the disposal or part disposal.

The gain is reduced by the multiple R/T where

R = the actual income tax reduction and

T = the tax at the SEIS rate (50%) on the amount subscribed for the issue.

R = £100,000 × 50% = £50,000

T = £130,000 × 50% = £65,000

227.2 LOSS ON DISPOSAL OF SEIS SHARES

[*TCGA 1992, s 150E(1)(3); FA 2012, Sch 6 paras 3, 23(1)*]

(A) Disposal more than three years after issue

Assuming the facts otherwise remain the same as in 227.1 above but that the shares are sold for £50,000 on 3 April 2022.

The allowable loss arising is calculated as follows

	£	£
Disposal proceeds		50,000
Less Cost	130,000	
Less Income tax relief given (and not withdrawn)	(50,000)	(80,000)
Allowable loss 2021/22		£(30,000)

Note

(a) Any loss arising is reduced by deducting the amount of the SEIS relief (given and not withdrawn) from the acquisition cost. On the question of income tax withdrawal, see note (b) to (B) below.

(B) Disposal within three years of issue

The facts are otherwise as in (A) above except that the shares are sold in an arm's length bargain on 3 April 2019, i.e. within three years after their issue.

Income tax relief given for 2018/19 is withdrawn as follows

Relief attributable (£100,000 @ 50%)	£50,000 (1)

Consideration

$$£50,000 \times \frac{50,000\ (£100,000\ @\ 50\%)}{65,000\ (£130,000\ @\ 50\%)}\ @\ 50\% \qquad £19,230\ (2)$$

The amount at (1) is greater than that at (2), so income tax relief of £19,230 is withdrawn. [*ITA 2007, ss 257FA, 257FB*].

The relief not withdrawn is therefore £(50,000 − 19,230) =	£30,770

The allowable loss arising is calculated as follows

	£	£
Disposal proceeds		50,000
Less Cost	130,000	
Less Income tax relief not withdrawn	(30,770)	(99,230)
Allowable loss 2018/19		£(49,230)

Notes

(a) For the purposes of computing an allowable loss, the consideration is reduced by the relief attributable to the shares. [*TCGA 1992, s 150E(1); FA 2012, Sch 6 para 3*]. The relief attributable is that remaining following any withdrawal of relief.

(b) A withdrawal of income tax relief arises on a disposal of SEIS shares within three years after their issue. [*ITA 2007, s 257FA; FA 2012, Sch 6 para 1*].

227.3 SEIS REINVESTMENT RELIEF

[*TCGA 1992, s 150G, Sch 5BB; FA 2012, Sch 6 paras 4, 5; FA 2013, s 57; FA 2014, s 55*]

On 1 June 2018, X sells an asset for £365,000. The asset had cost X £240,000 in 2007. X makes no other disposals in 2018/19. On 1 February 2019, X acquires by subscription 50,000 shares in ABC Ltd at a total price of £100,000. X claims SEIS income tax relief in respect of the acquisition.

If X makes a claim for SEIS reinvestment relief under *TCGA 1992, Sch 5BB* then his CGT position for 2018/19 is as follows

	£
Consideration	365,000
Less Acquisition cost	(240,000)
Gain	125,000
Less Reinvestment relief	(50,000)
Chargeable gain	75,000
Less annual exemption	(11,700)
Taxable gain 2018/19	£63,300

Notes

(a) SEIS reinvestment relief can be claimed where:

- an individual realises a chargeable gain on a disposal at any time in 2012/13 or a subsequent tax year (the 'relevant year'); and
- he is eligible for, and claims, SEIS income tax relief for the relevant year in respect of an amount subscribed for an 'issue of shares' in a company made to him (or treated as made to him) in that year.

(b) For 2013/14 onwards, the amount of relief is restricted to 50% of the amount on which SEIS income tax relief is claimed. For 2012/13, relief is available for 100% of that amount, subject to an overall limit of £100,000.

Where SEIS shares are treated as issued in the previous tax year as a result of a SEIS income tax relief carry-back claim under *ITA 2007, s 257AB(5)*, they will thereby qualify to be used in a reinvestment relief claim for the earlier year. (HMRC Capital Gains Manual VCM45010).

(c) A claim for SEIS reinvestment relief in respect of shares issued in 2018/19 must be made no later than 31 January 2025. [*TCGA 1992, Sch 5BB para 3; ITA 2007, s 257EA; FA 2012, Sch 6 paras 1, 5; FA 2013, s 57(2)*].

(d) If SEIS income tax relief attributable to shares is withdrawn, any SEIS reinvestment relief attributable to those shares is also withdrawn. If SEIS income tax relief attributable to shares is reduced, any SEIS reinvestment relief attributable to those shares is reduced in the same proportion. In either case, a chargeable gain is then deemed to accrue to the individual in the relevant year of an amount equal to the amount of reinvestment relief to be withdrawn or the amount by which reinvestment relief falls to be reduced. [*TCGA 1992, Sch 5BB para 5; FA 2012, Sch 6 para 5; FA 2013, s 57(4)*].

228 Settlements

Cross-reference. See **221.1** OFFSHORE SETTLEMENTS as regards capital gains of non-resident settlements.

228.1 ANNUAL EXEMPTIONS AND RATES OF TAX

[*TCGA 1992, ss 3, 4, Sch 1 paras A1, 2*]

The trustees of the E settlement, created in 1974, realise net chargeable gains and allowable losses as follows:

	Chargeable gain/ (allowable loss)
	£
2014/15	(2,250)
2015/16	3,100
2016/17	5,600
2017/18	3,200
2018/19	12,550

The trustees' capital gains tax liability is computed as follows

	£
2014/15	
Taxable amount	Nil
Losses carried forward	£2,250
2015/16	
Net chargeable gains	3,100
Losses brought forward	—
Taxable amount (covered by annual exemption of £5,550)	£(3,100)
CGT	Nil
Losses carried forward	£2,250
2016/17	
Net chargeable gains	5,600
Losses brought forward	(50)
Taxable amount (covered by annual exemption)	£5,550
CGT	Nil
Losses carried forward (£2,250 − £50)	£2,200

2017/18	
Net chargeable gains	3,200
Losses brought forward	—
Taxable amount (covered by annual exemption of £5,650)	£3,200
CGT	Nil
Losses carried forward	£2,200
2018/19	
Net chargeable gains	12,550
Losses brought forward	(2,200)
Chargeable gains	10,350
Deduct Annual exemption	(5,850)
Taxable gains	£4,500
CGT at 20% on £4,500	£900
Losses carried forward	Nil

Notes

(a) For 2016/17 onwards the rate of capital gains tax accruing to the trustees of any settlement is 20%, unless either the gains are upper rate gains (in which case the rate is 28%) or entrepreneurs' relief applies (in which case the rate is 10%). For previous years, the rate is 28%, or 10% where entrepreneurs' relief applies. [*TCGA 1992, s 4(3); FA 2016, s 83(5)(*]. For the meaning of 'upper rate gains' see **201.1**(C) ANNUAL RATES AND EXEMPTIONS.

(b) See *TCGA 1992, Sch 1 para 2(4)–(6)* for the annual exemption available to two or more settlements made by the same settlor after 6 June 1978.

228.2 TRUSTS WITH VULNERABLE BENEFICIARY

[*FA 2005, ss 23–45, Schs 1, 1A; FA 2013, Sch 44 paras 14–19; FA 2014, s 291*]

Harry was born in 2006. In June 2013 both of his parents are killed in a road accident. Neither parent has made a will, so that a statutory trust is established for Harry under the intestacy rules of *Administration of Estates Act 1925, ss 46, 47(1)*. The trustees and Harry's guardian make a vulnerable person election (by 31 January 2017) to take effect on 6 April 2014. On 16 May 2018, the trustees sell an asset, realising a chargeable gain of £20,000. The trustees (who are resident in the UK throughout) make no other disposals in 2018/19. Harry is resident in the UK throughout the tax year and has no personal chargeable gains. His taxable income for 2018/19 is lower than the amount of the personal allowance.

If the trustees make a claim for special tax treatment under *FA 2005, s 24* for 2018/19, their capital gains tax liability is calculated as follows.

	£
Gain	20,000
Annual exemption	(5,850)
Taxable gain 2018/19	£14,150
CGT £14,150 × 20%	2,830
Less reduction under *FA 2005, s 31*	(2000.00)
CGT payable by trustees	£830.00

The reduction under *FA 2005, s 31* is equal to:

TQTG – (TLVA – TLVB)

where

TQTG = the amount of capital gains tax to which the trustees would, apart from these provisions, be liable for the tax year in respect of qualifying trust gains;

TLVB = the total amount of capital gains tax to which the vulnerable person is liable for the tax year; and

TLVA = what TLVB would be if the qualifying trust gains accrued to the vulnerable person instead of the trustees, and no allowable losses were deducted from them.

In this case, TQTG = £2,830 (as above), TLVB is nil, and TLVA is calculated as follows.

	£
Gain	20,000
Annual exemption	(11,700)
Taxable gain	£8,300
CGT £8,300 × 10% (TLVA)	£830.00
The reduction is therefore £2,830 – (£830 – Nil) =	£2000.00

Notes

(a) The trustees are effectively able to make use of the beneficiary's annual exemption and, where applicable, lower rate of tax.

(b) A claim for special tax treatment applies to both income tax and capital gains tax. No separate claim can be made in respect of each tax.

(c) Where the vulnerable beneficiary is not UK resident, see *FA 2005, ss 32, 33, Sch 1.*

228.3 CREATION OF A SETTLEMENT

[*TCGA 1992, s 70*]

(A)

In December 2018, C transfers to trustees of a settlement for the benefit of his disabled daughter 10,000 shares in W plc, a quoted company. The value of the gift is £85,000. C bought the shares in 1981 for £20,000 and their value at 31 March 1982 was £35,000.

	£
Deemed disposal consideration	85,000
Market value 31.3.82	(35,000)
Chargeable gain	£50,000
Trustees' allowable cost	£85,000

Note

(a) If the transfer had been a chargeable lifetime transfer for inheritance tax purposes, or would be one but for the annual inheritance tax exemption and the settlement is not settlor-interested within *TCGA 1992, ss 169B–169G*, C could have elected under *TCGA 1992, s 260* to roll the gain over against the trustees' base cost of the shares. The trustees do not join in any such election.

(B)

In late April 2018 H settles farmland on trust for himself for life, with interests in reversion to his children. The land cost £20,000 in 1975 and its agreed values are £60,000 at 31 March 1982 and £125,000 at the date of settlement. H's interest in possession in the settled property is valued at £90,000.

The chargeable gain is computed as follows

	£
Deemed disposal proceeds	125,000
Market value 31.3.82	(60,000)
Chargeable gain 2018/19	£65,000

Notes

(a) The value of H's interest in the settled property is ignored and the transfer is not treated as a part disposal.

(b) As the settlement is settlor-interested, H cannot claim hold-over relief under *TCGA 1992, s 260* even though the transfer of the land into settlement is a chargeable lifetime transfer. See note (a) to (A) above.

228.4 PERSON BECOMING ABSOLUTELY ENTITLED TO SETTLED PROPERTY

[*TCGA 1992, s 71*]

(A)

M is a beneficiary entitled to an interest in possession in settled property, under a settlement made by her mother. The trustees exercise a power of appointment to advance capital to M, and, in September 2018, transfer to her a house valued at £80,000. The house was acquired by the trustees by gift from the settlor in 2003, when its value was £45,000.

The trustees realise a gain of £35,000 (£80,000 - £45,000) on the advancement of capital to M.

Note

(a) If, while it was settled property, the house had been occupied by M as her private residence with the permission of the trustees, then all or part of the gain would qualify for the private residence exemption under *TCGA 1992, s 225.*

(B) Transfer of settlement losses

[*TCGA 1992, s 71(2)–(2D)*]

F is the sole remaining beneficiary of an accumulation and maintenance settlement established under his late uncle's will and in which he became entitled to an interest in possession upon reaching the age of 18 in 1996. On 18 September 2003, his 25th birthday, he becomes absolutely entitled as against the trustees to the capital of the trust. At that date, the trust capital consists of the following

- cash of £12,000,
- 10,000 shares in ABC Ltd (purchased for £6,000 in May 2002 and currently valued at £11,000), and
- 15,000 shares in DEF Ltd (transferred into the trust at a CGT value of £27,000 but now valued at only £13,000).

On 30 June 2003, the trustees had sold shares in GHK Ltd at a gain of £3,000 (after deducting indexation allowance to April 1998). On 7 July 2003, they sold shares in LMN Ltd at a loss of £500. None of the above-mentioned trust investments were business assets for taper relief purposes. At 6 April 2003, the trustees had allowable capital losses of £1,000 brought forward from earlier years.

In December 2003, F sells the ABC Ltd shares for £11,600. He also disposes of other assets in 2003/04 realising chargeable gains of £9,400 (with no taper relief due). In 2018/19, he sells the DEF Ltd shares for £15,700 and also disposes of other assets realising chargeable gains of £19,000 and allowable losses of £1,500.

F takes over entitlement to trust losses as follows

	£	£
Loss on DEF Ltd shares transferred to F £(27,000 − 13,000)		14,000
Deduct Trustees' 'pre-entitlement gains'*:		
(i) gain on ABC Ltd shares transferred to F	5,000	
(ii) other gains in period 6.4.03–18.9.03	3,000	(8,000)
Loss treated as accruing to F (note (a))		£6,000

* See *TCGA 1992, s 71(2A)*

F's CGT position for 2003/04 and 2018/19 is as follows

2003/04

	£
Gain on sale of ABC Ltd shares £(11,600 − 11,000)	600
Other gains	9,400
	10,000
Deduct Annual exemption	(7,900)
Gains chargeable to tax 2003/04	£2,100
Ex-trust losses carried forward	£6,000

2018/19

	£	£
Gain on sale of DEF Ltd shares £(15,700 − 13,000)	2,700	
Deduct Ex-trust losses brought forward and treated as a loss for the year	(2,700)	—
Other gains	19,000	
Deduct Losses for the year	(1,500)	17,500
		17,500
Deduct Annual exemption		(11,700)
Gains chargeable to tax		£5,800

	£
Ex-trust losses brought forward	6,000
Utilised in 2018/19	(2,700)
Unused balance (note (b))	£3,300

Notes

(a) Trust losses of £1,000 brought forward and £500 accruing in 2003/04 cannot be transferred to F and in this case are wasted. The 'pre-entitlement gains' cannot be reduced by those losses before being set against the loss on DEF Ltd shares.

(b) In F's hands, the loss can only be set against a gain on the DEF Ltd shares on which it arose. As all those shares are sold in 2018/19, the loss cannot be carried forward any further and the unused balance of £3,300 is written off.

228.5 TERMINATION OF INTEREST IN POSSESSION ON DEATH

[*TCGA 1992, s 72; FA 2006, Sch 12 para 30(2)*]

(A)

K is entitled to an interest in possession under a settlement. The settled property consists of shares and cash. On K's death, L is entitled to a life interest in succession to K. K dies on 1 December 2018, when the shares are valued at £200,000. The trustees' allowable cost in respect of the shares is £40,000.

On K's death, the trustees are deemed to have disposed of and immediately reacquired the shares for £200,000, thus uplifting the CGT base cost, but no chargeable gain then arises.

Note

(a) Where the deceased became entitled to the interest in possession on or after 22 March 2006, the above treatment applies only if

(i) the deceased died under the age of 18 and, immediately before his death, *IHTA 1984, s 71D* (age 18 to 25 trusts) applies to the property in which the interest subsists; or

(ii) immediately before his death,

(a) the interest in possession is an immediate post-death interest within *IHTA 1984, s 49A*;

(b) the interest is a transitional serial interest within *IHTA 1984, s 49C*;

(c) the interest is a disabled person's interest within *IHTA 1984, s 89B(1)(c)(d)*; or

(d) *IHTA 1984, s 71A* (trusts for bereaved minors) applies to the property in which the interest subsists.

[*TCGA 1992, s 72(1)–(1C)*].

(B)

In 1976, E created a settlement for the benefit of his children M and N and his grandchildren, transferring an investment property valued at £10,000 to the trustees. The terms of the settlement were that M and N each have a life interest in half of the trust income, with the remainder passing to E's grandchildren. In 1990, N assigned his interest to P, an unrelated party, for £35,000, its then market value. In 2018, N dies. The value of a half share of the trust property is then £65,000.

On N's death, his life interest terminates. There is no effect on the trustees as N was no longer the person entitled to the life interest within the meaning of *TCGA 1992, s 72*.

Notes

(a) No chargeable gain arises on the disposal by N of his interest. [*TCGA 1992, s 76*].

(b) P may claim an allowable loss on extinction of the interest. For an example of the computation if the interest is a wasting asset, see **232.3** WASTING ASSETS.

229 Shares and Securities

Cross-references. See also **204** ASSETS HELD ON **6** APRIL **1965**, **205** ASSETS HELD ON **31** MARCH **1982**, **214** INDEXATION, **224** QUALIFYING CORPORATE BONDS and **230** SHARES AND SECURITIES — IDENTIFICATION RULES.

229.1 REORGANISATION OF SHARE CAPITAL — VALUATION OF DIFFERENT CLASSES OF SHARE ON SUBSEQUENT DISPOSAL

[*TCGA 1992, ss 126–131*]

(A) Unquoted shares

V acquired 10,000 ordinary shares in X Ltd, an unquoted trading company, in April 1999 at a cost of £15,000. In April 2007, as part of a reorganisation of share capital, V was additionally allotted 3,000 new 9% preference shares in X Ltd for which he paid £3,900. In June 2018, V sold his ordinary shareholding, in an arm's length transaction, for £20,000, but retained his preference shares, then valued at £4,000.

The chargeable gain on the disposal of the ordinary shares is calculated as follows

	£
Disposal consideration	20,000
Cost (£15,000 + £3,900) × $\frac{20,000}{20,000 + 4,000}$	(15,750)
Chargeable gain 2018/19	£4,250
Allowable cost of 3,000 preference shares (£15,000 + £3,900 − £15,750)	£3,150

Note

(a) The ordinary shares and preference shares held after the reorganisation (the 'new holding') constitute a single asset. [*TCGA 1992, s 127*]. A disposal of part of the new holding is thus a part disposal. If neither class of shares comprising the new holding is quoted on a recognised stock exchange at any time not later than three months after the reorganisation, acquisition cost on a part disposal is apportioned by reference to market values at the date of disposal. [*TCGA 1992, s 129*].

(B) Quoted shares

Assume the facts to be as in (A) above except that both the ordinary and preference shares are quoted on a recognised stock exchange. On the first day of dealing after the reorganisation took effect, the ordinary shares were quoted at £1.85 and the preference shares at £1.35. V's holdings were therefore valued at £18,500 and £4,050 respectively.

The chargeable gain on the disposal of the ordinary shares is calculated as follows

	£
Disposal consideration	20,000
Cost $(£15,000 + £3,900) \times \frac{18,500}{18,500 + 4,050}$	(15,506)
Chargeable gain 2018/19	£4,494
Allowable cost of 3,000 preference shares (£15,000 + £3,900 − £15,506)	£3,394

Note

(a) Where one or more of the classes of shares or debentures comprising the new holding is quoted on a recognised stock exchange at any time not later than three months after the reorganisation, acquisition cost on a part disposal is apportioned by reference to market values on the first day of dealing on which the prices quoted reflect the reorganisation. [*TCGA 1992, s 130*].

(C) Quoted shares — reorganisation after 31 March 1982, original holding acquired on or before that date

In 1980, W subscribed for 5,000 £1 ordinary shares at par in L plc, a quoted company. The value of his holding at 31 March 1982 was £8,000. In November 1990, L plc offered ordinary shareholders two 7% preference shares at £1 per share in respect of each five ordinary shares held. W took up his entitlement of 2,000 preference shares. On the first day of dealing after the reorganisation, the ordinary shares were quoted at £3.00 (making W's holding worth £15,000) and the preference shares at £1.02 (valuing W's holding at £2,040). In June 2018, W sells his preference shares on the market at £2.40 (total proceeds £2,800). (For simplicity, costs of acquisition and disposal are ignored in this example.)

The gain on the disposal of the preference shares is computed as follows

	£
Disposal consideration	4,800
(31.3.82 value £8,000 + cost £2,000) $\times \frac{2,040}{2,040 + 15,000}$	(1,197)
Chargeable gain 2018/19	£3,603

Note

(a) On a subsequent disposal of the ordinary shares, their cost would be £8,803 (£8,000 + £2,000 - £1,197).

229.2 BONUS ISSUES

[*TCGA 1992, ss 126–128, 130*]

(A) Bonus of same class

In October 2005, Y plc made a scrip issue of one ordinary share for every 10 held. L held 5,000 ordinary shares, which he acquired in May 1997 for £5,500, and therefore received 500 shares in the bonus issue. In October 2018, L sells 3,000 of his shares for £10,000.

Section 104 **holding**	Shares	Qualifying expenditure
		£
May 1997 acquisition	5,000	5,500
October 2005 bonus issue	500	—
	5,500	5,500
October 2018 disposal	(3,000)	(3,000)
Pool carried forward	2,500	£2,500

Calculation of chargeable gain	£
Disposal consideration	10,000
Allowable cost $\frac{3{,}000}{5{,}500} \times £5{,}500$	(3,000)
Chargeable gain 2018/19	£7,000

(B) Bonus of different class

On 6 April 1995, R bought 2,000 'A' shares in T plc for £3,800. In June 2000, R bought a further 500 'A' shares for £800. In October 2004 T plc made a bonus issue of 2 'B' shares for each 5 'A' shares held, and R received 1,000 'B' shares, valued at £1.20 each (total value £1,200) on the first dealing day after the issue. On the same day, the 'A' shares were quoted at £2 each (total value £5,000). In December 2018 R sells his 1,000 'B' shares for £4,000.

Section 104 **holding — 'A' shares**	Shares	Qualifying expenditure
		£
April 1995 acquisition	2,000	3,800
June 2000 acquisition	500	800
	2,500	4,600
October 2004 bonus issue of 'B' shares: transfer proportion of expenditure to 'B' shares (see note (a))		(890)
Pool of 'A' shares carried forward	2,500	£3,710

Section 104 **holding — 'A' shares**	Shares	Qualifying expenditure £
Section 104 **holding — 'B' shares**		
October 2004 bonus issue: proportion of pool		
transferred from 'A' shares holding	1,000	890
December 2018 disposal	(1,000)	(890)
	—	—

Calculation of chargeable gain on disposal of 'B' shares	£
Disposal consideration	4,000
Allowable cost (as allocated)	(890)
Chargeable gain 2018/19	£3,110

Notes

(a) The cost of the 'A' shares is apportioned between 'A' and 'B' shares by reference to market values on the first day of dealing after the reorganisation.

Proportion of qualifying expenditure $£4,600 \times \frac{1,200}{1,200 + 5,000}$ £890

(HMRC Capital Gains Manual CG51965 onwards.).

(b) A different basis of apportionment applies to unquoted shares (see HMRC Capital Gains Manual CG51919 onwards.).

229.3 RIGHTS ISSUES

[*TCGA 1992, s 42, s 123(1), s 128(4)*]

Cross-reference.
See **229.8(B)** below as regards sale of rights.

(A) Rights issue of same class

W plc is a quoted company which in June 2008 made a rights issue of one £1 ordinary share for every eight £1 ordinary shares held, at £1.35 payable on allotment. V, who held 16,000 £1 ordinary shares purchased in May 2000 for £15,000, took up his entitlement in full, and was allotted 2,000 shares. In December 2018, he sells 6,000 of his shares for £30,000.

'Section 104' **holding**	Shares	Qualifying expenditure
		£
May 2000 acquisition	16,000	15,000
June 2008 rights issue	2,000	2,700
	18,000	17,700
December 2018 disposal	(6,000)	(5,900)
Pool carried forward	12,000	£11,800

Calculation of chargeable gain	£
Disposal consideration	30,000
Allowable cost $\frac{6,000}{18,000} \times £17,700$	(5,900)
Chargeable gain 2018/19	£24,100

(B) **Rights issue of different class**

On 1 March 1998, A acquired 6,000 quoted £1 ordinary shares in S plc at a cost of £7,800. In October 2001, S plc made a rights issue of one 50p 'B' share for every five £1 ordinary shares held, at 60p payable in full on application. A took up his entitlement in full, acquiring 1,200 'B' shares. On the first dealing day after issue, the 'B' shares were quoted at 65p and the £1 ordinary shares at £1.50. A sells his 'B' shares in December 2018 for £20,000.

'Section 104' **holding — ordinary shares**	Shares	Qualifying expenditure
		£
March 1998 acquisition	6,000	7,800
October 2001 rights issue of 'B' shares	—	720
	6,000	8,520
Transfer proportion of expenditure to 'B' shares (note (a))		(680)
Pool carried forward	6,000	7,840

'Section 104' **holding — 'B' shares**	Shares	Qualifying expenditure
		£
October 2001 rights issue: proportion of pool transferred from ordinary shares holding	1,200	680
December 2018 disposal	(1,200)	(680)
Pool carried forward	—	—

Calculation of chargeable gain on disposal of 'B' shares	£
Disposal consideration	20,000
Allowable cost (as allocated)	(680)
Chargeable gain 2018/19	£19,320

Notes

(a) The cost of the original shares is apportioned between the original shares and the 'B' shares by reference to market values on the first day of dealing after the reorganisation.

Proportion of qualifying expenditure

$$£8,520 \times \frac{1,200 \times 0.65}{(1,200 \times 0.65) + (6,000 \times 1.50)} \qquad £680$$

(HMRC Capital Gains Manual CG51965 et seq.).

(b) A different basis of apportionment applies to unquoted shares (see HMRC Capital Gains Manual CG51919 et seq.).

(C) **Rights issue of same class: disposal out of *section 104* holding and 1982 holding**

G Ltd has purchased 100,000 25p ordinary shares in C plc as follows

Date	Number of shares acquired	Cost £
22.5.80	20,000	0.78
5.11.83	15,000	1.10
14.9.84	40,000	1.00
30.4.02	25,000	2.30

In May 1992, C made a rights issue of one ordinary share for every five held, at £1.50 payable in full on application. G took up its rights in full (15,000 ordinary shares). It sells 105,000 shares in August 2018 for £4.50 per share. The shares were quoted at 90p on 31 March 1982. Incidental costs of acquisition and disposal are disregarded for the purposes of this example.

Indexation factors	March 1982 to December 2017	2.501
	November 1983 to April 1985	0.094
	September 1984 to April 1985	0.052
	April 1985 to May 1992	0.470
	May 1992 to April 2002	0.261
	May 1992 to December 2017	0.996
	April 2002 to December 2017	0.583

Section 104 **holding**	Shares	Qualifying expenditure	In-dexed pool
		£	£
5.11.83 acquisition	15,000	16,500	16,500
Indexed rise: November 1983 to April 1985			
£16,500 × 0.094			1,551
14.9.84 acquisition	40,000	40,000	40,000
Indexed rise: September 1984 to April 1985			
£40,000 × 0.052			2,080
Pool at 6.4.85	55,000	56,500	60,131
Indexed rise: April 1985 to May 1992			
£60,131 × 0.470			28,262
May 1992 rights issue	11,000	16,500	16,500
	66,000	73,000	104,893
Indexed rise: May 1992 to April 2002			
£104,893 × 0.261			27,377
30.4.02 acquisition	25,000	57,500	57,500
	91,000	130,500	189,770
Indexed rise: April 2002 to December 2017			
£189,770 × 0.583			110,636
	91,000	130,500	300,406
August 2018 disposal	(91,000)	(130,500)	(300,406)
	—	—	—

1982 holding	Shares	Cost	Market value 31.3.82
		£	£
22.5.80 acquisition	20,000	15,600	18,000
May 1992 rights issue (note (a))	4,000	6,000	6,000
	24,000	21,600	24,000
August 2018 disposal	(14,000)	(12,600)	(14,000)
Pool carried forward	10,000	£9,000	£10,000

Calculation of chargeable gain

	£
(i) Identify 91,000 shares sold with *section 104* holding	
Disposal consideration 91,000 × £4.50	409,500
Allowable cost	(130,500)
Unindexed gain	279,000
Indexation allowance £300,406 − £130,500	(169,906)
Chargeable gain	£109,094

(ii) Identify 14,000 shares with 1982 holding

Without re-basing to 1982

	£
Disposal consideration 14,000 × £4.50	63,000
Cost $\frac{14,000}{24,000} \times £21,600$	(12,600)
Unindexed gain	50,400
Indexation allowance (see below)	(29,746)
Gain after indexation	£20,654

With re-basing to 1982

		£
Disposal consideration		63,000
Allowable expenditure $\frac{14,000}{24,000} \times £24,000$		(14,000)
Unindexed gain		49,000
Indexation allowance	£	
$£14,000 \times \frac{18,000}{24,000} \times 2.501$	26,260	
$£14,000 \times \frac{6,000}{24,000} \times 0.996$	3,486	
		(29,746)
Gain after indexation		£19,263
Chargeable gain		£19,254
Total chargeable gain £109,094 + £19,254		£128,348

Notes

(a) The 1982 holding cannot be increased by an 'acquisition', but can be increased by a rights issue as this is not treated as involving an acquisition. [*TCGA 1992, s 109(2), ss 127, 128*].

(b) See **230** SHARES AND SECURITIES — IDENTIFICATION RULES for further examples of the identification rules and the different rules applicable for capital gains tax purposes.

(c) Indexation allowance is frozen at its December 2017 level. No indexation allowance is available in respect of expenditure incurred after 31 December 2017, and for expenditure incurred on or before that date and falling to be deducted on a disposal after that date, indexation allowance is computed up to and including December 2017 only. [*TCGA 1992, ss 53(1)(1B), 54(1B); FA 2018, s 26(2)(3)(6)*].See **214.1** INDEXATION.

229.4 EXCHANGE OF SECURITIES FOR THOSE IN ANOTHER COMPANY

[*TCGA 1992, ss 135, 137, 138*]

(A) Takeover by quoted company

S was a shareholder in N Ltd, an unquoted company. He subscribed for his 20,000 50p ordinary shares at 60p per share in 1979 and the shares were valued at £3 each at 31 March 1982. In July 1987, the shareholders accepted an offer by a public company, M plc, for their shares. Each ordinary shareholder received one £1 ordinary M plc share plus 45p cash for every two N Ltd shares held. S acquired 10,000 M plc shares and received cash of £4,500. The M plc shares were valued at £7.50 each at the time of the acquisition. On 25 April 2018, S sells 4,000 of his 10,000 M plc shares for £84,000. The indexation factor for March 1982 to July 1987 is 0.281.

(i) *On the merger in 1987/88, S makes a disposal only to the extent that he receives cash*

	£
Disposal consideration	4,500
Allowable cost $\dfrac{4{,}500}{4{,}500 + (10{,}000 \times £7.50 = £75{,}000)} \times £12{,}000$	(679)
Unindexed gain	3,821
Indexation allowance £679 × 0.281	(191)
Chargeable gain 1987/88	£3,630

Note

(a) The fraction applied to allowable cost corresponds to 5.66%. If the percentage had not exceeded 5% the cash distribution of £4,500 would have been regarded as 'small' and could have been deducted from allowable cost (HMRC Capital Gains Manual CG52587, 57836). [*TCGA 1992, s 122*]. No gain would then have arisen in 1987/88, but the allowable cost would have been reduced by £4,500. See also **229.8(B)** below. (A distribution made after 23 February 1997 can additionally be regarded as 'small' if it does not exceed £3,000 — HMRC Capital Gains Manual CG57836.)

(ii) *The chargeable gain on disposal in 2018/19 is*

		£
Disposal consideration		84,000
Market value 31.3.82		
$£(20{,}000 \times £3) \times \dfrac{75{,}000}{75{,}000 + 4{,}500} \times \dfrac{4{,}000}{10{,}000}$	(note (b))	(22,642)
Chargeable gain 2018/19		£61,358

Notes

(a) The M plc shares are regarded as the same asset as the original N Ltd shares. [*TCGA 1992, ss 127, 135*]. Re-basing to 31 March 1982 thus applies, as the original shares were held on that date.

(b) Where there has been a part disposal after 31 March 1982 and before 6 April 1988 of an asset held on the earlier of those dates, and this is followed by a disposal after 5 April 1988 to which re-basing applies, the re-basing rules are deemed to have applied to the part disposal. [*TCGA 1992, Sch 3 para 4(1)*].

(B) Takeover by unquoted company

Y Ltd, a small unquoted company, is taken over in June 2008 by another unquoted company, C Ltd. The terms of the acquisition are that holders of £1 ordinary shares in Y Ltd receive two £1 ordinary shares and one £1 deferred share in C Ltd in exchange for every two ordinary shares held.

B acquired his holding of 500 Y Ltd shares on the death of his wife in May 1994, at probate value of £10,000. In May 2018, B sells his 250 C Ltd deferred shares for £4,500. The value of his 500 C Ltd ordinary shares is then £25,000.

There is no CGT disposal in 2008/09. The chargeable gain on the 2018/19 disposal is calculated as follows

	£
Disposal consideration	4,500
Allowable cost $\dfrac{4{,}500}{4{,}500 + 25{,}000} \times £10{,}000$	(1,525)
Chargeable gain 2018/19	£2,975
The allowable cost carried forward of the 500 C Ltd ordinary shares is (£10,000 − £1,525)	£8,475

(C) **Earn-outs**

K owns 10,000 ordinary shares in M Ltd, which he acquired for £12,000 in December 2007. In July 2017, the whole of the issued share capital of M Ltd was acquired by P plc. Under the terms of the takeover, K receives £2 per share plus the right to further consideration up to a maximum of £1.50 per share depending on future profit performance. The initial consideration is receivable in cash, but the deferred consideration is to be satisfied by the issue of shares in P plc. In December 2018, K duly receives 2,000 ordinary shares valued at £6 per share in full settlement of his entitlement. The right to future consideration is valued at £1.40 per share in July 2017.

If K elects to disapply *TCGA 1992, s 138A* the position would be

2017/18

	£	£
Disposal proceeds 10,000 × £2	20,000	
Value of rights 10,000 × £1.40	14,000	34,000
Cost		(12,000)
Chargeable gain 2017/18		£22,000

2018/19

	£
Disposal of rights to deferred consideration:	
Proceeds — 2,000 P plc shares @ £6	12,000
Deemed cost of acquiring rights	(14,000)
Allowable loss 2018/19	£(2,000)
Cost for CGT purposes of 2,000 P plc shares	£12,000

Without an election, the position would be

2017/18

	£
Proceeds (cash) (as above)	20,000
Cost $£12,000 \times \dfrac{20,000}{20,000 + 14,000}$	(7,059)
Chargeable gain 2017/18	£12,941
Cost of earn-out right for CGT purposes (£12,000 − £7,059)	£4,941

2018/19

The shares in P plc stand in the place of the right to deferred consideration and will be regarded as having been acquired in December 2007 for £4,941. No further gain or loss arises until a disposal of the shares takes place.

Notes

(a) Under *TCGA 1992, s 138A* the right to deferred consideration (the 'earn-out right') is treated as a security within *TCGA 1992, s 132*. The gain on the original shares (to the extent that it does not derive from cash consideration) can then be held over against the value of the new shares. This treatment is automatic where the conditions are satisfied, subject to the right to elect for such treatment not to apply.

(b) Various conditions must be satisfied for *section 138A* treatment to apply. In particular, the value or quantity of the securities to be received as deferred consideration must be 'unascertainable' (as defined). Any right to receive cash and/or an ascertainable amount of securities as part of the deferred consideration does not fall within these provisions and must be distinguished from the earn-out right, though this does not prevent these provisions from applying to the earn-out right.

(c) See **206.2** CAPITAL SUMS DERIVED FROM ASSETS above for deferred consideration generally.

229.5 SCHEMES OF RECONSTRUCTION

[*TCGA 1992, s 136; FA 2002, s 45, Sch 9 paras 2, 7*]

N Ltd carried on a manufacturing and wholesaling business. In 2010, it was decided that the wholesaling business should be carried on by a separate company. HMRC clearance under *TCGA 1992, s 138* was obtained, and a company, R Ltd, was formed which, in consideration for the transfer to it by N Ltd of the latter's wholesaling undertaking, issued shares to the shareholders of N Ltd. Each holder of ordinary shares in N Ltd additionally received one ordinary share in R Ltd for each N Ltd share he held. W, who purchased his 2,500 N shares for £10,000 in December 1993, received 2,500 R shares. None of the shares involved is quoted. In August 2018, W sells 1,500 of his N shares for £6 each, a total of £9,000, agreed to be their market value. The value of W's remaining 1,000 N shares is also £6 per share, and the value of his R shares is £4.50 per share.

	£
Disposal consideration	9,000
Allowable cost $£10,000 \times \dfrac{9,000}{9,000 + (1,000 \times £6) + (2,500 \times £4.50)}$	(3,429)
Chargeable gain 2018/19	£5,571

229.6 CONVERSION OF SECURITIES

[*TCGA 1992, s 132*]

N bought £10,000 8% convertible loan stock in S plc, a quoted company, in June 2006. The cost was £9,800. In August 2013, N exercised his right to convert the loan stock into 'B' ordinary shares of the company, on the basis of 50 shares for £100 loan stock, and acquired 5,000 shares. In June 2018, N sells 3,000 of the shares for £5.00 each.

		£
Disposal consideration		15,000
	Cost $\frac{3,000}{5,000} \times £9,800$	(5,880)
Chargeable gain 2018/19		£9,120

Notes

(a) The shares acquired on the conversion in 2013 stand in the shoes of the original loan stock. [*TCGA 1992, s 132*].

(b) The loan stock cannot be a corporate bond (and thus cannot be a qualifying corporate bond) as it is convertible into securities other than corporate bonds, i.e. into ordinary shares. [*TCGA 1992, s 117(1)*].

229.7 SCRIP DIVIDENDS

[*TCGA 1992, ss 141, 142; ICTA 1988, ss 249, 251(2)–(4)*]

D holds ordinary 20p shares in PLC, a quoted company. The company operates a scrip dividend (also known as a stock dividend) policy whereby shareholders are given the option to take dividends in cash or in new fully-paid ordinary 20p shares, the option being exercisable separately in relation to each dividend. D purchased 2,000 shares for £1,500 in March 1980 and a further 3,000 shares for £8,100 in May 1992 and up until the end of 1997 he has always taken cash dividends. In July 1998, he opts for a scrip dividend and receives 25 shares instead of a cash dividend of £100. On 20 April 2000, he purchases a further 1,000 shares for £3,950. He opts for cash dividends until, in July 2008, he opts for a scrip dividend of 44 shares instead of a cash dividend of £180. He opts for cash dividends thereafter. In May 2017, he sells 2,069 shares for £8,550 (ex div), leaving himself with a holding of 4,000.

In the case of both scrip dividends taken by D, the market value of the new shares is equivalent to the cash dividend forgone. The 'appropriate amount in cash' (see *TCGA 1992, s 142*) is thus the amount of that dividend. [*ICTA 1988, s 251(2)*]. The market value at 31 March 1982 of 20p shares in PLC is 80p.

The gain on the disposal in May 2018 is calculated as follows

The '*section 104* holding' is as follows.

	Shares	Qualifying expenditure
		£
March 1980 acquisition	2,000	1,600
May 1992 acquisition	3,000	8,100
July 1998 scrip dividend	25	100
April 2000 acquisition	1,000	3,950
July 2008 scrip dividend	44	180
	6,069	13,930
May 2018 disposal	(2,069)	(4,749)

	Shares	Qualifying expenditure
		£
Pool carried forward	4,000	9,181

Proceeds	8,550
Costs £13,930 × 2,069/6,069	(4,749)
Chargeable gain 2018/19	£3,801

Notes

(a) Scrip dividends after 5 April 1998 are treated as free-standing acquisitions. Previously, a scrip dividend received by an individual was treated as a reorganisation within *TCGA 1992, s 128* so that the new shares equated with those already held.

(b) See also **230.1** and **230.2** SHARES AND SECURITIES — IDENTIFICATION RULES.

229.8 CAPITAL DISTRIBUTIONS

(A)

[*TCGA 1992, s 122*]

T holds 10,000 ordinary shares in a foreign company M SA. The shares were bought in April 1996 for £80,000. In February 2019, M SA has a capital reconstruction involving the cancellation of one-fifth of the existing ordinary shares in consideration of the repayment of £10 to each shareholder per share cancelled. T's holding is reduced to 8,000 shares, valued at £96,000.

	£
Disposal consideration (2,000 × £10)	20,000
Allowable cost $\frac{20{,}000}{20{,}000 + 96{,}000} \times £80{,}000$	(13,793)
Chargeable gain 2018/19	£6,207
The allowable cost of the remaining shares is £80,000 − £13,793	£66,207

(B) Sale of rights

[*TCGA 1992, ss 122, 123*]

X is a shareholder in K Ltd, owning 2,500 £1 ordinary shares which were purchased for £7,000 in October 1996. K Ltd makes a rights issue, but X sells his rights, without taking them up, for £700 in August 2018. The ex-rights value of X's 2,500 shares at the date of sale was £14,500.

'*Section 104* holding' of K £1 ordinary shares	Shares	Qualifying expenditure
October 1996 acquisition	2,500	£7,000

HMRC cannot require the capital distribution to be treated as a disposal, as the £700 received for the rights does not exceed 5% of (£700 + £14,500) and in any case does not exceed £3,000 (see HMRC Capital Gains Manual CG57836). [*TCGA 1992, s 122(2)*]. If the transaction is not treated as a disposal, the £700 is deducted from the acquisition cost of the shares, leaving a balance of £6,300. If the transaction is treated as a disposal (possibly because X wishes to utilise part of his annual exemption), the computation is as follows.

	£
Disposal proceeds	700
Allowable cost $\frac{700}{700 + 14{,}500} \times £7{,}000$	(322)
Chargeable gain 2018/19	£378

The allowable cost of the shares is then reduced to £6,678 (£7,000 – £322).

230 Shares and Securities — Identification Rules

Cross-reference. See **229** SHARES AND SECURITIES.

230.1 CAPITAL GAINS TAX IDENTIFICATION RULES

Z, who is resident and ordinarily resident in the UK throughout, has the following acquisitions/disposals of ordinary 25p shares in MIB plc. MIB ordinary 25p shares were worth 210p per share at 31 March 1982. In 2018/19, Z made no disposals of chargeable assets other than as shown below.

Date	No. of shares bought/(sold)	Cost/ (proceeds)
		£
1 May 1980	1,000	2,000
1 October 1983	2,000	4,500
1 December 1996	500	1,800
1 May 2018	(1,000)	(3,900)
25 May 2018	2,000	7,600
2 January 2019	(3,000)	(18,000)
Remaining holding	1,500	

The disposal on 1 May 2018 is matched with 1,000 of the shares acquired on 25 May 2018 (under the 30-day rule — see note (a)). The resulting chargeable gain is as follows.

	£
Proceeds 1.5.18	3,900
Cost (£7,600 × 1,000/2,000)	(3,800)
Chargeable gain	£100

The disposal of 3,000 shares on 2 January 2018 is matched with 3,000 of the 4,500 forming the '*section 104* holding' as follows.

	No. of shares	Qualifying expenditure
		£
Shares acquired 1 May 1980 (note (b))	1,000	2,100
Additional shares 1 October 1983	2,000	4,500
Additional shares 1 December 1996	500	1,800
Additional shares 25 May 2018	1,000	3,800
	4,500	12,200
Disposal 1 January 2019	(3,000)	(8,133)
Pool carried forward	1,500	£4,067

The chargeable gain is as follows.

	£
Proceeds 2.1.19	18,000
Cost (£12,200 × 3,000/4,500)	(8,133)
Chargeable gain	£9,867
Total chargeable gains 2018/19 £100 + £9,867	£9,967

Notes

(a) For capital gains tax purposes, disposals are identified (1) with shares acquired on the same day (with certain limited exceptions by election); (2) with acquisitions in the following 30 days; (3) with the '*section 104* holding'; (4) with shares acquired after the disposal (and after the expiry of the 30-day period in (2)) taken in the order in which such acquisitions occur. [*TCGA 1992, ss 104, 105, 106A, 288(7B)*].

(b) Re-basing to market value at 31 March 1982 applies automatically for capital gains tax purposes. Accordingly, the qualifying expenditure included in the *section 104* holding in respect of the shares acquired on 1 May 1980 is the market value of those shares on 31 March 1982.

230.2 SHARE IDENTIFICATION RULES FOR COMPANIES

[*TCGA 1992, ss 104, 105–110*]

B Ltd has the following transactions in 25p ordinary shares of H plc, a quoted company.

		Cost/(proceeds)
		£
6.6.78	Purchased 500 at £0.85	425
3.11.81	Purchased 1,300 at £0.80	1,040
15.5.82	Purchased 1,000 at £1.02	1,020
8.9.82	Purchased 400 at £1.08	432
1.2.86	Purchased 1,200 at £1.14	1,368
29.7.87	Sold 2,000 at £1.30	(2,600)
8.6.90	Purchased 1,500 at £1.26	1,890
21.12.93	Received 1,000 from group company (cost £1,250, indexation to date £250)	1,500
10.4.18	Sold 3,900 at £4.00	(15,600)

The shares stood at £1.00 at 31.3.82.

Indexation factors	March 1982 to December 2017	2.501
	May 1982 to April 1985	0.161
	September 1982 to April 1985	0.158
	April 1985 to February 1986	0.019
	February 1986 to July 1987	0.054

July 1987 to June 1990	0.245
June 1990 to December 1993	0.120
December 1993 to December 2017	0.960

Disposal on 10 April 2018

The 'section 104 holding' pool immediately prior to the disposal should be as follows

	Shares	Qualifying expenditure	Indexed pool
		£	£
15.5.82 acquisition	1,000	1,020	1,020
Indexation to April 1985			
£1,020 × 0.161			164
8.9.82 acquisition	400	432	432
Indexation to April 1985			
£432 × 0.158			68
Pool at 6.4.85	1,400	1,452	1,684
Indexed rise: April 1985 – Feb. 1986			
£1,684 × 0.019			32
1.2.86 acquisition	1,200	1,368	1,368
	2,600	2,820	3,084
Indexed rise: February 1986 – July 1987			
£3,084 × 0.054			167
	2,600	2,820	3,251
29.7.87 disposal	(2,000)	(2,169)	(2,501)
c/f	£600	£651	£750
b/f	600	651	750
Indexed rise: July 1987 – June 1990			
£750 × 0.245			184
8.6.90 acquisition	1,500	1,890	1,890
	2,100	2,541	2,824
Indexed rise: June 1990 – December 1993			
£2,824 × 0.120			339
21.12.93 acquisition	1,000	1,250	1,500
	3,100	3,791	4,663
Indexed rise: December 1993 – December 2017			
£4,663 × 0.960			4,476
	3,100	3,791	9,139

The '1982 holding' is as follows

	Shares	Allowable expenditure
		£
6.6.78 acquisition	500	425
3.11.81 acquisition	1,300	1,040
	1,800	1,465

(i) Identify 3,100 shares sold with '*section 104* holding'

	£
Disposal consideration 3,100 × £4.00	12,400
Allowable cost	(3,791)
Unindexed gain	8,609
Indexation allowance £9,139 − £3,791	5,348
Chargeable gain	£3,261

(ii) Identify 800 shares sold with '1982 holding'

	£	£
Disposal consideration 800 × £4.00	3,200	3,200
Cost $\frac{800}{1,800}$ × £1,465	(651)	
Market value 31.3.82 $\frac{800}{1,800}$ × £1,800		(800)
Unindexed gain	2,549	2,400
Indexation allowance £800 × 2.501	(2,001)	(2,001)
Gain after indexation	£548	£399
Chargeable gain		£399
Total chargeable gain 10 April 2018 (£3,261+ £399)		£3,660

Notes

(a) Share disposals by companies are identified firstly with the '*section 104* holding' and secondly with the '1982 holding', both of which are regarded as single assets.

(b) On share disposals identified with shares held at 31.3.82, the re-basing provisions have effect, and indexation is based on the higher of cost and 31.3.82 value. If an irrevocable election is made under *TCGA 1992, s 35(5)* for all assets to be treated as disposed of and re-acquired at their market value on 31.3.82, indexation must be based on the 31.3.82 value even if this is less than cost. [*TCGA 1992, s 55(1)(2)*].

(c) Indexation allowance is frozen at its December 2017 level. No indexation allowance is available in respect of expenditure incurred after 31 December 2017, and for expenditure incurred on or before that date and falling to be deducted on a disposal after that date, indexation allowance is computed up to and including December 2017 only. [*TCGA 1992, ss 53(1)(1B), 54(1B); FA 2018, s 26(2)(3)(6)*]. See **214.1** INDEXATION.

231 Social Investment Relief

231.1 DISPOSAL OF SI ASSETS MORE THAN THREE YEARS AFTER ACQUISITION

[*TCGA 1992, ss 255B–255D; FA 2014, Sch 12 para 2*]

On 8 November 2018 Jon subscribes £1,350,000 for 900,000 shares in the community interest company, Snow Ltd, and obtains the maximum SI income tax relief of £300,000 (£1,000,000 × 30%) for 2018/19. On 3 April 2022 he sells the entire holding for £2,000,000.

The chargeable gain arising is calculated as follows

	£
Disposal proceeds	2,000,000
Cost	(1,350,000)
Gain	650,000
Less TCGA 1992, ss 255B, 255C exemption	
£650,000 × 300,000/405,000	(481,481)
Chargeable gain 2021/22	£168,519

Notes

(a) Gains arising on the sale more than three years after the acquisition of an asset qualifying for SI income tax relief are not chargeable gains unless the SI relief is fully withdrawn before disposal.

(b) Where the income tax relief is not given on the full social investment (otherwise than because of insufficient income), capital gains tax relief is given on a proportion of the gain on the disposal or part disposal.

The gain is reduced by the multiple D/I × R where

D = the actual income tax reduction;

I = the amount invested; and

R = the SI rate for the year of income tax relief.

In this example:

D = £1,000,000 × 30% = £300,000

I × R = £1,350,000 × 30% = £405,000

231.2 LOSS ON DISPOSAL OF SI ASSETS

[*TCGA 1992, s 255B(1); FA 2014, Sch 12 para 2*]

(A) Disposal more than three years after acquisition

Assuming the facts otherwise remain the same as in 231.1 above but that the shares are sold for £900,000 on 3 April 2022.

The allowable loss arising is calculated as follows

	£	£
Disposal proceeds		900,000
Less Cost	1,350,000	
Less Income tax relief given (and not withdrawn)	300,000	(1,050,000)
Allowable loss 2021/22		£(150,000)

Note

(a) Any loss arising is reduced by deducting the amount of the SI relief (given and not withdrawn) from the acquisition cost. On the question of income tax withdrawal, see note (b) to (B) below.

(B) Disposal within three years of acquisition

The facts are otherwise as in (A) above except that the shares are sold in an arm's length bargain on 6 April 2020, i.e. within three years after their issue.

Income tax relief given for 2018/19 is withdrawn as follows

Relief attributable (£1,000,000 @ 30%)	£300,000 (1)
Consideration £900,000 × (300,000 (i.e. £1,000,000 @30%)/405,000 (i.e. £1,350,000 × 30%) @ 30%	£200,000 (2)

The amount at (1) is greater than that at (2), so income tax relief of £200,000 is withdrawn. [*ITA 2007, ss 257R, 257RA*].

The relief not withdrawn is therefore £(300,000 − 200,000) =	£100,000

The allowable loss arising is calculated as follows

	£	£
Disposal proceeds		900,000
Less Cost	1,350,000	
Less Income tax relief not withdrawn	100,000	(1,250,000)
Allowable loss 2020/21		£350,000

Notes

(a) For the purposes of computing an allowable loss, the consideration is reduced by the relief attributable to the assets. [*TCGA 1992, s 255B(1); FA 2014, Sch 12 para 2*]. The relief attributable is that remaining following any withdrawal of relief.

(b) A withdrawal of income tax relief arises on a disposal of SI assets within three years of acquisition . [*ITA 2007, ss 257R, 257RA; FA 2014, Sch 11 para 1*].

231.3 SI DEFERRAL RELIEF

[*TCGA 1992, Sch 8B; FA 2014, Sch 12 paras 2, 3*]

On 1 August 2018, Robert realises a gain of £500,000 on the disposal of an asset he had owned since September 2005. Robert makes no other disposals in 2018/19. On 1 February 2020, Robert acquires shares in a community interest company for £400,000. Robert claims social investment income tax relief of £120,000 in respect of the investment. Robert makes a claim to defer the maximum £400,000 of the August 2018 gain against the qualifying investment.

On 1 July 2023, Robert sells 40% of his holding in the company for £199,200. He makes no other disposals in 2023/24.

Robert's CGT position for 2018/19 is as follows

	£
Gain	500,000
Less SI deferral relief	(400,000)
	100,000
Less annual exemption	(11,700)
Taxable gain 2018/19	£88,300

Robert's CGT position for 2023/24 is as follows

The gain of £199,200 on the shares in the SI company is exempt, the shares having been held for more than three years.

	£
Deferred gain brought into charge	
Total gain deferred	£400,000
Clawback restricted to expenditure to which disposal relates	£160,000
Taxable gain 2023/24 (subject to annual exemption)	(£160,000)
Gain remaining deferred until any future chargeable event (£400,000 − £160,000)	£240,000

Notes

(a) Only gains accruing on or after 6 April 2014 and before 6 April 2019 can qualify for SI deferral relief. [*TCGA 1992, Sch 8B paras 1(3), 2(2); FA 2014, Sch 12 paras 2, 3*].

(b) Where a disposal on or after 3 December 2014 qualifies for both ENTREPRENEURS' RELIEF (**211**) and SI deferral relief, deferral relief can be claimed and entrepreneurs' relief can then be claimed when the deferred gain comes back into charge on the happening of a chargeable event. [*TCGA 1992, ss 169T–169V; FA 2015, s 44*]. See **211.5** ENTREPRENEURS' RELIEF. Previously, the taxpayer had to choose between the reliefs.

232 Wasting Assets

Cross-references. See also **216.3** LAND, **226.3** ROLLOVER RELIEF — REPLACEMENT OF BUSINESS ASSETS.

232.1 GENERAL

[*TCGA 1992, ss 44–47; FA 2015, s 40*]

V bought an aircraft on 31 May 2013 at a cost of £90,000 for use in his air charter business. It has been agreed that V's non-business use of the aircraft amounts to one-tenth, on a flying hours basis, and capital allowances and running costs have accordingly been restricted for income tax purposes. On 1 February 2019, V sells the aircraft for £185,000. The aircraft is agreed as having a useful life of 20 years at the date it was acquired.

		£
Amount qualifying for capital allowances		
Relevant portion of disposal consideration $^{9}/_{10} \times$ £185,000		166,500
Relevant portion of acquisition cost $^{9}/_{10} \times$ £90,000		(81,000)
Chargeable gain 2018/19		£85,500
Amount not qualifying for capital allowances		
Relevant portion of disposal consideration $^{1}/_{10} \times$ £185,000		18,500
Relevant portion of acquisition cost $^{1}/_{10} \times$ £90,000	9,000	
Deduct wasted £9,000 $\times \frac{5y\ 8m}{20y}$	(2,550)	(6,450)
Gain		£12,050
The whole of the £12,050 is exempt.		
The total chargeable gain is therefore		£85,500

Note

(a) Gains on tangible movable property which are wasting assets not qualifying for capital allowances are exempt (and any losses would not be allowable). For disposals on or after 6 April 2015 (1 April 2015 for corporation tax purposes), the exemption does not apply where the asset has become plant as a result of its use for the purposes of a trade, profession or vocation carried on by a person other than the owner and it would not otherwise have been a wasting asset. This does not, however, apply if the asset is plant under a long funding lease and the disposal takes place during the term of the lease or it is a deemed disposal on termination of the lease. [*TCGA 1992, s 45; FA 2015, s 40*].

232.2 OPTIONS

[*TCGA 1992, ss 44, 46, 146*]

Cross-reference.

See also **203.1** ASSETS.

(A) Unquoted shares

On 1 July 2016, R grants C an option to purchase unquoted shares held by R. The cost of the option is £600 to purchase 10,000 shares at £5 per share, the option to be exercised by 31 December 2018. On 1 September 2018 C assigns the option to W for £500.

	£	£
Disposal consideration		500
Acquisition cost	600	
Deduct wasted £600 × $^{26}/_{30}$	(520)	(80)
Chargeable gain		£420

(B) Traded options

On 1 December 2018, C purchases 6-month options on T plc shares for £1,000. Two weeks later, he sells the options, which are quoted on the Stock Exchange, for £1,200.

	£
Disposal consideration	1,200
Allowable cost	(1,000)
Chargeable gain	£200

Note

(a) The wasting asset rules do not apply to traded options. [*TCGA 1992, s 146*].

232.3 LIFE INTERESTS

[*TCGA 1992, s 44(1)(d)*]

(A)

N is a beneficiary under a settlement. On 30 June 2004, when her actuarially estimated life expectancy was 40 years, she sold her life interest to an unrelated individual, R, for £50,000. N dies on 31 December 2018, and the life interest is extinguished.

R will have an allowable loss for 2018/19 as follows

		£	£
Disposal consideration on death of N			Nil
Allowable cost		50,000	
Deduct wasted			
	$\frac{14\text{y } 6\text{m}}{40\text{y}} \times £50,000$	(18,125)	
			(31,875)
Allowable loss			£31,875

Note

(a) The amount of the cost wasted is computed by reference to the predictable life, not the actual life, of the wasting asset.

(B)

Assume the facts to be as in (A) above except that the sale of the life interest was on 30 June 1981 and N's life expectancy *at that date* was 40 years. The value of the life interest remained at £50,000 at 31 March 1982.

		£	£
Disposal consideration			Nil
Market value 31.3.82		50,000	
Deduct wasted			
	$£50,000 \times \frac{36\text{y } 9\text{m } (31.3.82 - 31.12.18)}{39\text{y } 3\text{m } (\text{life expectancy at } 31.3.82)}$	(46,815)	
			(3,185)
Allowable loss 2018/19			£3,185

Note

(a) Where, by virtue of the re-basing rules, an asset is deemed to have been disposed of and re-acquired at its market value on 31 March 1982, that market value must be reduced in accordance with the period of ownership *after* that date and the predictable life of the wasting asset *at* that date.

Inheritance Tax

301 Accumulation and Maintenance Trusts

[*IHTA 1984, s 71; FA 2006, Sch 20 paras 2, 3*]

301.1 CHARGE ON FAILURE TO QUALIFY AS ACCUMULATION AND MAINTENANCE TRUST

On 1 January 1994 G settled £50,000 on trust equally for his great nephews and nieces born before 1 January 2014. The beneficiaries were to take absolute interests at age 18, income being accumulated for minor beneficiaries. By 2014 G had three great nephews and nieces, A (his brother's grandson) born in 1987 and B and C (his sister's grandsons) born in 2004 and 2007 respectively. The settlement was valued at £150,000 on 1 January 2019.

On 1 January 2019 the settlement fails to qualify as an accumulation and maintenance settlement as more than 25 years have elapsed since the date of settlement and the beneficiaries do not have a common grandparent. There will be a charge to IHT on the value of the settlement on 1 January 2019.

The rate of tax is the aggregate of

0.25% for each of the first	40	quarters	10%
0.20% for each of the next	40	quarters	8%
0.15% for each of the next	20	quarters	3%
	100		21%

The IHT charge is 21% × £150,000 = £31,500

Notes

(a) There was no charge to IHT on A becoming entitled to one-third on his eighteenth birthday in 2005.

(b) Settlements created on or after 22 March 2006 cannot qualify as accumulation and maintenance trusts. [*IHTA 1984, s 71(1A); FA 2006, Sch 20 para 2(3)*]. Accumulation and maintenance settlements created prior to that date continued to be treated under *IHTA 1984, s 71* until 6 April 2008 (unless they qualified as TRUSTS FOR BEREAVED MINORS (**323**)). From that date onwards any existing settlement must conform to revised rules to continue to receive *section 71* treatment: the beneficiary or beneficiaries must obtain a right to *capital* on or before the age of eighteen. No charge under *section 71* arose where as a consequence a settlement failed to qualify as an accumulation and maintenance trust on 6 April 2008. [*IHTA 1984, s 71(1)(a); FA 2006, Sch 20 para 3*].

(c) Settlements which failed to qualify as accumulation and maintenance trusts from 6 April 2008 as a result of the provisions in note (b) above are from that date either treated as 18-to-25 trusts (see 301.2 below) or taxed under the rules in **321** SETTLEMENTS: RELEVANT PROPERTY.

(d) See **323** TRUSTS FOR BEREAVED MINORS for certain settlements (including those created on or after 22 March 2006) which are taxed on a similar basis to accumulation and maintenance trusts.

301.2 PRE-22 MARCH 2006 SETTLEMENTS AFTER 5 APRIL 2008

(A) 18-to-25 Trusts

[*IHTA 1984, ss 71D–71G; FA 2006, Sch 20 para 1*]

On 30 April 1983 George, who had made no chargeable transfers in the previous seven years, settled £100,000 on trust equally for his grandchildren. The beneficiaries were to take absolute entitlements at age 25, income being accumulated for minor beneficiaries. George has two grandchildren; Alex, who is 25 on 28 February 2008, and Stephanie, born 27 September 1994. On Stephanie's 25th birthday on 26 September 2019 the remaining settlement property is valued at £600,000. It is assumed for the purposes of this example that the IHT threshold is then £350,000.

An exit charge arises under *IHTA 1984, ss 71F* on Stephanie becoming absolutely entitled to the settlement property on reaching age 25 on 26 September 2019 as follows.

	£
Assumed chargeable transfer	600,000
Assumed cumulative total	—
Deduct Nil rate band	(350,000)
	£250,000
IHT at lifetime rates	£50,000

$$\text{Effective rate } \frac{50,000}{600,000} = 8.33\%$$

Relevant faction

The number of complete quarters that have elapsed between the time of Stephanie's 18th birthday and the day before her 25th birthday is 28. The relevant fraction is therefore 28/40.

The IHT is charged at the relevant fraction of the effective rate on the property to which Stephanie becomes absolutely entitled

28/40 × 8.33% = 5.831%

IHT payable: 3/10 × 5.831% × £600,000	£10,496

Notes

(a) There is no charge to IHT on Alex becoming absolutely entitled to one half of the settled property on 28 February 2008.

(b) On 6 April 2008, the settlement ceases to be an accumulation and maintenance trust because the remaining beneficiary does not become entitled absolutely to settled property on or before attaining age 18 as required from that date (see note (b) to **301.1** above). No charge to IHT arises.

(c) From 6 April 2008 the settlement qualifies as an 18-to-25 trust because it has failed to qualify as an accumulation and maintenance trust by reason only of the change in rules on that date and the settlement secures that the remaining beneficiary becomes absolutely entitled to the settled property, any income arising from it and any accumulated income on or before attaining the age of 25. [*IHTA 1984, s 71D(4)(6); FA 2006, Sch 20 para 1*].

(d) No charge to tax would arise on a beneficiary becoming absolutely entitled before the age of 18. [*IHTA 1984, s 71E(2); FA 2006, Sch 20 para 1*].

(B) **Failure of 18-to-25 trust**

On 31 December 2005 Gilbert, who had made no cumulative chargeable transfers within the previous 7 years, settled £150,000 on an accumulation and maintenance settlement for his son Charles born on that date. The trust is contingent on Charles attaining the age of 25 years at which time he will become absolutely entitled to the settled property. If Charles dies before reaching age 25, Gilbert's nephew James, born on 22 March 1993, becomes the beneficiary, becoming absolutely entitled on attaining the age of 26. Charles dies on 6 April 2014. The settlement is valued at £640,000 on 30 December 2015. The property in the settlement is valued at £700,000 at 21 March 2019, the day before James's 26th birthday, when the funds are released to him.

Charges to IHT arise in respect of the settlement as follows.

Ten-year anniversary charge 31 December 2015

	£
Value of relevant property on 31.12.15	640,000
Less nil rate band £325,000	(325,000)
IHT at lifetime rates on £315,000 @ 20%	£63,000

$$\text{Effective rate } \frac{63{,}000}{640{,}000} = 9.84375\%$$

Appropriate fraction

The number of complete quarters that have elapsed between the date of Charles's death on 6 April 2014 and the tenth anniversary of the date of the settlement is 6. The appropriate fraction is therefore 6/40.

The IHT is charged at 30% of the appropriate fraction of the effective rate on the relevant property

IHT payable = 30% × 6/40 × 9.84375% × £640,000 = £2,835

Exit charge on James becoming absolutely entitled at 22 March 2019

Effective rate (as above, assuming no increase in nil rate band) = 9.84375%

The number of complete successive quarters between 31 December 2015 and 22 March 2019 is 12.

The proportionate charge is therefore:

9.84375% × 30% × 12/40 × £700,000 = £6,202

Notes

(a) The settlement qualifies as an accumulation and maintenance settlement until 5 April 2008 after which date it failed to qualify because Charles does not become absolutely entitled until age 25 (see note (b) to **301.1** above). No charge to IHT arose at that date.

(b) From 6 April 2008 the settlement is an 18-to-25 trust (see note (c) to A above). It ceases to qualify as an 18-to-25 trust on Charles's death on 6 April 2014 because the requirement for the beneficiary to become absolutely entitled on or before reaching age 25 is no longer met (James becomes absolutely entitled only at age 26). No charge to IHT arises on Charles's death. [*IHTA 1984, s 71E(2)(b); FA 2006, Sch 20 para 1*].

(c) Following Charles's death the settlement comes within the relevant property charging regime (see **321** SETTLEMENTS: RELEVANT PROPERTY) resulting in a 10-year anniversary charge on 31 December 2015 and an exit charge on 22 March 2019 when James reaches age 26.

302 Agricultural Property

[*IHTA 1984, ss 115–124B; FA 2009, s 122*]

302.1 RELIEF FOR TRANSFERS AND OTHER EVENTS

(A) Relief given at 100%

[*IHTA 1984, ss 116(1)(2)(7), 124A(1)(3)*]

X has owned since 1984 1,000 acres of land. In June 1993 he began to farm the land, utilising 800 acres for that purpose. The remaining 200 acres are not used for any business purposes. On 1 July 2018 X transfers all the land to his son, Y, at a time when its agricultural value was £1,000 per acre and its open market value £1,500 per acre. He had not used his annual exemptions for 2017/18 and 2018/19. X died on 6 September 2021. Y has continued to run the farm business since the date of the gift.

The value of the gift for inheritance tax purposes before relief is

	£	£
1,000 acres at £1,500 per acre		£1,500,000
The transfer subject to tax is		
(i) Agricultural value of land		
800 acres × £1,000	800,000	
Less agricultural property relief at 100%	(800,000)	—
(ii) Non-agricultural value of land		
800 acres × £500		400,000
(iii) Value of land not used in business		
200 acres at £1,500 per acre		300,000
		700,000
Deduct Annual exemptions (2017/18 and 2018/19)		(6,000)
Value transferred by PET becoming chargeable on death		£694,000

Notes

(a) Relief is at 100% because

(i) immediately before the transfer, X enjoyed the right to vacant possession;

(ii) X had farmed the land for two years before the transfer;

(iii) X had acquired the land more than seven years before the transfer and it had been farmed throughout those seven years (by X or any other person); and

(iv) the land was farmed by Y between the date of gift and X's death.

Note that although conditions (ii) and (iii) were both satisfied in this case, it is only necessary to satisfy one of them to qualify for 100% relief.

(b) Annual exemptions are deducted *after* deducting the agricultural property relief.

(c) Business property relief may be available in respect of the £400,000 excess of the open market value over the agricultural value.

(d) IHT will be charged at 80% of full rates as X died more than 3 but not more than 4 years after the gift.

(B) Transfer where land is held tenanted under an agricultural lease entered into on or after 1 September 1995

[*IHTA 1984, s 116(1)(2)(7)*]

A is the freehold owner of agricultural land which at current vacant possession value is estimated to be valued at £850,000. On 29 September 1992, he enters into an agricultural tenancy (with more than two years to run) with a farming partnership comprising his two sons and his grandson for a full market rental of £25,000 p.a. The tenanted value is estimated at £500,000.

In July 2017 his grandson is killed in a farming accident and a new letting agreement is made between the two sons and A for a full market rent of £35,000 p.a. on 15 September 2017.

A dies on 1 October 2018 when the tenanted value of the land has risen to £600,000.

	£
Transfer at death (tenanted valuation)	600,000
Deduct Agricultural property relief at 100%	(600,000)
IHT payable on	Nil

Notes

(a) No IHT charge arises on the grant of the lease to the partnership on the basis that it is for full consideration. [*IHTA 1984, s 16*].

(b) As A terminated the existing agricultural tenancy and entered into a new tenancy on or after 1 September 1995, agricultural property relief of 100% is available. Only 50% relief would have been available if the existing tenancy had continued, [*FA 1995, s 155; FA 1996, s 185*].

(C) Interaction with capital gains tax

A discretionary settlement has 400 acres of tenanted agricultural land, the tenancy having commenced before 1 September 1995. On 31 October 2016, the trustees appoint the agricultural land to a beneficiary who then becomes absolutely entitled to the land. 50% agricultural property relief is available. The value of the 400 acres as tenanted is £450,000. The trustees fail to pay the capital gains tax due of, say, £60,000 by 31 January 2019 and the beneficiary is assessed and pays the liability.

	£
Value transferred	450,000
Deduct Agricultural property relief at 50%	(225,000)
	225,000
Less Capital gains tax	(60,000)
Chargeable transfer (subject to grossing-up)	£165,000

Notes

(a) An election may be made for the CGT to be held over. [*TCGA 1992, s 260(1)–(5)*].

(b) If the trustees fail to pay all or part of the capital gains tax within twelve months of the due date, an assessment may be made on the beneficiary [*TCGA 1992, s 282*] and the amount of such tax borne by the donee is treated as reducing the value transferred. The beneficiary must become absolutely entitled to the property to obtain the relief. [*IHTA 1984, s 165*].

(c) If it were possible for the trustees to arrange for a new tenancy to begin after 31 August 1995 but before the transfer, the transfer would have attracted 100% agricultural property relief. [*FA 1995, s 155*]. This could possibly be achieved by terminating the existing lease and entering into a new lease with the same tenants, subject to the terms of the existing lease, the tenants' agreement and general legal requirements.

302.2 SHARES ETC. IN AGRICULTURAL COMPANIES

[*IHTA 1984, ss 122, 123*]

AC Ltd is an unquoted agricultural company of which A owns 60% of the shares.

	£
The company owns	
4,000 acres of — land agricultural value	4M
Other trading assets (net)	2M
Total value of company	£6M
A's shareholding is valued at	£4.5M

All necessary conditions for relief are satisfied.

If A were to die in, say, November 2018 the position as regards his shareholding would be as follows

	Total Value	Land	Other Assets
	£	£	£
Value of assets of company	6M	4M	2M
Value of shares, split in same proportions	4.5M	£3M	£1.5M
Deduct agricultural property relief (100% of £3M)	(3.0M)		
Deduct business property relief (100% of £1.5M)	(1.5M)		
Chargeable to IHT	Nil		

Notes

(a) Part of the value transferred is attributable to the agricultural value of agricultural property, so agricultural property relief is available. [*IHTA 1984, s 122*].

(b) The legislation appears to require that both agricultural property relief and business property relief be given, each against its appropriate part of the value. [*IHTA 1984, s 114*]. See also **304** BUSINESS PROPERTY.

303 Anti-Avoidance

303.1 ASSOCIATED OPERATIONS

[*IHTA 1984, s 268*]

(A)

H owns a set of four Chippendale chairs valued, as a set, at £6,000. Individually they would be valued at only £1,000, although a pair would be worth £2,500 and three £4,000.

He gives one chair to his son each year over four years, during which time all values increase at 10% p.a. (simple). In the fifth year H dies.

	£	£
Year 1		
Value of four chairs	6,000	
Deduct value of three	(4,000)	
Value transferred		2,000
Year 2		
Basic computation ignoring the associated operations rule		
Current value of three chairs	4,400	
Deduct value of two	(2,750)	
Value transferred	£1,650	
Revised to take account of associated operations rule		
Current value of four chairs	6,600	
Deduct value of two	(2,750)	
	3,850	
Deduct value transferred in Year 1	(2,000)	
		1,850
Year 3		
Current value of four chairs	7,200	
Deduct value of one	(1,200)	
	6,000	
Deduct value transferred in Years 1 and 2	(3,850)	
		2,150

	£	£
Year 4		
Current value of four chairs	7,800	
Deduct value transferred in Years 1, 2 and 3	(6,000)	
Value transferred		1,800
Total values transferred		£7,800

Note

(a) The normal rule would be that the transfer of value is the loss to the donor's estate, as in Year 1. However, if a series of transfers are treated as associated operations, the transfer is treated as if made at the time of the latest transfer, reduced by the value transferred by the earlier transfers.

(B)

If in (A) above H had wished to give away the chairs over two years instead of four, he might first have given two chairs to his wife, so that each could give the son one chair each year.

		£	£
Year 1			
(i)	Value transferred by husband to son		
	Value of two chairs (as half of a set of four linked by the related property rule)	3,000	
	Deduct value of one chair (as half of a pair)	(1,250)	
			1,750
(ii)	Value transferred by wife (similar calculation)		1,750
Year 2			
(i)	Value transferred by husband, applying the associated operations rule		
	Current value of four chairs	6,600	
	Deduct value transferred in Year 1 by H to son	(3,500)	
	Value transferred		3,100
Total values transferred			£6,600

Notes

(a) In this case, the total of the values transferred can exceed the value of the assets, although it must be doubtful whether HMRC would seek to apply the full rigours of the section unless the transfer by the wife in Year 1 had fallen within her annual exemptions, or she had survived seven years so that the gift was exempt.

(b) See *IHTA 1984, s 161* for the related property rule, and see also **326.2** VALUATION.

(c) The result above could have been achieved in another way. The first transfer by the husband to his spouse is quantified at £3,000 – the second to the son is quantified at £1,750 as in the example. If through *section 268* one looks at the position as if the transfer of value was made on the last of the operations, the calculation would be:

	£
Value in H's estate before any transfer	
(i.e. value of 4 chairs at the date of last transfer)	6,600
Value in husband's estate after all transfers	Nil
Value transferred	6,600
Deduct value of earlier operations:	
Transfer to wife disregarded *section 268(3)*	Nil
Transfer to son	(1,750)
Value transferred	£4,850

So the value transferred is £1,750 + £4,850 = £6,600. HMRC would not seek to raise a charge to tax on the actual transfers by the wife to the son.

HMRC may ask the District Valuer Service for the value effectively transferred by one transfer being the last of a series of associated operations. If any of the earlier operations were themselves transfers of value, other than transfers between spouses or civil partners [*IHTA 1984, s 18*], then the adjustment will be dealt with by HMRC.

304 Business Property

[*IHTA 1984, ss 103–114, 269*]

304.1 RELEVANT BUSINESS PROPERTY

(A) Shares in a holding company with a non-qualifying subsidiary

[*IHTA 1984, s 111*]

A owns 85% of the share capital of H Ltd, an unquoted company which has two wholly-owned subsidiary companies S Ltd and P Ltd. H Ltd and S Ltd are trading companies and P Ltd is a property investment company. The issued share capital of H Ltd is 100,000 ordinary shares of £1 each valued at £8 per share. The values of the issued shares in S Ltd and P Ltd are £250,000 and £300,000 respectively.

A gives 10,000 shares in H Ltd to his son in August 2016. He has already made chargeable transfers using up his basic exemptions. His son agrees to pay any IHT. A dies in January 2019, at which time his son still owns the shares. It is agreed that the fall in value in A's estate (reduction of a 85% holding to a 75% holding), by which the value of the gift for IHT purposes is measured, is equivalent to the actual value of the shares transferred.

	£	£
Value of gift		80,000
Deduct business property relief 100% × £80,000	80,000	
Less $100\% \times 80{,}000 \times \frac{300{,}000}{800{,}000}$	(30,000)	
		(50,000)
PET becoming chargeable transfer on death		£30,000

(B) Land used by a business

M has for many years owned a factory used in the business of Q Ltd, of which he has control. In September 2016, M gives the factory to his son S when its value is £740,000. He has made no previous chargeable transfer, but made a gift of £3,000 in 2016/17. M dies in October 2018, when the factory is being used for business purposes by S's partnership. S agreed to pay any IHT on the gift.

	£
Value of gift	740,000
Deduct business property relief (50%)	(370,000)
	370,000
Deduct annual exemption (2017/18)	(3,000)
PET becoming chargeable transfer on death	£367,000
IHT payable at full rates ((£367,000–325,000) × 40%))	
(death within 3 years)	£16,800

Notes

(a) If M wishes also to dispose of shares in Q Ltd by sale or gift after which he would no longer have control, he should give the factory to his son *before* disposing of the shares, or else the business property relief would not be available on the gift of the factory.

(b) If the factory had been used by Q Ltd at the date of M's death, no business property relief would be available on the gift since the factory would not be relevant business property in S's hands at the date of death.

(C) Land and buildings owned by trustees

X died in 1976 leaving a life interest in factory premises to his son A, with remainder to his grandsons B and C. A occupies the premises for the purposes of his trade, rent-free. In September 2017 A gives up his life interest when the value of the premises is £660,000. B and C agree to pay any IHT. A has already made chargeable transfers using up his annual exemptions. A dies in November 2018, when the factory is still being used in the trade which was then being carried on by B and C in partnership.

	£
Value of gift	660,000
Deduct business property relief (50%)	(330,000)
PET becoming chargeable transfer on death	£330,000
IHT payable at full rates ((£330,000–325,000) × 40%))	
(death within 3 years)	£2,000

(D) Further conditions for lifetime transfers

X transfers the share of his 25% interest in Amalgam Ltd (an AIM company) to his son Y and also transfers land and buildings in his partnership to his other son Z on 16 June 2015. X has already used his annual exemptions for 2015/16 and 2014/15. The shares are valued at £640,000 and the land and buildings at £676,000. In February 2017 Amalgam Ltd is quoted on the London Stock Exchange and Y's share value increases to £1 million.

Z sells the land and property to one of the partners in May 2017 and invests the whole proceeds in an unquoted company receiving shares to the value of £800,000. X dies on 6 June 2018.

Theoretical computation on death if shares in Amalgam Ltd had remained unquoted

	£	Gross	Tax
Value of shares to Y	640,000		
Deduct BPR 100%	(640,000)	Nil	Nil
Partnership assets to Z	676,000		
Deduct BPR 50%	(338,000)		
PET becoming chargeable transfer on death ((£338,000–325,000) × 40%))	338,000	£13,000	£5,200

Actual computation on death — tax payable on failed BPR and PETs that have become chargeable because of X's death within 7 years

	£	
Value of shares to Y	640,000	
Value of property to Z after BPR	338,000	
	978,000	
Less nil rate band	(325,000)	
	653,000	× 40% = £261,200

Apportionment of tax

Gift to Y	$£261{,}200 \times \dfrac{£640{,}000}{£978{,}000}$	=	£170,928
Gift to Z	$£261{,}200 \times \dfrac{£338{,}000}{£978{,}000}$	=	£90,272

Notes

(a) X's death within 3 years of the gift of the shares in Amalgam Ltd results in the loss of business property relief, because on a notional transfer by Y immediately before X's death, the shares, being a non-controlling shareholding in a quoted company, would not have qualified as relevant business property. [*IHTA 1984, s 113A(3)*]. In determining whether on the notional transfer an asset qualifies as relevant business property, the requirement for the asset to be held for two years by the transferor prior to the notional transfer is ignored.

(b) Z has sold the business assets in the partnership and reinvested the proceeds in other relevant business property which attracts 100% BPR (i.e. unquoted shares) as opposed to 50% for the original assets (i.e. land and buildings) in the partnership. Z's replacement of the partnership assets with unquoted shares qualifies for replacement property relief. [*IHTA 1984, s 113B*]. However, Z's position is affected by Y's loss of 100% BPR in respect of the transfer of shares to Y by X.

(c) Z could have taken the view that his position was vulnerable to Y's decision to accept quoted shares (with no control) and X's death within seven years of the gifts. Insurance on a reducing basis could have been taken out by Z to protect his position and cover the liability of £85,072 (i.e. £90,272 — £5,200).

305 Calculation of Tax

305.1 THE CUMULATION PRINCIPLE: POTENTIALLY EXEMPT TRANSFERS

[*IHTA 1984, ss 3, 3A, 7*]

On 1 May 2011 A gave £50,000 to his daughter, D, and on 1 May 2014 he gave £215,000 to his son, S. Both D and S agreed to pay any IHT due on the gifts.

On 7 March 2019 A died, leaving his estate, valued at £300,000, equally to D and S. The only other transfer made by A was an immediately chargeable transfer of £121,000 during 2009/10. A had sold his home in January 2015 and lived in a nursing home until his death.

Gift on 1 May 2011

The gift is a PET, which becomes exempt since A does not die within seven years of the date of the gift. No IHT is payable.

Gift on 1 May 2014

This PET becomes chargeable since A dies between 4 and 5 years after the gift. IHT is payable by S following the death at 60% of full rates on the basis of the Table of rates in force in 2018/19.

As this PET has become chargeable, it must be cumulated with other chargeable transfers made in the seven years before the date of the gift. The PET made on 1 May 2011 has become exempt and is excluded from the computation but the immediately chargeable transfer of £121,000 made during 2009/10 must be cumulated with the 2014 gift. Note that a transfer made more than seven years before the death of the transferor and which is not itself aggregated with the estate on death is thus brought into the computation of the IHT payable on the 2014 gift.

		£	£
Gift			215,000
Deduct annual exemptions	2014/15	(3,000)	
	2013/14	(3,000)	
			(6,000)
			£209,000

IHT on £209,000 charged in band £121,000 to £330,000

121,001–325,000 at nil%	—	
325,001–330,000 at 40%	2,000	
	£2,000	
IHT payable at 60% of full rates — £2,000 at 60%		£1,200

Death 7 March 2019

The chargeable transfers in the seven years prior to death comprise only the gift on 1 May 2014 of £209,000.

IHT on death on estate of £300,000 chargeable in band £209,001 to £509,000

	£
209,001–325,000 at nil%	—
325,001–509,000 at 40%	73,600
IHT payable	£73,600

Notes

(a) If A directs in his will that, despite the earlier agreement, any IHT due on the gift to S is to be borne by his estate, this amounts to a pecuniary legacy to S of the amount of the tax. The reduction in A's estate by the transfer is unchanged at £215,000 as is the tax of £1,200. The legacy is paid out of the death estate of £300,000 with previous chargeable transfers of £209,000. Since the whole of the estate is liable on death, the IHT remains at £73,600.

(b) If S has not by 1 April 2020 paid the IHT of £1,200 due on the gift from A, the personal representatives of A become liable for the tax as it has not been paid by S within 12 months after the end of the month in which A died. The IHT due remains £1,200 since the gross chargeable transfer is £209,000. A had no liability for the tax at the time the transfer was made and the reduction in value to his estate was, therefore, the amount of the gift to S, £215,000. The personal representatives have a right under general law to reimbursement for the tax from S. To the extent that reimbursement is probable, the tax is not a deduction from the estate. Since the personal representatives can claim reimbursement from the half estate due to S, no deduction will be given. Tax on the estate remains, therefore, at £73,600. [*IHTA 1984, ss 199, 204*]. If S had not benefited under A's will so that no assets were available to reimburse the personal representatives, the tax due of £1,200 might fall to be met from the estate.

(c) A's estate does not qualify for the additional residence nil-rate band because his home was sold before 8 July 2015. For examples on the residence nil-rate band see **310.5** EXEMPT TRANSFERS.

305.2 THE CUMULATION PRINCIPLE: GROSSING UP A CHARGEABLE TRANSFER

[*IHTA 1984, ss 3, 3A, 5, 7*]

(A)

On 13 July 2011 B gave £337,000 to his nephew N, who agreed to pay any IHT on the gift. On 24 December 2012 B settled £332,000 on discretionary trusts for his great-nephews and nieces, paying the IHT himself.

On 9 July 2018 B died with an estate worth £78,000, having made no other gifts.

Gift 13 July 2011

The gift is a PET but becomes chargeable since B dies between 6 and 7 years after the gift. The annual exemption for 2011/12, and that brought forward from 2010/11 are, however, available, reducing the chargeable transfer to £331,000.

IHT is charged on the transfer at 20% of full rates, using the Table of rates in force in 2018/19.

IHT on gift	£	
1–325,000 at nil%	—	
325,001–331,000 at 40%	2,400	
	£2,400	
IHT payable by N at 20% of full rates, i.e. 20% × £2,400		£480

Gift 24 December 2012

Initial liability

The gift to the discretionary trust is an immediately chargeable transfer on which the transferor, B, has agreed to pay the IHT. The annual exemption for 2012/13 is set against the chargeable transfer, reducing it to £329,000.

As B is paying the tax on the transfer, his estate is reduced by two amounts: the gross amount of the transfer itself (i.e. before deducting the annual exemptions) and by the tax due on the net transfer (i.e. after deducting the annual exemptions). The total tax will not merely comprise the tax due on the transfer, but the tax upon that tax, and so on. In order to determine the total tax due, where applicable the excess of the chargeable transfer above the nil rate band (or part thereof) is grossed up, using the following formula:

$$E \times \frac{100}{100 - T} \times T\% = G$$

E = excess over nil rate band

T = applicable rate of tax

G = tax due on gross chargeable transfer

In this example, as chargeable lifetime transfers are charged at 20%, being one half of the full death rates, 'T' will be 20. The computation therefore proceeds as follows.

	£
Value of transfer	332,000
Deduct Annual exemption	(3,000)
	329,000
IHT payable on gift	
$£(329{,}000 - 325{,}000) \times \frac{100}{100 - 20} \times 20\%$	1,000
B's gross chargeable transfer	£330,000

Revision on death

B's death occurs between 5 and 6 years after the gift, so the tax on the chargeable transfer is revised to the IHT payable at 40% of full rates. The PET on 13 July 2011 becomes chargeable, so IHT is charged on the gross chargeable transfer of £330,000 in the bracket £331,000 to £661,000.

	£
331,001–661,000 at 40%	132,000
IHT at 40% of £132,000	52,800
Less paid on chargeable lifetime transfer	(1,000)
Additional IHT payable following death	£51,800

Death 9 July 2018

Chargeable transfers in the seven years prior to death amount to £661,000, so IHT is charged on the death estate of £78,000 in the bracket £661,000 to £739,000.

IHT payable	
661,001–739,000 at 40%	£31,200

(B)

Facts are as in (A) above except that B died on 9 July 2019. It is assumed that the nil rate band remains unchanged after 6 April 2009.

The PET on 13 July 2011 is exempt and thus not cumulated when reworking the IHT on the chargeable transfer on 24 December 2012 or on death.

Gift 24 December 2012

IHT on gift, as before	£1,000

Following B's death between 6 and 7 years after the gift, IHT is reworked at 20% of full rates. IHT is charged on the gross chargeable transfer of £330,000 in the bracket £Nil to £330,000.

	£
325,001–330,000 at 40%	2,000
IHT payable at 20% of full rates, i.e. 20% × £2,000	£400
Deduct paid originally by B	(1,000)
	—

No further IHT is payable as the tax originally paid exceeds the IHT at the death rates.

Death 9 July 2019

Chargeable transfers in the previous 7 years amount to £330,000 so IHT is charged on the death estate of £78,000 in the bracket £330,000 to £408,000.

IHT payable	
330,001–408,000 at 40%	£31,200

Note

(a) No IHT is repayable in respect of the chargeable transfer on 24 December 2012, even though the IHT on death is less than the IHT originally paid on the gift.

305.3 PARTLY EXEMPT TRANSFERS

[*IHTA 1984, ss 36–42*]

(A) Where the only chargeable part of a transfer is specific gifts which do not bear their own tax

A, a widow, dies on 8 June 2018. Her estate is valued at £420,000 and her will provides for a tax-free legacy to her nephew of £348,000 and the residue of her estate to the National Trust. A had made no chargeable transfers during her lifetime.

Gross-up tax-free legacy at 'death' rates

	£
Tax-free legacy	348,000
Tax thereon	
$(348{,}000 - 325{,}000) \times \dfrac{100}{100-40} \times 40\%$	15,333
Gross chargeable transfer	£363,333

Calculation of net residuary estate	£
Value of estate	420,000
Deduct gross value of legacy	(363,333)
Residue	£56,667

Allocation of estate at death	
Nephew	348,000
National Trust	56,667
Tax	15,333
	£420,000

(B) Where tax-free specific gifts are not the only chargeable gifts

A dies on 1 January 2019 leaving a widow, son and nephew. His estate is valued at £560,000 before deduction of business property relief of £50,000 and his will provides for a tax-free legacy to his son of £360,000, a legacy to the nephew of £13,000 bearing its own tax, a bequest to charity of £26,000, with the residue shared three-quarters by his widow and one-quarter by the son. A had made no previous chargeable transfers.

Allocation of business property relief

[*IHTA 1984, s 39A*]

Since the will made no specific gifts of the business property, the business property relief is apportioned between each of the specific gifts and the residue, i.e. each is multiplied by

$$\frac{\text{Estate less business property relief}}{\text{Estate before business property relief}}$$

Son	£360,000	$\times \frac{510,000}{560,000} =$	£327,858
Nephew	£13,000	$\times \frac{510,000}{560,000} =$	£11,839
Charity	£26,000	$\times \frac{510,000}{560,000} =$	£23,678
Residue	£161,000	$\times \frac{510,000}{560,000} =$	£146,625
	£560,000		£510,000

Hypothetical chargeable estate	£	£	£
Tax-free legacy to son			327,858
Tax thereon			
$£(327,858 - 325,000) \times \frac{100}{100 - 40} \times 40\%$			1,905
			329,763
Legacy to nephew			11,839
			341,602
Chargeable residue:			
Gross estate		510,000	
Deduct gross legacies	341,602		
charity	23,678		
		(365,280)	
		£144,720	
Son's one-quarter share			36,180
Hypothetical chargeable estate			£377,782

Hypothetical chargeable estate — calculation of assumed tax rate

Tax on £377,782	
£(377,782 − 325,000) × 40%	£21,112

$$\text{Assumed rate } \frac{21{,}112}{377{,}782} \times 100 = 5.5884\%$$

Re-gross tax-free legacy to son using assumed rate

$$£327{,}858 \times \frac{100}{100 - 5.5884} \qquad £347{,}264$$

Calculate chargeable estate and tax thereon		£	£	£
Grossed-up value of tax-free legacy				347,264
Legacy to nephew				11,839
				359,103
Chargeable residue				
Gross estate			510,000	
Deduct	gross legacies	359,103		
	charity	23,678		
			(382,781)	
			£127,219	
Son's one-quarter share				31,804
Chargeable estate				£390,907
Tax on estate				
0–325,000 at nil %			—	
325,001–390,907 at 40%			26,362	
			£26,362	

$$\text{Estate rate is } \frac{26{,}362}{390{,}907} \times 100 = 6.7438\%$$

Calculation of residue		£	£
Gross estate			560,000
Specific legacies	— son	360,000	
	— nephew	13,000	
	— charity	26,000	
		399,000	

Tax on son's legacy

£347,264 at 6.7438%	23,418	
Legacies plus tax thereon		422,418
Residue		£137,582

Distribution of estate	£	£
Widow — three-quarters of residue		103,187
Son — specific legacy	360,000	
— one quarter share of residue	34,395	
	394,395	
Deduct tax on share of residue		
£34,395 × 6.7438%	2,319	
		392,076
Nephew — specific legacy	13,000	
Deduct tax thereon		
£11,839 × 6.7438%	798	
		12,202
Charity		26,000
Tax payable £(23,418 + 2,319 + 798)		26,535
		£560,000

(C) **As (B) above but with settled property**

The facts are as in (B) above except that in addition to his free estate valued at £560,000, A has a life interest acquired before 22 March 2006, worth £100,000 at 1 January 2019, in his late father's estate, with remainder to his son.

The hypothetical chargeable estate is £377,782 as in (B) above and thus the assumed rate remains at 5.5884%. The settled property is ignored at this stage — see note (a).

Calculate chargeable estate and tax thereon	£
Chargeable free estate as in (B) above	390,907
Settled property	100,000
Chargeable estate	£490,907

Tax on estate	
0–325,000 at nil %	—
325,001–490,907 at 40%	66,362
	£66,362

$$\text{Estate rate is } \frac{66,362}{490,907} \times 100 = 13.51824\%$$

Calculation of residue

		£	£
Gross estate			560,000
Specific legacies	— son	360,000	
	— nephew	13,000	
	— charity	26,000	
		399,000	
Tax on son's legacy			
£347,264 at 13.51824%		46,943	
Deduct Legacies plus tax thereon			(445,943)
Residue			£114,057

Distribution of estate

	£	£
Widow — three quarters of residue		85,543
Son — specific legacy	360,000	
— one quarter share of residue	28,514	
— settled property	100,000	
Deduct		
tax on share of residue		
£34,395 × 13.51824%	(4,649)	
tax on settled property		
£100,000 × 13.51824%	(13,518)	
		470,347
Nephew — specific legacy	13,000	
Deduct tax thereon		
£11,839 × 13.51824%	(1,600)	
		11,400
Charity		26,000
Tax payable (46,943 + 4,649 + 13,518 + 1,600)		66,710
		£660,000

Notes

(a) Where gifts take effect separately out of the deceased's free estate and out of a settled fund the provisions of *IHTA 1984, ss 36–39A* (partly exempt transfers) apply separately to each fund. [*IHTA 1984, s 40*]. HMRC take the view that the rate of tax to be used for grossing up, i.e. the 'assumed rate' in this example, should be found by looking at each fund separately and in isolation. Thus, the settled property is not taken into account above in the calculation of the assumed rate for gifts out of the free estate.

(b) The IHT on the settled property, payable by the trustees, is found by applying the estate rate of 13.51824% to the value of that property.

306 Charities

[*IHTA 1984, s 70*]

306.1 PROPERTY LEAVING TEMPORARY CHARITABLE TRUSTS

(A) Gross payment to beneficiaries

On 1 January 1974 A settled £100,000 on temporary charitable trusts. The income and capital were to be applied for charitable purposes only for a period of 25 years from the date of settlement, and thereafter could be applied for charitable purposes or to or for the settlor's grandchildren. On 1 January 2019 the trustees paid £50,000 to charity and the balance of the settlement, valued at £75,000, to the three grandchildren.

The relevant period is the period from settlement of the funds or, if later, 13 March 1975 to 1 January 2019, i.e. 175 complete quarters, and the amount on which tax is charged is £75,000 gross.

The rate of tax is

0.25% for 40 quarters	10.00%
0.20% for 40 quarters	8.00%
0.15% for 40 quarters	6.00%
0.10% for 40 quarters	4.00%
0.05% for 15 quarters	0.75%
	28.75%

IHT payable is 28.75% × £75,000 = £21,562

(B) Net payment to beneficiaries

Assume the same facts as in (A) above except that the trustees apply £75,000 net for the settlor's three grandchildren, and the balance to charity.

The rate of tax is, as before, 28.75%.

$$\text{IHT payable is } \frac{28.75}{100 - 28.75} \times £75{,}000 = £30{,}263$$

The gross payment to the beneficiaries is £75,000 + £30,263 = £105,263

307 Close Companies

[*IHTA 1984, ss 94–98, 102*]

307.1 VALUE TRANSFERRED

The ordinary shares of companies A and B are held as follows (in January 2019)

		A	B
Individuals	X	80%	
	Y	20%	
	Z		10%
Company	A		90%

Company B is non-resident and Z is domiciled in the UK. Company A sells a property valued at £220,000 to a mutual friend of X and Y for £20,000. The following month, company B sells a foreign property worth £100,000 to X for £90,000.

Company A

			£
The transfer of value is £220,000 − £20,000			200,000
Apportioned to	X	80% × £200,000	160,000
	Y	20% × £200,000	40,000
			£200,000

Company B

The transfer of value of £10,000 is apportioned

To X	80% × 90% × £10,000		7,200
	Deduct increase in X's estate		(10,000)
			—
To Y	20% × 90% × £10,000		1,800
To Z	10% × £10,000	note (c)	1,000
			£2,800

Notes

(a) If the sale by company A were to X (or Y), there would be no apportionment because the undervalue would be treated as a net distribution, thus attracting income tax.

(b) On the sale by company B, X would not be liable to income tax.

(c) If Z were not domiciled in the UK, his share of the transfer of value would not be apportioned to him. [*IHTA 1984, s 94(2)(b)*].

307.2 CHARGE ON PARTICIPATORS

Assume the values transferred by X, Y and Z in **307.1** above and that X and Y have each made previous chargeable transfers in excess of £325,000 since January 2012 and have used up their annual exemptions for 2017/18.

Company A

	X	Y	Z
	£	£	£
Value transferred	160,000	40,000	
Annual exemptions 2018/19	(3,000)	(3,000)	
	157,000	37,000	
Tax (25% of net)	39,250	9,250	
Gross transfer	£196,250	£46,250	
IHT thereon at 20%	£39,250	£9,250	
Company B			
Value transferred	7,200	1,800	1,000
Deduct increase in X's estate	(10,000)	—	—
		1,800	1,000
Deduct annual exemption		—	(1,000)
		1,800	—
Tax (25% of net)		450	
Gross transfer		£2,250	
IHT thereon at 20%		£450	

Note

(a) Although it is understood that HMRC would follow this method of calculation, there is an alternative view which follows the exact wording of *IHTA 1984, s 94(1)*. This view is that the grossing-up should take place before the increase in X's estate is deducted. In the above example, it makes no difference as the gross transfer would still be less than the increase in X's estate. But suppose that X held 90% of the ordinary shares in Company A. His value transferred would then be £8,100 (90% × 90% × £10,000) and this alternative method would proceed as follows.

	£
Value transferred	8,100
Tax (25% of net)	2,025
	10,125
Deduct increase in X's estate	(10,000)
	£125
IHT thereon at 20%	£25

307.3 ALTERATION OF SHARE CAPITAL

In January 2019 the share capital of company H, an investment company, is owned by P and Q as follows

P	600	
Q	400	
	1,000	ordinary £1 shares

The shares are valued at £10 per share for P's majority holding and £4 per share for Q's minority holding.

The company issues 2,000 shares at par to Q and the shares are then worth £3.50 per share for Q's majority holding and £1.50 per share for P's minority holding. P has previously made chargeable transfers in excess of £325,000 since January 2012 and has utilised his 2018/19 and 2017/18 annual exemptions.

The transfer of value for P is

	£
Value of holding previously	6,000
Less Value of holding now	(900)
Decrease in value	5,100
Tax (25% of net)	1,275
Gross transfer	£6,375
IHT thereon at 20%	£1,275

Notes

(a) P's transfer of value is *not* a potentially exempt transfer. [*IHTA 1984, s 98(3)*].

(b) An alternative charge may arise under *IHTA 1984, s 3(3)* (omission to exercise a right) but the transfer would then be potentially exempt and only chargeable if P died within seven years.

308 Deeds of Variation and Disclaimers

[*IHTA 1984, ss 17, 142, 218A; FA 2012, Sch 33 paras 9, 10*]

308.1 A died in December 2018 leaving his estate of £354,000 to his wife, B, absolutely. A and B had sold their house in June 2015 and moved in with one of their sons, C. B, having an index-linked widow's pension, agreed with her sons, C and D, that they could benefit from the estate to the extent of £325,000 in equal shares, i.e. £162,500 each. A deed of variation is duly executed, incorporating a statement that the variation is to have effect for inheritance tax purposes.

A had made no chargeable transfers before his death.

	£
Exempt transfer to B	29,000
Transfer to C	162,500
Transfer to D	162,500
	£325,000
IHT payable	Nil

Notes

(a) If B died 5 years later when her estate was valued at, say, £354,000, IHT payable would be £11,600 (assuming that the nil rate band was then £325,000). If no deed of family arrangement had been made, the personal representatives of B's estate would be entitled to claim A's unused nil rate band, (increased to the amount of the band at that time) and the total estate would potentially be covered by the two nil rate bands. The instrument has in this case potentially increased the IHT liability by £11,600 but has ensured that the sons received their £162,500 five years earlier than would have been the case if B had retained A's property until her death. [*IHTA 1984, s 8A; FA 2008, s 10, Sch 4 para 2*].

(b) The persons making an instrument of variation and (if additional tax results) the personal representatives, must include in the instrument a statement that the variation is to have effect for inheritance tax purposes. If additional tax results, the persons making the statement must deliver a copy of the instrument to HMRC and notify them of the additional tax payable. [*IHTA 1988, ss 142(2), 218A*]. For variations where the death of the deceased occurred on or after 6 April 2012, and where the variation is to any extent in favour of a charity or charitable trust, it is a requirement that the charity or charitable trustees must be notified of the existence of the variation. [*IHTA 1984, s 142(3A)(3B); FA 2012, Sch 33 paras 9, 10*].

(c) A's estate does not qualify for the additional residence nil-rate band because A and B's home was sold before 8 July 2015. For examples on the residence nil-rate band see **310.5** EXEMPT TRANSFERS.

309 Double Taxation Relief

[*IHTA 1984, s 159*]

309.1 UNILATERAL RELIEF

(A) Where property is situated in an overseas territory only

A, domiciled in the UK, owns a holiday home abroad valued at £396,000 which he gives to his brother in July 2018. He is liable to local gifts tax of, say, £8,830. He has made no previous transfers and does not use the home again at any time before his death in February 2023. It is assumed for the purposes of this example that the nil rate band is then £325,000.

		£	£
Market value of holiday home			396,000
Annual exemption	2018/19	(3,000)	
	2017/18	(3,000)	
			(6,000)
Chargeable transfer			£390,000
IHT payable at 60% of full rates by brother (death between 4 and 5 years after gift)			
£65,000 × 40% × 60%			15,600
Unilateral relief for foreign tax			(8,830)
IHT borne			£6,770

Note

(a) If the overseas tax suffered exceeded the UK liability before relief, there would be no IHT payable but the excess would not be repayable.

(B) Where property is situated in both the UK and an overseas territory

M, domiciled in the UK, owns company shares which are regarded as situated both in the UK and country X under the rules of the respective countries. On M's death in June 2018 the shares pass to M's son S. The UK IHT amounts to £5,000 before unilateral relief. The equivalent tax liability arising in country X amounts to £2,000.

$$\text{Applying the formula } \frac{A}{A+B} \times C$$

where

A = amount of IHT

B = amount of overseas tax

C = smaller of A and B

The unilateral relief available is

$$\frac{5{,}000}{5{,}000 + 2{,}000} \times £2{,}000 = £1{,}429$$

IHT payable = £5,000 − £1,429 = £3,571

(C) **Where tax is imposed in two or more overseas territories on property situated in the UK and each of those territories**

Assume the facts in (B) above except that a third country imposes a tax liability on the death as the shares are regarded as also situated in that country.

UK IHT before unilateral relief	£5,000
Tax in country X	£2,000
Tax in country Y	£400

$$\text{Applying the formula} \frac{A}{A + B} \times C$$

where

A = amount of IHT

B = aggregate of overseas tax

C = aggregate of all, except the largest, of A and the overseas tax imposed in each overseas territory

The unilateral relief available is

$$\frac{5{,}000}{5{,}000 + 2{,}000 + 400} \times (2{,}000 + 400) = £1{,}622$$

IHT payable £5,000 − £1,622 = £3,378

(D) **Where tax in one overseas territory is relieved against another overseas territory's tax**

Assume the same facts as in (C) above except that country X allows a credit for tax paid in country Y.

Unilateral relief for IHT

$$\frac{5{,}000}{5{,}000 + (2{,}000 - 400) + 400} \times £((2{,}000 - 400) + 400) = £1{,}429$$

IHT payable £5,000 − £1,429 = £3,571

310 Exempt Transfers

310.1 ANNUAL EXEMPTION

[*IHTA 1984, s 19*]

(A)

S, who has made no other transfers of value, made gifts to his sister of £5,000 on 1 June 2016 and £4,000 on 1 May 2017. S dies on 1 September 2018 with an estate valued at £325,000.

Annual exemptions are available as follows

2016/17	£	£
1 June 2016 Gift		5,000
Deduct 2016/17 annual exemption	3,000	
2015/16 annual exemption (part)	2,000	
		(5,000)
		Nil

2017/18	£
1 May 2017 Gift	4,000
Deduct 2017/18 annual exemption	(3,000)
PET becoming chargeable on death	£1,000

The PET, having become a chargeable transfer as a result of death within seven years, is covered by the nil rate band but is aggregated with the death estate in computing the IHT payable on death.

Note

(a) Although the annual exemption, to the extent that it is not fully utilised in the year, can be carried forward to the following year, the current year's exemption is treated as utilised before any exemption brought forward. [*IHTA 1984, s 19(1)(2)*]. If S had gifted £6,000 in 2016/17 and £3,000 in 2017/18, the total gifts would have been the same but they would have been fully covered by annual exemptions.

(B)

T made a gift to his son of £2,000 on 1 June 2018. On 9 November 2018, he settled £20,000 on a discretionary trust for his children and grandchildren. T had made no other gifts since 6 April 2018, but had used his annual exemptions in each year up to and including 2017/18. T died on 13 February 2024.

The gift on 1 June 2018 is a potentially exempt transfer which becomes chargeable since T died within seven years of the gift. The gift on 9 November 2018 is a chargeable transfer.

	£
1 June 2018 Gift to son — PET becoming chargeable	2,000
Deduct annual exemption 2018/19 (part)	(2,000)
	Nil
9 November 2018 Gift to trust	20,000
Deduct annual exemption 2018/19 (balance)	(1,000)
Chargeable transfer	£19,000

Note

(a) The annual exemption is allocated to earlier rather than later transfers within the same tax year regardless of whether they are PETs or chargeable transfers when made. Although this approach seems to render *IHTA 1984, s 19(3A)* otiose, *this is HMRC's current interpretation* (HMRC Inheritance Tax Manual, IHTM14143).

310.2 NORMAL EXPENDITURE OUT OF INCOME

[*IHTA 1984, s 21*]

A wife pays annual life assurance premiums on a policy in favour of her son. The income of her husband and herself for 2018/19 is

	£
Husband's salary	45,000
Wife's salary	6,600
	£51,600

Income levels are not expected to fluctuate wildly from year to year.

The wife's disposable income is

	£
Salary	6,600
Tax thereon (personal allowance £11,850)	Nil
Personal income	£6,600

Depending on her lifestyle, the wife is probably able to show that she has sufficient income to justify a 'normal expenditure' gift of, say, a £1,000 premium paid annually (and therefore habitual). In form P11 (Notes) HMRC state that, 'examples of usual expenditure are where the deceased was paying a regular premium on an insurance policy for the benefit of another person, or perhaps they were making a monthly or other regular payment.'

If the wife was also accustomed to pay personally for an annual holiday costing, say, £2,500, it might be difficult to show that the life assurance premium was paid out of income.

310.3 NIL RATE BAND — TRANSFER OF UNUSED AMOUNT TO SPOUSE OR CIVIL PARTNER

[*IHTA 1984, ss 8A–8C*]

(A)

John dies on 25 August 2008 with an estate of £312,000 and he leaves by his will £50,000 to each of his two grandchildren on discretionary trusts and the balance is left to his widow, Jean. He has made no transfers in the seven years prior to his death. Jean dies in October 2018 when the nil rate band is £325,000.

If Jean's personal representatives make a claim under *IHTA 1984, s 8A*, the nil rate band maximum available at the time of her death is as follows.

	£
Unused nil rate band at time of death	312,000
Less non-exempt transfers on John's death	(100,000)
Nil rate band unused by John	£212,000

The percentage increase to be made to Jean's nil rate band is therefore

$$\frac{£212,000}{£312,000} \times 100 = 67.95\%$$

Jean's nil rate band is increased to

£325,000 + (£325,000 × 67.95%) = £545,838

Notes

(a) Where a person dies on or after 9 October 2007, his nil rate band maximum at the time of death is, on a claim, treated as increased by the amount of the unused nil rate band of a predeceased spouse or civil partner. The nil rate band maximum is increased by the percentage given by the formula:

$$\frac{E}{NRBMD} \times 100$$

where

E = M - VT;

M = the maximum amount that could be transferred by a chargeable transfer on the predeceased person's death if it were to be wholly chargeable at the nil rate;

VT = value actually transferred by the chargeable transfer on the death of the predeceased person (or nil if applicable);

NRBMD = the nil rate band maximum applying at the time of the predeceased person's death.

[*IHTA 1984, s 8A(2)–(4)*].

(b) The increase in the surviving partner's nil rate band maximum is subject to a maximum of 100% of that band. This could apply where, for example, the person had more than one predeceased spouse or civil partner each of whom died with unused nil rate band. [*IHTA 1984, s 8A(5)*]. See (B) below for the maximum increase in the nil rate band maximum of the survivor.

(c) A claim under *IHTA 1984, s 8A* must be made by the personal representatives of the surviving partner within two years from the end of the month of death or, if later, within three months beginning with the date the personal representatives first act as such, or within such longer period as HMRC allow. If no such claim is made, a claim can be made by any other person liable to tax on the surviving partner's death within such period as HMRC allow. [*IHTA 1984, s 8B*].

(d) Similar provisions apply to allow unused residence nil-rate band (RNRB) to be transferred to a surviving spouse or civil partner who dies on or after 6 April 2017. Where the first death occurred before 6 April 2017, the survivor's RNRB is increased by 100% of whatever the value of the RNRB is at the time of the second death, provided that the value of the estate of the first to die did not exceed £2 million. See **310.5**(C) below.

(B)

Betty has been married and widowed twice before. Her first husband, David, died in October 1974 when estate duty applied. He left all his assets in his will to Betty having made no previous transfers. His estate was wholly within the £15,000 spouse's exemption applying at that time so that none of his tax free band was utilised in 1974. Betty's second husband Jack died on 18 June 2005 and left his assets to Betty excepting a £165,000 gift he made to his daughter in 2003. Betty died in December 2018. Jack and Betty had sold their house on 6 June 2015 and moved in with one of their sons.

If the personal representatives make a claim under *IHTA 1984, s 8A*, Betty's nil rate band maximum is increased as follows.

Increase in respect of David's nil rate band.

David used none of his nil rate band, and the percentage increase to Betty's maximum is therefore 100%.

Increase in respect of Jack's nil rate band.

	£
Unused nil rate band at time of death	275,000
Less non-exempt transfers on John's death	(165,000)
Nil rate band unused by Jack	£110,000

The percentage increase to Betty's maximum is therefore

$$\frac{£110{,}000}{£275{,}000} \times 100 = 40\%$$

The total increase to Betty's nil rate band maximum would therefore be (100% + 40% =) 140%. This is, however, restricted to 100%, making Betty's nil rate band maximum on death £650,000 (£325,000 + £325,000).

Notes

(a) The increase in the surviving partner's nil rate band maximum is subject to a maximum of 100% of that band. This could apply where, as in this example, the person had more than one predeceased spouse or civil partner each of whom died with unused nil rate band. [*IHTA 1984, s 8A(5)*].

(b) It is immaterial when the predeceased spouse or civil partner died. Unused nil rate bands can be transferred even if the death was before 25 July 1986 (i.e. when capital transfer tax or estate duty applied) and the provisions of *IHTA 1984, ss 8A–8C* apply as modified by *FA 2008, Sch 4 para 10* to enable this.

(c) Betty's estate does not qualify for the additional residence nil-rate band because Jack and Betty's home was sold before 8 July 2015.

(C) Charges subsequent to death of predeceased spouse or civil partner

[*IHTA 1984, s 8C*]

C died in August 2002 having made a conditionally exempt gift of heritage property to his brother, B. C left a property worth £125,000 to B and left the balance of his estate to his wife, D. In October 2008, the heritage property conditional exemption is breached when the property is valued at £104,000. D dies in February 2019.

If the personal representatives make a claim under *IHTA 1984, s 8A*, D's nil rate band maximum is increased as follows.

	£
Unused nil rate band at time of C's death	250,000
Less non-exempt transfers on C's death	(125,000)
Nil rate band unused by C	£125,000

The percentage increase to be made to D's nil rate band is therefore

$$\left(\frac{£125{,}000}{£250{,}000} - \frac{£104{,}000}{£312{,}000}\right) \times 100 = 16.67\%$$

D's nil rate band is increased to

£325,000 + (£325,000 × 16.67%) = £379,178

Notes

(a) Where, after the death of the first spouse or partner and before the death of the survivor, tax is charged on an amount under *IHTA 1984, ss 32* or *32A* (see **316** NATIONAL HERITAGE) or *s 126* (see **327** WOODLANDS) by reference to the rate that would have been applicable if the amount had been included in the estate of the first spouse or partner, *IHTA 1984, s 8A* applies using the following formula to replace that at (A) above:

$$\left(\frac{E}{NRBMD} - \frac{TA}{NRBME}\right) \times 100$$

where

E = M − VT;

M = the maximum amount that could be transferred by a chargeable transfer on the predeceased person's death if it were to be wholly chargeable at the nil rate;

VT = value actually transferred by the chargeable transfer on the death of the predeceased person (or nil if applicable);

NRBMD = the nil rate band maximum applying at the time of the predeceased person's death;

TA = the amount on which tax is subsequently charged;

NRBME = the nil rate band maximum at the time of the event giving rise to that charge.

[*IHTA 1984, s 8C(1)(2)*].

(b) If the tax is charged after the death of the survivor, it is charged as if the personal nil rate band maximum of the predeceased spouse or partner were reduced by the amount by which the survivor's nil rate band was increased under *IHTA 1984, s 8A*. [*IHTA 1984, s 8C(4)(5)*].

310.2 ELECTION TO BE TREATED AS DOMICILED IN THE UK

[*IHTA 1984, ss 267ZA, 267ZB; FA 2013, s 177*]

George is UK domiciled and his only asset is a house in the UK worth £3 million. His wife Monique is not domiciled in the UK for inheritance tax purposes and has only foreign assets worth £2 million. George dies on 1 August 2018 leaving his estate to Monique. The couple have no children.

If no election under *IHTA 1984, s 267ZA* is made, the IHT on the death of George is:

	£
Estate	3,000,000
Less spouse exemption	(325,000)
Nil rate band	(325,000)
	£2,350,000
Inheritance tax £2,350,000 @ 40%	£940,000

On the death of Monique on 1 September 2023 when her domicile status for IHT remains unchanged, IHT will once again be due on the UK house. Assuming that its value has not changed, and that the IHT on George's death was paid from her overseas assets, the IHT on Monique's estate will be:

Estate	3,000,000
Less nil rate band	(325,000)
	£2,675,000
Inheritance tax £2,675,000 @ 40%	£1,070,000
Total inheritance tax on George and Monique's deaths £940,000 + £1,070,000 =	£2,010,000

If Monique had elected, under *IHTA 1984, s 267ZA* and before 1 August 2020, to be treated as domiciled in the UK with effect from 1 August 2018, no IHT would be payable on George's death. On Monique's death, IHT would then be due on both her UK and foreign assets. If they remain unchanged from George's death and have the same values, and the nil rate band remains unchanged, the IHT liability would be:

	£
Estate	5,000,000
Less nil rate band	(650,000)
	£4,350,000
Inheritance tax £4,350,000 @ 40%	£1,740,000
Total inheritance tax on George and Monique's deaths	£1,740,000

Notes

(a) With effect from 6 April 2013 an individual who is not domiciled in the UK (disregarding the IHT deemed domicile provisions of *IHTA 1984 s 267*), but whose spouse or civil partner is so domiciled, may elect to be treated as UK domiciled. The election may be either:

- a 'lifetime election' made at any time when the person making the election is non-UK domiciled, or
- a 'death election' made within two years of the death on or after 6 April 2013 of the person's UK domiciled spouse or civil partner.

A death election may be made by the personal representatives of the non-UK domiciled spouse, in the event of that person's death.

An election has effect on the date specified in it, which must be on or after 6 April 2013. Subject to this, a lifetime election may specify a date which is within the period of seven years ending with the date on which it is made, and a death election may specify a date which is within the seven years ending with the date of the death of the UK domiciled spouse or civil partner. In both cases the parties must have been married or civil partners throughout the period covered by the election.

[*IHTA 1984, ss 267ZA, 267ZB; FA 2013, s 177*].

(b) Both elections are irrevocable, and apply only for IHT purposes. They have no application to the remittance basis rules for other tax purposes (see IT 23 and CGT 225 REMITTANCE BASIS).

(c) For transfers of value made on or after 6 April 2013, the exemption for transfers to a non-UK domiciled spouse or civil partner is equal to the nil rate band (currently £325,000). Previously the exemption was £55,000. [*IHTA 1984, s 18; FA 2013, s 178*].

310.5 RESIDENCE NIL RATE BAND

[*IHTA 1984, ss 8D–8M; F(No 2)A 2015, s 9; FA 2016, Sch 15*]

(A) Inheritance of house by direct descendant

John dies on 5 August 2018 and leaves his estate worth £550,000 to his children. This includes a house worth £150,000 to his son Rob, and other assets worth £400,000 shared equally between son Rob and daughter Ria. John has made no chargeable transfers in the seven years prior to his death.

	£
Estate	550,000
Less Residence nil rate band (Lower of £150,000 and £125,000)	(125,000)
Nil rate band	(325,000)
Taxable estate	£100,000
Inheritance tax £100,000 @ 40%	£40,000

Notes

(a) With effect for deaths on or after 6 April 2017 a residence nil rate band is available for transfers on death where the deceased's interest in a qualifying residential interest, which has been their residence at some point and is included in their estate, is inherited by one or more direct descendants on death, whether by will or on intestacy.

(b) A direct descendant is a child of the deceased, including a step-child, adopted child, foster child, and an infant subject to guardianship arrangement or a special guardianship order. Also included are the lineal descendants of any of these and a person who was the spouse or civil partner of a lineal descendant at the time of the death of the testator or where the descendant predeceased the testator, at the time of the descendant's death so long as such spouse or civil partner has not since remarried or become the civil partner of another.

(c) The maximum available residential nil rate band for 2018/19 is £125,000 (£100,000 for 2017/18). The maximum will increase to £150,000 for 2019/20 and £175,000 for 2020/21.

(B) Downsizing or disposal of house before death and inheritance by children

[*IHTA 1984, s 8FA; FA 2016, Sch 15 paras 1, 5*]

Monica lived in a house in London. On 10 April 2018 she sold her house for £120,000 and moved into a flat which she bought for £95,000. Monica dies on 15 July 2019. Her estate includes the flat which is now worth £105,000 and other assets worth £395,000 is shared equally between her children.

		£
Estate		500,000
Less Residence nil rate band (Lower of £105,000 and £150,000)	(105,000)	

Downsizing addition

Step 1: Former allowance as on 10 April 2018

$$\frac{120,000}{125,000} \times 100 = 96\%$$

Step 2: Percentage as on Monica's death on 15 July 2019

$$\frac{105,000}{150,000} \times 100 = 70\%$$

Step 3: Percentage of RNRB lost is 26% (96% - 70%)

Step 4: Lost RNRB amount $150,000 \times 26\%$	(39,000)	
		(144,000)
Nil rate band		(325,000)
Taxable estate		£31,000
Inheritance tax £31,000 @ 40%		£12,400

Notes

(a) A claim for the residence nil rate band may be made where a person has sold a home in lifetime which they lived in at some stage. The legislation envisages two different circumstances, first that where the deceased downsized from a more valuable residence and there is a less valuable residence left in the estate on death (as illustrated in this example), and second where a residence was previously sold and no other residence purchased. The personal representatives can nominate which former residence is to be used for this relief. The downsizing must have taken place on or after 8 July 2015; there is no relief for any downsizing before that date.

(b) Monica qualifies for the downsizing addition because she sold her house on 10 April 2018 i.e. on or after 8 July 2015, downsizing to a flat which remained in her estate until death but did not fully utilise the residential nil-rate band of £150,000 (see note (c) to (A) above). Both the flat and at least part of the remaining estate are inherited by Monica's children.

(c) The steps used to calculate the downsizing addition are those in *IHTA 1984, s 8FE(9)*.

(C) Transfer of unused band to spouse

[*IHTA 1984, ss 8G, 8L; F(No 2)A 2015, s 9; FA 2016, Sch 15 paras 1, 6*]

Mrs G died on 31 January 2015 leaving an estate worth £1,000,000 which includes a home worth £800,000. She left her estate to her husband Mr G. Mr G dies on 10 June 2018 leaving an estate of £1,500,000 after liabilities, including the interest in the home now worth £900,000 transferred to his daughter. He leaves legacies to friends, nephews and nieces of £400,000 and the residue to their two children in equal shares.

Estate	£1,500,000

Less Residence nil rate band (Lower of £900,000 and £125,000)	(125,000)	
Spouse's residence nil rate band transferred to Mr G	(125,000)	
Nil rate band	(325,000)	
Unused nil rate band brought forward	(325,000)	
Net amount available for claim		(900,000)
Taxable estate		£600,000
Inheritance tax £600,000 @ 40%		£240,000

Notes

(a) Unused residence nil rate band can be transferred between spouses and civil partners. This transfer is referred to in the legislation as 'brought-forward allowance'.

(b) The brought-forward allowance can be claimed where a person, who dies after 6 April 2017, has been pre-deceased at any time by one or more spouses or civil partners. It is based on the unused proportion of the RNRB at the time of the first death, calculated as follows:

(1) identify the actual amount of unused RNRB at the time of the first death;

(2) express this amount as a percentage of the residential enhancement available at the date of the first death;

(3) if the deceased has survived more than one partner, calculate the unused percentage for each one;

(4) add the percentages together but if the result is more than 100%, take 100%; and

(5) apply the total percentage calculated to the residential enhancement at the date of the later death to give the brought forward allowance.

Where the first death occurred before 6 April 2017 and the second death occurs during 2018/19, the actual amount of unused RNRB ((1) above) is deemed to be £125,000. The residential enhancement at the date of the earlier death ((2) above) is also assumed to be £125,000. The effect of this is that the survivor's RNRB is increased by 100% of whatever the value of the RNRB is at the time of the second death (£125,000 in this example).

(c) A claim under *IHTA 1984, s 8L* for a brought-forward allowance must be made within the two years from the end of the month in which the person dies, or if later the period of three months beginning with the date on which the personal representatives first act as such.

(D) Tapering for large estate

Robert dies on 10 October 2018 leaving an estate worth £2,100,000 to his two children, which includes main residence of £1,500,000 and other assets of £600,000. He had made no lifetime transfers.

£

Estate		2,100,000
Less Residential nil rate band		
Lower of £1,500,000 and £125,000	125,000	
RNRB restricted by $\frac{2,100,000 - 2,000,000}{2}$	50,000	(75,000)
Less Nil rate band		(325,000)
Taxable estate		£1,700,000
Inheritance tax £1,700,000 @ 40%		£680,000

Note

(a) The residential nil rate band is tapered away by £1 for every £2 that the value of the estate exceeds £2,000,000. [*IHTA 1984, s 8D; F(No 2)A 2015, s 9(1)(4); FA 2016, Sch 15 paras 1, 2*].

311 Gifts with Reservation

[*FA 1986, ss 102–102C, Sch 20; SI 1987 No 1130*]

311.1 GIFTS WITH RESERVATION

(A) Reservation released within seven years before death

On 19 June 2000 D gave his house to his grandson G, but continued to live in it alone paying no rent. The house was valued at £130,000. On 5 May 2014 D remarried, and went to live with his new wife F (in a home owned entirely by F). G immediately moved into the house, which was then valued at £333,000.

On 3 January 2019 D died, leaving his estate of £200,000 equally to his granddaughter H and his wife F.

Gift 19 June 2000

As the gift was made more than seven years before death, it is a PET which has become exempt.

5 May 2014 release of reservation

The release of D's reservation is a PET which becomes chargeable by reason of D's death between 4 and 5 years later. IHT is charged, at 60% of full rates on the basis of the Table of rates in force at the time of death, on the value of the house at the date of release of reservation.

		£	£
Gift			333,000
Deduct annual exemptions	2014/15	—	
	2013/14	—	
			—
Chargeable transfer			£333,000
Tax thereon)			
0–325,000 at nil%		—	
325,001–333,000 at 40%		3,200	
		£3,200	
IHT payable at 60% of full rates, 60% × £3,200			£1,920

Death 3 January 2019

IHT is charged at full rates on the chargeable estate of £100,000 (£100,000 passing to the wife is exempt) in the bracket £333,000 to £433,000.

Tax thereon

333,001–433,000 at 40%	£40,000

Notes

(a) HMRC consider that the annual exemption is not available against the deemed PET arising on the release of a reservation (HMRC Inheritance Tax Manual, IHTM14343).

(b) The additional residence nil-rate band is not available against a PET becoming chargeable on death. The band is also not available against the death estate. For the purpose of determining entitlement to the band, the house is deemed to have been disposed of when the reservation was released on 5 May 2014. [*IHTA 1984, s 8H(4D)(b); F(No 2)A 2015, s 9; FA 2016, Sch 15 para 7*]. The house was therefore disposed of before 8 July 2015. For examples on the residence nil-rate band see **310.5** EXEMPT TRANSFERS.

(B) Reservation not released before death

On 19 June 2013 X gave a painting to his grandson Y, but continued to hang it on the wall of his living room until he died on 3 January 2019. The painting was valued at £239,000.

On 3 January 2019 X died, leaving his estate of £200,000 (which did not include any residential property) equally to his granddaughter Z and his wife W. The painting was valued at £251,000 at the date of X's death.

Gift 19 June 2013

This is a potentially exempt transfer which becomes chargeable by reason of X's death within seven years.

Death 3 January 2019

As the reservation had not been released at the date of X's death, X is treated as beneficially entitled to the painting, which thus forms part of his chargeable estate on death.

A double charge would arise by virtue of the painting being the subject of a PET and a part of the chargeable estate on death. *The Inheritance Tax (Double Charges Relief) Regulations 1987* [*SI 1987 No 1130*] provide relief as follows.

First calculation under Reg 5(3)(a)

Charge the painting in the death estate and ignore the PET.

Chargeable estate	£
Free estate passing to Z	100,000
Painting	251,000
	£351,000

There are no chargeable transfers within the previous seven years.

IHT payable	£
0–325,000 at nil %	—
325,001–351,000 at 40%	10,400
	£10,400

Second calculation under Reg 5(3)(b)

Charge the PET and ignore the value of the painting in the death estate.

		£	£
Gift 19 June 2013			239,000
Deduct annual exemptions	2013/14	3,000	
	2012/13	3,000	
			(6,000)
Chargeable transfer			£233,000
Tax thereon			
0–233,000		Nil	

	£
Chargeable estate on death (excluding house)	100,000
IHT payable in the bracket £325,001 to £333,000	
325,001–333,000 at 40%	£3,200
Total IHT payable	£3,200

The first calculation yields the higher amount of tax (£10,400), so tax is charged by reference to the value of the gift with reservation in the estate, ignoring the PET.

Note

(a) The comparison between the two calculations is made *before* credit is given for tax already paid (should there be any) (see HMRC Inheritance Tax Manual, IHTM14712).

312 Interest on Tax

[*IHTA 1984, s 233; FA 1989, s 178; SI 1989 No 1297*]

312.1 B died on 10 February 2018. The executors made a payment on account of IHT of £70,000 on 30 June 2018 on delivery of the account. The final notice of determination was raised by HMRC Inheritance Tax on 19 June 2019 in the sum of £102,500. The rate of interest is assumed to be 5%.

Date of chargeable event (death)	10 February 2018
Date on which interest starts to accrue	1 September 2018

	£
IHT payable	102,500
Payment made on account 30 June 2018	(70,000)
Balance due	£32,500
Assessment raised by HMRC 19 June 2019	
Interest payable (1.9.18 to 19.6.19)	
£32,500 at 5% for 292 days	£1,300

Note

(a) Further interest may be charged if payment of the balance is not made promptly.

312.2 F gave his holiday home in Cornwall to his granddaughter G on 7 August 2014. On 23 May 2018 F died. He had made no use of the property at any time after 7 August 2014. G made a payment of £15,000, on account of the IHT due, on 1 January 2019. The liability was agreed at £27,000, and the balance paid, on 17 February 2019. The rate of interest is assumed to be 5%

Date of PET	7 August 2014
Date on which PET becomes chargeable	23 May 2018
Date on which IHT is due	1 December 2018

	£
IHT payable	27,000
Payment made on account 1 January 2019	(15,000)
Balance due	£12,000
Interest payable	
On £27,000 from 1.12.18–1.1.19	
£27,000 at 5% for 31 days	115
On £12,000 from 1.1.19–17.2.19	
£12,000 at 5% for 47 days	77
Total interest payable	£192

313 Liability for Tax

[*IHTA 1984, ss 199(1), 204(2)(3)(5)(6)*]

313.1 LIFETIME TRANSFERS

(A) Transferor

A settled £78,000 on discretionary trusts in December 2018, having previously made chargeable transfers on 31 March 2018 totalling £328,000.

A's liability is as follows	£
Gift	78,000
Deduct 2018/19 annual exemption	(3,000)
	£75,000
Grossed at 20%	£93,750
IHT thereon at 20%	£18,750

(B) Transferee

In example (A) above A pays only £10,000 of IHT and defaults on the balance of £8,750, so that the trustees become liable as transferee.

The trustees' liability is not however £8,750 but is as follows

	£
Original gross	93,750
Deduct IHT unpaid	(8,750)
Revised gross	£85,000
IHT thereon at 20%	17,000
Deduct Paid by A	(10,000)
Now due from trustees	£7,000

(C) Person in whom property is vested

In January 2019 C transferred to trustees of a discretionary trust shares in an unquoted property company worth, as a minority holding, £50,000. However, the transfer deprives C of control of the company with the result that the value of his estate is reduced by £210,000. He has already used his nil rate band and annual exemptions.

C's liability is as follows

Net loss to him	£210,000
Grossed at 20%	£262,500
IHT thereon at 20%	£52,500

C fails to pay so that the trustees become liable, as follows

	£
Original gross	262,500
Deduct unpaid IHT	(52,500)
	£210,000
IHT thereon at 20%	£42,000

Note

(a) The trustees' liability cannot exceed the value of the assets which they hold, namely the proceeds of sale of the shares, less any CGT and costs incurred since acquisition, plus any undistributed income in their hands.

313.2 TRANSFERS ON DEATH

[*IHTA 1984, ss 200(1)(3), 204(1)–(3)(5), 211*]

Personal representatives of E, who died on 30 September 2018, received the following assets:

	£
Free personal property	155,265
Land bequeathed to F (which, under the terms of the will, bears its own IHT)	29,735
Private residence, bequeathed to spouse	51,000

A trust in which E had a pre-April 2006 life interest was valued at £154,000. Under the will of E, legacies of £15,000, each free of IHT, were given to F and G and the residue was left to H. E had made no chargeable transfers during his lifetime.

	Persons liable		IHT
IHT is borne as to		£	£
chargeable transfer			
Free personal property	PRs	155,265	2,565
Land bequeathed to F	F	29,735	491
Private residence to spouse	—	Exempt	Nil
Trust fund	Trustees	154,000	2,544
		£339,000	£5,600

The residue left to H is as follows		
Free personal property		155,265
Deduct IHT	2,565	
Legacies to F and G	30,000	(32,565)
		£122,700

Note

(a) If the will had not directed that the IHT on the land bequeathed to F be borne by F, the IHT would be payable out of residue. [*IHTA 1984, s 211*].

313.3 LIFETIME TRANSFER WITH ADDITIONAL LIABILITY ON DEATH

[*IHTA 1984, ss 131, 199(2), 201(2)*]

(A)

On 31 December 2018, H, who had made no earlier chargeable transfers other than to utilise his annual exemptions for 2018/19 and earlier years, transferred £368,000 into a discretionary trust and, a month later, settled an asset worth £20,000 into the same trust. H paid the appropriate IHT. On 30 June 2021, H died. It is assumed that the nil rate band on 30 June 2021 is £350,000.

The trustees become liable to further IHT as follows

	£	£
Original net gift	£368,000	£20,000
Grossed-up at half of full rates	£378,750	£25,000
IHT (paid by H)	£10,750	£5,000
IHT at 80% of death rates applicable in June 2021 on original gross (death between 3 and 4 years after gifts)	5,760	8,000
Deduct paid originally by H	(10,750)	(5,000)
Now due from trustees	—	£3,000

Note

(a) The additional IHT on death is calculated using the rates in force at the date of death. Where the IHT at the new death rates, as tapered, is less than the IHT paid on the original chargeable transfer, there is no repayment.

(B)

The second gift in (A) above had fallen in value to £18,000 by the time of H's death.

The trustees may claim to reduce the IHT payable as follows

	£
Original gross gift	25,000
Deduct drop in value (£20,000 − £18,000)	(2,000)
Revised gross	£23,000
IHT thereon at 80% of death rate applicable in June 2021	7,360
Deduct paid by H	(5,000)
	£2,360

Note

(a) If the asset had fallen in value to £10,625 or less, so that the revised gross became £15,625 or less and the IHT at 80% of death rates £5,000 or less, the trustees would have no liability because H had already paid IHT of £5,000.

313.4 POTENTIALLY EXEMPT TRANSFER BECOMING CHARGEABLE ON DEATH

[*IHTA 1984, ss 199, 201, 204; FA 1986, Sch 19 paras 26–28*]

On 19 May 2015 M gave N £336,000. M died on 3 August 2018 having made no other gifts.

		£
Gift		336,000
Deduct annual exemptions	2015/16	(3,000)
	2014/15	(3,000)
		£330,000

The IHT at 80% of full rates on the gift to N is payable by N on 1 March 2019.

	£
0–325,000 at nil%	—
325,001–330,000 at 40%	2,000
	£2,000

IHT payable by N 80% × £2,000 = £1,600

Notes

(a) If N has not paid the IHT due of £1,600 by 1 March 2020 the personal representatives of M are liable, although their liability cannot exceed the death estate of M. The amount is a deductible liability from the estate only to the extent that reimbursement from N cannot be obtained.

(b) See also **305.1** CALCULATION OF TAX for liability to tax on potentially exempt transfers.

314 Life Assurance Policies

[*IHTA 1984, ss 21, 167*]

314.1 A has paid premiums of £2,000 p.a for 6 years on a policy on his own life. He gives the policy to his son B. The market value of the policy at the date of gift is £11,000. A also pays annual premiums of £2,000 on a policy on his life written in favour of his son.

Assignment of policy

The gift is valued either at

(i) market value (£11,000), or

(ii) the accumulated gross premiums paid (£12,000) if greater.

Annual premiums

The payment of an annual premium is regarded as an annual gift, the amount of the transfer being the gross premium (or, where due and payable before 6 April 2015, the net premium if paid after deduction of tax at source).

Notes

(a) The gifts are PETs. The assignment of the policy will only become chargeable if A dies within seven years, and only the annual premiums paid within seven years of A's death will be chargeable.

(b) Exemptions available for reduction of the chargeable transfer on assignment include the annual exemption and the marriage exemption.

(c) The normal expenditure exemption may be available to A for premiums paid and the annual exemption may also be claimed to exempt the gift in whole or in part. See also note (a) to **310.2** EXEMPT TRANSFERS.

(d) Normal expenditure relief is not available when a policy and annuity have been effected on a back-to-back basis (with certain exceptions).

315 Mutual Transfers

[*FA 1986, s 104; SI 1987 No 1130*]

315.1 POTENTIALLY EXEMPT TRANSFERS AND DEATH

A, who has made no previous transfers of value other than to use his annual exemptions for 2014/15 and 2015/16, makes a gift of £330,000 to B on 1 July 2015. On 15 July 2016 and 20 January 2017, he makes gifts of £238,000 and £96,000 respectively into a discretionary trust and the trustees pay the IHT due of £1,200 on the later transfer. On 2 January 2018, B dies and the 2014 gift is returned to A by virtue of B's Will. On 4 April 2019, A dies. His taxable estate on death is valued at £410,000 which includes the 2015 gift returned to him in 2018 which is still valued at £330,000. It is assumed that A's estate does not qualify for the additional residence nil-rate band.

First calculation under Reg 4(4)(a)

The gift in 2015 is a PET and would normally become a chargeable transfer by virtue of A's death within seven years of making the gift. However, for the purpose of this calculation, it is ignored and the returned gift is charged as part of A's death estate.

Additional tax due on chargeable lifetime transfers

		£
Gift on 15 July 2016		238,000
Deduct annual exemption 2016/17		(3,000)
		235,000
Gift on 20 January 2017		96,000
		£331,000
IHT at death rates on £331,000		2,400
IHT previously paid		(1,200)
Additional IHT payable by trustees		£1,200
Tax on death estate of £410,000 charged at 40%		
IHT payable	note (a)	£164,000
Total IHT payable as consequence of death (£1,200 + £164,000)		£165,200

Second calculation under Reg 4(4)(b)

The 2015 gift is charged as a PET but the returned gift is ignored in the death estate.

The tax due on PET of £330,000 at death rates

	£
0–325,000 at nil%	Nil
325,001–330,000 at 40%	2,000
	£2,000
IHT payable at 80% of full rates (death between 3 and 4 years after gift)	£1,600

Tax due on chargeable lifetime transfers of £331,000 (after annual exemption) charged at 40%

	£
IHT payable	132,400
IHT paid	(1,200)
Additional IHT payable	£131,200

Tax on death estate of £80,000 charged at 40%	
IHT payable	£32,000

Total IHT payable as consequence of death (£1,600 + £131,200 + £32,000)	£164,800

The first calculation gives the higher amount of tax, so the PET is ignored and the returned gift included in the death estate, the tax liabilities being as in the first calculation above.

Note

(a) Quick succession relief under *IHTA 1984, s 141* (see **319.1** QUICK SUCCESSION RELIEF below) might be due in respect of the returned PET by reference to any tax charged on that PET in connection with B's death. If, as a result of such relief, the first calculation produces a lower tax charge than the second, then the second calculation will prevail, i.e. the PET will be charged and the returned gift ignored in the death estate.

315.2 CHARGEABLE TRANSFERS AND DEATH

C, who had made no other transfer of value, gifted £320,000 on 31 May 2011 into discretionary trust, on which IHT of £400 was paid. On 5 October 2011, he gave D a life interest in shares worth £85,000; IHT of £17,000 was paid. On 3 January 2017, C makes a PET of £36,000 to E. On 31 December 2017, D dies and the settled shares return to C, the settlor (no tax charge arises on D's death). On 10 August 2018, C dies; his death estate is valued at £320,000 which includes the shares returned from D, now worth £60,000. It is assumed that C's estate does not qualify for the additional residence nil-rate band.

First calculation under Reg 7(4)(a)

The gift in October 2011 is ignored and the returned shares included as part of the taxable estate on death.

No additional tax arises on the May 2011 lifetime transfer of £314,000 (after annual exemptions) as it was made more than seven years before death.

Tax due on PET of £30,000 (after annual exemptions) made in January 2017 charged in band £325,001–344,000.

£19,000 at 40% = £7,600.

Tax on death estate of £320,000 charged in band £30,001 to £350,000 (the gift to the discretionary trust having fallen out of cumulation)

30,001–325,000 at nil%		
325,001–350,000 at 40%	£10,000	
Total IHT payable as consequence of death (£7,600 + £10,000) (but see note (a) below)		£17,600

Second calculation under Reg 7(4)(b)

The October 2011 gift is charged and the returned shares are excluded from the taxable estate on death.

Additional tax due on October 2011 transfer as a result of death — charged in band £325,001 to £399,000.

325,001–399,000 at 40%	£29,600
IHT payable at 20% of full rates (death between 6 and 7 years after gift)	5,920
IHT paid £17,000, but credit restricted to	(5,920)
Additional IHT	Nil

Tax due on PET of £30,000 (after annual exemptions) charged in band £399,001 to £429,000.

£30,000 at 40%	£12,000

Tax on death estate of £260,000 charged in band £115,001 to £375,000.

115,001–325,000 at nil %		
325,001–375,000 at 40%	£20,000	
Total IHT payable as consequence of death (£12,000 + £20,000)		£32,000

The second calculation gives the higher amount of tax so the returned gift is excluded from the death estate, the tax liabilities being as in the second calculation above.

Note

(a) If the first calculation had given the higher amount, a credit for IHT would have been due, restricted to the lower of

(i) the IHT paid on the lifetime transfer (i.e. £17,000); and

(ii) the IHT attributable to the returned shares on death, calculated as follows:

$$\text{Estate rate } \frac{10{,}000}{320{,}000} = 3.125\%$$

£60,000 × 3.125% = £1,875

The IHT actually payable as a consequence of death would have been £15,725 (£17,600 − £1,875).

316 National Heritage

[*IHTA 1984, ss 30–35, 57A, 77–79, 207, Sch 2 paras 5, 6, Sch 4, Sch 5; FA 2012, Sch 33 para 4*]

316.1 CONDITIONS FOR EXEMPTION

Lord A died in 1952 leaving Netherington Hall in Wiltshire to his son B together with all its contents. These contents included a painting by Whistler of Netherington Hall and also a rare painting of Mary Queen of Scots alongside Lord Bothwell her second husband. The pictures and other items in the Hall were all exempted from estate duty which, at the time Lord A died, was applied at a marginal rate of 80%.

Unfortunately the son Lord B dies in a hunting accident on Boxing Day 2017 and the Hall together with contents are left to his son, now Lord C. HMRC consider the painting by Whistler of the Hall to be pre-eminent for its artistic interest. The painting is accepted as pre-eminent and is re-exempted on the death of Lord B, subject to a contingent liability to IHT on any breach of undertaking or subsequent disposal by sale when the rate of IHT would be 40%.

HMRC do not consider the painting of Mary Queen of Scots, now valued at £5 million, to be pre-eminent.

As the Mary Queen of Scots painting fails the pre-eminence test IHT of £2 million (£5 million × 40%) is due and paid by the estate. Lord C sells the painting for £8 million (net of expenses and CGT) six months later in June 2018 thereby breaking the estate duty undertaking.

In view of HMRC's decision, there will be a tax charge calculated as follows:

	£
Estate duty at 80% on £8 million	6,400,000
Less credit for IHT paid on Lord B's death	(2,000,000)
Estate duty payable on sale	4,400,000

Note

(a) For claims made on or after 31 July 1998, any picture, print, book, work of art or scientific object, or any other thing not yielding income, or a collection or group of such objects, only qualifies (apart from by virtue of a historical connection with a building of outstanding historic or architectural interest) for conditional exemption, if it appears to HMRC to be *pre-eminent* for its national, scientific, historic or artistic interest [*IHTA 1984, s 31(1)(5)*]. Previously such objects simply had to appear to the Treasury to be of national, scientific, historic or artistic interest.

316.2 CONDITIONALLY EXEMPT TRANSFERS AFTER 6 APRIL 1976

(A) Chargeable event during lifetime of relevant person

C, who has made previous chargeable transfers during 2011 of £230,000, makes a conditionally exempt gift of property in February 2013. In October 2018, the property is sold for £500,000 and capital gains tax of £80,000 is payable.

			£
Cumulative total of previous chargeable transfers of relevant person			230,000
Net sale proceeds of conditionally exempt property		500,000	
Deduct Capital gains tax payable		(80,000)	
Chargeable transfer			420,000
Revised cumulative total for relevant person			£650,000
Inheritance tax payable (by reference to lifetime rates in October 2018)			
£325,000 at 20% =	£65,000		

(B) Chargeable event after relevant person is dead

D died in April 1999 leaving a taxable estate of £350,000 together with conditionally exempt property valued at £600,000 at the breach in October 2018.

	£
Value of relevant person's estate at death	350,000
Value of conditionally exempt property at date of breach	600,000
	£950,000

Inheritance tax payable (by reference to full rates applicable in October 2018).

£600,000 at 40% = £240,000

Notes

(a) As the chargeable event occurs after tax is reduced by the substitution of a new Table of rates, the new rates are used.

(b) Where a chargeable event arises in respect of property which was allowed conditional exemption on an earlier death, the lower 36% rate of inheritance tax cannot be claimed on that event even if the remaining estate had satisfied the conditions for that rate. [*IHTA 1984, s 33(2ZA); FA 2012, Sch 33 para 4*]. See **322.2** TRANSFERS ON DEATH.

(C) Multiple conditionally exempt transfers

D died in December 1988 leaving a conditionally exempt property to his son E. D's taxable estate at death was £230,000. In 1997 E gave the property to his daughter F. F gave the necessary undertakings so this transfer was also conditionally exempt. In December 2018 F sold the property for its market value of £500,000 and paid capital gains tax of £50,000. During 1997 E had made chargeable transfers of £20,000 and he has made no other transfers.

	£	£
Value of relevant person's estate at death		230,000
Net sale proceeds of conditionally		
exempt property	500,000	
Deduct capital gains tax	(50,000)	
Chargeable transfer		450,000
		£680,000
Inheritance tax payable by F		
£355,000 at 40% =		£142,000
Previous cumulative total of E		20,000
Add chargeable transfer		450,000
E's revised cumulative total		£470,000

Notes

(a) There have been two conditionally exempt transfers within the period of 30 years ending with the chargeable event in December 2018. HMRC may select either D or E as the 'relevant person' for the purpose of calculating the tax due. The IHT liability will be higher if D is selected. [*IHTA 1984, ss 33(5), 78(3)*].

(b) As F receives the proceeds of sale, she is the person liable to pay the IHT. [*IHTA 1984, s 207(1)*].

(c) Although the IHT is calculated by reference to D's cumulative total, it is E whose cumulative total is adjusted as he made the last conditionally exempt transfer of the property. [*IHTA 1984, s 34(1)*].

(d) As the chargeable event occurs after a reduction in the rates of tax, the new rates are used to calculate the tax payable. [*IHTA 1984, Sch 2 para 5*].

316.3 CONDITIONALLY EXEMPT TRANSFERS ON DEATH BEFORE 7 APRIL 1976

(A) Chargeable event more than 3 years after death

B died on 31 December 1975 leaving a taxable estate of £100,000 together with a conditionally exempt painting valued at £50,000. In June 2018 the painting was sold for £110,000.

		£
Value of deceased's taxable estate		100,000
Value of exempt property at date of chargeable event	note (a)	110,000
		£210,000
Recalculated IHT liability	note (b)	£90,750
IHT payable on conditionally exempt property		
$£90,750 \times \frac{110,000}{210,000}$		£47,536

No further liability accrues to the estate of the deceased.

Notes

(a) The value of the exempt property will be reduced by any capital gains tax chargeable in respect of the sale. [*TCGA 1992, s 258(8)*].

(b) The IHT liability is calculated using rates in force at the date of death.

(B) **Estate Duty**

Lord A dies in 1952 (see example at **316.1** above) leaving Netherington Hall and its contents to his son now Lord B. The paintings were exempted from estate duty which was at an 80% marginal rate at the time.

On Boxing Day 2018 Lord B dies in an accident and the Hall and contents are left to his son Lord C. The Executors omit to make claim within the two years to exempt the chattels even though these would have been considered to be pre-eminent under *IHTA 1984, s 31*. The sum of £2,400,000 is paid as IHT on the death in relation to the paintings' value of £6,000,000.

Lord C sells the paintings in the year 2019 for a total sum of £8,000,000 and estate duty at 80% becomes payable on these proceeds (net of expenses), and a credit for the tax previously paid of £2,400,000 is given.

	£
Estate duty 80% × £8m	6,400,000
Less credit for IHT paid on Lord B's death	(2,400,000)
Estate duty payable on sale	4,000,000

Note

(a) If a new exemption claim in respect of the paintings had been made on B's death then the old estate duty liability would have fallen out of account on the chargeable event as only IHT would have been relevant. [*IHTA 1984, Sch 6 para 4(2)(3)*]. The IHT due would have been £8m × 40% = £3,200,000.

316.4 CHARGE TO TAX

Tax credit

[*IHTA 1984, s 33(7)*]

Property inherited in 1984 from A's estate by B, who gave the necessary undertakings so that the property is conditionally exempt, is given in December 2018 by B to C. C agrees to pay any inheritance tax arising from the transfer but does not wish to give the necessary undertakings, so a chargeable event arises. B dies in March 2019.

	£
A's estate at date of death in 1984	180,000
B's cumulative chargeable transfers at date of chargeable event in December 2018 (all in 2017/18)	86,000
Value of property at date of chargeable event	250,000

Inheritance tax on chargeable event (subject to tax credit)

		£
Value of A's estate at date of death		180,000
Value of property at date of chargeable event		250,000
		£430,000
Inheritance tax payable		
£105,000 at 40%		£42,000
Inheritance tax on B's gift		
Cumulative total of previous transfers		86,000
Value of property gifted	250,000	
Deduct Annual exemption 2018/19	(3,000)	247,000
		£333,000
Inheritance tax arising on gift		£3,200
Tax credit		
IHT on B's gift		3,200
IHT on chargeable event	42,000	
Deduct tax credit	(3,200)	
		38,800
Total inheritance tax borne		£42,000

316.5 SETTLEMENTS — EVENTS AFTER 8 MARCH 1982

(A) Chargeable events following conditionally exempt occasions

A, who is still alive, settled property and investments on discretionary trusts in September 1988, conditional exemption being granted in respect of designated property. In April 2002, the designated property was appointed absolutely to beneficiary C who gave the necessary undertakings for exemption to continue. However, in October 2018, C sold the property for £135,000 net of costs, suffering a capital gains tax liability of £20,000. At the time of C's sale, A had cumulative chargeable transfers of £40,000.

			£
Cumulative total of previous chargeable transfers of relevant person			40,000
Net sale proceeds of conditionally exempt property			115,000
			£155,000
Inheritance tax payable by C			
£110,000	at nil%	—	
£5,000	at 20%	1,000	
£115,000		£1,000	£1,000

Notes

(a) A is the relevant person in relation to the chargeable event as he is the person to effect the only conditionally exempt transfer *and* the person who is settlor in relation to the settlement in respect of which the only conditionally exempt occasion arose. [*IHTA 1984, ss 33(5), 78(3)*].

(b) HMRC have discretion to select either the conditionally exempt transfer (by A to the trustees) in 1988 or the conditionally exempt occasion (from the trustees to C) in 2002 as the 'last transaction' for the purposes of determining who is the relevant person. A is the relevant person regardless of which is selected but HMRC are more likely to choose the earlier transfer as this will result in a greater amount of tax being collected. [*IHTA 1984, ss 33(5), 78(3)(4)*].

(c) The chargeable amount of £115,000 does not increase either A's cumulative total or that of the trustees for the purpose of calculating the IHT liability on any subsequent transfers. As the last conditionally exempt transaction before the chargeable event was a conditionally exempt occasion rather than a conditionally exempt transfer, the provisions of *IHTA 1984, s 34* (which allow for an increase in the cumulative total) do not apply. [*IHTA 1984, s 78(6)*].

(B) Exemption from the ten-year anniversary charge

[*IHTA 1984, s 79; FA 2006, Sch 20 para 34; F(No 2)A 2015, s 12*]

Trustees own National Heritage property for which the necessary undertakings have been given and the property has been designated by the Treasury. The property was settled in January 1975 and is the sole asset of the trust. No appointments or advances of capital have been made. On 30 October 2018, there is a breach of the undertakings. At this date the property is valued at £150,000.

Ten-year anniversary charge

There is no liability in 1985, 1995, 2005 or 2015.

Breach in October 2018

Value of property at time of event	£150,000

The relevant period is the period from the date of settlement or, if later, 13 March 1975 to 29 October 2018, i.e. 174 complete quarters.

The rate of tax is

0.25% for 40 quarters	10.00%
0.20% for 40 quarters	8.00%
0.15% for 40 quarters	6.00%
0.10% for 40 quarters	4.00%
0.05% for 14 quarters	0.70%
	28.70%

IHT payable is 28.70% × £150,000 = £43,050

316.6 MAINTENANCE FUNDS FOR HISTORIC BUILDINGS

[*IHTA 1984, Sch 2 para 6, Sch 4 paras 8, 12–14*]

On 1 January 1999 P settled £500,000 in an approved maintenance fund for his historic mansion during the lives of himself and his wife, W. P died in February 2002, his taxable estate and lifetime transfers chargeable on death amounting to £175,000. On 1 January 2019, the date of death of W, the fund, which has been depleted by extensive repairs to the mansion, is valued at £300,000. £80,000 is transferred to the National Trust, which also accepts the gift of the mansion, and the balance is paid to P's grandson G.

No IHT is payable on the £80,000 paid to the National Trust, but the balance passing to G is liable to IHT at the higher of a tapered scale rate (the 'first rate') and an effective rate calculated by reference to P's estate (the 'second rate'). [*IHTA 1984, Sch 4 paras 12–14*].

First rate

The property was comprised in the maintenance fund for 20 years, i.e. 80 quarters.

The scale rate is

0.25% for each of the first 40 quarters	10.0%
0.20% for each of the next 40 quarters	8.0%
	18.0%

Second rate

The effective rate is calculated, using half Table rates applying on 1 January 2019, as if the chargeable amount transferred (£220,000) had been added to the value transferred by P on his death (£175,000) and had formed the highest part of the total. Half Table rates are used because the fund was set up in P's lifetime.

		£
£150,000	at nil	—
£70,000	at 20%	14,000
£220,000		£14,000

$$\text{The effective rate is } \frac{14{,}000}{220{,}000} \times 100\% = \quad 6.36\%$$

As the second rate (6.36%) is lower than the first rate (18%) the first rate is used.

IHT payable is £220,000 at 18% = £39,600

317 Payment of Tax

[*IHTA 1984, ss 227, 228, 234*]

317.1 PAYMENT BY INSTALMENTS ON TRANSFER OR DEATH

(A)

F died on 17 December 2018 leaving a free estate of £395,000, including £75,000 (after business property relief at 50%) in respect of plant and machinery in a partnership. An election is made to pay inheritance tax on the plant and machinery by 10 equal yearly instalments.

Inheritance tax on free estate			£
On first	£325,000		Nil
On next	£70,000	at 40%	28,000
	£395,000		£28,000

IHT applicable to plant and machinery

$$\frac{75{,}000}{395{,}000} \times 28{,}000 \qquad £5{,}316$$

1st instalment due 1.7.19	£531
2nd instalment due 1.7.20	£531
and so on.	

Notes

(a) Instalments continue to be due at yearly intervals for 10 years or until the business property is sold, at which time all unpaid IHT becomes payable.

(b) Interest is payable on each instalment from the day it falls due. If payments are made on time, no interest is payable.

(B)

On 1 December 2018 G gave his land in a partnership of which G was a partner to his son S who agreed to pay any IHT on the transfer. The land was valued at £600,000. G had made prior chargeable transfers of £140,000, had already used his 2017/18 and 2018/19 annual exemptions, and he died on 31 December 2022.

S elected to pay the IHT by 10 yearly instalments and paid the first on 1 August 2023, and the second on 1 September 2024. On 1 December 2024 he sold the land, and paid the balance of the IHT outstanding on 1 February 2025. It is assumed that the rate of interest on unpaid inheritance tax is 3% throughout.

Inheritance tax on gift

		£
Value of land		600,000
Deduct business property relief at 50%		(300,000)
PET becoming chargeable on death		£300,000
IHT payable in the band £140,001–£440,000		
	£	
140,001–325,000 at nil%	Nil	
325,001–440,000 at 40%	46,000	
	£46,000	
Total IHT payable at 60% of full rates (death between 4 and 5 years after gift)		£27,600
1st instalment due 1.7.23	2,760	
Interest at 3% from 1.7.23 to 1.8.23		
$^{31}/_{366} \times$ £2,760 × 3%	7	
		2,767
2nd instalment due 1.7.24	2,760	
Interest at 3% from 1.7.24 to 1.9.24		
$^{62}/_{366} \times$ £2,760 × 3%	14	
		2,774
Balance due on sale on 1.12.24	22,080	
Interest at 3% from 1.12.24 to 1.2.25		
$^{62}/_{366} \times$ £22,080 × 3%	112	
		22,192
Total IHT and interest		£27,733

Note

(a) Interest on unpaid tax is calculated using 366 days as the denominator rather than 365 days.

318 Protective Trusts

318.1 FORFEITURE BEFORE 12 APRIL 1978

[*IHTA 1984, s 73*]

In 1951 X left his estate on protective trusts for his son Z. On 1 January 1978 Z attempted to assign his interest and the protective trusts were accordingly determined. On 1 May 1983 the trustees advanced £25,000 to Z to enable him to purchase a flat. At the same time, they also advanced £10,000 (net) to his granddaughter D. On 1 May 2018 Z died and the trust fund, valued at £200,000, passed equally to his grandchildren absolutely.

1 May 1983

There is no charge to IHT on the payment to Z, but a charge arises on the payment to D. The relevant period is the period from the determination of the protective trusts (1 January 1978) to 1 May 1983 i.e. 21 complete quarters.

The rate of tax is 0.25% for each of 21 quarters	5.25%

$$\text{IHT payable is } \frac{5.25}{100 - 5.25} \times £\,10{,}000 = \underline{£554}$$

The gross payment is £10,554

1 May 2018

There is a charge to IHT when the trust vests on the death of Z. 161 complete quarters have elapsed since the protective trusts determined.

The rate of tax is

0.25% for each of the first 40 quarters	10.0%
0.20% for each of the next 40 quarters	8.0%
0.15% for the next 40 quarters	6.0%
0.10% for the next 40 quarters	4.0%
0.05% for the next 1 quarters	0.05%
	28.05%

IHT payable is 28.05% × £200,000 = £56,100

318.2 FORFEITURE AFTER 11 APRIL 1978

[*IHTA 1984, s 88*]

Assume the same facts as in 318.1 above but that Z attempted to assign his interest on 1 January 1980.

1 May 1983

There is no charge to IHT on the payment to Z who is treated as beneficially entitled to an interest in possession under the trust. The payment to D is a chargeable transfer. Tax is charged at Z's personal cumulative rate of tax so that if he had made no previous transfers, the payment would be covered by his nil rate tax band. If the payment had been made after 16 March 1987, it would have been a potentially exempt transfer.

1 May 2018

There is a charge to IHT when the trust vests on the death of Z, calculated by aggregating £200,000 with all other chargeable property passing on his death and applying the normal death rates.

Notes

(a) For settlements created on or after 22 March 2006, *IHTA 1984, s 88* applies only if the interest of the principal beneficiary is an immediate post-death interest within *IHTA 1984, s 49A*, a disabled person's interest within *IHTA 1984, s 89B(1)(c)(d)* or a transitional serial interest within *IHTA 1984, ss 49B–49E*. [*IHTA 1988, s 88(4)–(6); FA 2006, Sch 20 para 24*]

(b) For settlements created before 22 March 2006, where the protective trusts fail or are determined on or after that date, for inheritance tax purposes the principal beneficiary is treated as if he became beneficially entitled to an interest in possession in the settled property before that date. [*IHTA 1984, s 88(3); FA 2006, Sch 20 para 24*]. Therefore the changes to the SETTLEMENTS: INTERESTS IN POSSESSION **(320)** provisions made by *FA 2006* do not apply and the beneficiary continues to be treated under *IHTA 1984, s 49* as beneficially entitled to the settled property concerned whether or not his interest is an immediate post-death interest, a disabled person's interest or a transitional serial interest.

319 Quick Succession Relief

[*IHTA 1984, s 141*]

319.1 TRANSFERS AFTER 9 MARCH 1981

On 1 January 2019 A died with a net estate valued at £400,000. In December 2014 he had received a gift from B of £20,000. B died in November 2016 and A paid the IHT (amounting to £8,000) due as a result of B's potentially exempt transfer becoming chargeable.

A was also entitled to an interest in possession in the whole of his father's estate. His father had died in February 2016 with a net estate of £331,000 on which the IHT paid was £2,400. On A's death, the property passed to A's sister and was valued at £145,000. A had made no previous transfers and left his estate to his brother.

	£
Free estate	400,000
Settled property	145,000
Taxable estate	£545,000

IHT on an estate of £545,000 = £88,000

Quick succession relief

The gift from B was made more than four but not more than five years before A's death so quick succession relief at 20% is available.

$$QSR = 20\% \times £8,000 \times \frac{12,000}{20,000} \qquad £960$$

Interest in possession in father's will trust	£
Net estate before tax	331,000
Tax	(2,400)
Net estate after tax	£328,600

A's death was more than two but not more than three years after his father's so relief is given at 60%.

$$QSR = 60\% \times £2,400 \times \frac{328,600}{331,000} \qquad £1,430$$

Tax payable on death of A	£	£
IHT on an estate of £545,000		88,000
Deduct QSR		
On gift from B	960	
On father's estate	1,430	
		(2,390)
IHT payable		£85,610

On free estate $\frac{400,000}{545,000} \times £85,610$ £62,833

On settled property $\frac{145,000}{545,000} \times £85,610$ £22,777

Note

(a) The relief is given only by reference to the tax charged on the part of the value received by the donee. Therefore, the tax paid must be apportioned by applying the fraction 'net transfer received divided by gross transfer made'.

320 Settlements: Interests in Possession

[*IHTA 1984, ss 49–49E, 51(1)–(1B), 52(1)(2A), 54A, 54B, 57; FA 2010, s 53*]

320.1 TERMINATION OF AN INTEREST IN POSSESSION

A had an interest in possession in a settlement valued at £222,000 with remainder to his son S for life. A's interest in possession commenced in 2002. On 1 July 2018, A released his life interest to S in consideration of S's marriage on 2 July 2018. A had made no gifts since 5 April 2018 but had used his annual exemptions prior to that date. His cumulative total of chargeable transfers at 5 April 2018 was £126,000, and these had all been made since 1 July 2011.

The release of A's life interest is an immediately chargeable transfer.

	£	£
Value of property		222,000
Exemptions		
Annual 2018/19	3,000	
In consideration of marriage	5,000	
		(8,000)
Chargeable transfer		£214,000

IHT on £214,000 is charged in the band £126,001 to £340,000.

	£
126,001–325,000 at nil%	Nil
325,001–340,000 at 20%	3,000
	£3,000

Tax payable by trustees as a consequence of A's release of his interest in possession	£3,000

Notes

(a) The annual gifts exemption and the exemption of gifts in consideration of marriage apply if notice is given to the trustees by the donor within 6 months of the gift.

(b) The tax payable is computed by reference to the transferor's cumulative total of chargeable transfers within the previous seven years, and the chargeable transfer forms part of his cumulative total carried forward.

(c) The interest in possession provisions apply in respect of interests to which a person becomes beneficially entitled on or after 22 March 2006 only if the interest is an immediate post-death interest within *IHTA 1984, s 49A* (see **320.3** below), a disabled person's interest within *IHTA 1984, s 89B(1)(c)(d)* or a transitional serial interest within *IHTA 1984, ss 49B–49E* (see **320.2** below). The provisions also apply where a UK-domiciled person becomes beneficially entitled to an interest in possession on or after 9 December 2009 by a disposition which is not a transfer of value as a result of *IHTA 1984, s 10* (dispositions not intended to confer gratuitous benefit). [*IHTA 1984, s 49(1A); FA 2010, s 53*]. Otherwise, an interest in possession to which a person becomes beneficially entitled on or after 22 March 2006 is treated as relevant property subject to the rules in **321** SETTLEMENTS: RELEVANT PROPERTY. [*IHTA 1984, s 59(1)(2); FA 2006, Sch 20 para 20*].

(d) As the release of A's life interest to S occurred after 5 October 2008, S's interest in possession is not a transitional serial interest and is subject to the rules in **321** SETTLEMENTS: RELEVANT PROPERTY. The release is an immediately chargeable transfer. See also **320.2** below.

320.2 TRANSITIONAL SERIAL INTERESTS

[*IHTA 1984, ss 49B–49E; FA 2006, Sch 20 para 5; FA 2008, s 141*]

Rick had an interest in possession in a settlement to which he became beneficially entitled in 1998. The terms of the settlement are that remainder goes to his son Robbie for life. Rick released his life interest to Robbie. At the date of the release, the settlement was valued at £350,000, Rick's cumulative chargeable transfers in the last seven years amounted to £130,000 and he had not used his annual exemptions for any year.

On the assumption that the release takes place on (i) 31 August 2007 and (ii) 5 November 2018, the IHT consequences for Rick are as follows.

(i) **Release on 31 August 2007**

Robbie's interest in possession is a transitional serial interest within *IHTA 1984, s 49C*. The transfer is therefore a potentially exempt transfer and will become chargeable only in the event of Rick's death within seven years.

(ii) **Release on 5 November 2018**

As the release occurs after 5 October 2008 Robbie's interest cannot be a transitional serial interest within *IHTA 1984, s 49C*. As his interest is not a transitional serial interest within *IHTA 1984, s 49D*, the relevant property regime (see **321** SETTLEMENTS: RELEVANT PROPERTY) applies to it. Rick's transfer is therefore a chargeable transfer and IHT is due as follows.

		£	£
Value transferred by Rick on 5 November 2018			350,000
Deduct annual exemptions	2018/19	3,000	
	2017/18	3,000	(6,000)
			£344,000

IHT on £344,000 is charged in the band £130,001 to £474,000.

	£
£130,001–325,000	Nil
£325,001–474,000 at 20%	29,800
IHT payable	£29,800

Notes

(a) The interest in possession provisions apply in respect of interests to which a person becomes beneficially entitled on or after 22 March 2006 only if the interest is a disabled person's interest within *IHTA 1984, s 89B(1)(c)(d)*, a transitional serial interest within *IHTA 1984, ss 49B–49E* or an immediate post-death interest within *IHTA 1984, s 49A* (see **320.3** below). The provisions also apply where a UK-domiciled person becomes beneficially entitled to an interest in possession on or after 9 December 2009 by a disposition which is not a transfer of value as a result of *IHTA 1984, s 10* (dispositions not intended to confer gratuitous benefit). [*IHTA 1984, s 49(1A); FA 2010, s 53*]. Otherwise, an interest in possession to which a person becomes beneficially entitled on or after 22 March 2006 is treated as relevant property subject to the rules in **321** SETTLEMENTS: RELEVANT PROPERTY. [*IHTA 1984, s 59(1)(2); FA 2006, Sch 20 para 20*].

(b) An interest in possession to which a person ('B') becomes beneficially entitled during the period 22 March 2006 to 5 October 2008 is a transitional serial interest if the settlement was created before 22 March 2006, immediately before that date a person was beneficially entitled to an interest in possession (the '*prior interest*'), and B became beneficially entitled to his interest on the prior interest coming to an end. B's interest must not be a disabled person's interest and the settlement must not be within the rules for TRUSTS FOR BEREAVED MINORS (**323**). [*IHTA 1984, s 49C; FA 2006, Sch 20 para 5; FA 2008, s 141*].

(c) Where a person ('C') becomes beneficially entitled to an interest in possession after 5 October 2008, that interest qualifies as a transitional serial interest only where the interest arises on coming to an end of a prior interest in possession on the death of C's spouse/civil partner. The prior interest must have been held by the spouse or civil partner immediately before 22 March 2006. C's interest must not be a disabled person's interest and the settlement must not be within the rules for TRUSTS FOR BEREAVED MINORS (**323**). [*IHTA 1984, s 49D; FA 2006, Sch 20 para 5; FA 2008, s 141*]. See also *IHTA 1984, s 49E* for treatment of an interest as a transitional serial interest where the settled property consists of rights under a life assurance contract.

320.3 IMMEDIATE POST-DEATH INTERESTS

[*IHTA 1984, s 49A; FA 2006, Sch 20 para 5*]

Garth, who is married to Maud, dies on 12 January 2017 having already made potentially exempt gifts on 21 May 2014 of £331,000. By his will he leaves his assets to Maud in trust for life and then on her death on trusts to his adult son Richard for life. His estate is valued at £760,000. Garth had made no gifts prior to 5 April 2014 other than to use his annual exemptions prior to 2013/14. Garth and Maud had sold their home in 2014 and moved into rented sheltered accommodation.

Maud dies on 8 January 2019 when the trust assets are valued at £800,000. Her free estate is valued at £100,000 and she has made no transfers in the preceding seven years, other than to utilise her annual exemptions.

IHT payable on death of Garth

		£	£
Value transferred on 21 May 2014			331,000
Deduct annual exemptions	2014/15	3,000	
	2013/14	3,000	(6,000)
			£325,000

IHT on chargeable gift of £325,000 is charged in the nil rate band up to £325,000. The balance of the estate left on trust for wife Maud is exempt under *IHTA 1984, s 18*. Garth has no unused nil rate band to transfer to Maud.

IHT payable on death of Maud

	£
Trust assets	800,000
Free estate	100,000
	900,000

	£
£0–325,000	Nil
£325,001–£900,000 at 40%	£230,000
IHT payable	£230,000

Notes

(a) The interest in possession provisions apply in respect of interests to which a person becomes beneficially entitled on or after 22 March 2006 only if the interest is a disabled person's interest within *IHTA 1984, s 89B(1)(c)(d)*, a transitional serial interest within *IHTA 1984, ss 49B–49E* (see 320.2 above) or an immediate post-death interest within *IHTA 1984, s 49A*. The provisions also apply where a UK-domiciled person becomes beneficially entitled to an interest in possession on or after 9 December 2009 by a disposition which is not a transfer of value as a result of *IHTA 1984, s 10* (dispositions not intended to confer gratuitous benefit). [*IHTA 1984, s 49(1A); FA 2010, s 53*]. Otherwise, an interest in possession to which a person becomes beneficially entitled on or after 22 March 2006 is treated as relevant property subject to the rules in **321** SETTLEMENTS: RELEVANT PROPERTY. [*IHTA 1984, s 59(1)(2); FA 2006, Sch 20 para 20*].

(b) An interest in possession in a settlement is an immediate post-death interest only if the settlement is effected by will or intestacy and the person holding the interest became beneficially entitled to it on the death of the testator or intestate. The interest in possession must not be a disabled person's interest and the settlement must not be within the rules for TRUSTS FOR BEREAVED MINORS **(323)**. [*IHTA 1984, s 49A; FA 2006, Sch 20 para 5*].

(c) Richard's interest in possession is not an immediate post-death interest as he did not become entitled to his interest in possession on the death of Garth. It is not a transitional serial interest (see note (c) to **320.3** above) or a disabled person's interest. His interest is therefore relevant property subject to the rules in **321** SETTLEMENTS: RELEVANT PROPERTY.

321 Settlements: Relevant Property

Where the value of trust property is given in an example, it is assumed, where relevant, that this includes any undistributed and unaccumulated income treated as included in trust property under *IHTA 1984, s 64(1A)*. Otherwise, such income is excluded as it is not treated as a taxable trust asset (Revenue Statement of Practice SP 8/86).

321.1 RATE OF TEN-YEAR ANNIVERSARY CHARGE

(A) Post-26 March 1974 settlements

[*IHTA 1984, ss 64, 66; FA 2014, Sch 25 para 4; F(No 2)A 2015, Sch 1 paras 3,7*]

On 1 May 1998 S settled £150,000 net, £100,000 to be held on discretionary trusts and £50,000 in trust for his brother B for life. At the date of the transfer S had a cumulative total of chargeable transfers of £67,000. £20,000 (gross) was advanced from the discretionary trusts to C on 1 March 2006.

The property held on discretionary trusts was valued at £187,000 on 1 May 2008.

On 1 January 2018 B died, when the property subject to his interest in possession was valued at £95,000. The whole trust property was valued at £322,000 on 1 May 2018 of which £105,000 derived from B's fund. The trustees had made no advances other than that to C.

It is assumed that rates of tax remain at the level for transfers after 5 April 2018.

1 May 2008 Ten-year anniversary charge

	£
Assumed chargeable transfer	
(i) value of relevant property immediately before the ten-year anniversary	187,000
(ii) value, at date of settlement, of property which was not, and has not become, relevant property	50,000
(iii) value, at date of settlement, of property in related settlement	—
	£237,000
Assumed transferor's cumulative total	
(i) value of chargeable transfers made by settlor in seven-year period ending on date of settlement	67,000
(ii) amounts on which proportionate charges have been levied in ten years before the anniversary	20,000
	£87,000

	Gross	Tax
	£	£
Assumed cumulative total	87,000	—
Assumed transfer	237,000	2,400
	£324,000	£2,400

$$\text{Effective rate of tax } \frac{2,400}{237,000} \times 100 = \underline{1.01266\%}$$

Ten-year anniversary charge

The IHT payable is at 30% of the effective rate on the relevant property

IHT payable = 30% × 1.01266% × £187,000 = £568

1 May 2018 Ten-year anniversary charge

	£
Assumed chargeable transfer (note (a))	
(i) value of relevant property immediately prior to the ten-year anniversary	322,000
(ii) value at date of settlement of property in related settlement	—
	£322,000
Assumed transferor's cumulative total	
(i) value of chargeable transfers made by settlor in seven-year period ending on date of settlement	67,000
(ii) amounts on which proportionate charges have been levied in ten years before the anniversary	—
	£67,000

	Gross	Tax
	£	£
Assumed cumulative total	67,000	—
Assumed transfer	322,000	12,800
	£389,000	£12,800

$$\text{Effective rate of tax } \frac{12,800}{322,000} \times 100 = \underline{3.97516\%}$$

Ten-year anniversary charge

Of the relevant property, £105,000 had not been relevant property for the period 1 May 2008–1 January 2018, i.e. 38 complete quarters.

IHT payable

			£
At 30% × 3.97516%	= 1.19%	on £217,000	2,582
At 30% × 3.97516%	= 1.19%		
Less 38/40 × 30% × 3.97516%	= 1.13%		
	0.06%	on £105,000	63
Total IHT payable			£2,645

Notes

(a) For charges arising on or after 18 November 2015, the assumed chargeable transfer is the aggregate of:

(i) the value of relevant property immediately prior to the ten-year anniversary;

(ii) the value at the date of settlement of relevant property in any related settlement;

(iii) the value of any same-day addition (as defined) to another settlement with the same settlor; and

(iv) where an increase in the value of any property in another settlement is represented by the value of a same-day addition within (iii) above and that other settlement is not a related settlement, the value at the date of settlement of the relevant property in that other settlement.

[*IHTA 1984, s 66(4); F(No 2)A 2015, Sch 1 paras 3, 7*].

(b) There is no same-day addition (see (a)(iii)(iv) above) if either or both of the settlements in question are 'protected settlements' which commenced before 10 December 2014. A settlement is a protected settlement if there have been no transfers of value by the settlor on or after 10 December 2014 as a result of which the value of the property comprised in the settlement was increased or if there has been such a transfer of value but that transfer was on the death of the settlor before 6 April 2017 and was effected by provisions of the settlor's will which were, in substance, the same as they were immediately before 10 December 2014. [*IHTA 1984, ss 62B(1)(c), 62C; F(No 2)A 2015, Sch 1 para 2*].

(B) Pre-27 March 1974 settlements

[*IHTA 1984, ss 64, 66; F(No 2)A 2015, Sch 1 para 3*]

On 1 June 1971 T settled property on discretionary trusts. The trustees made the following advances (gross) to beneficiaries

1.1.74	H	£10,000
1.1.77	B	£20,000
1.1.82	C	£60,000
1.1.88	D	£40,000
1.1.94	E	£80,000

On 1 June 1991 the settled property was valued at £175,000, on 1 June 2001 £180,000.

1 June 1991 Ten-year anniversary charge

Assumed chargeable transfer	£	
Value of relevant property		£175,000
Assumed transferor's cumulative total		
(i) Aggregate of distribution payments made between 1 June 1981 and 8 March 1982	60,000	
(ii) Aggregate of amounts on which proportionate charge arises between 9 March 1982 and 1 June 1991	40,000	£100,000

	Gross	Tax
	£	£
Assumed cumulative total	100,000	—
Assumed chargeable transfer	175,000	27,000
	£275,000	£27,000

$$\text{Effective rate of tax} = \frac{27{,}000}{175{,}000} \times 100 = \underline{15.429}\%$$

Ten-year anniversary charge

The IHT payable is at 30% of the effective rate on the relevant property.

IHT payable = 30% × 15.429% × £175,000 = £8,100

1 June 2001 Ten-year anniversary charge

Assumed chargeable transfer	
Value of relevant property	£180,000
Assumed transferor's cumulative total	
Aggregate of amount on which proportionate charge arises between 1 June 1991 and 1 June 2001	£80,000

	Gross	Tax
	£	£
Assumed cumulative total	80,000	—
Assumed chargeable transfer	180,000	3,600
	£260,000	£3,600

$$\text{Effective rate of tax} = \frac{3{,}600}{180{,}000} \times 100 = \underline{2}\%$$

Ten-year anniversary charge

The IHT payable is at 30% of the effective rate on the relevant property.

IHT payable = 30% × 2% × £180,000 = £1,080

1 June 2011 Ten-year anniversary charge

Not illustrated.

321.2 RATE OF PROPORTIONATE CHARGE BEFORE THE FIRST TEN-YEAR ANNIVERSARY

(A) Post-26 March 1974 settlements

[*IHTA 1984, ss 65, 68; F(No 2)A 2015, Sch 1 paras 4, 7*]

On 1 April 2009 M settled £60,000 (net) on discretionary trusts. His cumulative total of chargeable transfers (gross) prior to the settlement was £290,000. On 3 December 2017 he added £20,000 (net), having made no chargeable transfers since 1 April 2009.

On 11 October 2017 the trustees had advanced £40,000 to N, and on 1 March 2018 the trustees distributed the whole of the remaining funds equally to P and Q. The remaining funds were valued at £110,000, of which £88,000 derived from the original settlement, and £22,000 from the addition.

11 October 2017 proportionate charge

Assumed chargeable transfer

(i)	Value of property in the settlement at date of settlement	60,000
(ii)	Value at date of settlement of property in related settlement	—
(iii)	Value at date of addition of property added	—
		£60,000

Assumed transferor's cumulative total

Value of chargeable transfers made by settlor in seven year period ending on date of settlement	£290,000

	Gross (£)	Tax (£)
Assumed cumulative total	290,000	—
Assumed transfer	60,000	5,000
	£350,000	£5,000

$$\text{Effective rate of tax} = \frac{5,000}{60,000} \times 100 = \underline{8.33}\%$$

Appropriate fraction

The number of complete quarters that have elapsed between the date of settlement, 1 April 2009, and the advance on 11 October 2017 is 34.

IHT is charged at the appropriate fraction of the effective rate on the property advanced.

$$\text{IHT payable} = 30\% \times \frac{34}{40} \times 8.33\% \times £40{,}000$$
$$= 2.12\% \times £40{,}000$$
$$= £848$$

Had the advance of £40,000 been net, the IHT payable would be

$$\frac{2.12}{100 - 2.12} \times £40{,}000 = £866$$

and the gross advance would be £40,866

1 March 2018 proportionate charge

As property has been added to the settlement, the effective rate of tax is recalculated.

Assumed chargeable transfer	£
(i) Value of property in settlement at date of settlement	60,000
(ii) Value at date of settlement of property in related settlement	—
(iii) Value at date of addition of relevant property added	20,000
	£80,000

Assumed transferor's cumulative total	
Value of chargeable transfers made by settlor in seven-year period ending on date of settlement	£290,000

	Gross	Tax
	£	£
Assumed cumulative total	290,000	—
Assumed transfer	80,000	9,000
	£370,000	£9,000

$$\text{Effective rate of tax} = \frac{9{,}000}{80{,}000} \times 100 = 11.25\%$$

Appropriate fraction

The number of complete quarters that have elapsed between the date of settlement, 1 April 2009, and the advance on 1 March 2018 is 35.

The number of complete quarters that elapsed between the date of settlement, 1 April 2009, and 3 December 2017, the date on which property was added, was 34.

The IHT is charged at the appropriate fraction of the effective rate on the property advanced

			£
$30\% \times \frac{35}{40} \times 11.25\%$	on	£88,000 =	2,599

			£
$30\% \times \frac{(35-34)}{40} \times 11.25\%$	on	£22,000 =	19
		£110,000	
IHT payable on advance of £110,000			£2,618

Notes

(a) For charges arising on or after 18 November 2015, the assumed chargeable transfer is the aggregate of:

(i) the value of property in the settlement at the date of settlement;

(ii) the value at the date of settlement of property in any related settlement;

(iii) the value at the date of addition of property added to the settlement which was then relevant property (whether or not it has remained relevant property);

(iv) the value at the date it became relevant property of property either in the settlement at date of settlement or subsequently added which was not initially relevant property (whether or not it has remained relevant property);

(v) the value of any same-day addition (as defined) to another settlement with the same settlor; and

(vi) where an increase in the value of any property in another settlement is represented by the value of a same-day addition within (v) above and that other settlement is not a related settlement, the value at the date of settlement of the relevant property in that other settlement.

[*IHTA 1984, s 68(5); F(No 2)A 2015, Sch 1 paras 4, 7*].

(b) There is no same-day addition (see (a)(v)(vi) above) if either or both of the settlements in question are 'protected settlements' which commenced before 10 December 2014. A settlement is a protected settlement if there have been no transfers of value by the settlor on or after 10 December 2014 as a result of which the value of the property comprised in the settlement was increased or if there has been such a transfer of value but that transfer was on the death of the settlor before 6 April 2017 and was effected by provisions of the settlor's will which were, in substance, the same as they were immediately before 10 December 2014. [*IHTA 1984, ss 62B(1)(c), 62C; F(No 2)A 2015, Sch 1 para 2*].

(B) Settlor dies within 7 years of settlement — post-26 March 1974 settlement

On 1 July 2014 T settled £335,000 net on discretionary trusts. His only other transfer had been a gift of £70,000 to his brother B on 1 June 2013. On 7 March 2016 the trustees advanced £70,000 to B, who agreed to pay any IHT due. On 30 August 2018 T died.

Proportionate charge 7 March 2016

At the time of the advance, T had made no chargeable transfers in the seven years prior to the settlement (the gift to B being a PET).

Assumed chargeable transfer	
Value of property in the settlement at the date of settlement	£335,000
Assumed transferor's cumulative total	Nil
Tax on an assumed transfer of £335,000 =	£2,000

$$\text{Effective rate of tax} = \frac{2,000}{335,000} \times 100 = 0.60\%$$

Appropriate fraction

The number of complete quarters that have elapsed between the date of the settlement, 1 July 2014, and the advance on 7 March 2016 is 6.

IHT is charged at the appropriate fraction of the effective rate on the property advanced.

$$\text{IHT} = 30\% \times \frac{6}{40} \times 0.60\% \times £70,000$$

$$= 0.00027\% \times £70,000$$

$$= £19$$

On the settlor's death within seven years, the PET on 1 June 2013 becomes a chargeable transfer. There will be additional IHT payable by the trustees on the creation of the settlement, and additional IHT payable by B on the advance to him from the settlement.

The gross gift to the settlement, after deducting the 2014/15 annual exemption, was

Gross	Tax	Net
£	£	£
325,000	—	325,000
8,750	1,750	7,000
£333,750	£1,750	£332,000

Additional IHT is payable to increase the charge to 60% of full rates at the time of death (death between 4 and 5 years after gift), with a previous chargeable transfer to B of £67,000 (after deducting the 2013/14 annual exemption).

	Gross	Tax	Net
	£	£	£
Prior transfer	67,000	—	67,000
	333,750	30,300	303,450
	£400,750	£30,300	£370,450

	£
IHT at 60% of full rates 60% × £30,300	18,180
Deduct paid on lifetime chargeable transfer	(1,750)

	£
Additional IHT payable	£16,430

The additional IHT is payable by the trustees, reducing the value of property settled to £335,000 − £16,430 = £318,570

The IHT on the advance to B is recalculated

Assumed chargeable transfer	£318,570
Assumed transferor's cumulative total	
Chargeable transfers made by the settlor in 7 years prior to the settlement (gift 1 June 2013)	£67,000

	Gross	Tax
	£	£
Assumed cumulative total	67,000	—
Assumed transfer	318,570	12,114
	£385,570	£12,114

$$\text{Effective rate of tax} = \frac{12,114}{385,570} \times 100 = 3.14\%$$

The appropriate fraction is $^{6}/_{40}$ (unchanged).

$$\text{IHT borne} = 30\% \times \frac{6}{40} \times 3.14\% \times £70,000$$
$$= 0.1413\% \times £70,000$$
$$= £99$$

	£
IHT due	99
Deduct already paid	(19)
IHT payable	£80

321.3 RATE OF PROPORTIONATE CHARGE BETWEEN TEN-YEAR ANNIVERSARIES

[*IHTA 1984, ss 65, 69, Sch 2 para 3; F(No 2)A 2015, Sch 1 paras 5, 7*]

On 1 January 1999 G settled £70,000 (net) on discretionary trusts. His cumulative total of chargeable transfers at that date was £185,000. On 1 January 2009 the funds were valued at £150,000, no advances having been made. On 1 February 2011 the trustees advanced £30,000 (gross) to H. On 1 January 2012 G added £80,000 to the settlement, having made cumulative chargeable transfers in the previous seven years of £30,000. On 1 May 2018 the trustees advanced £40,000 to F from the funds originally settled.

It is assumed that rates of tax remain unchanged following the change of rates on 6 April 2010.

1 February 2011 advance to H

8 complete quarters have elapsed since the ten-year anniversary charge so the appropriate fraction is 8/40ths. The rate of tax is therefore 8/40ths of the rate at which IHT would have been charged on the last ten-year anniversary if the Table of Rates in force at 1 February 2011 had been in force at the date of the ten-year anniversary, 1 January 2009.

Tax would have been charged at the last ten-year anniversary as follows

Assumed chargeable transfer	£
(i) value of relevant property immediately before the ten-year anniversary	150,000
(ii) value, at date of settlement, of property which was not, and has not become, relevant property	—
(iii) value at date of settlement of property in related settlement	—
	£150,000

Assumed transferor's cumulative total	£
(i) value of chargeable transfers made by settlor in seven-year period ending on date of settlement	185,000
(ii) amounts on which proportionate charges have been levied in ten years before the anniversary	—
	£185,000

	Gross	Tax
	£	£
Assumed cumulative total	185,000	—
Assumed transfer	150,000	2,000
	£335,000	£2,000

$$\text{Effective rate} = \frac{2,000}{150,000} \times 100 = 1.333\%$$

Rate of tax at ten-year anniversary = 30% × 1.333% = 0.4%

Therefore rate of tax on advance to H

= 8/40 × 0.4%

IHT payable = 8/40 × 0.4% × £30,000 = £24

1 May 2018 advance to F

Since property has been added to the settlement, a hypothetical rate of tax at the previous ten-year anniversary must be recalculated as if the added property had been added prior to the anniversary.

		Gross	Tax
	£	£	£
Assumed cumulative total		185,000	—
Assumed transfer			
property at anniversary	150,000		
added property	80,000	230,000	18,000
		£415,000	£18,000

Effective rate = 18,000/230,000 × 100 = 7.83%

Rate of tax that would have been charged at the ten-year anniversary
= 30% × 7.83%
= 2.3%

The advance to F took place 37 complete quarters after the ten-year anniversary. The rate of tax is 37/40 × 2.3% = 2.128%

If the advance to F was £40,000 gross

IHT payable = £40,000 × 2.128% = £851

If the advance to F was £40,000 net

IHT payable = 2.128/(100 – 2.128) × £40,000 = £870

The gross distribution would then be £40,870.

322 Transfers on Death

322.1 POTENTIALLY EXEMPT TRANSFER FOLLOWED BY LOAN FROM DONEE TO DONOR

[*FA 1986, ss 103, 104; SI 1987 No 1130, Reg 6*]

X gives cash of £330,000 to Y on 1 November 2012. On 20 December 2012, Y makes a loan of £330,000 to X. On 31 May 2013, X makes a gift of £20,000 into a discretionary trust. X dies on 15 April 2018, his death estate is worth £345,000 before deducting the liability of £330,000 to Y which remains outstanding. X has made no lifetime transfers other than those specified, except that he has used his annual exemptions for all relevant years. It is assumed that rates of tax remain unchanged following the change made on 6 April 2010.

First calculation under Reg 6(3)(a)

The transfer of £330,000 in November 2012 is a PET which becomes chargeable by virtue of X's death within seven years. However, for the purpose of this calculation the PET is ignored but no deduction is allowed against the death estate for the outstanding loan.

No IHT is due in respect of the chargeable transfer in May 2013 as it is covered by the Nil rate band.

The estate of £345,000 is charged in the band £20,001 to £365,000.

		£
20,001–325,000	at nil%	Nil
325,001–365,000	at 40%	16,000
IHT due		£16,000

Second calculation under Reg 6(3)(b)

The PET in November 2012 is charged on death in the normal way and the loan is deducted from the death estate.

The PET is charged in the band £0 to £330,000.

		£
0–325,000	at nil%	Nil
325,001–330,000	at 40%	2,000
		£2,000
IHT at 40% of full rates (death between 5 and 6 years after transfer)		£800

Additional tax is due on the chargeable transfer in May 2013, £20,000 is charged in the band £330,001 to £350,000.

20,000 at 40%	£8,000
IHT at 60% of full rates (death between 4 and 5 years after transfer)	£4,800

Tax is charged on the death estate of £15,000 (£345,000–330,000) in the band £350,001 to £365,000.

350,001–365,000 at 40%	£6,000
Total IHT due £(800 + 4,800 + 6,000)	£11,600

The first calculation gives the higher amount of tax, so the PET is ignored and no deduction is allowed for the outstanding loan against the death estate.

Notes

(a) If the PET had exceeded the loan, the excess would not be ignored for the purpose of the first calculation above.

(b) If X had made more than one PET to Y and the total PETs exceeded the amount of the loan, only PETs up to the amount of the loan are ignored for the purpose of the first calculation above, later PETs being disregarded in preference to earlier ones.

322.2 REDUCED RATE FOR ESTATES WITH 10% GIFTS TO CHARITIES

[*IHTA 1984, Sch 1A; FA 2012, s 209, Sch 33*]

(A)

The estate of Percival who died on 30 April 2018 is valued at £425,000, comprising quoted investments and cash. He leaves a legacy of £10,000 to the National Trust and the residue of £415,000 less inheritance tax passes to his children. Percival had made no chargeable transfers in the seven years before his death.

Percival's estate consists of only one component (see note (b)), the general component, and its baseline amount is calculated as follows.

	£
Step 1. Determine value transferred by chargeable transfer attributable to component	
Estate	425,000
Less gift to charity	(10,000)
	415,000
Step 2. Deduct available nil-rate band	(325,000)

	£
	90,000
Step 3. Add back gift to charity	10,000
Baseline amount	£100,000

As the donated amount (£10,000) is at least 10% of the baseline amount for the general component, that component (and in this case the entire estate) qualifies for the 36% rate of inheritance tax.

The inheritance tax due on the chargeable estate (£425,000 – £10,000) is charged in the band £Nil to £415,000.

		£
Nil–325,000	at nil%	Nil
325,001–415,000	at 36%	32,400
IHT due		£32,400

Notes

(a) For deaths on or after 6 April 2012, inheritance tax is charged on the net chargeable value of any component (see note (b)) of an estate at a rate of 36% where 10% or more of the 'baseline amount' of that component has been left to charity. [*IHTA 1984, Sch 1A paras 1, 2; FA 2012, Sch 33 paras 1, 10*].

(b) An estate can consist of up to three components:

- the survivorship component, consisting of any joint or common property liable to pass on death by survivorship;
- the settled property component, consisting of settled property comprised in the estate by virtue of an interest in possession to which the deceased was beneficially entitled; and
- the general component, consisting of all other property comprised in the estate other than gifts with reservation.

[*IHTA 1984, Sch 1A para 3; FA 2012, Sch 33 para 1*].

(c) The steps taken in calculating the baseline amount are those set out in *IHTA 1984, Sch 1A para 5*. In this simple example the deduction of the gift to charity in step 1 followed by its adding back in step 3 appears redundant but where there is more than one component, this is necessary in apportioning the nil-rate band between components. See (B) below.

(d) The gift to charity reduces the residue by only £2,400 (£10,000 gift less IHT reduction (£40,000 – £32,400)).

(e) Where the conditions are satisfied, the reduced rate applies automatically. An election can, however, be made to disapply the reduced rate for all or any components of the estate. Such an election must be made within two years after the death by all the appropriate persons (as in note (b) to (B) below). [*IHTA 1984, Sch 1A paras 8, 9; FA 2012, Sch 33 para 1*].

(B) **Election to merge parts of the estate**

The facts are as in (A) above, except that Percival's legacy to the National Trust is £25,000 and he has also had an interest in possession since 2000 in a settlement valued at death at £100,000.

If no election is made under *IHTA 1984, Sch 1A para 7*, the inheritance tax position is as follows.

General component

	£
Step 1. Determine value transferred by chargeable transfer attributable to component	
Estate	425,000
Less gift to charity	(25,000)
	400,000
Step 2. Deduct appropriate proportion of available nil-rate band*	(260,000)
	140,000
Step 3. Add back gift to charity	25,000
Baseline amount	£165,000

*£325,000 × (£400,000/£500,000) = £260,000

As the donated amount (£25,000) is at least 10% of the baseline amount for the general component (£16,500), that component qualifies for the 36% rate of inheritance tax. No gift to charity is made out of the settled property component, so that component does not qualify for the lower rate. Inheritance tax is chargeable as follows.

	£
Free estate	425,000
Interest in possession	100,000
	525,000
Less gift to charity	(25,000)
	500,000
Less nil-rate band	(325,000)
	175,000
£140,000 @ 36%	50,400
£35,000 @ 40%	14,000
	£64,400

If an election is made under *IHTA 1984, Sch 1A para 7*, the inheritance tax position is as follows.

Merged components

	£
Step 1. Determine value transferred by chargeable transfer attributable to merged components	
Free estate	425,000
Interest in possession	100,000
	525,000
Less gift to charity	(25,000)
	500,000
Step 2. Deduct available nil-rate band*	(325,000)
	175,000
Step 3. Add back gift to charity	25,000
Baseline amount	£200,000

As the donated amount (£25,000) is at least 10% of the baseline amount for the merged components (£20,000), those components qualify for the 36% rate of inheritance tax. Inheritance tax is chargeable as follows.

	£
Free estate	425,000
Interest in possession	100,000
	525,000
Less gift to charity	(25,000)
	500,000
Less nil-rate band	(325,000)
	175,000
£175,000 @ 36%	£63,000

Notes

(a) Where an estate includes more than one component and one of the components qualifies for the reduced rate, an election may be made to treat that component and one or more other eligible parts as one single component. If the 10% test is met for the merged component, then the reduced rate applies to the whole of the merged component. The parts that are eligible to be merged with the qualifying component are the other two components and all the property forming part of the estate by reason of the gifts with reservation provisions. [*IHTA 1984, Sch 1A para 7(1)–(5); FA 2012, Sch 33 para 1*].

(b) The election must be made within two years after the death by all those who are appropriate persons with respect to the qualifying component and each of the eligible parts to be included. The appropriate persons are:

- in relation to the survivorship component, all those to whom the property in the component passes;

- in relation to the settled property component, the trustees;
- in relation to the general component, all the personal representatives (or, if there are none, all those who are liable to inheritance tax attributable to the property in the component); and
- in relation to property forming part of the estate under the gifts with reservation provisions, all those in whom the property concerned is vested when the election is to be made.

[*IHTA 1984, Sch 1A paras 7(6)(7), 9; FA 2012, Sch 33 para 1*].

(c) Where there is more than one component, the available nil-rate band is apportioned between the components for the purposes of step 2, in proportion to the amounts determined at step 1 for each component. [*IHTA 1984, Sch 1A para 5; FA 2012, Sch 33 para 1*].

323 Trusts for Bereaved Minors

[*IHTA 1984, ss 71A–71H; FA 2013, Sch 44 paras 2–6, 9*]

323.1 TRANSITIONAL PROVISIONS FOR PRE-22 MARCH 2006 TRUSTS

(A)

Jacob dies in 2002. Under the terms of his will he leaves his estate on accumulation and maintenance trusts for the benefit of his two children, Lisa and Luke, then aged one and two. The children are to become absolutely entitled to their share of the settled property at 18.

From its creation in 2002 until 21 March 2006 the trust is within the regime for ACCUMULATION AND MAINTENANCE TRUSTS **(301)**.

On and after 22 March 2006 the trust is a trust for bereaved minors within *IHTA 1984, ss 71A–71C*. No IHT charges will arise on the children becoming absolutely entitled, on the death of either of the children, or on the settled property being paid or applied for their advancement or benefit.

Notes

(a) To qualify as a trust for a bereaved minor, the settlement (whether the settled property is settled before, on or after 22 March 2006), must be for the benefit of a bereaved minor and must be established under the will of a deceased parent (including a step-parent or other person with parental responsibility) of the minor, on the intestacy of a parent or under the Criminal Injuries Compensation Scheme. The minor must become absolutely entitled to the settled property and any income arising (including accumulated income) on or before attaining the age of 18. [*IHTA 1984, s 71A*].

(b) Existing accumulation and maintenance trusts which meet the above conditions are treated as trusts for bereaved minors from 22 March 2006. [*IHTA 1984, s 71(1B)*].

(B)

The facts are as in (A) above, except that the children become absolutely entitled only at 25.

From its creation in 2002 until 5 April 2008 the trust is within the regime for ACCUMULATION AND MAINTENANCE TRUSTS **(301)**.

On and after 6 April 2008, the trust is an 18-to-25 trust within *IHTA 1984, ss 71D–71G*. See **301.2(A)** ACCUMULATION AND MAINTENANCE TRUSTS.

Notes

(a) The settlement does not qualify as a trust for bereaved minors as the beneficiaries do not become entitled absolutely to settled property on or before attaining age 18.

(b) On its failure as an accumulation and maintenance settlement, the trust qualifies as an 18-to-25 trust under both the transitional provisions of *IHTA 1984, s 71D(3)(4)* and the bereaved minors provisions of *IHTA 1984, s 71D(1)(2)*.

(c) On 6 April 2008, the settlement ceases to be an accumulation and maintenance trust because the remaining beneficiaries do not become entitled absolutely to settled property on or before attaining age 18 as required from that date (see note (b) to **301.1** ACCUMULATION AND MAINTENANCE TRUSTS). No charge to IHT arises and the settlement becomes an 18-to-25 trust.

(C)

The facts are as in (A) above, except that the children become entitled only to an interest in possession on attaining the age of 18.

From its creation in 2002 until 5 April 2008 the trust is within the regime for ACCUMULATION AND MAINTENANCE TRUSTS (**301**).

On and after 6 April 2008, the trust is a relevant property trust, subject to the rules in **321**SETTLEMENTS: RELEVANT PROPERTY.

Note

(a) After 5 April 2008, the settlement does not qualify as an accumulation and maintenance settlement, a trust for bereaved minors or an 18-to-25 trust as the beneficiaries take only an interest in possession at age 18.

324 Trusts for Disabled Persons

[*IHTA 1984, ss 74, 89, 89A; FA 2013, Sch 44 paras 6–10*]

324.1 PROPERTY SETTLED BEFORE 10 MARCH 1981

In 1973 Q settled £50,000 in trust mainly for his disabled son P, but with power to apply property to his daughter S. On 1 January 2019 the trustees advanced £5,000 gross to S on her marriage.

There will be a charge to IHT on the payment to S.

The relevant period is the period from settlement of the funds or, if later, 13 March 1975, to 1 January 2019, i.e. 175 complete quarters.

The rate of IHT is the aggregate of

0.25% for each of the first	40	quarters	10.00%
0.20% for each of the next	40	quarters	8.00%
0.15% for each of the next	40	quarters	6.00%
0.10% for each of the next	40	quarters	4.00%
0.05% for each of the next	15		0.75%
	175		28.75%

IHT payable is £5,000 × 28.75% = £1,438

324.2 PROPERTY SETTLED AFTER 9 MARCH 1981 AND BEFORE 8 APRIL 2013

Assume the facts in 324.1 above except that the settlement was made on 1 July 1982.

If the trust secures that not less than half the settled property which is applied during P's life is applied for his benefit, then P is treated as beneficially entitled to an interest in possession in the settled property. The transfer to S is a potentially exempt transfer which may become chargeable in the event of P's death within seven years of the transfer. The gift in consideration of marriage exemption applies (£1,000 on a gift from brother to sister) subject to the required notice.

Otherwise, the trust is discretionary and the IHT liability, if any, would be calculated under the rules applying to SETTLEMENTS: RELEVANT PROPERTY **(321)**.

324.3 PROPERTY SETTLED AFTER 7 APRIL 2013

Assume the facts in 324.1 above except that the settlement was made on 1 July 2013.

The trustees have the power to apply amounts otherwise than for the benefit of the disabled person in excess of the annual limit. The annual limit is the lower of £3,000 and 3% of the maximum value of the settled property in the period in question (in this case £1,500).

The trust is discretionary and falls within the rules applying to SETTLEMENTS: RELEVANT PROPERTY **(321)**.

324.4 SELF-SETTLEMENT BY PERSON WITH CONDITION EXPECTED TO LEAD TO DISABILITY

[*IHTA 1984, s 89A; FA 2013, Sch 44 paras 7, 9*]

On 31 July 2018 X, who is in the early stages of Alzheimer's disease and currently resides in a care home, settles £300,000 into discretionary trust for his benefit in the future.

X is treated as beneficially entitled to an interest in possession in the settled property. The transfer into settlement of the property is a potentially exempt transfer which may become chargeable in the event of X's death within seven years of the transfer.

325 Trusts for Employees

[*IHTA 1984, s 72; FA 2006, Sch 20 para 21*]

325.1 POSITION OF THE TRUST

A qualifying trust for employees of a close company was created on 1 July 1989. On 4 May 1999, £15,000 is paid to a beneficiary who is a participator in the close company and holds 15% of the issued ordinary shares. On 4 August 2018, the whole of the remaining fund of £200,000 ceases to be held on qualifying trusts.

4 May 1999

There is a charge to IHT. The relevant period is the period from 1 July 1989 to 4 May 1999, i.e. 39 complete quarters.

The rate of tax is

0.25% for 39 quarters = 9.75%

$$\text{IHT payable is } \frac{9.75}{100-9.75} \times £15{,}000 = \underline{£1{,}620}$$

1 July 1999 and 1 July 2009

There is no liability at the ten-year anniversaries.

4 August 2018

There is a charge to IHT. The relevant period is the period from 1 July 1989 to 4 August 2018, i.e. 116 complete quarters.

The rate of tax is

0.25% for 40 quarters =	10.00%
0.20% for 40 quarters =	8.00%
0.15% for 36 quarters =	5.40%
	23.40%

IHT payable is £200,000 × 23.4% = £46,800

326 Valuation

326.1 LAND SOLD WITHIN FOUR YEARS OF DEATH

[*IHTA 1984, ss 190–198*]

(A)

A (a bachelor) died on 1 May 2015 owning four areas of land, as follows.

(i) 10 acres valued at death £20,000

(ii) 15 acres valued at death £30,000

(iii) 20 acres valued at death £30,000

(iv) 30 acres valued at death £40,000

He also owned a freehold house valued at death at £50,000.

In the four years following A's death, his executors made the following sales.

(A) Freehold house sold 15.11.15, proceeds £53,000, expenses £2,000.

(B) Land area (iii) sold 1.6.17, proceeds £29,500, expenses £1,500.

(C) Land area (ii) sold 8.8.18, proceeds £27,000, expenses £1,000.

(D) Land area (iv) sold 19.9.18, proceeds £42,000, expenses £3,000.

The following revisions must be calculated on a claim under IHTA 1984, Pt VI, Chapter IV

	£	
Gross sale proceeds of house	53,000	
Deduct probate value	(50,000)	£3,000
Gross sale proceeds of land area (ii)	27,000	
Deduct probate value	(30,000)	£(3,000)
Gross sale proceeds of land area (iii)	29,500	
Deduct probate value	(30,000)	£(500)

Notes

(a) The sale of area (iii) is disregarded as the loss on sale (before allowing for expenses) is less than 5% of £30,000 (£1,500) and is also lower than £1,000. [*IHTA 1984, s 191*].

(b) The overall allowable reduction on all sales is therefore nil even though there is a loss after expenses.

(c) For deaths after 15 March 1990, a sale *for less than the value at death* which is made in the fourth year after death is treated as having been made in the three years after death. [*IHTA 1984, s 197A*].

(B) **Further purchases of land**

A died on 30 June 2018 owning a house and a seaside flat.

At death the valuations were

	£
House	50,000
Flat	30,000
	£80,000
Sales by the executors realised (gross)	
House proceeds 1.7.19	42,000
Flat proceeds 1.12.19	33,000
	£75,000

On 1 May 2019, the executors bought a town house for the daughter for £40,000 (excluding costs).

Initially relief is due of £(80,000 − 75,000)	£5,000

Recomputation of relief

$$\text{Appropriate fraction} = \frac{\text{Purchase price}}{\text{Selling price}} = \frac{40,000}{75,000} = \frac{8}{15}$$

		House		Seaside Flat
	£	£	£	£
Value on death		50,000		30,000
Sale price	42,000			
Add (£50,000 − £42,000) × 8/15	4,267			
Revised value for IHT		(46,267)		
Sale price			33,000	
Deduct (£33,000 − £30,000) × 8/15			(1,600)	
Revised value for IHT				(31,400)
Revised relief		£3,733		£(1,400)
Total			£2,333	

Note

(a) The purchase is taken into account because it is made within the period 30 June 2018 (date of death) and 1 April 2020 (four months after the last of the sales affected by the claim). [*IHTA 1984, s 192(1)*]. If a sale made in the fourth year after death was affected by the claim (under *IHTA 1984, s 197A*), it would *not* be taken into account in determining the above-mentioned period. [*IHTA 1984, s 197A(3)*].

326.2 RELATED PROPERTY

[*IHTA 1984, s 161*]

On the death of a husband on 31 October 2018, the share capital of a private company was held as follows.

	Shares	
Issued capital	10,000	
Husband	4,000	40%
Wife	4,000	40%
Others (employees)	2,000	20%
	10,000	100%

The value of an 80% holding is £80,000, while the value of a 40% holding is £24,000. In his Will, the husband left his 4,000 shares to his daughter.

The related property rules apply to aggregate the shares of

Husband	4,000	
Wife	4,000	
Related property	8,000	shares

Chargeable transfer on legacy to daughter

IHT value of 8,000 shares (80%)	£80,000
IHT value attributed to legacy of husband's shares (4,000)	£40,000

(Subject to 100% business property relief if conditions satisfied).

326.3 SHARES AND SECURITIES

Quoted shares sold within twelve months after death

[*IHTA 1984, ss 178–189*]

An individual died on 30 June 2018 and included in his estate was a portfolio of quoted investments. The executors sold certain investments within twelve months of death. The realisations were as follows

	Probate Value	Gross Sales
	£	£
Share A	7,700	7,200
Share B	400	600
Share C	2,800	2,900
Share D	13,600	11,600
Share E	2,300	2,300
Share F	5,700	5,100
Share G	19,400	17,450
Share H	8,500	8,600
	£60,400	55,750
Incidental costs of sale		(2,750)
Net proceeds of sale		£53,000

On 1 September 2018, share J, having a probate value of £200 and still held by the executors was cancelled.

On 1 December 2018, share K, having a probate value of £1,000 has its stock exchange quotation suspended. On 30 June 2019, the investment is still held by the executors, its estimated value is £49 and the quotation remains suspended.

On 30 April 2019, the executors purchased a new holding for £1,750.

The executors would initially be able to claim a reduction of
(£60,400 − £55,750) + (£200 − £1) + (£1,000 − £49) = £5,800

After the purchase, the reduction is restricted as follows

$$\text{Relevant proportion} = \frac{\text{Reinvestment}}{\text{Total sales}} = \frac{1{,}750}{£55{,}750 + £1 + £49} = \frac{1{,}750}{55{,}800}$$

Original relief restricted by

$$\frac{1{,}750}{55{,}800} \times £5{,}800 = £182$$

Total relief £5,800 less £182 £5,618

Notes

(a) No costs of selling investments may be deducted from the sale proceeds.

(b) The cancelled shares are treated as sold for £1 immediately before cancellation. The suspended shares are treated as sold on the first anniversary of death at their value at that time (provided that value is less than their value on death). [*IHTA 1984, ss 186A, 186B*].

(c) The purchase is taken into account as it is made during the period beginning on date of death and ending two months after the end of the last sale taken into account (including deemed sales as in (b) above).

(d) The probate value of each of the investments sold will be adjusted, both for CGT and IHT purposes, to the gross sale proceeds plus the relevant proportion of the fall in value. Thus the probate value of share A will be revised from £7,700 to

$$£7{,}200 + \left(\frac{1{,}750}{55{,}800} \times (7{,}700 - 7{,}200)\right) = £7{,}216$$

(e) Although excluded from computation of the loss on sale for inheritance tax purposes, incidental costs of sale are deductible from proceeds in calculating CGT.

327 Woodlands

[*IHTA 1984, ss 114(2), 125–130, 208, 226(4), Sch 2 para 4*]

327.1 TAX CHARGE

(A)

A died owning woodlands valued at £275,000 being land valued at £200,000 and trees growing on the land valued at £75,000. The woodlands passed to his son D. The executors elected to exclude the value of the trees from the taxable estate on A's death. D died six years later leaving the woodlands to his daughter E. They were then valued at £400,000 being land at £250,000 and trees at £150,000. The rate of tax which would have applied to the value of trees on D's death was 40%, but once again the executors elected to exclude the value of the trees from his estate.

E sold the woodlands for £500,000, including trees valued at £180,000, four years later.

The IHT on the trees is payable when the trees are sold. The trustees of the settlement pay IHT at what would have been the marginal rate on D's death had the tax scale at the time of the sale applied on D's death, e.g. 40% on £180,000 (the proceeds of sale) = £72,000.

Note

(a) If D had gifted the land (with the trees) just before his death, the IHT would have become payable on the trees at what would have been the marginal rate on A's death had the scale at the time of the gift applied on A's death, on the value of the trees at the date of the gift. IHT would also have been payable on D's lifetime transfer (this being a PET but becoming chargeable by virtue of D's death shortly afterwards) but the value transferred by this transfer would have been reduced by the deferred IHT charge. See (B) below.

(B)

B died in 1985 leaving woodlands, including growing timber valued at £100,000, to his daughter C. The executors elected to exclude the value of the timber from the taxable estate on B's death. B had made prior transfers of £50,000 and his taxable estate (excluding the growing timber) was valued at £310,000.

On 1 February 2013 C gave the woodlands to her nephew N, when the land was valued at £355,000 and the growing timber at £125,000. N agreed to pay any IHT on the gift. C died in January 2019, and had made no prior transfers other than to use her annual exemptions each year. It is assumed that IHT rates remain at their current level.

IHT on B's death

No IHT is payable on the growing timber until C's disposal when tax is charged on the net value at that time. The rates are those which would have applied (using the death scale applying on 1 February 2013) if that value had formed the highest part of B's estate on death. The tax was payable on 1 September 2013.

Deferred IHT payable £125,000 at 40%	£50,000

IHT on C's lifetime transfer

IHT is payable on C's gift to N as C died within 7 years of the gift. The deferred IHT is deducted from the value transferred.

		£
Value of land and timber		480,000
Deduct deferred IHT		(50,000)
Chargeable transfer		£430,000
IHT at death rates		
On first	£325,000	—
On next	£105,000 at 40%	42,000
	£430,000	£42,000
IHT payable at 20% of full rates (death between 6 and 7 years after gift)		£8,400

Total IHT payable	
Deferred IHT	50,000
Lifetime transfer	8,400
	£58,400

Note

(a) In the above calculations it has been assumed that the woodlands were not run as a business either at the time of B's death or at the time of C's gift. If B had been running the woodlands as a business, such that business property relief would have been available on his death, the amount chargeable on C's disposal would have been reduced by 50%, i.e. to £62,500, on which IHT payable would have been £25,000. [*IHTA 1984, s 127(2)*]. If C ran the woodlands as a business (whether or not B had done so), business property relief would be available on her gift to N provided N also ran the woodlands as a business, but would be given after the credit for the deferred IHT. (With business property relief now usually at 100%, the order of set-off is not so relevant).

		£
Value of land and timber		480,000
Deduct deferred IHT	say	(25,000)
		455,000
Deduct business property relief at, say, 100%		(455,000)
Chargeable transfer		Nil

Value Added Tax

401 Bad Debt Relief

[*VATA 1994, s 36; SI 1995 No 2518, Regs 165–172E; VAT Notice 700/18/13*]

401.1 PART PAYMENTS AND MUTUAL SUPPLIES

W Ltd has supplied goods to A Ltd. The sales ledger reveals the following amounts due

	Gross	Net	VAT
Invoice	£	£	£
16159 dated 31.7.18	487.39	406.16	81.23
15874 dated 12.7.18	364.19	364.19	—
14218 dated 12.6.18	238.04	238.04	—
14104 dated 10.6.18	256.58	213.82	42.76
	1,346.20	£1,222.21	£123.99
Less paid on account on 14104	(100.00)		
Amount due from A Ltd	£1,246.20		

A Ltd was, however, used by W Ltd for delivery work and there is one unpaid invoice for £143.75.

The bad debt relief claimable is as follows

	£
Amount due from A Ltd	1,246.20
Less amount due to A Ltd	(143.75)
Debt due from A Ltd	£1,102.45

The debt is attributed to

	Gross	VAT
	£	£
Invoice 16159	487.39	81.23
Invoice 15874	364.19	—
Invoice 14218	238.04	—
Invoice 14104 (part) *	12.83	2.14
	£1,102.45	£83.37

The amount of bad debt relief claimable is £83.37.

*12.83 / 256.58 × £42.76 = £2.14

Notes

(a) Relief can be claimed provided the debt has been written off as a bad debt in the supplier's accounts and provided six months have elapsed from the date of supply and from the time when the consideration became due and payable.

(b) Where payments on account are specifically allocated by the customer, this allocation must be followed provided the amount paid covers the full value of the supply. General payments on account must be allocated to earliest supplies first, supplies on the same day being aggregated. Where the claimant owes money to the purchaser which can be set off, the amount of the debt for bad debt relief purposes must be reduced by the amount so owed.

401.2 SECOND-HAND GOODS

B, a second-hand dealer, buys a table for £400 and sells it for £500 under the margin scheme, i.e. his profit margin is £100.

If the customer only pays £450, bad debt relief claimable is

1/6 × £50 = £8.33

If the customer only pays £350, bad debt relief claimable is

1/6 × £100 = £16.67

Note

(a) Where a bad debt arises on goods sold under the margin scheme,

- (i) if the debt is equal to or less than the profit margin, relief may be claimed on the VAT fraction of the debt; and
- (ii) if the debt is greater than the profit margin, relief is limited to the VAT fraction of the profit margin.

401.3 REPAYMENT OF REFUND

In July 2018 a business sells goods for £120 (£100 plus £20 VAT). It receives no payment by the relevant date and claims bad debt relief of £20. It subsequently receives £75.00 from the customer for the goods.

The business must repay to HMRC the VAT element of the £75 received, calculated as follows.

$$\frac{75}{120} \times £20 = £12.50$$

402 Capital Goods

402.1 THE CAPITAL GOODS SCHEME

[*SI 1995 No 2518, Regs 112–116; VAT Notice 706/2/17*]

On 1 July 2011, A Ltd, a partly exempt business, acquired the freehold of a five storey office block, incurring VAT of £112,500. The premises are used as the head office administration block for the whole company. On 1 October 2018 the building is sold at a profit for £1.5 million to a company which only makes exempt supplies. The option to tax is not exercised.

A Ltd's partial exemption year runs to 31 March. Its claimable percentage of non-attributable input tax is as follows.

Year ended			
31 March 2012	80%	31 March 2016	75%
31 March 2013	90%	31 March 2017	85%
31 March 2014	75%	31 March 2018	90%
31 March 2015	60%	31 March 2019	95%

The input tax position is as follows

Year ended 31 March 2012 (Interval 1)

Initial input tax claim £112,500 × 80% = £90,000

Year ended 31 March 2013 (Interval 2)

Additional input tax claimed

$$\frac{112{,}500}{10} \times (90 - 80)\% = \quad £1{,}125$$

Year ended 31 March 2014 (Interval 3)

Input tax repayable

$$\frac{112{,}500}{10} \times (80 - 75)\% = \quad (£562.50)$$

Year ended 31 March 2015 (Interval 4)

Input tax repayable

$$\frac{112{,}500}{10} \times (80 - 60)\% = \quad (£2{,}250)$$

Year ended 31 March 2016 (Interval 5)

Input tax repayable

$$\frac{112{,}500}{10} \times (80 - 75)\% = \qquad \underline{(£562.50)}$$

Year ended 31 March 2017 (Interval 6)

Additional input tax claimed

$$\frac{112{,}500}{10} \times (85 - 80)\% = \qquad \underline{£562.50}$$

Year ended 31 March 2018 (Interval 7)

Additional input tax claimed

$$\frac{112{,}500}{10} \times (90 - 80)\% = \qquad \underline{£1{,}125.00}$$

Year ended 31 March 2019 (Interval 8)

Additional input tax claimed

$$\frac{112{,}500}{10} \times (95 - 80)\% = \qquad \underline{£1{,}687.50}$$

Adjustment in respect of Intervals 9 and 10

Input tax repayable

$$2 \times \frac{112{,}500}{10} \times (80 - 0)\% = \qquad \underline{(£18{,}000.00)}$$

(£16,312.50)

Notes

(a) The adjustment period for buildings is normally ten years.

(b) For the interval in which the building is sold, the adjustment is calculated in the normal way as if it had been used for the whole of the interval. This applies whether it was sold on the first or last day of the interval. For the remaining intervals, the recovery percentage is nil as the option to tax has not been exercised and the supply of the building is therefore exempt.

(c) If the option to tax is exercised on the sale of the building in Interval 8, instead of input tax of £18,000 being repayable in respect of Intervals 9 and 10, further input tax is claimable of

$$2 \times \frac{112,500}{10} \times (100 - 80)\% = \quad \underline{£4,500}$$

On the other hand, VAT of £300,000 is chargeable on the sale which is not recoverable by the exempt company, increasing the effective price to £1,800,000 which might not be acceptable to the purchaser.

(d) See IT 4.7 CAPITAL ALLOWANCES ON PLANT AND MACHINERY for the interaction between the VAT Capital Goods Scheme and capital allowances on assets within the scheme.

403 Catering

403.1 SPECIAL METHOD FOR CATERERS

[*SI 1995 No 2518, Regs 66–75; VAT Notice 727/12, paras 8.3–8.8*]

A fish bar sells both fried fish and chips and wet fish and seafoods. It also has a small restaurant. It is impractical for the owner to keep a record of each sale as it takes place. He can, however, note his zero-rated supplies over a representative period which are

	£
Receipts from wet fish rounds	724
Shops sales of wet fish and seafoods	285
Sundries (cold leftovers)	28
	£1,037
Overall gross takings	£7,580

At the end of a given quarterly tax period, gross takings total £24,016.28.

Standard-rated percentage is

$$\frac{(7,580 - 1,037)}{7,580} \times 100 = 86\%$$

Output tax for the VAT period is

£24,016.28 × 86% × $^1/_6$	£3,442.33

Notes

(a) If each sale can be recorded as it takes place, the normal method of accounting can be used. Otherwise either the Point of Sale scheme or, if the business can satisfy HMRC that it is unable to operate the Point of Sale Scheme, the above catering adaptation can be used.

(b) It is not necessary to include the cost of food used for free meals for family and staff but the full cost of any standard-rated items of food taken out of business stock for own or family use should be included.

(c) The representative period chosen depends on the nature of the business but HMRC must be satisfied that it takes account of hourly, daily and seasonal fluctuations. Details of the sample, including dates and times, must be retained and a new calculation must be carried out in each VAT period.

404 Hotels and Holiday Accommodation

404.1 STAYS OVER FOUR WEEKS.

[*VATA 1994, Sch 6 para 9; VAT Notice 709/3/13*]

In 2018 weekly terms for accommodation, facilities and meals in a hotel are £720.00 (£600.00 plus £120.00 VAT) of which £288.00 (£240.00 + £48.00 VAT) represents the charge for meals.

For the first four weeks, the VAT charge is the full £120.00 but thereafter a reduced VAT value may be calculated in one of the following ways. The proportion for meals has been taken to be 40% but this will not always be so.

(a) **If charges are expressed in VAT-exclusive terms**

	£	£
Total VAT-exclusive weekly charge	600.00	
Less VAT-exclusive charge for meals	(240.00)	48.00
	£360.00	
VAT-exclusive value of facilities		
(20% minimum)	72.00	14.40
VAT due		£62.40

Weekly terms are therefore £600 + £62.40 VAT.

(b) **If charges are expressed in VAT-inclusive terms and the total amount charged to the guest is reduced to take account of the reduced element of VAT**

VAT is as under (a) above but the calculation is

	£	£
Total VAT-inclusive charge	720.00	
Less VAT-inclusive charge for meals	(288.00)	48.00
VAT-inclusive charge for facilities		
and accommodation	432.00	
Less VAT included 1/6 × £432	(72.00)	
Balance (exclusive of VAT)	£360.00	
VAT-exclusive value of facilities	72.00	14.40
(20% minimum)		
VAT due		£62.40

The weekly terms are £600 + £62.40 VAT.

(c) **If charges are expressed in VAT-inclusive terms but the total amount charged to the guest is not reduced to take account of the reduced element of VAT**

	£	£
Total VAT inclusive charge	720.00	
Less VAT-inclusive charge for meals	(288.00)	48.00
VAT-inclusive charge for facilities and accommodation	432.00	
Less VAT included *4/104 × £432	(16.62)	16.62
VAT-exclusive charge for facilities and accommodation	£415.38	
Total VAT		£64.62

The weekly terms are not reduced (i.e. £720.00 including £64.62 VAT).

Notes

(a) *At least 20% of the VAT-exclusive charge, after deducting meals, must be treated as being for standard-rated facilities. In this example, the 20% minimum has been used, hence the fraction

$$\frac{20 \times \text{facilities element}\%}{100 + (20 \times \text{facilities element}\%)} = \frac{20 \times 20\%}{100 + (20 \times 20\%)} = \frac{4}{104}$$

If the true value of facilities is more than 20%, the higher value must be used. At a specialist hotel, such as a health farm, the charge for facilities could be as high as 40% and the VAT charge would then be correspondingly higher.

(b) The taxable turnover of a hotel with many long stay guests is very different from its gross takings. It may not therefore need to apply for registration.

405 Input Tax

405.1 REPAYMENT OF INPUT TAX WHERE CONSIDERATION NOT PAID

[*VATA 1994, s 26A; SI 1995/2518, Regs 172F–172J; VAT Notice 700/18/13*].

(A)

In 2018 B purchases goods for £1,200 (£1,000.00 plus £200.00 VAT) and reclaims the full amount of VAT. By the relevant date (see note (a)), it has only paid £500.00 (leaving £700 unpaid).

It must make a repayment of input tax to HMRC of

$$200 \times \frac{700}{1{,}200} = £116.67$$

(B)

After making the repayment of £116.67 to HMRC, B subsequently makes a further payment of £300 for the goods.

B can now reclaim VAT from HMRC of

$$116.67 \times \frac{300}{700} = £50.00$$

Notes

(a) Where a customer claims VAT on a supply as input tax and all or part of the amount due for that supply is not paid to the supplier within six months of

(i) the date of the supply, or

(ii) if later, the date on which the consideration for the supply becomes payable

the customer must make a refund to HMRC for the VAT period in which the end of the relevant six-month period falls. This does not apply where the cash accounting scheme is used (so that the date for the recovery of input tax is the date of payment).

(b) Where a customer is in dispute with the supplier, and the supplier agrees to extend the due date for payment of the amount in dispute, repayment is not required until six months after the agreed extended date for payment.

(c) Where, subsequent to making a refund to HMRC under (a) above, a customer pays the whole or part of the consideration for the supply in relation to which the input tax repayment was made, his entitlement to input tax on the supply is restored in proportion to the amount of consideration paid.

405.2 NON-BUSINESS ACTIVITIES

[*VATA 1994, s 24(5); VAT Notice 700, paras 32.1–32.7*]

A church receives income not only by way of donations, but also through the sale of books, cards and light refreshments in its bookcentre and coffee shop. For the first quarter its total income is £34,671.49 of which £15,246.22 is donations. VAT on purchases directly attributable to religious activities is £217.95, VAT on purchases related to the bookcentre and coffee shop is £738.95, VAT on general repairs, maintenance and overheads is £2,185.27.

Input tax is calculated as follows	£
VAT on purchases related to business activities	738.95
Add proportion of VAT on general repairs etc.	
$\frac{(34{,}671.49 - 15{,}246.22)}{34{,}671.49} \times £2{,}185.27$	1,224.33
	£1,963.28

Notes

(a) VAT on purchases directly attributable to religious activities (non-business) is not input tax and cannot be recovered.

(b) The calculation continues in the same way, quarter by quarter, until the VAT year end when an annual adjustment is made by applying the same calculation to the total figures for the year.

(c) There is no UK legislation covering the apportionment of VAT to arrive at input tax. If computations based on times, attendance, floor areas, etc. produce a fairer result, they can be used.

(d) If some element of business income arises from exempt supplies, input tax may have to be further apportioned to arrive at deductible input tax. See **408** PARTIAL EXEMPTION.

406 Motor Cars

[*VAT Notice 700/64/14*]

406.1 SCALE CHARGE FOR PRIVATE FUEL

[*VATA 1994, ss 56, 57, Schs 4, 6; FA 2013, Sch 38*]

L Ltd provides its employees with cars and pays all day-to-day running expenses, including the cost of any petrol used for private motoring. Each employee submits a monthly return showing opening and closing mileage, together with fuel and servicing receipts for the period. The company chooses to assess the VAT on petrol used for private motoring using the scale charge.

T, the sales director, has a car with CO_2 emission of 220g/km and puts in a monthly claim for April 2018 which includes petrol used for private motoring. He supports this with petrol bills totalling £176.49 and a service invoice for £288.00 (£240.00 plus VAT £48.00). The company prepares monthly VAT returns.

The company should code the expenses claim as follows

Debit			£
Servicing			240.00
Fuel £176.49 × $^5/_6$		147.08	
Scale charge note (a)		26.50	
			173.58
Input VAT	— on service	48.00	
	— on petrol £176.49 × $^1/_6$	29.42	
			77.42
			£491.00
Credit			
Expenses reimbursed to T			
£176.49 + £288.00			464.49
Output VAT			26.50
			£490.99

Note

(a) A fuel benefit scale can be used to assess a VAT charge where any petrol or other motor fuel is provided by registered traders for private journeys made by employees, directors, partners or proprietors. Where a trader opts to use the scale charge, all supplies of private fuel must be accounted for on that basis for the prescribed accounting period. The monthly scale charge for prescribed accounting periods beginning after 1 May 2017 for a car with CO_2 emission of 220g/km is £159. The VAT charge is therefore £159 × $^1/_6$ = £26.50.

407 Output Tax

[*VAT Notice 700, para 31.2*]

407.1 MIXED SUPPLIES

(A) Apportionment based on cost of both supplies: VAT-inclusive price

In July 2018 a VAT-inclusive price of £140 is charged for a supply of zero-rated goods which cost £23 and standard-rated goods which cost £40 (excluding VAT).

$$\text{Proportion of the total cost represented by standard-rated goods} = \frac{(40 + \text{VAT})}{(40 + \text{VAT}) + 23} = \frac{48}{71}$$

VAT-inclusive price of standard-rated goods = $^{48}/_{71}$ × £140 = £94.65

VAT included = £94.65 x 1/6 = £15.78

Tax value of zero-rated supply = £140 − £94.65 = £45.35

The total price is therefore apportioned

Value of standard-rated supply	78.87
VAT on standard-rated supply	15.78
Value of zero-rated supply	45.35
	£140

(B) Apportionment based on cost of both supplies: VAT-exclusive price

In July 2018 a VAT-exclusive price of £126 is charged for a supply of zero-rated goods which cost £23 and standard-rated goods which cost £40 (excluding VAT).

Proportion of the total cost represented by standard-rated goods = $^{40}/_{63}$

VAT-exclusive value of standard-rated goods = $^{40}/_{63}$ × £126 = £80

VAT on standard-rated goods = £80 × 20% = £16

Tax value of zero-rated supplies = £126 − £80 = £46

The total price is therefore apportioned

Value of standard-rated supply	80
Value of zero-rated supply	46
	126
VAT on £80 at 20%	16
	£142

(C) **Apportionment based on the cost of one supply only**

In July 2018 a VAT-inclusive price of £142 is charged for a supply of zero-rated goods which cost £26 and standard-rated services, the cost of which cannot be identified. A fair and reasonable uplift on the zero-rated goods, consistent with actual profit margins of the business, is 50%.

Value of zero-rated supplies = £26 + 50% = £39

VAT-inclusive price of the standard-rated goods = £142 − £39 = £103

VAT on standard-rated goods = £103 × $^{1}/_{6}$ = £17.17

The total price is therefore apportioned

Value of zero-rated supply	39.00
Value of standard-rated supply (103 − 17.17)	85.83
	124.83
VAT on £85.83 at 20%	17.17
	£142.00

(D) **Apportionment based on the cost of one supply only: annual calculation (Method 1)**

Assume that the figures in (C) above are representative of similar transactions and the total VAT-inclusive income from such transactions in the year is £25,000.

Zero-rated percentage = $^{39}/_{142}$ × 100 = 27.465%

Value of zero-rated supplies in year = £25,000 × 27.465% = £6,866

Consideration for standard-rated supplies in year = £25,000 − £6,866 = £18,134

Output tax due = £18,134 × $^{1}/_{6}$ = £3,022.33

(E) **Apportionment based on the cost of one supply only: annual calculation (Method 2)**

VAT-inclusive subscription income of £400,000 is received in a year in respect of supplies of zero-rated literature with direct costs of £42,000 and standard-rated services, the direct cost of which cannot be identified. The total costs of the business (excluding depreciation) amount to £250,000 in the year. A fair and reasonable uplift to the direct costs of the zero-rated goods to allow for indirect costs is 100%.

Direct cost of zero-rated supplies	42,000
Uplift of 100%	42,000
Full cost of providing zero-rated supplies	£84,000

Proportion of costs attributable to zero-rated supplies

$$\frac{84{,}000}{250{,}000} \times 100 = 33.6\%$$

Proportion of costs attributable to standard-rated supplies = 66.4%

Consideration for standard-rated supplies = £400,000 × 66.4% = £265,600

Output tax = £265,600 × $^1/_6$ = £44,266.66

(F) **Apportionment based on normal selling prices (market values): VAT-inclusive price**

A VAT-inclusive price of £200 is charged for a zero-rated supply (which would separately be charged at £50) and a standard-rated supply (which would separately be charged at £200 including VAT).

Proportion of the total normal price represented by standard-rated goods =

$$\frac{200}{200 + 50} = \frac{4}{5}$$

VAT-inclusive price of standard-rated goods = $^4/_5$ × £200 = £160

VAT included = £160 × $^1/_6$ = £26.67

Tax value of zero-rated supply = £200 − £160 = £40

The total price is therefore apportioned

Value of standard-rated supply (£160 − £26.67)	133.33
VAT on standard-rated supply	26.67
Value of zero-rated supply	40.00
	£200.00

408 Partial Exemption

408.1 STANDARD METHOD

[*SI 1995 No 2518, Regs 99–109; VAT Notice 706*]

In its tax year X Ltd makes the following supplies

	Total supplies (excl VAT)	Standard rated supplies (excl VAT)	Exempt supplies
	£	£	£
First quarter	442,004	392,286	49,718
Second quarter	310,929	266,712	44,217
Third quarter	505,867	493,614	12,253
Fourth quarter	897,135	876,387	20,748
	£2,155,935	£2,028,999	£126,936

Input tax for the year is analysed as follows

	Attributable to taxable supplies	Attributable to exempt supplies	Remaining input tax	Total input tax
	£	£	£	£
First quarter	36,409	4,847	11,751	53,007
Second quarter	20,245	311	5,212	25,768
Third quarter	34,698	1,195	10,963	46,856
Fourth quarter	69,707	5,975	9,357	85,039
	£161,059	£12,328	£37,283	£210,670

The proportion of residual input tax attributable to taxable supplies is calculated using the ratio of

$$\frac{\text{Value of taxable supplies}}{\text{Value of all supplies}}$$

expressed as a percentage and, if not a whole number, rounded *up* to the next whole number.

	£	£
First quarter		
Input tax attributable to taxable supplies	36,409	
Proportion of residual input tax deductible		
$\frac{392,286}{442,004} = 88.75\%$		
£11,751 × 89% =	10,458	
		46,867
Second quarter		
Input tax attributable to taxable supplies	20,245	
Proportion of residual input tax deductible		
$\frac{266,712}{310,929} = 85.78\%$		
£5,212 × 86% =	4,482	
	£24,727	
The value of exempt input tax is £1,041 (311 + [5,212 − 4,482]). As this is not more than £625 per month on average and is less than 50% of all input tax in the quarter, all input tax in the quarter is recoverable.		
Deductible input tax		25,768
Third quarter		
Input tax attributable to taxable supplies	34,698	
Proportion of residual input tax deductible		
$\frac{493,614}{505,867} = 97.58\%$		
£10,963 × 98% =	10,744	
	£45,442	

	£	£
The value of exempt input tax is £1,414 (1,195 + [10,963 − 10,744]). As this is not more than £625 per month on average and is less than 50% of all input tax in the quarter, all input tax in the quarter is recoverable.		
Deductible input tax		46,856
Fourth quarter		
Input tax attributable to taxable supplies	69,707	
Proportion of residual input tax deductible		
$\frac{876,387}{897,135} = 97.69\%$		
£9,357 × 98% =	9,170	
		78,877
		£198,368

Annual adjustment

At the end of the tax year the company carries out an annual adjustment.

	£
Input tax attributable to taxable supplies	161,059
Proportion of residual input tax deductible	
$\frac{2,028,999}{2,155,935} = 94.11\%$	
£37,283 × 95% =	35,419
Deductible input tax for year	196,478
Deducted over the four quarters	(198,368)
Under declaration to be paid to HMRC	£(1,890)

408.2 SPECIAL METHOD

[*SI 1995 No 2518, Regs 99–109; VAT Notice 706*]

The facts are the same as in **408.1** above except that HMRC allow X Ltd to use a special method and calculate the proportion of remaining input tax attributable to taxable supplies by the formula

$$\text{Residual input tax} \times \frac{\text{Input tax attributable to taxable supplies}}{\text{Total input tax}}$$

	£	£
First quarter		
Input tax attributable to taxable supplies	36,409	
Proportion of residual input tax deductible		
$£11{,}751 \times \frac{36{,}409}{53{,}007} =$	8,071	
		44,480
Second quarter		
Input tax attributable to taxable supplies	20,245	
Proportion of residual input tax deductible		
$£5{,}212 \times \frac{20{,}245}{25{,}768} =$	4,095	
	£24,340	
The value of exempt input tax is £1,428 (311 + [5,212 − 4,095]). As this is not more than £625 per month on average and is less than 50% of all input tax in the quarter, all input tax in the quarter is recoverable.		
Deductible input tax		25,768
		70,248

	£	£
Third quarter		
Input tax attributable to taxable supplies	34,698	
Proportion of residual input tax deductible		
$£10,963 \times \frac{34,698}{46,856} =$	8,118	
		42,816
Fourth quarter		
Input tax attributable to taxable supplies	69,707	
Proportion of residual input tax deductible		
$£9,357 \times \frac{69,707}{85,039} =$	7,670	
		77,377
		£190,441

Annual adjustment

At the end of the tax year the company carries out an annual adjustment.

	£
Input tax attributable to taxable supplies	161,059
Proportion of residual input tax deductible	
$£37,283 \times \frac{161,059}{210,670} =$	28,503
Deductible input tax for year	189,562
Deducted over the four quarters	(190,441)
Under declaration to be paid to HMRC	£(879)

Note

(a) In fact, this special method leaves X Ltd worse off than in **408.1** above, but is included here for illustration purposes.

409 Records

409.1 ADJUSTMENTS OF ERRORS ON INVOICES

[*VAT Notice 700, para 19.10; VAT Notice 700/45/17, paras 3.1–3.3*]

F sells a vast range of foodstuffs. Due to a programming error some wholesale packs of citric acid are incorrectly invoiced as zero-rated 'lemon flavouring'. The company decides not to raise supplementary invoices.

The following adjustment is required

	£
Citric acid sales	1,725.00
VAT charged	64.70
	£1,789.70
£1,789.70 × $^{1}/_{6}$ =	298.28
Less VAT charged	(64.70)
Additional VAT payable	£233.58

Note

(a) With many computer systems it is difficult to raise invoices or credit notes for VAT only. It is essential to ensure that any VAT amount will appear in the correct position on the documentation and will be posted by the system to the VAT account.

410 Reduced Rate Supplies

410.1 GRANT-FUNDED INSTALLATION OF HEATING EQUIPMENT

[*VATA 1994, s 29A, Sch 7A Group 3; VAT Notice 708/6/14*]

(A) Full grant received covering all work

A builder installs reduced rate heating equipment to a value of £300 and carries out other building work to a value of £700 (both excluding VAT) for C in his main residence. A grant is received to cover the full cost of the work.

	£	£
Value of reduced rate supplies	300	
VAT thereon (5%)	15	
		315
Value of other supplies	700	
VAT thereon (20%)	140	
		840
Total cost covered by grant		£1,155

(B) Apportionment where partial grant received which the grant-awarding body allocates to the installation of reduced rate heating equipment

The facts are as in (A) above except that C receives a grant of £200 towards the installation of the reduced rate supplies and pays for the rest of the work himself.

	£	£
Value of reduced rate supplies which are grant-funded	200	
VAT thereon (5%)	10	
		210
Value of other supplies	800	
VAT thereon (20%)	160	
		960
Total cost including VAT		1,170
Less Grant received		(200)
Contribution from C		£970

(C) **Apportionment where partial grant received which the grant-awarding body does not allocate**

The facts are as in (A) above except that C receives a grant of £200 towards the total cost and pays for the rest of the work himself.

Proportion of total grant allocated to reduced rate supplies

$$£200 \times \frac{300}{1000} = £60$$

	£	£
Value of reduced rate supplies which are grant-funded	60	
VAT thereon (5%)	3	
		63
Value of other supplies	940	
VAT thereon (20%)	188	
		1,128
Total cost including VAT		1,191
Less Grant received		(200)
Contribution from C		£991

411 Retail Schemes

[*VATA 1994, Sch 11 para 2(6); SI 1995 No 2518, Regs 66–75; VAT Notice 727*]

411.1 POINT OF SALE SCHEME

[*VAT Notice 727/3/13*]

N Ltd is a garden centre selling plants and gardening equipment. It also sells gardening books and magazines and barbecue supplies. Due to the product mix, the company splits takings at the time of sale using multi-button tills. At the end of its VAT period, standard-rated takings totalled £125,639.34, zero-rated sales of books, etc. totalled £1,549.28 and reduced rate sales of barbecue fuels totalled £194.32.

Output tax for the period is

(£125,639.34 × $^1/_6$) + (£194.32 × $^1/_{21}$) = £20,939.89 + £9.25 = £20,949.14

Notes

(a) The method of calculation is the same for all VAT periods.

(b) Taxable turnover must not exceed £130 million.

411.2 APPORTIONMENT SCHEME 1

[*VAT Notice 727/4/13*]

B Ltd has figures for the four quarterly periods in a VAT year as follows.

	Cost of standard-rated goods for resale (incl VAT)	Cost of reduced rate goods for resale (incl VAT)	Total cost of goods for resale (incl VAT)	Gross takings
	£	£	£	£
First quarter	9,429	78	15,701	21,714.55
Second quarter	10,418	124	17,840	24,316.51
Third quarter	9,972	312	15,919	21,899.29
Fourth quarter	7,076	25	11,293	16,149.61
	£36,895	£539	£60,753	£84,079.96

First quarter

Standard-rated sales are

$$\frac{9{,}429}{15{,}701} \times £21{,}714.55 = £13{,}040.35$$

Reduced rate sales are

$$\frac{78}{15,701} \times £21,714.55 = £107.87$$

Output tax =(£13,040.35 × 1/6) + (£107.87 × 1/21) =	£2,178.53

By similar calculations output tax in the remaining quarters is

Second quarter	2,374.73
Third quarter	2,306.80
Fourth quarter	1,688.21
	£8,548.27

Annual adjustment

Standard-rated sales for the year are

$$\frac{36,895}{60,753} \times £84,079.96 = £51,061.35$$

Reduced rate sales for the year are

$$\frac{539}{60,753} \times £84,079.96 = £745.96$$

Output tax = (£51,061.35 × 1/6) + (£745.96 × 1/21) = £8,545.75

£2.52 must be added to the amount of VAT deductible for the fourth quarter.

Notes

(a) VAT-exclusive retail sales must be less than £1 million.

(b) Any supplies of services, home-grown or self-made goods, or supplies of catering must be dealt with outside the scheme.

(c) The annual adjustment must be made on 31 March, 30 April or 31 May each year, depending upon the VAT return periods. The first adjustment may therefore cover less than a full year.

411.3 APPORTIONMENT SCHEME 2

[*VAT Notice 727/4/13*]

Z Ltd owns a store and can analyse all purchases of stock for resale. It decides to use Apportionment Scheme 2 and calculates that the expected selling price, including VAT, of stock for retail sale at the commencement of using the scheme is £818,703, of which £331,379 represents standard-rated lines. Trading figures for the first four quarters under the scheme are

	ESP of standard-rated goods received for resale (incl VAT)	Total ESP of goods received for resale (incl VAT)	Gross takings
	£	£	£
First quarter	393,741	1,009,199	835,265
Second quarter	400,829	891,685	829,524
Third quarter	314,227	905,859	1,018,784
Fourth quarter	493,207	1,235,087	1,486,381

Output tax is calculated as follows

First quarter

Opening stock	331,379	818,703	
First quarter	393,741	1,009,199	
	£725,120	£1,827,902	

$$\text{Standard-rated sales} = \frac{725,120}{1,827,902} \times £835,265 = £331,345$$

Output tax = £331,345 × 1/6 — £55,224.16

Second quarter

Opening stock	331,379	818,703	
First quarter	393,741	1,009,199	
Second quarter	400,829	891,685	
	£1,125,949	£2,719,587	

$$\text{Standard-rated sales} = \frac{1,125,949}{2,719,587} \times £829,524 = £343,435$$

Output tax = £343,435 × 1/6 — £57,239.17

Third quarter

Opening stock	331,379	818,703	
First quarter	393,741	1,009,199	
Second quarter	400,829	891,685	
Third quarter	314,227	905,859	
	£1,440,176	£3,625,446	

$$\text{Standard-rated sales} = \frac{1,440,176}{3,625,446} \times £1,018,784 = £404,702$$

Output tax = £404,702 × 1/6 — £67,450.33

	ESP of standard-rated goods received for resale (incl VAT)	Total ESP of goods received for resale (incl VAT)	Gross takings
	£	£	£
Fourth quarter			
First quarter	393,741	1,009.199	
Second quarter	400,829	891,685	
Third quarter	314,227	905,859	
Fourth quarter	493,207	1,235,087	
	£1,602,004	£4,041,830	

$$\text{Standard-rated sales} = \frac{1,602,004}{4,041,830} \times £1,486,381 = £589,136$$

Output tax = £589,136 × $^1/_6$ £98,189.33

Notes

(a) For the fifth quarter, the method of calculation continues as in the fourth quarter above, the first quarter's figures being dropped and the fifth quarter's added to produce a rolling average across the last year.

(b) VAT-exclusive retail sales must be less than £130 million.

(c) Any supplies of services or supplies of catering must be dealt with outside the scheme.

(d) If it is not possible to perform a physical stock-take on the date of starting to use the scheme, the ESP values of goods received for resale in the previous three months may be used.

411.4 DIRECT CALCULATION SCHEME 1

[*VAT Notice 727/5/13*]

K runs a newsagent's shop. In addition to sales of newspapers and magazines (zero-rated), he also sells confectionery and tobacco (standard-rated), a limited range of food items (zero-rated) and barbecue fuels (reduced rate supplies). At the end of a VAT period, gross takings are £18,714.55. The expected selling prices of purchases in the period are £11,236.19 for standard-rated goods, £8,154.27 for zero-rated goods and £157.93 for reduced rate goods.

The minority goods are zero-rated and reduced rate supplies (i.e. the main goods are standard-rated).

Output tax is calculated as follows.

	£	£
Gross takings		18,714.55
Expected selling prices of zero-rated goods	8,154.27	
Expected selling prices of reduced rate goods	157.93	
		(8,312.20)
Standard-rated element of takings		£10,402.35
Output tax = (£10,402.35 × $^1/_6$) + (£157.93 × $^1/_{21}$) =		£1,741.25

Notes

(a) VAT-exclusive retail sales must be less than £1 million.

(b) Minority goods are those at the rate of VAT which forms the smallest proportion of retail supplies or, where goods are supplied at three rates of VAT, which forms the two smallest proportions.

(c) Supplies of services with the same liability as the minority goods must be dealt with outside the scheme, as must supplies of catering.

(d) If the minority goods are standard-rated and reduced rate supplies (i.e. the main goods are zero-rated) output tax is simply:

(ESP of standard-rated goods × $^1/_6$) + (ESP of reduced rate goods × $^1/_{21}$)

411.5 DIRECT CALCULATION SCHEME 2

[*VAT Notice 727/5/13*]

K decides to use Direct Calculation Scheme 2. When he starts to use the scheme, his opening stock, valued at expected selling prices, is

	£
Standard-rated goods	3,145.91
Zero-rated goods	2,250.34
Reduced rate goods	142.51

For the first four quarters, his relevant details are

	ESP of standard-rated goods purchased	ESP of zero-rated goods purchased	ESP of reduced rate goods purchased	Gross takings
	£	£	£	£
First quarter	11,236.19	8,154.27	157.93	18,714.55
Second quarter	9,075.02	11,667.67	259.32	20,726.40
Third quarter	9,872.90	10,124.75	137.54	20,855.88
Fourth quarter	11,431.39	11,008.62	21.43	22,649.04
	£41,615.50	£40,955.31	£576.22	£82,945.87

At the end of the fourth quarter, his closing stock, valued at expected selling prices, is

	£
Standard-rated goods	4,217.22
Zero-rated goods	3,151.44
Reduced rate goods	119.19

First quarter

The minority goods are zero-rated and reduced rate supplies. Output tax is calculated as follows.

	£	£
Gross takings		18,714.55
ESP of zero-rated goods	8,154.27	
ESP of reduced rate goods	157.93	
		(8,312.20)
Standard-rated element of takings		£10,402.35

Output tax = (£10,402.35 × $^1/_6$) + (£157.93 × $^1/_{21}$) = £1,741.25

Second quarter

The minority goods are standard-rated and reduced rate supplies. Output tax is calculated as follows.

(£9,075.02 × $^1/_6$) + (£259.32 × $^1/_{21}$) = £1,524.85

Third quarter

The minority goods are standard-rated and reduced rate supplies. Output tax is calculated as follows.

(£9,872.90 × $^1/_6$) + (£137.54 × $^1/_{21}$) = £1,652.03

Fourth quarter

The minority goods are zero-rated and reduced rate supplies. Output tax is calculated as follows.

	£	£
Gross takings		22,649.04
ESP of zero-rated goods	11,008.62	
ESP of reduced rate goods	21.43	
		(11,030.05)
Standard-rated element of takings		£11,618.99
Output tax = (£11,618.99 × $^1/_6$) + (£21.43 × $^1/_{21}$) =		£1,937.52

The annual adjustment is as follows

The minority goods are zero-rated and reduced rate supplies. Output tax is calculated as follows.

	£	£
Gross takings		82,945.87
Less zero-rated goods		
opening stock	2,250.34	
ESP of goods purchased	40,955.31	
	43,205.65	
closing stock	3,151.44	
		(40,054.21)
		42,891.66
Less reduced rate goods		
opening stock	142.51	
ESP of goods purchased	576.22	
	718.73	
closing stock	119.19	
		(599.54)
Standard-rated element of takings		£42,292.12
Output tax = (£42,292.12 × $^1/_6$) + (£599.54 × $^1/_{21}$) =		7,077.24
Output tax already calculated		
£1,741.25 + £1,524.85 + £1,652.03 + £1,937.52		6,855.65
Additional VAT payable with return for fourth quarter		£221.59

Notes

(a) VAT-exclusive retail sales must be between £1 million and £130 million.

(b) Minority goods are those at the rate of VAT which forms the smallest proportion of retail supplies or, where goods are supplied at three rates of VAT, which forms the two smallest proportions.

(c) Supplies of services with the same liability as the minority goods must be dealt with outside the scheme, as must supplies of catering.

412 Second-Hand Goods

412.1 PART EXCHANGE

[*VAT Notice 718, para 13.6*]

A car dealer sells a car for £2,000 cash plus a car for which £1,000 is allowed in part exchange.

Selling price. A selling price of £3,000 must be entered in the stock book.

Purchase price. As the car taken in exchange is eligible to be resold under the scheme, the amount allowed in part exchange (£1,000) is the purchase price. The purchase must also be recorded in the stock book.

412.2 GLOBAL ACCOUNTING SCHEME — NEGATIVE MARGIN

[*SI 1995/1268, Art 13; SI 1999/3120; VAT Notice 718, para 14.8*]

A dealer starts to use the global accounting scheme and values his opening stock on hand at £10,000. In the first VAT period, his total purchases from his purchase summary are £2,000 and his sales from his sales summary are £8,000. In his second VAT period purchases are £1,000 and sales are £7,000.

The margin for the first VAT period is

£8,000 − (£10,000 + £2,000) = (£4,000)

There is a negative margin and no VAT is due. The negative margin is carried forward to the next period.

The margin for the second VAT period is

£7,000 (£4,000 + £1,000) = £2,000

VAT due = £2,000 × $^1/_6$ = £333.33

Notes

(a) If there is a negative margin (because total purchases exceed total sales), no VAT is due and the negative margin is carried forward to the following VAT period for inclusion in the calculation of the total purchases of that period.

(b) A negative margin cannot be set off against other VAT due in the same VAT period on transactions outside the global accounting scheme.

412.3 AUCTIONEERS' SCHEME

[*SI 1992/3122, Art 8(7); SI 1995/1268, Art 12(7); VAT Notice 718, paras 11.1–11.4*]

Goods are sold at auction for £1,000 (the hammer price). Commission is charged to the seller at 10% net of VAT and a buyer's premium is charged of 15% net of VAT.

Commission = (£1,000 × 10%) + 20% VAT =	£120
Purchase price = £1,000 − £120 =	£880
Buyer's premium = (£1,000 × 15%) + 20% VAT =	£180
Selling price = £1,000 + £180 =	£1,180
Margin = £1,180 − £880 =	£300
Output tax = £300 × $^1/_6$ =	£50

Note

(a) The purchase price, selling price, margin and VAT due are calculated from the successful bid price (hammer price) and commission and other charges.

'*Purchase price*' is the hammer price less commission payable to the auctioneer under his contract with the seller for the sale of the goods.

'*Selling price*' is the hammer price plus the consideration for any supply of services by the auctioneer to the purchaser (e.g. buyer's premium) in connection with the sale of the goods.

The margin is the difference between the purchase price and the selling price. The margin is regarded as being VAT-inclusive i.e. the VAT included is VAT-inclusive margin × VAT fraction (currently $^1/_6$).

National Insurance Contributions

501 Age Exception

501.1 PERSONS OVER PENSIONABLE AGE

[*SSCBA 1992, s 6(3); SI 2001 No 1004, Regs 7, 28, 29*]

(A)

Gail is approaching state pensionable age on 6 November 2018. She currently works full time earning £500 per week as a PA to the managing director. Although she will attain state pension age in November 2018 both she and the wages clerk are unsure what the position will be if she goes part time for three days of the week from that date earning £300 per week. The managing director is also keen to know whether he will have to pay more Class 1 secondary contributions by employing Jean for the other two days she is away on a wage of £200.

Gail must present her birth certificate or passport to her employer so that the company has proof that age exception is warranted. If it is found that no proof has been obtained then the employer is entirely liable for any underpayment. If Gail does not want her employer to see her birth certificate or passport, HMRC will send her a letter to show them instead. Gail should write to National Insurance Contributions and Employers Office, HM Revenue and Customs BX9 1AN explaining why she doesn't want her employer to see her birth certificate or passport. Although Class 1 primary contributions will cease, the employer must continue to deduct secondary contributions even though Gail is over pensionable age.

		Weekly class 1 liabilities before job sharing arrangement in force			
		Primary*		Secondary†	
	£	%	£	%	£
Gail	500.00	Nil/12	40.56	Nil/13.8	46.64
		Weekly class 1 liabilities when job sharing arrangement in force			
Gail	300.00	Nil	Nil	Nil/13.8	19.04
Jean	200.00	Nil/12	4.56	Nil/13.8	5.24
	£500.00		£4.56		£24.28

(* Nil% × £162, 12% × remainder.) († Nil% × £162, 13.8% × remainder.)

The employer will save £22.36 (i.e. £46.64 – £24.28) each week in secondary contributions under the job sharing arrangement.

Notes

(a) An employed earner who attains pensionable age is excepted from liability for Class 1 primary contributions on any earnings paid to him or for his benefit after the date he attains pensionable age. The exception does not apply to earnings which would normally have fallen to be paid to him or for his benefit before that date. Earnings which, though paid before he attains pensionable age, would normally fall to be paid to him in a subsequent tax year are within the exception. [*SSCBA 1992, s 6(3); SI 2001 No 1004, Regs 28, 29*].

(b) See (B) below for the age at which a person attains state pensionable age.

(B) Pensionable age

Imogen was born on 29 March 1954. Applying the table in *Pensions Act 1995, Sch 4 Part 1*, she attains pensionable age on 6 September 2019.

Note

(a) Pensionable age is, in the case of a man born before 6 December 1953, 65, and in the case of a woman born before 6 April 1950, 60. For women born after 5 April 1950 and before 6 October 1954, and for men born after 5 December 1953 and before 6 October 1954, pensionable age rises on a sliding scale contained in *Pensions Act 1995, Sch 4 Pt 1*. For men and women born after 5 October 1954 and before 6 April 1960 pensionable age is 66. A sliding scale under *Sch 4 Pt 1* again applies to gradually increase the pensionable age for men and women born after 5 April 1960 and before 6 March 1961, so that for men and women born after 5 April 1961 pensionable age is 67. A further phased increase applies to those born on or after 6 April 1977 and before 6 April 1978, so that the pensionable age for those born after 5 April 1978 will be 68. The Government has announced that it intends to amend the law so that the increase in pensionable age to 68 will apply to those born after 5 April 1970.

502 Aggregation of Earnings

502.1 EMPLOYMENT UNDER THE SAME EMPLOYER

[*SSCBA 1992, Sch 1 para 1(1)(a); SI 2001 No 1004, Reg 14*]

(A) Earnings paid for different periods

Arnold is employed by Bauble Bros as a sales representative. He receives a weekly salary, quarterly commission and an annual bonus. Under the earnings period rules, his earnings period is a week (unless HMRC has directed otherwise). In the week ended 13 July 2018, Arnold receives:

	£
Salary for the week ended 13 July 2018	100
Commission for the quarter ended 30 June 2018	387
Bonus for the year ended 31 December 2018	3,300
	£3,787

By virtue of *SSCBA 1992, Sch 1 para 1(1)(a)*, the contribution liabilities of Arnold and of Bauble Bros for that week will be assessed by reference to a single amount of earnings of £3,787.

Notes

(a) All earnings paid to an earner in a given earnings period in respect of one or more employed earner's employments under the same employer are aggregated and treated as a single payment of earnings in respect of one such employment. [*SSCBA 1992, Sch 1 para 1(1)(a); SI 2001 No 1004, Reg 14*]. See **511.1(A)(B)** EARNINGS PERIODS for the rules which determine the earnings period where there are multiple regular pay patterns.

(b) Aggregation does not take place if it is not reasonably practicable. [*SI 2001 No 1004, Reg 14*].

(c) See **502.5** below where an earner has been, but is no longer, a director of a company.

(B) More than one contract

Throughout 2018/19, Cyril is employed by the Dainty Dish Restaurant under two separate contracts of service. As barman, he is paid earnings of £150 per week and, as wine waiter, he is paid earnings of £200 per week.

The total weekly Class 1 liability is as follows.

			£
Primary	£162	@ Nil	Nil
	£188	@ 12%	22.56
	£350		22.56
Secondary	£162	@ Nil	Nil
	£188	@ 13.8%	25.94
	£350		£25.94
			£48.50

Notes

(a) Because C's two employments are under the same employer, all his earnings in respect of those employments are aggregated and treated as a single weekly payment of £350 in respect of a single employment. [*SSCBA 1992, Sch 1 para 1(1)(a)*].

(b) See notes (b) and (c) to (A) above.

502.2 DIFFERENT EMPLOYMENTS, SECONDARY CONTRIBUTORS IN ASSOCIATION

[*SSCBA 1992, Sch 1 para 1(b); SI 2001 No 1004, Reg 15(1)(a)*]

Throughout 2018/19, Edward is paid earnings of £165 per week in respect of his employment with Fabrications Ltd; £167 per week in respect of his employment with Gudroofs; £88 per week in respect of his employment with Homemakers Ltd and £103 per week with Interiors Ltd. H is in voluntary liquidation under John, a liquidator, but is continuing to play its part in a joint project with F, G and I involving the development of a residential building site. Edward is employed by G, H and I in connection with that joint project but his employment with F is in connection with unassociated activities in which that company is involved.

There are four secondary contributors who pay earnings to Edward: F, G, J (as liquidator of H) and I, but of these only F, G and I are carrying on business in association (J, as liquidator, is not), and of these only G and I are doing so in respect of Edward's employments. Accordingly, only the earnings Edward receives from G and I fall to be aggregated, with Class 1 contribution liabilities arising as follows.

		Primary*		Secondary†	
	£	%	£	%	£
F	165.00	Nil/12	0.36	Nil/13.8	0.41
G	167.00				
I	103.00				
	270.00	Nil/12	12.96	Nil/13.8	14.90
J	88.00	Nil	Nil	Nil	Nil

(* Nil% × £162, 12% × remainder.)
(† Nil% × £162, 13.8% × remainder.)

Notes

(a) All earnings paid to an earner in a given earnings period in respect of more than one employed earner's employments by different secondary contributors who, in respect of those employments, carry on business in association with each other, are aggregated and treated as a single payment of earnings in respect of one such employment. [*SSCBA 1992, Sch 1 para 1(1)(b); SI 2001 No 1004, Reg 15(1)(a)*].

(b) See notes (b) and (c) to **502.1**(A) above.

502.3 DIFFERENT EMPLOYMENTS, DIFFERENT EMPLOYERS ONE OF WHOM IS SECONDARY CONTRIBUTOR

[*SSCBA 1992, Sch 1 para 1(1)(b); SI 2001 No 1004, Reg 15(1)(b)*]

From 6 April 2018, Keith is employed by the Lively Lazarites Central Fund as an accountant at a salary of £172 per week. He is also remunerated by that fund at the rate of £165 per week as minister of the LL Free Church in Lincoln.

Under the provisions of *SSCBA 1992, s 6(4)* (which require the earnings from each employment to be viewed in isolation from the other) Class 1 contribution liabilities of £1.20 primary and £1.38 secondary would arise on the earnings of £172 per week. On the earnings of £165 per week, Class 1 contribution liabilities of £0.36 primary and £0.41 secondary would arise. As the fund is not only Keith's employer, however, but also the secondary contributor as regards the earnings paid to him as a minister of religion, his earnings must, by virtue of *SI 2001/1004, Reg 15(1)(b)*, be aggregated and, in consequence, Class 1 contributions of £21.00 primary and £24.15 secondary will be payable on the combined earnings of £337.

502.4 DIFFERENT EMPLOYMENTS, SECONDARY CONTRIBUTOR OTHER THAN ONE OF THE EMPLOYERS

[*SSCBA 1992, Sch 1 para 1(1)(b); SI 2001 No 1004, Reg 15(1)(c)*]

In 2018/19, Marveltipe Agency obtains temporary employment for Norma, a secretary, with O Ltd, P Ltd and Q Ltd. Through Marveltipe, Norma is paid weekly earnings of £98 from O, £108 from P and £78 from Q. Marveltipe also obtains work for Jean with O, P and Q. Through Marveltipe, Jean is paid monthly earnings of £2,500, £1,900 and £1,100 respectively.

Although the earnings are in respect of different employments and are paid by different persons, Marveltipe (though not itself one of Norma or Jean's employers) is the secondary contributor as regards those earnings (see *SI 1978 No 1689, Sch 3 para 2(a)*). Both

Norma's and Jean's earnings must therefore be aggregated. Class 1 contributions for Norma will therefore be payable on earnings of £284 per week as if it were a single payment in respect of one employment. Class 1 contributions for Jean will likewise be payable on earnings of £5,500 per month.

Notes

(a) All earnings paid by different persons to an earner in a given earnings period in respect of more than one employed earner's employments where some other person is, by regulation, treated as the secondary contributor in relation to those earnings, are aggregated and treated as a single payment of earnings in respect of one such employment. [*SSCBA 1992, Sch 1 para 1(1)(b); SI 2001 No 1004, Reg 15(1)(c)*].

(b) But for the requirement to aggregate Norma's earnings, they would have escaped liability as each amount falls below the 2018/19 weekly earnings thresholds of £162. In Jean's case, primary Class 1 contributions would have been 12% of the earnings (less £702 threshold) from each source – subject to the annual maximum. Aggregation results in a single calculation on the combined earnings so that only 2% is deducted on earnings of £1,637 (total earnings £5,500 less UEL £3,863).

502.5 EARNINGS RELATING TO PERIODS OF FORMER DIRECTORSHIP

[*SI 2001 No 1004, Reg 8(5)(a)*]

Throughout 2018/19, Richard is employed by Stiffs Ltd as an embalmer at a salary of £2,000 per month. Until 31 December 2017 he had been a director of the company but had, on that date, resigned because of worsening health. In September 2018, the board votes him a bonus of £7,000 in respect of his services as director during the year ended 31 December 2017 and a further £5,000 in respect of his services as embalmer during the same period.

Class 1 contributions are as follows.

		Primary		Secondary	
Salary		%	£	%	£
£702		Nil		Nil	
£1,298		12	155.76	13.8	179.12
£2,000					
	(less than *monthly* UEL for primary contribution purposes £3,863)				
Bonuses					
£8,424		Nil		Nil	
£3,576		12	429.12	13.8	493.49
£12,000					
	(less than *annual* UEL for primary contribution purposes £46,350)				
Total			£584.88		£672.61

Notes

(a) Where an earner who was, but is no longer, a director of a company receives earnings in any tax year after that in which he ceased to be a director, those earnings, insofar as they are paid in respect of any period during which he was a director, are not to be aggregated with any other earnings with which they would otherwise fall to be aggregated. [*SI 2001 No 1004, Reg 8(5)(a)*].

(b) An annual earnings period applies to the earnings relating to the period when Richard was a director. [*SI 2001 No 1004, Reg 8(5)(b)*].

(c) Were it not for *Reg 8(5)(a)*, Richard's earnings in September 2018 would fall to be aggregated as the amounts are derived from different employments under the same employer (see **502.1**(B) above).

502.6 AGGREGATION WITH GRATUITIES ETC. PAID SEPARATELY

Anthony runs a small hotel in which he employs Bonnie and Clyde as waiters. For the week ending 23 June 2018, Bonnie's earnings are £146 and Clyde's earnings are £192. On the face of it, no contribution liabilities arise as regards Bonnie's earnings as they fall below the thresholds of £162, and liability for primary and secondary Class 1 contributions as regards Clyde's earnings are at only 12% primary and 13.8% secondary on the earnings over £162. In the week concerned, however, guests have asked for tips of £50 to be added to their bills and Anthony has passed those tips to David, the hall porter, instructing him that Bonnie is to receive £25 and Clyde is to receive £25. In those circumstances, contribution liabilities for which Anthony is accountable are as follows:

		£		£
Bonnie	Class 1 primary:	162	@ Nil%	0.00
		9	@ 12%	1.08
		171		1.08
	Class 1 secondary:	162	@ Nil%	0.00
		9	@ 13.8%	1.24
		171		1.24
Clyde	Class 1 primary:	162	@ Nil%	0.00
		55	@ 12%	6.60
		217		6.60
	Class 1 secondary:	157	@ Nil%	0.00
		55	@ 13.8%	7.59
		217		7.59

Note

(a) Where tips, gratuities etc. are earnings for contributions purposes and their allocation is not carried out by the person who is the secondary contributor as regards the ordinary earnings of the employed earner to whom they are allocated, the secondary contributor must nevertheless aggregate the tips etc. with the ordinary earnings and account for Class 1 contributions on the aggregate amount. See HMRC leaflet CWG2 (2018), para 2.8.

502.7 AGGREGATION FOR CLASS 4 PURPOSES

[*SSCBA 1992, s 15*]

Francis is in business as an interior decorator and as a furniture renovator. He is also an equal partner in a firm that supplies fitted kitchens. His interior decorating business was established several years ago with a 31 October accounting date but the furniture renovating business commenced on 1 May 2013 with a 30 April accounting date. The fitted kitchen partnership is long-established (with a 31 December accounting date) and F's share of profits one-half. Trading results adjusted in accordance with the tax and Class 4 rules are as follows

Year ended	Trade	
31 October 2015	Interior decorator	£10,000
31 October 2016	Interior decorator	£12,500
31 October 2017	Interior decorator	£13,500
31 October 2018	Interior decorator	£14,500
30 April 2015	Furniture renovator	£1,200
30 April 2016	Furniture renovator	£1,350
30 April 2017	Furniture renovator	£1,550
30 April 2018	Furniture renovator	£1,950
31 December 2015	Fitted kitchens	£28,500
31 December 2016	Fitted kitchens	£29,000
31 December 2017	Fitted kitchens	£32,000
31 December 2018	Fitted kitchens	£34,000

The amount of trading income chargeable to income tax, and in respect of which Class 4 contributions are calculated, for 2015/16 is as follows

	£
Interior decorator (current year basis)	10,000
Furniture renovator (current year basis)	1,200
Fitted kitchens (current year basis split according to profit share in 2015/16:1/2 × £28,500)	14,250
	£25,450

The amount of trading income chargeable to income tax, and in respect of which Class 4 contributions are calculated, for 2016/17 is as follows

	£
Interior decorator (current year basis)	12,500
Furniture renovator (current year basis)	1,350
Fitted kitchens (current year basis split according to profit share in 2016/17:1/2 × £29,000)	14,500
	£28,350

The amount of trading income chargeable to income tax, and in respect of which Class 4 contributions are calculated, for 2017/18 is as follows

	£
Interior decorator (current year basis)	13,500
Furniture renovator (current year basis)	1,550
Fitted kitchens (current year basis split according to profit share in 2017/18:1/2 × £32,000)	16,000
	£31,050

The amount of trading income chargeable to income tax, and in respect of which Class 4 contributions are calculated, for 2018/19 is as follows

	£
Interior decorator (current year basis)	14,500
Furniture renovator (current year basis)	1,950
Fitted kitchens (current year basis split according to profit share in 2018/19:1/2 × £34,000)	17,000
	£33,450

Note

(a) Class 4 contributions are payable in respect of all profits which are immediately derived from the carrying on or exercise of one or more trades, professions or vocations and are profits chargeable to income tax under *ITTOIA 2005, Pt 2 Ch 2*. [*SSCBA 1992, s 15(1)*]. Profits must therefore be aggregated, but time apportionment to the tax year is not required. See also **513** PARTNERS.

503 Annual Maximum

503.1 CLASS 1 AND CLASS 2 LIMITATION

[*SI 2001 No 1004, Reg 21*]

For the whole of 2018/19, Finch is employed by Grebe at a salary of £3,100 per month, and was paid an annual bonus in March of £8,000. She was also employed by Heron at a salary of £1,875 per month. The Class 1 primary contributions paid on her earnings from her employed earner's employments are as follows

	£			£	£
Grebe	702.00	(monthly earnings threshold)	@ Nil%	0.00 × 11 =	0.00
(First 11 months)	2,398.00		@ 12%	287.76 × 11 =	3,165.36
	3,100.00				3,165.36
(March)	680.00	(monthly earnings threshold)	@ Nil%	0.00 × 1 =	0.00
	3,161.00		@ 12%	379.32 × 1 =	379.32
	3,863.00	(monthly UEL)			
	7,237.00		@ 2%	144.74 × 1 =	144.74
	11,100.00				524.06
(Total)					3,689.42
Heron	702.00	(monthly ET)	@ Nil%	0.00 x 12 =	0.00
	1,173.00		@ 12%	140.76 x 12 =	1,689.12
	1,875.00				1,689.12
Total Class 1 paid:					5,378.54

On the face of it, F has paid excessive contributions since the notional annual maximum for 2018/19 is £4,642.80. It is therefore necessary to consider Finch's personalised maximum using the following numbered steps.

Step		£	£
1.	Calculate 53 × (UEL − primary threshold), i.e. 53 × (£892 − £162)		38,690.00
2.	12% thereof		4,642.80
3.	Earnings from each employment that falls between primary threshold and UEL: £2,398 × 11 = £26,378 £3,161 × 1 = £3,161		

Step		£	£
	£1,173 × 12 = £14,076	43,615	
4.	Deduct figure in step 1. from 3. (£43,615 − £38,690)	4,925.00	
5.	As the line above gives a positive figure, multiply by 2%		98.50
6.	Earnings from each employment which exceeds UEL	Nil	
7.	Multiply step 6 result by 2%		Nil
8.	Add steps 2, 5, 7 – this gives the personalised annual maximum		£4,741.30

The contributions paid do exceed this personalised maximum and, provided the necessary conditions are met, the excess, suitably adjusted, will be repayable.

Note

(a) Where an earner is employed in more than one employment (including self-employments), liability in any tax year for primary Class 1 contributions and, where payable, Class 2 contributions, cannot exceed an amount equal to 53 primary Class 1 contributions at the primary percentage payable on earnings at the upper earnings limit together with such other liabilities which arise at the additional 2% rate. [*SI 2001 No 1004, Reg 21*]. *Reg 21* sets out an eight step process for calculating an individual's personal maximum, as illustrated in this example.

503.2 CLASS 4 LIMITATION

[*SI 2001 No 1004, Reg 100; SI 2016 No 352, Reg 15*]

(A) Case 1

Kate is a self-employed artist with profits chargeable to income tax for 2018/19 (and requiring no further adjustment) of £15,500. She also pays Class 2 contributions for the year. Throughout 2018/19 she is also a director of Kate's Krafts Ltd. Her earnings from the company during the year were £13,450. Contributions are paid as follows:

		£
Class 1 primary	£8,424 × Nil%	0.00
	£5,026 (£13,450 − £8,424) × 12%	603.12
Class 2	£2.95 × 52 Note: As there are 52 Sundays in 2018/19 only fifty-two weeks of Class 2 is payable	153.40
		£756.52

Her Class 4 liability is not to exceed the amount determined using the following steps:

Step		£	£
1.	Subtract the Class 4 lower profits limit from upper profits limit i.e. £46,350 – £8,424		37,926.00
2.	9% thereof	3,413.34	
3.	Add 53 times the weekly rate of Class 2 i.e. 53 × £2.95	156.35	3,569.69
4.	Subtract from Step 3 the amount of Class 2 paid and Class 1 paid at the main percentage rate (i.e. other than 2%)		
	Class 1	603.12	
	Class 2 – £2.95 × 52	153.40	(756.52)
			2,813.17
	This produces a positive result which must be compared with Class 1 and Class 4 – payable at the main rate – and Class 2:		
	Class 1	603.12	
	Class 2	153.40	
	Class 4 (£15,500 – £8,424) × 9%	636.84	
		£1,393.36	
	As £2,813.17, is more than these potential liabilities, the figure of Class 4 payable at the main rate (i.e., 9%) is the figure calculated above (i.e. £636.84). This is a 'Case 1' situation and no further steps are necessary, because there is no liability at the additional rate of 2%.		
	Class 4 contributions ('Case 1', so equal to Step 4)		£636.84

Note

(a) Where for any year Class 4 contributions are payable in addition to primary Class 1 contributions and/or Class 2 contributions, the liability for Class 4 contributions is not to exceed the amount which, when added to the primary Class 1 and Class 2 contributions (after applying the limitation in 503.1 above) equals the sum of the amount of Class 4 contributions which would be payable on profits equal to the upper annual limit plus 53 times the amount of a Class 2 contribution, plus an amount in respect of the additional 2% rate. [*SI 2001 No 1004, Reg 100*]. *Reg 100* sets out a multi-step process for calculating each earner's personal maximum, with different further steps for each of three possible results at step four. See (B) and (C) below for cases 2 and 3.

(B) **Case 2**

Iris is a self-employed dressmaker with profits chargeable to income tax for 2018/19 (and requiring no further adjustment) of £19,250. She pays Class 2 contributions for the year. Intermittently, when business is poor, she supplements her income by taking employment with Jeans Ltd. Her earnings from Jeans Ltd during the year were 32 weeks at £627. Contributions are paid as follows

		£
Class 1 primary	£162 × Nil% × 32	0.00
	£465 × 12% × 32	1,785.60
Class 2 Note: As there are 52 Sundays in 2018/19 only fifty-two weeks of Class 2 is payable	£2.95 × 52	153.40
		£1,939.00

In the absence of a relieving provision, Class 4 contributions of £974.34 (i.e. (£19,250 - £8,424) @ 9%) would also be payable. However, the Class 4 liability is not to exceed the amount determined following the numbered steps in the legislation as follows:

Step		£	£
1.	Subtract the Class 4 lower profits limit from upper profits limit i.e. £46,350 − £8,424		37,926.00
2.	9% thereof	3,413.34	
3.	Add 53 times the weekly rate of Class 2 i.e. 53 × £2.95	156.35	3,569.69
4.	Subtract from Step 3 the amount of Class 2 paid and Class 1 paid at the main percentage rate (i.e. other than 2%)		
	Class 1	1,785.60	
	Class 2 − £2.95 × 52	153.40	(1,939.00)
	This produces a positive result which must be compared with Class 1 and Class 4 – payable at the main rate – and Class 2:		1,630.69
	Class 1	1,785.60	
	Class 2	153.40	
	Class 4 (£19,250− £8,424) × 9%	974.34	
	As £1,630.69 is less than these potential liabilities, this is the figure of Class 4 payable at the main rate (i.e. 9%) – a 'Case 2' situation.	2,913.34	

Step		£	£
5.	Multiply the result of Step 4 (i.e. £1,630.69) by 100/9	18,119	
6.	Subtract the lower profits limit from the lesser of the upper profits limit and the amount of assessable profits	10,826	
7.	Subtract the answer in 5 from the answer in 6. (If negative, treat as nil.)	Nil	
8.	Multiply the above by 2%		Nil
9.	Multiply the profits less the upper profits limit by 2%		Nil
	Class 4 contributions ('Case 2', so add 4, 8 and 9)		£1,630.69

In consequence, Iris's liability is limited to that of someone deriving equivalent total earnings exclusively from self-employment.

(C) Case 3

Jan is a self-employed printer with profits chargeable to income tax for 2018/19 (and requiring no further adjustment) of £47,000. Throughout the year she pays Class 2 contributions. Throughout the year she is also a director of Jan's Jeans Ltd. Her earnings from the company during the year were £47,200. Contributions are paid as follows:

		£
Class 1 primary	£8,424 × Nil%	0.00
	£37,926 (£46,350 − £8,424) × 12%	4,551.12
	£850 (£47,200 − £46,350) × 2%	17.00
Class 2	£2.95 × 52 Note: As there are 52 Sundays in 2018/19 only fifty-two weeks of Class 2 is payable	153.40
		£4,721.52

Her Class 4 liability is not to exceed the amount determined using the following numbered steps:

Step		£	£
1.	Subtract the Class 4 lower profits limit from upper profits limit i.e. £46,350 – £8,424		37,926.00
2.	9% thereof	3,413.34	
3.	Add 53 times the weekly rate of Class 2 i.e. 53 × £2.95	156.35	3,569.69
4.	Subtract from Step 3 the amount of Class 2 paid and Class 1 paid at the main percentage rate (i.e. other than 2%)		
	Class 1	4,551.12	
	Class 2 – £2.95 × 52	153.40	4,704.52
			(1,134.83)
	This produces a negative result, called 'Case 3' in the legislation – see Step 9 also. No Class 4 contributions are payable at the main (9%) rate.		
	The consequence is that the result of this Step 4 is treated as nil.		Nil
5.	Multiply the result of Step 4 by 100/9	Nil	
6.	Subtract the lower profits limit from the lesser of the upper profits limit and the amount of assessable profits	37,926	
7.	Subtract the answer in 5 from the answer in 6. (If negative, treat as nil.)	37,926	
8.	Multiply the above by 2%		758.52
9.	Multiply the profits less the upper profits limit by 2%		
	i.e. £47,200 – £46,350 × 2%		17.00
Class 4 contributions ('Case 3', so add 4, 8 and 9)			£775.52

504 Class 1 Contributions: Employed Earners

Cross-reference. See also 502 AGGREGATION OF EARNINGS.

504.1 RATES

[*SSCBA 1992, ss 8, 9*]

Kevin employed Glenn at a rate of £900 per week from 26 March to 7 April 2018, making payment on Saturday each week.

Primary contributions due are:

Week ended 31 March 2018	157 ×	Nil%	Nil
	709 ×	12%	85.08
	34 ×	2%	0.68
			£85.76
Week ended 7 April 2018	162 ×	Nil%	Nil
	730 ×	12%	87.60
	8 ×	2%	0.16
			£87.76

Kevin's secondary contributions in respect of Glenn's employment are as follows:

Week ended 31 March 2018	157 ×	Nil%	Nil
	743 ×	13.8%	102.53
			£102.53
Week ended 7 April 2018	162 ×	Nil%	Nil
	738 ×	13.8%	101.84
			£101.84

Notes

(a) Most secondary contributors are entitled to an '*employment allowance*' for a tax year which is deducted from the amount due from secondary Class 1 contributions. The allowance is the lower of £3,000 and the amount of the contributions. See *National Insurance Contributions Act 2014, ss 1–8*. The allowance is ignored for the purpose of this example (and all of the examples in this work).

(b) An age-related secondary contribution rate of 0% applies to payments to any earner under the age of 21 on the date of payment, unless the earnings payment exceeds the relevant upper earnings limit for the earnings period, in which case the standard employer rate applies to any earnings above that limit. From 6 April 2016, the 0% rate applies also to payments to relevant apprentices under the age of 25. [*SSCBA 1992, ss 9A, 9B; National Insurance Contributions Act 2014, s 9; National Insurance Contributions Act 2015, s 1*]. The primary contribution rate is unaffected, as are the Class 1A and Class 1B rates.

505 Class 1A Contributions: Benefits in Kind

505.1 THE PERSON LIABLE

[*SSCBA 1992, ss 10–10ZB; FA 2015, Sch 1 para 23*]

(A) Benefits provided by third party

Avant is a sales representative. Throughout 2018/19, his contract of service is with Ballade and they pay Avant his salary and commission, he is provided with a car and private medical insurance; but the car he uses is owned and made available to him by Cavalier, Ballade's parent company and they also pay the medical insurance premium. Because Avant has been provided with benefits and private use of the car, he is chargeable to income tax on an amount arrived at under *ITEPA 2003, ss 201–203*, and, in consequence, a Class 1A contribution is payable for 2018/19 in respect of Avant and the benefits provided to him. But, because the secondary Class 1 contribution on the last payment of earnings made to Avant in 2018/19 is paid by Ballade, Ballade must pay the Class 1A contribution even though Cavalier, not Ballade, is the person who owns the car and paid for the medical insurance.

(B) Two or more employers in tax year

Herald works for Integra until 5 January 2019 when he changes jobs and takes up employment with Jetta. He is provided with a car (which is available for his private use) in each job. A tax charge will arise in respect of each car for 2018/19 so a Class 1A contribution will be payable in respect of each car for that year. Integra will pay secondary Class 1 contributions in relation to Herald's last earnings in his employment with Integra so Integra will be liable to pay a Class 1A contribution in respect of the car provided in that job, while Jetta will pay secondary Class 1 contributions in relation to Herald's last earnings in the tax year so Jetta will be liable to pay a Class 1A contribution in respect of the car provided in the second job.

(C) Person succeeding to a business

Orion works for Panda by whom he is provided with a car which is available for his private use. In October 2018, Panda sells his business to Quinta and Quinta continues to employ Orion and to allow him the private use of the car. As Quinta will pay a secondary Class 1 contribution in relation to Orion's last payment of earnings in 2018/19 in respect of the employment by reason of which the car is made available, he (to the exclusion of Panda) will be liable to pay the entire Class 1A contribution for the year in respect of the car – and any other benefits in kind – provided throughout the year.

If, of course, Orion had left Panda's employment before the change took place, the Class 1A liability in respect of the car provided to Orion from 6 April 2018 to the date of his leaving would rest with Panda.

505.2 CARS PROVIDED FOR THE PRIVATE USE OF THE EMPLOYEE

(A) Reduction for periods when car not available for use

[*ITEPA 2003, s 143*]

Kadette takes up employment by Legend on 2 June 2018 and a new petrol driven, 1,800 cc car, with carbon dioxide emissions of 125 g/km costing £15,000 is made available for his business and private use. Petrol is also provided. On 15 June, Kadette is involved in an accident and the car is off the road until 8 July. On 21 September, Kadette is involved in another accident and this time the car is off the road until 29 October. On 2 November, Kadette is moved into a clerical post within the company where he no longer has the use of a company car.

The cash equivalent of the car and fuel benefits for 2018/19 are £3,900 (£15,000 × 26%) and £6,084 (£23,400 × 26%) respectively, but the car is unavailable for 57 days at the start of the tax year, for 37 days in September/October, and for 155 days at the end of the tax year. The period of repair in June/July does not count as unavailability because it lasted for only 22 consecutive days. The cash equivalents of £3,900 and £6,084 are, therefore, reduced by $^{249}/_{365}$ to £1,239 and £1,934.

(B) Car made available by reason of more than one employment

[*SI 2001 No 1004, Reg 36*]

Robin works for Senator, Trevi and Uno and, by reason of those three employments, is provided with a petrol driven car costing £22,500 and with carbon dioxide emissions of 99 g/km. This is available for his private use but fuel is not provided. In 2018/19 the car benefit of £4,500 (20% × £22,500) is reduced by deducting from it

$$\pounds 4,500 \times \frac{3-1}{3} = \pounds 3,000$$

In other words, each employer will be liable for a Class 1A contribution on £1,500 and the aggregate of those reduced scale amounts (3 × £1,500) is £4,500, i.e. the scale amount on which a single employer of Robin would have been liable for a Class 1A contribution.

(C) Shared cars

[*SI 2001 No 1004, Reg 36*]

Accord, Bacara and Clio work for Dedra and, by reason of their employments, are concurrently provided with one car for private use costing £15,790 and with carbon dioxide emissions of 94 g/km. This is available for private use but fuel is not provided. The scale charge in each case is £3,000 (£15,790 × 19%) but these three amounts are then each reduced by deducting

$$\pounds 3,000 \times \frac{3-1}{3} = \pounds 2,000$$

In other words, Dedra will be liable for three Class 1A contributions on £1,000 and the aggregate of those reduced scale amounts (3 × £1,000) is £3,000, i.e. the car benefit on which he would have been liable for a Class 1A contribution if he had made the car available to just one employee.

506 Class 1B Contributions: PAYE Settlement Agreements

506.1 CALCULATION OF CONTRIBUTIONS

[*SSCBA 1992, s 10A*]

Benevolent Ltd has 500 employees who are all provided with late night taxis each year prior to Christmas when a large, regular and anticipated order is placed by an overseas customer that is time sensitive. The taxi fares amount to an average of £50 per employee during the year ended 5 April 2019. Of the employees affected, 400 are basic rate taxpayers and the other 100 are higher rate (but not additional rate) taxpayers. Also, 100 employees receive expenses amounting to £2,000 in total relating to home to work travel (all higher rate taxpayers). Benevolent Ltd seeks a PSA for 2018/19 onwards. The PSA negotiation might be as follows:

Tax due under PSA.	£	
Value of benefits provided to basic rate taxpayers		£
(400 × £50)	20,000.00	
Tax thereon @ 20%	4,000.00	
Gross up tax $£4,000 \times \dfrac{100}{100-20}$		5,000.00
Value of benefits provided to higher rate taxpayers		
(100 × £50)	5,000.00	
Value of expenses provided to higher rate taxpayers	2,000.00	
	7,000.00	
Tax thereon @ 40%	2,800.00	
Gross up tax $£2,800 \times 100 / 100 - 40$		£4,666.67
Total tax		£9,666.67
NICs due under PSA.		
Value of expenses otherwise liable for Class 1 NICs	2,000.00	
Class 1B NICs due @ 13.8% on £2,000		276.00
Value of benefits otherwise liable to Class 1A NICs	25,000.00	
Class 1B NICs due @ 13.8% on £25,000		3,450.00
Tax paid by employer liable to Class 1B charge	9,666.67	
Class 1B NICs due re tax paid by employer @ 13.8%		1,334.00
Total NICs and tax payable by Benevolent Ltd		£14,726.67

The tax and Class 1B is payable to HMRC on or before 19 October 2019 (22 October 2019 if paid electronically).

Note

(a) For 2018/19 onwards, the requirement for employers to agree annually with HMRC which employee expenses and benefits may be included in a PAYE settlement agreement is removed. Employers can submit their PSA request at the year end (before 6 July) and make ad hoc requests during the year. Where an employer entered into a PSA for 2017/18, HMRC sent a new PSA for 2018/19 automatically before April 2018, simply requiring the employer to sign the new agreement. Once a PSA is in place for 2018/19 it will continue for subsequent tax years until either the employer or HMRC cancel it or the employer needs to change it.

507 Class 4 Contributions: On Profits of a Trade etc.

Cross-reference. See also **502** AGGREGATION OF EARNINGS; **510** EARNINGS FROM SELF-EMPLOYMENT.

507.1 EXCEPTION OF CLASS 1 CONTRIBUTORS FOR EARNINGS CHARGEABLE TO TAX AS TRADING INCOME

[*SI 2001 No 1004, Reg 94*]

Ariadne is a practising solicitor and also the company secretary of Web Ltd. Her accounting year ends on 30 June and her 2018/19 assessable profits for Class 4 purposes (based on her accounts to 30 June 2018 under *ITTOIA 2005, ss 198(1), 200(3), 201(1)*) are £33,000. During 2018/19 she is paid secretarial fees (under deduction of standard rate primary Class 1 contributions, as appropriate) on a quarterly basis as follows.

	Gross fees	*Class 1*	
	£	£	
June 2018	500.00	—	(below earnings threshold)
September 2018	500.00	—	(below earnings threshold)
December 2018	2,200.00	Nil	(Nil% on [£8,424 ÷ 4 = £2,106])
		11.28	(12% on remainder [£2,200 − £2,106 = £94])
March 2019	14,000.00	Nil	(Nil% on [£8,424 ÷ 4 = £2,106])
		1,137.78	(12% on remainder up to the UEL [£46,350 ÷ 4 = £11,587.50] less £2,106)
		48.25	(2% on the remainder up to £14,000 = £2,412.50).
	£17,200.00	£1,197.31	

As these fees are included gross in Ariadne's accounts (the Class 1 contributions being correctly debited to drawings), the amount of £17,200 is deducted from the profits on which Class 4 contributions would be payable. The position for 2018/19 will be:

	£
Profits as stated	33,000
Less: Class 4 exception	(17,200)
	15,800
Less: lower annual limit	(8,424)
	£7,376
Total Class 4 liability	
£7,376 × 9% =	£663.84

508 Company Directors

Cross-reference. See also **502** AGGREGATION OF EARNINGS; **511** EARNINGS PERIODS.

508.1 EARNINGS

[*SI 2001 No 1004, Reg 22(2)*]

(A)

Gary Newsmith is a director of Lesstain Ltd, which has an accounting date of 5 July. Gary has no balance standing to his credit with the company at 6 July 2018 and fees already voted and paid have exactly equalled his drawings up to that date. G has substantial earnings from other sources and takes only one payment annually from L in respect of his services. A meeting is held on 2 April 2019 at which Gary's fees for the year ending 5 July 2019 are determined at £50,000, but this amount is neither credited to his current account nor made available to him. Due to cash flow problems and the desire to tie Gary to the company, it is agreed that Gary will only become entitled to his emoluments on 4 October 2020.

Gary is taxable on these earnings in 2019/20, since that is the year in which the end of the accounting period falls, and Lesstain Ltd has to apply PAYE to the general earnings on 5 July 2019, despite the fact that Gary may not draw the general earnings before 4 October 2020. When that date arrives, the company must deduct and account for National Insurance contributions, since it is only then that the money is put unreservedly at Gary's disposal.

Note

(a) Fees voted to a director in advance become earnings for contribution purposes on the date the director has an unreserved right to draw on them. (*Garforth v Newsmith Stainless Ltd* [1979] 2 All ER 73).

(B) **Fees voted in advance**

Dawn is a director of East Ltd. On 31 March 2018 E votes fees to D of £8,000 payable on the last Friday in each month for the next twelve months. D will have earnings for contribution purposes thus:

27 April 2018	£8,000
25 May 2018	£8,000
29 June 2018	£8,000
Etc.	

(C) **Fees credited to overdrawn account**

Sherlock is a director of Homes Ltd. On 16 July 2018, his current account with the company is overdrawn by £2,800, of which £2,000 has been treated as earnings for contribution purposes. On 20 July 2018 fees of £30,000 are voted to him and credited to the account. £28,000 of those fees are earnings for contribution purposes.

Note

(a) To the extent that items creating an overdrawn account have already been treated as earnings for contribution purposes, the fees etc. credited will not be earnings for contribution purposes, but any other part of the amount credited will be. [*SI 2001 No 1004, Sch 3 Part X para 2*].

508.2 CALCULATION OF CONTRIBUTIONS

[*SI 2001 No 1004, Regs 8, 22(2)*]

Frederick is appointed a director of Great Ltd on 1 November 2018. Earnings are paid to Frederick as follows:

Date	*Payment*	*Cumulative*
	£	£
30 November	700	700
31 December	800	1,500
31 January	5,000	6,500
28 February	900	7,400
31 March	13,600	21,000

There are 23 whole or part contribution weeks left in 2018/19, not counting for this purpose the one day which constitutes week 53 (Leaflet CA 44, Para 25 and page 27). His earnings period as a director is therefore 23 weeks. As the weekly earnings thresholds and the upper earnings limit for 2018/19 are £162.00 (employee), £162.00 (employer) and £892.00 respectively, Frederick's earnings thresholds and upper earnings limit are £3,726.00 (i.e. £162 × 23), £3,726.00 (i.e. £162 × 23) and £20,516.00 (i.e. £892.00 × 23). (The calculation of these limits and thresholds is necessary only if contributions in respect of earnings are to be calculated by use of the modified exact percentage method.)

Contributions can be calculated by use of either the *modified exact percentage method* or the *modified tables method*.

The *modified exact percentage procedure* would operate as follows:

Cum. Pay			Cum. Primary	Primary payable	Cum. secondary	Secondary payable
£			£	£	£	£
700	Nil%	× £700				
1,500	Nil%	× £1,500				
6,500	Nil%	× £3,726				
	12%	× £2,774	332.88	332.88		
	Nil%	× £3,726				
	13.8%	× £2,774			382.81	382.81
7,400	Nil%	× £3,726				
	12%	× £3,674	440.88	108.00		
	Nil%	× £3,726				
	13.8%	× £3,674			507.01	124.20
21,000	Nil%	× £3,726				
	12%	× £16,790				
	2%	× £484	2,024.48	1,583.60		
	Nil%	× £3,726				
	13.8%	× £17,274			2,383.81	1,876.80
				£2,024.48		£2,383.81

Alternatively, the *modified tables procedure* could have operated, thus:

Cum.Pay ÷ 23	Weekly table band	Primary per table × 23	Primary payable	Secondary per table × 23	Secondary payable
£	£	£	£	£	£
30.43					
65.22					
282.61	282.00	332.58	332.58	382.49	382.49
321.74	321.00	440.22	107.64	506.23	123.74
913.04	892+21	2,024.46	1,584.24	2,383.72	1,877.49
			£2,024.46		£2,383.72

Note

(a) The above procedures are set out in HMRC booklet CA 44, Paras 41 to 44. It will be noted that there are only minor discrepancies between the two results.

509 Deferment of Payment

509.1 CLASS 1 DEFERMENT

[*SSCBA 1992, s 19(1)(2); SI 2001 No 1004, Regs 68, 84*]

Eel is employed by Flounder Ltd, Grunion Ltd and Hake Ltd. In March 2018, when his earnings from the three companies were £630, £300 and £580 per week respectively, he applied for Class 1 deferment for 2018/19.

As his anticipated earnings from Flounder Ltd and Hake Ltd together (£1,510) exceeded the required amount for 2018/19 (£892, plus £162 per additional employment) deferment was granted in respect of the primary Class 1 contribution liability which would otherwise have arisen on his earnings from Grunion Ltd.

If, when the year ends, it is found that earnings from Flounder Ltd and Hake Ltd, contrary to expectations, have not together reached the upper earnings limit throughout the year, HMRC will issue a demand for the balance of contributions due (relating those contributions to Eel's earnings from Grunion Ltd but calculating the amount by reference to his actual total earnings in the year). If (as is more likely), however, the earnings from Flounder Ltd and Hake Ltd have together exceeded the upper earnings limit throughout the year, any excess contributions paid on those earnings will be refunded and the earnings from Grunion Ltd will be automatically excepted from the liability at the main rate which, until its exception, had been merely deferred.

Note

(a) In making application for deferment, a contributor has to agree to pay any amount by which contributions fall short of the total liability within 28 days of demand (see form CA 72A).

510 Earnings from Self-Employment

Cross-reference. See also **507** CLASS **4** CONTRIBUTIONS: ON PROFITS OF A TRADE ETC.

510.1 EARNINGS FOR CLASS 4 PURPOSES — LOSS RELIEF

[*SSCBA 1992, Sch 2 para 3(1)(4)*]

Kit has a sportswear business. His trading results (adjusted for tax purposes) are

Year to		£
5 July 2015	Profit	12,000
5 July 2016	Loss	(17,200)
5 July 2017	Profit	4,000
5 July 2018	Profit	19,400

K's assessable amounts of profit and other income are

	Trade Profit	Investment Income
	£	£
2015/16	12,000	1,500
2016/17	Nil	1,700
2017/18	4,000	1,800
2018/19	19,400	2,200

If K claims relief for his 2016/17 loss of £17,200 under *ITA 2007, s 64*, it will be apportioned against 2015/16 earned income i.e. £12,000 profits, then against 2015/16 investment income i.e. £1,500 and then against 2016/17 investment income i.e. £1,700. The balance of the loss (£2,000) is then carried forward against profits of the same trade only This will result in revised assessable amounts of profit and income, thus

	Trade Profit	Investment Income
	£	£
2015/16	Nil	Nil
2016/17	Nil	Nil
2017/18	2,000	1,800
2018/19	19,400	2,200

For Class 4 purposes, however, only £14,000 of the loss has been relieved (£12,000 in 2015/16 and £2,000 in 2017/18) and the remaining £3,200 must, therefore, also be carried forward to 2017/18 (and subsequent years, if necessary, as in the example), giving revised Class 4 profits as follows

	Class 4
	£
2015/16	Nil
2016/17	Nil
2017/18	Nil
2018/19	18,200

Notes

(a) Loss relief available for income tax purposes under *ITA 2007, s 83* (carry-forward against subsequent profits) and *s 89* (carry-back of terminal loss) is also available for Class 4 purposes. Relief under *ITA 2007, ss 64, 72* (set-off against general income) is also so available provided that the loss arises from activities of which any profits would have been earnings for Class 4 purposes (and see note (*b*) below). [*SSCBA 1992, Sch 2 para 3(1)*]. See also **IT 15** LOSSES.

(b) Where a loss deducted for income tax purposes is deducted from income other than trading profits, the loss is, to that extent, carried forward for Class 4 purposes and set off against the first available trading profit for subsequent years. [*SSCBA 1992, Sch 2 para 3(4)*].

511 Earnings Periods

511.1 PAY PATTERNS

[*SI 2001 No 1004, Regs 2–9*]

(A) Multiple regular pay pattern

Clive is a salesman for Dubbleglays Ltd. He is paid a monthly salary, a quarterly commission and an annual bonus and has, therefore, three regular pay intervals: a month, a quarter and a year.

As the shortest of these is a month, Clive's earnings period is a month and all the earnings paid to him in a year will be related to one or other of the twelve such periods it contains. If, therefore, he is paid £830 commission on 8 May for the quarter ended 31 March, £500 salary on 15 May for the month of May and £2,500 bonus on 29 May for the year ended 31 December of the preceding year, his earnings for the earnings period from 6 May to 5 June (PAYE month 2) will be £3,830, irrespective of the fact that only £500 of the total is earned within the month and the remainder relates to previous tax years and was earned over a period of between three and twelve months.

Notes

(a) Where two or more regular pay patterns run concurrently, the earnings period is normally the length of the shorter or shortest interval at which any part of the earnings is paid. [*SI 2001 No 1004, Reg 3(1)(2)*].

(b) See (B) below for the power for HMRC to direct that the longer or longest interval should be the earnings period.

(c) See **502.1(A)** AGGREGATION OF EARNINGS for the aggregation of earnings where two or more regular pay patterns run concurrently. See also **502.6**, **502.7** AGGREGATION OF EARNINGS for circumstances in which a common earnings period must be determined for related employments.

(B) Multiple regular pay pattern — HMRC direction

For the tax year, Everard (one of Clive's colleagues—see (A) above) had total earnings of £15,200 comprising:

	£	Pay interval
Salary	7,200	month
Commission	4,000	quarter
Bonus	4,000	year

A similar pattern had subsisted during the preceding two tax years.

If HMRC direct on, say, 5 June that, from the date of the direction onwards, and for all future years, E is to have an annual earnings period, E's earnings periods for the tax year would be:

month to	5 May
1 month to	5 June
44-week period to	5 April

and his earnings period for the next and all future tax years would be the tax year concerned.

Note

(a) Where two or more regular pay patterns run concurrently and it appears to HMRC that the greater part of earnings is normally paid at intervals of greater length than the shorter or shortest, HMRC may, by notifying the earner and secondary contributor, specify the longer or longest pay interval as the earnings period. [*SI 2001 No 1004, Reg 3(2A)–(3)*].

(C) Irregular payments

On 15 July, Jack is employed by Kwest Films Ltd as a researcher but, because of his age, is not entitled to the adult minimum wage. He is to be paid £5 per hour and to work in his own time and at his own convenience. He has, however, to meet the following deadlines

'Health Service' material	31 August
'Aids' material	28 October
'Disarmament' material	31 October

Jack works 106 hours on the first project, 151 hours on the second and 12 hours on the third. Earnings periods and earnings will be as follows

	£
48 days from 15 July to 31 August	530
58 days from 1 September to 28 October	755
Week ended 1 November (though only a four-day fixed period)	60

Note

(a) Where earnings are paid at irregular intervals and neither follow nor can be treated as following a regular pay pattern, the earnings period is the length of that part of the employment for which the earnings are paid or a week, whichever is the longer. [*SI 2001 No 1004, Reg 4(a)*].

511.2 CHANGE OF REGULAR PAY INTERVAL

[*SI 2001 No 1004, Reg 18*]

(A) Change to longer interval

Nuthatch and Osprey are both employed by Partridge Ltd. N is paid £400 per week and O is paid £250 per week. In June 2018, they become salaried employees and begin to be paid monthly at £1,800 and £1,050 per month, respectively. The last weekly wage is paid to each of them on 7 June and their first monthly salaries are paid on 28 June.

The first new earnings period is the month from 6 June to 5 July and their last payments of weekly wage fall within this period. Contributions have already been calculated on that wage as follows.

		Primary*		Secondary*	
		%	£	%	£
N	£400	Nil/12	28.56	Nil/13.8	32.84
O	£250	Nil/12	10.56	Nil/13.8	12.14

If contributions on the payment of salary on 5 July are calculated without regard to that wage payment, those contributions will be

		Primary*		Secondary*	
		%	£	%	£
N	£1,800	Nil/12	131.76	Nil/13.8	151.52
O	£1,050	Nil/12	41.76	Nil/13.8	48.02

If, however, contributions are calculated on the total payments in the earnings period, contributions will be

		Primary*		Secondary*	
		%	£	%	£
N	£2,200	Nil/12	179.76	Nil/13.8	206.72
O	£1,300	Nil/12	71.76	Nil/13.8	82.52

**First £702 (monthly) or £162 (weekly) at Nil%.

Under *SI 2001/1004, Reg 18(3)*, the contributions due on the two separate parts of earnings are not to exceed the contributions due on the total and they do not.

However, HMRC guidance requires the recalculation to be performed regardless of any comparison and thus, N's separate contributions (primary, £28.56 + £131.76 = £160.32 and secondary, £32.84 + £151.52 = £184.36) become primary, £179.76 and secondary £206.72, and O's separate contributions (primary £10.56 + £41.76 = £52.32 and secondary, £12.14 + £48.02 = £60.16) are to be uplifted to £71.76 primary and £82.52 secondary. Thus, according to HMRC, primary contributions of £151.20 (£179.76 - £28.56) and secondary contributions of £173.88 (£206.72 - £32.84) are to be paid on the first payment of monthly salary to N, while primary contributions of £61.20 (£71.76 - £10.56) and secondary contributions of £70.38 (£82.52 - £12.14) are to be paid on the first payment of monthly salary to O. The legal validity of HMRC's instruction in these circumstances is questionable.

Notes

(a) An earner's earnings period may be changed as a result of a change in the regular pay interval. If the new earnings period is longer than the old, then where a payment of earnings at the old interval falls within the first new earnings period, contributions on all payments made during the new earnings period are not to exceed the contributions which would have been payable had all those payments been made at the new interval. [*SI 2001 No 1004, Reg 18(3)*].

(b) In such circumstances HMRC instruct employers to calculate contribution liabilities on the total of all payments of earnings made in the new earnings period and then to deduct from those amounts the contribution liabilities already calculated on payments of earnings made at the old interval within the new earnings period. (HMRC Leaflet CWG2 (2018), para 1.10).

(B) Change to shorter interval

Snipe is employed by Teal Ltd at a salary of £800 per month. He receives £800 on 6 August 2018 but then, from 1 September 2018, his pay arrangement is changed to one under which he receives a weekly wage of £200. His first weekly wage under the new arrangement is paid on 2 September 2018. It follows that, in the contribution month ended 5 September, S has received two payments of earnings.

The payments are not aggregated so that liabilities are as follows:

Primary	(on a monthly earnings period basis)	£800 @ Nil%/12% =	£11.76
	(on a weekly earnings period basis)	£200 @ Nil%/12% =	£4.56
			£16.32
Secondary	(on a monthly earnings period basis)	£800 @ Nil%/13.8% =	£13.52
	(on a weekly earnings period basis)	£200 @ Nil%/13.8% =	£5.24
			£18.76

Note

(a) Where an employed earner's regular pay interval is changed so that the new interval is shorter than the old interval and, as a result, the first of the new earnings periods is contained within the last of the old earnings periods, the two payments are treated separately. (HMRC Leaflet CWG2 (2018), para 1.9).

511.3 HOLIDAY PAY

[*SI 2001 No 1004, Reg 19*]

Utrillo and Vermeer are both employed by Whistler Ltd. Each is paid a wage of £260 and holiday pay (for the following two weeks) of £250 each per week on 28 June 2018. U works during his holiday period and earns £180 paid to him on 5 July and £220 paid to him on 12 July. His wage on 19 July is £260. V takes his holiday but £140 in overtime pay becomes due for payment to him on 5 July. This is paid (along with a wage of £260) on 19 July after his return to work.

If W adopts *method A*, final calculations will be as follows.

U	£	*Primary*	£	*Secondary*	£
28 June 2018	260	Nil%/12%	11.76	Nil%/13.8%	13.52
5 July 2018	430	Nil%/12%	32.16	Nil%/13.8%	36.98
12 July 2018	470	Nil%/12%	36.96	Nil%/13.8%	42.50
19 July 2018	260	Nil%/12%	11.76	Nil%/13.8%	13.52
	£1,420		£92.64		£106.52

V	£	*Primary*	£	*Secondary*	£
28 June 2018	260	Nil%/12%	11.76	Nil%/13.8%	13.52
5 July 2018	390	Nil%/12%	27.36	Nil%/13.8%	31.46
12 July 2018	250	Nil%/12%	10.56	Nil%/13.8%	12.14
19 July 2018	260	Nil%/12%	11.76	Nil%/13.8%	13.52
	£1,160		£61.44		£70.64

If W adopts *method B*, final calculations will be as follows.

U	£	*Primary*	£	*Secondary*	£
28 June 2018	760 ÷ 3 = 253	Nil%/12%	10.92 × 3 = 32.76	Nil%/13.8%	12.56 × 3 = 37.68
5 July 2018	180	Nil%/12%	2.16	Nil%/13.8%	2.48
12 July 2018	220	Nil%/12%	6.96	Nil%/13.8%	8.00
19 July 2018	260	Nil%/12%	11.76	Nil%/13.8%	13.52
	£1,420		£53.64		£61.68

V	£	*Primary*	£	*Secondary*	£
28 June 2018	760 ÷ 3 = 253	Nil%/12%	10.92 × 3 = 32.76	Nil%/13.8%	12.56 × 3 = 37.68
5 July 2018	—	—	—	—	—
12 July 2018	—	—	—	—	—
19 July 2018	400	Nil%/12%	28.56	Nil%/13.8%	32.84
	£1,160		£61.32		£70.52

Note

(a) Where a payment of earnings includes a payment in respect of one or more week's holiday, the earnings period may be the length of the interval in respect of which the payment is made ('*method B*'). Alternatively, the holiday pay may simply be treated for contribution purposes as pay in the weeks in which earnings would normally have been paid ('*method A*'). Method B cannot be used in respect of a payment on termination of employment which includes a payment in respect of such holiday. [*SI 2001/1004, Reg 19*]. If method B is used and the length of the interval in respect of which the payment is made includes a fraction of a week, that fraction is treated as a whole week.

511.4 PAYMENTS TO DIRECTORS AND EX-DIRECTORS

[*SI 2001 No 1004, Reg 8*]

Anchovy is a director of Barracuda Ltd. His drawings (treated as earnings) are £3,600 per month. On 30 June 2018 he resigns his office and begins to work as an ordinary employee of Carp Ltd (a completely unconnected company) who pay him a weekly wage. In May 2019 Anchovy is paid a bonus of £10,000 by B in respect of the year ended 31 March 2019.

An earnings period of one year is to apply to his earnings for the months April, May and June 2019 of £10,800 from B. A weekly earnings period will then apply in respect of his earnings from C. The £10,000 bonus will attract an annual earnings period.

Notes

(a) Where a person is a company director at the beginning of a tax year, the earnings period in respect of his earnings is that tax year. If a person is appointed as a company director during a tax year, the earnings period is the number of weeks remaining in the tax year. [*SI 2001 No 1004, Reg 8(2)(3)*].

(b) Where any payments are made to an ex-director in any year *after* that in which his directorship ceased the earnings period is the tax year in which they are paid if they are in respect of any period during which he was a company director. [*SI 2001 No 1004, Reg 8(5)*].

(c) See also **508** COMPANY DIRECTORS.

512 Intermediaries

Cross-reference. See also **IT 20** PERSONAL SERVICE COMPANIES ETC.

512.1 CALCULATION OF DEEMED PAYMENT

[*SI 2000 No 727*]

Graham is an IT consultant working through his own service company and has secured a job with Benevolent Ltd through an agency to work on the computerised accounts system for seven months from October 2018 to April 2019 inclusive. In accounts, a team leader (another IT contractor) tells Graham what work he is to carry out but he is left to his own experience to determine 'how' the work is carried out. Graham is expected to be in attendance at Benevolent Ltd a regular 40 hours per week. Graham's company is paid an hourly rate for his services at 1.5 times the normal hourly rate. Billed monthly, Benevolent Ltd pays the agency who in turn are invoiced by Graham's company. The total invoices for the seven months will amount to £35,000. Graham draws a salary of £10,000 from his company over the period. Allowable expenses up to 5 April 2019 amount to £750 and there are pension contributions of £2,000. The main indications that self-employment arises here is the minimal financial risk from invoicing, the ability to work for others and the existence of Graham's company. In contrast, the engagement is relatively long and he must carry out the services personally. Also Benevolent Ltd provides the equipment and working accommodation and he works the usual working hours of the client. The engagement with Benevolent Ltd would appears to have been an employment had it been between Graham and the client direct rather than through the service company. The intermediary rules therefore apply for 2018/19 as follows:

Relevant income received (October, November, December, January, February; March not paid as at 5 April 2019; April 2019 not yet invoiced)		£25,000
Deduct		
Pension contributions paid	£2,000	
Expenses paid (allowable)	£750	
Flat rate allowance (5% of £25,000)	£1,250	
Salary paid in year to 5 April 2018	£10,000	
Class 1 NICs paid and due on salary paid in year (on £10,000)	£217	(£14,217)
Net deemed payments before NICs		£10,783
Employer's NICs (£10,783 × 13.8/113.8)		(£1,308)
Deemed payment		£9,475

Notes

(a) The post-expense figure before NICs (i.e. £10,783) is multiplied by 100/113.8 to reach the deemed payment figure since the earnings threshold has already been taken into account on the £10,000 salary. Clearly, an adjustment will be necessary if none or only part of the earnings threshold has not been set against salary payments already made in the tax year in question.

(b) For 2017/18 onwards, different rules apply where the engagement via the intermediary is with a public authority. In such cases, the liability to pay employment taxes and NICs moves to the public sector body or agency/third party paying the intermediary.

513 Partners

Cross-reference. See also IT 18 PARTNERSHIPS.

513.1 CLASS 4 CONTRIBUTIONS

[*SSCBA 1992, Sch 2 para 4*]

(A)

Alder, Birch and Cypress are in partnership as arboriculturists. Their profit for the year ended 30 June 2018 is £34,000 and during that year C is a salaried partner while A and B share the remaining profit in equal shares. The tax assessment for 2018/19 is £34,000. Although A and B continue to share profits on the same basis, however, C's salary for the year ended 30 June 2019 is £12,000 and for the year ended 30 June 2019 is £14,000. For Class 4 purposes the 2018/19 assessment is to be

			£
C		=	12,000
A	1/2 × (£34,000 − £12,000)	=	11,000
B	1/2 × (£34,000 − £12,000)	=	11,000
			£34,000

Note

(a) Where a trade or profession is carried on in partnership, the liability of any partner in respect of Class 4 contributions arises in respect of his share of the profits of that trade or profession. [*SSCBA 1992, Sch 2 para 4(1)*]. The share of profits is determined on the basis of the profit sharing arrangements in the basis period for the year concerned. See also IT 18 PARTNERSHIPS

(B)

Diamond and Emerald are in partnership as jewellers sharing profits in the ratio of 1:1 until 30 September 2016 and in the ratio of 1:2 after that date. Diamond also runs a nightclub. The partnership profits for the years to 30 September 2016, 30 September 2017 and 30 September 2018 are £36,000, £38,000 and £34,000. D's profits from his nightclub are £28,000 for 2016/17, £24,000 for 2017/18 and £34,000 for 2018/19.

D and E will each separately self-assess their income tax and Class 4 National Insurance liabilities. In the case of D, this will be based on the total income from both sources of self-employment income.

D's Class 4 liability for 2016/17 is

		£
£36,000 × 1/2		18,000
Nightclub		28,000
		46,000
Less: Excess over upper annual limit (£43,000)		3,000
		43,000
Less: Lower annual limit		8,060
		£34,940
Class 4 contributions due:		
£34,940 @ 9% =	£3,144.60	
£3,000 @ 2%	60.00	
	£3,204.60	

E's Class 4 liability for 2016/17 is

		£
£36,000 × 1/2		18,000
Less: Lower annual limit		8,060
Class 4 contributions due:		£9,940
£9,940 @ 9% =	£894.60	

D's Class 4 liability for 2017/18 is

		£
£38,000 × 1/3		12,667
Nightclub		24,000
		36,667
Less: Lower annual limit		8,164
Class 4 contributions due:		£28,503
£28,503 @ 9% =	£2,565.27	

E's Class 4 liability for 2017/18 is

		£
£38,000 × 2/3		25,333
Less: Lower annual limit		8,164
Class 4 contributions due:		£17,169
£17,169 @ 9% =	£1,545.21	

D's Class 4 liability for 2018/19 is

		£
£34,000 × 1/3		11,333
Nightclub		34,000
		45,333
Less: Lower annual limit		8,424
Class 4 contributions due:		£36,909
£36,909 @ 9% =	£3,321.81	

E's Class 4 liability for 2018/19 is

		£
£34,000 × 2/3		22,666
Less: Lower annual limit		8,424
Class 4 contributions due.		£14,242
£14,242 @ 9% =	£1,281.78	

D and E's Class 4 liabilities for 2016/17 were payable in two equal interim instalments on 31 January 2017 and 31 July 2017 based on the 2015/16 self-assessments, with the balance payable on 31 January 2018. Similarly, their Class 4 liability for 2017/18 is payable in two equal instalments on 31 January 2018 and 31 July 2018 based on the 2016/17 self-assessment, with the balance payable on 31 January 2019 and so on.

The self-assessment payments will, therefore, include the following amounts in relation to Class 4 contributions.

	D	E
	£	£
31 January 2018 (2017/18 POA)	1,602.30	447.30
31 July 2018 (2017/18 POA)	1,602.30	447.30
31 January 2019 (2017/18 repayment/balance)	(639.33)	650.64
31 January 2019 (2018/19 POA)	1,282.64	772.61
31 July 2019 (2018/19 POA)	1,282.64	772.60
31 January 2020 (2018/19 repayment/balance)	756.53	(263.46)
31 January 2020 (2019/20 POA)	1,660.91	640.89
31 July 2020 (2019/20 POA)	1,660.91	640.89

Notes

(a) See note (a) to (A) above.

(b) Where a trade or profession is carried on in partnership, the liability of any partner in respect of Class 4 contributions is calculated by aggregating his share of the profits with his share of the profits of any other trade or profession. [*SSCBA 1992, Sch 2 para 4(1)*].

Index

This index is referenced to chapter and paragraph number within the six main sections of the book. The entries in bold capitals are chapter headings in the text.